Combined edition for 1st and 2nd Year

FITTER

SHOP THEORY

For Fitter Trade of I.T.I., A.T.I., Apprenticeship *etc. and*
also useful for
Turner, Machinist, Instrument Mechanic, Tool and Die Maker *etc.*

by

KAPIL DEV

An ISO 9001 : 2008 Certified Company
COMPUTECH PUBLICATIONS LIMITED
4591/15, Aggarwal Road (Near Happy School) Darya Ganj,
New Delhi - 110002 (India)
Division - ASIAN PUBLISHERS
Buy books online : www.computechpublications.com

Latest Edition

Price : **₹ 187.50**

ISBN 978-81-7317-027-0

Published by :

Computech Publications Ltd. (*Division* – **Asian Publishers**)
4591/15, Aggarwal Road (Near Happy School)
Darya Ganj, New Delhi – 110002 (India)
Phone : 011-43080162, 43080163, 43080164 *Fax* : 011-43080165
WhatsApp : +91-9716836703
E-mail : nap@newasianpub.in ; info@computechpublications.in
Buy books online : www.computechpublications.in

Buy books online : www.computechpublications.com

Laser Typesetting : ANP Graphics and Software, DELHI

PREFACE TO REVISED EDITION

Encouraged by the overwhelming response given by trainees and teachers to this book, I feel pleasure in presenting this revised edition in which sketches of all types of tools and other drawings throughout the book have been improved. This will help the trainees in understanding the subject more clearly and easily. Now it is hoped that trainees and teachers will find this book most suitable among the books available in the market on this subject for their training.

Valuable suggestions from teachers and trainees will be thankfully acknowledged.

— Author

PREFACE

"FITTER" is one of the most important trades, which are being taught at various Industrial Training Institutes and other training centres all over India. Fitter trade has very vast scope, and there is no single book on Fitter theory covering the full knowledge on the subject. To fullfil the needs of the trainees, this book has been written.

This book covers complete syllabus of Fitter trade formulated by N.C.V.T. Theory and several practicals have been described with the help of neat diagrams in very easy language so that an average student can easily understand the subject matter.

It is hoped that trainees as well as Instructors would take full advantage of this book; which is useful for C.T.I., M.T.I., G.I.T.I. and apprenticeship trainees as well.

I am grateful to all those who gave their valuable suggestions for making this work of good-standard; I am also grateful to all those persons and agencies, to whom it is not possible to acknowledge here individually due to pausity of space, from whom help is taken in making figures in this book.

I am greatly thankful to Mr. R.K. Mehta, the Publisher, for his co-operation and hard-work for bringing out this book in such a nice get-up.

I would be thankful to those instructors and readers who send their useful suggestions for further improvement of this book.

— Author

CONTENTS

Chap. No.	Description	Page No.
1.	Fitter Trade and its Introduction	1
2.	Safety Precautions	2 - 7
3.	Measurements, Weights and their Units	8 - 10
4.	Hand Tools for Measuring	11 - 17
5.	Precision Measuring Tools	18 - 35
6.	Gauge and Indicator	36 - 55
7.	Marking Tools and Equipments	56 - 64
8.	Cutting Tools	65 - 102
9.	Dismantling, Assembling and other Tools	103 - 116
10.	Threads	117 - 123
11.	Limits, Fits and Tolerances	124 - 129
12.	Fasteners	130 - 147
13.	Jigs and Fixtures	148 - 151
14.	Sheet Metal Work	152 - 160
15.	Blacksmithy and Forging	161 - 167
16.	Lathe Machine	168 - 182
17.	Grinding and Grinding Machines	183 - 194
18.	Honing, Lapping and Surface Finishing	195 - 197
19.	Engineering Metals	198 - 212
20.	Heat Treatment	213 - 217
21.	Anti-corrosive Treatment	218 - 219
22.	Lubricants and Coolants	220 - 225
23.	Mechanical Power Transmission	226 - 235
24.	Bearings	236 - 238
25.	Pipe and Pipe Fittings	239 - 244
26.	Welding Process and their Introduction	245 - 246
27.	Gas and Arc Welding Tools	247 - 252
28.	Electric Arc Welding Processes	253 - 255
29.	Welding Joint, Bead and Preparation of Edges	256 - 258

1

Fitter Trade and Its Introduction

In this progressive age, a kind of revolution has taken place in industries all over the world. In order to meet our day to day material needs a number of new machines have been invented and produced. These machines have become an integral part of our life. How difficult our life would become without these machines can be well imagined ! Right from dawn to dusk we have to use a number of machines daily. It may be a stove, bicycle, sewing machine, television, aeroplane *etc*. All these things are manufactured in different workshops in different countries. These workshops and factories vary in size according to our needs and their utility. These may be small, medium or large scale industries but basis of production in all industries is the technicians who work there. Be it a developed or a developing country, every nation needs technicians for production and repair of various machines. In order to meet the demand for technicians, most of the countries have arrangements for proper and efficient training of these technicians. Fitter is one of the trades in which training is given to the technicians. In simple words. Fitter is a technician who fits something. But this definition is not adequate. In fact, Fitter trade is a wide field. Under this trade, we can have three broad categories :

(*i*) **Machine Fitter.** Technicians who fit different parts and assemble or produce a machine, come under this category. These parts might have been made by a technician of some other trade or by the fitter himself.

(*ii*) **Bench Fitter.** Technicians who make or repair a part of a machine by using different kinds of hand tools, generally come under this category.

(*iii*) **Pipe Fitter.** As is clear from the name itself, a Pipe Fitter is one who performs all kinds of pipe-fitting jobs. These may be pipes used for taps in houses, pipes used in cold storages or pipes used in boilers.

In the Industrial Training Institutes, syllabus for the Fitter Trade has been formulated keeping in view the requirements mentioned in the above three categories of Fitter. Along with the main trade of Fitter, side by side training is also given in the allied fields of plumber, sheet metal, blacksmithy and turner. These fitters can efficiently work as Machine Fitter, Bench Fitter and Pipe Fitter in different types of industries. In fact, an efficient Fitter is the very basis of efficient working in a workshop. The most significant thing about a Fitter is that he can fit, make, or repair a machine or any of its part, efficiently by using different hand tools and machines.

2

Safety Precautions

There is no doubt that invention and production of a large number of machines have proved a blessing to the mankind by enabling us to meet our day to day needs of materials. Machines help us in quick production of different things. But the same machines have also proved dangerous as far as the life of those working on them is concerned. Day in and day out, accidents take place in factories and workshops. Many lives are lost. Some workers become permanently handicapped. Some are seriously injured. With the increase in number of new machines, the number of accidents caused by machines is also growing. Life is a valuable gift. It is necessary to take all necessary precautions to save it. "Safety First" is considered as the golden rule of preventing accidents. The number of accidents can be reduced to a great extent, if before doing anything due care is taken to prevent accidents. "Some accidents are averted by the grace of God. But the possibility of accidents can be reduced to the minimum by taking proper care at the time of work." If we analyse the factors responsible for accidents in technical jobs, the following causes can be listed :

(*i*) Inadequate knowledge of the job.

(*ii*) Lack of suitable working environments and proper facilities for work.

(*iii*) Urge to do a job hurriedly.

(*iv*) To work more than one's capacity.

(*v*) Urge to earn maximum money in minimum time.

(*vi*) Lack of proper machines and tools.

It is clear from the above facts that if adequate safety measures are taken before doing a particular job, the number of accidents in the workshops and factories can be reduced.

Different types of machines are produced and repaired in workshops by the technicians with the help of different machines and tools. In order to make these technicians efficient, training in different trades is given in the Industrial Training Institutes. The trainees acquire practical knowledge from these training institutes. Therefore, it is essential that they should take necessary precautions for safety. These precautions for safety can be divided into three sections :

(*i*) Safety precautions for self

(*ii*) Safety precautions for the job

(*iii*) Safety precautions for the protection of tools and machinery

Safety for Self

First of all each worker should take care to protect his body from accidents. A slight negligence can make a worker handicapped or disabled. In order to ensure personal safety, the following important points should be borne in mind :

(*i*) While working in a workshop one should always wear only fit clothes and avoid wearing loose ones like dhoti, kurta, payjama *etc.* because loose clothes carry the risk of being caught in the running belts of machines.

(*ii*) Use of neckties and muffler should be avoided in the workshop.

(*iii*) While a machine is in motion, one should not unnecessarily touch any of its parts. There are chances of accidents.

(*iv*) Belt guard should be used on machines run by belts. The belt guards should not be removed while the machine is in operation.

(*v*) Lubrication should be done only after putting off the machine. It should not be done while the machine is in operation. If lubrication is done while the machine is in operation, oil-cane or the lubricating equipment may hit a moving part of the machine or it may cause spray of the oil and the oil drops may fall into your eyes, causing damage.

(*vi*) Adequate provision of light and air should be there at the site of work.

(*vii*) One should not move bare-footed in workshops or factories. Tiny iron particles can cause damage to a bare foot.

(*viii*) One should not touch cutting chips with hands, while working on a machine.

(*ix*) If you do not have knowledge about working of a machine, you should not operate it without the help of a person who knows its working.

(*x*) One should not look at the bright flame of welding instrument as it is harmful for eyes. Welding should be done by using special glasses meant for this purpose.

(*xi*) One should neither take up nor do anything which is beyond one's capability. Little knowledge is always a dangerous thing.

(*xii*) We should concentrate on work while working in workshop. If our attention is diverted, it can prove dangerous. Therefore, one should not indulge in any activity which causes loss of concentration.

(*xiii*) One should neither use a defective machine nor any defective tools.

(*xiv*) A tool should be used only for the purpose for which it is intended, not for other purposes.

(*xv*) In the event of an accident in the workshop, immediate arrangements for first aid and treatment should be made.

(*xvi*) While using tools care should be taken to ensure that there is no grease, oil or any oily substance, on the handle of the hammer. Do not use a file or scraper without its handle.

(*xvii*) Eye-glasses should be used while using a grinder.

(*xviii*) After using tools, these should be properly washed and cleaned.

Safety for Job

Production or repair of a machine or any part of a machine costs a lot of money. If we do a job carelessly it would further increase its cost. Therefore, it is also essential that one should do the job with due care and precautions for safety. The following safety measures are necessary to ensure safety for job :

(*i*) Before taking up any job in the workshop, it is necessary to plan the operation of work and job should be performed accordingly otherwise it may result in loss of time and money and the job would not be done satisfactorily.

(*ii*) If a machine is required to be used for doing a job, it should be ensured that job is carried out properly on the machine.

(*iii*) While cutting a particular object one should not make a deep cut.

(*iv*) Coolant and lubricants should be used according to the nature of metal, while doing a cutting job so that there is not much change in its natural properties.

(*v*) Proper tools, with sharp edges, should be used for cutting jobs otherwise it would spoil the job.

(*vi*) Proper arrangements should be made to fasten heavy jobs on machines.

(*vii*) Use of right types of tools and machines for various jobs is very important for proper results. If right kind of tools and machines are not used it may prove harmful and spoil the job.

Safety for Tools and Machines

Various operations are carried out and various types of tools and machines are used for production and repair of each machine or part of a machine, it is equally important to protect these tools and machines from loss or damage. In this connection, the following important points should be borne in mind :

(*i*) Each tool and machine has been made to perform certain specific jobs. It is important from the point of their safety that these tools and machines should be used only for the specific purposes for which these are meant. Otherwise, tools and machines would be damaged.

(*ii*) A file to be used for filing, should not have any grease or oily substance on it. Nor we should use file in place of a hammer.

(*iii*) While using a chisel care should be taken to hit at its centre, otherwise its head would become mushroomed.

(*iv*) The wires used in electrical jobs should be properly insulated. If the insulation has become weak, it should be changed. Wire with damaged insulation carry the risk of producing sparks and result in fire when they come in touch with each other.

(*v*) While using hacksaw, the blade should not be tightened too much, otherwise there are chances that it would break.

(*vi*) Coolant should be used while doing cutting job with a hacksaw blade, else it would get hot and its edge would be spoiled.

(*vii*) Cutting tools such as file, chisel, scraper, *etc.* should be kept separate from other tools. These tools can cause scratches on other tools if mixed with other tools.

(*viii*) Tools meant for precision measurements should be used carefully. Detailed precautions needed for handling these tools are given in the next chapter.

(*ix*) Never use a new machine, whose function and operation is not known to you else it may damage the machine.

(*x*) If a machine suddenly creates unusual noise, in such cases, the machine should be stopped then and there and efforts should be made to locate its fault. It is not advisable to use the machine until the fault is located and machine is repaired.

(*xi*) Before using a machine, proper cleaning, greasing and oiling should be done.

(*xii*) A defective machine must be repaired before using it otherwise it may get more damaged.

(*xiii*) As far as possible, gears of a running machine should not be changed nor these should be touched.

(*xiv*) If it is necessary to leave, after putting a machine into operation, first the machine should be put off and then one should leave.

(*xv*) In case of sudden failure of electricity, machine should be switched off.

(*xvi*) No machine should be given more than the load fixed for its operation.

(*xvii*) For heavy jobs special arrangements should be made with machines.

(*xviii*) Foundation of machines should be according to their weight, speed and function.

If the above mentioned precautions are taken, a number of accidents in the workshops can be avoided. But fire is another big cause of accidents in workshops. It can cause loss of human lives as well as property. Fire can damage even the adjoining buildings, whether they are workshops or residential buildings. Following precautions are necessary to avert fire accidents in factories and workshops :

Possible cause of Fire and steps to prevent Fire :

Different kinds of inflammable materials like lubricants, acids *etc.* are used in the workshops. A slight negligence can cause fire. In addition electric sparks are also a major cause of fire in workshops. There are following main causes of fire which should be avoided :

(*i*) Oil-soaked pieces of clothes should not be thrown here and there in the workshops and factories. These can cause fire. These oil-soaked pieces of clothes should either be kept in a covered tin box or thrown at a safe distance from the workshop, if those are not needed.

(*ii*) Kerosene and other inflammable oils should be kept in separate store so that they don't catch fire, in case fire accident occurs in a workshop.

(*iii*) All electric connections and fittings should be properly joined. Loose fittings and electric connections can cause sparks and fire.

(*iv*) Electric and power wires should be properly insulated. If the insulation becomes weak, the wiring should be changed. Otherwise, when two such wires join, they cause sparking and can result in causing fire.

(*v*) Electric supply companies give electric current of specific load. Therefore, it is not advisable to put more load. By doing so, there are chances of fire in the workshop.

(*vi*) Smoking is one of the major causes of fire in workshops. The small burning butts of cigarettes, bidis, *etc.* cause fire. Therefore, if possible there should be no smoking in the workshops or if it is done, due care should be taken.

(*vii*) Gas cylinders used for welding should be kept at a safe place.

Measures to put off Fire

Inspite of care, there are chances of fire in workshops and factories. It is therefore necessary that there should be proper arrangements to extinguish fire. Buckets full of water, sand, fire extinguishers, *etc.* should be readily available in workshops. In the event of fire in the workshop, the following steps should be taken :

(*i*) Fire brigade should be immediately informed about the fire accident in the factory or workshop.

(*ii*) Fire caused by electricity should not be extinguished with water, because it can cause current.

(*iii*) If fire is caused by electricity the electric supply should be immediately cut so that it does not cause current.

(*iv*) As far as possible, costly articles should be removed and carried to a safe place.

(*v*) If a person catches fire, he or she should not run but lie down on the ground and try to extinguish fire by turning sides.

(*vi*) If one gets surrounded by fire on all sides one should try to come out by rolling down on the ground.

(*vii*) One should not loose mental balance, in event of fire. Nervousness or anxiety can cause more damage. Instead one should try to whatever is possible to extinguish fire and save whatever can possibly be saved,

First Aid

We have discussed various precautions needed to avert accidents in factories and workshops. A slight negligence in these precautions can prove dangerous. Accident in workshops directly affect the workers. While loss of property can be made up later on, it is essential to take steps to treat the injured persons immediately. One does not know when an accident will occur in a workshop but all workshops cannot have medical staff for quick treatment at the site. Only a few big industrial houses have made available medical facilities to deal with accidental cases. Therefore, it is very important to provide First Aid facilities in all workshops. Training should be given to the employees of workshop so that they can provide first aid relief to the injured, in case of an accident. If necessary, after giving first aid, treatment can be had from a doctor or a doctor can be called on the site, if situation demands. The following things should be available in the workshop to provide First Aid facilities :

(*i*) Tincture Iodine
(*ii*) Tincture Benzene
(*iii*) Mercurochorome
(*iv*) Detlol
(*v*) Burnol
(*vi*) Pain relieving tablests
(*vii*) Medicine to treat unconsciousness
(*viii*) Dressing material
(*ix*) Meshed cloth
(*x*) Cotton
(*xi*) Safety pin
(*xii*) Raw Plaster
(*xiii*) Small wooden strips
(*xiv*) Dropper
(*xv*) Glass for administering medicine
(*xvi*) Glass for washing eyes
(*xvii*) Strature *etc.*

With the help of above things, first aid can be provided to an injured person and he may get cured or get temporary relief.

Artificial Respiration

At times, because of electric shock or some other accident, breathing of a worker can stop, posing danger to his life. In such cases, artificial respiration is very essential to save his life. For giving artificial respiration, the following three methods are commonly used :

(*i*) Shafers Process
(*ii*) Sylvestor's Process
(*iii*) Lawbord Process.

Shafers Process. Under this process, the person who requires artificial respiration should be laid on the ground in such a way that his mouth and nose should not touch the ground. You should sit keeping your head towards patient's shoulder near his head as shown in Fig.2.1.

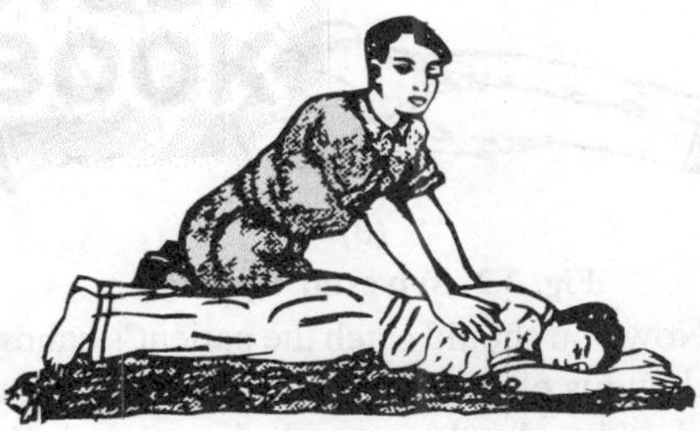

(A)

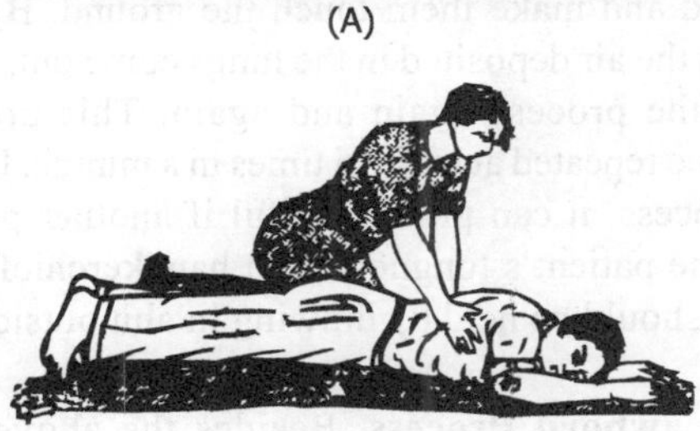

(B)

Fig. 2.1. Shafers process

Place your palms on the patient's back in such

a way that the lower part of the hands remains a bit above his hips, your thumbs should touch each other and your fingers should lean towards both the sides of the patient's back. Now, you should gradually lay the weight of your body on his back but do not give any jerks. In this way, the patient's stomach will be pressed and his wind pipe will be cleared of any obstruction like water, air, phlegm *etc.* Now you should withdraw your weight from his back and again repeat the same process, which can enable the patient to start respiration. This process should be done at least 20 times in a minute.

Sylvestor's Process. Under this process the patient should be laid down in a straight position. We should make his clothes loose. A pillow or support of some folded cloth should be kept under his back. You should sit on your knees towards the patient's head as shown in Fig. 2.2

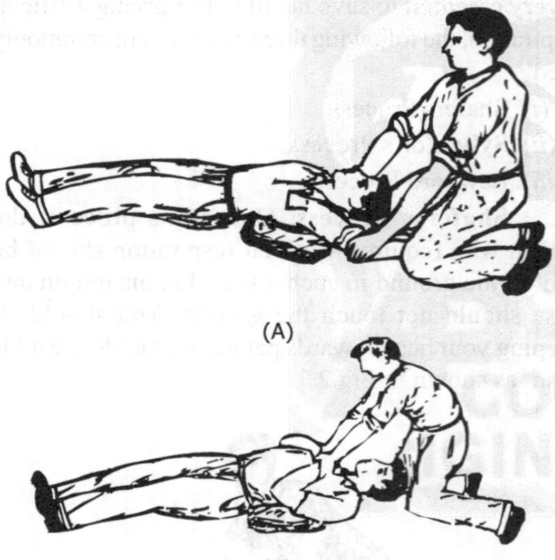

(A) (B)

Fig. 2.2. Sylvestor's process

Now you should catch the patient's hands from a bit below his elbows and then bring them towards his head and make them touch the ground. By this process the air deposited in the lungs come out. Now, repeat the process again and again. This process should be repeated at least 15 times in a minute. Under this process, it can prove helpful if another person holds the patient's tongue with a handkerchief. The tongue should be held by drawing in abit outside the mouth.

Lawbord Process. Besides the above two processes, this is third process. It is compatatively easier. Under this process, the patient should be laid in a straight position and his mouth should be cleared. You should sit by his side, holding your hand beneath his head and blow air into his mouth with your mouth as shown in Fig. 2.3.

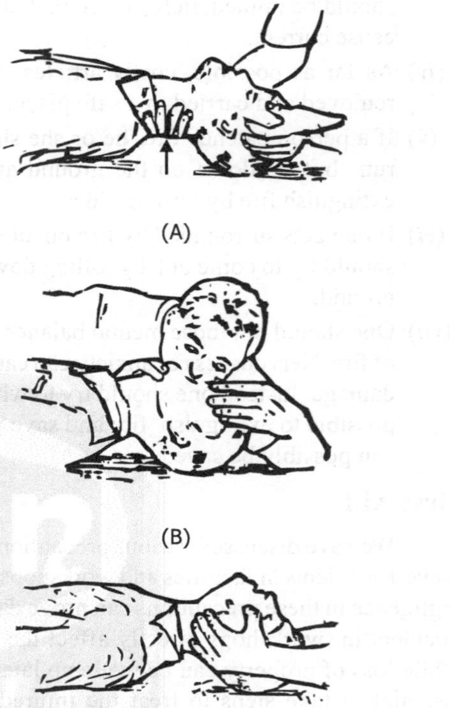

(A) (B) (C)

Fig. 2.3. Lawbord process

After once blowing air into patient's mouth in the above manner remove your mouth from his month and keep it away till the air blown into his mouth comes out. Then repeat the process.

By following the above processes, the stuck up air can be cleared and the patient can start breathing again, if the patient fails to respond by breathing again, a doctor should be immediately called and only after he declares the patient as dead we should take the person as dead.

Important points regarding First Aid

(*i*) We should not get nervous at the sight of patient's injury or pain. Nor we should try to escape from the site.

(*ii*) Instead of going into the questions of how the accident occurred, when it happened and why it happened, we should immediately arranage to provide first aid to thc patient. The above investigations can be done later on. First Aid should be our first concern in case of an accident.

(*iii*) We should check up properly how much pain the accident-victim is feeling and where. This is important for providing proper first aid.

(*iv*) If the patient is unconscious and blood is coming out, immediately steps should be taken to stop it.

(*v*) Before stopping the blood, the direction of blood in the nerves should be ascertained.

(*vi*) If the accident has been caused by electricity, fire, gas or oil, first efforts should be made to get the patient rid of these painiful agents.

(*vii*) The patient should be immediately removed from the accident site and taken to a comfortable place. There, he can be put on the bed or asked to sit, depending upon his condition.

(*viii*) Until a doctor declares an accident victim as dead, first aid relief should be continued.

(*ix*) It should be ensured that crowd does not gather around a patient.

(*x*) While trying to stop blood, pressure should not laid on any of the accident victims as we may not be sure whether any of his bone's has been broken. Otherwise his pain will grow because of burden or pressure.

(*xi*) An accident patient can be given hot milk or tea but not water or intoxicating things.

(*xii*) Efforts should be made to preserve the proof of accident, if available. We should not let such important proofs be destroyed.

(*xiii*) If it is felt necessary to put off a patient's clothes, these should be put off in such a careful manner that the patient does not feel it.

(*xiv*) If an accident victim has got burn injuries, he should not be allowed to remain in open air but a blanket should be srapped round his body.

(*xv*) We should arrange to call a doctor immediately or try to carry the accident victim to a doctor, if the situation demands.

Questions

1. What are the main reasons of accidents in workshops ?
2. What safety precautions should be taken to prevent accidents ?
3. List the safety precautions that should be taken for safety for self.
4. Describe the main safety measures for safety of jobs and tools.
5. What are the reasons for fire accidents in workshops? (1972)
6. What measures are necessary for extinguishing fire in the workshop ? (1972)
7. What do you understand by First Aid ? Describe in detail.
8. What are the important precautions to be taken while grinding the lathe cutting tool ? (1979)
9. What safety precautions are necessary while doing reaming ? (1974)
10. What safety measures should be taken while doing the job of chipping ? (1974)

3

Measurements, Weights and their Units

In all kinds of technical jobs as well as in our daily life, we have to measure and weigh a number of things. In order to meet this necessity, all countries have adopted measurement and weight system according to their needs. As India remained under the British rule for a long time, it was but natural that British measurement and weight system had its impact on India. Even today this system is being followed in several fields. This British system is known as F.P.S. The Government of India realised the importance of easy measurement and weight system and entrusted the job of framing new system to Indian Standards Institute. The I.S.I. approved the C.G.S. system.

F.P.S. System

This system remained prevalent in India and several other countries. In this system, Foot, Pound and Second were used, that is why it is named as F.P.S. system. For measuring length, units of inch, foot, yards and mile are used. For weighing purposes, dram, ounce and pound units are used. For measurement of time units of second, minute and hours are used. This system was evolved by the British Standard Institute and as such it is also known as B.S.I. system.

Under the F.P.S. system the following units are used :

Units of Measurement of Length

8 gauges = 1 inch
12 inches = 1 foot
3 feet = 1 yard
220 yards = 1furlong
8 Furlong or 1760 Yards = 1 Mile

Units of Weight Measurement

16 drams = 1 ounce
16 ounces = 1 pound
28 pounds = 1 quarter
4 quarters = 1hundred weight
20 hundred weight = 1 ton

Measurement of Capacity

4 gills = 1 pint
2 pints = 1 quarter
4 quarters = 1 gallon

Other Units

8 ratti = 1 masha
12 masha = 1 tola
5 tolas = 1chhatank
16 chhatanks = 1 seer
40 seer = 1 maund

Measurement of Time

60 seconds = 1 minute
60 minutes = 1 hour
24 hours = 1day

C.G.S. System

This system is also known as French or Metric system. This is an international system for measurement and weighing physical things. The Indian Standards Institute has approved this system for adoption. Under this system, for measurement of lenght centimetre, for weight gram, and for time second have been taken as the basis. Under C.G.S. system the following units are used :

Measurement of Length

10 millimetres = 1 centimetre
10 centimetres = 1 decimetre
10 decimetres = 1 metre
(or 100 centimetres)
10 metres = 1 decametre
10 decametres = 1 hectometre
(or 100 metres)

10 hectometres	= 1 kilometre (or 1000 metres)

Measurement to Weight

10 milligrams	= 1 centigram
10 centigrams	= 1 decigram
10 decigrams	= 1 gram
10 grams	= 1 decagram
10 decagrams	= 1 hectogram
10 hectograms	= 1 kilogram
100 kilograms	= 1 quintal
10 qunitals	= 1 metric tonne

Measurement of Capacity

10 mililitres	= 1 centilitre
10 centilitres	= 1 decilitre
10 decilitres	= 1 litre
10 litres	= 1 decalitre
10 decalitres	= 1 hectolitre
10 hectolitres	= 1 kilolitre

Measurement of Time

60 seconds	= 1 minute
60 minutes	= 1 hour
24 hours	= 1day
7 days	= 1 week
30 days	= 1 month
12 months (or 365 days)	= 1 year

Apart from F.P.S system and C.G.S. system for measurement at large scale, MKS system is also prevalent in India.This system is almost similar to CGS system. For measuring length metre is used. For weighing things kilogram and for measuring time seconds unit is used.

Area Measurement (British System)

144 sq. inch	= 1 sq. foot
9 sq. foot	= 1 sq. yard
4840 sq. yards	= 1 acre
640 acres	= 1 sq. mile

Area Measurement (Metric System)

100 sq. milimetres	= 1 sq. centimetre
100 sq. centimetres	= 1 sq. decimetre
100 sq. decimetres	= 1 sq. metre
100 sq. metres	= 1 are
100 are (or 10000 sq. m.)	= 1 hectare
100 hectares (or 100000 sq. ares)	= 1 sq. kilometre

Measurement of Volume (British System)

1728 cubic inches	= 1 cubic foot
27 cubic feet	= 1 cubic yard

Measurement of Volume (Metric System)

1000 cubic mm	=1 cubic centimetre
1000 cubic cm	=1 cubic decimetre
1000 cubic decimetres	=1 cubic metre
1000 cubic metres	=1 decametre
1000 cubic decametres	=1 cubic hectometre
1000 cubic hectometres	=1 cubic kilometre

Temperature and its Units

Temperature indicates the level of heat of an article. Organs of our body cannot measure the heat of a thing. If we put our finger in hot water and then put it into cool water, we shall observe that our finger remains hot for some time even after putting the finger into cold water. Therefore, we cannot depend on our body organs for knowing the temperature of an article. For this purpose a thermometer containing mercury is used. These are used as a scales between two stages of temperature. Normally Celsius (Centigrade) and Fahrenheit thermometres are used. In centigrade thermometers the melting point at atmospheric pressure is 0°C and the boiling point is at 100°C. These degrees can be conveniently divided into equal parts. In the same way, at atmospheric pressure in Fahrenheit thermometer, the melting point of ice is 32°F and boiling point of water is 212°F. These degrees are divided into equal parts and indicated on the thermometer.

For meeting the technical and other needs now these degrees are converted into one another. For this purpose, the following formula is applied :

Temperature Conversion Formula :

From Centigrade to Fahrenheit,

$$°C = \frac{5}{9}(°F - 32)$$

From Fahrenheit to Centigrade,

$$°F = \frac{9}{5}(°C + 32)$$

Example (*i*) Conversion of 32° Centigrade into Fahrenheit.

$$32°C = \frac{5\,(F - 32)}{9}$$

$$F - 32 = \frac{32 \times 9}{5}$$

$$F = \left(\frac{32 \times 9}{5}\right) + 32$$

$$= 57.6 + 32$$

$$= 89.6° \text{ F}$$

Example (*ii*) Conversion of 110° Fahrenheit into Centigrade.

$$\frac{C}{5} = \frac{110 - 32}{9} = \frac{78}{9}$$

$$9C = 78 \times 5$$

$$C = \frac{78 \times 5}{9} = \frac{390}{9}$$

$$= 43.33° \text{ C}$$

Questions

1. Which is the approved measurement and weight system in India ?
2. What do you understand by F.P.S. and C.G.S. ?
3. What is the formula for converting inch into millimetre ?
4. Which formula is used for converting Centigrade into Fahrenheit ?
5. Convert 30° Centigrade into Fahrenheit.

4

Hand Tools for Measuring

As already said, a Fitter is a practical person, who fits different parts of a machine with the help of hand tools, makes certain parts of a machine or repairs these parts. In doing so, a Fitter has to use different types of hand tools, depending upon the job in hand. Dismantling or assembling can be done with the help of tools like, spanner, hammer, pliers and screw-driver. But the job of making a new machine requires some more tools. There are at least four different activities in making a new thing. For example, if we wish to make a shoe, first of all we will have to measure the size of foot. So we require measuring tape and a paper. Secondly, according to the measurement and design we have to make markings on the leather piece. For this purpose marking material is required. After the marking is over, the leather is cut with a scissor *etc*. With the help of a form the upper part of a shoe is prepared. Likewise for making a new part of a machine, first measurement of the part is taken. Then marking is done on the metal. According to the marking the metal is brought into the required shape through cutting, filing *etc*. When the part is ready it is fitted into the machine. In this way, we have observed that a Fitter uses four kinds of tools for any kind of job. In other words, we can divide the tools used by a Fitter into the following four categories :

(*i*) Measuring Tools
(*ii*) Marking Tools
(*iii*) Cutting Tools
(*iv*) Dismantling and Assembling Tools

Measuring Tools. For making a new part or repairing a worn out part, first of all we need measuring tools. Right measurement is the basis of making a tool. These measuring tools can be further divided into following categories :

(*i*) Direct Measuring Tools
(*ii*) Indirect Measuring Tools

The above two categories of measuring tools can further be divided as under :

(*i*) Simple Measuring Tools
(*ii*) Precision Measuring Tools

All the above categories can be included into the following kinds of tools :

(*i*) Foot rule
(*ii*) Outside Calliper
(*iii*) Inside Calliper
(*iv*) Outside Micrometer
(*v*) Inside Micrometer
(*vi*) Depth Micrometer
(*vii*) Vernier Calliper
(*viii*) Vernier Height Gauge
(*ix*) Vernier Depth Gauge
(*x*) Combination Set
(*xi*) Vernier Bevel Protractor
(*xii*) Dial Test Indicator

Foot Rule

Foot Rule is used for physically measuring any article. These are made of wood, cardboard, plastic, aluminium, spring steel or stainless steel. In engineering line generally foot rules made of spring steel or stainless steel are used. Foot rules, of whatever material these are made of, are of the size of 6″, 12″, 24″, 36″ and 48″. Foot rules of 12″ size are most widely used. Companies who manufacture Foot Rules, indicate inches or millimetres or both, and divisions of inches and milimetres on the foot rules. Generally foot rules indicate division markings at each distance of an inch. An inch is divided into 8 equal parts. In this way, each marking represents $\frac{1}{8}$ inch, which is known as 'SOOT'. $\frac{1}{8}$ is divided into two parts marking of $\frac{1}{16}$ inches. Further, $\frac{1}{16}$ is divided into $\frac{1}{32}$ inch and $\frac{1}{64}$ inch parts. Foot rule with this graduation is shown in Fig. 4.1 below :

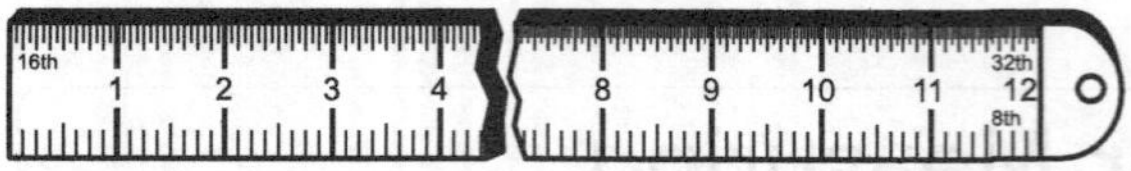

Fig. 4.1. Foot rule

This foot rule can be used to measure minimum upto $\frac{1}{64}$ inch. The graduation can be indicated on one edge or both the edges of the foot rule. Some foot rules have signs on one edge only and on the other edge there is marking of metric system. These foot rules are more useful as we can measure in British as well as metric system with these foot rules. On the edge where millimetre graduation is indicated signs at every centimetre are indicated. Each centimetre is divided into ten equal parts to indicate a millimetre. Each sign of millimetre is also divided into two equal parts. Thus we can measure upto $\frac{1}{2}$ millimetre from this edge. This type of graduation has been shown in the Foot Rule Fig. 4.1. "Brown and Sharp" tool company has made foot rules with 8 types of standard graduation. The following graduation is indicated on these foot rules on two or all the four edges of a foot rule.

Standard Combination Number	*First edge*	*Second edge*	*Third edge*	*Fourth edge*
1.	10, 20, 50, 100	12, 24, 48	14, 28	16, 32, 64
2.	8	10, 20, 50, 100	12, 24, 48	16, 32, 64
3.	10	50	32	64
4.	8	16	32	64
5.	16	32	64	100
6.	32	34	—	—
7.	64	100	—	—
8.	50	100	—	—

Among the standards of graduation indicated in the above table, number 4 graduation is widely used. The graduation indicated on its four edges has been illustrated in Fig. 4.2.

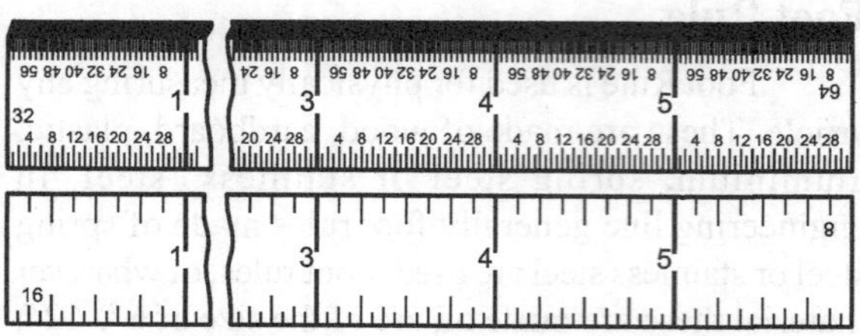

Fig. 4.2. Brown and Sharp standard 4 graduation

As is evident from the above figure on this type of foot rule graduation is indicated on all the four edges of the foot rule. On the first edge graduation is indicated in inches and each inch is also sub-divided in 8 equal parts. On the other edge each inch is divided into 16 equal parts. On the third edge each inch is further divided into 32 equal parts. On the fourth edge each inch is divided into 64 equal parts and their graduation is indicated.

The above mentioned foot rules of different graduations, which are used according to convenience, are of the following types :

(*i*) Flexible steel rule	(*ii*) Hook rule
(*iii*) Narrow rule	(*iv*) Shrink rule
(*v*) Short rule	(*vi*) Key-set rule
(*vii*) Calliper rule	(*viii*) Steel tape rule
(*ix*) Folding rule	(*x*) Canvas tape rule.

Flexible Rule. This rule is used for measuring spherical or hemispherical jobs. These are of 6″ to 12″ in size. These are made from spring steel sheet of $\frac{1}{64}$ thickness so that it attains the property of elasticity. Its use has been shown in Fig. 4.3.

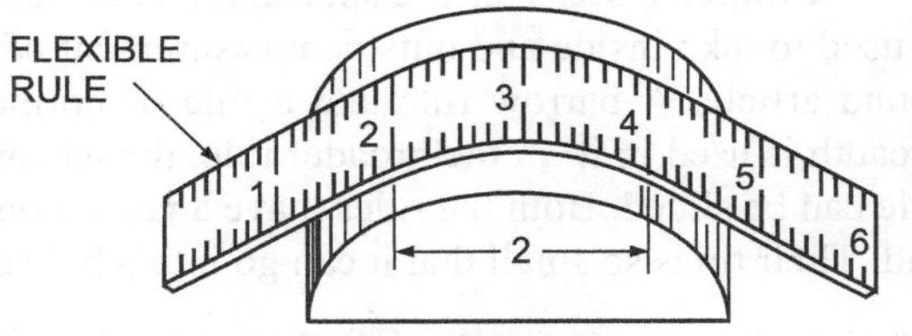

Fig. 4.3. Flexible rule

This rule contains measurement both in inches and millimetres. First two inches are divided into equal parts of $\frac{1}{32}''$ and the third inch is divided into equal parts of $\frac{1}{64}''$. On rest of the rule each inch is divided into eight equal parts. In the same way on the other side of the rule marking is indicated in centimetres. One centimetre is divided into ten equal parts whose one part is equal to one millimetre. This one part is also divided into two and the marking is indicated on the rule.

Hook Rule. This rule is also made of spring steel but a hook is attached to its one end. It is used to measure special type of spaces. Suppose there is a groove inside a hole and we have to measure the remaining part (leaving aside the groove) or to measure the remaining part of a round job leaving aside its step as shown in Fig. 4.4.

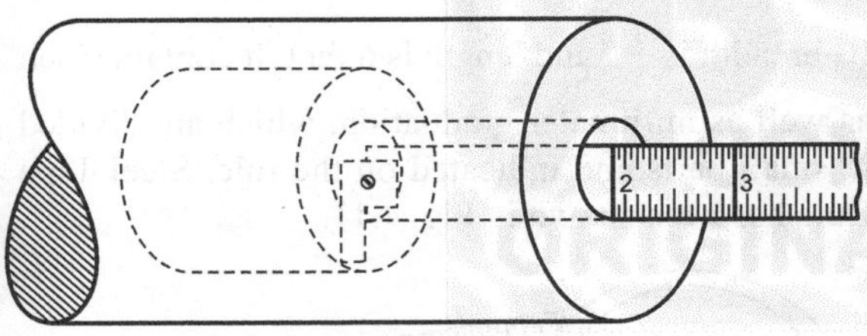

Fig. 4. 4. (*a*) Method of taking internal measurement with a hook rule

If the Hook Rule is a narrow rule, we can measure a hole of $\frac{3}{8}''$ thickness from inside. Hook rule can be of the size of 6″, 12″ or more.

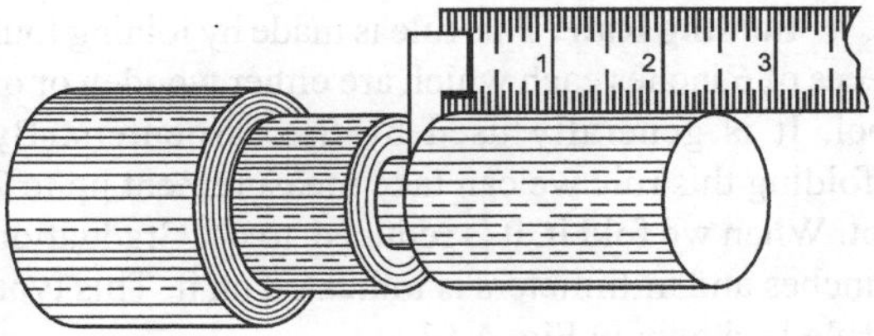

Fig. 4. 4. (*b*) Method of measuring external surface of a job with hook rule

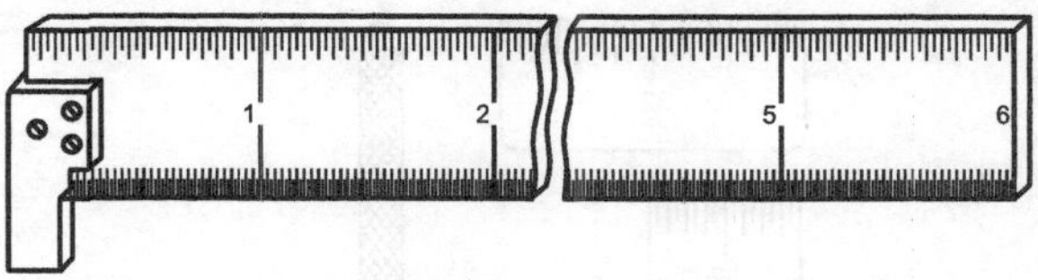

Fig. 4. 4. (*c*) Hook rule and its use

Narrow Rule. Narrow Rule is like a flexible rule but it is smaller and less in breadth. Its breadth is $\frac{1}{4}''$. A clip is attached to it with which it can be hanged with a pocket. Marking in inches and millimetres is indicated on one end of this rule as shown in Fig. 4.5.

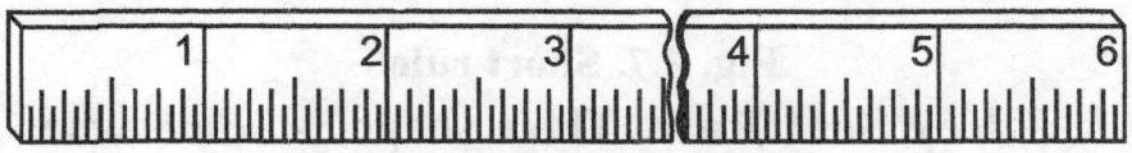

Fig. 4. 5. Narrow steel rule

It can be generally used for all type of jobs but it is especially used to measure slit, slot or thin pipe *etc.*

Shrink Rule. This rule is generally used in Pattern Maker's trade. This is used by the Pattern Maker when making patterns in order to properly allow for the shrinkage of the metal in which the pattern is to be cast. There its marking of $\frac{1}{8}''$, $\frac{1}{16}''$, $\frac{1}{32}''$ and $\frac{1}{64}''$ on this rule but this marking is slightly more than actual inch. It is written with the proportion for one inch as $\frac{1}{10}''$ to $\frac{7}{16}''$. Because of its enlarged size patterns get shrink allowance.

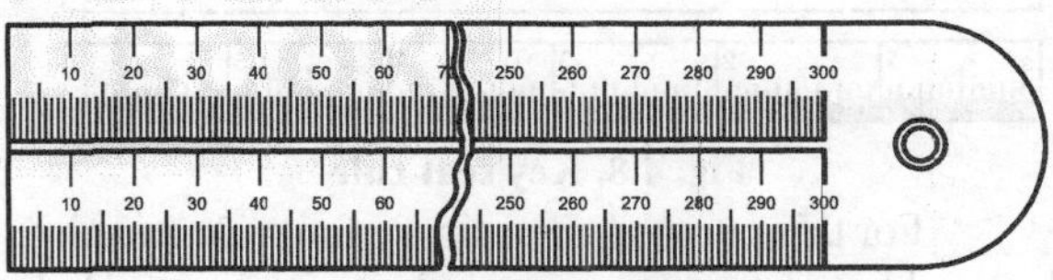

Fig. 4.6. Shrink allowance

Short Rule. This rule is used by the machinists and die-makers for measuring small gaps, slots *etc.* It is a set of small rules, which are made of steel leaves.

Each rule contains marking wherein an inch is divided into 32 equal parts ($\frac{1}{32}''$). The length of these rules is $\frac{1}{4}''$, $\frac{3}{8}''$, $\frac{1}{2}''$, $\frac{3}{4}''$ and 1″. A special holder is used to handle these rules as shown in Fig. 4.7.

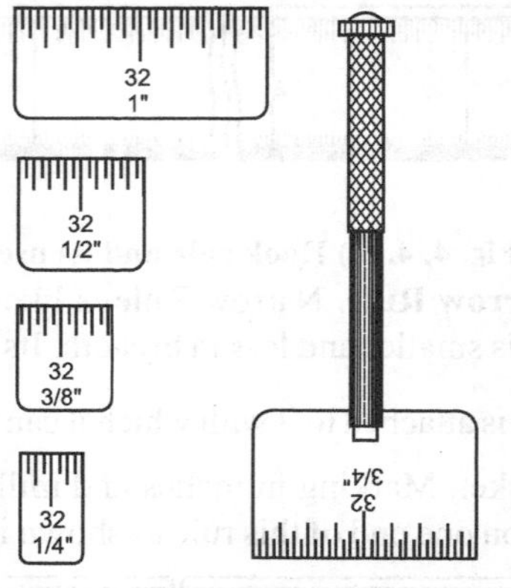

Fig. 4.7. Short rule

Key Seat Rule. Their shape is some what different from ordinary rules. It is almost like angle iron, having both beams at 90° angle. It is used to measure the spherical and hemi-spherical things which cannot be measured with ordinary rules because this can be adjusted on those round things easily. These are particularly made to measure marking of "key way" rules one is plain and the other contains marking of inches or millimeter which are divided in $\frac{1}{32}''$, $\frac{1}{64}''$, or $\frac{1}{2}''$ mm. It has been shown in Fig. 4.8.

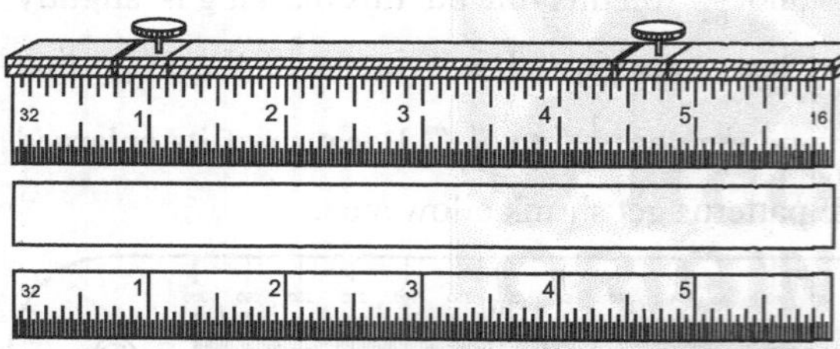

Fig. 4.8. Key seat rule

For this purpose an ordinary foot rule can also be used but in that case a seat clamp is also needed. This clamp is in the form of a pair. Both the clamps have grooves to fit in steel foot rules at equal height. In order to keep the foot rules held into the grooves, knurled nuts are fixed on the clamps, which can be tightened or taken out easily with hands. A pair of key seat clamp has been shown in Fig. 4.9.

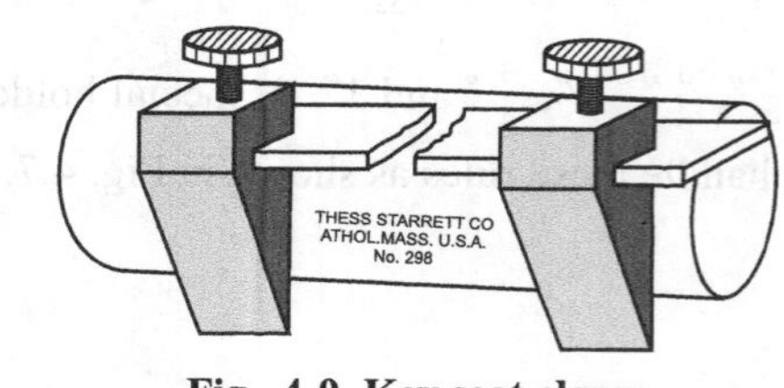

Fig . 4-9. Key seat clamp

Caliper Rule. This is a special type of rule. It is used to take inside and outside measurement of a round article. A narrow rule and a rule of normal breadth is used in it. In the broader rule, the narrow rule can be slided. Both the rules have a jaw on one end. Their tip is so small that it can go into a hole of $\frac{1}{8}''$ size. A screw is fixed on the broader rule wilh which narrow rule can be adjusted and can be locked in position. These rules contain both the Metric system and the British system of graduation. Caliper rule has been illustrated in Fig. 4.10.

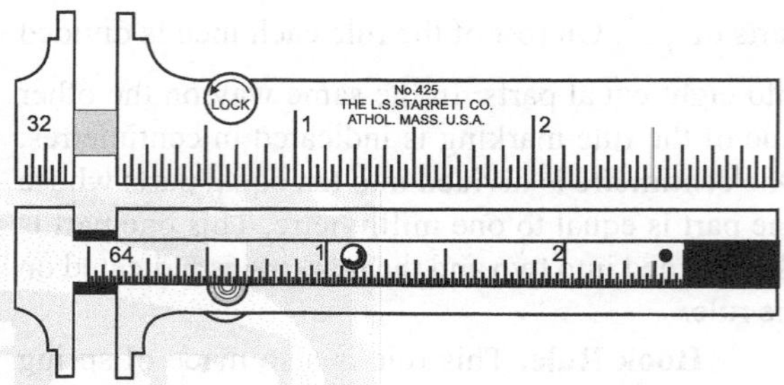

Fig. 4.10. Calliper rule

Steel Tape Rule. It is often difficult or rather impractical to carry long foot rules. For the purpose of convenience steel tape rules have been made.

This is made of spring steel and has elasticity. It can be rolled packed into a round tiny box (case). Its breadth is $\frac{1}{2}''$ and length is 6 feet. It contains inch as well as millimeter graduation, which are divided in small parts and indicated on the rule. Steel Tape Rule has been shown in Fig. 4.11.

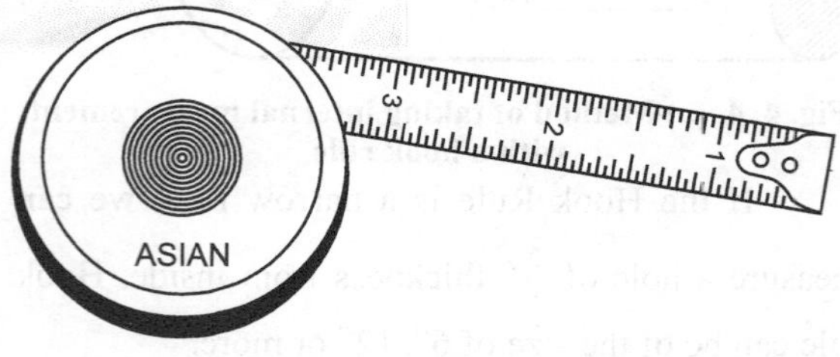

Fig. 4.11. Steel tape rule

Folding Rule. This rule is made by joining four pieces of 6 inches each which are either wooden or of steel. It is generally used by the carpenters. By unfolding this rule we can take measurement up to 2 foot. When we fold it, it is reduced to 6″. Graduation in inches and millimeters is indicated on it. This type of rule is shown in Fig. 4.12.

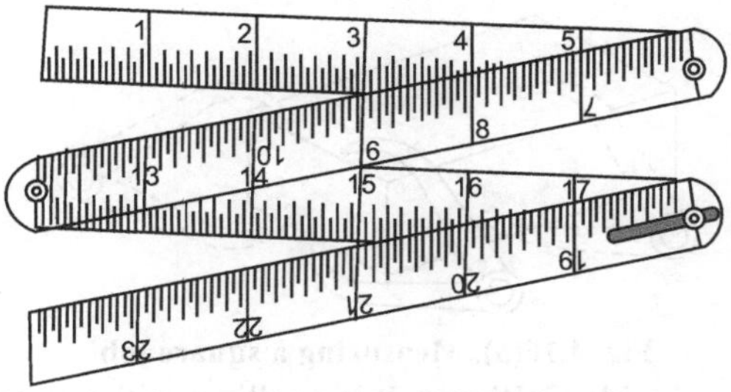

Fig. 4.12. Folding rule

Canvas Tape Rule. For measuring greater lengths this type of rule is used. This is made of a long canvas tape, which can be rolled and packed in a small leather or steel box. A ring is attached to its one end. By pulling this ring we can pull out the tape according to our need. For folding it a small handle is also provided. These tape rules are generally made of 50 feet or 100 feet length. Canvas Tape Rule has been shown in Fig. 4.13.

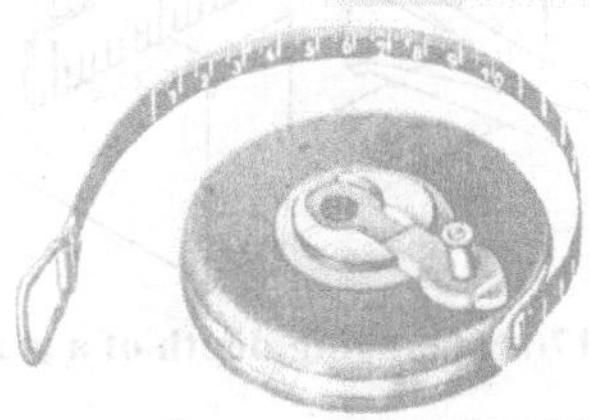

Fig. 4.13. Canvas tape rule

With all types of foot rules described above, we can measure a job or take their help in marking them. This measurement is taken directly. Foot rule is a simple tool but only by using it properly we can make the job of proper size or its right measurement can be taken. In Fig. 4.14 some right and some wrong methods have been shown.

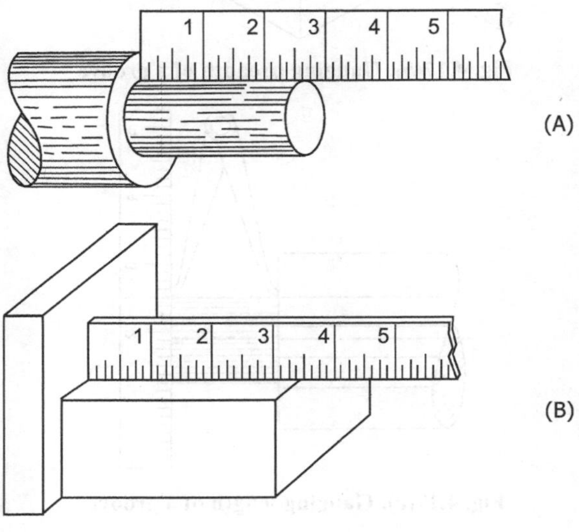

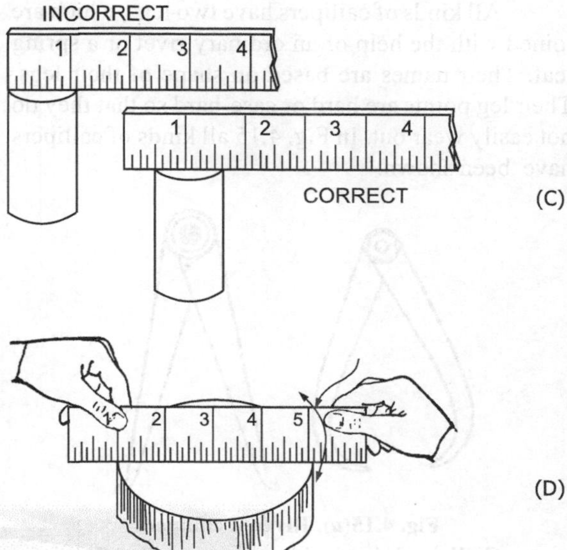

Fig. 4.14 Methods of taking measurement

The following points should be borne in mind while taking measurement with a steel foot rule :

1. Measurement should be taken by keeping the steel foot rule erect on the job and not by laying it down on the job.
2. As far as possible measurement should be taken from the corner of the steel foot rule.
3. We should save the steel foot rule from getting rusted.
4. Steel foot rule should be kept separate from other tools so that it does not get any scratches.
5. Steel foot rule should not be used as a screw driver otherwise its corners would be spoiled.
6. Steel foot rule should not be hit at a hard thing.
7. After using it steel foot rule should be cleaned properly and kept at its place.

Callipers

We can easily take measurement of a rectangular job with any foot rule but it requires a great deal of experience to take outside and inside measurement of a round job. Even there is doubt regarding the accuracy of measurement taken in this manner. Therefore, callipers are used for taking measurement of round jobs. Calliper is one of the measuring tools, which takes measurement in an indirect way. This is generally made from mild steel or carbon steel. Callipers are of two kinds :

1. Outside calliper
2. Inside calliper.

All kinds of callipers have two legs, which are joined with the help of an ordinary rivet or a spring leaf. Their names are based on shape of their legs. Their leg points are hard or case-hard so that they do not easily wear out. In Fig. 4.15 all kinds of callipers have been shown.

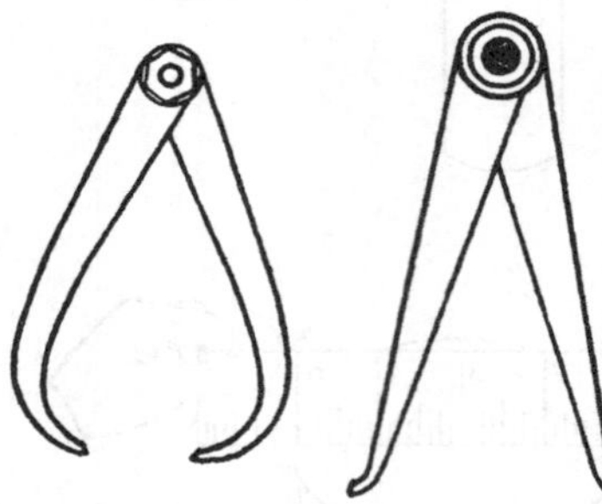

Fig. 4.15(*a*). Riveted calliper

Callipers joined with rivets are called firm joint callipers. Their legs can be adjusted with hands. The legs of spring joint callipers are joined with a pin at the centre, which has a spring in the form of a leaf. Its legs are regulated by a nut mounted on its screw. Its special feature is that its measurement remains static unless its nut is moved. Callipers are used in 6″ and 8″ size.

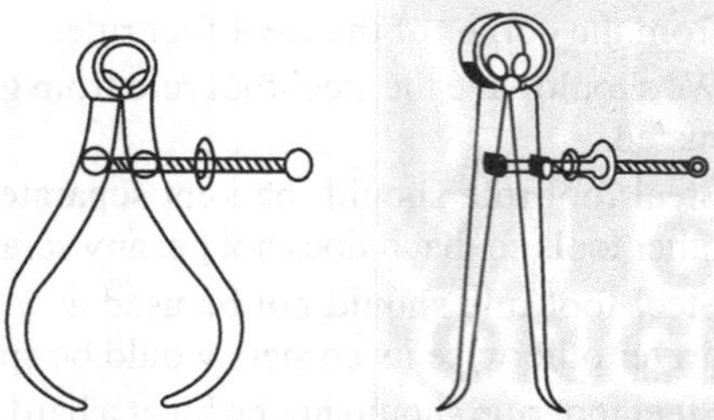

Fig. 4.15(*b*) Spring calliper

Outside Callipers. It is a calliper used for gauging outside measurements or sizes of round jobs. We can also gauge breadth and thickness with it. Both its legs are turned inwards in a round shape. Between these legs the measurement of a job is taken as shown in Fig. 4.16.

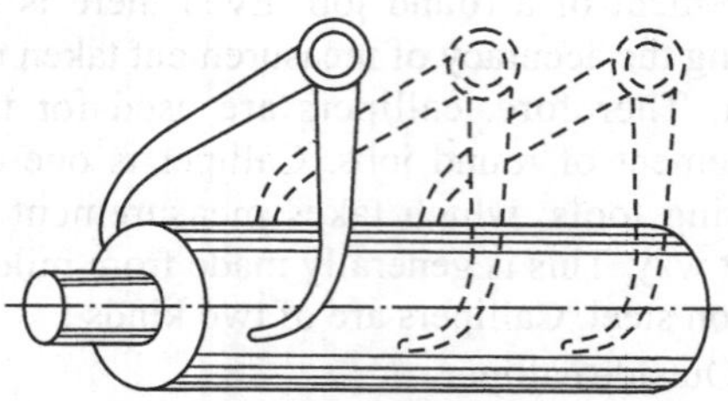

Fig. 4.16(*a*) Gauging measurement of a round job

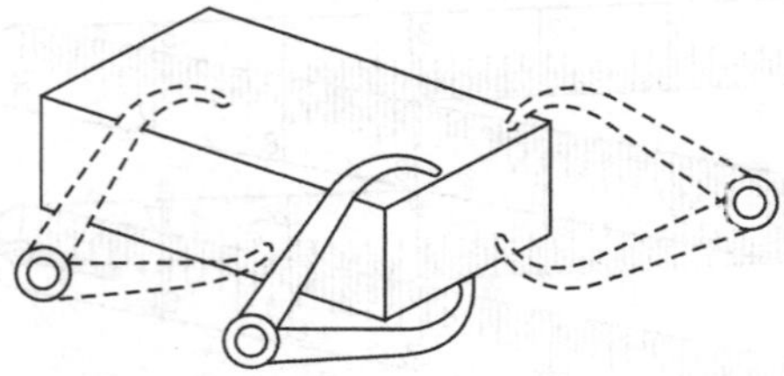

Fig. 4.16(*b*). Measuring a square job

Inside Callipers. It is a calliper with points at the end of the legs turned outward instead of inward, so that it may be used for gauging inside diameters. But we can also gauge the breadth and depth of a slot or slit groove *etc*. Some uses of this caliper have been shown in Fig. 4.17.

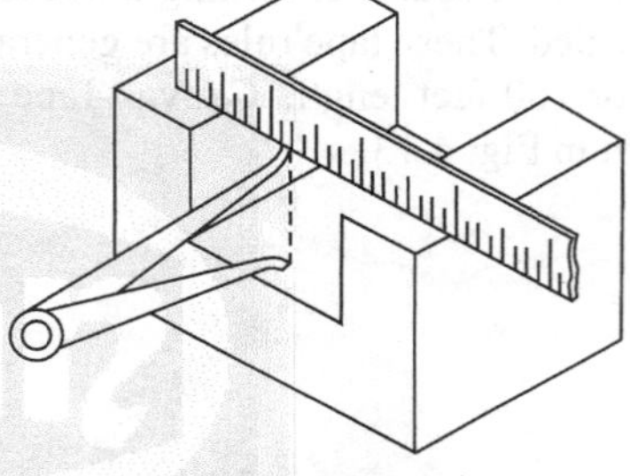

Fig. 4.17(*a*). Gauging depth of a groove

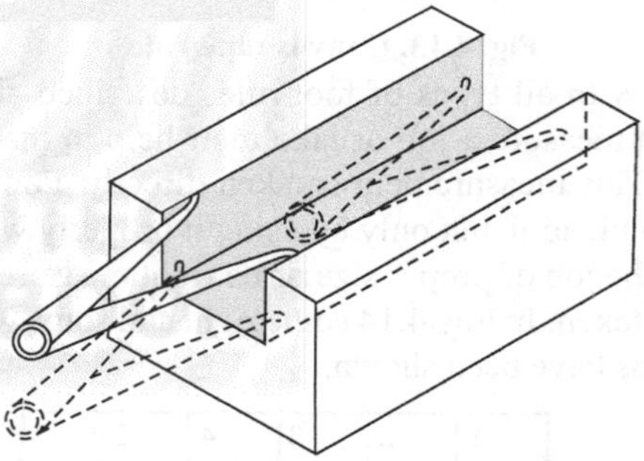

Fig. 4.17(*b*). Gauging breadth of a groove

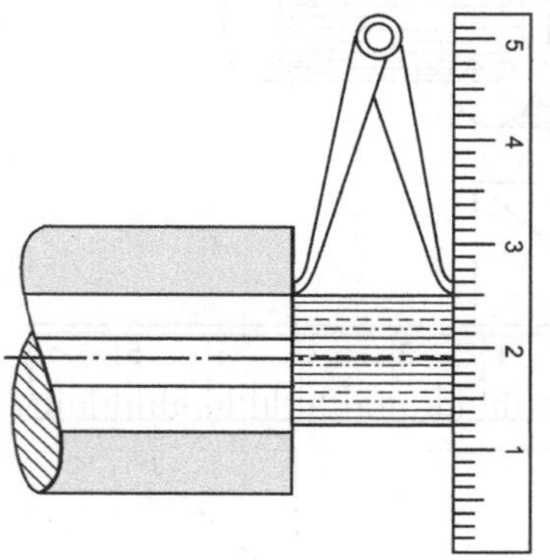

Fig. 4.17(*c*). Gauging length of a groove

Use of Calipers and Precautions

1. Select the calipers according to the job.
2. Open the calipers roughly according to the job.
3. Set the calipers in such a mannner that its legs have only a mild touch with the job.
4. While opening and closing the calipers with firm joint it should be ensured that we do not strike it on any other metal except wood. Otherwise its points would be damaged and we would not be able to gauge correct measurement with it.
5. Spring Calipers should be handled (picked up) in such a way that we are able to move its nut with our thumb and forefinger.
6. After taking correct measurement we should read from the steel rule as shown in Fig. 4.18.

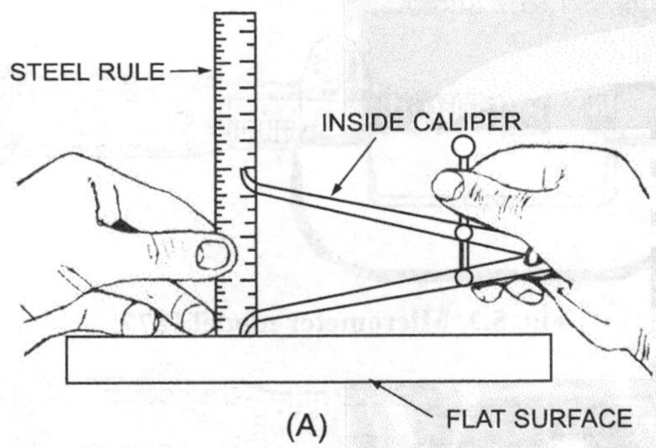

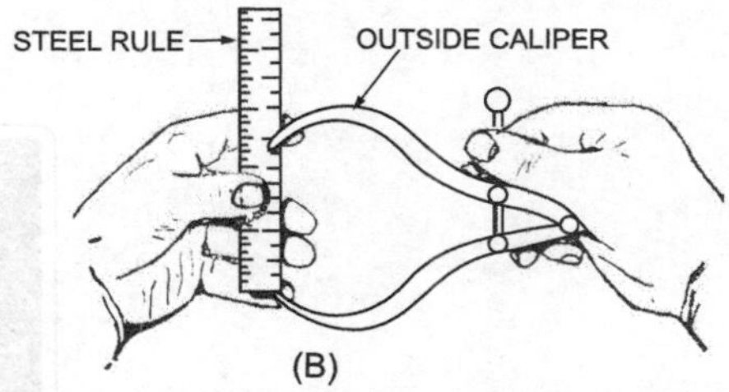

Fig. 4.18. Reading Callipers measurement on rule

7. Measurement with calipers should be taken thrice to get actual measurement.
8. We should not measure a fixed part on a moving machine because by doing so the calipers can fall down and get damaged.
9. At times, for certain purposes, measurement has to be transferred from one caliper to another. In such cases, it should be ensured that the tips of legs of both the calipers meet at the same point as shown in Fig. 4.19.

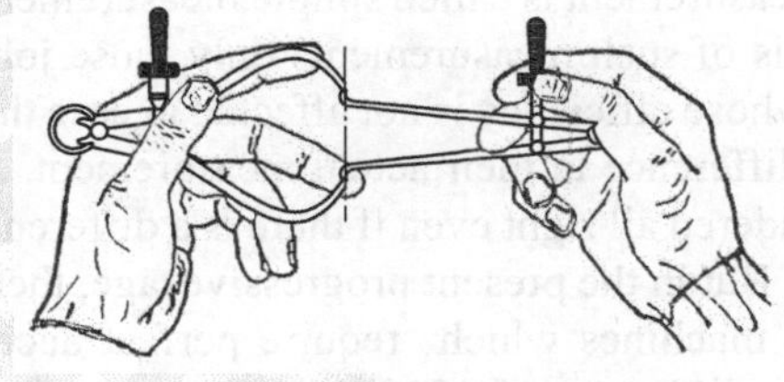

Fig. 4.19. Transferring measurement from one caliper to another

10. Do not tighten or make loose the joint of calipers.

Questions

1. In how many categories the tools used in the fitter trade have been divided ? List them.
2. What are the different types of foot rule ? To what minimum extent graduation is indicated on the steel foot rule ?
3. Name the different types of calipers.
4. What is the method of taking measurement with outside and inside caliper ?
5. What function is performed by Jenny Caliper ? How does it function ? What is its other name ?

5

Precision Measuring Tools

In the previous chapter foot rule and caliper were discussed. These instruments are generally used in the workshops to measure different jobs. We can measure the job with the aid of these tools minimum upto $\frac{1}{64}''$ or half milimeter *i.e.,* 0.5 mm. This measurement is called simple measurement. On the basis of such measurements only those jobs are made whose efficiency is not affected in case there is slight difference in their actual measurement. A job is considered all right even if there is a difference of 0.010″. But in the present progressive age, there are several machines which require perfect accuracy. Even the difference of 0.010″ in their measurement is not acceptable. For obtaining such perfect accuracy precision measuring tools are manufactured. Micrometer is one such precision measuring tool for taking direct measurement.

History of Micrometer. Micrometer was invented in 1848 by a scientist named Jean Palmar in France who had settled in America. Production of micrometer was taken up in 1870 in England by Brown and Sharp Company and named it after the name of its inventor as "Palmar Micrometer". In 1877 it was available in improved form and a model or sample of micrometer was made on this basis the modern micrometer began to be manufactured in different countries all over the world. The model of the micrometers mentioned above have been shown in Figs. 5.1, 5.2 and 5.3.

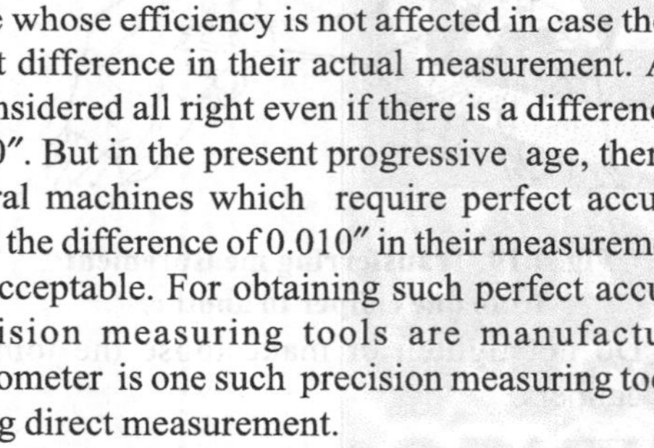

Fig. 5.1. Palmer micrometer

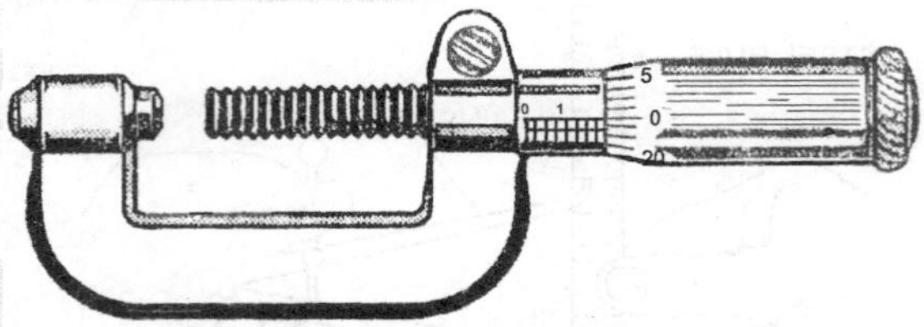

Fig. 5.2. Micrometer model 1877

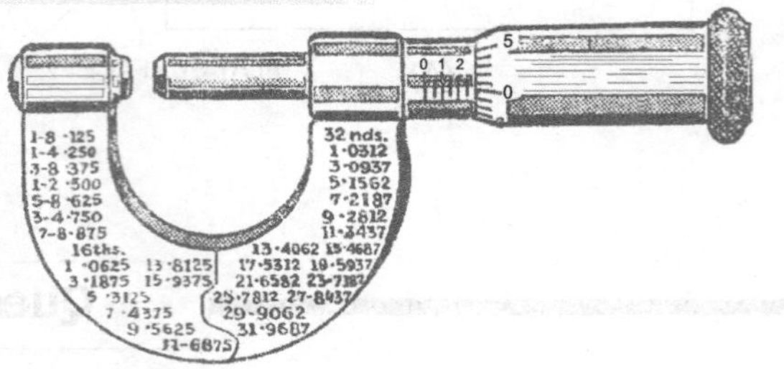

Fig. 5.3. Micrometer model 1885

Principle of Micrometer. Micrometer is made on the basis of nut and screw bolts. You must be familiar with the screw bolt. It contains threads cut at an equal distance. Likewise threads are also there at equal distance in the nut. When we fit the nut on the bolt and revolve it, it starts advancing forward or backward. The distance from a point on a screw thread to a corresponding point on the next turn is called the pitch of the screw. In a single thread the pitch is the amount of advance in one revolution.

In other words, the "pitch" of a "single" type thread is the distance of the centre of one thread from the centre of an adjoining one. The bolt having a single start and its lead and pitch are equal. The distance a screw advances when given a single complete turn is called lead.

In actual micrometer this principle has been adopted on the basis of Fig. 5.4.

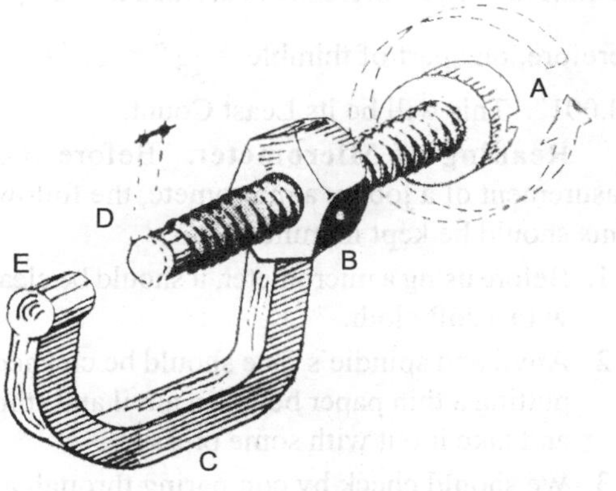

Fig. 5.4. Design of the basis of measurement

In Fig. 5.4, bolt "A" is fitted in nut "B". With nut B, frame C is joined. When head of bolt A completes a turn, the end D of bolt moves towards or opposite anvil E in linear motion. Thus space for measuring of job is created between the bolt edge D and anvil E.

Construction of Micrometer. When we look at a micrometer (outside), we observe that five parts are visible in it. These have been illustrated in Fig. 5.5 below :

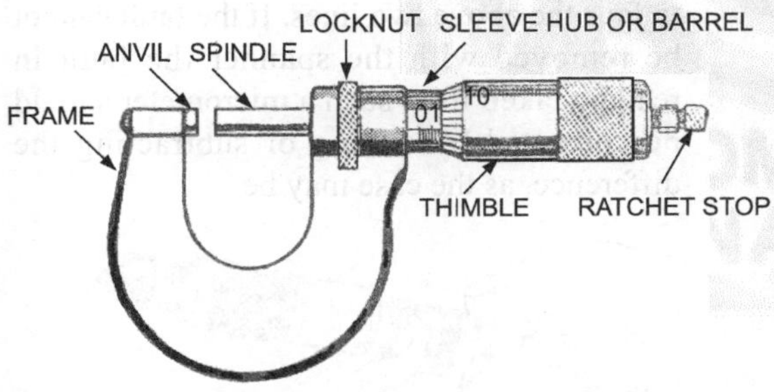

Fig. 5.5. Outside micrometer

1. Frame	2. Anvil
3. Spindle	4. Sleeve or Barrel
5. Thimble	6. Lock nut
7. Ratchet stop.	

1. **Frame.** This part is in "U" shape or in a shape according to our needs. This is one of the main parts of a Micrometer. This is made of cast steel, aluminium, alloy or cast-iron. It is galvanised or it has some other anti-corrosive treatment to save it from rusting. At one end on the frame there is an anvil and the other end has a hole, from where spindle comes out. The range of measurement of the frame is indicated on the frame itself. At times, it also contains a conversion table of inches into decimals for our convenience.
2. **Anvil.** It is a small round part made of hard steel. It is finished with high accuracy. The job is measured by placing it between anvil and spindle. Both have tips made of chromium in order to avoid wear out.
3. **Spindle.** This part is according to the diameter of the anvil but is more than anvil's length. Nearly half of spindle is outside the frame and the rest has 40 threads per inch (T.P.I.). On the part having thread there is a thimble and a ratchet is fixed on the other edge.
4. **Sleeve or Barrel.** It is a hollow part which meets at frame towards spindle. It has threads at the scale of 40 threads per inch (T.P.I.). On these threads the spindle moves forward backwards. There is a line drawn towards outside, which is known as Datum line. (Datum line is any base or fundamental line from which dimensions are taken or graphic calculations are made.). This line has a marking based on an inch divided in 10 parts *i.e.*, one part is equal to $\frac{1}{10}''$. This $\frac{1}{10}$ part is further divided into 4 parts and indicated on the line. This part is equal to $\frac{1}{10}'' \times \frac{1}{4}'' = \frac{1}{40}''$ or 0.025.
5. **Thimble.** This is also a hollow part. It remains fixed on spindle. Its edge on the spindle side has bevel or taper and this end is divided into 25 or 50 equal parts and indicated there. Each fine marking signs are indicated in *local measurements*. On the other end knurling on about $\frac{2}{3}$ part which enables it to revolve is done. When it is revolved, the spindle too revolves with it and it gains linear motion *i.e.*, it moves onwards or backwards.
6. **Lock Nut.** Lock nut is provided to keep the micrometer fixed so that reading can be done easily and without any difficulty. It is fixed on the edge, on the spindle side of the frame in the form of *asterisk* round ring. It is knurled towards the outside. By using a lock nut, we do not need to set micrometer again and again for the same measurement.
7. **Ratchet Stop.** At the last end of the micrometer this part is fixed duly knurled. When the correct

measurement of the job is indicated on the micrometer (after the movement of the thimble) this part gives the sound, of kit kit. In the absence of the ratchet stop one may take the reading by exerting more pressure on thimble or the pressure may less. In this case, there is possibility of difference in measurement. Ratchet stop ensures same measurement whosoever takes it.

Micrometer Graduation. As already mentioned, graduation is indicated at two places on a micrometer :

1. Barrel or Sleeve Graduation.
2. Thimble graduation.

Barrel or Sleeve Graduation. In metric micrometer, on datum line 25 mm is divided into 25 equal parts. Local scale is indicated after each 5 such parts. This graduation is above the line. Milimeter is divided into two parts and marking indicated below the datum line which are equal to $\frac{1}{2}$ mm. The marking above the datum line is called Main Division and the small marking below the datum line are called Sub Division. Similarly, in inch micrometer, an inch is divided into 10 equal parts and its marking is indicated which have the local measure or scale. The parts are called Main Division. This main division is further divided into four equal parts and marked. Its one part is called Sub Division.

Thimble Graduation. In metric micrometer, a buck shot can be divided into 0 to 50 parts. Local scale is marked on its each 5th mark. One such mark is called a Thimble Division. Similarly, in Inch Micrometer, the circumference of thimble can be divided into 25 equal parts. Local scale is also marked on its each fifth part.

Least Count. The smallest measurement that can be measured with an instrument is called Least Count.

Least Count of Metric Micrometer. As already told in graduation, if we give one full round to thimble, its spindle moves $\frac{1}{2}$ mm forward or backward. Therefore, one part of thimble = $\frac{1}{2} \times \frac{1}{50} = \frac{1}{100}$ or 0.001 mm. This is its least count.

Least Count of inch Micrometer. As already told in graduation, one complete round of thimble moves its spindle $\frac{1}{40}''$ forward or backwards and thimble's circumference is divided into 25 parts.

Therefore, one part of thimble = $\frac{1}{40}'' \times \frac{1}{25}'' = \frac{1}{1000}''$ or 0.001″. This will be its Least Count.

Reading of Micrometer. Before taking measurement of a job by a micromete, the followmg points should be kept in mind :

1. Before using a micrometer, it should be cleaned with a soft cloth.
2. Anvil and spindle's face should be cleaned by putting a thin paper between anvil and spindle and take it out with some pressure.
3. We should check by comparing through anvil and spindle face ratchet stop whether the base line tallies with the "0" line made on the thimble edge or not when the ratchet produces sound. If both the lines are straight in one direction then we should take the micrometer as faultless. If these lines do not tally then we should take the micrometer is having some fault and try to remove the fault. Each micrometer has a "C" or hook spanner, which is fixed in the hole provided in the sleeve and thimble and the defect should be removed by comparing face to face the above two lines. If the fault cannot be removed with the spanner the fault in reading taken from such a micrometer should be corrected by adding or subtracting the difference, as the case may be.

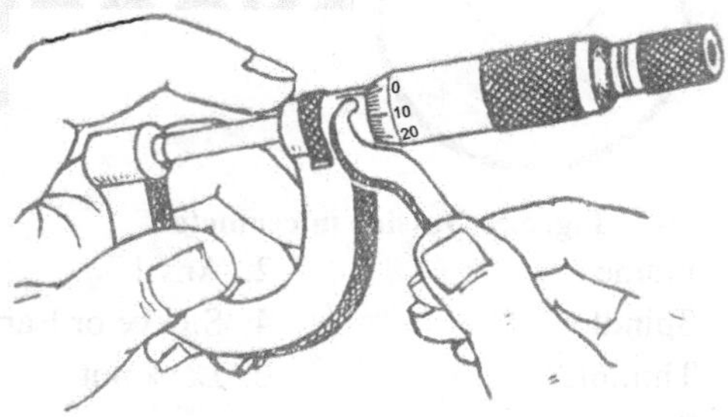

Fig. 5.6. Correction of fault

4. Before taking measurement with a micrometer we should open it slightly more than the size of the job.
5. The job should be brought between spindle and the anvil and then with the help of ratchet the thimble should be moved. When the ratchet stop starts producing sound, lock nut should be tighten and reading should be taken.

Range of Micrometer. The limit of measurement of an outside micrometer is upto one inch or 25 mm. For reading beyond this limit, other micrometers of different limits are used which can take measurement upto 24″. These micrometers take measurement upto the limit 0 to 1″, 1″ to 2″ and 2″ to 5″. Similarly, the metric micrometers take measurement upto the limit of 0 to 25, 25 to 50 mm *etc.* According to the size of the job, we select the micrometer.

Reading. For taking reading from an inch micrometer, first of all we should write down the minimum measurement of its limit, multiply fully open main division of the barrel or sleeve with 0.1 and multiply the fully opened sub division of the barrel by 0.025. Now we should multiply the point meeting at the base line of the thimble by 0.001. Similarly, in order to take measurement from a mm micrometer, first we take down the minimum measurement of its limit, write the main division of the barrel, multiply the sub division of the barrel by 0.5, multiply the point meeting at the base line of thimble by 0.1. Some example of recording the reading of micrometers is given below :

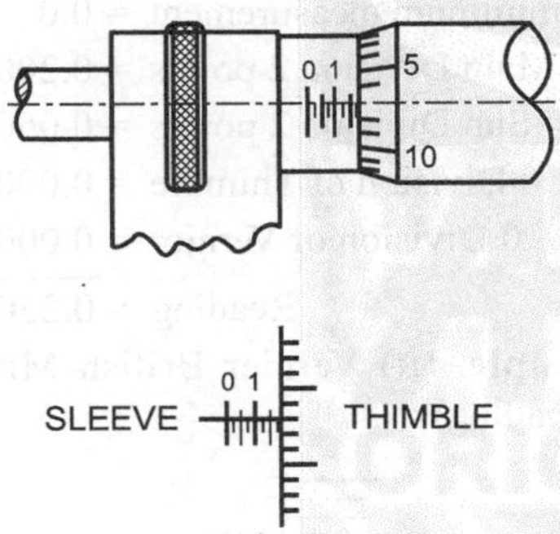

Fig. 5.7. Example (*i*)

Example. (*i*) British Micrometer (0.178″ Reading). According to Figure :

Minimum measurement = 0.0
One main division = 0.100
Three sub divisions = 0.075
Three divisions of thimble = 0.003
Reading = 0.178″

Example. (*ii*) British Micrometer (0.596″ Reading). As per figure :

Minimum measurement = 0.0
Five main divisions = 0.500
Three sub divisions = 0.075
21 divisions of thimble = 0.021
Reading = 0.596″

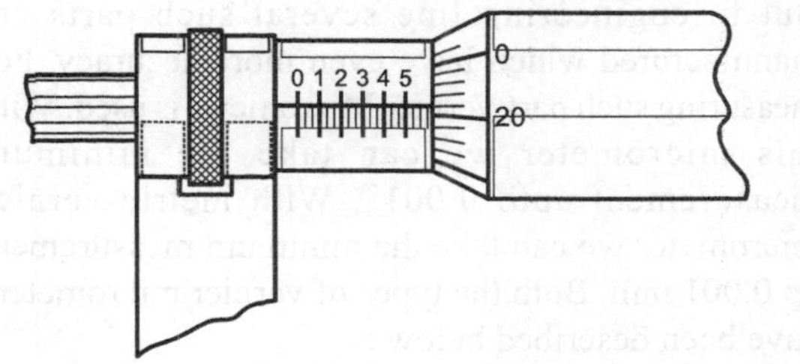

Fig. 5.8. Example (*ii*)

Example. (*iii*) Metric Micrometer (7.47 mm Reading)

Minimum measurement = 0.00
7 main divisions = 07.00
0 Sub division = 00.00
47 divisions of thimble = 00.47
Reading = 7.47

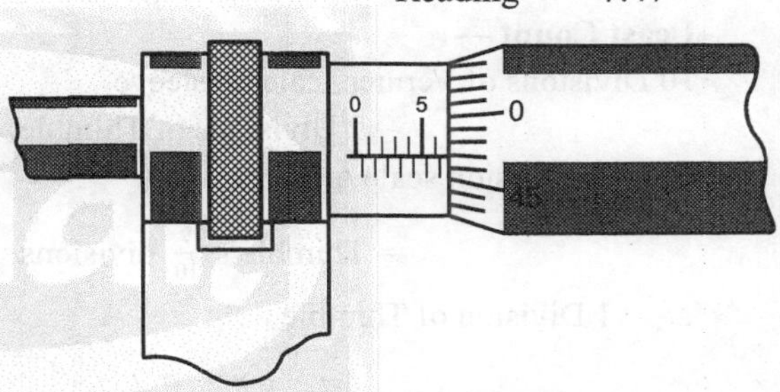

Fig. 5.9. Example (*iii*)

Example. (*iv*) Metric Micrometer (5.78 mm Reading) :

Minimum measurement = 0.0
5 Main divisions = 5.0
1 Sub division = 0.50
28 Divisions of thimble = 0.28
Reading = 5.78 mm.

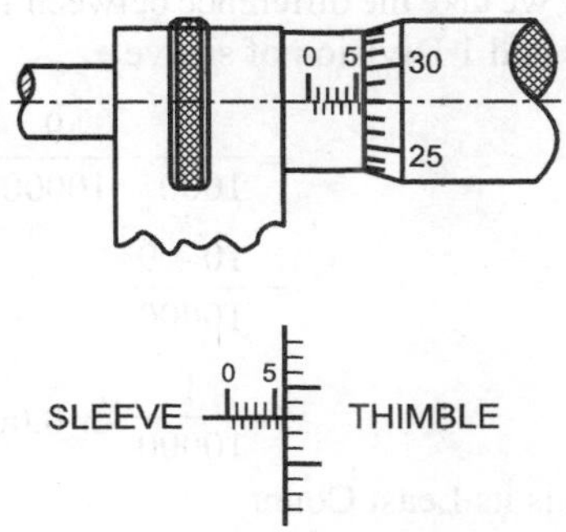

Fig. 5.10. Example (*iv*)

Vernier Micrometer. The micrometer mentioned above can take minimum measurement upto 1000th part of an inch *i.e.* $\frac{1}{1000}$″ or 0.001 mm.

But in engineering line several such parts are manufactured which have even more accuracy. For measuring such part Vernier Micrometer is used. With this micrometer we can take the minimum measurement upto 0.001″. With metric vernier micrometer we can take the minimum measurement up 0.001 mm. Both the types of vernier micrometers have been described below :

British or Inches Vernier Micrometer. Its make-up is similar to the ordinary micrometer. Graduation on sleeve and thimble is also similarly marked but above the Datum line on the sleeve itself 10 lines are drawn parallel to the Datum line. This type of micrometer is called Vernier Micrometer. This scale made by dividing the distance of a parts of thimble into 10 equal parts. On the basis of the difference between these two scales readings taken.

Least Count —

10 Divisions of Vernier scale on sleeve

$$= 9 \text{ Divisions of Thimble}$$

$\therefore$ 1 Division scale on sleeve

$$= \text{Thimble's } \frac{9}{10} \text{ divisions}$$

$\therefore$ 1 Division of Thimble

$$= \frac{1}{1000}''$$

$\therefore$ $\frac{9}{10}$ Divisions of Thimble

$$= \frac{1}{1000} \times \frac{9}{10}$$

$$= \frac{9}{10000}$$

Now we take the difference between 1 Division of Thimble and 1 Division of sleeve

$$= \frac{1}{1000} - \frac{9}{10000}$$

$$= \frac{10-9}{10000}$$

$$= \frac{1}{10000} \text{ or } 0.0001''$$

This is its Least Count.

Method of reading British Vernier Micrometer

(*i*) For taking reading of this micrometer, write the minimum measurement according to the limit.

(*ii*) Write down the main part of the sleeve which is outside the thimble.

(*iii*) Write down the open sub-parts on the sleeve.

(*iv*) Write down that parts of thimble which is joined to the Datum Line. If no part is joined to the Datum Line then write the part, which has crossed the Datum Line.

(*v*) The line from vernier calliper which meets thimble's part, write its value as divided by 10000. You will get the measurement by adding them all.

Example. (*i*) British Micrometer (0.2500" Reading)

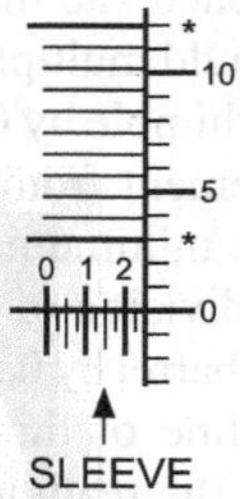

Fig. 5.11. Example (*i*)

The minimum measurement	= 0.0
Main Division 2 points	= 0.2000
Sub Division 2 points	= 0.0500
0 Division of Thimble	= 0.0000
0 Division of Vernier	= 0.0000
Reading	= 0.2500″

Example. (*ii*) Vernier British Micrometer (0.2507″ Reading)

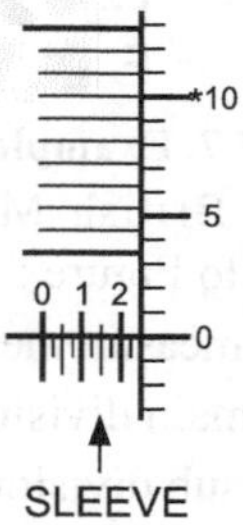

Fig. 5.12. Example (*ii*)

The minimum measurement	= 0.0
Main Division 2 Points	= 0.2000
Sub Division 2 Points	= 0.0500
0 Division of Thimble	= 0.0000
0 Division of Vernier	= 0.0007
Reading	= 0.2507″

Metric Vernier Micrometer. This micrometer is also similar to the ordinary metric micrometer. The only difference is that 10 lines are drawn parallel to the Datum Line on the sleeve. These 10 lines are equal to the 9 divisions of thimble or 0.09 mm. We can take the minimum measurement upto $\frac{1}{1000}$ mm or 0.001 mm. This is called its least count.

Least Count

$\therefore$ 10 divisions of vernier scale on the sleeve

= Thimble's 9 divisions

$\therefore$ 1 division of vernier scale on sleeve

$= \frac{9}{10}$ division of thimble

Because 1 division of thimble

$= 0.01$ mm or $\frac{1}{100}$ mm.

$\therefore$ 9 Divisions of Thimble

$$= \frac{1}{100} \times \frac{9}{10} = \frac{9}{1000} \text{ mm}$$

Now take the difference between 1 division of thimble and 1 division of vernier scale

$$= \frac{1}{100} - \frac{9}{1000}$$

$$= \frac{10-1}{1000} = \frac{1}{1000} \text{ mm}$$

This is its Least Count

The Method of reading Metric Vernier :

(1) Write the open parts on the sleeve.

(2) Write the sub part on the sleeve.

(3) Write the signs of the periphery of the thimble.

(4) Write the division of vernier scale.

Example. (*i*) Vernier Metric Micrometer (4.600 mm Reading)

4 Points of the Main Division	=	4.000
1 Point of the Sub-Division	=	0.500
10 Divisions of Thimble	=	0.100
0 Division of Vernier	=	0.000
Reading	=	4.600 mm.

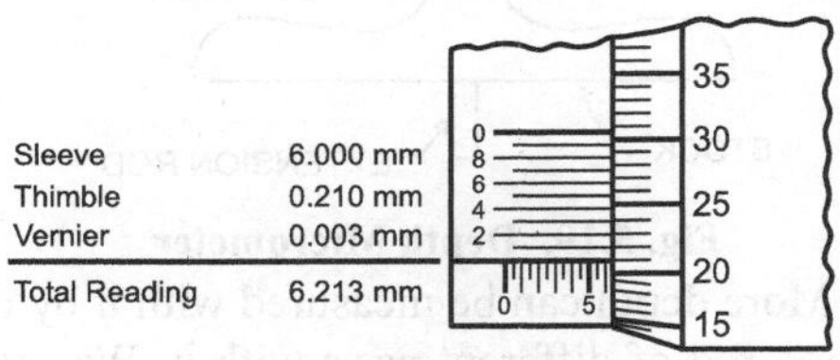

Fig. 5.13. Example (*i*)

Example. (*ii*) Vernier Metric Micrometer (6.213 mm reading)

6 Divisions of Main Division	=	6.000
0 Divisions of Sub Division	=	0.000
21 Divisions of Thimble	=	0.210
3 Divisions of Vernier Scale	=	0.003
Reading	=	6.213 mm

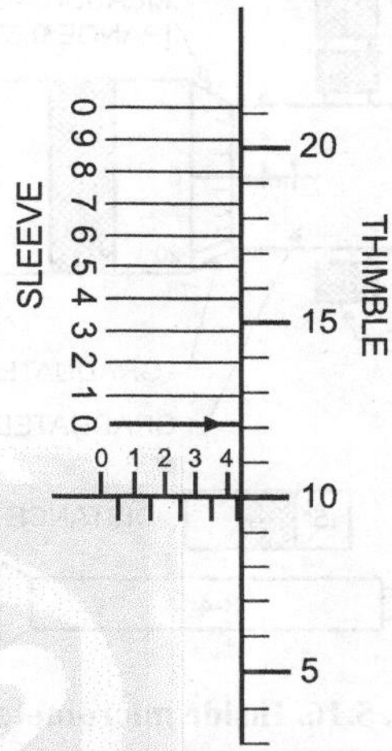

Fig. 5.14. Example (*ii*)

Example. (*iii*) Vernier Metric Micromete (4.007 mm reading)

4 Divisions of Main Division	=	4.000
0 Division of Sub Division	=	0.000
0 Division of Thimble	=	0.000
7 Divisions of Vernier Scale	=	0.007
Reading	=	4.007 mm

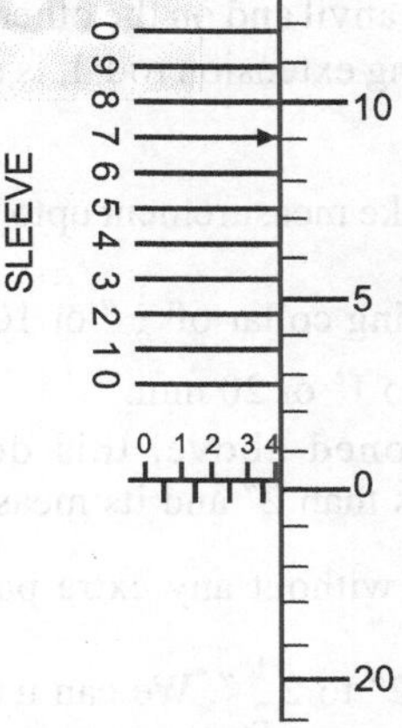

Fig. 5.15. Example (*iii*)

Inside Micrometer. For taking minute or very minute measurement of a job, from outside especially a round job, micrometer is used. In the same way, for taking the inside measurement of a job inside micrometer is used. But an ordinary inside micrometer can not take the minimum measurement of 2 inches or 50 mm. Inside micrometer contains the following parts, which have been shown in Fig. 5.16 :

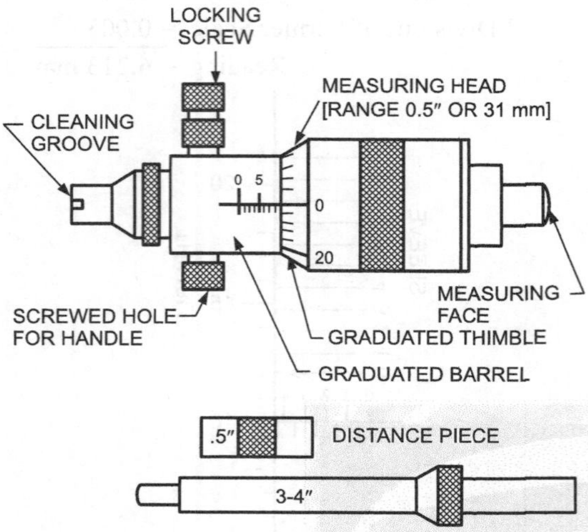

Fig. 5.16. Inside micrometer

1. Handle
2. Extension Rod
3. Spacing Socket or Collar
4. Sleeve
5. Thimble
6. Anvil
7. Locking Screw.

In Fig. 5.16 in the Inside Micrometer sleeve and thimble also look like Outside Micrometer. On the one end it has anvil and on the other end there is a provision for fixing extension rod. It is used by fixing a handle.

This can take measurement upto $\frac{1}{2}$″ or 10 mm.

After fixing spacing collar of $\frac{1}{2}$″ or 10 mm we take measurement upto 1″ or 20 mm.

As mentioned above, this does not take measurement less than 2″ and its measuring limit is $\frac{1}{2}$″. In this way, without any extra part it can take measurement of 2″ to $2\frac{1}{2}$″. We can use the spacing collar for measuring 2″ to 3″. For taking further measurements extension rod has to be used at distance of every inch, which are 2″ to 3″, 3″ to 4″, 4″ to 5″ and 5″ to 6″.

Example. Reading 0.2505.

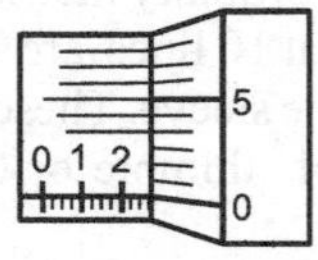

Fig. 5.17. Example (*i*)

Small Inside Micrometer. This micrometer is used for measurement less than those mentioned above. It can take the minimum measurement of 0.200″ or 5 mm. Its sleeve and thimble are similar to that of an outside micrometer and two jaws are there in place of the frame. Graduation is in the opposited directions as shown in Fig. 5.18.

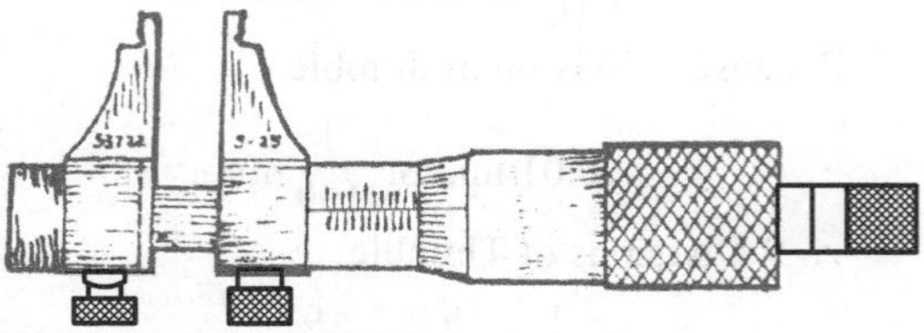

Fig. 5.18 Small Inside Micrometer

This micrometer is available in different measuring limits. For example, 0.200″ to 1″, 1″ to 2″ and 2″ to 3″ *etc.* and in metric system 5 to 25, 25 to 50 and 50 to 75 mm. *etc.*

In addition to the above mentioned inside and outside micrometers, there are some more micrometers for performing specific purposes.

Depth Micrometer. It is used for measuring the depth of a hole, slot and groove. Its thimble and sleeve are similar to outside micrometer but graduation on the sleeve is reverse. Instead of frame it has a steel base, which stays onto the jobs.

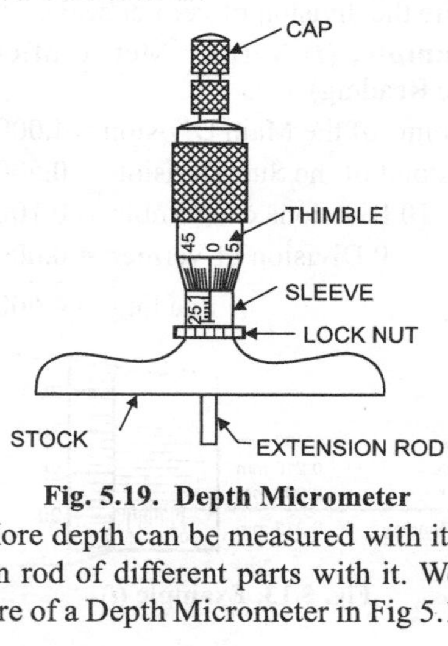

Fig. 5.19. Depth Micrometer

More depth can be measured with it by using extension rod of different parts with it. We can see the picture of a Depth Micrometer in Fig 5.19 above.

Screw Thread Micrometer. We can measure pitch diameter of "V" shaped threads with this micrometer. It is of the same shape as an outside micrometer but its spindle is built in 55° angle in conical shape as shown in Fig. 5.20. In the same way, anvil is also conical. Thus spindle and anvil can go into the complete depth of the thread groove. Generally one can take measurement of 3-4 types of threads with this micrometer. For the remaining types of threads different micrometers are used.

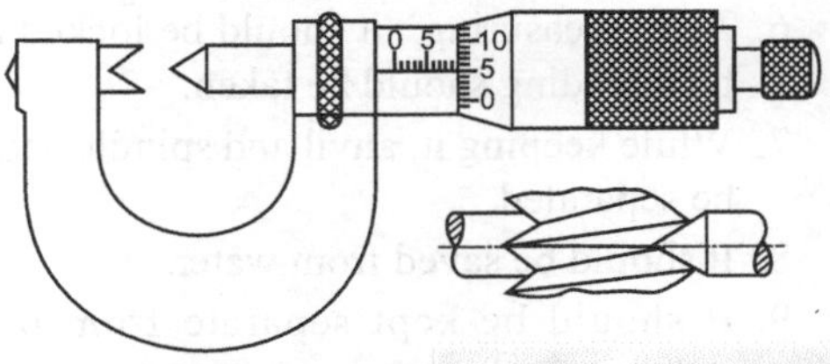

Fig. 5.20. Screw Thread Micrometer

Tube Micrometer. Tubes and thin pipes are measured with this tube micrometer. In this micrometer anvil is fitted to the frame at 90° angle and it is slightly more in length as shown in Fig. 5.21. Measuring process is similar to that of outside micrometer.

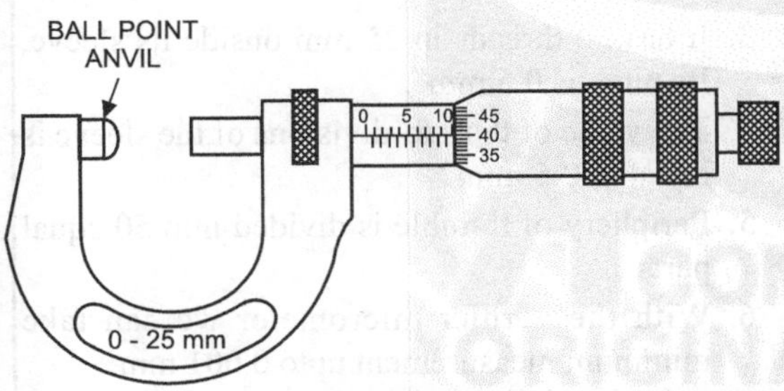

Fig. 5.21. Tube Micrometer

Sheet Micrometer. This is a special type "U" shape micrometer. Its depth is 2″ or 4″.

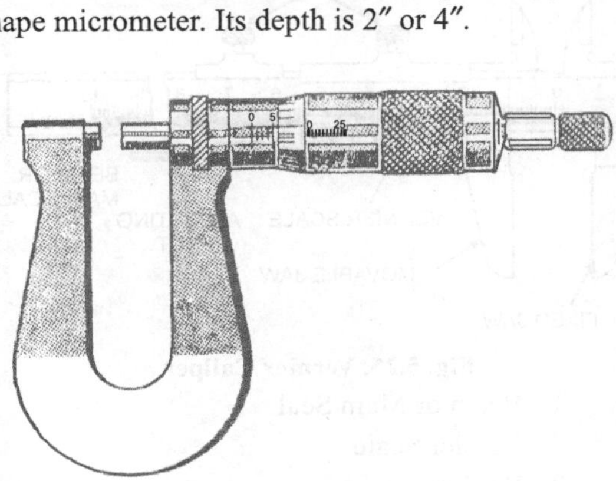

Fig. 5.22. Sheet Micrometer

Its frame is made of steel after forging. We can take measurement of sheets. The measuring limit of 2″ deep micrometer is $\frac{1}{2}$ ″ or 0.5″. Measuring limit of 4″ deep micrometer is 1″. Metric micrometer of this type are also available in metric units. Sheet micrometer has been shown in Fig. 5.22.

Paper Micrometer. This micrometer is used in the paper industry. Its shape is almost similar to the outside micrometer but pads are built over spindle and anvil. Between these we can easily measure the paper. Like other micrometers graduation is indicated in British system *i.e.,* inch or metric system. This has been illustrated in Fig. 5.23.

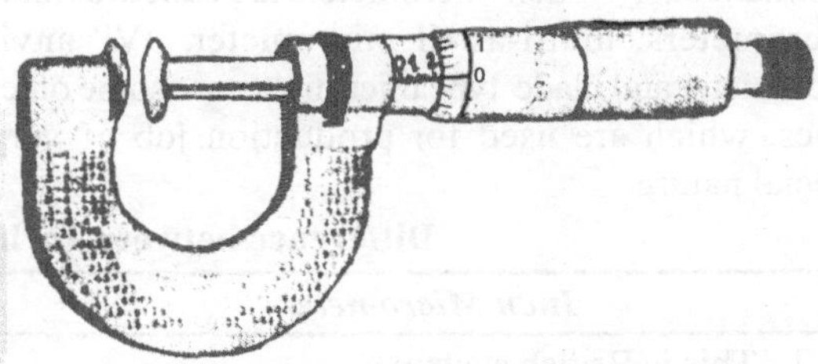

Fig. 5.23 Paper Micrometer

Digit Micrometer. From the point of view of easiness this micrometer is very useful. Its frame is similar to outside micrometer which has a dial on the side of spindle. This dial is connected to spindle through gears. When a job is measured with this micrometer, along with sleeve and thimble, its reading can be had from dial also. This type of micrometers are also available in inches and milimeters. The main advantage of this micrometer is that there are no chances of mistake in addition as the measurement is indicated on its dial itself. Even if there is less lights reading on this micrometer can be clearly read. It takes less time as well.

Indicator Micrometer. This micrometer works like a comparator. In production works this is used to find limit of the jobs. Its make up is like an outside micrometer and there is an indicator on its frame which has 0 in the centre and graduation on both the sides. On one side sign (–) is indicated and on the other side (+) is indicated and there are two indicators as shown in Fig. 5.24.

When we use it we set the thimble according to the job and lock it and the needles are set according to high and low limit. If there is a difference in the job, these indicator needles indicate it in (–) or (+) while using it we need not set the measurement again and again. Therefore, besides efficiency in production, it saves time also.

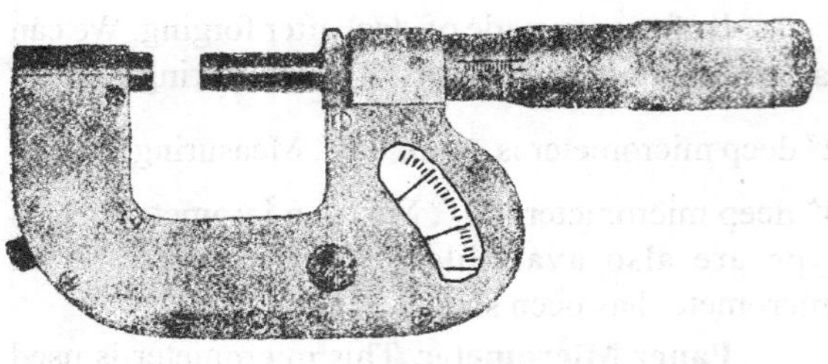

Fig. 5.24. Indicator Micrometer

In addition to these micrometers, adjustable micrometers where anvils of different sizes can be fixed are also used. For certain jobs Hub micrometers are also used. There are other micrometers which can take measurements in inches and milimeters simultaneously. Such micrometers are called combi-micrometers, multi-anvil micrometer, "V" anvil micrometer and blade type micrometer are some other types, which are used for production job of very special nature.

Precautions for Micrometers

1. Before using it, it should be properly cleaned with a soft cloth.
2. Before use, it should be ensured that it is faultless.
3. It should not be used on machines in operation or on rough surface.
4. Before measuring, job should be properly cleaned.
5. For setting it, Ratchet Stop should be used.
6. After measuring, it should be locked and then reading should be taken.
7. While keeping it, anvil and spindle should be separated.
8. It should be saved from water.
9. It should be kept separate from other ordinary tools.
10. We should never put heavy oil in it.

Difference between Inch and Millimetre Micrometer

Inch Micrometer	*Milimeter Micrometer*
1. This is British system.	1. This is an international system.
2. The minimum measurement that can be taken with this mnicrometer is 0.001″.	2. This can take the minimum measurement upto 0.01 mm.
3. There is a thread of 40 T.P.I. in its sleeve and its pitch is 1/40″.	3. It has 50 threads in 25 mm onside its sleeve. Its pitch is 0.5 mm″.
4. The value of the sub-divisions of the sleeve is equal to 0.025.	4. The value of the sub-divisions of the sleeve is equal to 0.5 mm.
5. Periphery of thimble is divided into 25 equal parts.	5. Periphery of thimble is divided into 50 equal parts.
6. The minimum measurement that can be taken with a vernier micrometer is 0.001″.	6. With the vernier micrometer we can take minimum measurement upto 0.001 mm.

Vernier Caliper. It is an instrument for measuring precision jobs. We can take measurement in metric as well as British system with this micrometer. It can take measurement of internal and external length, breadth *etc.* upto 0.001″ in British system and upto 0.002 mm in Metric system. This instrument was invented in 1630 A.D. by a great mathematician Parry Vernier in France. The instrument has been named after his name. Its measuring limit is far greater in comparison to a micrometer. These are made in the range of 6 to 48″ *i.e.,* 150 mm to 1200 mm such as 6″, 8″, 10″ *etc. i.e.,* with difference of 2″ each and so on and 150, 200, 250 mm *etc. i.e.,* with difference of 50 mm each.

Vernier caliper is made by assembling several different parts. It contains the following main parts, which have been shown in Fig. 5.25.

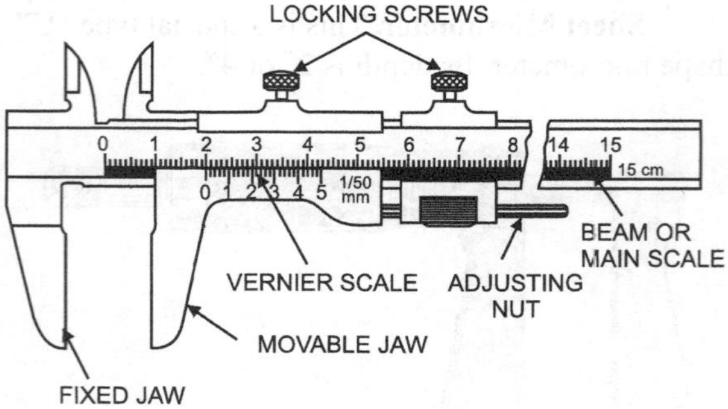

Fig. 5.25. Vernier Caliper

1. Beam or Main Seal
2. Vernier Scale
3. Fix Jaw
4. Movable Jaw

5. Locking Screw
6. Adjusting Nut
7. Fine Adjusting Unit.

Beam or Main Scale. This is a "L" shaped hand made of stainless steel or good alloy steel. It contains main graduation. The graduation on the complete scale is divided by marking at every inch. One inch is divided into ten equal parts. Local scale is also written. This one part is further divided into four equal parts and thin marking is indicated but these signs have no local scale written there.

Vernier Scale. This is an important part of the vernier caliper. It contains vernier scale.

Movable Jaw is attached to it. This scale is divided into 25 equal parts which are equal to 24 parts of the main scale.

Fix Jaw. Built at 90° angle on an edge of the beam, this part remains stationary at the time of measurement. Its jib is built in such a way that it can take inside as well as outside measurement easily.

Movable Jaw. This jaw remains with vernier scale. It also contains a jib made like a fixed jaw for touching the job.

Locking Screw. After setting the movable jaw on the job with the help of these screws the jaw is locked so that reading remains permanent otherwise there are chances of its change.

Adjusting Nut. It is also called fine adjusting nut. It connects the fine adjusting unit with the vernier scale. It is used for pushing vernier scale to take precision measurement.

Fine Adjusting Unit. Movable jaw is set for precision measurement, with the help of adjusting nut after making this unit stationary.

Principle of Vernier Caliper. It is a measuring tool with which measurement of a job is taken on the basis of difference between two different scales of a measuring tool.

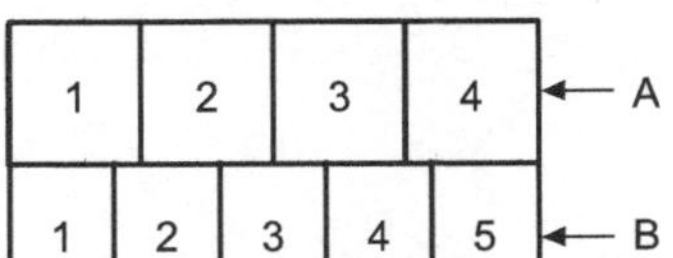

Fig. 5.26. Principle of Vernier Caliper

Out of the two scales of the measuring tool, one is more or less than the other. For example, on the main scale 1 inch has been divided into 4 equal parts and distance of 1 inch on the small vernier scale has been divided into 5 equal parts as shown in Fig. 5.26.

According to the above figure one part of the scale = 1/4″ and one part on the vernier scale = 1/5″.

Therefore difference between the two parts :

$$= \frac{1}{4} - \frac{1}{5} = \frac{5-4}{20} = \frac{1}{20} \text{ or } 0.05''$$

If the lower vernier scale's first part is moved so as to correspond with the first part of the main scale then the lower scale will be pushed 1/20″ towards the right hand. Similarly, if the second part of the lower scale is moved and corresponded with the second part of the upper scale, then the lower scale will be moved 2/20″ = 1/10″ or 0.1. Based on this principle Vernier Caliper has been designed.

In this manner two different scales are used in vernier caliper. Signs of inch and millimeter are indicated on these scales. On the main scale local measurement is indicated at each inch and is divided into 10 equal parts and their local scale is also indicated. Each small part is further divided into 4 parts. Thus distance of an inch is divided into $10 \times 4 = 40$ parts and its smallest part is equal to

$$= \frac{1''}{40} \text{ or } 0.025''$$

Graduation is indicated by dividing the vernier scale into 25 equal parts and the main scale has 24 equal parts. Their difference is known as the least count of the vernier caliper.

Least Count —

$\therefore$ One of the main scales $= \frac{1''}{40}$

24 divisions of the main scale

$$= \frac{1}{40} \times 24 = \frac{24''}{40}$$

$\therefore$ 25 divisions of vernier $= \frac{24''}{40}$

$\therefore$ One divisions of vernier $= \frac{24}{40} \div 25$

$$= \frac{24}{40} \times \frac{1}{25} = \frac{24''}{1000}$$

Now let us see the difference between main scale and vernier scale (least count) :

$$\frac{1}{40} - \frac{24}{1000} = \frac{25-24}{1000} = \frac{1}{1000} \text{ or } 0.001''$$

This is its least count.

In Metric Scale — Generally its least count is 1/50 or 0.02 mm. On the main scale parts of 1/2 mm are indicated. Graduation is done by dividing the distance of 24 divisions of the main scale into 25 divisions of the vernier scale.

$\therefore$ One division of the main scale $= \frac{1}{2}$ mm

$\therefore$ 25 divisions of the vernier scale
= 24 parts of the main scale
or $\frac{24}{2}$ mm

$\therefore$ One division of vernier $= \frac{24}{2} \div 25$

$$= \frac{24}{2} \times \frac{1}{25} = \frac{24}{50} \text{ mm}$$

Now let us find out the difference between main scale and vernier scale (least count) :

$$= \frac{1}{2} - \frac{24}{25} = \frac{25-24}{50} = \frac{1}{50} \text{ or } 0.02 \text{ mm}$$

Method of taking reading from Vernier Caliper

1. Write that part of the scale which contains inch signs and which is on the left hand side of 0, on the vernier scale.
2. Look at the divisions of central distance. How many of them are on the left hand side of 0 of the vernier?
   Their value is 0.1″, 0.2″ *etc.* respectively.
3. Write the small parts of the main scale. Their value is 0.025.
4. Write down the part of the vernier scale which corresponds with the main scale after carefully watching it.
5. The sum total of all the four items written above is reading of the vernier caliper.
   Example. (*i*) 3.565″ Reading

Divisions of an inch on main scale	= 3.000″
5 central divisions on main scale	= 0.500″
2 small divisions on main scale	= 0.050″
15th division of vernier coincides	= 0.015″
Reading	= 3.565″

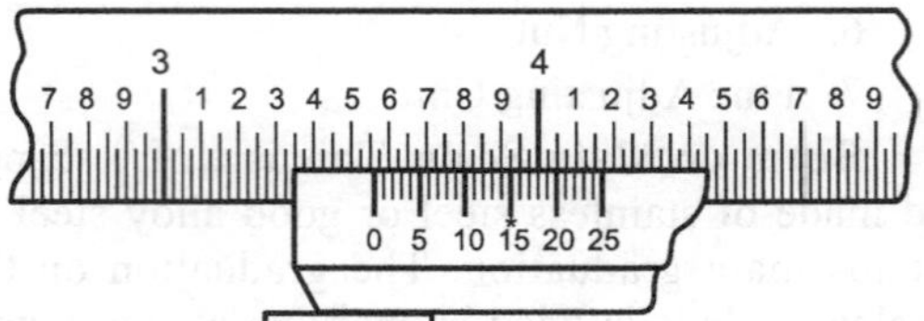

Fig. 5.27. Example (*i*)

Example. (*ii*) 15.38 mm.

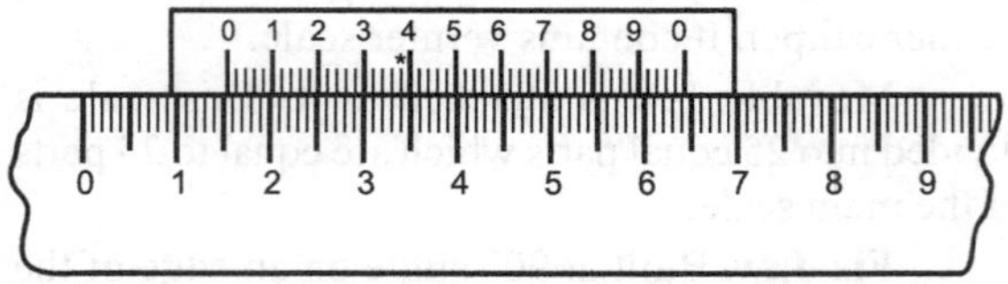

Fig. 5.27. Example (*ii*)

Precautions for Vernier Caliper

1. It is necessary that there is no play in its beam and movable jaw and it could be easily.
2. After long use, the jaw-edges wear out. In such cases, it should be regrinded.
3. A job fixed on a machine in operation should not be measured with it.
4. It should always be kept away from the cutting tools.
5. It is difficult to see the part of vernier scale which meets the main scale. Therefore, it is advisable to use a magnifying glass.
6. Some experience is required for taking measurement with a Vernier Caliper as it is difficult to maintain the contact between jaw and job at the same level throughout. Therefore, we should take reading at least three times.
7. After using it, we should clean it with thinner and keep it in the case.

Difference between Caliper and Micrometer

Vernier Caliper	*Micrometer*
1. Its range varies from 0″ to 48″ or 0 to 1200 mm.	Its range is limited from 0″ to 1″ or 0 to 23 mm. For measurement beyond this we require other micrometers.
2. With this we can measure both the external and internal jobs.	Different micrometers are needed for taking measurement.
3. We can take measurements in inches and mm simultaneously.	Different micrometers are required for measurement in inch and mm.
4. It is easy to make and also costs less.	It is difficult to make and it costs more.
5. Measurement taken by Vernier Caliper is not considered very exact because its touch is not always equal.	Its measurement is considered exact because appropriateness of touch is controlled by ratchet stop.
6. Experience is required to take measurement with this caliper.	It is easy to measure with the micrometer.
7. Its least count is 0.02 mm.	Its least count is 0.01 mm.

Different types of Vernier Calipers. As mentioned above, we can measure all kinds of jobs with the Vernier Calipers. Its jaws are made of different forms, keeping in view the easiness of the job, accuracy of measurement and its utility. On the basis of jaws, vernier calipers are classified as under:

Flat Edge Vernier Caliper. This type of vernier is used for normal functions. This has been illustrated at Fig. 5.27. We can take outer measurement of a job's length, breadth, thickness and diameter *etc*. As the jib of its edge is of special tpye, inner measurement can also be taken with it. But from that measurement the job's breadth has to be substracted. This measurement is often written on the jaw otherwise it should be measured with a micrometer.

Knife Edge Vernier Caliper. The edge of this Vernier Caliper is like a knife. Other parts of this Vernier Caliper are like other Vernier Calipers as shown in Fig. 5.29.

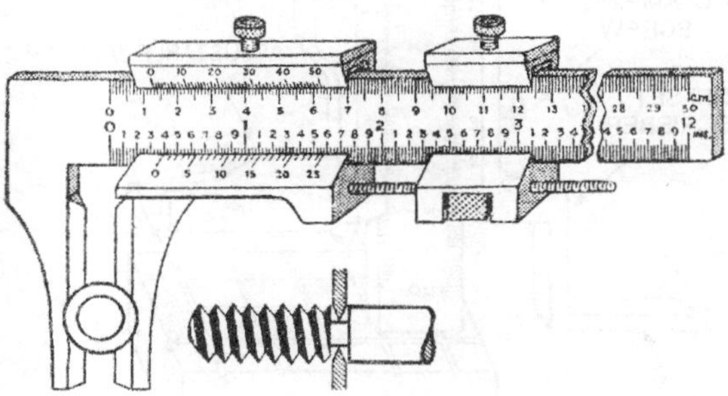

Fig. 5.29. Knife edge vernier caliper

This Vernier Caliper is used for measuring narrow space, distance of holes of I bolt *etc*. Its main shorts-coming is that because of thin edge of its jaw, it wears out quickly and it starts giving inaccurate measurement. It should be used sparingly and carefully.

Flat and Knife Edge Vernier Caliper. Some companies also make Vernier Calipers which have their jaw like an ordinary Vernier Caliper from one side but have knife-edge jaw at the other side, as shown in Fig. 5.30.

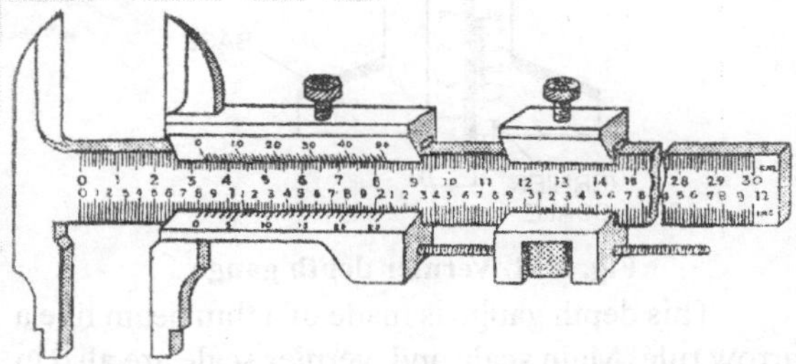

Fig. 5.30. Flat and Knife edge vernier caliper

With this Vernier Caliper all types of jobs can be measured easily.

Gear Tooth Vernier Caliper. This is a special type of instrument, which is made like a combined form of two vernier calipers. It contains two separate scales vertical and horizontal as shown in Fig. 5.31.

With the Vernier Caliper, thickness of a tooth of a gear can be taken from its pitch circle. In other words, Vernier Caliper is used to measure different parts of a gear.

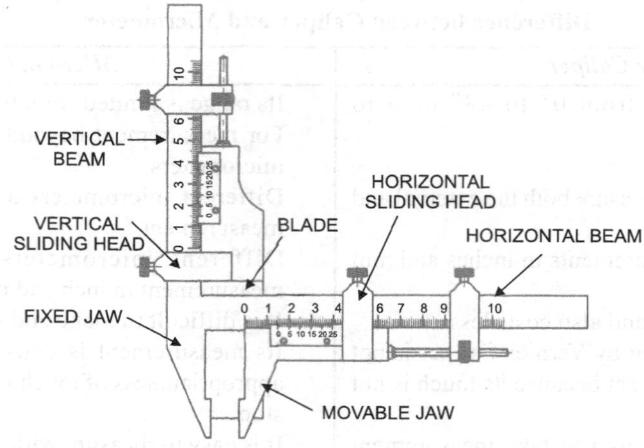

Fig. 5.31. Gear tooth vernier caliper

Vernier Depth Gauge. As is evident from its name, this instrument is used for measuring depth of slot of a job, its hole or groove. This is almost similar to Vernier Caliper. Its reading is also taken in the same way. But instead of a jaw a flat shaped base is used in it as shown in Fig. 5.32.

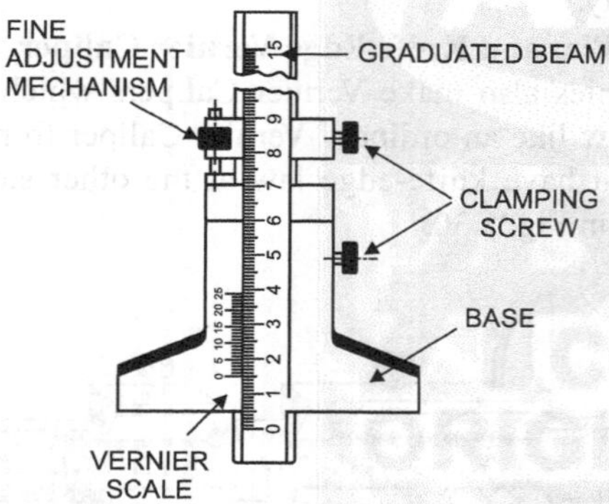

Fig. 5.32. Vernier depth gauge

This depth gauge is made of a thin beam like a narrow rule. Main scale and vernier scale are also in inch or metric system in it. Its speciality is that we can take measurement of three types with it :

(*i*) Its main scale is marked in parts of inches which is divided into 64 sub-sections

(*ii*) The other end is divided into 40 sub-sections and every fourth line is slightly bigger. It contains local size in 1, 2, 3 to 9. On the same end, there is a vernier scale, with whose help a minimum of 0.001″ measurement can be taken.

(*iii*) On its back graduation is in mm which can take minimum measurement of 0.02 mm with the help of a vernier scale.

Vernier Height Gauge. It is used for taking accurate measurement of height of a job or for marking. It is almost similar to vernier caliper but it is used by attaching some additional attachments. Beam remains fitted on a base in length form. Off-set scriber is fitted on the beam itself with which height of a job is measured or marking is done. Its bases are of two types :

(*i*) Solid Base (*ii*) Moveable Base

In Vernier Height Gauge, slide base remains joined with the beam permanently as shown in Fig. 5.33.

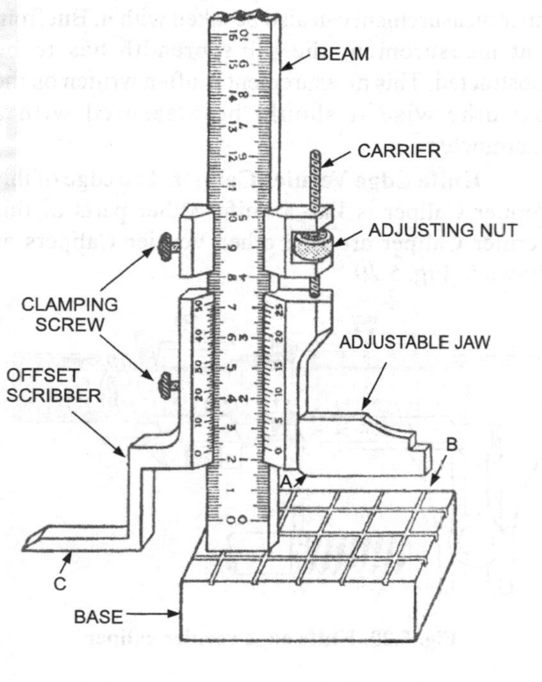

Fig. 5.33 Solid base vernier height gauge

In this type of Vernier Height Gauge there is no facility to set the beam or base according to the requirement of the job. In Movable Base Verniers this facility exists. This type of Vernier Height Gauge is in the form of a set, which has base, vernier caliper, offset scriber fixing screw *etc*. All its parts have been shown in Fig. 5.34.

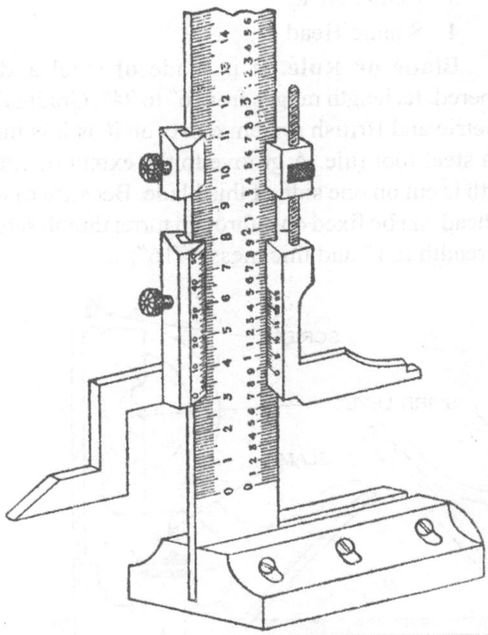

Fig. 5.34 Moveable base vernier height gauge

This type of vernier height gauge can be used as an ordinary vernier caliper by separating its base. While using both types of vernier height gauges, it is necessary to keep in mind the following points :

1. It should always be used on the plain surface of the job.
2. While marking, excessive pressure should not be exerted on its scriber.
3. It should be used on a surface plate only.
4. It should be used only for precision marking or measurement.
5. Its reading should be noted down.

Vernier Dial Caliper. In ordinary vernier calipers there are chances of mistake as far as clear reading is concerned. For this purpose, now a days Vernier Dial Calipers are being used. In place of vernier scale, it contains a graduated dial as shown in Fig. 5.35.

Like vernier calipers, it can measure in inches as well as in millimeters. Like a dial test indicator, rack and pinion are used in it. Rack remains on the main scale which is connected to pinion of the dial. For using it movable jaw is moved by the thumb roller. For taking reading, we have to check how many main and sub marks an inch the bevel edge of the movable jaw has crossed and add the reading, the needle on the dial gives.

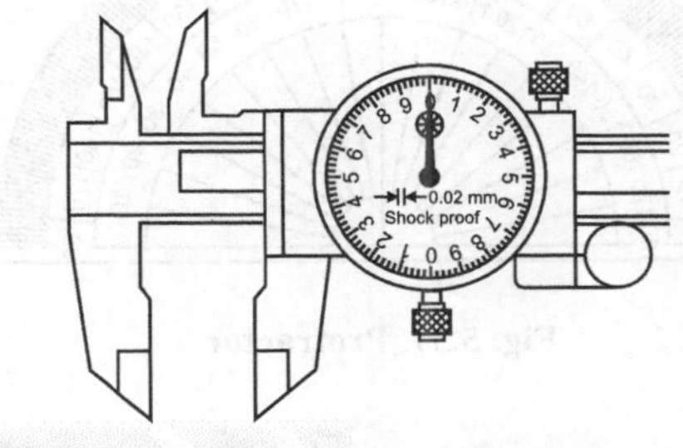

Fig. 5.35. Vernier dial caliper

Telescope Gauge. Like an ordinary caliper, this instrument is used for indirect but precision measurement. Measurement of a hole, bore, slot *etc*. is taken with it. It is of "T" shape and its rod is knurled.

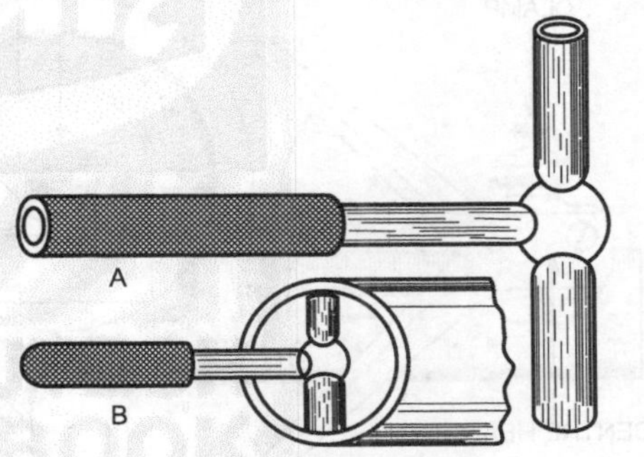

Fig. 5.36 Telescope gauge

The rod on the lower side is in two parts. One part is movable while the other is stationary. In the stationary part there is a spring which pushes the other part towards outside. For taking measurement of a job, we press the movable against the spring and put it in the hole or slot. There is provision for lock on the rod, through which it is locked. Now the length of both the parts is accurately equal to its hole or slot. This length can be read with the help of vernier caliper. An ordinary vernier caliper here cannot get as accurate friction or touch as the two parts of the lower rod get through the spring. There are different distance pieces available with it in the range of 150 mm. With their help we can take further measurement as shown in Fig. 5.36.

Combination Set. We need a protractor to measure an angle or mark it on a job. There is marking at each degree on the protractor. On the centre of the protractor there is an angle of 90° and on both the sides 0° and 180° angles are indicated. With the central point we can measure angles on both the sides. It is semi-circular in shape.

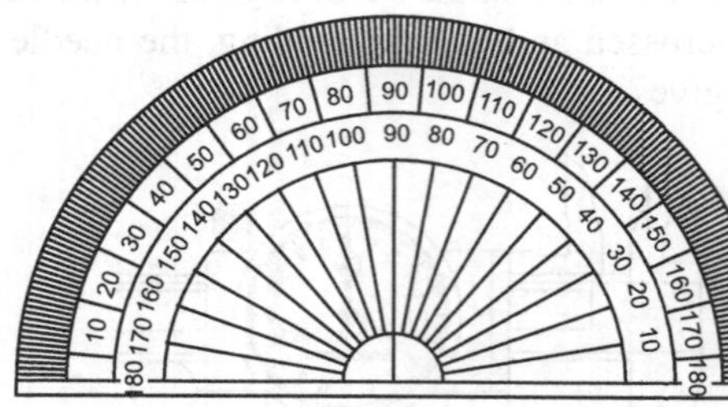

Fig. 5.37. Protractor

These are made either of steel or plastic. These are generally used in ordinary jobs. In the fitter trade, combination set is used for measuring angles or indicating them on the job. In fact, it is an instrument which has the following four parts :

1. Blade or Rule
2. Protractor Head
3. Centre Head
4. Square Head

Blade or Rule. It is made of steel and is tampered. Its length ranges from 6″ to 24″. Graduation in metric and British system exists on it as it is there on a steel foot rule. A groove to the extent of entire length is cut on one side of this blade. Because of this any head can be fixed on it through turret thumb screw. Its breadth is 1″ and thickness 1 /16″.

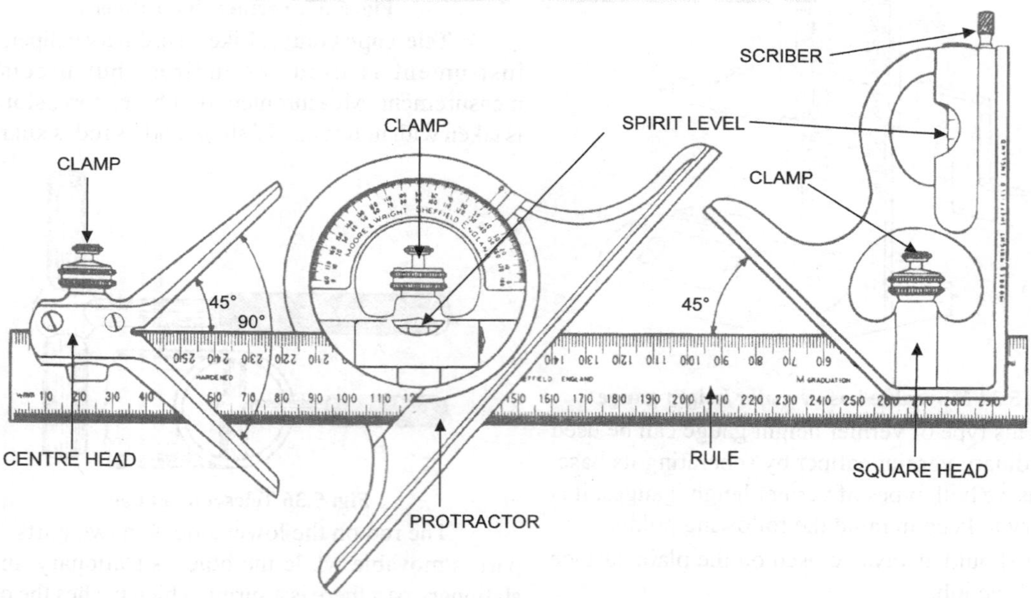

Fig. 5.38. Combination Set

Protractor Head. It is made of steel or drop forge steel. It is fitted with the blade with the help of knurled nut which is at the centre of protractor dial. It contains two dials. One contains graduation up to 180°. At every tenth part local scale is indicated. This dial revolves in the other outer dial. Two screws are fitted on it, through which the inner dial is set. On the outer dial, a line is marked, which acts as a basis for setting the angle. Through this we can measure an angle of the job or mark it. On the inner dial, there is a spirit label through which surface cut in angle can be measured without blade. Protractor Head and blade's use has been shown in Fig. 5.39.

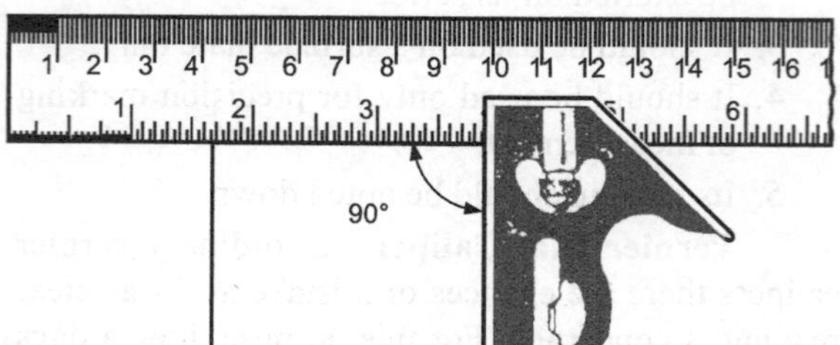

(*a*)

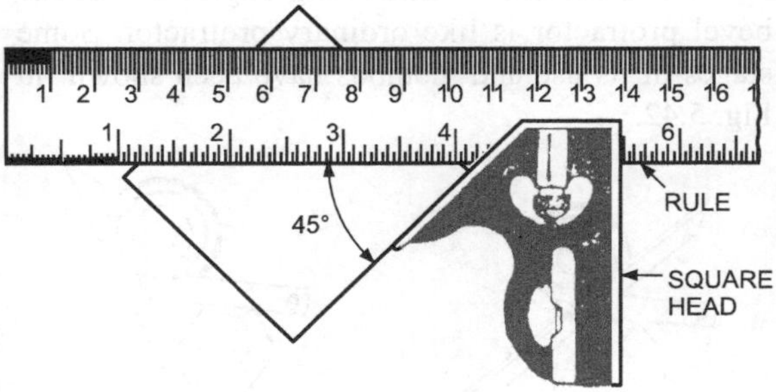

(b)

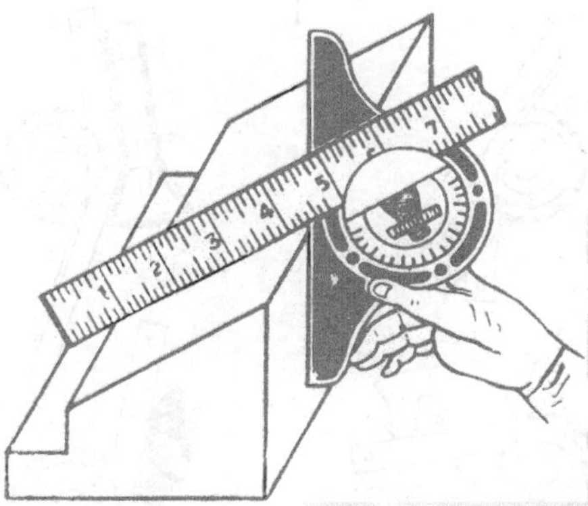

(c)

Fig. 5.39. Protractor head's use

Centre Head. Its shape is like the English letter "V". The angle between its two legs is of 90°. It can be set anywhere on the blade through lock screw. With it we can find the central point of a round job. Radial lines can be drawn on the job.

Square Head. This attachment can be used for different functions. One of its arms is built at 45° angle and the other at 90° angle. Through it we can verify 45° and 90° angles of a job. It can also be used as depth gauge and Height gauge forms. A scriber is also attached to it, which is fitted in the hole of head. Therefore head can be set at the proper place and marking can be done. It also contains a spirit label, with its help we can verify the accuracy of any surface.

Vernier Bevel Protractor. With the help of this instrument, we can measure or mark angle of a taper at 1/ 12° or 5 minute accuracy. While we can take measurement with an ordinary protractor or combination set only up to 1° like other vernier scales. This instrument can also take measurement on the difference of two scales. Different parts of a vernier bevel protractor have been shown in Fig. 5.40.

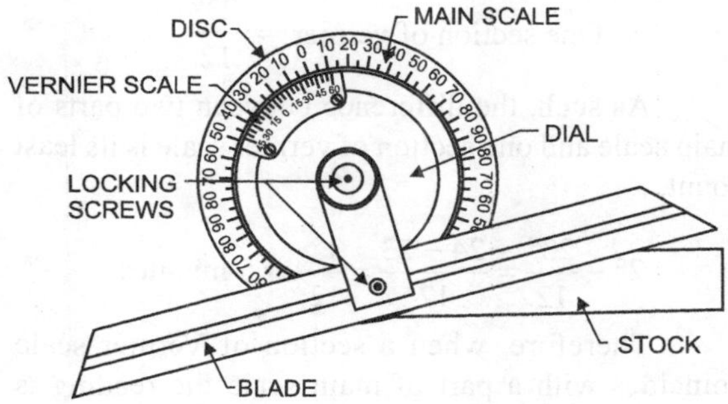

Fig. 5.40. Vernier bevel protractor

Base or Stock. This is made of thick or thin metal sheet in rectangular shape, which has a complete groove at a length of about 3″ so that blade can slide in it. Its length is 4″. Measurement or marking can be done by sticking it to the surface of the job and joining the blade with the other surface.

Blade. It is made of high carbon steel and is hardened or tempered, the metal sheet is 1/2″ in breadth and 1/10″ in thickness. It contains a groove covering its complete length. In this groove blade can be adjusted at any distance with clamping screw with the dial. On both the sides of the blade, there are bevel-cut edges. One edge has an angle of 45° while at the other edge the angle is of 60°.

Dail or Main Scale. This part is round in shape and is joined to the stock. Marking is done on it in two ways. Some dials are in semi circular shape, having graduation upto 180°. In the centre there is a marking of 90° and on its both sides there is marking of angles from 90° to 0°. After every 10 markings local scale is also indicated. The fully circular dials have marking upto 360°. This marking is indicated four times 0° to 90° by treating the line coming parallel to stock as 0.

Dial Clamping Screw and Nut. A stud is fitted in the dial. The dial revolves on its axis. It is fixed on one side of the dial. With its help dial can be set in any desired position.

Blade Clamping Screw. With the help of this screw, dial or scale can be set in any position in the groove of the blade.

Vernier Scale. In the centre of this scale zero (0°) sign is indicated. On both the sides of zero, there are 12 sections, each section is smaller than the two parts of main scale by 1/12° or 5 minute because these 12 sections of vernier scale are equal to 23° of the main scale.

$\because$ 12 sections of Vernier $= 23°$ of main scale

$$\therefore \text{ One section of vernier } = \frac{23°}{12}$$

As such, the difference between two parts of main scale and one section of vernier scale is its least count.

$$2° - \frac{23°}{12} = \frac{24 - 23}{12} = \frac{1°}{12} \text{ or 5 minutes}$$

Therefore, when a section of Vernier scale coincides with a part of main scale the reading is 5 minute or 1/12°. On both sides of 0° on the vernier scale, 15, 30, 45 and 60 is written.

Reading of Vernier Bevel Protractor. In order to measure angle of a job, we note the degrees by which zero sign of vernier scale is ahead on the main scale. Then we observe that which part of vernier scale is meeting the part of main scale.

Now the line which meets is multiplied by 5. This product of multiplication indicates the measurement in minutes. If we add the reading already taken to it this would be the measurement of the angle.

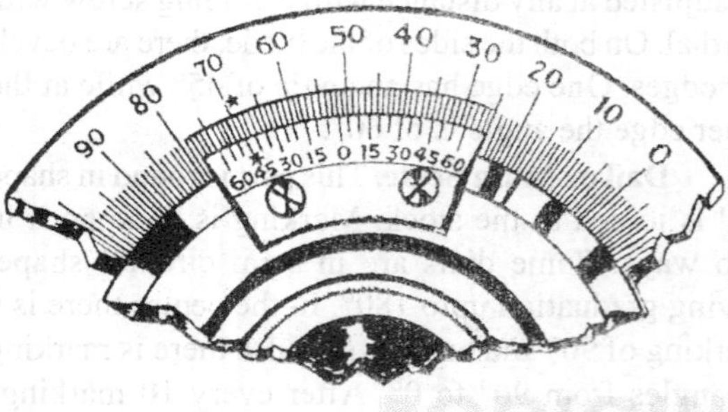

Fig. 5.41. Vernier bevel protractor (Example)

Example. Look at Fig. 5.41 above. We observe that there are 51 divisions between 0° of main scale and "0" Line of Vernier scale. Therefore, we note its degree as 51°. Now ninth part of vernier scale meet the main scale part, which has been starred. Therefore, its reading is 9 × 5 = 45 minutes. Total of both the readings 51° 45″ is the accurate reading of vernier bevel protractor or accurate measurement of the angle made by its blade and stock.

The method of measuring angles by vernier bevel protractor is like ordinary protractor. Some stages of its use and methods have been shown in Fig. 5.42.

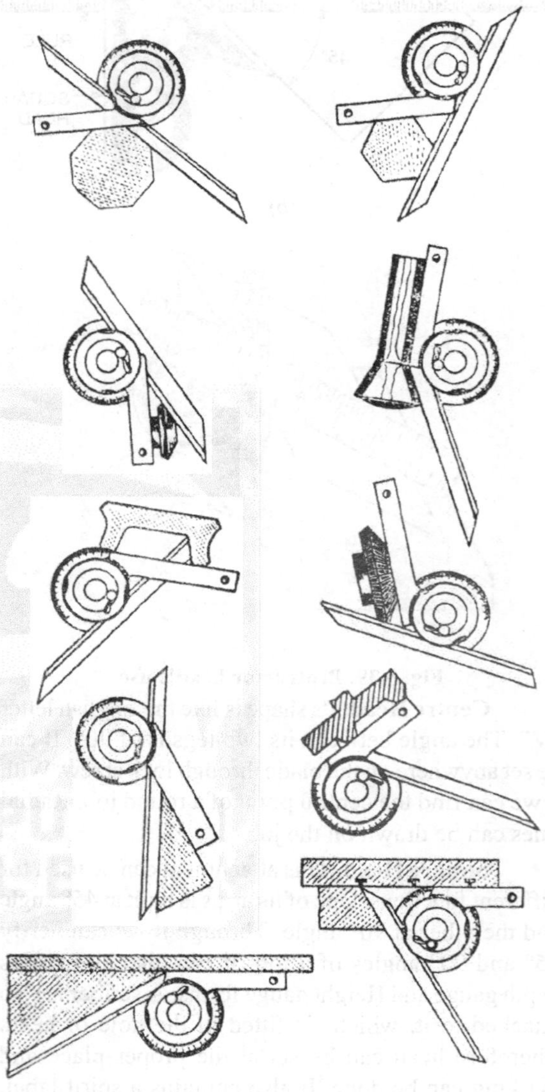

Fig. 5.42. Different stages of use of vernier bevel protractor

Questions

1. What is the working principle of Micrometer ?
2. Draw a sketch of Side Micrometer and show its parts.
3. What do you understand by zero error ?
4. Explain Micrometer least count.
5. Draw a sketch showing reading of 0.792″ in an outside micrometer.
6. What is the least count of Vernier Micrometer? Explain.
7. What is the function of Depth Gauge Micrometer ? How is it different from an outside micrometer ?
8. Explain with the help of a sketch, the makeup of Inside Micrometer and how to use it.
9. Explain the principle of Vernier Caliper with the help of a sketch.
10. What are the different kinds of Vernier Caliper ? Name them alongwith their uses.
11. How to find the least count of Vernier Caliper ? Explain.
12. What is the difference between Vernier Caliper and Micrometer ?
13. Comment on Telescopic Gauge.
14. Explain in detail the Combination Set.
15. Draw a sketch of Vernier Bevel Protractor showing all its parts.
16. How reading is taken from a Vernier Bevel Protractor ? Explain with examples.
17. Why Vernier Bevel Protractor is used ?
18. How can we find the least count of Vernier Bevel Protractor ?

6

Gauge and Indicator

In the previous chapter, we read about precision measuring tools. Through these measuring tools different parts of machines can be produced, inspected or tested. These tools take a specific accurate measurement, therefore, the machine parts manufactured with their help are of accurate measurement. But still there is probability of some difference in them. In this way, while taking up production at a large scale there is difference in size, which poses difficulty in the mass production. Now parts of similar machines can be manufactured in the national and international workshops and their standards are maintained at the same level. If there is any defect in the machine parts then it would be difficult to fit these parts in a machine manufactured in another workshop. Therefore for manufacturing different types of machine parts tolerance is fixed. Machine parts made with this tolerance can be used anywhere with ease because these machines contain the property of "interchangeability". But there is difficulty in securing this quality or a lot of time is wasted in this regard, because of exact measurement by micrometers. Therefore for high scale production gauges are used. These gauges are made in different rates of tolerance, in different shapes and designs. There are following advantanges from their uses :

1. Their use saves time as a number of jobs can be checked in little time.
2. Semi-skilled technicians can also help in production by using these gauges.
3. Jobs done with these gauges have the property of interchangeability.
4. It takes little time in joining these jobs.
5. Jobs are produced of proper tolerance.
6. There is no need of employees for inspection and examination at production stage.
7. There is little possibility of defects in the jobs.
8. Rate of production is increased.
9. As the cost on the job is reduced, its price can be reduced.
10. Those who produce such parts gain in the market trustworthiness.

Construction of Gauges. In shape and design gauges are made in such a way that they can measure and check length, thickness, depth and slanting of a job easily and accurately. These are generally made of high carbon steel and they are made hard and accurately grinded. In addition, some gauges which are widely used are made of vanadium steel or chromium steel. For making these gauges, hardening, grinding, lapping and finishing is done and then for seasoning these are kept in hot water for 10 or 12 hours. Strict checking is done to ensure that the size of the gauge is accurate. Electroplating is done on gauges so that their size do not change because of long use. If there is a reduction in their size, it is brought to the desired size through electroplating or through lapping.

Classification of Gauges. In different types of machine parts, different kind of accuracy is required. Therefore, gauges are made according to these requirements. Gauges can be classified into the following three categories according to their use and accuracy :

(i) Worker gauge. This type of gauge is used by the technicians at the time of production of jobs. By using this gauge we need not set the tools repeatedly or reading. These gauges are made generally to cheek the measurement with accuracy upto 0.0005″ or 0.00025 mm.

(*ii*) Inspection gauge. In various jobs made by the technicians for use, some shortcomings are possible in them. Therefore, it is necessary to get the jobs made by them checked by inspectors. Checking by gauges is done by the inspectors. This gauge can check the jobs with accuracy to the extent of 0.0003.

(iii) **Master Inspection gauge.** This type of gauges are also known as Reference gauges.The veracity of inspection gauges is verified with it from time to time because the inspection gauges also wear out and there is possibility of their giving inaccurate results. Master inspection gauges can check the inspection gauges with accuracy to the extent of 0.0001″.

Types of Gauges. As described above gauges are used to measure length, breadth, depth and slant of a job. Therefore, gauges are made according to requirements of the different jobs, in different shapes and sizes. For inspection of different kinds of jobs, the following types of gauges are generally used :

1. Plug gauge
2. Ring gauge
3. Snap gauge
4. Radius gauge
5. Profile gauge
6. Centre gauge
7. Receiving gauge
8. Caliper gauge
9. Drill gauge
10. Drill point gauge
11. Feeler gauge
12. Screw Pitch gauge
13. Angle gauge
14. Taper gauge
15. Wire gauge
16. Gauge block
17. Indicator gauge
18. Sin bar

Plug Gauge. This type of gauge is used to verify measurement of different kinds of holes. These gauges are manufactured according to different job requirements and are known by their shape and use such as :

1. Cylindrical plug gauge
2. Taper plug gauge
3. Thread plug gauge
4. Square plug gauge
5. Hexagonal plug gauge *etc.*

Different types of plug gauges have been shown in Fig. 6.1 below :

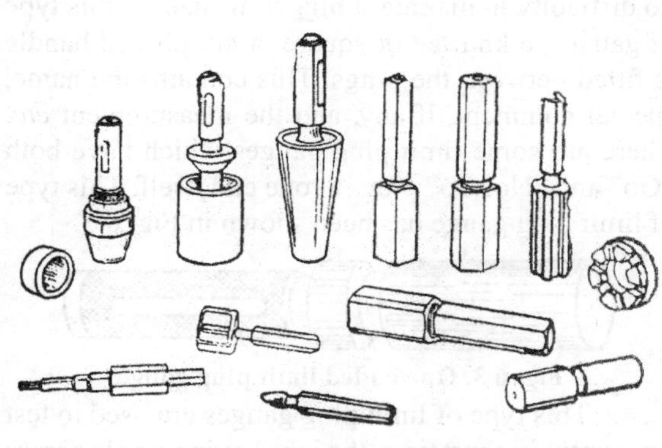

Fig. 6.1. Different types of plug gauges

All these plug gauges are one-ended. The inspcction plugs are made as per the actual measurement of the job and this measurement is indicated on the plug itself. These gauges are called Nominal size plug gauge. These are used to verify (or test) the inspection gauges. Thus these gauges are used as Reference Gauges.

In construction jobs, the workers generally make use of double-ended plugs. On one end of this type of plug "Go" is written while on the other end "Not Go" is indicated. In Fig. 6.2, a cylindrical plug with two ends has been shown.

Fig. 6.2. Cylindrical plug gauge

Both its ends "Go" and "Not Go" are made according to the limit of the hole of the job which is to be tested. The size of "Go' end is kept slighly more than the low limit and the measurement of the "Not Go" end is kept slightly more than high limit. For example, if we have to measure a hole of size 2″ and its approved tolerance is + 0.003 or – 0.002, the "Go" end of the checking plug gauge should be (2″ – 0.002 = 1.998″). In the same way, the "Not Go" end should be (2″ + 0.003″ = 2.003″).

While checking the bore (hole), the "Go" end of the plug gauge should go inside the hole and the "Not Go" end should not go inside the hole. Therefore, this type of gauges are called Limit Plug Gauge. For the purpose of convenience, the plug with "Go" indication is made smaller or short. Contrarily, the plug with "Not Go" indication is made bigger or longer in comparison. As such it takes little time in recognising the "Go" and "Not Go" ends. As the "Go" end has to be inserted in the hole, therefore, it is made in length, as per the job. On the other hand, "Not Go" end is not be inserted in the hole, there is no difficulty in making it bigger in size. In this type of gauges, a knurled or square or six-phased handle is fitted between the plugs. This contains the name, special comment, if any, and the measurement *etc.* There are some limit plug gauges which have both "Go" and "Not Go" plugs at one end itself. This type of limit plug gauge has been shown in Fig. 6.3.

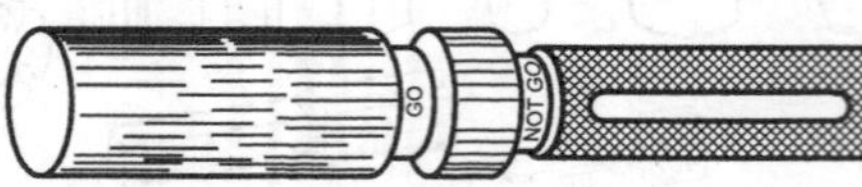

Fig. 6.3. One ended limit plug gauge

This type of limit plug gauges are used to test (or verify) in short time the jobs having a hole across them. But we cannot check the closed holes with these limit, plug gauges.

Plug gauges having diameter upto 2″ are made in solid form along with the handle but in plug gauges of measurement exceeding 2″, handles and plugs are built separately and these are fitted together through threads. In order to reduce the weight of bigger plug gauges, drill holes are made. The most important thing in these gauges is that since the "Go" end is inserted in the hole this end wears out more than any other part. Therefore, by replacing or repairing only one part, the plug gauge becomes fit for accurate checking.

Use and Precautions. For using plug gauges these should be moved inside the job in revolving motion. The hole of the job should be properly cleaned before using the plug gauge. Before and after using the plug gauge, it should be properly cleaned.

Ring Gauge. This gauge is used for checking external diameters of round and cylindrical jobs. The diameter of the hole is made accroding to the actual measurement of the job. Their outer part is knurled so that these can be handled easily.

In any round job, there are generally four types of external surfaces. According to these surfaces, these gauges are also of four types :

(*i*) **Plain Ring Gauge.** This gauge is used for checking the external measurement of a round or cylindrical job. This has been shown in Fig. 6.4.

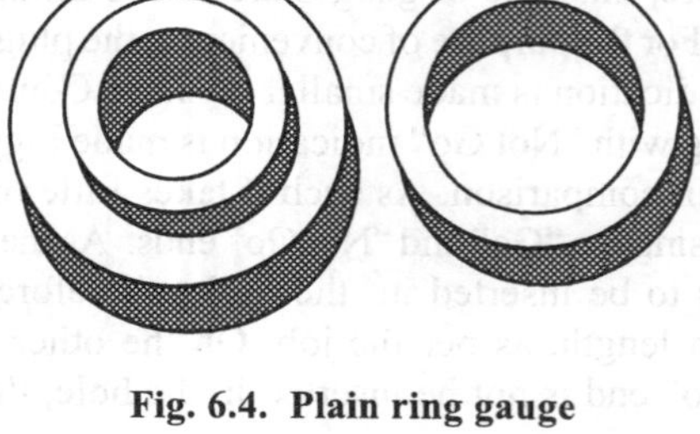

Fig. 6.4. Plain ring gauge

(*ii*) **Thread Ring Gauge.** This type of gauge is used to check the external threads cut on a cylindrical job. This has been shown in Fig. 6.5.

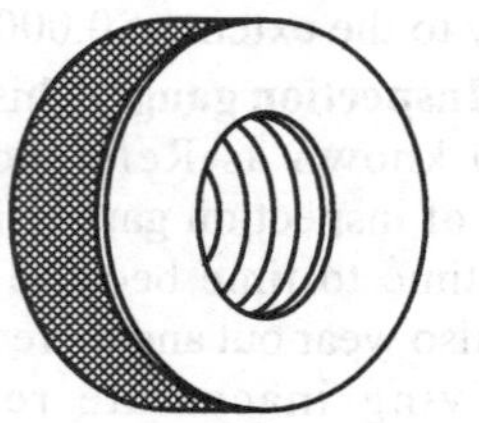

Fig. 6.5. Thread ring gauge

(*iii*) **Taper Ring Gauge.** These gauges are used for checking the externaal taper angles of round or cylindrical job.

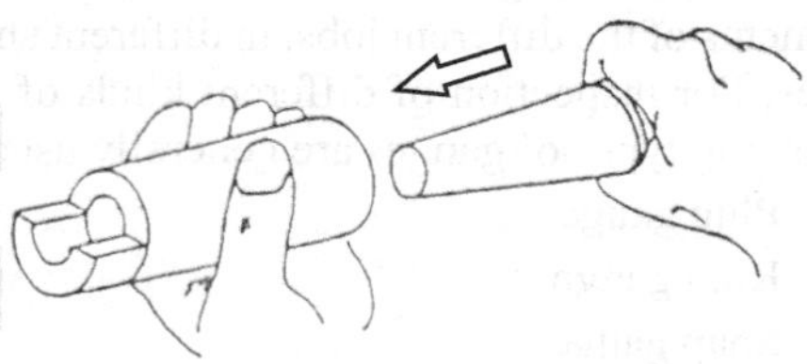

Fig. 6.6. Taper ring gauge

(*iv*) **Form Ring Gauge.** Form ring gauge is used especially for external measurement of those jobs which have abnormal shapes.

Some ring gauges are made according to the gauge limits also. Such gauges are made of rectangular steel by making holes on both the sides. On one end "Go" is indicated while on the other "Not Go" is written.

The holes on both these ends are made according to the job limit.

Snap Gauges. This is a non-adjustable gauge for checking length, breadth, thickness or its external diameter. These gauges are broadly of two types :

(*i*) **Solid Snap Gauge.** This type of gauge is almost similar in shape to the English alphabet 'C'. This is available in the form of one end and two-ends limit snap gauge. The checking sides of this gauge have very plain surface which is made very smooth and accurate.

In Fig. 6.7 two types of solid snap gauges have been shown :

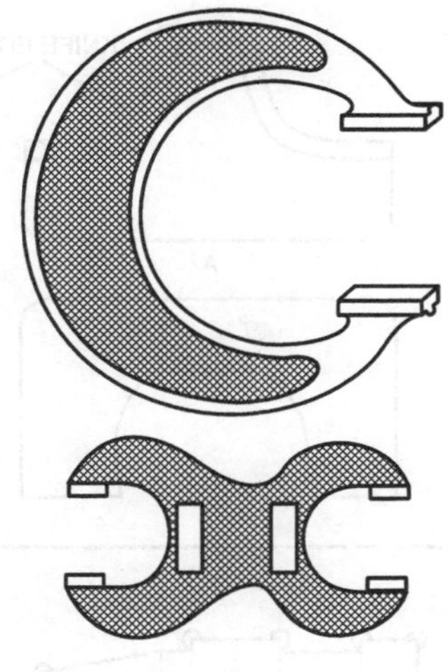

Fig. 6.7. Solid snap gauge

One-end gauge is meant for checking the actual size and two-end gauge is known as limit snap gauge. With this gauge, checking can be done as per limit of the job. "Go" is indicated on its one end and "Not Go" is written on the other end. Their size is also indicated. While checking the size of a job, the job should go into the "Go" end. If it does not go into the "Go" end, it means the size of job is larger. The job should not go into "NOT GO" end, if it goes, it means that the size of the job has become less than the actual size.

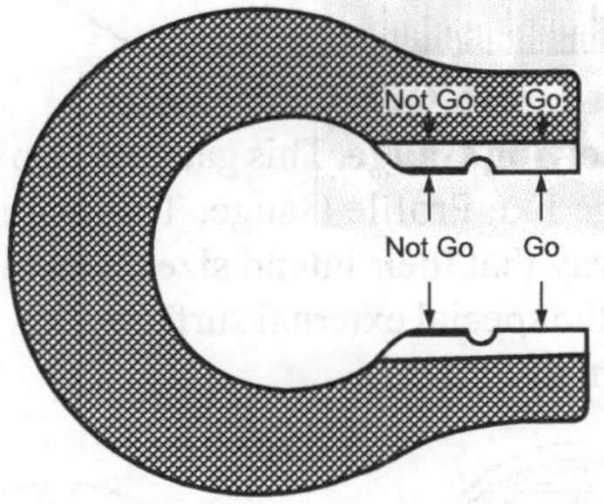

Fig. 6.8. One end limit snap gauge

Some snap gauges have one end and are in "C" shape but these are made according to the limit of the job. This type of snap gauge has been shown in Fig. 6.8.

In this type of snap gauge both "Go" and "Not Go" sizes are at one end. The main advantage of these gauges is that it saves time to check the size with them.

(ii) **Adjustable Snap Gauge.** This gauge is also of "C" shape like one-ended solid snap gauge. On their inspecting surface three or four anvils are fitted. These anvils are adjusted with the help of screw in proper size. Therefore, we can check different jobs according to their limit, with this snap gauge. In order to control the size, gauge block is used. This type of gauge with four anvils has been shown in Fig. 6.9.

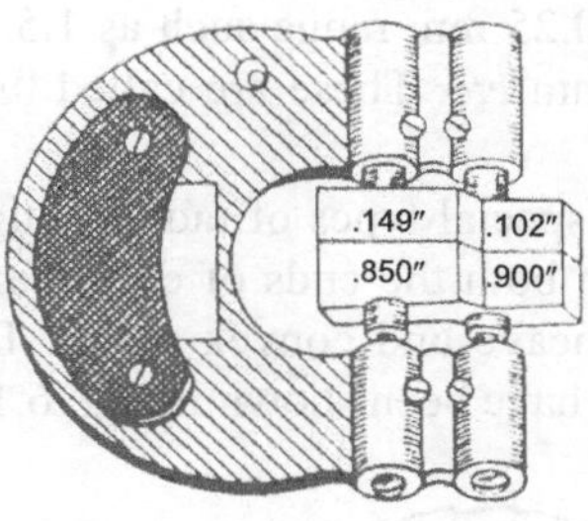

Fig. 6.9. Adjustable snap gauge

At the time of checking a job, the job should go into the external pair of anvils but it should not go into the internal pair of anvils. This gauge can be adjusted upto $\frac{3}{4}''$.

Radius Gauge. Shape of this gauge is like a small pocket knife having a number of leaves fixed on both its ends with a screw or a rivet. These leaves have concave or convex shape at their ends. Size of their radius is indicated on the leaves. With this gauge the radii of fillets and rounded corners can be measured. It is also known as Fillet gauge. One radius gauge has leaves of one range. Different ranges of radius are available. Few radius gauges have been shown in Fig. 6.10.

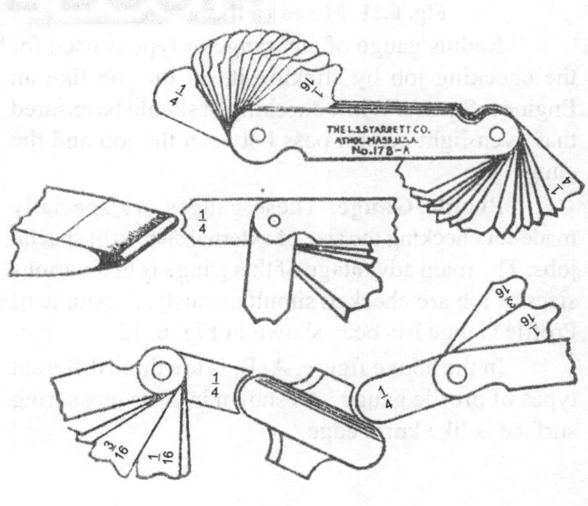

Fig. 6.10. Radius gauge

Radius gauges are classified in several ways according to their ranges. These are available both in English as well as Metric ranges. English radius gauges are in range of $\frac{1}{64}''$ such as $\frac{1}{8}''$, $\frac{9}{64}''$, $\frac{5}{32}''$, $\frac{11}{64}''$ and $\frac{3}{16}''$ *etc.* Similarly, Metric radius gauges are available in 0.25 mm range such as 1.5, 1.75, 2.25, 2.75 and 3 mm *etc.* These are called "A" and "B" sizes.

Some special types of radius gauges are also available. On both the ends of each leaf, there is a radius of concave and convex range. This type of radius gauge have been shown in Fig. 6.11

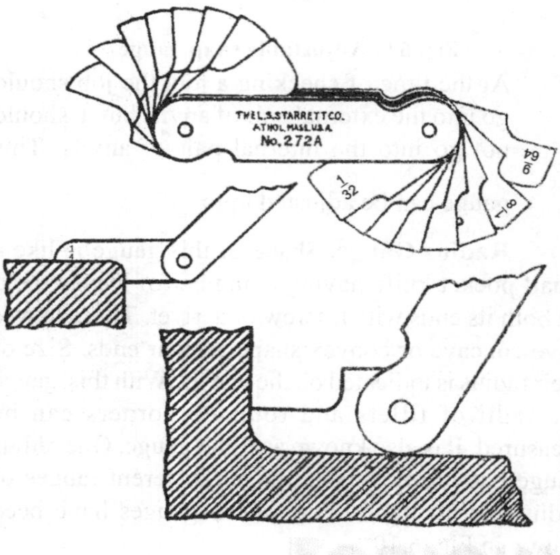

Fig. 6.11. Mixed radius gauge

Radius gauge of any range or type is used for the checking job by sticking it, on the job like an Engineer Square. While checking, it should be ensured that even light cannot pass between the job and the gauge.

Profile Gauge. These gauges are specially made for checking the size of external shapes of special jobs. The main advantage of this gauge is that various sizes of job are checked simultaneously. A sample of Profile Gauge has been shown in Fig. 6. 12.

In the above figure, A, B, C are three different types of profile gauge. As shown in A its measuring surface is like knife edge.

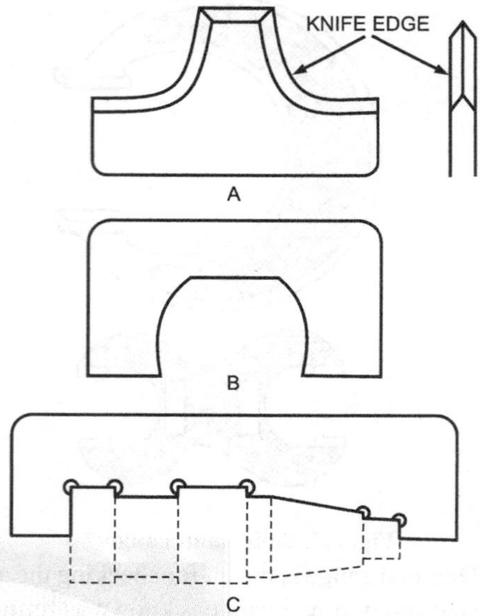

Fig. 6.12. Profile gauge

Centre Gauge. It is a flat gauge used for setting a tool for the cutting of "V" threads. This is made of spring steel. "V" is made of angles of 60°, 55° and 29°. This type of gauge has been shown in Fig. 6.13.

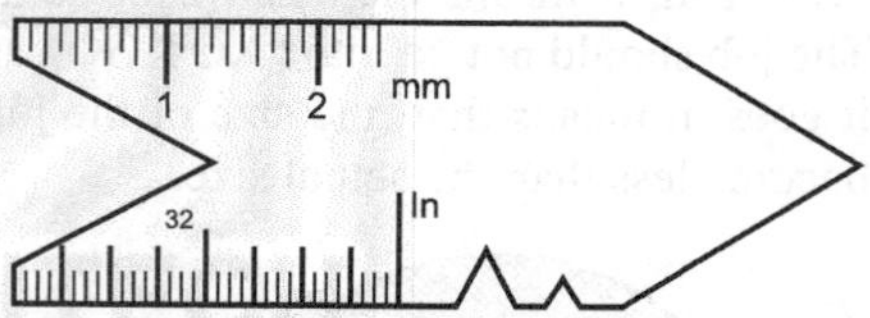

Fig. 6.13. Centre gauge

Receiving Gauge. This gauge is also especially made gauge like Profile Gauge. These are designed in such a way that their intend size checking surface can check the special external surface. This gauge has been shown in Fig. 6.14.

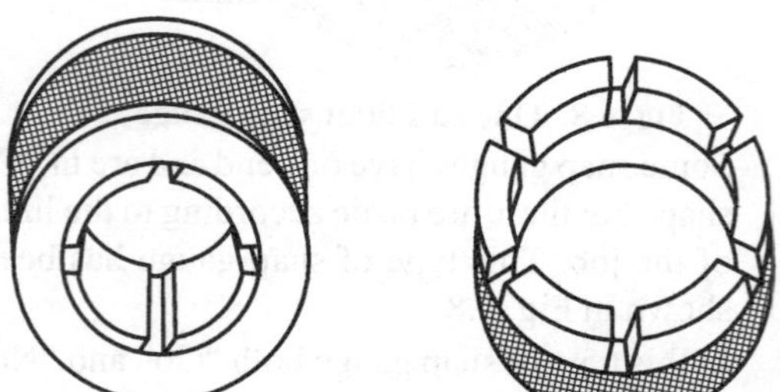

Fig. 6.14. Receiving gauge

Caliper Gauge. The main feature of this gauge is that we can check the internal or external size of a job with one gauge. Its shape is almost similar to the snap gauge but on one of its end there are jaws for checking internal size and on the other end, there is an anvil for checking the external size.

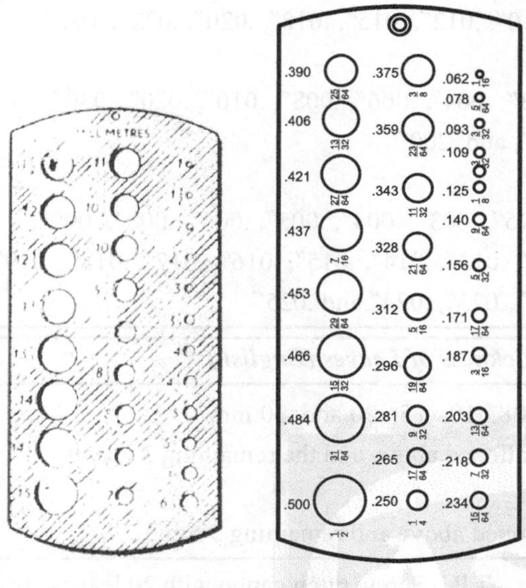

Fig. 6.15. Drill gauge (Metric and English)

Drill Gauge. It is a flat steel plate drilled with holes of different sizes and properly marked so that the size of a drill may be easily determined by fitting it to the plate. Its size is $6\frac{1}{4}'' \times 2\frac{5}{16}'' \times \frac{5}{64}''$. Its length is measured by its radius from both the sides. The size of the holes is indicated according to the drill. We can measure the size of those drills with this gauge, which have lost their size indication because of long use. These gauges are available both in Metric as well as Brtish system. In addition Letter drill and Number drills are also available. Metric and English drill gauges have been shown in Fig. 6.15.

Drill Point Gauge. In order to drill properly and make hole of proper size, it is essential that drill is grinded at proper angle and both its lip centres are equal from the centre line. After grinding the drill, drill point gauge is used to check them.

It has two parts : (*i*) Steel Rule (*ii*) Gauge, which can be set anywhere with a thumb screw. It has been illustrated in Fig. 6.16. This gauge can be used like other measuring tools as well such as Depth Gauge, Engineers Square and Hook Rule *etc*.

Feeler Gauge. This gauge is also like a small knife, which contains leaves of different thickness fitted on it with a screw or a revet. Thickness is written on the leaves itself. The size of small gaps and clearance is determined with this gauge. The number of leaves in a Feeler gaug depends on the companies manufacturing them. These gauges are available in eight types of standards. These are made in both English as well as Metric measurements.

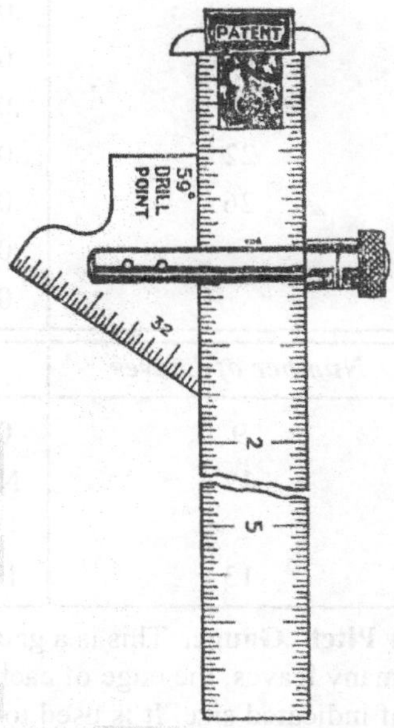

Fig. 6.16. Drill point gauge

English Feeler gauges have five sets. These can be known from the following two tables shown on next page :

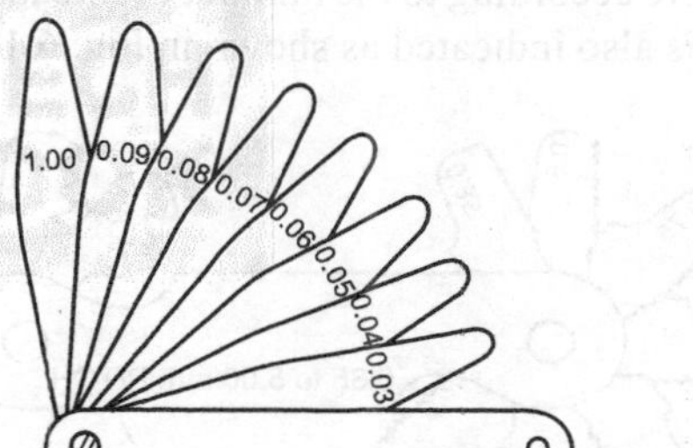

(a) Feeler gauge of tapered leaves

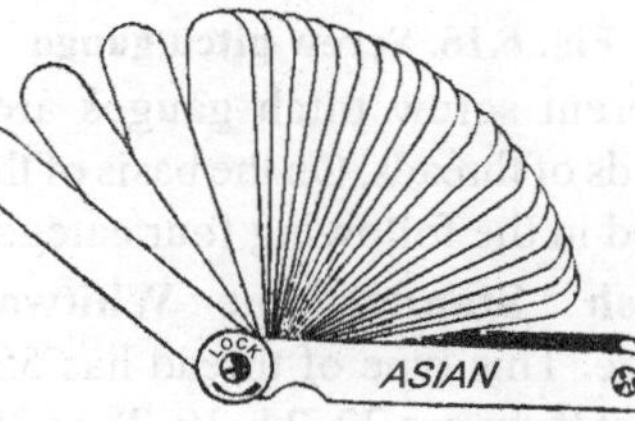

(b) Feeler gauge (Englidh) of parallel leaves

Fig. 6.17. Feeler gauge

The leaves of the feeler gauge can be parallel in breadth or in taper.

S. No.	Number of Leaves	Thickness of Leaves (English)
1.	6	.0015″, .002″, .003″, .004″, .005″, .006″ and .015″
2.	9	.0015″, .002″, .003″, .004″, .006″, .008″, .010″, .012″ and .015″, .015″ *or* .010″, .012″, .015″, .018″, .020″, .022″, .025″ .030″ and .035″
3.	13	.0015″, .002″, .003″, .004″, .006″, .008″, .010″, .020″, .030″, .040″, .075″, .100″, and .200″
4.	22	.004″ to .025″
5.	26	.0015″, .002″, .0025″, .003″, .004″, .005″, .006″, .008″, .009″, .010″, .011″, .012″, .013″, .014″, .015″, .016″, .017″, .018″, .019″, .020″, .021″, .022″, .023″, .024″ and .025″

S. No.	Number of Leaves	Thickness of Leaves (English)
1.	9	.04, .05, .06, .07, .08, .10, .15, .20 and .30 mm
2.	12	Nine leaves as mentioned above and the remaining 3 leaves 1, 2 and 3 mm.
3.	13	12 leaves as mentioned above and remaining 5 mm.

Screw Pitch Gauge. This is a gauge usually made up of many leaves, the edge of each being cut to a thread of indicated size. It is used to determine the number of threads per inch on given screw, bolt or nut. This gauge is also like a radius gauge or filler gauge in shape. In a set a number of leaves are fitted on either end of the gauge. In these leaves grooves are there according to the number of threads and their pitch is also indicated as shown in Fig. 6.18.

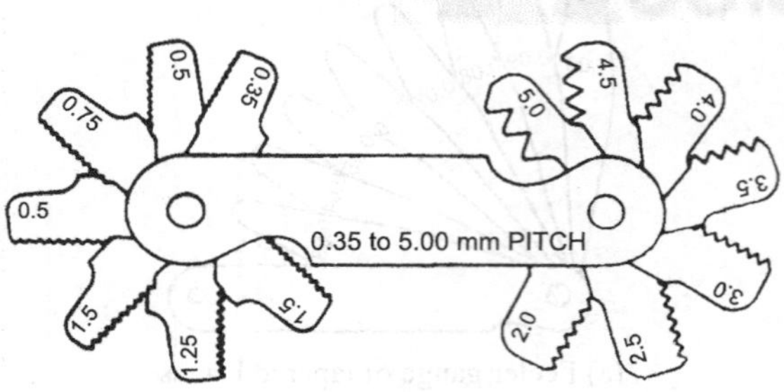

Fig. 6.18. Screw pitch gauge

Different screw pitch gauges are made for different kinds of threads. On the basis of threads these are classified in the following four categories :

(i) **British Standard or Whitworth Pitch Gauge.** This type of thread has 55° angle. In one set there are 22, 24, 26, 28 or 30 leaves. In a screw pitch gauge with 22 leaves, leaves are from 9 T.P.I. to 30 T.P.I. Leaves in the screw pitch gauge with 24 leaves, are of 4 T.P.I. to 30 T.P.I. Screw pitch gauge with 20 leaves are of two kinds. In one set there are leaves of 4 T.P.I. to 60 T.P.I. and in the other set 32 T.P.I. to 80 T.P.I. In screw pitch gauge with 28 leaves, leaves are form 4 T.P.I. to 62 T.P.I. Screw pitch gauge with 30 leaves, have leaves of two sets.

In one type the leaves are of $3\frac{1}{2}$ to 60 T.P.I. and in the other set from 4 to 42 T.P.I.

(ii) **American National Standard Screw Pitch Gauge.** This type of thread has an angle of 60°. This gauge has 27 leaves. These leaves are of $2\frac{1}{4}$ T.P.I.to 28 T.P.I.

(iii) **Bicycle Screw Pitch Gauge.** This type of threads are made for electrical goods and cycle part. There are 22 leaves with it. These leaves are of 32 T.P.I. to 74 T.P.I.

(iv) **Metric Screw Pitch Gauge.** These are of two kinds. First set has 28 leaves, which have leave of pitch ranging from 25 to 250 mm. In the second set there are 22 leaves with pitch ranging from 1 mm to 11.5 mm.

(v) **International Standard Screw Pitch Gauge.** With this gauge, threads of international standard are measured. There are 17 leaves in this gauge. Its leaves are of 5 mm to 7 mm pitch.

Angle Gauge. This gauge also belongs to the

class of gauge made of steel leaves. In a case like a knife, it contains leaves on both the ends. Their ends are made on angles and the degree of these angles is written there. These leaves are made of steel and are duly tapered. Their size is $\frac{9}{32}'' \times 1\frac{1}{16}'' \times 4\frac{3}{16}''$. One set contains 18 leaves, 9 leaves on one end and 9 on the other. We can check angles of 1°, 2°, 3°, 4°, 5°, 7°, 8°, 9°, 10°, 12°, 14°, $14\frac{1}{2}$°, 15°, 20°, 25°, 30°, 35° and 45° with this angle gauge. This type of angle gauge has been shown in Fig. 6.19 below :

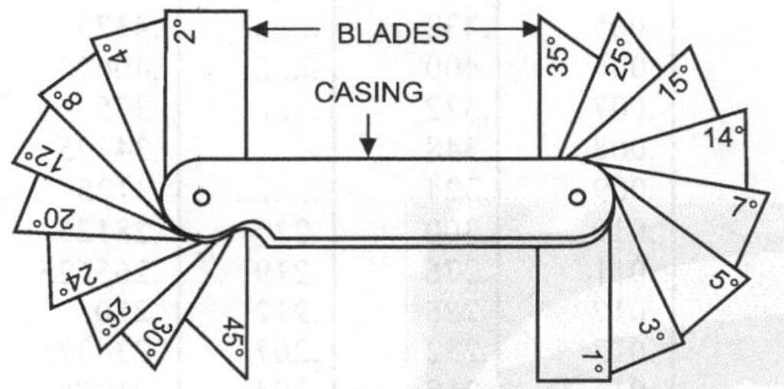

Fig. 6.19. Angle gauge

Taper Gauge. It is a gauge for testing the accuracy of tapers, either inside or outside as well as to measure a slot or internal or external diameter of a pipe. Its shape is $\frac{1}{16}''$ in breadth, $6\frac{1}{4}''$ in length. It is made of tool steel. Its thickness is in taper. In Fig. 6.20 (*A*), a taper gauge has been shown. On one side from 0.10″ to .150″ division is indicated, each part is bigger to the other by .001″ on the other side, difference between each part is of $\frac{1}{20}$ mm and parts are indicated from $\frac{3}{10}$ mm to 4 mm. Besides this, another type of taper gauge is also made. This type of taper gauge has been shown in Fig. 6.20 (*B*). In this type of set there are four or eight leaves. These leaves are made of .012 thick spring steel and their shape is tapered towards the ends.

Taper gauge with eight leaves has being shown in Fig. 6.20 (*C*). Leaves of set *A* are $2\frac{1}{2}''$ in length. We can test the accuracy of measurement of taper from $\frac{1}{10}''$ (.100″) to $\frac{1}{2}''$ (.500″) upto .001″. The leaves of Set *B* are $2\frac{3}{4}''$ in length. We can measure taper from $\frac{1}{2}''$ (.500″) to 1″. For measuring taper, leaf of appropriate size is put inside the holes. At this moment, both sides of the gauge leaf should be stuck to the job. We can determine or read accurately the measurement of outside caliper with taper gauge.

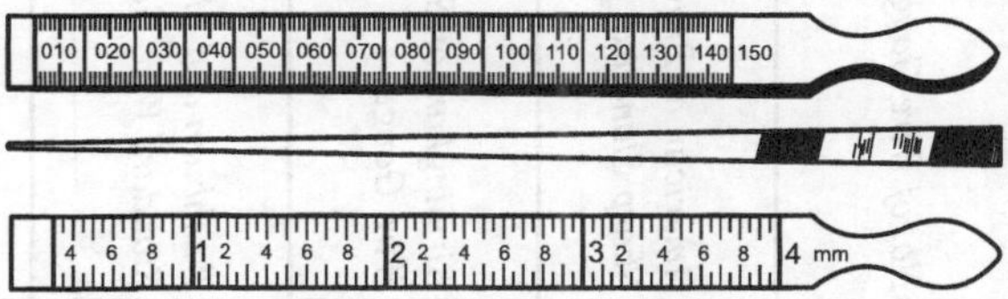

(*A*) Taper gauge

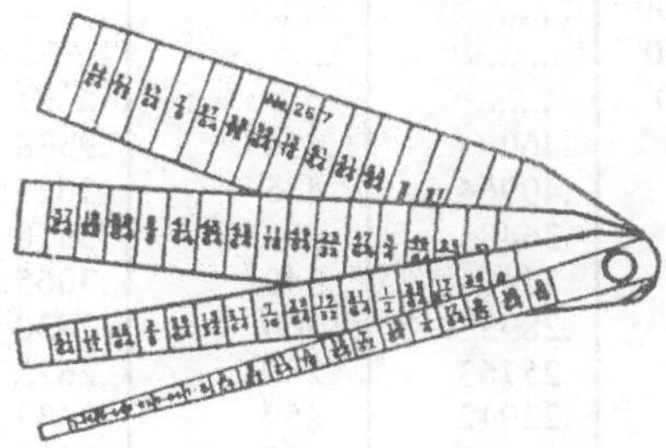

(*B*) Pipe measuring taper gauge of four leaves

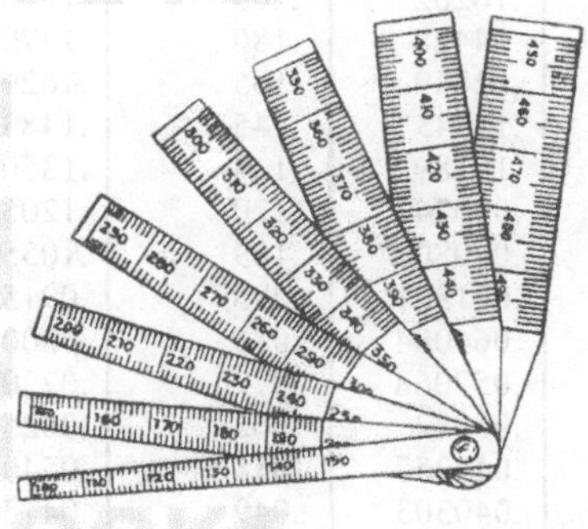

(*C*) 8 leaves taper gauge for measuring of holes or pipes

Fig. 6.20.

Wire Gauge. It is a notched plate having a series of gauged slots. These are numbered according to the sizes of wire and sheet metal manufactured. These are

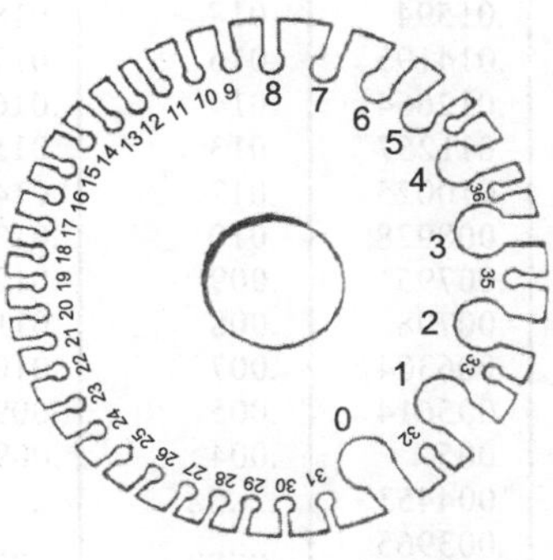

Fig. 6.21. Wire gauge

Number of different Standard Wire Gauges and their sizes in inches

No. of Wire Gauge	American or Brown and Sharp Standard	Birmingham or Sub Iron Wire Gauge	Washburn and Moyen Standard Wire Gauge	Washburn and Moyen Steel Music Wire Gauge	American S & W Co. Music Wire Gauge	Imperial Standard Wire Gauge	Stubs Steel Wire Gauge	U.S. Standard Gauge
00000000	....	....	....	.0083	....	....	....	....
0000000	....	....	....	.0087	....	....	....	....
000000	....	....	....	.0095	.004	.464	....	.46875
00000	....	....	....	.010	.005	.432	....	.4375
0000	.460	.454	.9338	.011	.006	.400	....	.40625
000	.40964	.425	.3625	.012	.007	.372	....	.375
00	.3648	.380	.3310	.0133	.008	.348	....	.34375
0	.32486	.340	.3065	.0144	.009	.324	....	.3125
1	.2893	.300	.2830	.0156	.010	.300	.227	.28125
2	.25763	.284	.2625	.0166	.011	.276	.219	.265625
3	.22942	.259	.2437	.0178	.012	.225	.212	.250
4	.20431	.238	.2253	.0188	.013	.232	.207	.234375
5	.18194	.220	.2070	.0202	.014	.212	.204	.21875
6	.16202	.203	.1920	.0215	.016	.192	.201	.203125
7	.14428	.180	.1770	.023	.018	.176	.199	.1875
8	.12849	.165	.1620	.0243	.020	.160	.197	.171875
9	.11443	.145	.1483	.0256	.022	.144	.194	.15625
10	.10189	.134	.1350	.027	.024	.128	.191	.140625
11	.090742	.120	.1205	.0284	.026	.116	.188	.125
12	.080808	.109	.1055	.0295	.029	.104	.185	.109375
13	.071961	.095	.0915	.0314	.031	.092	.182	.09375
14	.064084	.083	.0800	.0326	.033	.080	.180	.078125
15	.057068	.072	.0720	.0345	.035	.072	.178	.0703125
16	.05082	.065	.0625	.036	.037	.064	.175	.0625
17	.045257	.058	.0540	.0377	.039	.056	.172	.05625
18	.040303	.049	.0475	.0395	.041	.048	.168	.050
19	.03589	.042	.0410	.0414	.043	.040	.164	.04375
20	.031961	.035	.0348	.0434	.045	.036	.161	.0375
21	.028462	.032	.03175	.046	.047	.032	.157	.034375
22	.25347	.028	.0286	.0483	.049	.028	.155	.03125
23	.022571	.025	.0258	.051	.051	.024	.153	.028125
24	.0201	.022	.0230	.055	.055	.022	.151	.025
25	.0179	.020	.0204	.0586	.059	.020	.148	.021875
26	.01594	.018	.0181	.0626	.063	.018	.146	.01875
27	.014195	.016	.0173	.0658	.067	.0164	.143	.0171875
28	.0126641	.014	.0162	.072	.071	.0149	.139	.015625
29	.011257	.013	.0150	.076	.075	.0136	.134	.0140625
30	.010025	.012	.0140	.080	.080	.0124	.127	.0125
31	.008928	.010	.0132	....	.085	.0116	.120	.0109375
32	.00795	.009	.0128	....	.090	.0108	.115	.01015625
33	.00708	.008	.0118	....	.095	.0100	.112	.009375
34	.006304	.007	.0104	....	....	.0092	.110	.00859375
35	.005614	.005	.0095	....	....	.0084	.108	.0078125
36	.005	.004	.0090	....	....	.0076	.106	.00703125
37	.004453	....	....	....	....	.0068	.105	.006640625
38	.003965	....	....	....	....	.0060	.101	.00625
39	.003531	....	....	....	....	.0052	.099	....
40	.003144	....	....	....	....	.0048	.097	....

used for measuring the diameter of wire. The number of the slot in which wire or sheet fits properly, is its gauge. A standard wire gauge has been shown in Fig. 6.21. There are eight types of standard gauges :

1. **American (Brown and Sharp) Standard Wire Gauge** : These gauges are used for measuring copper, brass, aluminium and all non-ferrous metal wires, sheets and plates. This gauge contains slots of numbers from 0000 to 40.
2. **The Bermingham or Stubs Iron Wire Gauge:** It is used for measuring the hot and cold rolled steel and sheets. It contains slots of numbers 0000 to 36.
3. **Washburn and Moyen Standard Wire Gauge :** With this gauge we can measure drill rods, in addition to wires and sheets of 0000 to 36 number.
4. **Washburn and Moyen Steel Music Wire Gauge :** With this gauge we can measure special wire which are used in musical instruments. Slots of numbers ranging from 00000000 to 36 are cut in this gauge.
5. **S.W. American Music Wire Gauge :** This gauge is also used for measuring wires used in musical instruments but it contains slots of numbers ranging from 000000 to 33.
6. **Imperial Standard Wire Gauge :** This contains slots of numbers ranging from 000000 to 40 for measuring wires or sheets.
7. **Stubs Steel Wire Gauge :** Slots from number 1 to 40 are cut in this gauge.
8. **United States Standard Wire Gauge :** Iron and steel plates are measured with this gauge. Slots of numbers from 000000 to 38 exist in this gauge.

In all the wire gauges, slot numbers have their own standard sizes. Except in the case of music wire gauge, in all other wire gauges as the number of the slot increases the size decreases. Only in W. and M. Steel Wire Gauge and American S.W. Co. Musical gauge, as the number of the slot increases so does the size of the slot. In the above table, measurement of all kinds of standard wire gauges has been given. We can find out the different gauges of different standards for slot of one particular number.

Slip Gauge or Gauge Block. It is necessary to obtain accuracy in sizes in production of different machine parts. This accuracy depends upon the approved limit of job to be manufactured. In ordinary jobs where limit is upto $\frac{1}{64}''$ (+) or (–), it can be measured with ordinary steel foot rule. But in the production of various tools and machine parts where limit of tolerance is .0001 cannot be measured with foot rule. In certain jobs the limit of tolerance is approved to a very small extent. For measuring or checking the size of such jobs slip gauges are used. These are generally made of tool steel. Their shape is square, rectangular or triangular. Their gauging surface is quite plain. Such is the extent of their accuracy that when two pieces of gauges are kept properly one over the other through proper ringing action, they stick to each other because of vacuum. In such a state, not even a ray of light can pass through them.

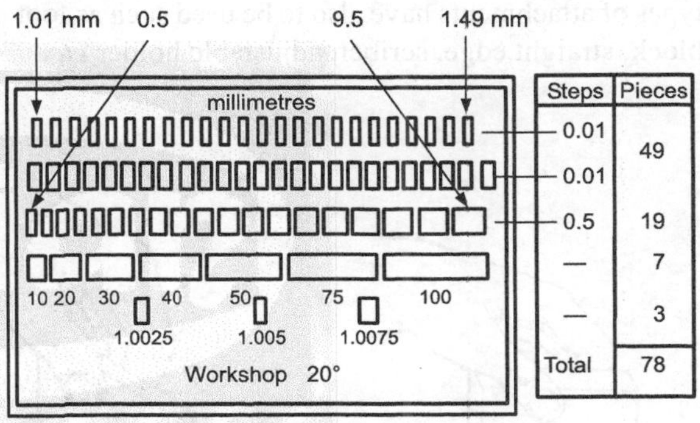

Fig. 6.22. Slip gauge set

Their manufacturing process is also different from that of ordinary gauges. These are cut by machines with appropriate allowance and then machining is done. They are manfactured in almost correct size and the seasoning is done in natural or artificial way. After seasoning, tempering, grinding and lapping is done. One slip gauge set has been shown in Fig. 6.22.

These slip gauges are always in sets. In one set there are 5 to 103 gauge blocks. In each set-range, size is chosen in such a way that gauge can be prepared to take any measurement within that range, by adding the gauges through the gauge ringing method. These gauges have been divided into three different sections on the basis of their utility and accuracy. These are "B", "A" and "AA".

1. **Worker Slip Gauge Set.** This gauge belongs to the "B" class. It is used by the technicians in workshops. This gauge is for accuracy of .000008″.
2. **Inspection Slip Gauge Set.** This gauge belongs to the "A" class. This is used by the

inspectors to test the accuracy of the jobs made by the workers. These are made for accuracy of .000004″.

3. **Master Slip Gauge Set.** This gauge belongs to "AA" class. It has the highest accuracy. These are made for .000002″ accuracy. The accuracy of other gauges and tools is tested with these gauge sets.

Shapes of gauges. According to the job and utility of testing, the shapes of gauges are of three types :

1. Rectangular gauge block
2. Square gauge block'
3. Angle gauge block

For using the above gauge blocks, different types of attachments have also to be used such as foot block, straight edge, scriber, adjustable holder *etc.*

Uses of Slip Gauge. This gauge is generally used for the following functions :

1. To inspect (or verify) micrometer and Vernier Calipers.
2. To set adjustable gauges such as snap gauges.
3. To use sin bar.
4. For exact marking of a job.
5. To make solid snap gauges and caliper gauges.
6. To verify measurement of a job with the help of comparator.
7. To have comparative measurement of any job, with the help of an indicator.

For using slip gauge in any kind of job, more than one gauge blocks are joined. The act of joining gauge blocks is known as ringing. It has been illustrated in Fig. 6.23.

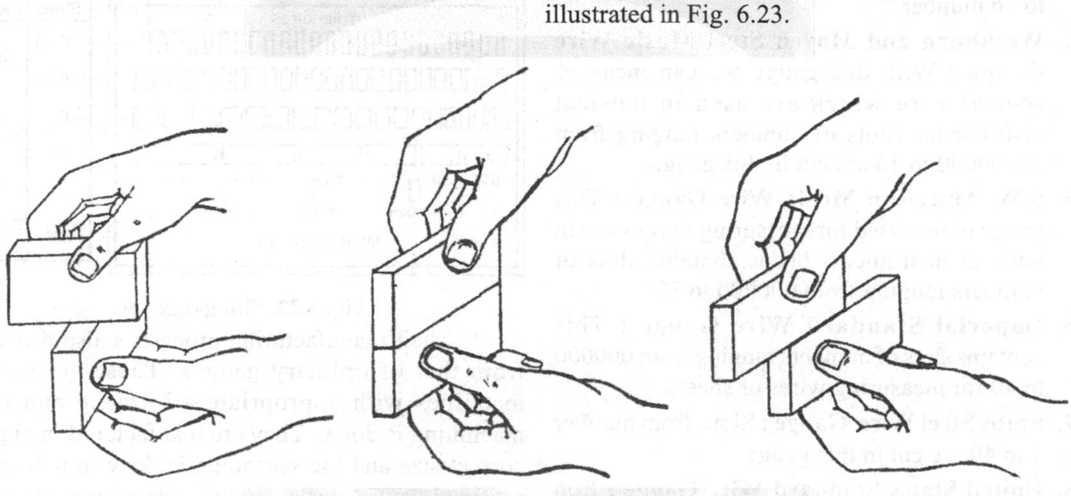
(*a*) (*b*) (*c*)

Fig. 6.23. Ringing action of gauge blocks

Ringing action. Two or more gauge blocks are joined in the following manner :

1. The gauging surface of the gauge blocks should be cleaned properly with tissue paper or chamois leather. At times, carbon tetrachloride is also used to clean these blocks.
2. The gauging surface of both the gauge blocks should be kept in a crossed manner as shown in Fig. 6.23(*a*).
3. Now the gauge blocks should be turned in such a way that their gauging surfaces come in a line as shown in Fig. 6.23(*b*).
4. Again, the gauge blocks should be withdrawn and brought out to about fifty percent as shown in Fig. 6.23(*c*).
5. Now again, the upper gauge block should be pushed back and brought back to parallel position as shown in Fig. 6.23 (*b*).

After this action both the gauge blocks will stick with each other and even air cannot pass through these blocks. If we want to separate them by pulling them directly, we cannot do so. These gauge blocks can only be separated by pushing them back. In the same way, other gauge blocks can also be joined. When all the blocks stick together they are in a position to stick together when they are hanged.

Metric Slip Gauge. Apart from inch measurement gauges, Metric slip gauges are generally used in most of the countries throughout the world. This type of block gauges are also available in sets. One set consists of 113, 111, 88, 86 or 45 slip gauges. With these gauges measurement from 0.001 mm to 200 mm can be taken. Measurement of the slip gauges depends upon the slip gauges available in the set. For example, measurement of 111 and 45 number has been given below :

Set of 111 Slip Gauges

No. of gauges	*Measurement in mm*	*Limit in mm*	*Class*
9	1.001 to 1.009	0.001	First
49	1.01 to 1.49	0.01	Second
49	1.5 to 24.5	0.05	Third
4	25 to 100	25	Fourth

Set of 45 Slip Gauges

No. of gauges	*Measurement in mm*	*Limit in mm*	*Class*
9	1.001 to 1.009	0.001	First
9	1.01 to 1.09	0.01	Second
9	1.1 to 1.9	0.1	Third
9	1 to 9	1	Fourth
9	10 to 90	10	Fifth

In the above mentioned and other sets measurement marking is indicated on each part. With help of these slip gauges with accuracy of 0.01 mm measurement can be taken by joining one or several parts.

In the above mentioned sets and similarly in all sets their size is indicated there on. With the help of these sets we can take measurement with 0.001 mm accuracy either with a single set or by joining several sets together.

Method of Use. While using slip gauges it should be insured that as far as possible minimum number of sets should be used. While selecting the sets first of all we should start by locating the 1000th part of mm secondly 100th part, thirdly 10th and finally 1 mm. Two examples have been given below :

Example 1. For checking measurement of 43.489 mm with slip gauge containing 45 sets, gauges would be selected as under :

Number 9 block in first class	=	1.009 mm
Number 8 block in second class	=	1.080 mm
Number 4 block in third class	=	1.400 mm
Number 4 block in fifth class	=	40.000 mm
Total 4 blocks	=	43.486 mm

Example 2. For testing measurement of 91.701 mm with slip gauge of 111 sets, selection of gauges would be as under :

Number 1 block in first class	=	1.001 mm
Number 20 block in second class	=	1.200 mm
Number 29 block in third class	=	14.500 mm
Number 3 block in fourth class	=	75.000 mm
Total 4 blocks	=	91.701 mm

Indicator Gauge. This gauge inspects minutely the surface of different types of jobs. We can inspect parallelism, flatness, taper, ovalness, straightness, high point *etc.* of surface of a job with accuracy of 0.001″ or 0.01 mm. In these jobs phase gauge can also be used but we do not get accurate results with phase gauges. As there is a graduation dial on the indicator, we can see the difference accurately and in a direct manner.

Indicators are mainly of four types :

1. Universal junior indicator
2. Universal test indicator
3. Last word indicator
4. Dial test indicator

Universal Junior Indicator. This is a flexible and delicate gauge. We can inspect the jobs with this indicator upto the limit of 0.012″ because on both the sides of zero marks upto 0.006″ are indicated. Generally it is used by fitting it in the tool post of lathe machine. With the universal junior indicator, we can verify a job accurately.

Universal Test Indicator. This is also a gauge of simple structure and is very useful. For contact there are three contact points in it, which are at equal distance from the fulcrum. By contact with any one of them its lever hand acquires speed and on the basis of proportion of contact power the difference is indicated on the graduated gauge. The limit of its inspection is 0.030″ because on both the sides of zero there is indication upto 0.015″

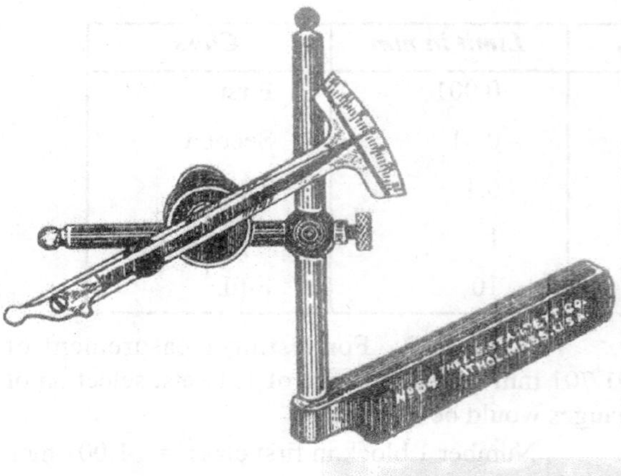

(*a*) **Universal test indicator**

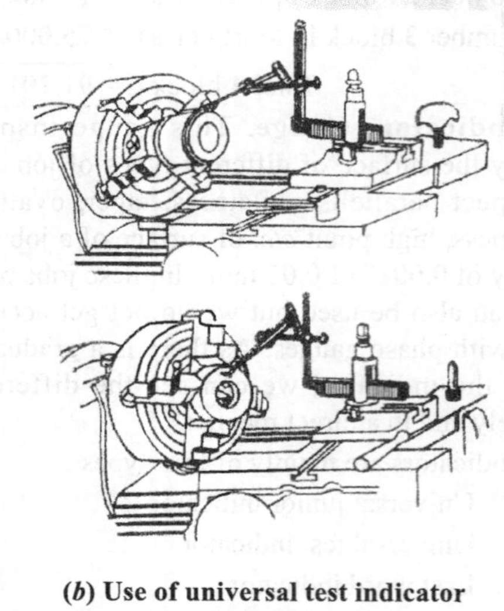

(*b*) **Use of universal test indicator**

Fig. 6.24.

The scale indicated on this has least count of 0.001″ or 0.02 mm. It is also mainly used for inspecting a job built or mounted on a lathe machine. This type of universal test indicator and its uses on lathe has been shown in Fig. 6 24. With this we can inspect the job externally or internally. These are of two types. The first type has only a gauge. The second type has a dial gauge. With the graduated dial gauge even slight difference in surface is also known through the needle.

Last Word Indicator. This type of indicators are available in five different kinds. Of these only "F" model last word indicator is highly used. It also contains graduated dial. Its contact point is ratchet joint, therefore, it can be fitted as per requirement without opening the spring clip. Its limit is also 0.030″ and it can indicate difference in 0.01 mm.

Dial Test Indicator. This is a very useful dial test indicator which is used for accurate checking and measuring gauge. With it we can know difference in surface. These are made to check accuracy upto 0.0001″ in English system and 0.001 in millimeters. A dial test indicator has been shown in Fig. 6.25.

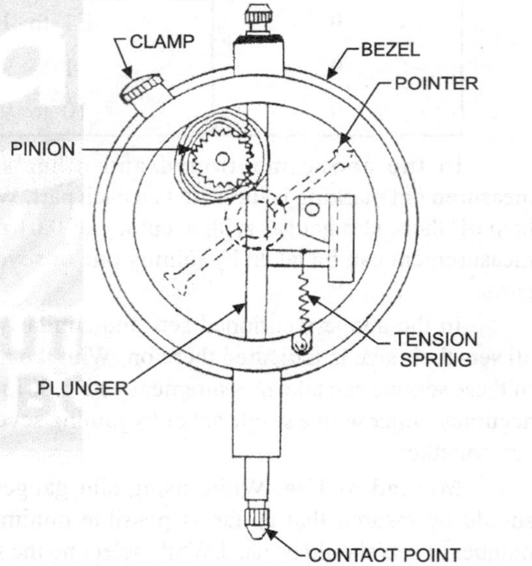

Fig. 6.25. Dial test indicator

It has the following main parts :

1. Case or housing
2. Cover
3. Bejel
4. Dial
5. Indicator needle
6. Revolution counter
7. Rack and plunger
8. Stem
9. Contact point
10. Dust cap
11. Crystal

Working Principle of Dial Gauge. The working principle of dial gauge has been shown in Fig 6.26. Only working of few parts has been illustrated in it. A plunger (A) is fixed in indicator's stem. A rack with pitch of 1 mm is fixed in it. A small gear (B) is also united. This gear has 10 teeth. The shaft on which gear (B) is fixed on the same shaft another gear (C′) with 100 teeth is united. Another gear (D′) is united with gear (C). On the axis of gear (D) needle is fixed. Marking from 0 to 100 at equal distance is indicated on the dial. To revert back the rack again to its original position, a spring is also attached.

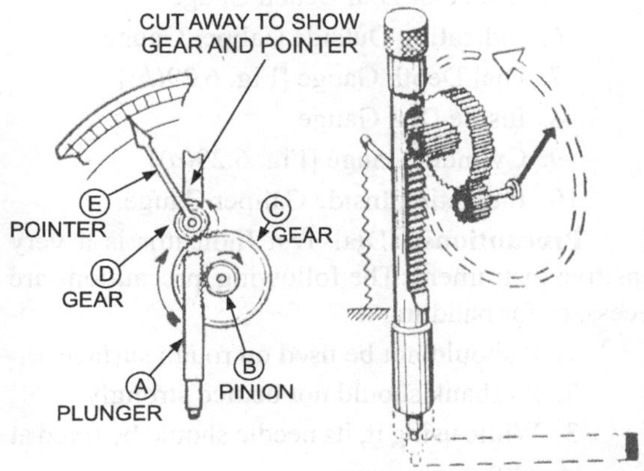

Fig. 6.26. Dial gauge indicator's working principle

When there is pressure on the contact point of gauge, rack moves up or down. Thus, when one tooth of rack moves up or down, a tooth of gear (B) also moves. In other words, when the rack rises up or comes down completely then gear (B) completes one full round. And with it, gear (C) also moves one complete round. Gear(C) with 100 teeth moves gear (D) 10 rounds because it has only 10 teeth. In this way when gear (D) completes ten rounds, it means rack rises up 10 mm or comes down. If gear (D) completes one round rack rises up or comes down $\frac{10}{10}$ = 1 mm. The needle fixed on the axis of gear (D) takes one round of the dial, which contains 100 markings at equal distance from one another. Thus we can say that when the needles move on 100 marks rack rises up or comes down by 1 mm.

Therefore its least count 100 points = 1 mm

$$\therefore \quad \text{One point of the dial} = \frac{1}{100}$$

$$= 0.001 \text{ mm.}$$

English Dial Test Indicator. Besides indicators of metric system other indicators of English system can measure or check with accuracy of 0.001. Value of one part of the dial in these indicators is equal to $\frac{1}{1000}$″. This also works like a metric system. The only difference in this indicator is that there are 40 teeth per inch. The gear joined to the rack has 40 teeth, with this another gear with 100 teeth is also joined. This gear remains joined with the gear with 100 teeth in the same manner. On the axis of this small gear a needle is fixed. This needle moves on the same dial on which 100 points are indicated at equal distance from each other.

In the English Dial Test Indicator when pressure is exerted on the contact point, gear (C) completes one round and because of it gear (D) completes ten rounds. In other words, when gear (D) moves ten rounds, rack goes up or down one inch. If gear (D) moves one round, rack also moves $\frac{1}{10}$″ =0.01″ up or down. Thus when the needle moves on the dial one round, rack moves only 0.1″. Therefore, the least count of indicator is :

$$100 \text{ points of Dial} = 0.1''$$

$$\text{Therefore} \quad 1 \text{ point of Dial} = \frac{0.1}{100} = 0.001''$$

In the above working principle, the number of teeth of gears and racks is given. These are not in the Dial Test indicators. It is decided by the dial manufacturing company. If we divide each part of the dial with 100 prints, then that gauge would give minimum measurement of 0.0005″. Similarly, division of points can be done in other ways also. Dial test indicators can be divided into two parts according to the difference in their dials and functioning.

Balanced Dial Test Indicator. In this type of dial test indicator, division of points is indicated on both sides of zero as shown in Fig. 6.27. On both

Fig. 6.27. Balanced dial test indicator

sides of zero line points upto 0.025″ are indicated. If the needle takes one round, its value or measurement is equal to 0.050″. In this type of dial, on both the sides of zero line points from 0.015″ to 0.05″ are indicated. Thus its limit is from 0.030" to 0.100″.

Continuous Dial Indicator. In this type of dial units division starts from one side of zero and continues upto the other side of zero as shown in Fig. 6.28.

Fig. 6.28. Continuous dial indicator

Dial test indicator of any kind is used alongwith a number of attachments for different functions.

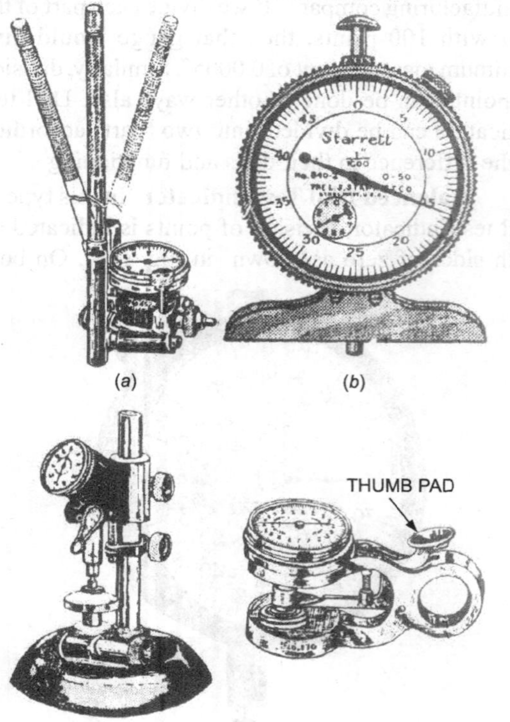

Fig. 6.29. Different types of dial indicators

Their names are according to the nature of their job and combination of attachments. Some of these sets have been named as under and illustrated in Fig. 6.29.

1. Test Set Dial Indicator
2. Universal Dial Test Indicator
3. Dial Bench Gauge [Fig. 6.29(*c*)]
4. Dial Sheet Gauge [Fig. 6.29(*d*)]
5. Inspector Dial Bench Gauge
6. Indicating Outside Caliper Gauge
7. Dial Depth Gauge [Fig. 6.29(*b*)]
8. Inside Dial Gauge
9. Cylinder Gauge [Fig. 6.29(*a*)]
10. Indicating Inside Caliper Gauge.

Precautions. Dial Test Indicator is a very sensitive instrument. The following precautions are necessary for handling it :

1. It should not be used on rough surface.
2. Its shank should not be tied strongly.
3. While using it, its needle should be fixed at zero.
4. It should be saved from pushes and jolts.
5. Plunger should always be kept clean.
6. According to the nature of work, proper combination should be used.
7. It should be kept separately from other tools.
8. Its repair should be done only by experienced mechanics.

Sine Bar. As we all know, with a protractor we can measure or indicate angle upto the acccuracy of 1°. For above this, angle protractor, universal bevel protractor and vernier bevel protractor can be used upto $\frac{1}{2}$° to 5 minutes. But for measurement or indication with accuracy of five minutes by Vernier bevel protractor is a very difficult act, which requires experience.

In various jobs we have to measure and mark the angles with the accuracy of a minute. For this purpose sine bar is used.

Working Principle of Sine Bar. Sine bar is based on the sine angle of a right angled triangle, that is why it is known as Sine Bar. Under this principle, in order to find out sine of an angle of a right angled triangle its perpendicular is divided by hypotenuse. In the triangle shown in Fig. 6. 30, if we want to know the sine of angle A, its perpendicula (*a*) will be divided by hypotenuse (*c*). Similarly, if sine of angle B is to be found, the opposite side B will be divided by hypotenuse (a).

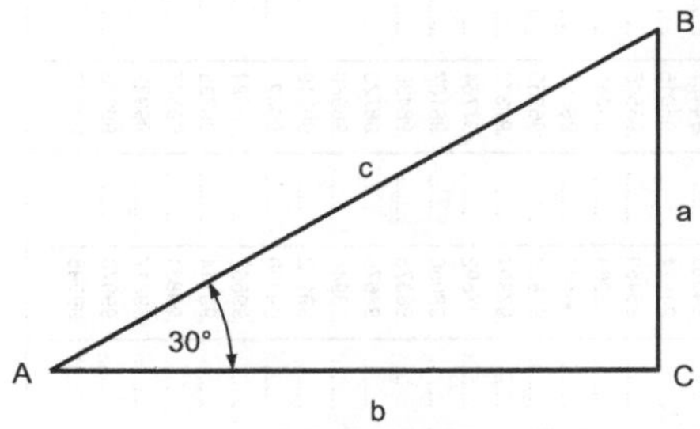

Fig. 6.30. Principle of sine bar

In this way, $\sin B = \frac{\text{Perpendicular}}{\text{Hypotenuse}}$

These are of three types :

1. Plug type.
2. Roller type.
3. Sine table type.

Structure. Its structure is very simple. It is made of steel and is hardened. Proper ground and lapping is done to make it highly plain. Two rollers or plugs of the same type of finishing done on them are fixed on them. These plugs are fixed in three ways. These three types of sine bars have been shown Fig. 6.31.

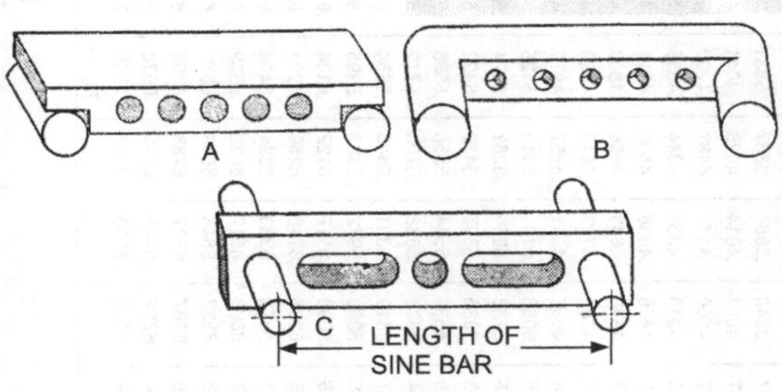

Fig. 6.31. Sine bar

The upper and lower surfaces of sine bar are parallel to each other and in the same way the centre lines of the plugs are also parallel to each other. The distance from the centre to centre of the plugs is the limit of that sine bar. These are normally available in size of 5″, 10″ and 20″.

On the basis of their accuracy they have been divided into two classes. Accuracy of class "A" is 0.00001″ per inch, while that of class "B" is accurate upto 0.00210″ per inch.

Method of Measuring with Sine Bar. For making measurement with sine bar, surface plate, gauge block, indicator set and clamp used for holding jobs, are used alongwith sine bar. Surface plate acts as a base and gauge lock acts as perpendicular and sine bar acts as a length of hypotenuse. The job which is to be measured should be kept on the sine bar and placed on the surface plate as shown in Fig. 6.32.

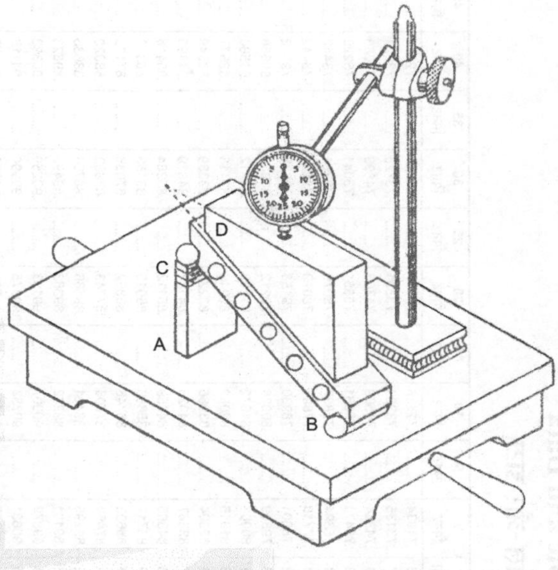

Fig. 6.32. Measurement by sine bar

Now gauge blocks are attached below the sine bar plug on the side of the angle of the job which is to be measured. These gauge blocks are fixed such an extent that the upper surface of the job becomes parallel to the surface plate. Dial test indicator is used to check it. When the surface of the job becomes parallel to the surface of the surface plate with the help of the gauge blocks, the measurement of those blocks is totalled. Thus their sum total is equal to perpendicular and sine bar's measurement is hypotenuse. So this total is divided by hypotenuse or the measurement of sine bar. In this way we find out the sine of that angle of the job. The measurement of this sine is known by sine table in degrees and minutes.

Example. (*i*) In Fig. 6.32, four gauge blocks have been used. Its sum total is 3.337″ and the length of sine bar is 5″

$$\therefore \quad \sin B = \frac{\text{Perpendicular}}{\text{Hypotenuse}} = \frac{3.337}{5}$$
$$= 0.66674$$

On finding out the measurement of 0.66674 from the sine bar table we came to know it as 41° 49′ which means angle B whose perpendicular is AC, block is of 41° 49′. But the accuracy of this

Natural Sine Table and Data
प्राकृतिक साइन टेबल और डाटा

डिग्री	0 मिनट	5 मिनट	10 मिनट	15 मिनट	20 मिनट	25 मिनट	30 मिनट	35 मिनट	40 मिनट	45 मिनट	50 मिनट	55 मिनट
0	....	.0015	.0029	.0044	.0058	.0073	.0087	.0102	.0116	.0131	.0145	.0160
1	.0175	.0189	.0204	.0218	.0238	.0247	.0262	.0276	.0291	.0305	.0320	.0334
2	.0349	.0364	.0378	.0393	.0407	.0422	.0436	.0451	.0465	.0480	.0494	.0509
3	.0523	.05538	.0552	.0567	.0581	.0596	.0610	.0625	.0640	.0654	.0669	.0683
4	.0698	.0712	.0727	.0741	.0756	.0770	.0785	.0799	.0815	.0828	.0843	.0857
5	.0872	.0886	.0901	.0915	.0930	.0944	.0958	.0973	.0987	.1002	.1016	.1031
6	.1045	.1060	.1074	.1089	.1103	.1118	.1132	.1147	.1167	.1175	.1190	.1204
7	.1219	.1233	.1248	.1262	.1276	.1291	.1305	.1320	.1334	.1349	.1363	.1377
8	.1392	.1406	.1421	.1435	.1449	.1464	.1478	.1493	.1507	.1521	.1536	.1550
9	.1564	.1579	.1593	.1607	.1622	.1636	.1650	.1665	.1679	.1694	.1709	.1722
10	.1736	.1751	.1765	.1779	.1794	.1808	.1822	.1834	.1851	.1865	.1879	.1894
11	.1908	.1922	.1937	.1951	.1965	.1979	.1994	.2008	.2022	.2036	.2051	.2065
12	.2079	.2093	.2108	.2122	.2136	.2150	.2164	.2179	.2193	.2207	.2221	.2235
13	.2250	.2264	.2278	.2292	.2306	.2320	.2334	.2349	.2363	.2377	.2391	.2405
14	.2419	.2433	.2447	.2462	.2476	.2490	.2504	.2518	.2532	.2546	.2560	.2574
15	.2588	.2602	.2616	.2630	.2644	.2658	.2672	.2686	.2700	.2714	.2728	.2742
16	.2756	.2770	.2784	.2798	.2812	.2826	.2840	.2854	.2868	.2882	.2896	.2910
17	.2924	.2938	.2952	.2965	.2979	.2993	.3007	.3021	.3035	.3049	.3063	.3076
18	.3090	.3104	.3118	.3132	.3145	.3159	.3173	.3187	.3201	.3214	.3228	.3242
19	.3256	.3269	.3283	.3297	.3311	.3324	.3338	.3352	.3365	.3379	.3393	.3407
20	.3420	.3434	.3448	.3461	.3475	.3488	.3502	.3516	.3529	.3543	.3557	.3570
21	.3584	.3597	.3611	.3624	.3638	.3652	.3665	.3679	.3692	.3706	.3719	.3733
22	.3746	.3760	.3773	.3787	.3800	.3813	.3827	.3840	.3854	.3867	.3881	.3894
23	.3907	.3921	.3934	.3947	.3961	.3974	.3987	.4001	.4014	.4028	.4041	.4054
24	.4067	.4081	.4094	.4107	.4120	.4134	.4147	.4160	.4173	.4187	.4200	.4213
25	.4226	.4239	.4253	.4266	.4279	.4292	.4305	.4318	.4331	.4344	.4358	.4371
26	.4384	.4397	.4410	.4423	.4435	.4449	.4462	.4475	.4488	.4501	.4514	.4527
27	.4540	.4553	.4566	.4579	.4592	.4605	.4617	.4630	.4643	.4656	.4669	.4682
28	.4695	.4707	.4720	.4733	.4746	.4759	.4772	.4784	.4797	.4810	.4823	.4835
29	.4848	.4861	.4873	.4886	.4899	.4912	.4924	.4937	.4949	.4962	.4975	.4987
30	.5000	.5013	.5025	.5038	.5050	.5053	.5075	.5088	.5100	.5113	.5125	.5138
31	.5150	.5163	.5175	.5188	.5200	.5213	.5225	.5238	.5250	.5262	.5274	.5287
32	.5299	.5311	.5324	.5336	.5348	.5361	.5373	.5385	.5397	.5410	.5422	.5434
33	.5446	.5459	.5471	.5483	.5495	.5507	.5519	.5531	.5544	.5556	.5568	.5580
34	.5592	.5604	.5616	.5628	.5640	.5652	.5664	.5676	.5688	.5700	.5712	.5724
35	.5736	.5748	.5760	.5771	.5783	.5795	.5807	.5819	.5831	.5843	.5854	.5866
36	.5878	.5890	.5901	.5913	.5925	.5936	.5948	.5960	.5972	.5983	.5995	.6006
37	.6018	.6030	.6041	.6053	.6064	.6076	.6088	.6099	.6117	.6122	.6134	.6145
38	.6157	.6168	.6179	.6191	.6202	.6214	.6225	.6236	.6248	.6259	.6271	.6283
39	.6295	.6304	.6316	.6327	.6338	.6349	.6361	.6372	.6383	.6394	.6406	.6417
40	.6428	.6439	.6450	.6461	.6472	.6483	.6494	.6506	.6517	.6528	.6539	.6550
41	.6561	.6572	.6582	.6593	.6604	.6615	.6626	.6637	.6648	.6659	.6670	.6681
42	.6691	.6702	.6713	.6724	.6734	.6745	.6756	.6767	.6777	.6788	.6799	.6808
43	.6820	.6831	.6841	.6852	.6862	.6873	.6884	.6894	.6905	.6915	.6926	.6937
44	.6947	.6957	.6967	.6978	.6988	.6999	.7009	.7019	.7030	.7040	.7055	.7053
45	.7071	....	.70916	....	.71121	....	.7133	....	.71529	....	.71732	....

डिग्री	0 मिनट	5 मिनट	10 मिनट	15 मिनट	20 मिनट	25 मिनट	30 मिनट	35 मिनट	40 मिनट	45 मिनट	50 मिनट	55 मिनट
46	.71934	....	.72136	....	.72337	....	.7254	....	.72731	....	.72937	....
47	.73135	....	.73333	....	.73531	....	.73728	....	.73924	....	.74120	....
48	.74314	....	.74509	....	.74703	....	.74896	....	.75088	....	.75280	....
49	.75471	....	.75661	....	.75851	....	.76041	....	.76229	....	.76417	....
50	.76694	....	.77897	....	.78079	....	.78261	....	.78442	....	.78622	....
51	.77715	....	.77897	....	.78079	....	.78261	....	.78442	....	.78622	....
52	.78601	....	.78930	....	.79158	....	.79335	....	.79512	....	.79688	....
53	.79869	....	.80038	....	.80212	....	.80386	....	.80558	....	.80730	....
54	.80902	....	.81072	....	.81292	....	.81412	....	.81580	....	.81748	....
55	.81915	....	.82082	....	.82246	....	.82413	....	.82577	....	.82741	....
56	.82904	....	.83066	....	.83228	....	.83389	....	.83549	....	.83708	....
57	.83867	....	.84025	....	.84182	....	.84339	....	.84495	....	.84650	....
58	.84805	....	.84959	....	.85112	....	.85264	....	.85416	....	.85562	....
59	.85717	....	.85866	....	.86015	....	.86163	....	.86310	....	.86457	....
60	.86603	....	.86748	....	.86892	....	.87036	....	.87178	....	.87321	....
61	.87462	....	.87603	....	.87743	....	.87882	....	.88020	....	.88158	....
62	.88295	....	.88431	....	.88566	....	.88701	....	.88835	....	.88968	....
63	.89101	....	.89232	....	.89363	....	.89493	....	.89623	....	.89753	....
64	.89879	....	.90007	....	.90153	....	.90259	....	.90383	....	.90507	....
65	.90631	....	.90753	....	.90875	....	.90996	....	.91116	....	.91236	....
66	.91355	....	.91472	....	.91590	....	.91706	....	.91822	....	.91936	....
67	.92090	....	.92164	....	.92276	....	.92388	....	.92499	....	.92609	....
68	.92718	....	.92827	....	.92935	....	.93042	....	.93118	....	.93253	....
69	.93358	....	.93462	....	.93565	....	.93667	....	.93769	....	.93869	....
70	.93969	....	.94068	....	.94167	....	.94464	....	.94361	....	.94457	....
71	.94552	....	.94646	....	.94740	....	.94832	....	.94924	....	.95015	....
72	.95106	....	.95195	....	.95284	....	.95372	....	.95459	....	.95545	....
72	.95630	....	.95715	....	.95799	....	.95882	....	.95964	....	.96045	....
74	.96126	....	.96205	....	.96285	....	.96363	....	.96440	....	.96517	....
75	.96593	....	.96667	....	.96742	....	.96815	....	.96887	....	.96959	....
76	.97030	....	.97100	....	.97169	....	.97237	....	.97304	....	.97371	....
77	.97437	....	.97502	....	.97566	....	.97630	....	.97692	....	.97754	....
78	.97815	....	.97875	....	.97934	....	.97992	....	.98050	....	.98107	....
79	.98163	....	.98218	....	.98272	....	.98325	....	.98378	....	.98436	....
80	.98481	....	.98531	....	.98580	....	.98629	....	.98676	....	.98723	....
81	.98769	....	.98814	....	.98858	....	.98902	....	.98944	....	.98986	....
82	.99027	....	.99067	....	.99106	....	.99144	....	.99182	....	.99219	....
83	.99255	....	.99290	....	.99324	....	.99357	....	.99390	....	.99421	....
84	.99452	....	.99482	....	.99511	....	.99540	....	.99567	....	.99594	....
85	.99619	....	.99644	....	.99668	....	.99692	....	.99714	....	.99736	....
86	.99756	....	.99776	....	.99795	....	.99813	....	.99831	....	.99847	....
87	.99863	....	.99878	....	.99892	....	.99904	....	.99917	....	.99929	....
88	.99939	....	.99949	....	.99958	....	.99966	....	.99973	....	.99975	....
89	.99985	....	.99989	....	.99993	....	.99996	....	.99998	....	1.0000	....
90	1.0000	....		....		....		....		....		....

Fig. 6.34.

measurement depends upon the fact that the grip between job and sine bar should be so tight that even a ray of light should not pass through it. For this purpose light or filler gauge is used.

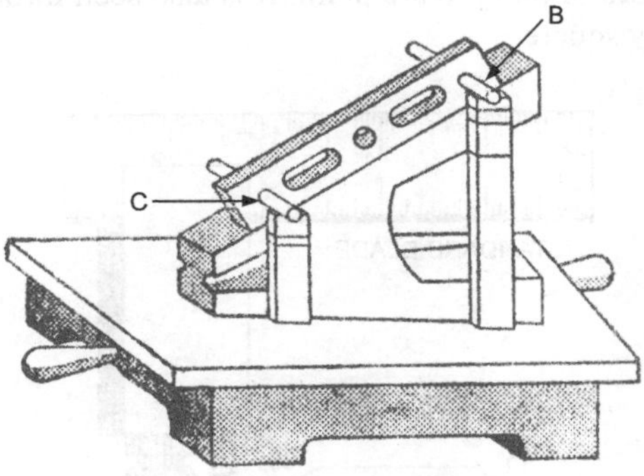

Fig. 6.33. Other use of sine bar

In the above example, job is placed over the sine bar to find out its angle. But for some other jobs, setting is done in a different way. In Fig. 6.33 a sine bar has been shown as fitted over the job. In such cases, it is essential that the upper surface remains stuck to sine bar and the lower surface should be united with the surface plate. We do not require dial test indicator in this case. Gauge blocks are fixed under the plugs in the same manner. In Fig. 6.33 there is a bracket. It does not have a place to keep sine bar on it so over both the plugs on one side of the sine bar in the job and below both the plugs gauge plugs are provided. The total of gauge blocks is 1.109″ and 2.9887″ and length of the sine bar is 5″.

Thus sine A = (2.9887″ – 1.109″)

$$= \frac{1.8797}{5} = 0.37594$$

On checking the value of 0.37594 in the Sine Bar Table (Fig. 6.34) measurement of angle "A' is equal to 22° 5'.

Precautions :

1. In order to find out angle of a job through sine bar, sine bar should be set on a good surface plate.
2. Great precautions are needed in using sine bar. While setting it, job sine bar and surface plate should be joined at their correct place otherwise the measurement of angle would become inaccurate.
3. It is necessary to take special care of sine bar. In order to protect it from rust, grease or oil should be used on it.
4. It should be kept away from other tools, particularly cutting tools.
5. Before using sine bar, it should be thoroughly cleaned.

Try Squares. We take assistance of try squares while marking a job or measuring or checking them. It is actually used to check whether the angle made by the two sides of square is a right angle (90°) or not. We can also check plainers and straighteners with it.

It is also known as Engineers' Square. In Fig. 6.35 an ordinary try square has been shown. It has two parts, (*i*) Blade, (*ii*) Stock or beam. Thin portion is called blade and the thick part is called stock. Blade and stock are made of steel and are hardened and grinded. These are joined with each other at 90° (right) angle. Ends of stock and blade are accurately parallel to each other at 0.0001″. The blade contains graduation in inches and millimeters. Similarly, there is a "L" square in which the thickness of the blade and the stock is the same. It is used in sheet motal, carpentary and building construction. Try squares used in engineering line can be divided into three parts :

1. Solid Try Square.
2. Adjustable Try Square.
3. Diemakers Try Square.

1. Solid try square. Their limit is between 100 mm to 150 mm. They are of two types. In the first type we include those try squares whose blade and stock have same thickness, which are generally made from onepiece, at the right angle.

In the other type, blade is comparatively thinner than the stock, these are joined at right angle through a rivet. Their size is known on the basis of the length of the blade. Their edge is bevel edge.

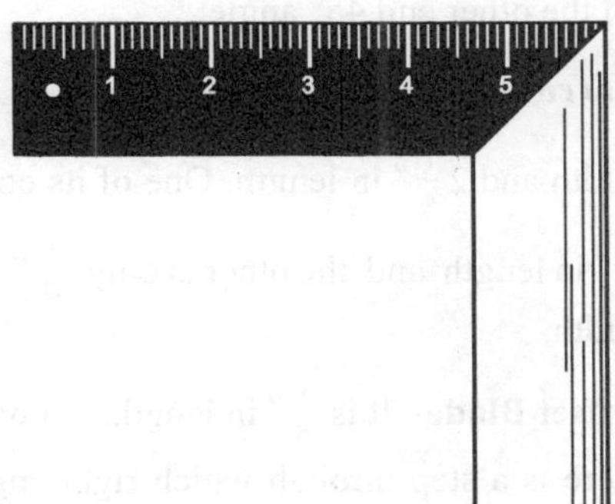

Fig. 6.35 Engineer / Try square

Adjustable Try Square. This type of try square has been shown in Fig. 6.36. In this try square stock can be fitted anywhere at any distance on the blade. Thus a right angle is formed on both sides of the stock. For fitting the stock on the blade there is a provision of knurled nut and thumb screw. There is a groove on the complete length of the blade, in which thumb screw's hook is fixed. In some adjustable try squares there is a provision of a set of two or three blades. Their length is from 4″ to 12″.

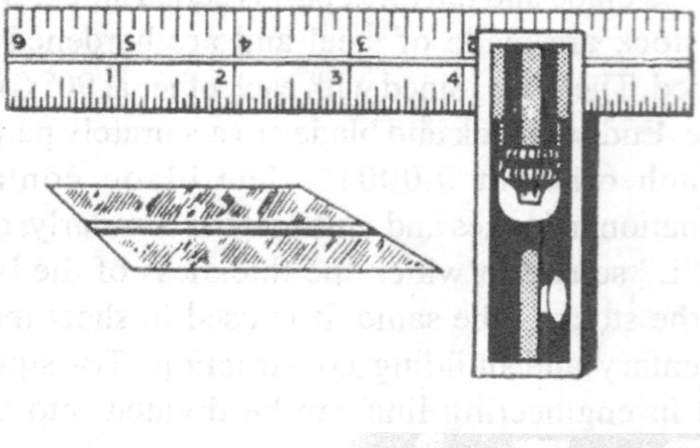

Fig. 6.36. Adjustable try square

Die Makers Try Square. This try square is almost similar to Adjustable Try Square. But there is another small screw on its stock. A special feature of this try square is that apart from setting it at right angle, it can be set upto 30°. It is also manufactured in the form of a set, which contains the following four types of blades :

1. **Standard Blade.** This is an ordinary blade. It is $\frac{1}{2}$″ in width and $2\frac{1}{2}$″ in length. It contains inch or mm signs. An inch is divided in 32 parts and indicated on it.
2. **Bavel Blade.** In this type of blade, bavel is made in the form of on one end 30° angle and on the other end 45° angle.
3. **Narrow Blade.** This type of blade is $\frac{5}{32}$″ in width and $2\frac{1}{4}$″ in length. One of its corner is $\frac{5}{8}$″ in length and the other is only $\frac{3}{32}$″ inch in width.
4. **Offset Blade.** It is $\frac{1}{8}$″ in length. On one side there is a step through which right angles of unusual jobs can be measured.

Procedures for use of Try Square. Try square is often used for checking or verifying the right angle of any angle made by any two sides of a job. For verifying right angle, it is essential that both the surfaces of that job are plain. It is also seen through the try square.

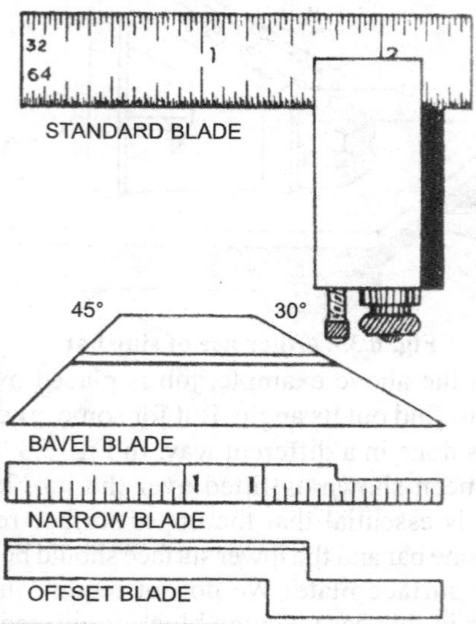

Fig. 6.37. Die makers try square

In order to check the plainers of surface of a job, we should place the blade upside down. The edge of the blade should be completely touched to the surface of the job. If even rays of light pass through it, it means the surface of the job is not plain. Similarly, in order to verify the right angle of a job, place the try square. Both the sides of the job should remain stuck to the blade and stock of the try square. Even rays of light should not pass through it. The accuracy of a internal right angle of a job can also be measured with the medium of light.

Precautions :

1. We should not use try square as a hammer *i.e.,* we should not use it to hit any job otherwise its accuracy is spoiled.
2. Try square should be kept away from cutting tools.
3. It should be cleaned properly before use.
4. After making its use, it should be kept after applying grease.

Questions

1. What are the uses of Gauges in workshops ?
2. Which are the main gauges used by a Fitter ?
3. How do we classify gauge ?
4. Why do we use Master Inspection Gauge ?
5. What is the difference between gauge and other measuring tools ?
6. Briefly describe Plug gauge, Ring gauge and Span gauge.
7. What are the different types of Radius gauge ?
8. What is the difference between drill gauge and point gauge ?
9. Draw a sketch of Filler Gauge and describe.
10. What is the use of screw Pitch Gauge ?
11. What is the working principle of Dial Test Indicator ? Explain with the help of sketch.
12. Explain the use of Sine Bar with the help of a sketch.
13. Of how many types wire gauges are there and what are their uses ?
14. Draw a sketch of Try Square and mention its uses.
15. What do you mean by GO and NOT GO Gauges ?
16. Comment on the following :

    (*a*) Centre gauge

    (*b*) Receiving gauge

    (*c*) Caliper gauge

    (*d*) Angle gauge

    (*e*) Taper gauge

7

Marking Tools and Equipment

For making any new article (job), it is necessary to have correct marking, according to its blue print or drawing. If the marking is not exact, the job will not be according to the drawing measurements. We can well imagine the difficulty in using a machine part made with wrong measurements. A lot of time is wasted in fitting a wrong part. For exact marking, the following important points should be kept in mind :

1. Before marking, drawing of the job should be carefully read.
2. While reading the drawings its measurement should be carefully noted.
3. According to the measurement, the required tools should be kept ready in advance.
4. Only correct and genuine tools should be used for marking.
5. Before making the marking permanent through dot-punching, the marking lines should be checked once again.
6. The place, at which drilling is to be done, should be marked with centre-punch. For different kinds of job, different types of marking is needed. The following kinds of tools and instruments are used for different markings, according to drawings :
   1. Marking Table
   2. Surface Plate
   3. Angle Plate
   4. Odd Leg or Jenny Caliper
   5. Divider
   6. Scriber
   7. Surface Gauge
   8. Universal Surface Gauge
   9. Trammel
   10. V. Block
   11. Punch.

Marking Table

A special marking-out table is often used in almost all workshops for undertaking marking jobs. This is rectangular or circular as shown in Fig. 7.1.

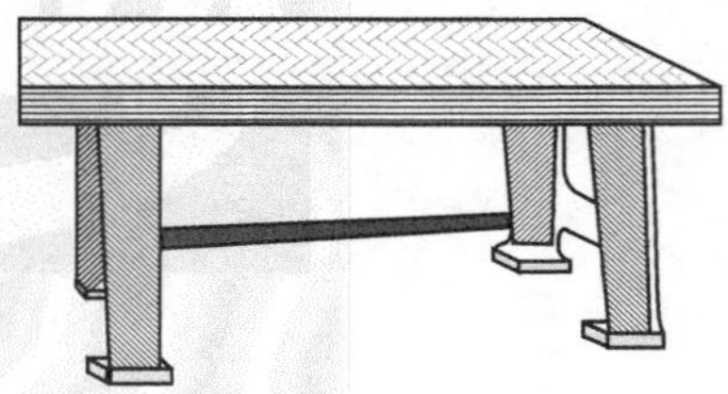

Fig. 7.1. Marking Table

Its breadth is from 4′ to 5′ and length is 6′ to 10′. The upper part of this table is generally made plain. This table is used for simple and routine marking jobs, where general tools such as steel foot-rule scriber and odd-leg caliper is used. In addition, it is also used for punching and chipping job.

Surface Plate

For jobs which require exact markings, surface plate is used. Like the marking table, this table is also either rectangular or circular. These plates are made of close grain-cast iron and these are kept out at least

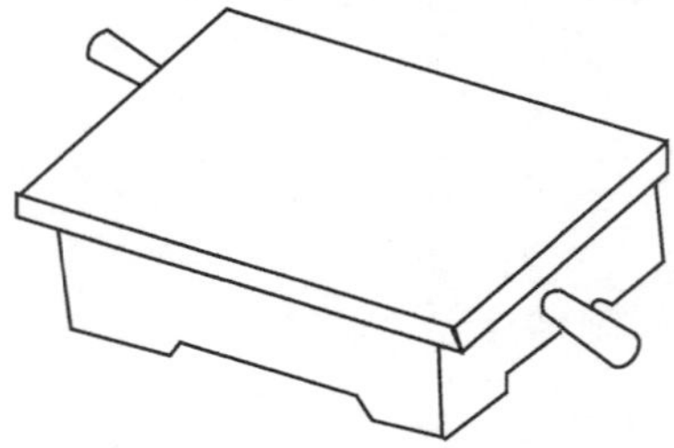

Fig. 7.2. Surface plate

for one year for the purpose of seasoning. Their upper surface has fine finish which may contain 10 per cent to 20 per cent high spots. For convenience there are two handles on opposite sides. There are ribs on the inner side of the plates, which make them more strong. The main plate *extends beyonds* its base frame as shown in Fig. 7.2.

Considerable care is required for making surface plate. After its moulding and seasoning it is cut or scratched according to the size on the plainer machine. Its surface is almost made plain and through scrapping, it gives its true form. Master plate is used for this purpose. Lead oxide is applied on the surface plate and then rubbed on the master plate. The spots which are higher than the basic principle/original surface, their lead oxide is wiped and their high spots are levelled by scrapping. Similarly, lead oxide is applied to two new surface plates and their high spots are plained after detecting them.

Use of Surface Plate. Surface Plate is generally used for jobs which are required to be made accurate straight or parallel lines are drawn on any job with the help of vernier height gauge and surface gauge. A pair of "V" blocks is kept on it, marking of centre of a round job is also done. Besides these, surface plate is used for the following jobs :

1. To measure the smoothness of the job with the main surface of the surface plate.
2. To measure the right angle of a job.
3. To measure or mark angle of a job with the help of sine bar.
4. To check the jobs produced, in less time.
5. To measure a job with a Dial Test Indicator.

Precautions. Before and after using the surface plate, the following precautions should be taken:

1. Before marking or measuring a job, its surface should be properly cleaned with a soft paper.
2. While using it, it should not be hit as there are chances of damage to its surface.
3. In order to make the marking of the job permanent it should not be used as a table.
4. Cutting tool should never be used on it.
5. It should be kept separately in the furnace.
6. After using it, oil or grease should be applied and it should be covered with a lid and kept safely.

Angle Plate

This plate is made of good cast iron. It is built at 90° angle. It has rectangular grooves. Both its outer surfaces are accurately plained by the scraper. If we place it on the surface plate, it makes an angle of 90°. It is used to provide support to the job from behind while measuring. In heavy jobs, nut bolts are fitted in its grooves and marking is done or they are tied on the angle plate for other machining activity is done.

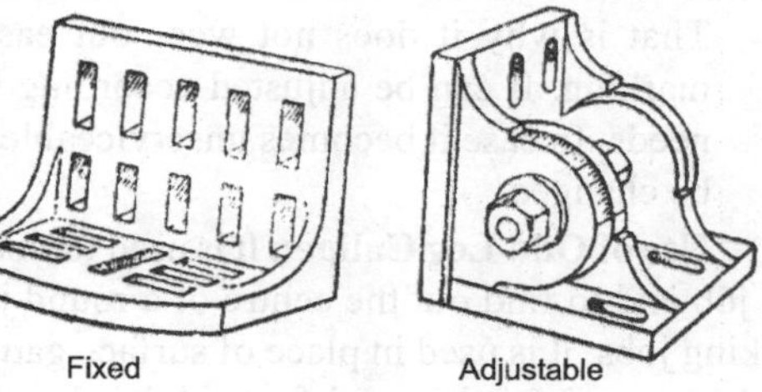

Fig. 7.3. Angle plate

Angle plate is of two types in big and small size as shown in Fig. 7.3 above.

1. **Fixed Angle Pate.** It is used to give support to the job at the right angle. Job is fixed on it for carrying other machining activities.
2. **Adjustable Angle Plate.** It is used for doing angular marking or measurement.

Odd Leg Caliper

It is also known as Jenny Caliper or Hermaphrodite Caliper. One of its legs is straight and the other is bent about $\frac{1}{8}''$ to $\frac{1}{4}''$ towards inside as shown in Fig. 7.4.

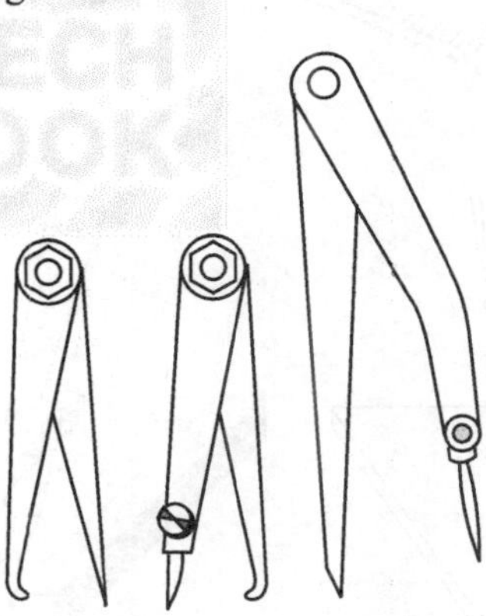

Fig. 7.4. Odd leg caliper

Both the legs are joined with a rivet or a spring. With slight pressure we can increase or decrease distance between these two legs. These are made of mild steel and their points are case-hardened. According to their makeup these are of the following two types :

1. **Fixed-Point Odd-Leg Caliper.** This type of caliper has been shown in Fig. 7.4. The working leg of this caliper remains fixed.
2. **Adjustable Point Odd Leg Caliper.** This type of caliper has been shown in Fig. 7.4 (B). One end of this working leg is fitted with a screw and a nut. This point is made of tool steel wire. That is why it does not wear out easily in marking. It can be adjusted according to our needs. In case it becomes unserviceable it can be changed.

Use of Odd Leg Caliper. It is used for marking of a job and to find out the centre of a round job. In marking jobs, it is used in place of surface gauge. Its measurement is set by steel foot rule's edge. While setting the size it should be ensured that the bent leg should be kept on the side of steel foot rule and the pointed leg should be slipped to appropriate distance as shown in Fig. 7.5(A).

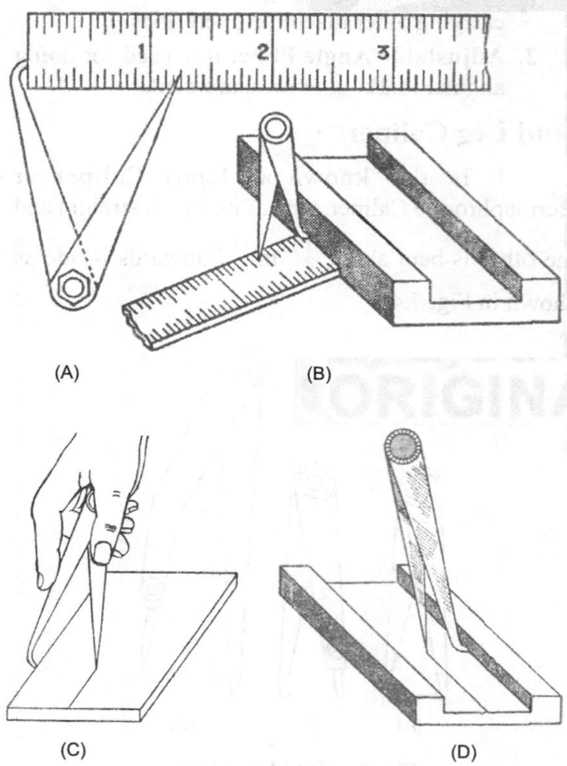

Fig. 7.5. Use and method of marking

But in case a parallel line is to be drawn in a groove, the bent leg of the caliper should be stuck with some wall-like straight surface and the pointed leg should be adjusted according to need for setting measurement as shown in Fig. 7.5(B). It is an important act to hold the caliper. If we do not hold it properly, the marking can be wrong. Caliper should be held as shown in Fig. 7.5(C). While marking, the bent leg should be stuck to one finish side of the job and we should draw the line with the pointed leg. The caliper should be slightly inclined in the same direction in which the line proceeds. While drawing lines in a grooved job, the bent leg of the caliper should be stuck to the finished wall as shown in Fig. 7.5(D).

Determining Centre of a Cylindrical Job. For determining centre of a job in the form of a cylindrical stick, the odd leg caliper should be opened to the extent of nearly half of the size of stick's diameter. Now the bent leg of the caliper should be stuck anywhere and a chop should be drawn with the pointed leg. In the same manner, we should draw four chops by turning the caliper. At the points where the chop markings intersect we should draw straight lines intersecting each other. The point where both the lines meet is treated as the centre of the job. Three ways of drawing a chop have been illustrated in Fig. 7.6.

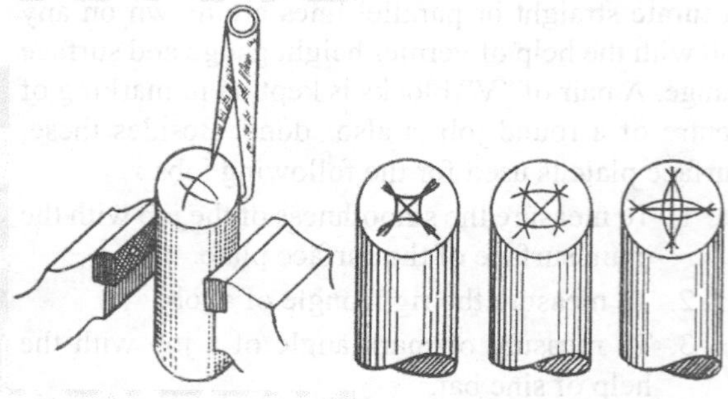

Fig. 7.6. Determining centre of a cylindrical stick

Dividers

Dividers are used to draw circle on a job, chop or to divide a line into equal parts and to mark them. These are generally made of mild steel. Its pointed ends are case hardened so that they do not wear out easily.

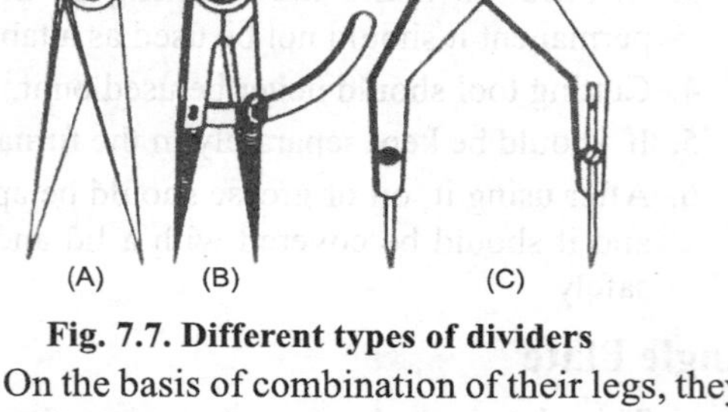

Fig. 7.7. Different types of dividers

On the basis of combination of their legs, they are classified into two parts :

1. **Firm joint-dividers.** In this type of dividers, their legs are joined by a rivet and washer at the top. But the rivet is not fixed tightly so that its legs can be opened easily. Different types of firm joint-dividers are shown in Fig. 7.7.
2. **Spring Joint-Dividers.** In this type of dividers, both the legs are tightened on a pin with a spring. Their legs are also joined with each other by an extra screw and split nut as shown in Fig. 7.8. Their legs can be easily opened or closed as required, by moving its nut. A knurled stud is often fixed in the centre of the spring. We hold it at the time of marking. After once setting it we can check the job several times because its size does not change itself easily. It saves time and makes the job accurate.

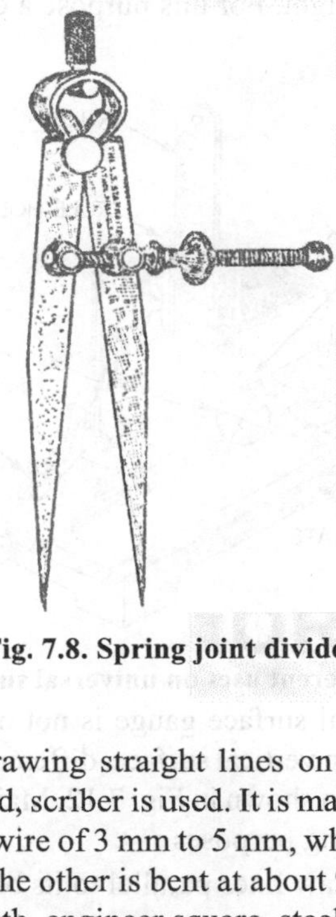

Fig. 7.8. Spring joint dividers

Scriber

For drawing straight lines on jobs made of metal or wood, scriber is used. It is made of a steel or carbon steel wire of 3 mm to 5 mm, whose one end is straight and the other is bent at about 90° angle. It is used alongwith engineer square, steel foot rule, and straight edge. Its length varies from 150 mm to 300 mm. Both its ends are pointed. For special use in various jobs, other types of improved scribers are also used. These are of the following five types as shown in Fig. 7.9 :

1. Ordinary scriber
2. Improved scriber
3. Adjustable sleeve scriber
4. Pocket scriber
5. Knok scriber

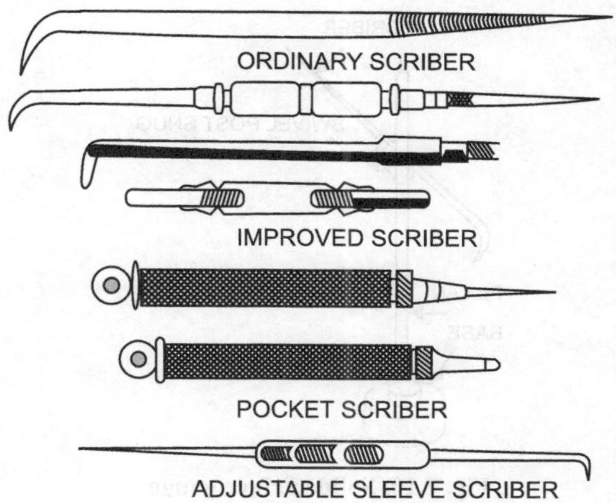

Fig. 7.9. Different types of scribers

Use and Precautions. Before drawing lines on a job coating of Persian blue, copper sulphate or chalk should be done on its surface and it should be allowed to get dried. We should cover the point, which is not to be used with a piece of cloth, cork *etc.* so that its point does not hurt our fingers. We should check the point of the leg, if it needs to be sharpened we must sharpen it with a file before using it. We should not exert excess pressure at the time of drawing lines. Scriber should be slightly bent in the direction in which the line is being extended.

Surface Gauge

It is also known as Marking Block or Scribing Block. With the scriber and odd leg caliper we can do marking on ordinary jobs but for drawing parallel lines with high accuracy surface gauge is used. These are of the following two types :

1. Solid Surface Gauge
2. Universal Surface Gauge

Solid Surface Gauge. In the beginning this gauge was used for accurate marking. This was made on a solid base which had a rod fixed in its centre.

Scriber was fixed by fitting a snug bolt in this pillar. For making use of it, it was adjusted with hand and drawn near the steel foot rule. It is used to take more time and there was no provision of placing it on a round job. Moreover its pillar (rod) used to remain erect. As such it could not be set in an angular position. Thus, several difficulties were experienced in its use. It has been shown in Fig. 7.10.

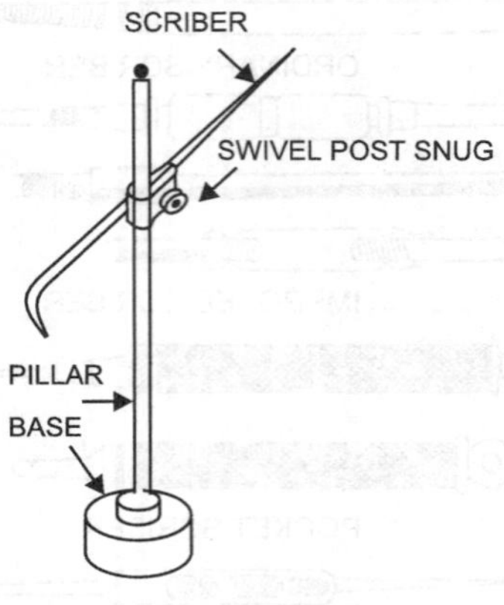

Fig. 7.10. Solid surface gauge

Universal Surface Gauge. For accurate marking in less time and without difficulty universal surface gauges were made and came into use. With this gauge accurate marking can be done on almost all types of jobs. It contains the following parts as shown in Fig. 7.11.

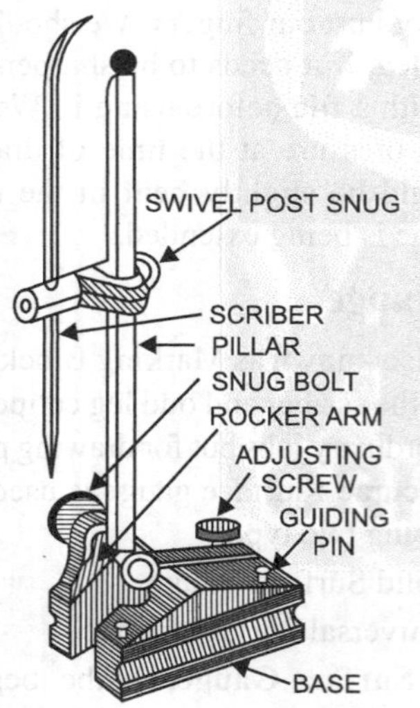

Fig. 7.11. Universal surface gauge

1. Base
2. Rocker Arm
3. Snug Bolt
4. Pillar or Rod
5. Adjustable Screw
6. Guide Pin
7. Swivel Post Snug
8. Scriber

The base of universal surface gauge is made of good cast iron in rectangular form. It is slotted in "V" shape throughout its length. On the upper surface of its base, two guide pins are fixed. These pins are used for marking like an odd leg caliper for sticking it a machined surface. Because of "V" shaped slots this does not stick to the surface plate. Thus it can be easily pushed ahead or pulled backwards. Besides, this dirt and filth of the surface plate does not have any effect on the marking because that dirt can be transferred to the slots. It can be easily placed on the round rod. On one side of the base rocker arm is tightened with a screw. On one side of this rocker arm, pillar is fixed with a snug bolt. With help of bolt this pillar can be bent at any angle. Scriber's point can be easily matched with any part of the steel foot rule through the adjusting screw. Scriber is fitted in the pillar with the help of the snug bolt, which does the actual marking. Swivel post snug can be set on the pillar at any height. For this purpose a clamping nut is fixed.

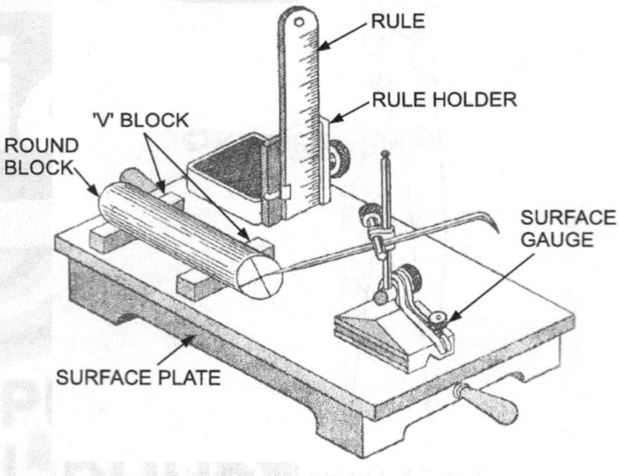

Fig . 7.12. Different uses on universal surface gauge

Universal surface gauge is not only used for drawing lines on vertical surface, different uses of this gauge have been shown in Fig. 7.12. Mainly it is used for the following purposes :

1. To draw lines parallel to its base.
2. To find out the centre of cylindrical and square rods.
3. To draw lines parallel to plain arm of a job.
4. To properly focus the job on the lathe.
5. To draw parallel line like height gauge on normal job.

Precautions :

1. We should keep the swivel post snug of surface gauge tight.
2. Scribed should be bent (inclined) atless than 90°.

3. While drawing similar parallel lines, we should check them from time to time.

4. Scriber should not be kept excessively outside the snug.

Trammel

Like a divider, a trammel is also used for drawing a circle chop or two parallel lines. It has a round or square rod, which is called a trammel bar or beam.

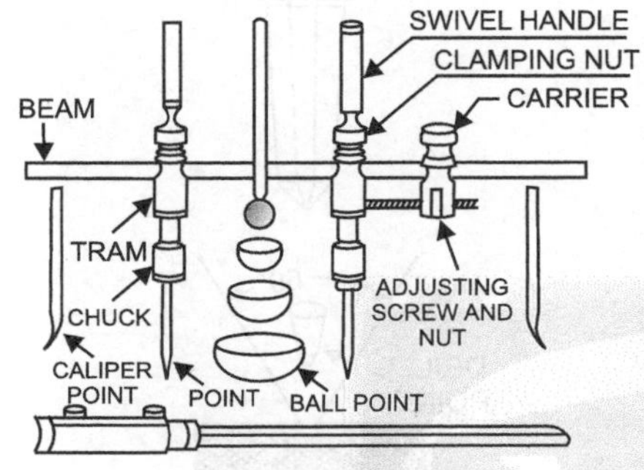

Fig. 7.13. Trammel

There are two movable trams on this beam. This can also be used as an inside or outside caliper by fixing points of different types. It has the following main parts, which has been shown in Fig. 7.13.

1. Beam
2. Tram
3. Clamping nut
4. Chuck
5. Point
6. Carrier
7. Adjusting screw
8. Swivel handle

Beam is generally 15 mm to 50 mm in length. In good trammels graduation is indicated in millimeters. Ball point is fitted in its tram, from a bored centre a circle or chop is drawn. For extraordinary big jobs additional beams are also attached.

"V" Block

For marking on a round or rectangular job, "V" block is used to clamp it. With its help drilling, punching and other machining operations are easily carried out on such jobs. It is made of cast iron or tool steel. Its surfaces are well machined and grinded. A "V" shaped slot of 90° angle is made in the centre on both sides. On the remaining two sides rectangular grooves are made in which clamp is fixed. These are generally of the following three types and are available in pairs.

Simple "V" Block. This is rectangular block which has a "V" shaped groove on its upper surface as shown in Fig. 7.14 (*a*).

Heavy round jobs are kept over it for marking or machining. There is no provision to clamp the job since because of heavy weight of the job, it remains fixed.

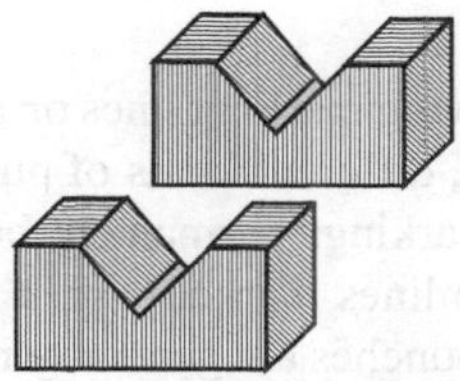

Fig. 7.14. (*a*) Simple "V" block

Clamping "V" Block. It is also a rectangular block. A "V" shape groove is cut on two surfaces, facing each other and on the remaining two surfaces rectangular grooves are cut, in which clamp is fixed. Job is kept on the "V" groove and clamp is fixed with the clamping screw. These are generally used in pairs as shown in Fig. 7'14 (*b*).

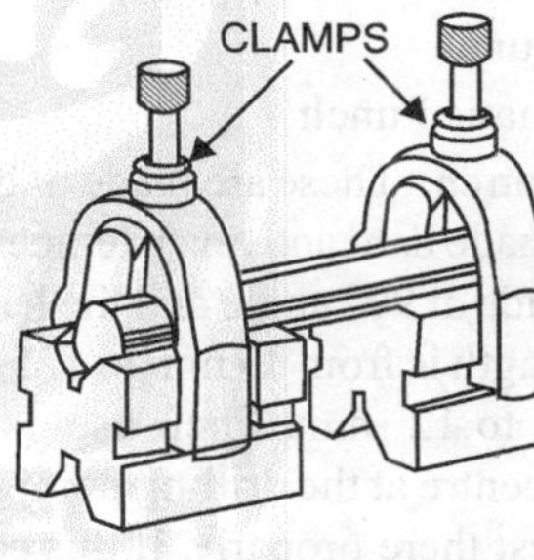

Fig. 7.14. (*b*) Clamping "V" Block

Its distinct feature is that while carrying out any operation on a round job, the job does not move or shake.

Magnetic "V" Block. In this "V" block which looks like an ordinary "V" block, provision of

Fig. 7.14 (*c*). Magnetic "V" block

magnetic power is made. Because of magnetic effect the job remains stuck to the block.

A switch is provided to start or put off the magnetic effect. When we put the switch in "on" condition the job gets stuck to the block and in "off ' condition the magnetic effect ends. This type of "V" block has been shown in Fig. 7.14 (*c*).

Punch

After drawing marking lines on a job by scriber or surface gauge, different kinds of punches are used to make these markings permanent, because there is possibility of the lines marked with a scriber getting affected. These punches are generally made of carbon steel or tool steel. Mainly the following punches are used :

1. Centre Punch
2. Dot Punch
3. Prick Punch
4. Solid Punch
5. Hollow Punch
6. Pin Punch
7. Bell Punch
8. Automatic Punch

Centre Punch. These are made of high carbon steel. These are made hard and given temper treatment. Their point is made at 90° angle and the handling part is knurled. Its length is from 35 mm to 125 mm and its width is from 4 to 12 mm. Their use is generally made to make a centre at the drilling point so that drill bit's point can rest there properly. If this centre is not made by the centre punch, there are chances of slipping of the point and drilling at a wrong point. This type of centre has been illustrated in Fig. 7.15.

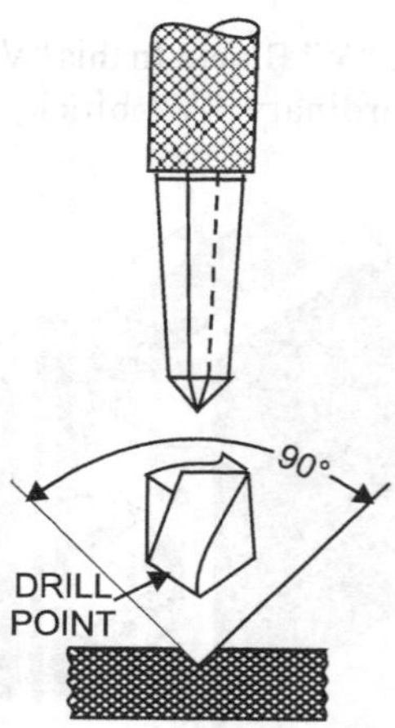

Fig. 7.15. Centre punch

Dot Punch. This is by and large similar to the Centre Punch. The main difference is that its point is at 60° angle. It is used to make permanent the marking done by scriber so that these lines do not obliterate at the time of work. Its length is from 80 mm to 100 mm and its thickness from 3 mm to 5 mm. It has been illustrated in Fig. 7.16.

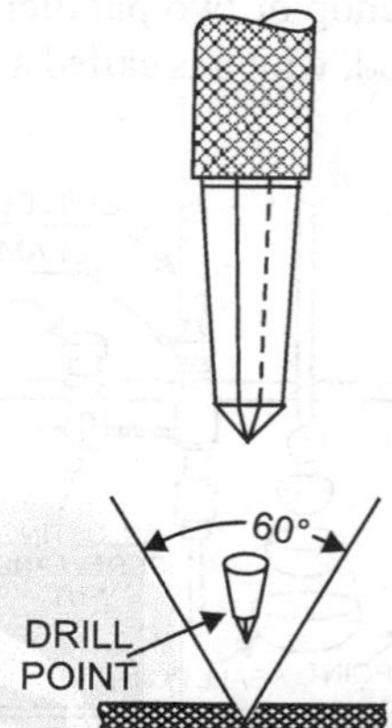

Fig. 7.16. Dot punch

Prick Punch. This is also made of high carbon steel. Prick punch is also made hard and tempered. Its point is made at 30° angle. It is used for marking on jobs of thin metal sheets or to make holes in them. It has been shown in Fig. 7.17.

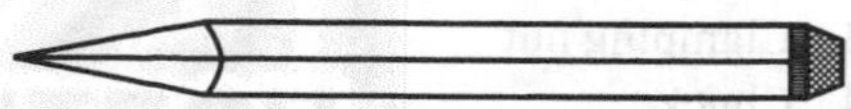

Fig. 7.17. Prick punch

Solid Punch. Solid punch is used for boring holes in blacksmithy and sheet metal. These are used in different measurements according to the jobs. These are made of high carbon steel, hardened and tempered. While using these in hot jobs it is essential to cool them in cold water. These are used in rough works because holes made with solid punch are not exactly according to measurements and are not clean.

Hollow Punch. It is a special type of a hardened steel punch with hollowness as shown in Fig. 7.18. It is used for cutting holes in metal, cardboard, fabric. These are available in different sets for holes of different sizes. As they are hollow, the metal which is cut with them falls out through the grooves built on its side. Thus, we can make a number of holes in little time and the holes are quite clear.

Fig. 7.18. Hollow punch

Pin Punch. This punch is somewhat different from other punches. It is comparatively larger in length. Instead of being pointed in shape these are parallel. It is used for tight fitting pins. A pin punch has been shown in Fig. 7.19.

Fig. 7.19. Pin punch

Bell Punch. As per its name it is like a small bell in shape. Its size is considered according to circumference of the bell. It is used to find out the centre of round jobs and for light marking. In this circumference a punch is fixed with the help of a spring, which is like a centre punch. For using it its head is hit with a hammer and because of punch spring it raises alone.

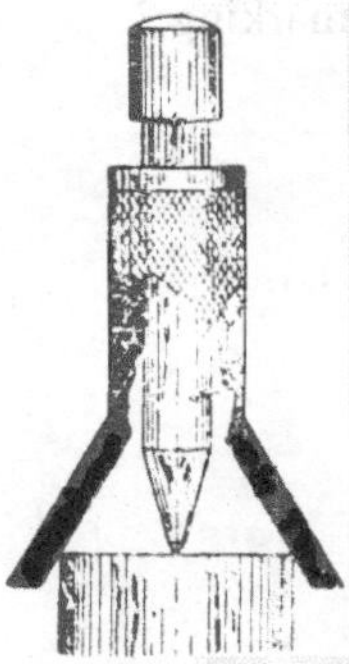

Fig. 7.20. Bell punch

Automatic Punch. This is also a special kind of punch. It is made of high carbon steel which is hardened or tapered. There is no need for a hammer *etc.* for using this punch.

A main punch is fitted with its body with a spring. Spring remains settled through a lever head. When marking is to be done, its lever head is pressed. Through this pressure main punch would be pressed and do the marking. The blow of the punch can be limited or controlled with the lever head. Its main punch is built at 60° or 90° angle. This type of punch has been illustrated in Fig. 7.21.

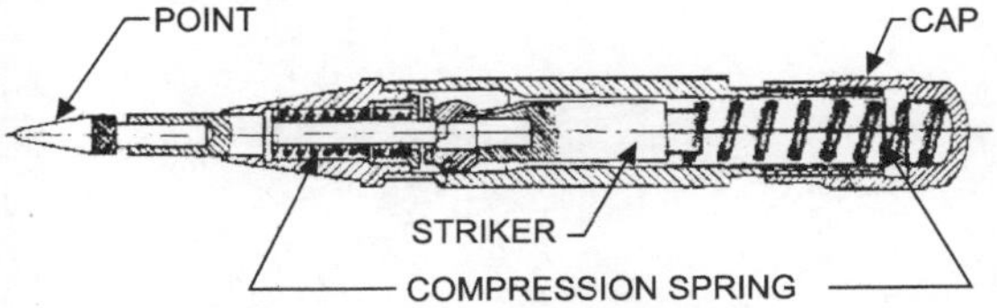

Fig. 7.21. Automatic punch

Precautions. In order to ensure correct and accurate marking with any type of punch, the following precautions should be taken :

1. Selection of punch should be made according to the make-up of the job or metal.
2. Light hammer should be used for a light punch.
3. Do not use an ordinary punch or a hard metal.
4. Use a punch after seeing its angle.
5. If point of the punch is damaged, it should be repaired and then the punch should be used.
6. Hollow punch should not be used on thick sheets.

Method of Marking

The efficiency of a job depends to a considerable extent, on the marking done on a job, before it is machined. If marking is not accurate, the job would be of wrong size, it may become slightly more or less than the size requircd. In a way, marking job is a matter of experience and different methods have been evolved for marking on different types of jobs. There are different methods for marking a round and a square job. Although no specific rules can be framed for marking yet for general marking the following methods are adopted :

1. We should keep the drawing of job which we are suppose to make and understand it properly.
2. Before marking, two adjoining sides and a surface of the job should be well prepared after filling, scraping and other machining.
3. The marking surface should be coated with a thin paste of persian blue, copper sulphate or chalk and desired before marking.
4. If a surface gauge or vernier gauge is to be used for marking, the job should be properly placed on the surface plate, with angle plate and "V" block.
5. Marking scriber or punch should be pointed.
6. Marking tools should be selected according to the job.
7. In case a chop or circle is to be drawn on the job, a deep mark should be made at the centre of the job with the help of a centre punch otherwise there are chances of slipping of divider.
8. If drill marking is necessary, we should draw a circle of the same size outside the centre and from the same centre another bigger circle should also be drawn so that we can know that drill is being done at the proper place.
9. If a line has to come upto a cut or slot then we should fill this gap with lead *etc.*

10. For marking of a circle, four marks should be made opposite each other with a dot punch at its circumference.
11. After marking is done according to the drawing, it should be checked again.
12. When marking is done accurately, it should be made permanent with a dot punch or any other punch, as the case may be. But before making the marking permanent, other helping lines should be erased.

Questions

1. What is the importance of marking tools in making a job ?
2. List the marking tools used by a Fitter.
3. Draw a sketch of Surface Plate and explain it.
4. Explain the uses of an Odd Leg Caliper.
5. Draw a sketch of *Trammel* and explain its functions.
6. How do we find out the centre of a stick by using a divider ?
7. In what ways a divider is different from a *Trammel* ?
8. Explain briefly the different types of punches.
9. What are the functions and advantages of a Universal Surface Gauge ?
10. Why the use of "V" block is essential ?
11. What are the important points to be kept in mind while marking ?

8

Cutting Tools

For making any type of new job, after marking, it is prepared in the desired form with the help of cutting tools. Besides this, cutting tools are also in repairing jobs for cutting, scraping or chipping. Different kinds of cutting tools are used according to the needs of different jobs. Exactnees of the job largely depends on the use of proper and right kind of cutting tools. Therefore, it is very essential for us to have adequate knowledge about the different kinds of cutting tools. For cutting, scraping, chipping or drilling a fitter, turner or machineman uses the following tools :

1. Chisel
2. File
3. Scraper
4. Hacksaw
5. Drill
6. Tap
7. Die
8. Reamer
9. Stud extractor

Chisel

Chisel is used to cut flat, round or angle iron and $\frac{1}{8}$″ thick metal sheets. It is also used to remove the unwanted metal from the surface of a job by cutting it in bits and small pieces. This act is known as chipping. Cutting done by a chisel is rough. Therefore, there is need for finishing after chipping done by chisel. It saves time. Chisels are used both on hot and cold metals. As such chisels have been divided into two categories :

1. **Hot Chisel.** Hot chisel is used for cutting hot metals in *blacksmith's* workshop. There is a hole in a chisel in which a wooden handle is fixed. Sometimes an iron handle is also used. Their cutting edge is made at an angle of 30°. While using this part, it is frequently dipped into water for making it cold so that its edge remains intact. This type of chisel is illustrated in Fig. 8.1 below.

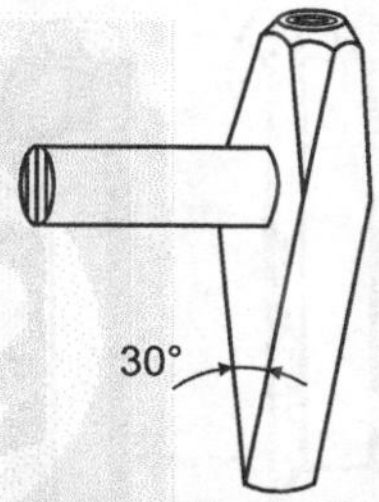

Fig. 8.1. Hot Chisel

2. **Cold Chisel.** Cold chisels are generally used in sheet metal and fitter trade workshops. With cold chisel cutting or chipping of metals can be done when these metals are in cold condition. This is available with 4 sides, 6 sides or 8 sides. These are made of high carbon steel, which contain 0.75% to 1.00% of carbon. Its length for various jobs varies from 50 mm to 200 mm. Generally chisel of 150 mm length is

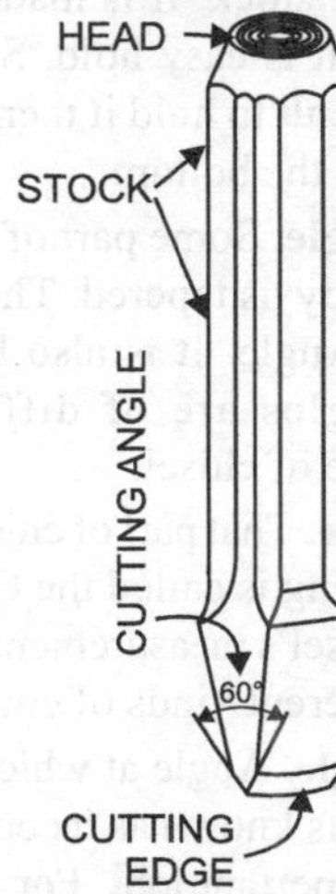

Fig. 8.2. Parts of chisel

used. Practically, chisel's measurement is known from the width of chisel's cutting edge. A chisel has the following main parts which have been illustrated in Fig. 8.2 :

1. Head
2. Body
3. Forging Angle
4. Cutting Edge
5. Cutting Angle

Head. The top-most part of a chisel is called "Head". It is a bit sunk in the middle so that the blow of hammer strikes at the centre of the chisel. Body and head of the chisel is not tempered. Thus, because of repeated blows, its head becomes *mushroom* as shown in Fig. 8.3.

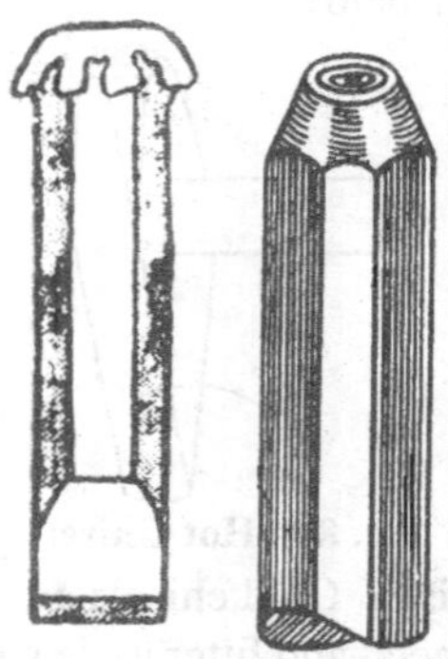

Fig. 8.3.

In this case, chisel's head should be set right by grinding. While making head the upper part of the body should be 10° to 20°.

Body. That part of a chisel from which we hold it, is called body or stock. It is made of four, six or eight sides so that it is easy hold. Some chisels are round but it is difficult to hold it them. Body is made somewhat flat from the bottom.

Forging Angle. Some part of the flat position below a chisel's body is tapered. This angle of taper is called Forging Angle. It is also known as Draw Angle. These angles are of different degrees, according to the use of chisel.

Cutting Edge. That part of chisel that performs the function of cutting is called the Cutting Edge. Its width is taken as chisel's measurement. Different types of chisels have different kinds of cutting edges.

Cutting Angle. Angle at which a cutting edge of chisel is grinded is known as its cutting angle. The cutting is highly important job. For cutting different types of metals, different suitable angles are given. For cutting hard metal, cutting angle is more and for cutting soft metals the cutting angle is less. If a chisel meant for cutting less hard metal is used for cutting hard metal, it will take larger time and the cutting too will not be clean. While grinding chisels for cutting various kinds of metals their angles should be as under :

1. Mild Steel = 55°
2. Cast Iron = 60°
3. Tool Steel = 65° to 70°
4. Copper = 45°
5. Aluminium = 30°
6. Brass = 50°

Grinding and Cutting Edge. Unless the cutting edge is properly grinded it will take longer to cut anything with it and it would be damaged as well. While grinding the cutting edge, it should be ensured that the edge should be grinded a bit in convex shape. In this way, when we hit the chisel with a hammer its protruding part touches the surface first of all. Thus there is no likelihood of its slipping from the surface as well as its edge-ends do not break. While grinding an old edge, first its old edge should be levelled. While doing so it should be ensured that there should be enough pressure on the chisel so that it remains in contact with the grinding wheel because it should not be allowed to jump otherwise some stairs are left on the chisel. While making a new edge, the tool rest of the grinding wheel should be brouight quite close to the wheel. Chisel should be properly placed at the tool rest and grinding should be done at appropriate angle. For having a proper edge it is essential that at the time of grinding, chisel should first be brought into contact with the centre of the grinding wheel. Then we should move the chisel on both the ends of the wheel turn by turn while placing it on the tool rest. The edge would take a round shape. Again, we should repeat this process after changing the side of chisel. Chisel edge should be made cold intermittantly.

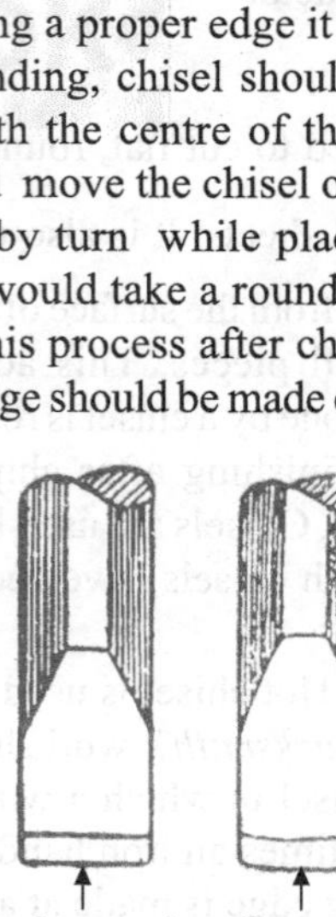

Fig. 8.4. Edge of chisel

Hardening and Tempering of Chisel. In order to make the cutting edge last longer even the tapered part of a chisel is made hard and the edge is tempered. For this purpose, chisel should be heated at appropriate temperature upto half of its length and this edge part of the chisel should be cooled in clean water. This would make that particular part of chisel hard. Then its edge part should be cleaned with a sand-paper. Again it should be heated at appropriate temperature. Now the colour of this part would start changing and when it turns into appropriate colour, it should be cooled down in lime-water. This would temper the chisel's cutting edge and it would work for longer period. This requires considerable experience. It has been explained in detail in the chapter on "Heat Treatment".

1. **Flat Chisel.** It is an all-metal chisel used for obtaining a flat surface on metal by chipping. This chisel is used to cut wires, thin sheets and round rods *etc*. This chisel's edge is in "V" shape and is flat, which is raised from the centre. Because of this projected part, it does not get stuck into the cut surface, while chipping. Old rivets and jammed nut and bolts are cut with the chisel.

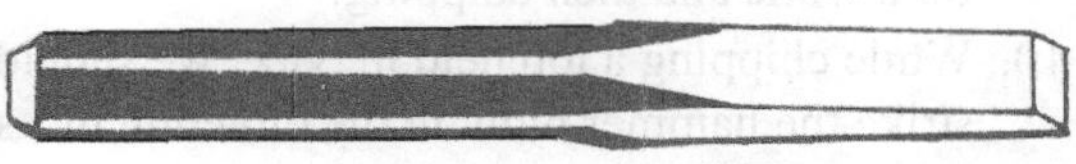

Fig. 8.5. Flat chisel

2. **Cross Cut Chisel.** It is mainly used to cut square slits and channels. Keyway on a shaft is made with this chisel. Its use has been illustrated in Fig. 8.7 below. Its cutting edge

Fig. 8.6. Cross cut chisel

Fig. 8.7. Cross cut Chisel in use

is from 3 mm to 12 mm in width. In order to ensure that this chisel does not get stuck into the grooves and slits while using it in the grooves and slits, the part behind its edge is made comparatively thin

3. **Side Cut Chisel.** Where other types of chisels cannot be used easily, side cut chisels are used. The key-way and cotter-way is cleaned with this chisel. It is almost similar to the flat chisel but the part which performs the function of cutting is turned to one side. It is turned at 90° angle and then forged. Its cutting angle is generally at 60° and forging angle at 25° angle.

Fig. 8.8. Side cut chisel

4. **Round Nose Chisel.** Its edge is round. It is used for making an oil groove in a bearing and for cutting slits at corners. Its forging angle is at 30° and cutting angle is of 35° to 40°. In such jobs where drill is dislocated at the time of drilling and some substance is left, the left over metal is set right with this chisel.

Fig. 8.9. Round nose chisel

5. **Diamond Point Chisel.** This is made of good quality steel. Its shape is square and it is tapered. Its edge is pointed and of the shape of a diamond. On the basis of its square ends, its measurement is determined. Square corners and triangular corners are cleaned with it. We can make groove in plain surface with this chisel.

Fig. 8.10. Diamond point chisel

6. **Cow Mouth Chisel.** Its shape is like that of a broad mouth of a cow. That is why it is known as Cow Mouth Chisel. Edges of the protruding parts of plain metal and rivet heads and big round holes are made with it. Its forging angle is at 25°.

Fig. 8.11. Cow mouth chisel

Method of Using Chisel. Chisel is used for cutting and chipping a thin metal sheet, plate, round rod and such other material. In Fig. 8.12 cutting of a metal plate has been illustrated. The following points should be kept in mind while using a chisel :

1. Accurate marking should be done on the metal to be cut.
2. Always hold the chisel properly with your left hand and the hammer in your right hand.
3. Set the chisel properly on the marked line then strike the hammer on its head. Before striking the second blow on the chisel, it should be set again.
4. While cutting with a chisel we should concentrate on its cutting edge.
5. Strike the hammer blow at the centre of the head of chisel.

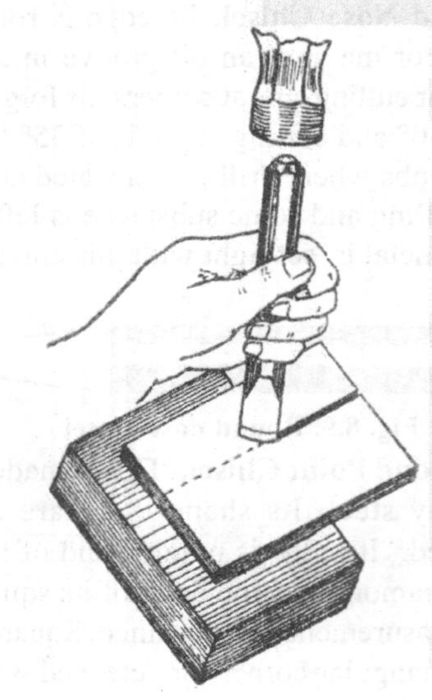

Fig. 8. 12. Cutting a metal plate

Method of Chipping. Chipping is done to chip a metal about 6 mm deep. For this purpose cold chipping is done. The following points should be borne in mind while carrying out chipping operation :

1. Select the chisel with appropriate cutting angle according to the metal.
2. If job is small in size, and it has to be held in a vice, we should use a wooden block under the job.
3. While chipping we should stand to the left of vice and near the bench as shown in Fig. 8. 13.
4. We should hold handle of the hammer from its end, raise it up to the height of our neck and then strike a blow.
5. Chisel should be inclined towards the user at an angle of 40°, while chipping.
6. At a time we should not chip any metal more than 2 to 3 mm. Otherwise the edge of chisel may be damaged.

Fig. 8.13. Method of chipping

7. If the surface to be chipped is broad, before using a cross cut chisel, we should make a groove on the job by making a cut.
8. Only a flat chisel should be used for chipping.
9. While chipping after hiting the chisel with a hammer three-four times, we should withdraw for a while and then chipping.
10. While chipping a job held in vice, we should strike the hammer blow in the direction of its stationary jaw.

Precautions :

1. At the time of chipping we must always use safety goggles.
2. Keep your face towards the wall while chipping.
3. If someone is working in your front, you should fix chipping guard in the rear of vice so that chips do not hit him.
4. Mushroom head chisel should never be used for chipping.
5. There should not be any greasy substance on the chisel head and face of the hammer being used for chipping.
6. An extraordinarily long chisel should not be used for chipping.
7. While chipping we should keep on applying grease on the edge of the chisel.

Files

A file is used to cut, trim or finish a job of metal or wood, in order to give them a shape according to our needs such as making the job round, square or angular. File is a hard steel instrument with numerous cutting points. Metal is cut in small or tiny particles with the help of a file. Therefore, mostly a file is used for giving final finishing touches to a job of metal or wood. After chipping a job of metal generally becomes rough and a file is used to make it smooth. In case a machine part is larger in size than the required size, a file is used to make it suitable. In addition, a file is used where other cutting tools cannot be used. Files are also used for sharpening the edge of some other cutting tools.

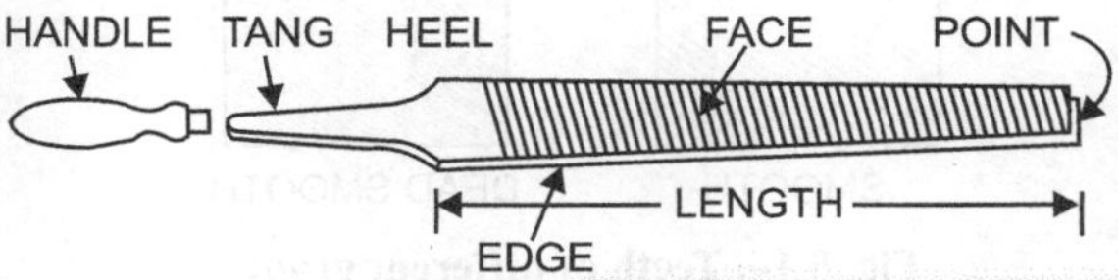

Fig. 8.14. File

File is made from high carbon steel. File is first made hard and then tempered except its tang part. It has the following main parts :

(1) Handle
(2) Tang
(3) Heel
(4) Face
(5) Edge
(6) Tip or Point

A wooden handle is fitted in its tang. Teeth are cut on its face and edge so that it can perform the job of cutting The part having no teeth is called as heel. Thick side of file is called edge and its lower end is known as tip or point.

Classification of files. Files of different types are used in various jobs for different purposes. These are specifically made for certain purposes. While making a selection of file for a specific job, some important points should be considered. In other words, we can say that files can be classified into the following categories :

I. On the basis of length
II. On the basis of shape
III. On the basis of grades
IV. On the basis of cut

I. Classification according to length. A file is measured according to its length. This length includes whole file except its tang portion *i.e.*, length from heel to tip is the measurement of the file. In fitter trade, files of 100 mm to 450 mm length are used.

II. Classification according to shape. Files of different shapes are used for jobs of different shapes but in fitter trade, the following types of files are mostly used :

(1) Flat file
(2) Round file
(3) Half-round file
(4) Triangular file
(5) Square file
(6) Hand file
(7) Knife file

Flat File. This file is of rectangular cross-section in shape. It is made slightly tapered both in width and thickness. Two-third part of this file is parallel and the rest one-third is tapered. Double cut teeth are cut on the face and simple-cut teeth are cut on the edge. These are used to reduce flat surface by filing or finishing (Fig. 8.15 A).

Round File. This type of file has round section. Like flat file $\frac{2}{3}$ of the file is parallel and the rest $\frac{1}{3}$ is tapered. It is used for *rubbing* or finishing key hole of small diameter. (Fig. 8.15 B).

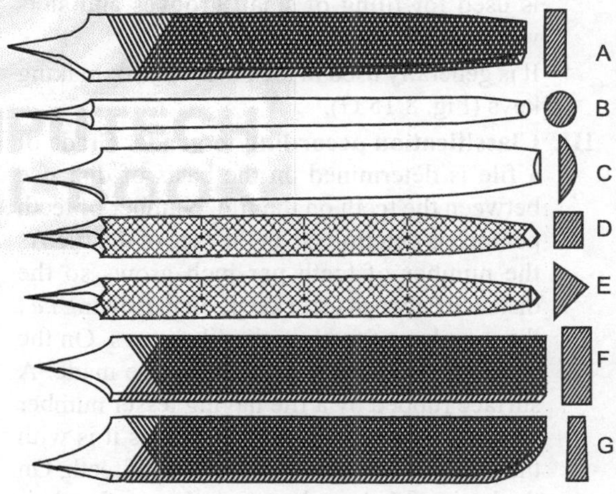

Fig. 8.15. Files of different shapes

Half-Round File. It is a file which is flat on one side and $\frac{1}{3}$ curved on the other side. The amount of convexity never equals a semi-circle. Double cut dents are cut on it and like a round file it is also tapered. With this file the damaged hole can be set in order again. (Fig. 8.15 C).

Triangular File. It is triangular in shape. Its

angles are of 60°. It is also parallel in $\frac{2}{3}$ part and is tapered in $\frac{1}{3}$ part. Filing of "V" slot job, square and rectangular jobs of above 60° and below 90° angle is done with this file. It is also known as three square file. Teeth of the saw with which we cut wood can also sharpened with this file (Fig. 8.15 E).

Square File. It is square in shape and is somewhat tapered. Its measurement is taken from its square. Filing of rectangular, square groove, slot and key-way is done with this file (Fig. 8.15 D).

Hand File. This file is almost similar to the flat file. The only difference is that there is no taper in its width, which means it is parallel. But its edge is tapered from the bottom. Besides this, either one or both of its edges do not have grooves, it is used for filing of internal right angle side of a job. In such a case, one side of the job remains intact and it is not damaged, that is why it is also called Safe Edge File (Fig 8.15 F).

Knife Edge File. Its shape is like the edge of a knife. Its thin edge is at about 10° angle. Teeth are cut on its face as well as its edge. It is used for filing of small grooves and slots whose angle is less than 60°.

It is generally used in lock industry for making keys (Fig. 8.15 G).

III. Classification according to grade. Grade of a file is determined on the basis of distance between the teeth on the file. Number of teeth per inch is determined on the face of the file. As the number of teeth per inch grows so the distance between teeth keeps on narrowing *i.e.,* the number of teeth in the file grows. On the basis of these teeth their grades are made. A surface rubbed by a file having lesser number of teeth is not that plain and fine as it is with that of a file having more number of teeth. On the basis of the number of teeth on a file their classification is done as under :

Rough File. In this type of file, teeth are of big size and less in number. It is used for cutting soft materials because its cutting is rough. Because of rough cutting, it cannot be used for hard metal. Filing done with rough file is coarse (Fig. 8.16).

Bastard File. Teeth of this file are comparatively smaller than those of the rough file. It is used initially to shed metal (through filing) in large quantity (Fig. 8.16).

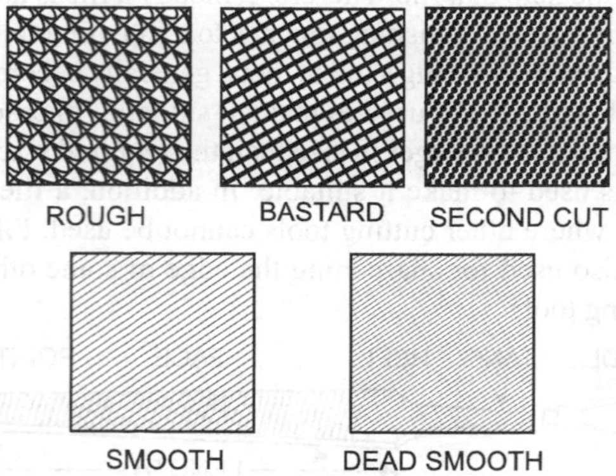

Fig. 8.16. Teeth of different grades

Second-cut File. This is a file of medium grade. In the Fitter Trade this file is mostly used to bring the job in the proper size. As compared to bastard file, filing done with this file makes the surface plain (Fig. 8.16).

Smooth File. This file makes the surface quite plain, in addition to making a job of accurate size through filing (Fig. 8.16)

Dead Smooth File. For normal filing, this type of file is generally not used. Its teeth are very close to each other and it rubs off the metal in very little quantity. It is used for bringing shinning on the job after finishing has been done.

Number of teeth on file. On files of different grades teeth are cut in the following manner :

S.No.	*Grade of file*	*Number of teeths*
1.	Rough file	20 to 25 teeths per inch
2.	Bastard file	25 to 30 teeths per inch
3.	Second cut file	35 to 40 teeths per inch
4.	Smooth file	40 to 65 teeths per inch
5.	Dead smooth file	25 to 30 teeths per inch

IV. Classification of files on the basis of cut. The teeth cut on the files are of different shapes and types. According to the cut they are classified as under :

Single-cut File. This file has parallel lines of teeth running diagonally across its face in one direction only, at an angle of 65° degrees to 85° degrees as distinguished from a double cut file, which has a double series of teeth crossing each other at an oblique angle. Metal surface is rubbed in little quantity and thus the surface becomes smooth. Therefore it is used for hard metal and for finishing (Fig. 8.17 A).

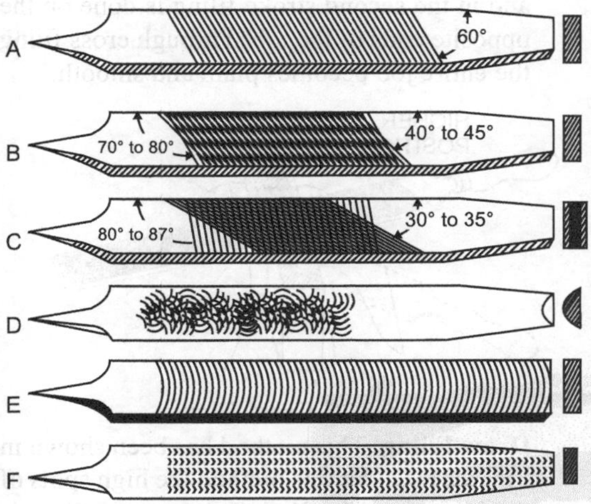

Fig. 8.17. Different cuts on files

Double-cut File. This file has two rows of teeth crossing each other at an angle of 40° to 45° and the other row has angles of 70° to 80°. Because of double teeth, this file cuts metal quickly but it cannot make surface very smooth. That is why it is generally used for normal filing. This has been shown in Fig. 8.17 (B). This cut is called coarse type. Second cut file is also for finishing. In this file, one row of teeth is at an angle of 30° to 35° and the other row is of 80° to 87° angle as shown in Fig. 8.17 (C).

Curved-cut File. It is also known as Vixen file. It is used for filing of wide surface of soft metals like aluminium, zinc, copper and brass. It has circular teeth as shown in Fig. 8.17 (C).

Spiral-cut File. This type of teeth are cut in round or semi-round files. The shape of their teeth is like that of threads.

Rasp-cut File. This is a file of special thick teeth. These teeth are of triangle shape and are in bulging state. It is flat, half-round and round. It is used for jobs of wood, plastic, fibre, hard rubber and job of horns and hoof of animals (Fig. 8.17 F).

Thus selection of a file is done after considering the following four points and the utility of the job :

1. Shape of file
2. Cut of the file-teeth
3. Grade of the file on the basis of number of its teeth.

While taking a file the following points should be ascertained :

Convexity and taper in Files. Face of the file is not made completely flat but has some protruding roundness which means it is convex. Similarly, both edges of file are tapered towards tips instead of being parallel. There are three advantages of its being convex :

(1) At the time of filing, the entire surface of the job does not come into contact. Therefore there is less exertion.

(2) If the pressure is in the centre, both ends of the job are equally rubbed. If the file is used in a flat manner it is difficult to keep equal pressure on both the ends.

(3) An entirely flat file carries the risk of being bent when it is hardened.

Besides convexity, files are tapered towards the lower part breadthwise. While filing, the taper of the front side can also go into a narrow place *e.g.*, $\frac{1}{2}$ round file can be used in less than $\frac{1}{2}''$ because its taper is less than $\frac{1}{2}''$.

Filing

The removal of material in the form of tiny particles by using a file is called filing. In order to get proper surface through filing, the following points needs consideration :

1. Choose the right type of file, according to the job.
2. There should be handle fitted on the tang of the file. In small files, a small handle should be fitted and a larger handle in larger file. Otherwise the balance of the file would not be proper and power would be unnecessarily wasted.
3. Hold the handle of the file with the right hand and keep the file end balanced with the left hand.
4. At the time of filing, left leg should be kept ahead and the right leg a little behind as shown in Fig. 8.18.
5. Pressure on the file should be exerted while moving it ahead, not while driving it back.

6. Only your hands should move with the file and not your whole body. As far as possible, keep rest of your body still.

Fig. 8.18. Filing

7. Speed of moving the file should be at the rate of 30 to 35 strokes per minute.

   Filing is done in three different positions :

   1. Straight filing
   2. Cross filing
   3. Draw filing

Straight filing. This method has been shown in Fig. 8.19. Under this method we should stand almost in front of vice and file is moved in the straight direction of the vice. Through straight filing method the metal is quickly cut. But there is a great need for alertness to keep the balance of file. If a file of large size is being used, then the left hand should be kept as shown in Fig. 8.19 (A or B). If finishing work is being done then file should be held in the left hand as shown in Fig. 8.19 C.

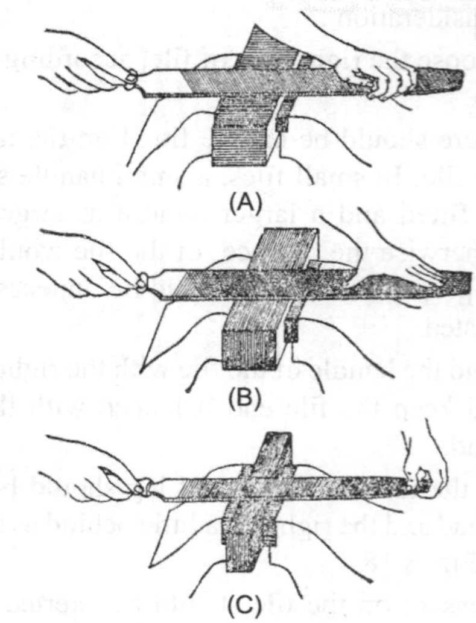

Fig. 8.19. Straight filing

Cross Filing. This method has been illustrated in Fig. 8.20. Under this method file is moved from one end to other end of job in one stroke and in the second stroke filing is done on the opposite ends of the job. Through cross filing the entire job becomes plain and smooth.

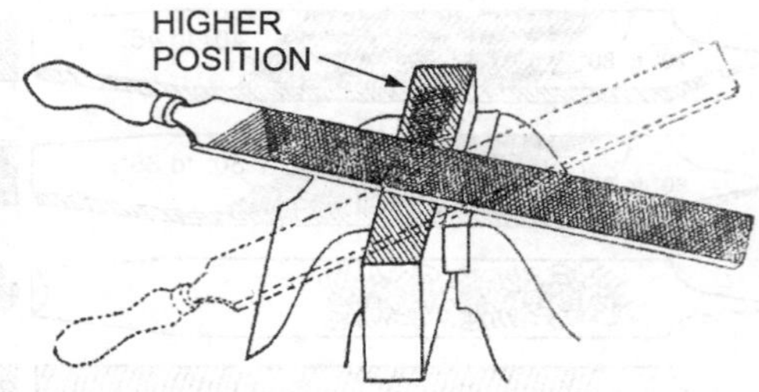

Fig. 8.20. Cross filing

Draw Filing. This method has been shown in Fig. 8.21. Under this method the high spots of the job are easily filed. This type of filing is done to bring finishing on the job which shines.

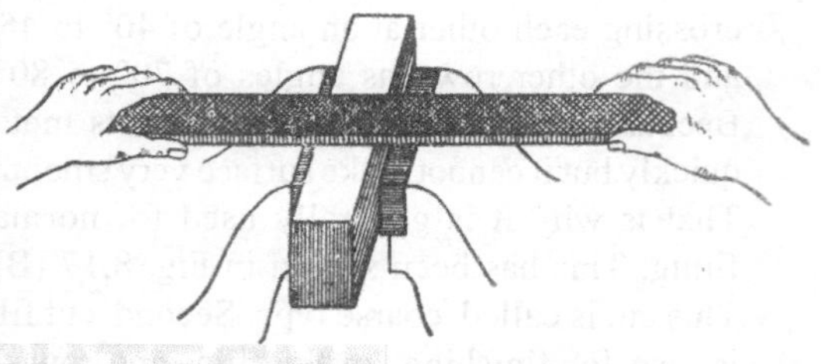

Fig. 8.21. Draw Filing

While doing this type of filing handle is taken out. In draw filing chalk is rubbed on the face of the file so that the particles cut by the file are not left in the file itself. Otherwise the file would leave some marks on the metal when filing is done on it.

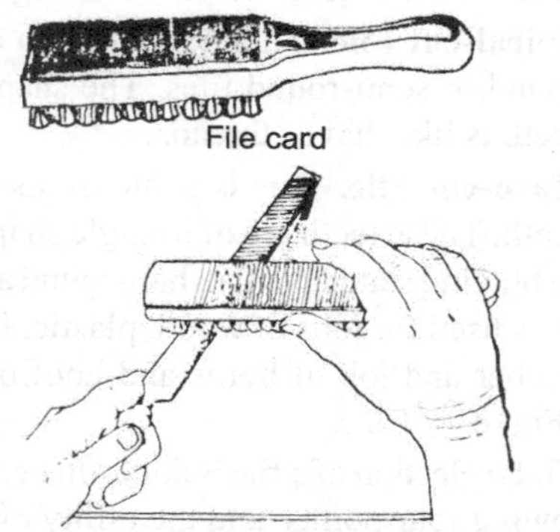

Fig. 8.22.

Pinning Fault of Files. While rubbing or cutting any material with a file, tiny particles of metal get entrapped in the dents of file. These particles leave signs of scratching on the job while filing and affect their size. These faults are called pinning. To remove this fault, file card is used. File card is like hard wire brush. It is rubbed on the file as shown in Fig. 8.22 to clear the particle of material from the dents of file. Besides this, if dry chalk is rubbed on the file, there would be less pinning.

Special Files

Where the above mentioned files do not serve the purpose of filing, special type of files are used for special jobs. These special flies are of various types. Here we have mentioned only those special files which are used widely.

Needle File. This type of files are usually made in sets. In one set there are 8, 10 or 12 files. One set of 12 files has been shown in Fig. 8.23. These files are different in shapes and grades. Their length ranges between 100 mm to 200 mm. There is no need to add a handle separately to the files since their tang is made like a handle. These are very delicate files and they should be used with care. There is risk of their being broken because of little carelessness. These files are used by the watch makers, tool and diemakers and goldsmiths.

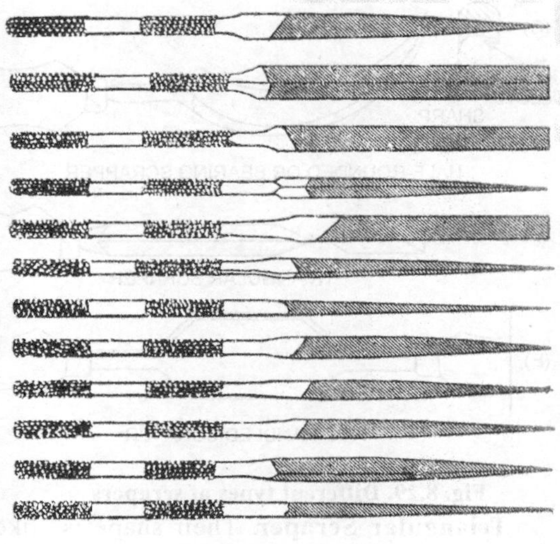

Fig. 8.23. Needle file set

Warding File. This type of file has been shown in Fig. 8.24. This is almost like a flat file. It is very thin, parallel in thickness and its tip is pointed. It is used for filing of jobs having narrow grooves. Particularly these are used by lock and key makers and watchmakers.

Fig. 8.24. Warding file

Mill File. This file is almost similar to the hand file. It contains only single cut dents. It is used for polishing of brass jobs and for filing on the lathe machines.

Pillar File. This file is also like a hand file. Its breadth is in parallel and thickness is in taper. It is used for filing of right angled corners of jobs. Besides this, where square file and hand file cannot be used a pillar file is used.

Die-sinker Riflers. This is a special type of file which is crooked and circular in shape. Dents are cut on both of its ends and the middle portion is made plain for holding it. With it filing can be done in deep spaces like die or mould (Fig. 8.25.)

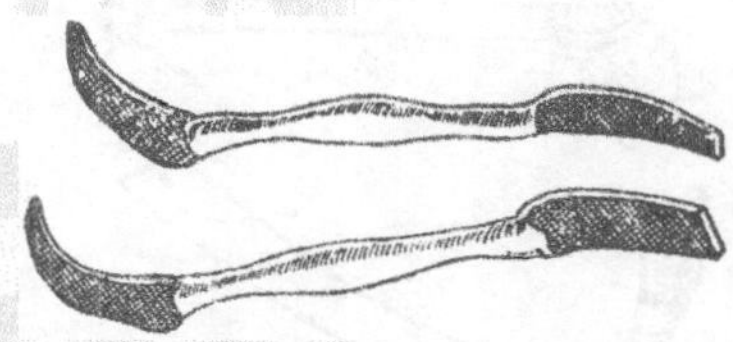

Fig. 8.25. Die-sinkers Riflers

Setting File. This is a sort of flat file, which can be bent according to needs. With it the inside surface of a key-way is filed (Fig. 8.26).

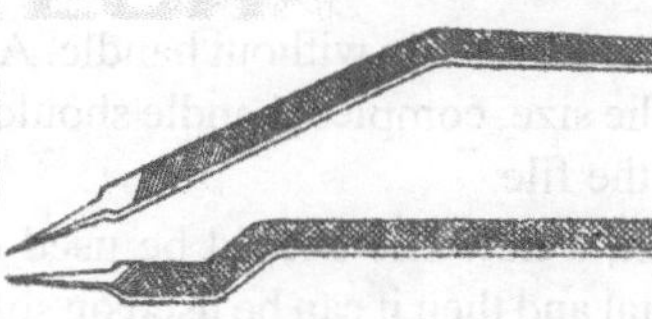

Fig. 8.26. Setting File

Barret File. This file is triangular in shape. Its two sides are short and one side is large. It is also called cantt file. It is used for enlarging the inside angle.

Swiss Pattern File. These files are more or less similar to the warding files. Their tip is also pointed. But they have more dents cut per inch. The watch makers and other technicians doing precision work make use of these files.

Rotary File and Burrs. This file is made by hand in different shapes as shown in Fig. 8.27. A rod is attached to them, which is fitted in drill chuck, lathe chuck, or any other type of drilling machine and then used. It is used by the pattern makers and die makers, for enlarging a hole, convex surface *etc*.

Fig. 8.27.

Flexible File. There is no tang in this type of file and both the ends are holed. A special type of handle is fixed in it and filing of circular jobs is done (Fig. 8.28).

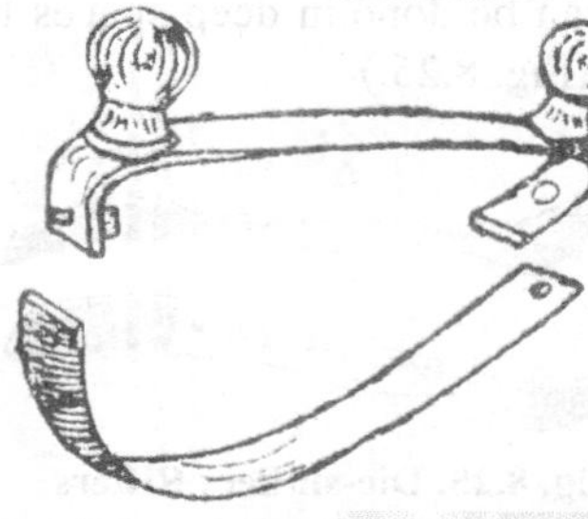

Fig. 8.28. Flexible File

Precautions :

1. Select the file according to the job.
2. Do not use a file without handle. According to the size, complete handle should be fixed on the file.
3. First, a new file should be used on a soft metal and then it can be used on solid metal.
4. If substantial material is to be cut then first chipping should be done and then filing.
5. For filing of sheet metal jobs, the job should be fixed in a vice by using wood on both its sides. It should also be ensured that sheet should not be higher than vice.
6. While filing a sheet, we should cut it in length.
7. We should make use of chalk in order to save the job from pinning. If there are metal particles on the file these should be cleaned with a brush.
8. Keep the file away from other tools. They should not be heaped together.
9. File should not be heated.
10. Do not apply oil or grease on the file.

Scrapers

This is a cutting hand tool. It is used to remove the high spots left after maching has been done on a job. These are made of steel or alloy steel and their culling edge hardened and tapered. Material upto 0.002 ″ to 0.003″ should be scratched. It is different in shape and it is used like a file by using a handle in the tang. Square, triangular and round surfaces are scrapped with these scrapers. Mainly the following types of scrapers are used whose length is from 100 mm to 250 mm and their thickness varies from 1 mm to 3.5 mm :

Flat Scraper. Shape of this type of scraper is like a flat file. But its cutting edge is more in breadth than its body and is very slightly rounded. Its edge is made at about 80° angle. It is used for scrapping high spots lift on the plain surface of the material (Fig. 8.29 A).

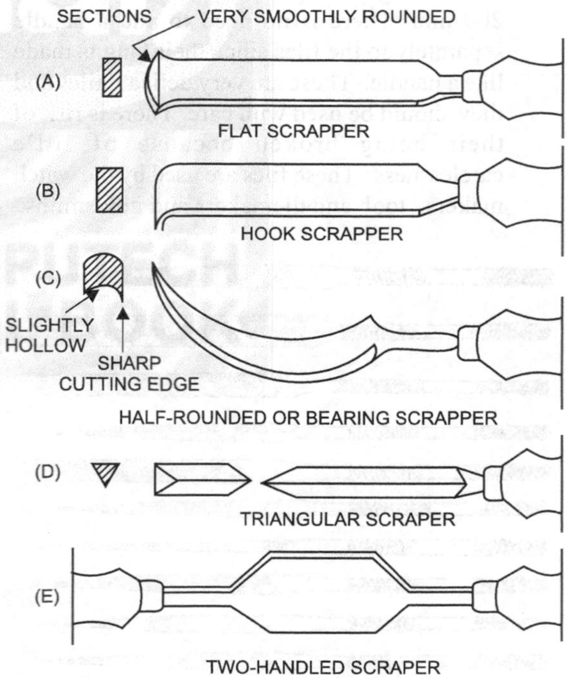

Fig. 8.29. Different types of scrapers

Triangular Scraper. Their shape is like triangular file. But it is pointed towards the lower side. These are used to clean the corners (Fig. 8.29 D).

Hook Scraper. This is a special type of scraper. Its lower portion is bent and the rest is like a flat scraper. It is used to scrap the plain surface of a metal, where flat scraper cannot work (Fig. 8.29 B).

Half Round Scraper. Its shape is like a half round file. But its body is hollow from inside. It is used for scraping the high spots between bearings and bushes made in two pieces. Cutting edge is grinded on both the sides of the body (Fig. 8.29 C).

Double Handle Scraper. In this type of scrapers handles are fitted on both ends of the scrapers. It is used for scraping broad surfaces like draw filing. This saves time (Fig. 8.29 E).

Method of Scraping. Scraping is a process by which the high spots left on a job after the machine are removed by using different scrapers through scratching. For the scraping process, Persian blue or red lead paste is applied on the lathe surface plate equal to the surface of the job. Square jobs are rubbed on this paste. Thus only at the high spots the paste sticks. After ascertaining these high spots, these are removed by scraping them.

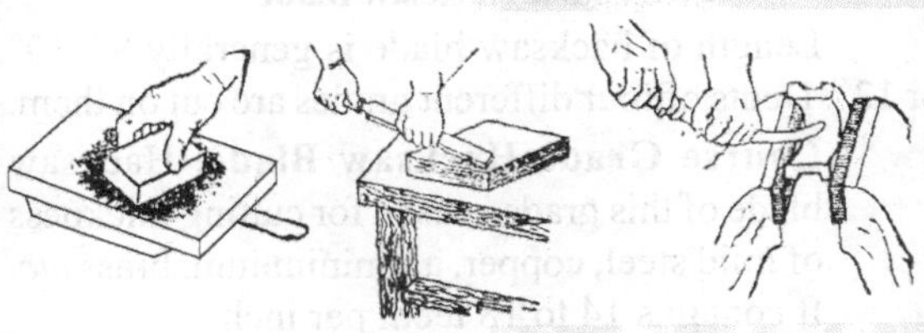

Fig. 8.30 Scrapping process

The method of ascertaining the high spots on the square jobs and scraping them is shown in Fig 8.30 (A). If we have to scrap a bearing of two pieces of a shaft, the above paste should be applied to the bearing surface. The bearing should be tied and their meter shaft is revolved. By this process the paste will stick on the high spots of the bearing and then they are scratched with a scraper. Surface of a scraped job becomes completely accurate. The method of scrapping a bearing has been shown in Fig. 8.30 (B).

The following points should be borne in mind while using a scraper :

(1) We should have our right hand on its handle and left hand on its body.

(2) While using a scraper it should be bent at about 30° angle.

(3) We should not keep a stroke of the scraper too long.

(4) After scraping once, scraper should be driven at right angle.

(5) Persian blue or red paste should be applied at appropriate place. It is a must.

(6) Scraping is appropriate for metal of 0.002″ to 0.003″. For scraping of high spots, filing should be done again.

(7) In order to find out high spots scraper should be rubbed on the surface plate and on shaft *etc.* intermittantly.

(8) Scraping should be considered accurate only when the colour of paste start appearing on the entire surface.

Precautions :

(1) Select the scraper according to the requirement of the job.

(2) Scraper should have proper edge.

(3) Our hands should be free from any sticky substance while scraping.

(4) Scraper should not be used without handle.

(5) We should neither touch scraper's edge nor move hands on its surface.

(6) Different places of surface plate should be used to obtain high spots.

(7) After scraping surface should be properly cleaned.

(8) Scraper should be kept separate from other tools.

Hacksaw

In order to cut metal, rods, pipes, plates or sheets of varied thickness a hacksaw is used. It can be operated by hand or by power. Less metal is wasted by cutting it with a hacksaw and the cut edges are more clean than those cut with a chisel. Hacksaw is built by fitting two parts :

(1) Hacksaw Frame

(2) Hacksaw Blade.

Hacksaw Frame. In shape it looks like the English letter "C". But both its arms are bent at the right angle. On one end of these arms a handle is fixed and on the other end a pin is fixed. A pin each is fixed on handle and sliding screw itself in which Hacksaw Blade is fitted. These pins are also known as "Prong". Hacksaw Blade is fitted on these pins and then it is tightened according to need with fly nut or wing nut. Mainly Hacksaw frames are of two types :

Fixed Hacksaw Frame. For making this type of hacksaw frame, one piece flat iron strip or pipe is bent at right angle. In these frames only hacksaw blades of a specific size can be fixed, not of short size or long size. Two types of handles are used : (1) Straight Handle and (2) Pistol Type Handlewhich have been shown in Fig. 8.31 and Fig. 8.32.

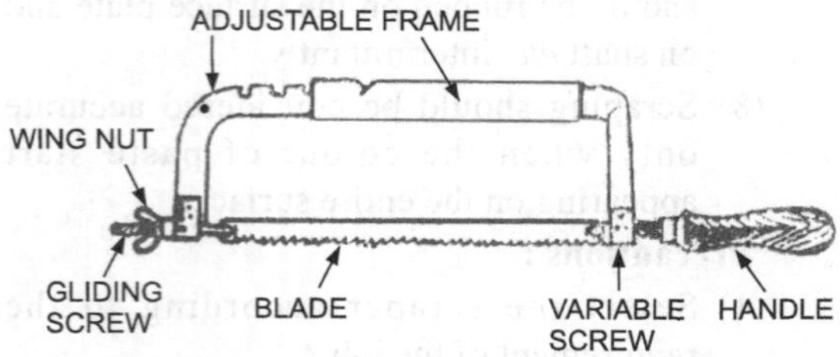

Fig. 8.31. Straight hacksaw frame

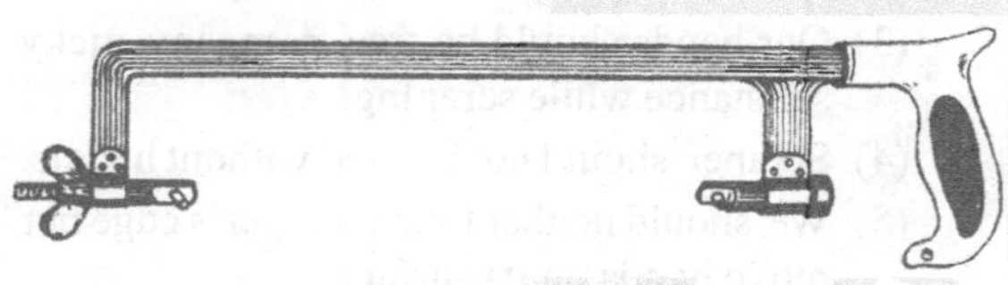

Fig. 8.32. Pistol type handle frame

Adjustable Hacksaw. Its structure is a bit different from a fixed frame. The frame is made in two parts. These parts can be adjusted at different distances. Therefore in these adjustable hacksaws, big and small hacksaw blades of different standard can be used. There is adquate provision of pin and grooves to pull, adjust and set them. These types of handles are used in this hacksaw : (1) Straight Handle, (2) Pistol Type Handle and (3) Tublar Type Handle which have been shown in Figs. 8.33, 8.34 and 8.35 :

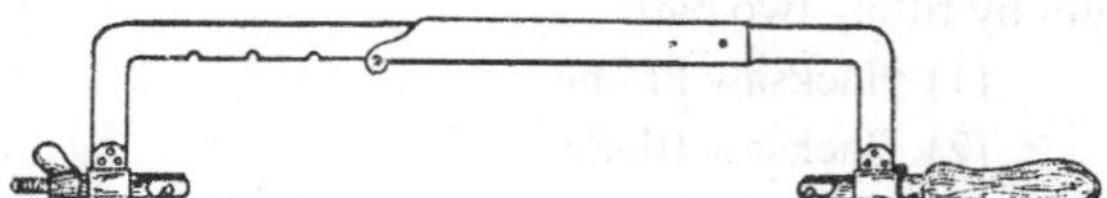

Fig. 8.33. Straight handle adjustable frame

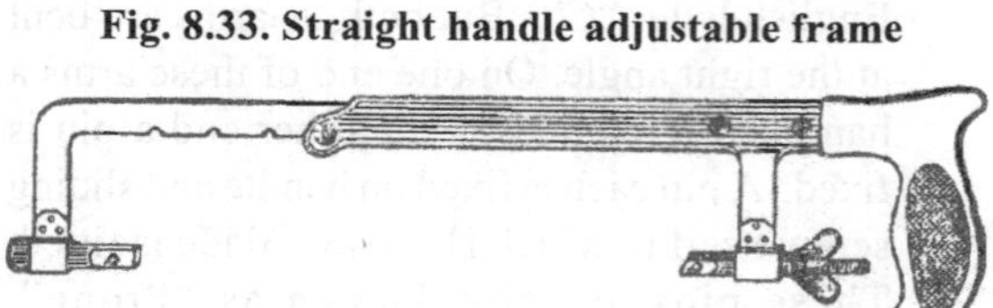

Fig. 8.34. Pistol type adjustable frame

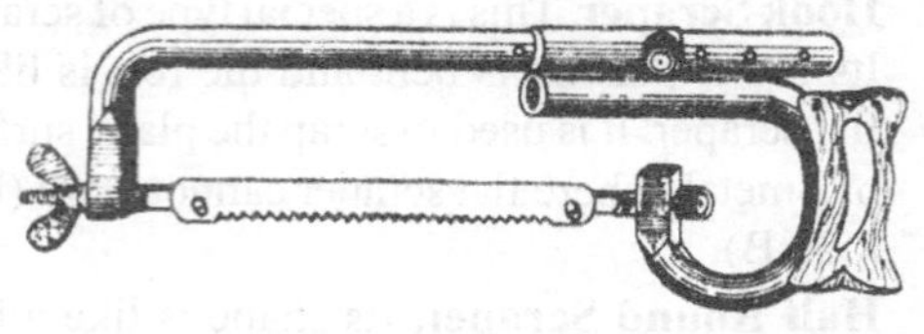

Fig. 8.35. Tublar Type adjustable frame

These frames are generally made of flat strip or thin pipes and their handle are made of wood or aluminium.

Hacksaw Blade. On the basis of metal of the job, different types of hacksaw blades are used in a hacksaw. These are made of tungsten steel, high speed steel and they are hardened and tampered. Their classification depends on three points : (1) Size of the blade, (2) Number of dents cut on the blade per inch and (3) Nature of the blade.

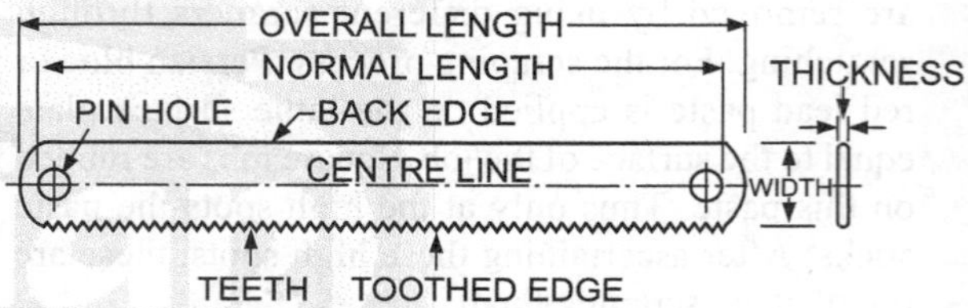

Ftg. 8.36. Hacksaw blade

Length of hacksaw blade is generally 8″, 10″ or 12″. Dents of four different grades are cut on them.

Course Grade Hacksaw Blade. Hacksaw blade of this grade is used for cutting thickness of mild steel, copper, aluminiunium, brass *etc*. It contains 14 to 18 teeth per inch.

Medium Grade Hacksaw Blade. Hacksaw blade of this type is used for cutting all kinds of metals such as cast iron, tool steel, aluminium, brass, high carbon steel *etc*. From 20 to 24 teeth per inch are cut in this hacksaw blade.

Fine Grade Hacksaw Blade. This type of hacksaw blade is mainly used to cut thin pipes, sheets, tubes *etc*. It has 24 to 30 dents per inch.

Superfine Grade Hacksaw Blade. For cutting extraordinary solid metals and thin metal sheets, this type of hacksaw blade is used. There are 30 to 32 dents per inch in this type of hacksaw blade.

In all the hacksaw blades of various grades, mentioned above, teeth are cut on one or both the edges. These blades are hardened in two different processes and on these depend their nature.

All Hard Blade. Blades of this nature are hardened and tampered only except the ends having holes. These are used for cutting articles cast iron or mould iron *etc.*

Flexible Blade. In Blades of this nature only the cutting teeth and nearby part is hardened and tempered. By this process they become elastic and there is less risk of their being broken in the event of a shock. These blades are used for cutting thin sheets, pipes, curves *etc.*

Setting of Teeth. Teeth of hacksaw blades are also bent to left or right side as in the case of ordinary saw used for cutting wood. Bending of teeth is known setting of teeth. With this setting of teeth the hacksaw blade cuts slot in the metal of slightly more thickness than that of the blade. Therefore, because of this slot the blade does not get stuck while operating it. If this setting is not done, there is great risk that the blade would get stuck in the metal and get broken. Setting of teeth in a blade is done in three ways.

Regular or Single Setting. In this type of setting, one tooth is bent to the left and the next tooth to the right and every fifth tooth is kept straight. This tooth helps in cleaning the metal particles from the slot. This type of setting has been shown in Fig. 8.37.

Fig. 8.37. Staggered setting of teeth

Double Alternate Setting. In this type of setting, two teeth are turned to the right and two to the left and one dent between them is left straight, which performs the function of clearing the metal particles from the slot.

Zig-Zag or Wave Setting. In this type of setting a few teeth are bent to the right and a few to the left. Thus it looks like a wave. This type of setting is done on blades of line grade and super fine grades. It has been illustrated in Fig. 8.38.

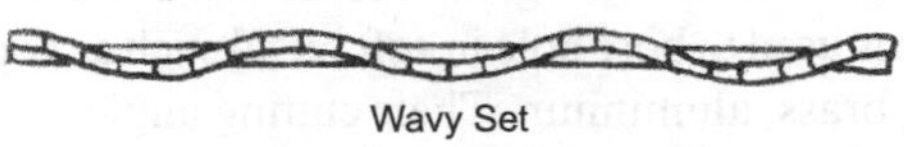

Fig. 8.38. Wave setting of teeth

Method of Using Hacksaw. Pipes, plates, sheets *etc.* made of metal can be easily and clearly cut with a hacksaw. But for efficient cutting the following points should be borne in mind :

(1) Selection of hacksaw blade should be done according to the metal for which it is to be used.

(2) While fixing the blade on the frame it should be ensured that its teeth should cut the metal when they are driven forward.

(3) Job should be held in the vice in such a way that its cutting lines are clearly visible.

(4) Before starting a cut with hacksaw blade, blade should be kept on the marking line, the left hand thumb should be placed with its support as shown in Fig. 8.39. It would ensure that the blade would move only on the line, there would be no risk of its slip.

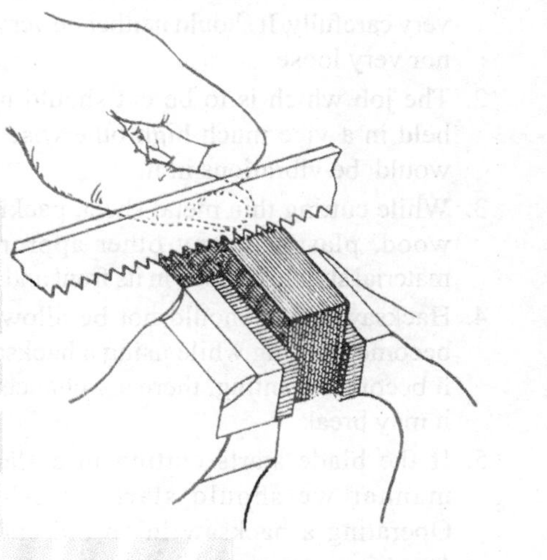

Fig. 8.39. Starting a hacksaw

(5) After marking with the support of thumb we should hold the handle with the right hand palm and fingers and with the left hand palm and fingers we should hold the other end of the hacksaw frame as shown in Fig. 8.40.

Fig. 8.40 Operating the hacksaw

(6) You should stand on the left hand of the vice and keep your right foot backward and the left foot a little ahead of the right.

(7) Contact between blade and the job should be in such a way that atleast two teeth should remain in contact with the surface of the job.

(8) The speed of operating hacksaw should be 40 to 50 strokes per minute.

(9) Pressure should be exerted on forward stroke and it should be withdrawn on backward stroke.

(10) Before finishing cutting with a hacksaw the cutting speed should be slowed down.

Precautions :

1. Hacksaw blade should be fitted on the frame very carefully. It should neither be very tight nor very loose.
2. The job which is to be cut should not be held in a vice much high otherwise there would be vibrations in it.
3. While cutting thin metal sheet, packing of wood, plastic or any other appropriate material should be used in its front and back.
4. Hacksaw blade should not be allowed to become slanting while using a hacksaw. If it becomes slanting, there are chances that it may break.
5. If the blade starts cutting in a slanting manner we should start a fresh cut. Operating a hacksaw in an old cut may *break* it.
6. If a blade get broken while working, then we should replace it with a blade which has been used almost for the same period rather than using a brand new blade. The new blade can break if it is operated in that old slot.
7. If necessary, water should be used as a coolant.
8. After using a hacksaw either its blade should be taken out or it must be made lose.

Drill and Drill Machine

In order to bore round holes in different jobs, drill and drill machines are used. The tool used for boring hole is called drill. The machine with whose help the drill is moved is called drill machine. The process of boring holes with drill and drill machine is called drilling.

Drill. These are made of carbon steel, high speed steel and alloy steel. Drill is of three different shapes :

1. Flat Drill
2. Straight Fluted Drill
3. Twist Drill

Flat Drill. This type of drill is generally made by beating slender sticks of high carbon steel. Its cutting edge is grinded and then hardened and tampered. It can he made easily in any shape or size. It is not used for boring holes in iron. It is usually used for boring holes in carpentary work and soft metals. Cutting point is kept at 90° angle.

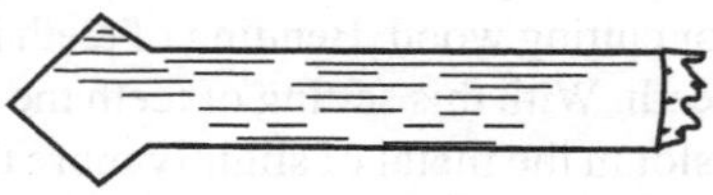

Fig. 8.41 Flat drill

But it has the following shortcomings :

1. Holes bored by this drill are neither round nor in one direction.
2. Holes are made of bigger diameter than the drill's size.
3. For boring holes with flat drill much pressure and power is needed.
4. Chips cut by this drill do not come out of the holes themselves.
5. Coolant is not able to reach upto the cutting edge. Therefore, soon it becomes hot and starts getting damaged.
6. By excessive grinding of it, the diameter of the cutting edge gets reduced.

Flat drill has some advantages also. These are:

1. On those solid metals where other drills get broken, this drill can be used after properly hardening and tempering.
2. These are made in different sizes after forging them.
3. These drills are very cheap.

Straight Fluted Drill. In this type of drill two grooves from top to bottom are cut opposite to each other. This groove is known as flute. This is used to bore hole in soft metal such as copper, brass, aluminium. Their cutting angle is made differently according to the metal. As compared to flat drills, holes can be bored with it cleanly and in a beter shape. For different types of small holes which are needed in spray nozzel *etc.* Special drills are used of straight flute which is known as Eureka Drill.

Twist Drill. Now a days, twist and thick drills are used for boring holes quickly, clean and of accurate size. These are often made of slender sticks of high speed steel and alloy steel. Then cutting edge is made on bottom end and a twisted groove is cut on its body from top to bottom which is known as flute. Because of this twisted flute it is called Twist Drill. It contains the following main parts as shown in Fig. 8.42 :

1. Tang, 2. Shank, 3. Body, 4. Point, 5. Neck

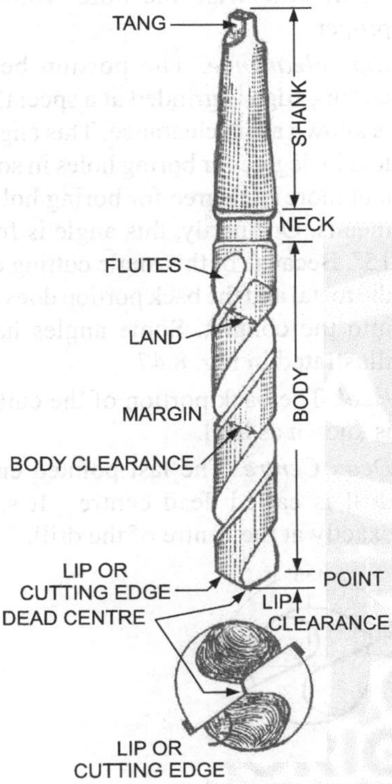

Fig. 8.42. Twist drill

Tang. The upper most part of the twist drill is called tang. It is small and flat in shape. It is driven into the handle. With its help it is easy to fit the drill.

Shank. Shank is the portion of the drill by which it is held and driven. It is held in a socket drill chuck. Shanks are of the following four types :

Taper Shank. In large size drills taper shank is made. It contains a Morse taper. A drill with this type of shank can be easily fitted in the drilling machine. That is why this type of shank drills are commonly used. There is negligible risk of their being slipped because at the time of giving pressure, their hold in the spindle or socket is strengthened.

Straight Shank. This type of shanks are generally made in drills of less than $\frac{1}{2}$ diameter. These are gripped in drill chucks.

Ratchet Shank. This type of shanks are square but these are tapered. They are used after fitting them in brace chuck. Since there is taper in the spindle of ratchet, this type of shank is properly held in it.

Taper shank

Fig. 8.43

Straight shank

Fig. 8.44

Bit Shank. This type of shanks are mostly used in carpentary. These are also held straight in ratchet brace *etc.*

Ratchet shank

Fig. 8.45

Bit shank

Fig. 8.46

Body. It is the main part of the drill. It extends from the extreme cutting end to the beginning of the shank. Hole is bored with this part. Different types of spiral grooves are cut in the body. It is known with the following names :

1. Flute	2. Land
3. Margin	4. Body Clearance
5. Web (or core)	6. Point

Flute. The spiral grooves in the body of the drill are called flutes. These grooves are made by milling machine. Cutting edge is made on their boarder. These grooves act as an outlet passage for clearing the chips cut by the drill. Through these grooves the coolant reaches the point.

Land. The projected part between the grooves on the body is called land. These are cylindrically ground surfaces on the leading edges of the drill-flutes. The width of the land is measured at right angles to the flute.

Margin. On the verge of flutes a bright line is visible, which extends to the entire length. It is known as margin. At the time of boring a hole, only this part come into contact of the job. The diameter of the drill measured according to this margin.

Body Clearance. The other projected part on the body except margin, is called body clearance. Its diameter is less than that of the margin. This portion of the body surface is reduced in diameter to provide diametrical clearance. Thus, at the time of boring a hole it does not move by rubbing the surface of the job and saves the drill from getting hot and damage.

Web. The central portion of the drill situated between the "roots" of the flutes and extending from the point end towards the shank is known as web. The point end of the web forms the chisel edge.

Point. The lower portion of drill is called point. It is made in the form of an angle. Different angle is made for different metals. Its point is generally grinded at 118° angle. On a minute analyses of the point, it can be further divided into four parts :

1. *Lip.* The cutting edge of the drill known as lip. This edge is there with each flute of the drill. The length and angle of lip should be equal otherwise the hole would not be proper.
2. *Lip clearance.* The portion behind the cutting edge is grinded at a special angle. It is known as lip clearance. This angle is kept less in degree for boring holes in solid metal and more in degree for boring holes in soft metals. Ordinarily, this angle is from 8° to 15°. Because of this angle cutting edge cuts the metal and the back portion does not come into the contact. Some angles have been illustrated in Fig. 8.47.
3. *Heel.* The back portion of the cutting edge is known as heel.
4. *Dead Centre.* The last pointed end of the drill is called dead centre. It should be exactly at the centre of the drill.

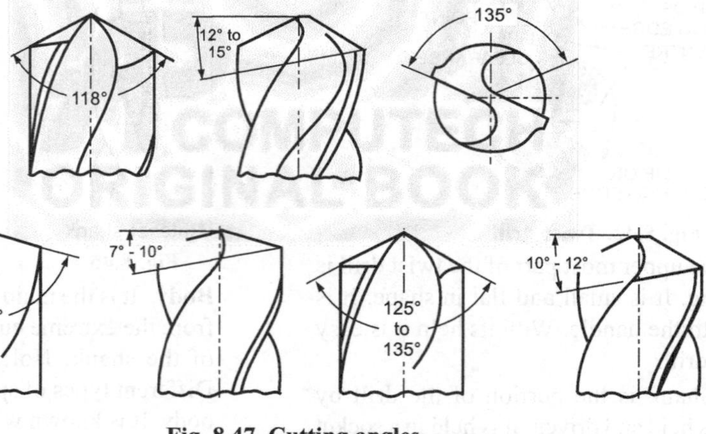

Fig. 8.47. Cutting angles

Measurement of Twist Drill. For holes of different sizes, drills are made in different measurements. These measurements are made in the following four standards :

1. Inch or fraction size drill
2. Millimeter size drill
3. Number size drill
4. Letter size drill

Inch or Fraction Size Drill. These drills have measurement in inches or fractions. These have diameter of $\frac{1}{64}''$ to 3″. Drills of $\frac{1}{64}''$ to 1″ are available in increasing order from $\frac{1}{64}''$ to 1″ such as $\frac{1}{64}''$, $\frac{1}{32}''$, $\frac{3}{64}''$, $\frac{1}{16}''$, *etc.* Likewise drills of 1″ to 3″ diameter are available in increasing order starting from $\frac{1}{32}''$, such as, 1″, $1\frac{1}{32}''$, $1\frac{1}{16}''$ *etc.*

Millimeter Size Drill. ISI has recommended their measurement. According to I.S. 5101–1969, the measurement of straight shank or parallel shank is as under :

0.20, 0.22, 0.25, 0.28, 0.30, 0.32, 0.35, 0.38, 0.40, 0.42, 0.45, 0.48, 0.50, 0.52, 0.55, 0.58, 0.60, 0.62, 0.65, 0.68, 0.70, 0.72, 0.75, 0.78, 0.80, 0.82, 0.85, 0.88, 0.90, 0.92, 0.95 and 0.98 mm.

From 1 mm to 3 mm in increasing order of 0.05 mm.

From 3 mm to 14 mm in increasing order of 0.1 mm.

From 14 mm to 16 mm in increasing order of 0.25 mm.

According to I.S. 5103–1969, taper shank drills are made in the following measurement :

From 3 mm to 14 mm — 3, 3.2, 3.5, 3.8, 4, 4.2, 4.5 *etc.*

From 14 mm to 32 mm in increasing order of 0.25 mm.

From 32 mm to 51 mm in increasing order of 0.5 mm.

From 53 mm to 120 mm in increasing order of 1 mm.

Number Size Drill. The measurement of some drills can be known from their numbers. There are drills from number 1 to 80. The larger the number of drill, the thinner is its drill. In other words, drill of 1 number will be of the larger diameter and drill of 80 number is of minimum diameter. We can find out their actual size in decimal inches from the following table.

Conversion table of Number Drill

No.	*Decimal*	*No.*	*Decimal*	*No.*	*Decimal*	*No.*	*Decimal*	*No.*	*Decimal*
1.	.2280″	17.	.1730″	33.	.1110″	49.	.0700″	65.	.0350″
2.	.2210″	18.	.1695″	34.	.1100″	50.	.0670″	66.	.0330″
3.	.2130″	19.	.1660″	35.	.1065″	51.	.0635″	67.	.0312″
4.	.2090″	20.	.1610″	36.	.1040″	52.	.0595″	68.	.0310″
5.	.2055″	21.	.1590″	37.	.1015″	53.	.0570″	69.	.0293″
6.	.2040″	22.	.1570″	38.	.0995″	54.	.0550″	70.	.0280″
7.	.2010″	23.	.1540″	39.	.0980″	55.	.0520″	71.	.0260″
8.	.1990″	24.	.1520″	40.	.0960″	56.	.0465″	72.	.0250″
9.	.1960″	25.	.1495″	41.	.0935″	57.	.0430″	73.	.0240″
10.	.1935″	26.	.1470″	42.	.0893″	58.	.0420″	74.	.0226″
11.	.1910″	27.	.1440″	43.	.0860″	59.	.0410″	75.	.0210″
12.	.1890″	28.	.1405″	44.	.0820″	60.	.0400″	76.	.0196″
13.	.1850″	29.	.1360″	45.	.0810″	61.	.0390″	77.	.0180″
14.	.1820″	30.	.1285″	46.	.0785″	62.	.0380″	78.	.0160″
15.	.1800″	31.	.1160″	47.	.0760″	63.	.0370″	79.	.0145″
16.	.1770″	32.	.1130″	48.	.0730″	64.	.0360″	80.	.0135″

Letter Size Drill. In certain drills, instead of size or number English letters from A to Z are indicated. We come to know their actual size only from these letters. Drill of letter "A" which is of "234" is of the minimum diameter. Drill of letter "Z", which is of "413" of the maximum diameter. Actual size of the drills with letters from A to Z can be known in inch-decimals from the following table :

Conversion table of Letter Drill

Letter	*Decimal Equivalent*	*Letter*	*Decimal Equivalent*	*Letter*	*Decimal Equivalent*	*Letter*	*Decimal Equivalent*	*Letter*	*Decimal Equivalent*
A	.234″	G	.261″	M	.295″	S	.348″	Y	.407″
B	.238″	H	.266″	N	.302″	T	.358″	Z	.413″
C	.242″	I	.272″	O	.316″	U	.368″		
D	.246″	J	.277″	P	.323″	V	.377″		
E	.250″	K	.287″	Q	.332″	W	.386″		
F	.257″	L	.290″	R	.339″	X	.397″		

Special Drill

Apart from the above drills there are some special twist drills also. Some of the main drills belonging to this category are :

1. Double Fluted Drill
2. Multi-Fluted Drill
3. Centre Drill
4. Counter Sinking Drill
5. Counter Boring Drill
6. Oil Hole or Tube Drill
7. Spirec Drill
8. Shell Drill
9. Step Drill

Doable Fluted Drill. This type of drill is the best and strongest. Two flutes opposite to each other are cut in this drill. It is used almost in all type of work.

Multi-Fluted Drill. For certain special jobs this drill is used. There are more than two flutes in this drill. Its distinguished feature is that because of its bigger cutting edge, hole is bored quickly and it is clean.

Centre Drill. It is also known as combination drill. On both its ends a cutting point is made and its middle portion is plain. Drilling and counter sinking can be performed simultaneously with this drill. It is used for fastening the lengthy job from centre to centre on the lathe machines and also to do centre drill in a rod. It has been shown in Fig. 8.48.

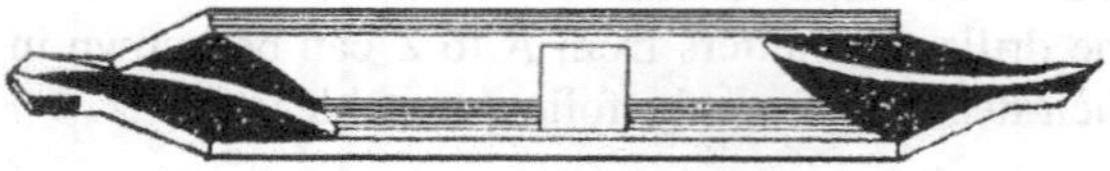

Fig. 8.48. Centre drill

Counter Sinking Drill. At places where counter head screws are to be fitted, after making holes with drill, counter sinking is done with this drill. In this way, the head job of screw fits well. This is a multi-fluted drill in which four flutes are cut. Its cutting point is grinded at 60° or 82°. In Fig. 8.49 this type of drill and a screw fitted in a hole bored by it has been shown.

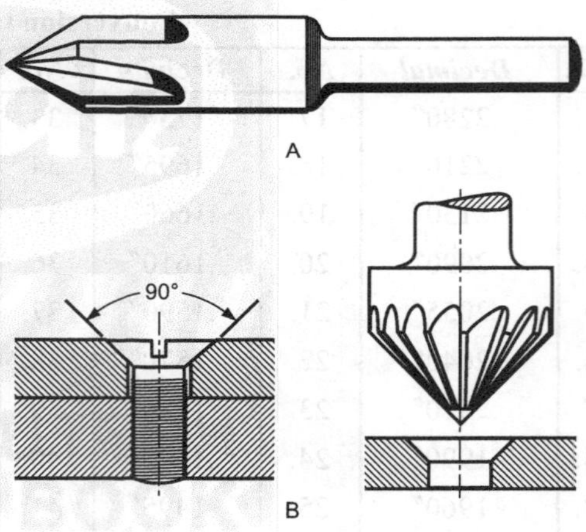

Fig. 8.49. Counter sinking drill

Counter Boring Drill. Where Alien screws are fitted counter boring is done with this drill. These types of screws are also fitted like the counter screw in the surface of the job. It is

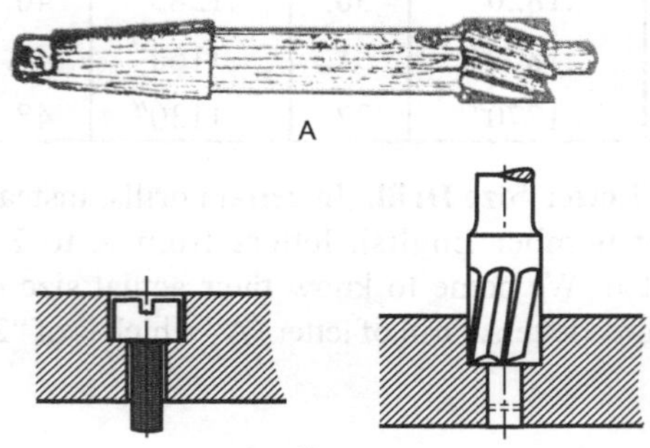

Fig. 8.50. Counter boring drill

used to enlarge a hole. Boring in a hole is done from the upper side upto the height of screw head. For fitting this type of screw the surface of the job remains similar to plain surface. The screw head does not pose any hinderance in its functioning.

Note. A noteworthy point is that in counter sinking the hole is cut slanting at 60° or 82° angle from the top whereas in counter boring the hole is made deeper in the increased size upto the height of screw head. The drill used for counter boring is also called counter boring cutter. A pilot is built on its lower side. This pilot sets in the hole and helps in straight counter boring.

Oil Hole or Tube Drill. There is need for coolant or lubricant at the time of boring hole with a drill which ensures that the drill point does not lose its capacity to cut after becoming hot.

Fig. 8.51. Oil hole or tube drill

Apart from ordinary drills there are other drills in which a hole is made from shank to cutting point for providing lubricant upto the cutting point.

Spirec Drill. These are very delicate drills. These are used for boring very minute holes in spray pump nozzle, store nipple *etc*. Their size ranges from 0.0086″ to 0.0984″. These are available in numbers.

Shell Drill. This is a different type of drill. Its shape is like side and Face Cutter is used in milling works. There are four flutes made on it. Its upper part is $\frac{1}{3}$″ per foot in taper. For using it a mandrel is required. It is used for enlarging a hole.

Cutting and Clearance Angle of Drill. The cutting angle of drill is at 118° *i.e.,* 59° at one side. In special works it can be increased or decreased. The clearance angle of drill is kept at 8° to 15°. If the clearance angle is more the cutting would be fast but there would be risk to the point. It may break. If the clearance angle in low, the points would not cut properly. Besides this, the length of lips should also be equal otherwise the hole would become large.

Method of Drill Grinding :

1. For grinding the drill, it should be held in such a manner that in one hand we should have its shank and in the other its body.

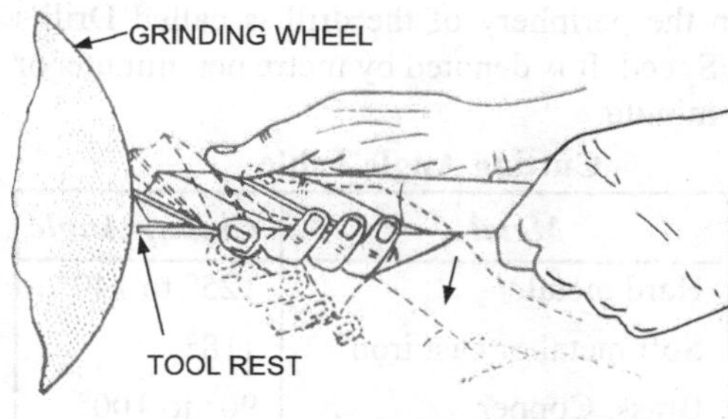

Fig. 8.52. Method of drill grinding

2. Drill grinder should be placed on the tool rest in such a way that its point should touch the grinding wheel at 59° angle as shown in Fig. 8.53.

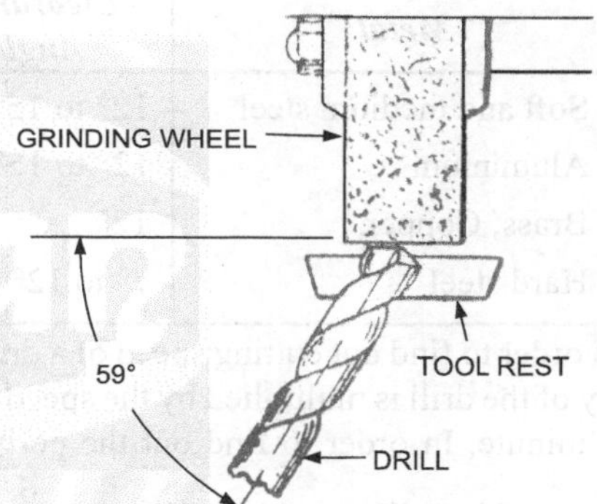

Fig. 8.53. Method of drill grinding

3. While grinding, the cutting edge of the drill should be pressed and drill should be rotated only upto 50 percent.
4. For lip clearance, lip should be raised up.
5. While grinding the lips, both the lips should be gradually grinded one by one.
6. After grinding, the lips should be measured. They should be of equal size.
7. We must check the angle with the drill angle gauge
8. Cutting angle of drill differs from metal. It can be known from the Table given on the next page.

Cutting Speed and Feed. The number of revolutions a rotating article revolves per minute is known as its speed. Therefore, speed of a revolving article is denoted by Revolutions Per Minute (R.P.M.). The distance a drill penetrates into the workpiece in a revolution is called "Drill Feed". This feed is expressed in inches or millimeters. The total distance covered in total revolutions made in a minute by a point on the periphery of the drill is called Drill's Cutting Speed. It is denoted by metre per minute or feet per minute.

Cutting Angle Table

S. No.	*Metal*	*Cutting Angle*
1.	Hard metal	125° to 140°
2.	Soft metal or cast iron	118°
3.	Brass, Copper, Aluminium	90° to 100°
4.	Bakelite, Fibre, Wood	70° to 80°

Note : 118° angle can be used for all.

Table of Clearance Angle

S. No.	*Metal*	*Clearance Angle*
1.	Soft and medium steel	12° to 15°
2.	Aluminium	12° to 15°
3.	Brass, Copper,	12°
4.	Hard steel	7° to 12°

In order to find out cutting speed of a drill, the periphery of the drill is multiplied by the speed of the drill per minute. In order to find out the periphery, the diameter of the drill is multiplied by $(\pi) = \frac{22}{7}$. This measurement is in inches or millimeters. Therefore, in order to find out speed of inch drill, the following formula is applied.

Formula :

$$\text{Speed} = \frac{D \times \pi}{12} \times \text{R.P.M.} \quad (D = \text{dia. of drill})$$

$$\text{or} \quad = 0.26 \times D \times \text{R.P.M.}$$

Similarly, if the speed of drilling is known, in order to find its F.P.M. the following formula is used :

Formula : $\frac{\text{F.P.M.} \times 12}{\pi \times D}$ or $\frac{3.8 \times \text{F.R.M.}}{D}$

What should be the speed of drill, should be determined by keeping the following points in mind :

1. Solidity of the metal to be drilled. For solid metal the speed is kept low. For soft metal speed is fast.
2. If the hole is to be bored deep, speed should be slow and if the hole is to be bored less deep, the speed would be fast.
3. For drills of big size speed is kept low. For drill of less diameter speed is high.
4. If lubricant or coolant is being properly supplied then speed can be kept high.
5. Speed can also be kept fast, if job has been gripped (held) firmly.
6. Efficiency of the machine also affects its speed. On an efficient machine drill can be operated at a high speed.

In order to find out the speed of drills with diameter in millimeters the following formula is used :

Formula :

$$\text{Speed} = \frac{\pi \times D \times \text{R.P.M.}}{1000}$$

(D = Diameter of drill in millimetres)

Example. In a job of mild steel a hole is to be bored with a drill of 21 mm. Find out its cutting speed when it has 500 R.P.M.

Solution : By taking the actual scale in the formula :

$$\text{Cutting Speed} = \frac{22 \times 21 \times 500}{7 \times 1000}$$

$$= 33 \text{ metres per minute}$$

Example. If a hole of $\frac{3}{4}''$ is to be bored in a job of brass, find out its R.P.M. when its speed is 99 per minute.

Solution : By taking the actual scale in the formula :

$$\text{R.P.M.} = \frac{99 \times 12}{\frac{22}{7} \times \frac{3}{4}}$$

$$= 504 \text{ revolutions per minute}$$

Right Cutting Speed for Different Metals

S. No.	Name of metal	Cutting Speed (M. per min.)	Cutting Speed (Ft. per min.)	Coolant
1.	Aluminium and Alloy	60 to 90	200 to 300	Kerosene oil or Soluble oil
2.	Brass and soft Bronze	30 to 90	100 to 300	Dry or soluble oil
3.	High tensile Bronze	21 to 36	76 to 120	Soluble oil
4.	Cast Iron :			
	1. Soft	30 to 45	100 to 150	Dry
	2. Medium	21 to 30	70 to 100	Dry
	3. Hard	12 to 18	40 to 60	Dry
5.	Copper	18 to 24	40 to 60	Soluble oil
6.	Malleable iron	24 to 27	80 to 90	Soda water or soluble oil
7.	Steel :			
	1. Mild steel	24 to 39	80 to 130	Soluble oil
	2. Carbon steel	18 to 27	60 to 90	Soluble oil
	3. High carbon steel	15 to 18	50 to 60	Soluble oil
	4. Tool steel	12 to 24	40 to 80	Mineral oil
	5. Alloy steel	12 to 18	40 to 60	Lord oil or Mineral oil

Feed of Drills of Different Diameters

S. No.	Diameter of Drill (in inches)	Feed per Revolution
1.	$\frac{1}{8}''$ or less	0.001″ - 0.002″
2.	$\frac{1}{8}''$ to $\frac{1}{4}''$	0.002″ - 0.004″
3.	$\frac{1}{4}''$ to $\frac{1}{2}''$	0.004″ - 0.007″
4.	$\frac{1}{2}''$ to $\frac{3}{4}''$	0.007″ - 0.011″
5.	$\frac{3}{4}''$ to 1″	0.011″ - 0.015″
6.	1″ or more	0.015″ - 0.025″

Method of Drilling :

1. Drill should be choosen according to the material and the hole to be bored in it. It should have appropriate edge and all its angles should be well grinded.
2. Drill should be properly fitted in the spindle or chuck of the drilling machine.
3. Speed of the machine should be set according to the metal of the job and diameter of the drill.
4. Job should be properly gripped in the machine vice or other medium.
5. At the place where hole is to be made, marking should be done with the central punch.
6. Place the drill straight in the place of centre punch and check.
7. If a blind hole is to be bored, set the depth of the drill with the machine.
8. Place the drill exactly in the centre of drill punch mark.
9. If the drill is operating exactly in the centre, speed can be given.
10. Use of lubricant and coolant is essential to get clean and proper finish and to save the drill from getting hot.

Precautions :

1. Cutting angle and clearance angle *etc.* of the drill should be grinded according to the material.
2. Speed on the machine should be set according to the metal and the diameter of the drill.
3. Lips of the drill should be similar.
4. If a hole of large diameter is to be bored, first the hole should be bored with a small drill.
5. Sleeve or spindle should be cleaned before fitting the drill.
6. While drilling, a wooden socket should be placed below the job so that drill may not damage the machine bed by going across.

7. Drilling should not be done without properly clamping the job.
8. Drift should be used to separate drill from the machine.

At times, because of defective drilling either drill gets damaged quickly or the hole bored in the job would get damaged. The causes and remedies of such defects are given below :

Drills becomes Defective Soon

Defects	*Causes*	*Remarks*
1. Breaking of cutting edge	1. Different clearance angle.	1. Correct the clearance angle by grinding it again.
	2. Because of blow hole or solidity in the metal.	2. Before drilling, the metal should be checked and drilling with low feed speed should not be done.
	3. Because of drilling at a higher speed and with blunt point.	3. Grind the drill again or reduce the speed.
	4. Cutting angle may be of more degrees than it should be.	4. Cutting angle should be suitably grinded.
	5. Drill may not be fitted properly.	5. Fit the drill properly.
	6. Coolant may not be reaching the cutting adge.	6. Supply coolant properly.
2. Drill gets broken from the front side	1. Edge of the drill might have finished.	1. Grind the edge of the drill.
	2. Spindle of the drill machine might be loose.	2. Repair the machine.
	3. Feed of the drill or pressure or both may be less.	3. Give proper feed and pressure.
	4. Job may not be properly clamped.	4. Clamp the job properly.
	5. Chips might have blocked in the flutes.	5. Clear the chips from the flutes.

Hole of the Job Becomes Defective

Defects	*Causes*	*Remarks*
1. Hole is of coarse surface	1. Edge of the drill may not be proper.	1. Grind the drill properly.
	2. There might be excessive pressure on the drill.	2. Reduce the pressure on the drill.
	3. Adequate coolant might not have been used.	3. Use proper coolant.
	4. Drill might have been fixed wrongly.	4. Fix the drill properly.
2. When the drill bores a hole of larger diameter than needed.	1. Diameter of the drill might be larger.	1. Take a drill of proper diameter.
	2. There may be difference between length and angle of the lips.	2. Grind the drill properly.
	3. Drill's hold may not be proper.	3. Tight the drill suitably.
	4. Drill or machine spindle may be curved.	4. Take a straight drill and repair the machine.

3. Hole is not bored at the right point and is deeper.	1. Careless drilling.	1. Drill carefully.
	2. Job may not be set properly.	2. Set the job properly before drilling.
	3. Drill is not grinded properly.	3. Grind the drill properly.
	4. Depth of drill may be set wrongly.	4. Set the drill depth correctly.

Drilling Machine

For boring holes in metal or wood, drill and drilling machine is used. Drill is a tool which is fitted in a drill machine and then moved. When the drill rotates on the metal it bores a hole. As different types of drills are used for boring holes in different metals likewise there are different types of drilling machines. These machines can be divided into two parts :

Portable Drill Machine. For boring holes in small jobs, this type of drill machine is used. Besides it is used for those jobs which cannot be brought to the other fixed drill machines. The portable drill machines are generally of five types. These can be easily moved from one place to another.

1. **Hand Drill Machine.** It is driven with the hand power. It has a handle on the upper side, which we catch with our left hand. Pressure is given with this handle. A chuck is fixed in the spindle on the lower side to hold the drill. In between a gear is fixed in which a handle is attached for driving the drill. When we move this handle, drill moves through the medium of a small gear. This type of hand drill machine has been shown in Fig. 8.54. Holes can be bored with this upto $\frac{1}{4}$ ″.

Fig. 8.54. Hand drill machine

2. **Breast Drill Machine.** This drill is bigger in size and capacity in comparison to hand drill machine. Its shape is like a hand drill machine. But instead of a handle on the upper side there is a covered iron breast plate. This breast plate is pressed with breast and pressure is exerted on the drill. Two additional bevel gears are also provided which are fitted in spindle in order to increase the speed. It is generally used in repair works. This type drill machine is shown in Fig. 8.55. Holes upto $\frac{1}{2}$ ″ diameter can be bored with this machine.

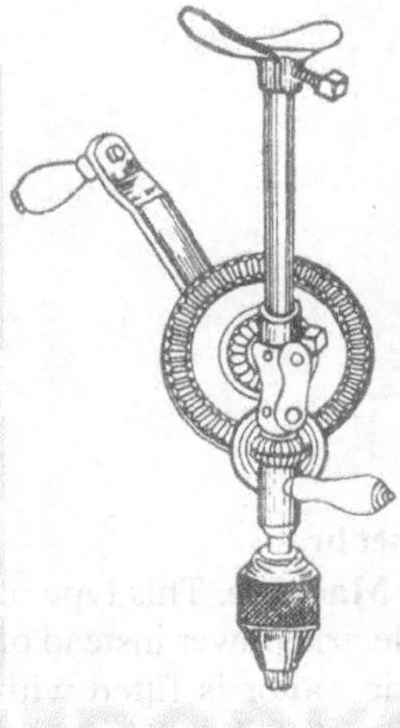

Fig. 8.55. Breast drill machine

Fig. 8.56. Use of breast drill machine

3. **Ratchet Brace.** Its capacity is more than hand drill machine and breast drill machine. It is used for boring holes in those heavy jobs which cannot be fitted on the fixed drill machines. In this type of drill machines ratchet shank twist is used which is square and also tapered. In this machine, in place of chuck, tapered square hole is there in its spindle in which ratchet shank drill fits easily. A straight drill post is fitted in its base plate. There is an arm on its drill post with which it can be set at the desired height. Ratchet and drill is also attached to the arm. It is driven (or operated) with a handle of 2 to 4 feet in length. Two powls are there in its handle, which fit in the ratchet and move trhe spindles and the drill. When the drill

is moving with the powl, if we move the handle in the opposite direction the powl ratchet slips and for that period the spindle remains fixed. In this way, slowly holes are made in the heavy jobs. In order to give feed to the machine, a sleeve having threads is fitted above the spindle which is gradually moved with hands.

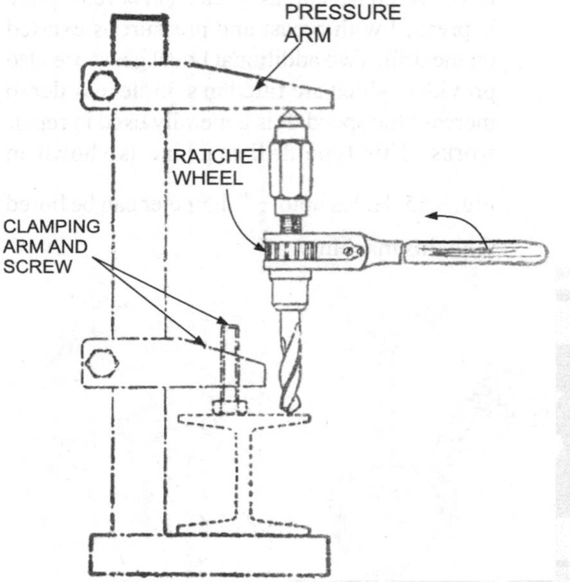

Fig. 8.57. Ratchet brace

4. **Electrical Hand Drill Machine.** This type of machine is driven by electric power instead of hand power. An electric motor is fitted with this machine. A spindle is fitted on its motor-shaft with the help of a few gears. On this spindle the drill chuck is mounted. On one side a handle is built according to convenience and a switch to put on and off the machine is fitted within the reach of fingers. These machines can be driven both with A.C. and D.C. current.

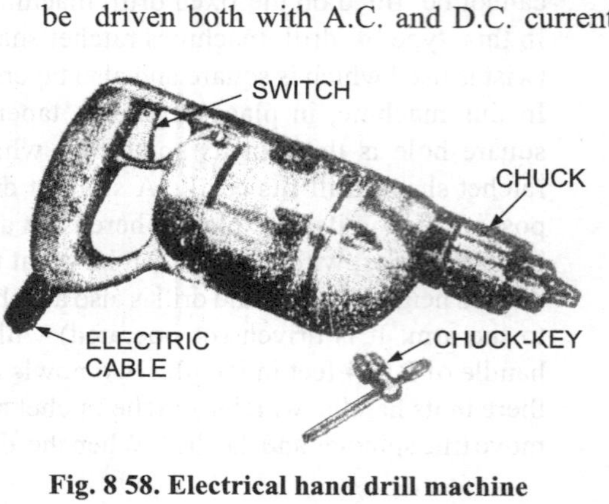

Fig. 8 58. Electrical hand drill machine

According to their working capacity they are of two types : (1) Light duty electrical hand drill machines, in which drills of $\frac{1}{2}''$ diameter are used; (2) Heavy duty electrical hand drill maching in which drills of 1″ diameter are used. Neat and clean holes are bored with these machines without using much power. These can also be used for other works such as by fitting a rotary file or grinding wheel for filing or grinding purposes.

5. **Pneumatic Drill Machine.** Its construction and way of working is almost similar to the electrical hard drill machine. The only difference is that it does not have electrical motor and wires *etc*. Drill is moved with the compressed air power. To provide air, air valve and plunger is fitted. Air is supplied by an air compressor which is connected with the pressure line. An air valve is provided on the handle itself to start or stop the supply of air. Where use of electrical hand drill is risky, pneumatic drill machine is used *e.g.,* in the sea or other places of water.

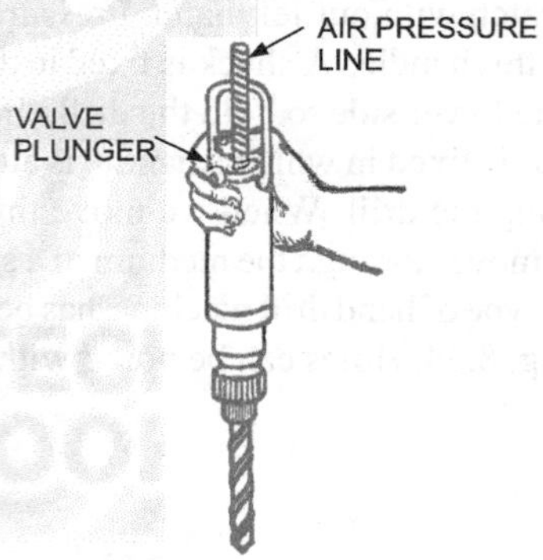

Fig. 8.59. Pneumatic drill machine

Stationary Drill Machine. Those machines which can be fixed at one place on the foundation, are called stationary or fixed drill machines. These are used for drilling, reaming and taping *etc*. of heavy jobs. These are of small and big capacity. For using these machines it is necessary to bring the jobs to the machine table.

These drill machines are of the following types :

1. Sensitive Drill Machines
2. Pillar Type Drill Machines
3. Column Type Drill Machines
4. Radial Drill Machines
5. Gang Drill Machines
6. Multi Spindle Drill Machines.

1. **Sensitive Drill Machine.** This is a medium class drill machine. Its speed is comparatively very fast. These are of hand-operated as well as electrically operated types. These are generally fixed on work bench by bolt-nut. These machines are considered best for drilling and lapping. There is no provision for self-regulating give feed. Therefore, feed is given by hand with the help of rack and pinion. Because in this machine the feed depends on the alertness of the worker that is why it is also called the sensitive drill machine. It is of two type :

   (1) Bench Type (2) Floor Type.

   Bench Type Sensitive Drill Machine. This type of machine has been shown in Fig. 8.60. It can be operated by hand as well as by electric power. In this machine head can be fixed in any direction and at any height. In this way, apart from drilling of ordinary jobs drilling can be done in long rods also.

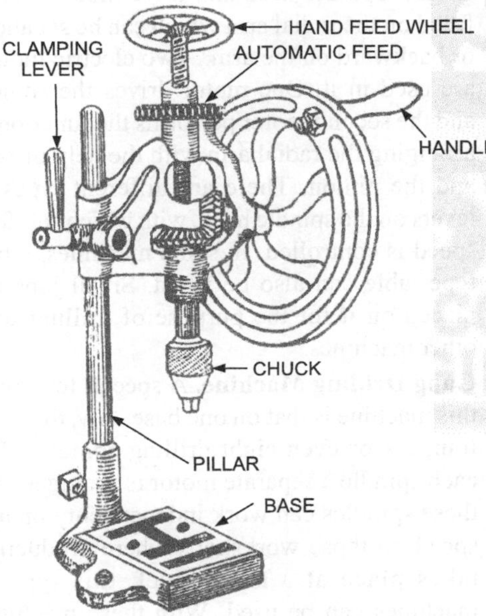

Fig. 8.60. Bench type sensitive drill machine

   Floor Type Sensitive Drill Machine. It is driven with an electric motor. But this machine is established at one place on the ground by foundation bolts in place of work bench.

2. **Pillar Type Drill Machine.** This type of machines are highly used in the workshops. Holes upto diameter of 25 mm. can be done with this machine. It contains the following main parts :

   1. Main Drive 2. Spindle 3. Pillar 4. Feed Drive 5. Working Table.

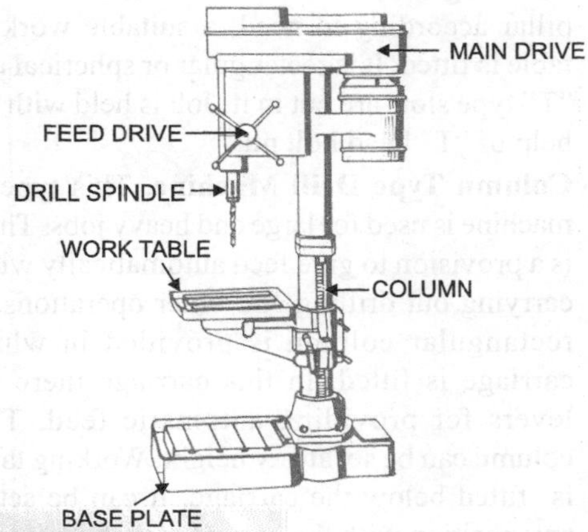

Fig. 8.61. Pillar type drill machine

   Main Drive. This machine is operated by an electric motor. The electric motor is fitted in a bracket on the spindle head. Two step pulleys are separately fitted in the opposite direction to each other on spindle and motor shaft *i.e.,* in the pulleys in one pulley small step is kept above and in the other pulley big step is kept above. The motor pulley revolves on the spindle pulley on the "V" belt. If the step of the motor pulley is small and that of spindle pulley is larger, the speed will be low. On the other hand, if the step of motor pulley is bigger than that of the spindle pulley, speed would be more. Drilling speed is set by it. Belt and pulley is covered with a cover.

   Spindle. In this drill machine standard morse taper is cut inside the spindle. Taper snank drill of large diameter can be fitted in this easily. Drills of small diameter can be fitted with the help of drill chucks.

   Pillar. This is a hollow pipe of cast-iron or mild steel. On one side of the pillar groove like the rack are cut, with its help working table can be fitted at any height. On the upper part of the pillar spindle head is fitted. There is a provision to join the pillar to the base plate of the machine.

   Feed Drive. In order to provide feed to the drill, rack teeth are cut on the spindle sleeve. As a result, a pinion is joined which revolves with the help of head lever. Lever feed is called lever. When it revolves, spindle moves up and down. A gauge is fixed near the lever to set the depth. On setting it the drill does not go that much deep.

Working Table. To set the machine on the pillar according to need, a suitable working table is fitted. It is rectangular or spherical and "T" type slots are cut in it. Job is held with the help of "T" head bolt nut.

3. **Column Type Drill Machine.** This type of machine is used for large and heavy jobs. There is a provision to give feed automatically while carrying out drilling and other operations. A rectangular column is provided in which carriage is fitted. In this carriage there are levers for providing automatic feed. This column can be set at any height. Working table is fitted below the carriage. It can be set in any position with the help of elevating screw.

4. **Radial Type Drill Machine.** For small and medium size jobs any other type of machines can be used. But for drilling of very heavy and such jobs which cannot be set on any other machine's working table, Radial type drill machines are used. On any other machine to bore accurate holes through supplements or to have these holes at the fixed place. Radial type drilling machine is a very large and accurate drilling machine. A special feature of this machine is that unlike other machines job is not fitted on it but it is set by moving the radial arm. Thus it is easy to carry out drilling and other similar operations even on the heaviest jobs. It contains the following main parts :

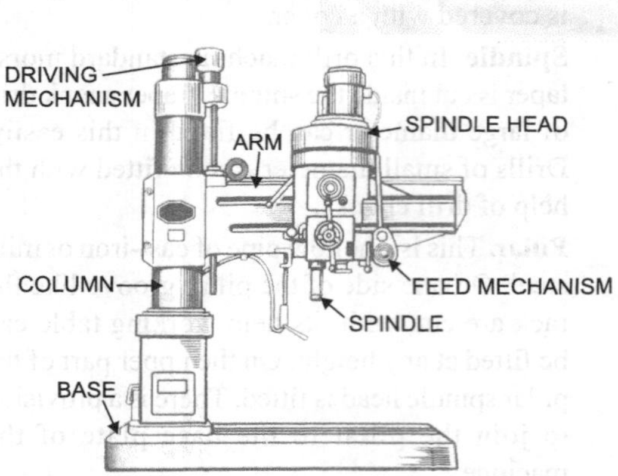

Fig. 8.62. Radial type drill machine

1. Column
2. Radial arm motor
3. Spindle motor
4. Base
5. Auxiliary box table
6. Drill
7. Spindle
8. Radial arm
9. Spindle head
10. Star head wheel
11. Fine feed wheel
12. Spindle head screw
13. Spindle head operating wheel
14. Speed lever
15. Reversing lever
16. Radial arm clamping lever.

On the lower side of this machine, a heavy base made of cast iron is attached which is fixed on the ground with the foundation nut-bolts. Towards an end of this base a pillar is fixed. Radial arm is fixed on this pillar. There is a provision to set it in desired direction and height. Spindle head and drive mechanism is fitted on the radial arm which can be set ahead or backward on the arm. Two electric motors are used in it. One motor drives the spindle and the second motor performs the function of arranging the radial arm with the help of rack and the pinion. There are different types of levers on the spindle head, with which self feed speed is controlled. In some machines, a box type table can also be fitted. Small jobs are placed on it for the purpose of drilling with other machines.

5. **Gang Drilling Machine.** A special feature of this machine is that on one base only, there are four, six or even eight drilling spindles. For each spindle a separate motor is provided. All these spindles can work independenty on any speed, in those workshops where production takes place at a mass level, this type of machines can be used. With these machines some other operations in addition to drilling can be performed on the same table by pulling the job to the other drill spindle. These machines save time considerably and these machines can perform several operations one after the other.

6. **Multi Spindle Drill Machine.** On this type of machine also a number of operations can be performed like drilling, reaming and tapping on one place itself. The main spindle is driven

by one motor. With this main spindle 8 to 10 spindles are driven which perform several operations such as drill, lap *etc*. Its spindles can also be set according to the needs.

Uses of Drill Machine. Although mainly drilling is done with the drill machines but the following jobs are also performed with these machines :

Counter Boring. Under this operation, a hole is made deeper so that after tapping in this hole allen screw *etc*. can be fitted on the surface of the job at the equal level. For this purpose, counter boring drill is used on the drill machine.

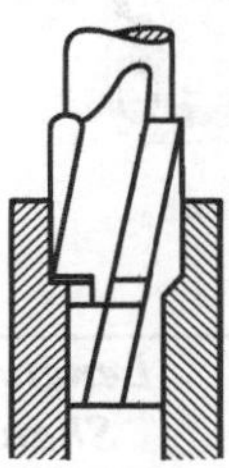

Fig. 8.63. Counter boring

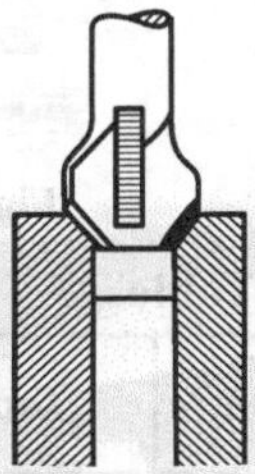

Fig. 8.64. Counter sinking

Counter Sinking. Under this operation, a hole already bored is cut in slanting manner from the top at an angle of 60° 82° or 92°. With this operation, the machine-screw is fitted in the hole evenly.

Tapping. The process of cutting threads with a tap is known as tapping. In this operation in an already bored hole tap is revolved with the help of machine according to its size and thus threads are cut.

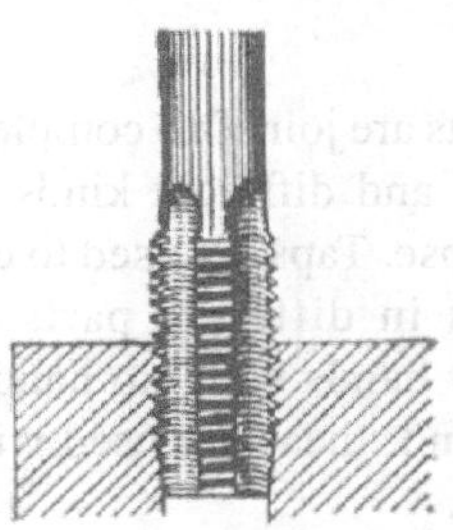

Fig. 8.65. Tapping

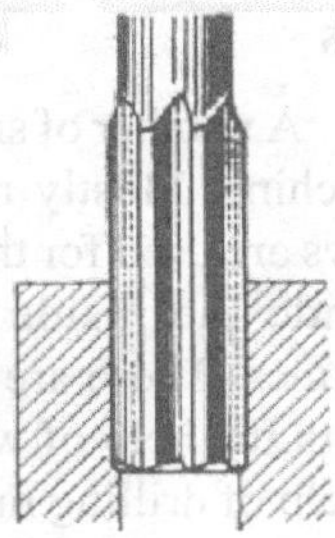

Fig. 8.66. Reaming

Reaming. The process of smoothing the surface of holes with a reamer is known as reaming. Under this process, a hole is enlarged, finished straightened or tapered.

Trepanning. The process of cutting a groove on a circular hole is called trepanning. Under this process, with a special tool big holes are bored or cut in round shape. Two cutting bits are provided in this tool in a special holder at an equal distance from the centre, which cut according to their diameter.

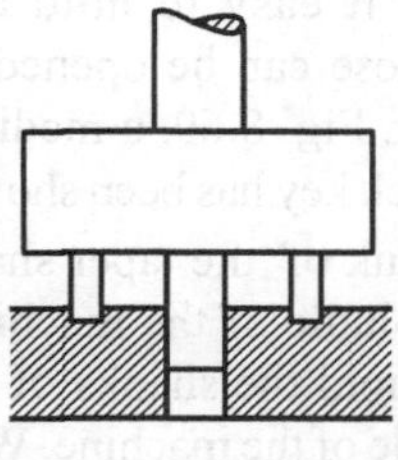

Fig. 8.67. Trepanning

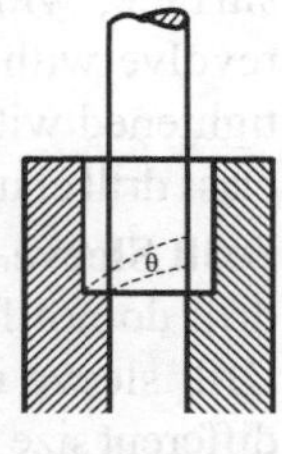

Fig. 8.68. Boring

Boring. Under this process a small hole is enlarged with the help of a boring tool and it is finished.

Supplementary Tools of Drill Machine

In addition to drill machine, the following supplementary tools are also used for boring holes :

Drill Chuck. In small drill machines small drill chucks are fitted in the machines. In such machines without the help of chuck it is not possible to hold any drill. But in big and medium drill machines spindle is cut in taper so we can hold taper shank drills without the help of chucks. But the straight shank drills are held in these machines with the drill chucks. These drill chucks are of different diameters and are of different capacity such as upto $\frac{1}{4}$″ and upto $\frac{1}{2}$″. In these drill chucks a taper shank is made which fits in the drill machines properly.

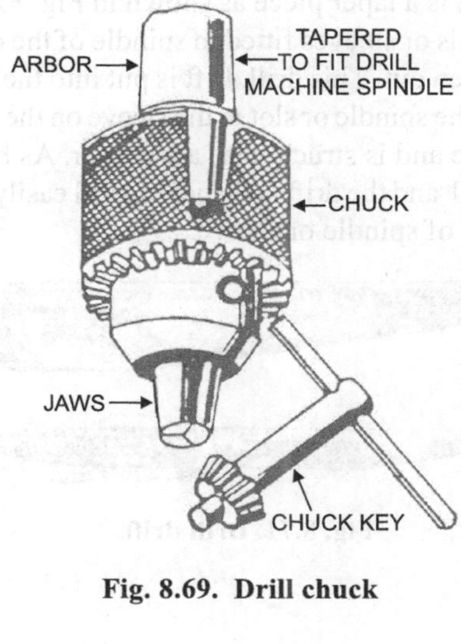

Fig. 8.69. Drill chuck

Their taper is morse taper. There are three jaws in a drill chuck. In the big chucks jaws can be opened or tightened with the chuck-key but in small chucks knurling is done on the outer surface, which makes it easy to hold and revolve with hand. These can be opened or tightened with hands. In Fig. 8.69, a medium class drill chuck and chuck key has been shown.

Drill Sleeve. Every shank of the taper shank drill do not fit in the spindle of the machine. Drill sleeve is used to hold the shanks of the different size from spindle of the machine. With its help shanks of different tapers — big or small can be easily fit in the spindle of the machine. These sleeves, made in tapers, on the upper side plain tangs are made a bit below the tang a groove is made across the sleeve. Their body is in taper. Their upper part is greater in size but the lower part is comparatively smaller in size. These are available in different numbers which are appropriate for different drills. Their numbers are like 0-1, 1-2, 2-3, 3-4 *etc.* The first number indicates the measurement of inside taper of sleeve and the second number indicates the outside taper size of the sleeve. It has been shown in Fig. 8.70.

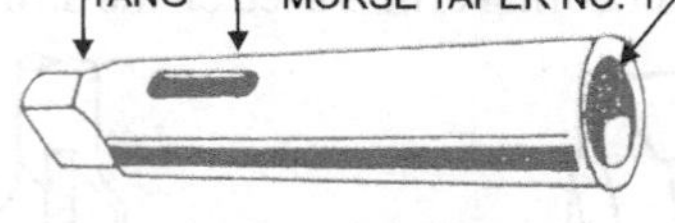

Fig. 8.70. Drill sleeve

Sleev's Morse Taper Table

Taper No.	*Small Diameter*	*Big Diameter*	*Tapper per inch*	*Taper per foot*	*Length of Shank*
0.	0.252″	0.3561″	0.052050″	0.62460′	$2\frac{11}{32}$ inch
1.	0.369″	0.475″	0.049882″	0.59858′	$2\frac{9}{16}$ inch
2.	0.572″	0.700″	0.049951″	0.59941′	$3\frac{1}{8}$ inch
3.	0.778″	0.938″	0.050196″	0.60235′	$3\frac{7}{8}$ inch
4.	1.020″	1.231″	0.051038″	0.62326′	$4\frac{7}{8}$ inch
5.	1.475″	1.748″	0.052626″	0.63151′	$6\frac{1}{8}$ inch
6.	2.116″	2.494″	0.052137″	0.62565′	$8\frac{9}{16}$ inch

Drill Drift. This drill is made of mild steel and is a taper piece as shown in Fig. 8.71. Big drills or sleeves fitted in spindle of the drill are taken out. This drill drift is put into the groove in the spindle or slot in the sleeve on the tapered side and is struck with a hammer. As both the drill and the drift are tapered, drill easily passes out of spindle or sleeve.

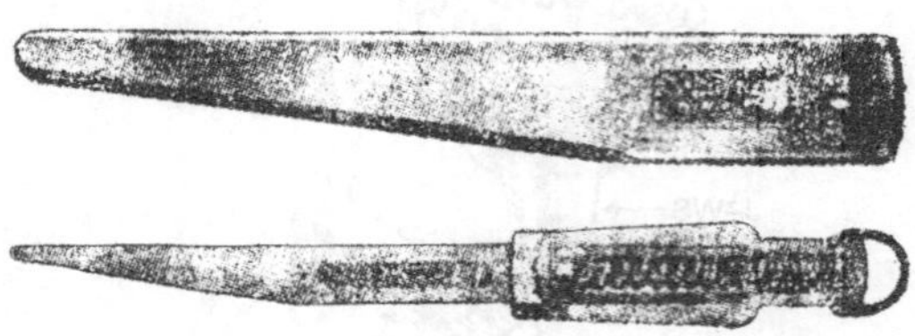

Fig. 8.71. Drill drift

Taps

A number of small parts are joined to complete a machine. Mostly nut, bolt and different kinds of screws are used for this purpose. Taps are used to cut or undo the inside threads in different parts of machines. These are used by hands with tap handle or with the help of wrench and these are used with the help of drilling machines.

Taps are made of high carbon steel, high speed steel, alloy steel *etc.* These are hardened and tapered. Their shape is almost like a headless bolt with full threads. The upper portion is square and four flutes are made on the entire part in which threads are there.

Different parts of tap have been shown in Fig. 8.72. These are as under :

1. Body
2. Shank
3. Tang
4. Land

5. Mutes 6. Heel
7. Cutting Face 8. Chamfer

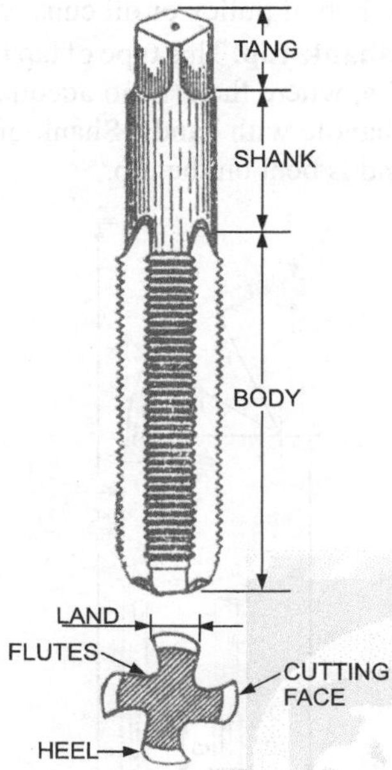

Fig. 8.72. Tap

Body. That part of tap on which threads are cut is called body.

Shank. The smooth part above the part on which threads are cut, is called shank. It is round and the pitch of threads which are to be cut by shank is indicated on it.

Tang. The part above shank is called tang. It is square in shape. It is revolved by holding it in a tap handle.

Land. Space between flutes *i.e.,* where threads are cut is called land. This part is slightly projected.

Flutes. On the entire body of tap the grooves cut on the space between two lands, are called flutes. These are made in length from top to bottom. The particles of metal cut while cutting threads are come out of these flutes and these are also used for supplying lubricant inside.

Heel. The tilted part behind the threads cut on the land is called heel.

Cutting Face. The face of the cutting tool against which the material is moved is called the cutting face.

Chamfer. The lower part of the threads cut by tap is in taper. This is called chamfer.

Types of Taps. For cutting inside threads in different types of jobs, the following kinds of taps are used :

1. Hand tap 2. Gas Tap
3. Master Tap 4. Machine Tap
5. Machine Screw Tap 6. Extension Tap
7. Bend Shank Tap 8. Stay Bolt Tap
9. Spiral Fluted Tap 10. Fluteless Tap

Hand Tap. These taps are used in the form of a set. This set includes three taps.

(1) *Taper Tap* in which 8 to 10 threads are rubbed and chamfered on the lower side. These are easily set in the drill holes and perform the job of starting a thread. The lower end of this tap is equal to tap size drill.

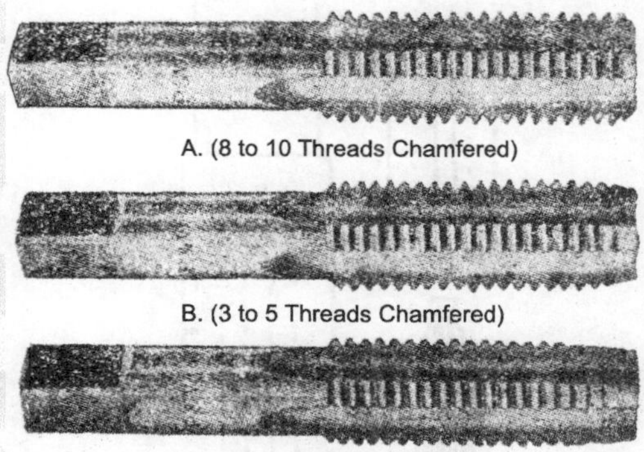

Fig. 8.73. Hand tap set

(2) *Intermediate Tap.* It is also known as second tap. Taper upto 3 to 5 threads is made on the lower side in this tap. It is used to provide proper depth and shape to threads which have been made by the taper tap. If threads are to be cut through the drill hole then only these two taps are used.

(3) *Bottom Tap or Finishing Tap.* This is the third tap of the set. It is used after using the above mentioned taps, at places where the hole is not across the job. Besides, it is also used for cleaning and finishing of the threads which are cut through the entire drill. Taper is cut at its end on one or one and a halt thread.

Gas Tap. It is used for cutting gas type threads, for fitting at places where any liquid or gas passes through the pipes. In this type of tap $1\frac{1}{2}$

threads towards the lower portion is chamfered and there is some taper in the body length. It is $\frac{3}{4}$ taper per foot. That's why gas does not leak.

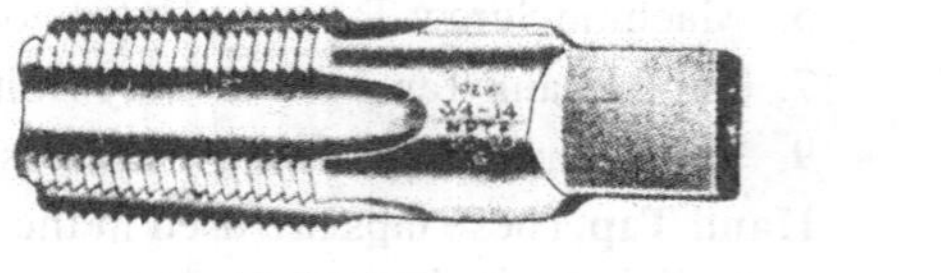

Fig. 8.74. Gas tap

Master Tap. This tap is almost similar to the hand tap but it has 6 to 10 flutes because of which it contains more cutting faces. With this tap the thread is accurate and clean. In thread ring gauge and similar inspection tools threads are cut only with this tap.

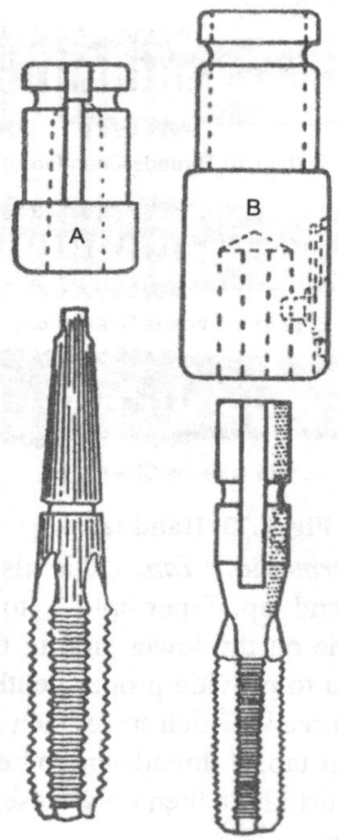

Fig. 8.75. Master tap

Machine Tap. This type of taps are used for cutting threads with tap drill machine. They are used by holding them in a special holder. It is necessary to have reverse speed in the drill machine so that tap can be extracted from the job easily.

Machine Screw Tap. Taps with which threads are cut in the holes of less than $\frac{1}{4}''$ diameter, are called Machine Screw Taps. Two or four threads are chamfered on the lower side.

Extension Tap. This type of tap is like an ordinary hand tap but its shank is considerably long. It is used for cutting threads in deep places such as hub of pulley or oil cups *etc.*

Bend Shank Tap. This type of tap is used with a handle, where there is no adequate place to move handle with hands. Shank of this tap is long and is bent on the top.

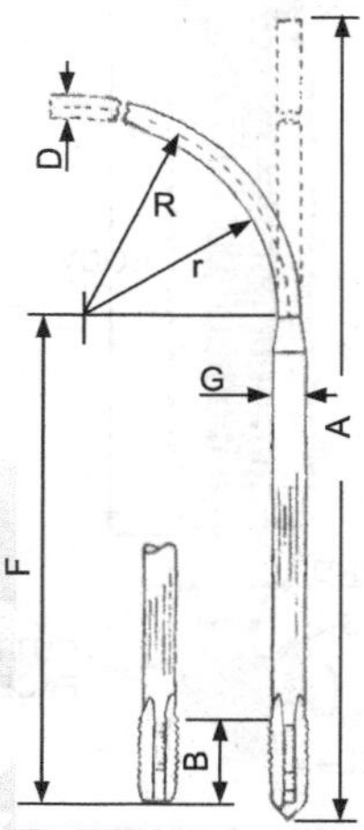

Fig. 8.76. Bend shank tap

Stay Bolt Tap. This one is also a special quality tap which performs three functions. The lower plain portion of this tap which is equal to the diameter of the hole of job helps in keeping the tap straight. In the middle of this tap, a reamer is built which helps in making the job of clean and of accurate size. Tap is built above the reamer which is used for cutting accurate threads.

Spiral Fluted Tap. This type of tap is used where slots or grooves are to be cut such as key-way. Its special feature is that in this tap instead of straight flutes these are cut spiral. Because their being spiral flutes these taps do not get caught in the edges of slot. On its edge two or three threads are chamfered.

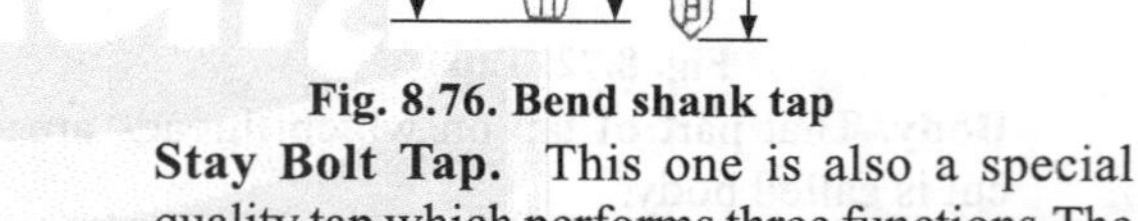

Fig. 8.77. Spiral fluted tap

Fluteless Tap. This type of taps are used to cut threads like thread rolling process in soft metals like brass, copper, aluminium *etc.* It does not cut any material. One distinguished feature of this tap is that there are no flutes in this tap but threads are cut on its entire body.

Fig. 8.78. Fluteless tap

Appropriate size of hole for the tap. Before driving the tap for cutting inside threads of a job a hole of the appropriate size is bored with the drill. The size of the drill should be equal to the core diameter of the tap. If the size of the drill is greater the threads would not be of the proper depth. If the size of the drill is less there would be difficulty in cutting threads and there would be danger of tap being broken. Thus, it is essential that the drill should be of proper size. Size of drill is called tap size drill. In order to determine it, the following formula is used :

$$\text{Size of the drill} = \text{Size of tap} \times \frac{7}{8} - \frac{1}{32}$$

Example. Find out the appropriate size of the drill for 1″ B.S.W. tap.

Solution : $1 \times \frac{7}{8} - \frac{1}{32}$

$$= \frac{7}{8} - \frac{1}{32} = \frac{27''}{32} \text{ or } 0.843''$$

approx. size of the drill.

Formula for Metric Tap.

Size of the drill = size of tap – 1.23 × Pitch.

Example. Find out the appropriate size of drill for a tap of 20 mm while the pitch is 1 5.

Solution : Size of the drill

$= 20 - 1.23 \times 1.5$

$= 20 - 1.845$

$= 18.155 = 18.25$

drill of the nearest size.

Tap Handle. For cutting threads in a job by hand with the help of tap; tap is moved in the hole with the tap handle. These tap handles are of three types :

1. Solid Tap Handle
2. Adjustable Tap Handle
3. "T" Type Handle

Solid and Adjustable Tap Handle. Solid tap handle is made solid. On both sides handles are fixed for convenience. In the middle rectangular part, two separate rectangular grooves are cut across the tap. Taps of two sizes can be moved in these. In adjustable tap in the middle part, a set of two pieces is there which are held by the adjusting screw and taps of different sizes can be moved as shown in Figs. 8.79 and 8.80.

Fig. 8.79. Solid tap handle

Fig. 8.80. Adjustable tap handle

"T" Type handle. It is in fact a kind of chuck in which three jaws are fitted. Different types of small taps are held in this chuck. A hole is bored on the upper side of its shank and a rod is put across, with its help the tap tied to the rod can be easily moved.

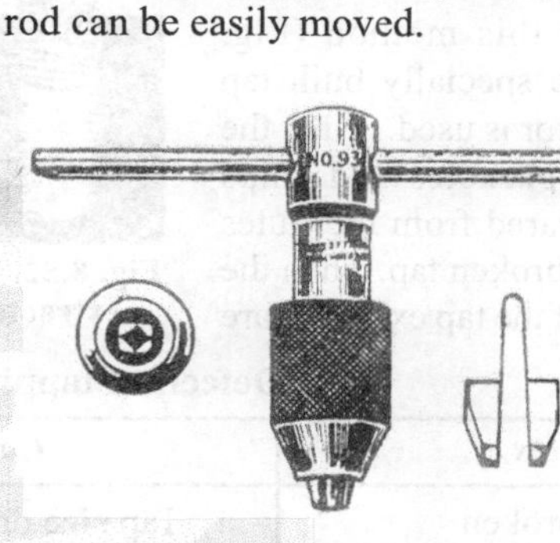

Fig. 8.81. "T" type handle

Method of cutting threads with tap :

1. Bore a tap drill hole of appropriate size for the tap.
2. Chamfer or file the drill at the tap.
3. Hold the job firmly in vice *etc.*
4. First of all, use the taper tap for cutting threads.
5. After moving two or three threads ensure through the try square that tap is moving straight.
6. Tapping should be done by moving the tap forward and backward.
7. Adequate lubricant should be used while tapping.
8. After moving the taper tap, intermediate and finishing tap should be moved.
9. While cutting threads in blind hole in between tap should be taken out to clean the metal particles.

Precautions :

1. Tap drill hole of appropriate size is essential before lapping.
2. Tap should be properly cleaned before using the tap.

3. Use tap handle according to the tap.
4. Keep equal pressure of hand on both the ends of tap handle.
5. Tap should be moved forward and backwards and we should prevent any jolts.
6. Tap should be cleaned properly and kept safely.

Method to extract a broken tap from a job. If the tap gets broken in the job itself, it can be extracted by the following methods :

Tap Extractor Method. Under this method (Fig. 8.82) a specially built tap extractor is used. First, the metal particles and chips are cleared from the flutes of the broken tap. Then the jaws of the tap extractor are put in them and the broken tap is extracted by moving the extractor in reverse direction.

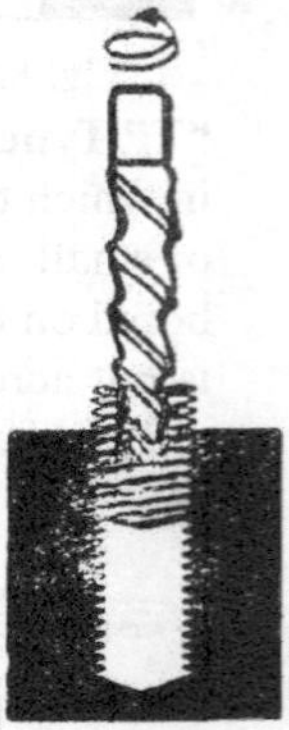

Fig. 8.82. Tap extractor

Nose Plier Method. This is the easiest method. Nose plier's ends are put in the flutes of the tap and revolve it in a reverse direction. But this method is suitable only to extract big taps because the nose plier ends need adequate place.

Hammer and Punch Method. A pointed punch is used to revolve the tap in the reverse direction, with the help of a hammer.

Acid Method. Under this method, nitric acid is poured over tap. With this the material on the edge of the threads on the job and on the circumference of the tap is burnt. Thus the tap becomes loose in the hole and it can be extracted with a plier.

Apart from the above method, we extract a broken tap by a stud extractor also, which has some left hand helical threads, by drilling.

Defects of tapping — its Causes and Remedy

Defects	*Causes*	*Remarks*
1. Tap is broken	1. Tap size drill being short.	1. Bore a hole of the right size.
	2. Lower position of the tap being defective.	2. Tap should be revolved in the reverse order quickly.
	3. Tap does not move straight.	3. Move the tap straight.
2. Thread of the tap's end gets broken.	1. Lack of lubrication.	1. Apply proper lubrucants.
	2. Chips stuck in the broken threads.	2. After cutting some threads chips should be cleared.
	3. Metal is very hard.	3. Check the metal.
	4. Because of exerting more pressure than the needed.	4. Do not exert excess pressure on the tap.
3. Threads are cut beyond the required size.	1. Tap of greater size is used.	1. Use tap of proper size.
	2. Because of excessive pressure on the tap.	2. Tap should be moved with adequate pressure.
	3. There may be play in the tap handle or machine spindle.	3. Remove the defect of the defective tool through verification.

Dies

Dies are used for cutting threads on the outside surface on pipe, round rods *etc.* It is operated with hand and for this purpose die stock is used. These are made of high carbon steel, high speed steel and alloy steel. These are made of circular and square shape. Threads of proper size are cut in the die which are chamfered from one side upto certain length which facilitate to start thread. For different purposes, mainly the following types of dies are used :

1. Round Split Die
2. Adjustable Die
3. Die Nut
4. Die Plate
5. Pipe Die
6. Acron Die

Round Split Die. These are also known as Slide Die. This is a one-piece die, which is cut from one end. This die is fitted on the die stock in such a way that all the three screws of the stock are set on the seat built on it This checks the die from rotating in the stock. After fitting it on the job, centre screw is tightened before cutting threads. These dies are used for small jobs. A round split die has been shown in Fig. 8.83.

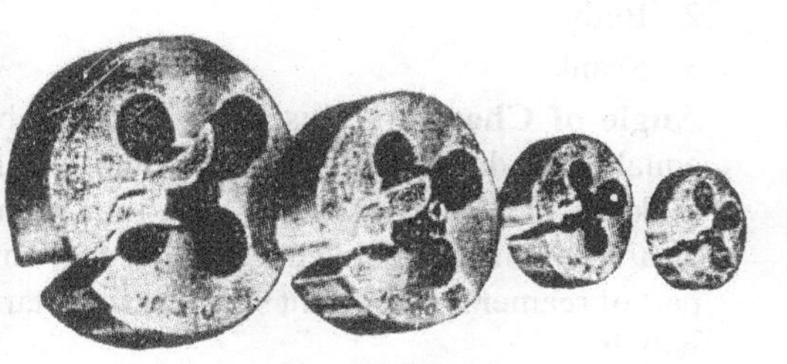

Fig. 8.83. Round split die

Adjustable Die. This die is in two pieces. In both the pieces threads are cut inside. In these threads round grooves are cut which perform the job of cutting edge. These pieces bear Number 1 or 2. There is a provision for adjusting distance among them with the outside screw. For this purpose there is a seat of the screw. Threads can be cut on the big jobs with this die. First hight threads are cut by slightly tightening both the pieces and after tightening it further deep threads are cut. This type of die has been shown in Fig. 8.84.

Fig. 8.84. Adjustable die

Die Nut. Its shape is square or like a six-phased nut as shown in Fig. 8.85. In the threads cut inside it, four or six flutes are cut which make a cutting edge. It is used for repairing the old threads. It can be moved with an ordinary spanner.

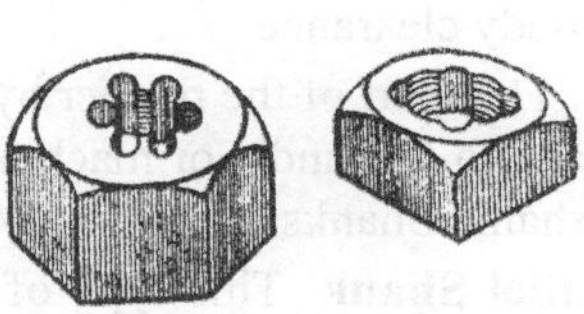

Fig. 8.85. Die nut

Die Plate. This is a plate made of steel and is hardened and tapered; which has a handle on one side as shown in Fig. 8.86. In this plate, for cutting small threads of different diameters, holes with threads are cut. Threads upto $\frac{1}{8}''$ on a screw can be cut with it, which are used in radio and electrical jobs.

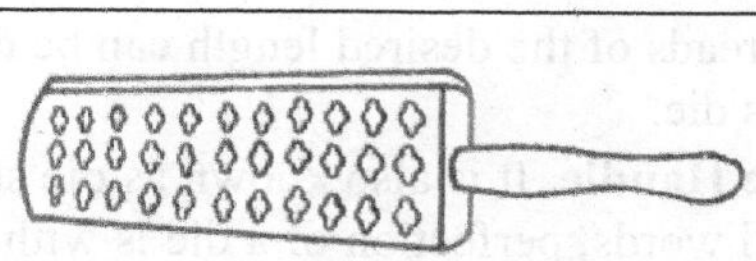

Fig. 8.86. Die plate

Pipe Die. This die is specially used for cutting threads on water pipes, gas and oil pipes *etc.* Dies of two to four pieces are used in it, which are fitted in different types of die handles as shown in Fig. 8.87. An adjusting screw is provided on stock or handle for adjusting the die. A guide is fitted in this stock or handle, which guides the die to move in the straight direction of the pipe. Threads cut with this die are of a special type because this die cuts threads in taper. This is why the sockets fitted on these pipes become gas and liquid proof.

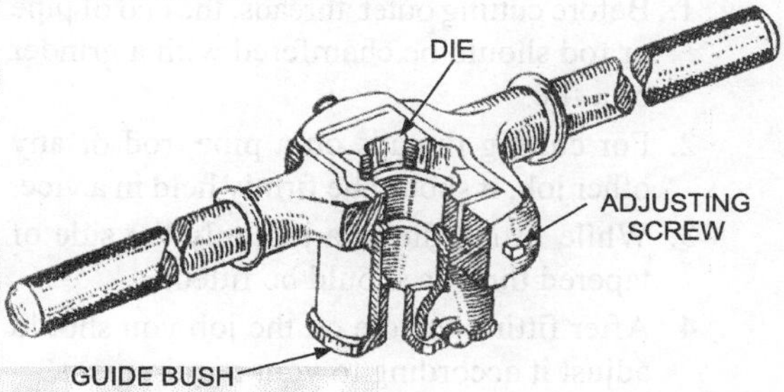

Fig. 8.87. Pipe die

Acron Die. This is the modern form of die. This type of die is used for cutting outside threads on a pipe fitted in a groove or a hole. This die is also like a nut in which threads are cut inside and it is cut intermitantly as shown in Fig. 8.88. For the purpose of convenience, this is tapered from one end. It is moved by holding it in a holder of special type.

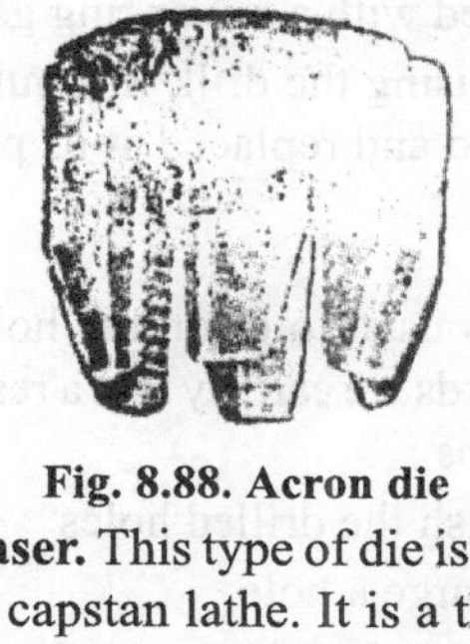

Fig. 8.88. Acron die

Die Chaser. This type of die is used with turret lathe or capstan lathe. It is a threaded section of a screw cutting die. Like a machine chuck, six skids are fixed there on which dents for cutting threads are cut. These skids can be adjusted with the handle on the die head.

Threads of the desired length can be cut with this die.

Die Handle. It is also known as die stock. In real words, perfection of a die is with skid of the die and this handle. The die skids are fitted in this handle or the stock. For dies of varying sizes, die handles of different range are used. These can be divided into the following two parts :

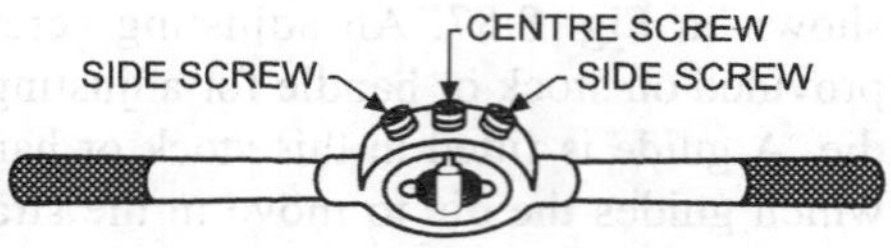

Fig. 8.89. Die handle

1. Adjustable Die Handle
2. Solid Die Handle

Method of Using Die :

1. Before cutting outer threads, the end of pipe or rod should be chamfered with a grinder or a file.
2. For cutting threads on a pipe, rod or any other job, it should be firmly held in a vice.
3. While fitting die in a job only the side of tapered threads should be fitted.
4. After fitting the die on the job you should adjust it according to your requirement.
5. Keep on moving the die forward and backwards.
6. Equal pressure should be exerted on the die handle.
7. Jobs of large diameter, threads should be cut after adjusting two-three cuts.
8. Proper lubrication should be used while cutting threads.
9. After cutting the threads, it should be checked with a nut or ring gauge.
10. After using the drill, it should be properly cleaned and replaced at its proper place.

Reamer

Reamer is used to clean the holes made by a drill. In other words we can say that a reamer performs the following jobs :

1. To finish the drilled holes
2. To enlarge a hole
3. To taper a hole
4. To straighten a curved hole

Reamers are made of high carbon steel, hard speed steel or alloy steel. It is made by cutting several straight grooves or flutes. The process of using a reamer is called reaming.

A reamer has the following parts :

1. Angle of Chamfer
2. Body
3. Shank

Angle of Chamfer. This angle is made by equally grinding each end of the flute. While making it care is taken to see that some clearance is made behind the cutting edge. This part of reamer is important since cutting starts with it.

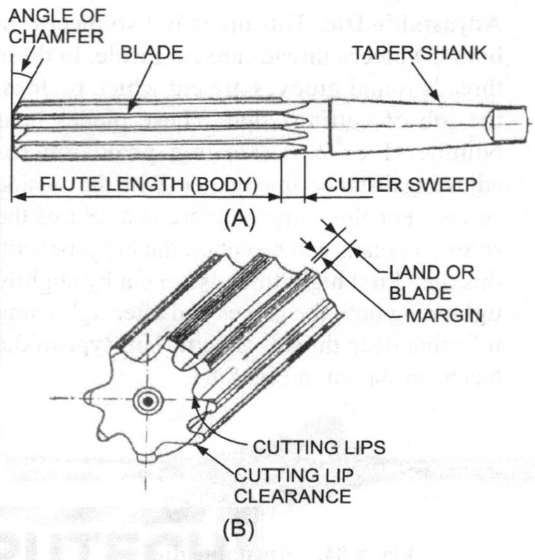

Fig. 8.90. Reamer

Body. The part where many flutes are made is called body. The part between two flutes is called land. Above the land, the protruding and shining part of flute is called margin. The part behind it is slightly shortened, which makes body clearance.

Shank. That part of the reamer by which it is connected to its handle or machine spindle is called shank. Shanks are of two types :

1. **Parallel Shank.** This type of shanks are square and can be easily moved with reamer handle.
2. **Taper Shank.** This type of shank is round but is given *moarse* taper. These are held in machine spindle *etc*.

Kinds of Reamer. For different types of jobs, different kinds of reamers are used. They are of the following types :

1. Hand Reamer
2. Machine Reamer
3. Shell Reamer
4. Adjustable Reamer
5. Expansion Reamer
6. Taper Reamer
7. Pilot Reamer

Hand Reamer. It is a cutting tool of accurate size. It is used for finishing drilled holes. Straight or spiral grooves or flutes are cut on its body. A square tang is made on the upper side of the shank in which handle is fixed to move it. That is why this is called a Hand Reamer.

Fig. 8.91. Hand Reamer

Machine Reamer. It is used in the production jobs with the help of machines. These are held in the machine with the drill chuck or sleeve. Machine reamers are of the following two types :

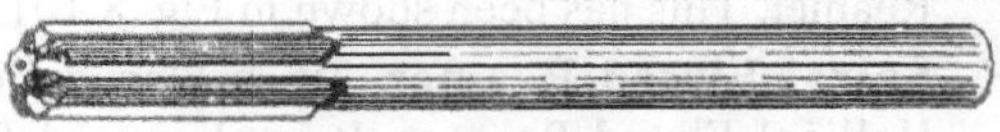

Fig. 8.92. Machine Reamer

1. **Fluted Reamer.** Its special feature is that it has cutting grooves in large number. Therefore, its land is less broad. Its shank can be in taper or straight. With its use finishing is accurate and shining.

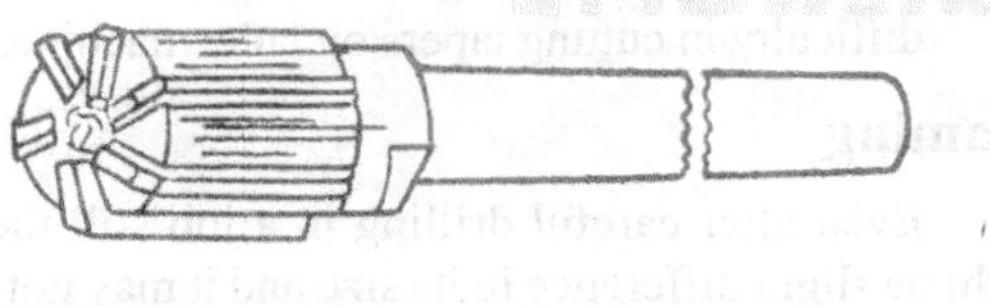

Fig. 8.93. Fluted Reamer

2. **Rose Reamer.** This reamer contains less number of teeth as compared to the fluted reamer and the breadth of land is more. There is more taper at its end and in the rest of the body there is 0.001″ taper, which saves it from being broken. The size of hole is made accurate with this reamer but it does not provide polish.

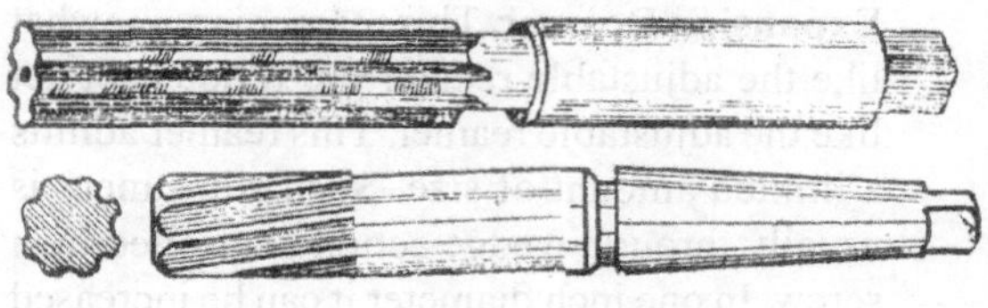

Fig. 8.94. Rose Reamer

Shell Reamer. This type of reamer is used on the machine with the help of arbot. Teeth like those on the fluted reamer and those on the rose reamer are cut on this reamer. Besides, this teeth can be made straight or spiral. These are available in different sizes. Their distinguished feature is that in case of damage, only body of the reamer is changed while the same arbot is used.

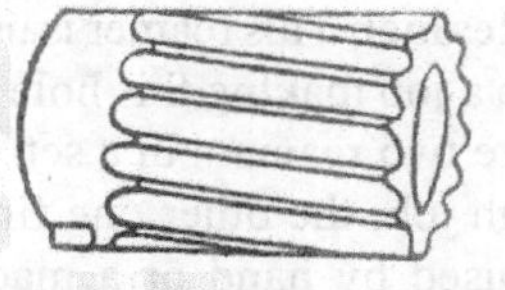

Fig. 8.95. Shell Reamer

Adjustable Reamer. This is the most useful reamer. This can be increased or decreased in size according to range. Threads are cut in its body and grooves are tapered in which blades are fixed. These blades are moved up and down through the adjusting nuts and thus the size of the reamer can be increased or decreased. This size can be increased or decreased up to $\frac{1}{32}$″. By using it, gradually the size can be increased and metal can be cut easily. If its edge becomes blunt, these blades can be taken out and their edge can be sharpened.

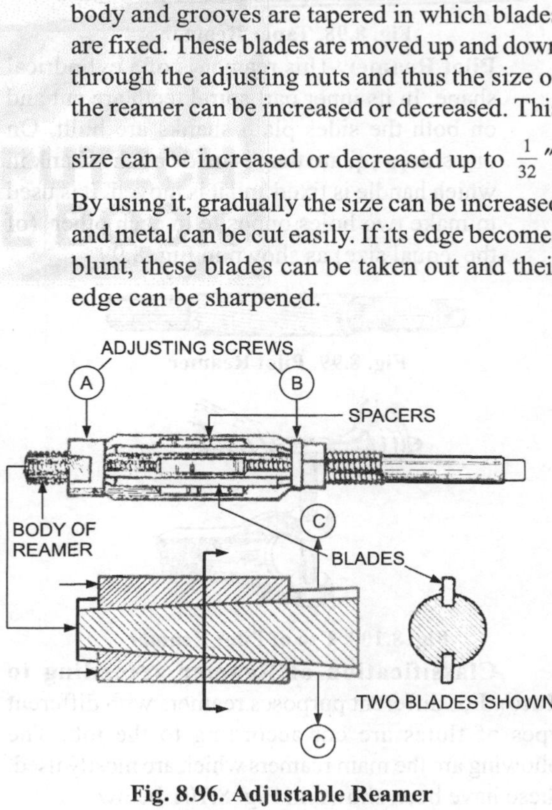

Fig. 8.96. Adjustable Reamer

Expansion Reamer. This reamer is somewhat like the adjustable reamer but it does not act like the adjustable reamer. This reamer admits a limited amount of size. Such adjustment is usually through wedge action controlled by a screw. In one inch diameter it can be increased or decreased only upto 0.005″. A taper hole is there in its body. A taper plug having threads is fitted on it. Head of the plug is square which can be moved by a wrench or a spanner. Size is increased or decreased because of it. It is mostly used for surface finishing.

Fig. 8.97. Expansion Reamer

Taper Reamer. This reamer is used for drilling a hole in a job making this hole a tapered one. There are two reamers in a set. One performs the rough job, the other one finishing. These can be used by hand or a machine because these are made of straight shank or taper shank.

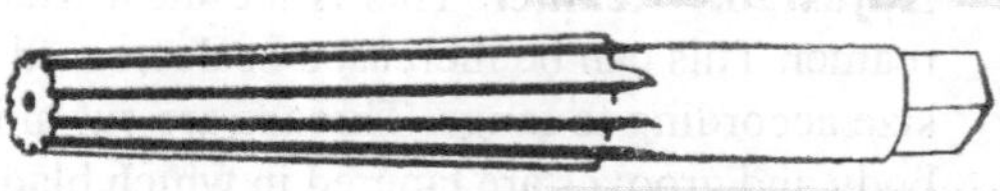

Fig. 8.98. Taper Reamer

Pilot Reamer. This reamer is of a cylindrical shape. In its inner part spiral teeth are cut and on both the sides plain shanks are built. On one side, a square tang is made on the shank in which handle is fixed and it is moved. It is used to make two holes opposite to each other (of the equal size) as shown in Fig. 8.99.

Fig. 8.99. Pilot Reamer

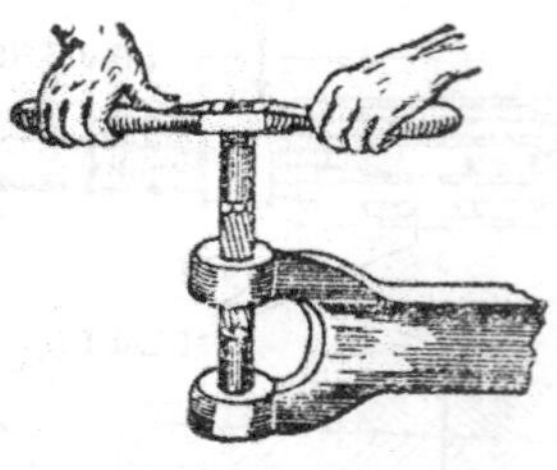

Fig. 8.100. Use of Pilot Reamer

Classification of Reamer according to Flutes. For different purposes reamers with different types of flutes are cut according to the job. The following are the main reamers which are mostly used. These have been shown in Fig. 8.101 below.

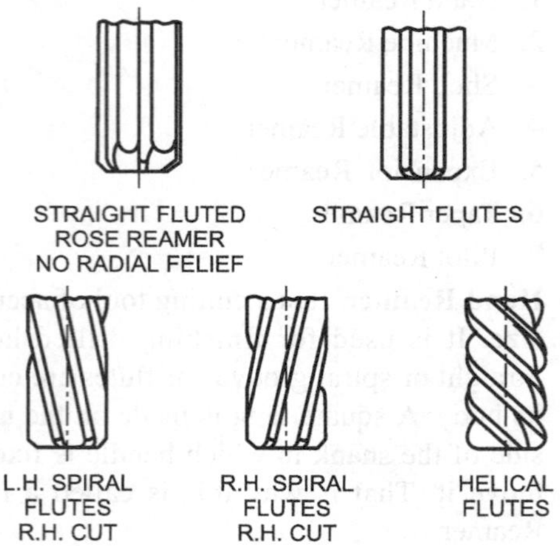

Fig. 8.101. Reamer flutes

1. Parallel Fluted Reamer
2. Spiral Fluted Reamer.
3. Spiral Fluted Taper Reamer.

Parallel Fluted Reamer. Straight flutes are cut in this type of reamers. It is used for cleaning the ordinary holes. For this type of flute there is a special reamer, which is known as Rose Reamer. This has been shown in Fig. 8.101.

Spiral Fluted Reamer. It is also called Hellical Fluted Reamer. It is also used for cleaning oil grooves and keyways. It cuts metal quickly and easily.

Spiral Fluted Taper Reamer. In this type of reamer flutes are made in taper. It is used to taper the small and large holes. It is especially used for tapering the small holes because we face difficulty in cutting tapers on lathe machine.

Reaming

Even after careful drilling in a job still there might be slight difference in its size and it may not be polished. Such holes are made of the proper size and smoothed by using a reamer. The process of smoothing the surface of holes with a reamer is called reaming. The hole can be enlarged or polished through reaming. According to the size of the job, metal from 0.001″ to 0.005″ is left in the hole for reaming purpose. Reaming operation can be done by hand or machine. In order to avoid chattering, the reamer should be moved slowly. Care should also be taken to ensure proper lubrication at the time of reaming.

Stud Extractor

If a bolt, drill or screw *etc.* gets broken in a job, a stud extractor is used to take out the broken part. Stud extractor is fixed on the broken bolt or drill and moved in the reversed order. It gets fixed through the threads and takes out the broken bolt or screw as shown in Figs. 8.102 and 8.103.

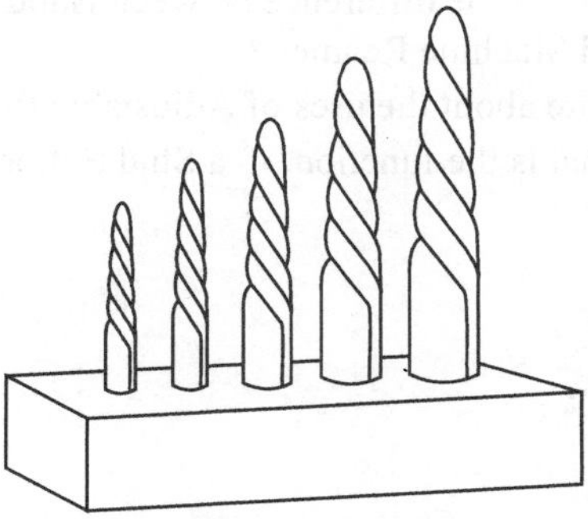

Fig. 8.102. Stud extractor

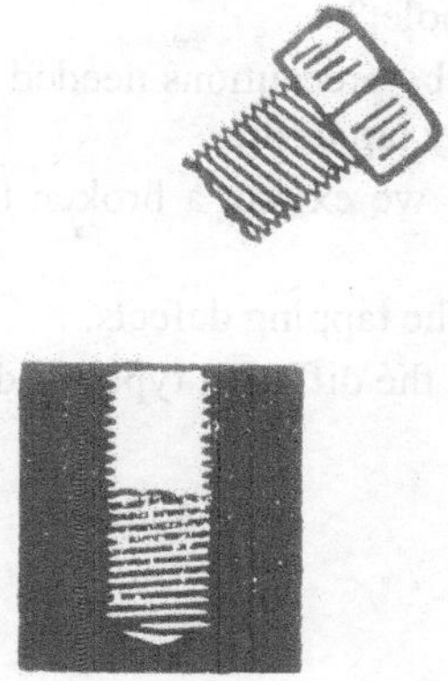

Fig. 8.103. Use of stud extractor

Questions

1. Name the tools used under the category of "Cutting Tools".
2. What is meant by hot chisel and cold chisel ?
3. Draw a sketch of chisel, showing its different parts.
4. What is the importance of chisel's cutting angle ? What should be the angle for cutting mild steel, cast-iron, tool steel, brass, aluminium and copper ?
5. Describe chipping process. What precautions are necessary for this process ?
6. What are the different kinds of files and on what basis files are classified ?
7. What is the difference between double cut and second cut ?
8. Why taper is given in flat file ?
9. Comment on the following :
   (*a*) Pinning
   (*b*) File card
   (*c*) Draw file
   (*d*) Needle file
   (*e*) Rasp cut file.
10. What is the function of a scraper ? How many kinds of scrapers are there ? Draw a sketch of a scraper.
11. Write a brief note about the types of Hack-saw frames.
12. What is the basis for classification of Hacksaw blades ?
13. What precautions are necessary for Hacksaw ?
14. What is meant by setting of Hacksaw blade ?
15. What are the different types of drills ?
16. Draw a sketch of twist drill and explain its parts.
17. What are the causes of defects in a drill ?
18. Explain the functions of each part of drill.
19. Give a summarized account of cutting angle of drill for different materials.
20. What precautions are necessary while drill grinding ?
21. What is meant by drill's feed and speed ? What purpose these serve for different materials ?
22. What cause defects in a drill ?
23. Which are the different types of drills ?
24. What are the special features of radial drill machine ? Draw a sketch of radial drill and explain its working process.
25. What is the difference between Gang drill machine and Multi spindle drill machine ?
26. What functions does a drill machine perform ?
27. What is the difference between Counter Boring and Counter Sinking ?
28. Comment on the following :
   (*a*) Drill chuck (*b*) Drill sleeve
   (*c*) Drill drift.
29. What are the functions of Tap and Die?
30. Draw a sketch of Tap and show its parts.
31. What are the different types of tap ?

32. What are the different sources of finding out tap size hole ?
33. List out the precautions needed while cutting threads by tap or die.
34. How can we extract a broken tap out of the job?
35. Explain the tapping defects.
36. What are the different types of die ?
37. Give brief account of Plate die and Die chaser.
38. What are the uses of Reamer ?
39. Draw a sketch of Reamer, showing all its parts.
40. What are the different types of Reamer ?
41. What is the difference between Hand Reamer and Machine Reamer ?
42. Write about the uses of Adjustable Reamer.
43. What is the function of a Stud Extractor ?

9

Dismantling, Assembling and other Tools

Apart from using measuring, marking and lifting tools, required for general use or repair of a machine, we also require dismantling and assembling tools. In the previous chapters, we have already discussed measuring, cutting and marking tools. In this chapter we shall discuss dismantalling and assembling tools. In addition, other important tools used in workshops have also been described in details. These tools are as under :

1. Screw Driver
2. Plier
3. Spanner
4. Wrench
5. Hammer
6. Vice
7. Clamp

Screw Driver

Screw Driver is used for tightening or loosening screw. A round rod with flat end, having a handle at the other end is called a screw driver. A screw driver has three main parts, as shown in Fig. 9.1 below :

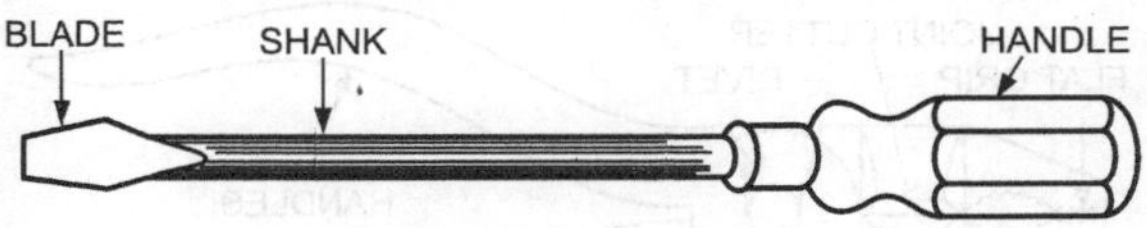

Fig. 9.1. Screw driver

(1) Handle, (2) Shank, (3) Blade.

Handle. Generally wooden or plastic handles are fixed to the screw drivers. In order to save the wooden handle from being broken, an iron ring is fixed to the handle.

Shank. The middle part between the blade and the handle is called shank. On its lower part tip or blade is made. On the upper part either there is a hole through which a wire is passed or this end is made flat so that when this part is fixed to handle it does not allow the shank to move separately. These are generally made of carbon steel.

Blade. Blade is the lower part of the shank. It is also known as tip. This part is hardened and tempered.

Length of Screw Driver. Length of a screw driver is measured excluding handle. The length of a screw driver varies from 50 millimeter *i.e.,* 2″ to 18″. Screw drivers are of following kinds :

1. Ordinary Flat Screw driver
2. Offset Screw Driver
3. Ratchet Screw Driver
4. Philips Screw Driver
5. Watch Maker Screw Driver
6. Carpenter Screw Driver

Ordinary Flat Screw Driver. As its name indicates, this type of screw driver is used for tightening or loosening different types of screws. These are available in small as well as larger sizes. These screw drivers *have* a handle of wood or plastic fixed to them. According to needs, there are light duty screw drivers or heavy duty screw drivers. They have a flat tip.

Offset Screw Driver. These screw drivers have also flat blade. But no handle is used in these screw drivers. Their shank is turned at 90° angle at both the ends and bits are made on both the ends. In cases of narrow or slanting spaces, where ordinary flat screw driver cannot work, This offset screw driver is used. It is shown in Fig. 9.2.

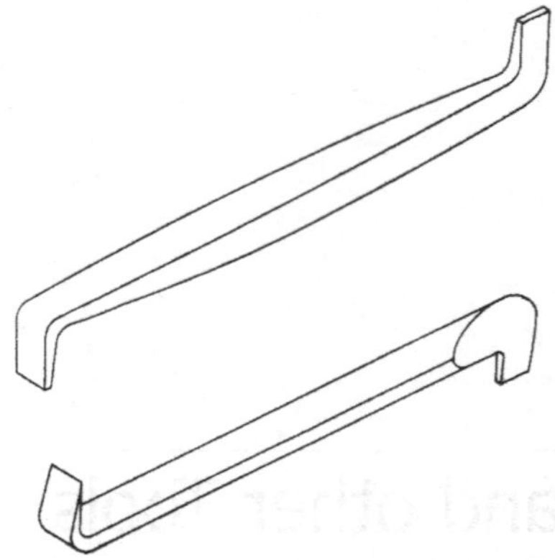

Fig. 9.2. Offset screw driver

Ratchet Screw Driver. In this type of screw driver a spring or ratchet is fitted in the handle. There is a button at its handle. When this button is pressed, shank of the ratchet screw starts revolving through the spring. When the button is left free again the shank comes to its original position. With its help screws can be quickly tightened or loosened.

Philips Screw Driver. Tip of this type of screw driver is different from that of others. This tip is pointed and is made after cutting four flutes. Such screw drivers are used where the screws have T cross-shaped groove at their heads. These screws are available in varying number measurements.

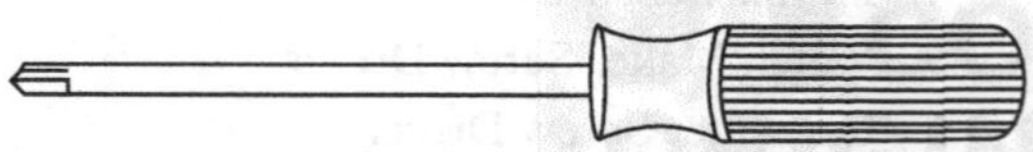

Fig. 9.3. Philips screw driver

Watch Maker Screw Driver. These screw drivers are available in sets. In a set there are six screw drivers, having number markings from 0 to 5. The smaller the number of the screw driver, the smaller and thinner is its bit. In place of handle, a cap is fixed to the shank. The cap is fixed to the shank in such a way that both cap and the shank can be moved independently. For tightening or loosening a screw, tip is placed at the head of the screw and cap is pressed with one finger, while with other fingers shank is rotated. Watch Maker Screw Driver can be used in all kinds of instruments and watches. In appearance, it looks as shown in Fig. 9.4 below :

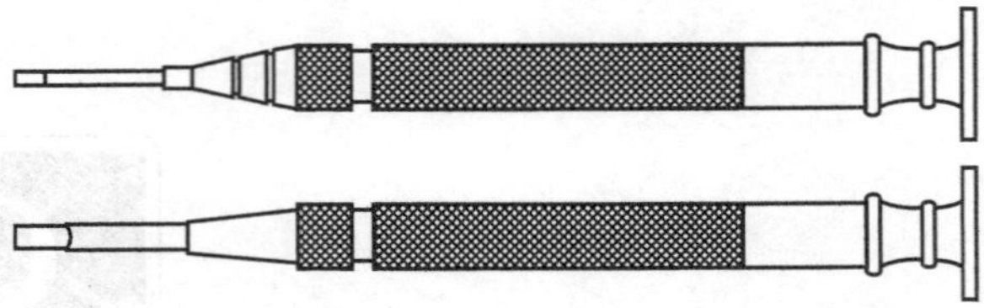

Fig. 9.4. Watch maker screw driver

Carpenter Screw Driver. This is made of a round rod and flat tip. Its handle is made flat from two sides (as shown in Fig 9.5). This enables the worker to exert full force on the screw driver.

Fig. 9.5. Carpenter screw driver

This screw driver is used by the carpenters in their day to day work.

Plier

Plier is a very useful tool. With the help of a plier small jobs and articles can be held. It is also used to cut or turn wires. Its jaws are hardened and tempered. Size of a plier varies from 4″ to 10″. For different kind of job, the following types of pliers are used :

Flat or Combination Plier. This plier has flat jaws. One side of the jaw is sharp for cutting purpose. These pliers are useful in a large number of jobs like cutting wires, turning nails, and to catch small jobs. Pliers used in electrical jobs have insulated handles. Combination plier should not be used for cutting a very hard metal else its edge would be spoiled. For strong grip of jobs *parallel* slots are made on inner side of its jaws.

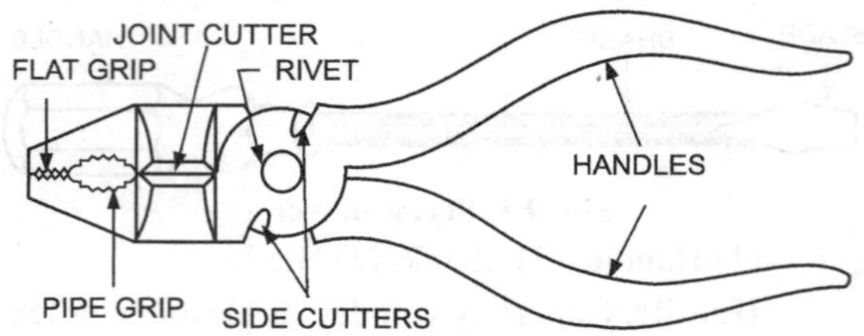

Fig. 9.6. Combination plier

Long Nose Plier. The jaws of this type of pliers are tapered in length and are *conical*. These pliers do not have a cutting edge. These are used where there is no adequate space for combination plier. They are mainly used in gold smithy, radio and T.V. jobs for making hooks of wires or bending wires. Bearing locks can also be opened with it.

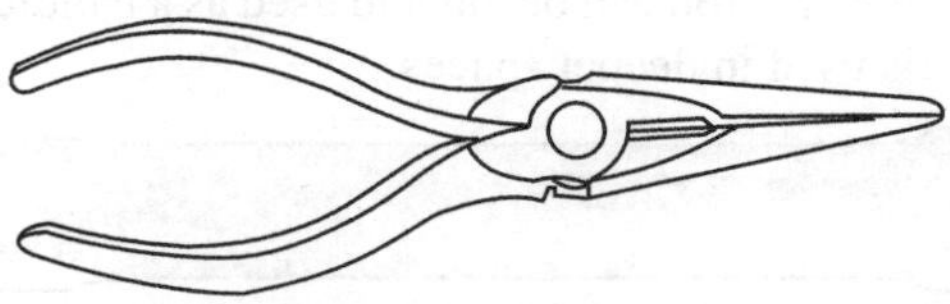

Fig. 9.7. Long nose plier

Slip Joint Pliers. As per their name these are pliers which permit adjustment to a greater range of opening by slipping motion of the two halves about the pin or rivet which connects them. Their jaws are square so they can hold only square jobs. They can not cut wires *etc.*

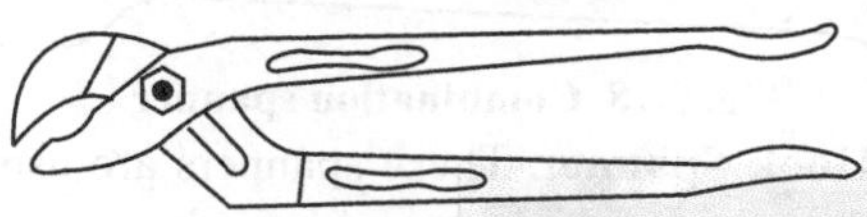

Fig. 9.8. Slip joint plier

Gas Pliers. This type of pliers are used to open nuts fixed on gas and oil pipes *etc.* Its opening can be enlarged or closed as per requirement like the slip joint pliers.

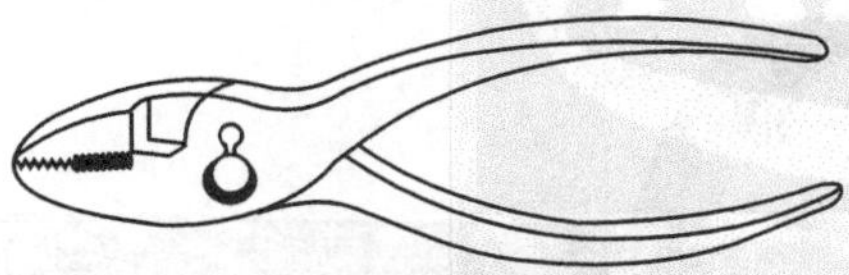

Fig. 9.9. Gas plier

Side Cutting Pliers. This type of pliers are generally used for cutting thin electrical wires. We cannot grip articles or bend them with this plier.

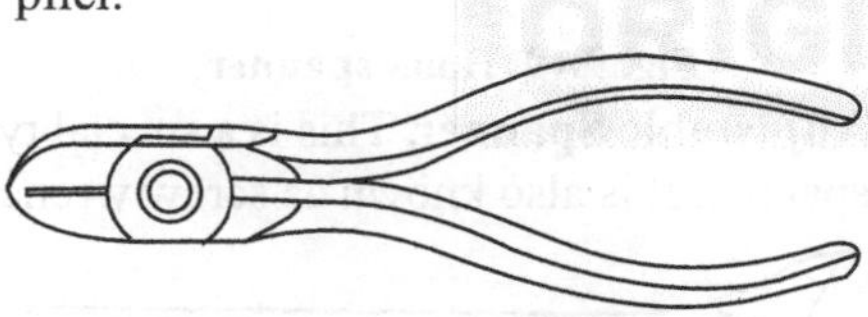

Fig. 9.10. Side cutting plier

Pincer Pliers. It is used for pulling out nails. Their jaws are in round shape and their ends are tapered. Their one leg is flat from the backside and slot is made in its centre. Even small nails can be taken out with these pliers.

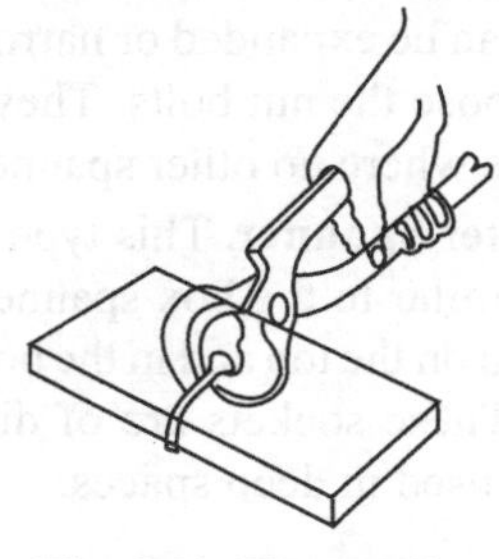

Fig. 9.11. Pincer plier

Vice Grip Pliers. This is a highly useful plier. The opening of its jaws can be enlarged or reduced. It is also used as a wrench or a vice also.

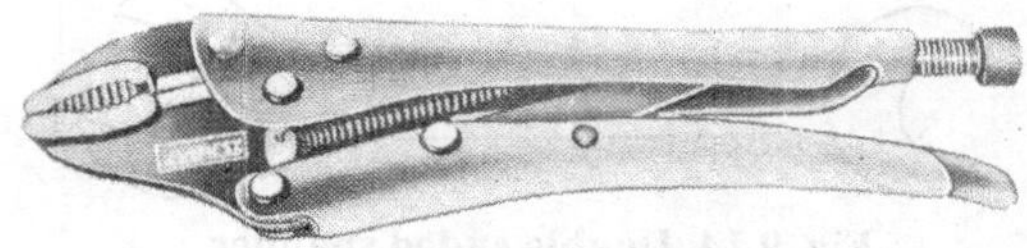

Fig. 9.12. Vice grip plier

Precautions

1. Pliers should not be used in place of hammer, spanner or wrench.
2. For different types of job, different pliers should be used.

Spanner

Spanners are used more than any other tool for tightening or opening different jobs. These are generally made of drop forge steel or carbon steel. These are made in different shapes and sizes, according to requirements. In the workshops usually the following types of spanners are used :

1. Open end or single-end spanner
2. Double ended spanner
3. Ring Spanner
4. Socket Spanner
5. Box Spanner
6. Combination Spanner
7. Hook Spanner
8. Adjustable Spanner
9. "T" Socket Spanner'
10. Magneto Spanner
11. Alien Key
12. Pin Face Adjustable Spanner

Open end Spanner. In this type of spanner only one end is open, in which nut or bolt head is gripped to loose or tight it. It is also known as single end spanner. Their size is taken from the distance between their jaws. Thus selection of a spanner is made according to the distance between the opposite sides of nut or bolt (Fig. 9.13).

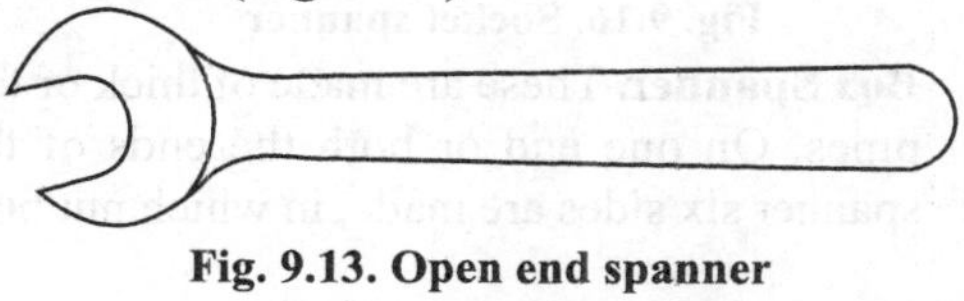

Fig. 9.13. Open end spanner

Double ended Spanner. In this type of spanner open ends are made at both the ends to hold nuts or bolt heads in them. These two ends are made at angles of 15° to 30° from the in-between body. This type of spanners are most widely used.

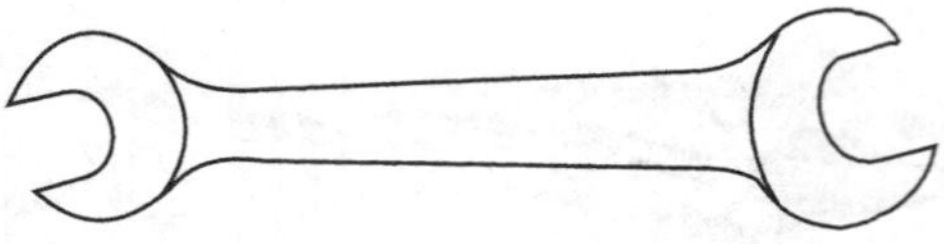

Fig. 9.14. Double ended spanner

Ring Spanner. In this type of spanner on one or both the ends round rings are made to grip nuts and bolts in order to tight or loose them. These rings are bent down in opposite direction from each other. Inside these rings projected teeth are built with which six sided nut bolts can be easily gripped. As it grips all the sides it does not slip. There are some ring spanners whose ends are not bent (Fig. 9.15).

Fig. 9.15. Ring spanner

Socket Spanner. This type of spanners are in the form of round sockets. On one end of this spanner a square hole is made. On the other end, grooves are cut outside in nut-bolt size, as in a ring spanner. In the square hole, Tommy bar is fixed whose shape is also square. These spanners are used where because of paucity of space ring spanners cannot be used. Beside this, socket spanners are also used where nut bolts are to be tightened by measuring them with torque wrench. These are available in small and big size in form of sets. Tommy bar, Universal Tommy and Ratchet Tommy alongwith these spanners. With their help nut bolts of slanting, straight or congested space can be made tight or loose.

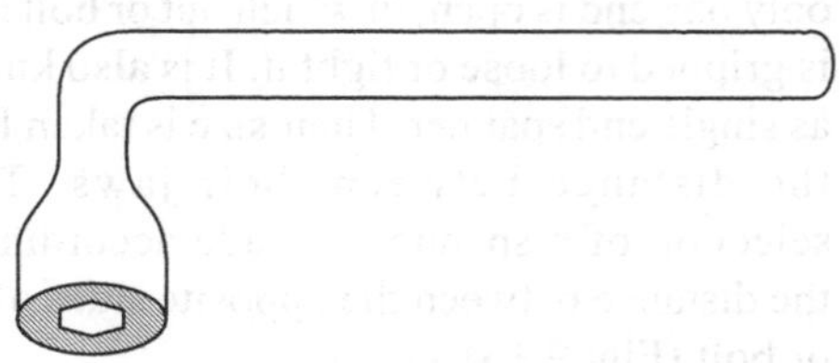

Fig. 9.16. Socket spanner

Box Spanner. These are made of thick or thin pipes. On one end or both the ends of this spanner six sides are made, in which nut bolts with six phases are easily gripped. Holes are made across the rod on one or both the ends in which a rod can be put and used as a handle. It is used in deeper spaces.

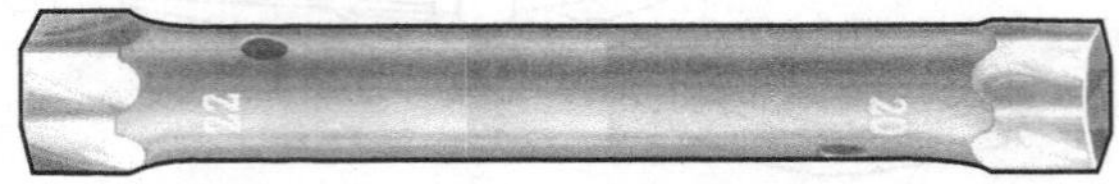

Fig. 9.17. Box spanner

Combination Spanner. On one end of this spanner an open end spanner and on the other end a ring spanner is made. At both these ends, the spanners are of equal size.

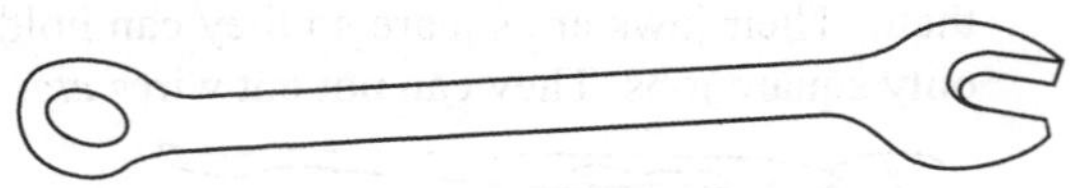

Fig. 9.18. Combination spanner

Hook Spanner. These spanners are used for those nuts which do not have holes on their periphery. There are no faces on these nuts. Thus the pin of this spanner gets fixed in the hole and performs the function of revolving it for opening or tightening it.

Fig. 9.19. Hook spanner

Adjustable Spanner. This is a special type of spanner. It is also known as screw wrench.

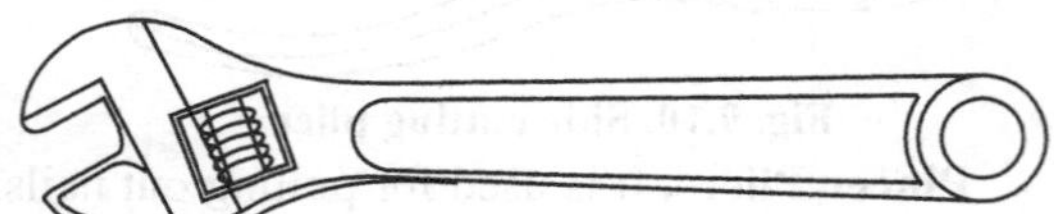

Fig. 9.20. Adjustable spanner

Its jaws can be expanded or narrowed down to tight or loose the nut bolts. They are used for those nuts where no other spanner fits well.

"T" Socket Spanner. This type of spanner is almost similar to the box spanner but it has a fixed hand on the top and in the bottom a socket is built. These sockets are of different sizes. They are used in deep spaces.

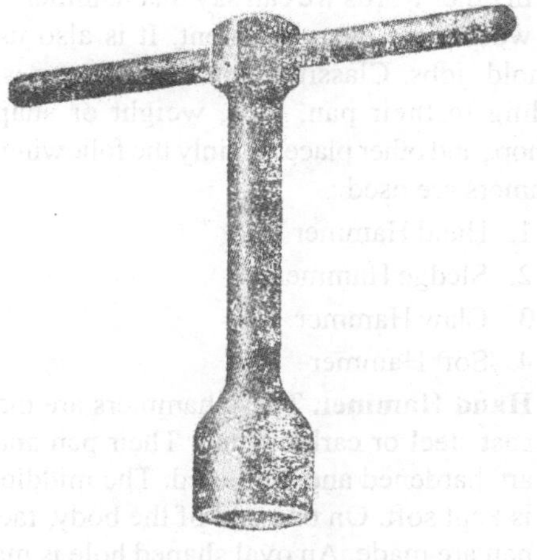

Fig. 9.21. "T" Socket spanner

Magneto Spanner. It is a bunch of small sized single-end spanner. Spanners of different sizes are tied together for tightening or opening small nut bolts.

Allen key. These are thin steel rods with six faces which are bent at 90° angle from one end. These are used to open such bolts whose heads are made round. They have a hole of six faces on the upper side. Such bolts perform the function of tightening while keeping the job's surface equal. These are available in numbers and sets of different sizes.

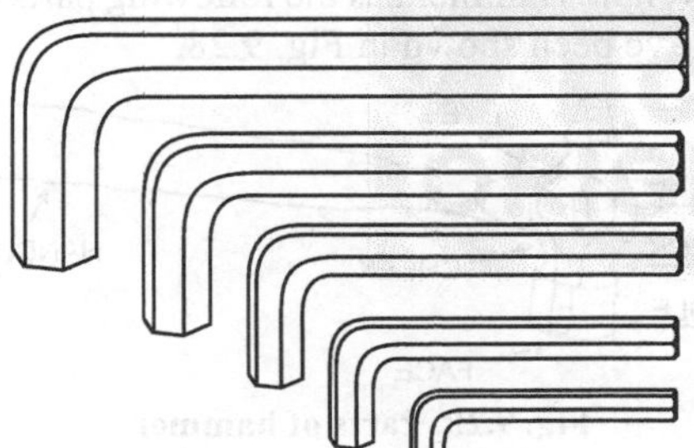

Fig. 9.22 Allen Key

Pin Face Adjustable Spanner. This type of spanner is made by joining two legs with a rivet. At the end of its legs a pin is fitted on each leg. It is used on round nuts having holes in the periphery to receive the spanner pin. The distance between its legs can be enlarged or narrowed down to use it on all type of nuts.

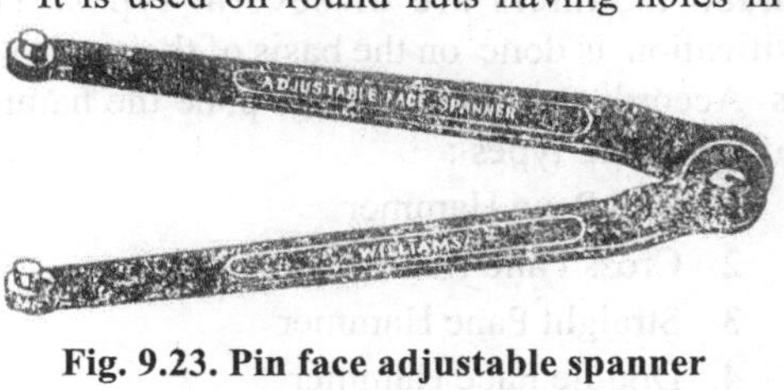

Fig. 9.23. Pin face adjustable spanner

Size of the spanner. All kinds of spanners are used to dismantle or tight nut or bolts of specific sizes. All spanners are in units of mm, inches and ww. Milimetre spanners are availeble in variations of 7 mm. Similarly, inch spanners are available in $\frac{1}{16}''$ and double ended and ring spanners are mostly in sets of 6, 8, 12 and 36″.

In a set of 6 spanners in inch spanners, the double ended and ring spanners are available in the following sizes :

$$1'' \times \frac{15''}{16},\ \frac{7''}{16} \times \frac{13''}{16},\ \frac{3''}{4} \times \frac{11''}{6},\ \frac{5''}{8} \times \frac{19''}{32},$$

$$\frac{1''}{2} \times \frac{9''}{16} \text{ and } \frac{3''}{8} \times \frac{7''}{16}$$

Similarly, millimetre spanners are in numbers. In double-ended and ring spanners on the one side one number is written and on the other one number more than that is written. Socket spanners are available in different sizes.

Wrenches

For fastening and dismentling bolts and pipes, apart from the spanners different types of wrenches are used. Most of these wrenches are adjustable, with different opening ranges. Mainly the following types of wrenches are used :

Pipe wrench. As per its name this spanner is used to fasten or dismantle pipes and their units. Its jaw is made of forging tough steel. On its movable jaw flat threads are cut and on its fixed jaw a plate is joined with a groove in it.

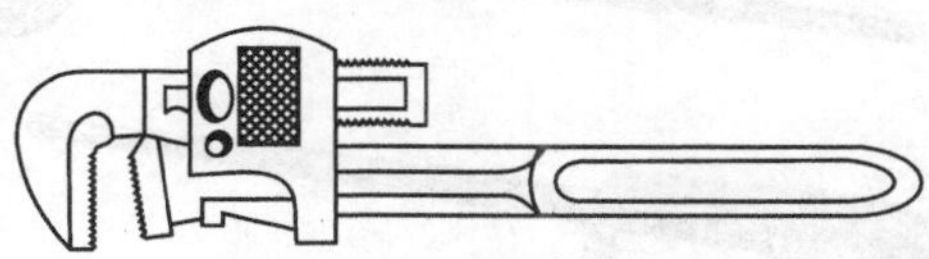

Fig. 9.24. Pipe wrench

A knurled round nut is fitted in this groove. On revolving this nut, the movable jaw increases or reduces the size by moving up or down. A spring is fixed between fixed and the movable jaw, which helps in proper grip of the job. Pipe wrenches are made of 6″, 9″ and 18″.

Monkey Wrench. It is also like an adjustable spanner. Its bigger jaw is built with handle itself. The other jaw is movable on which threads are cut as in the pipe wrench. Its jaws are of plain surface like lhat of open end spanner. These can be adjusted with a round nut. It is also used like a screw wrench.

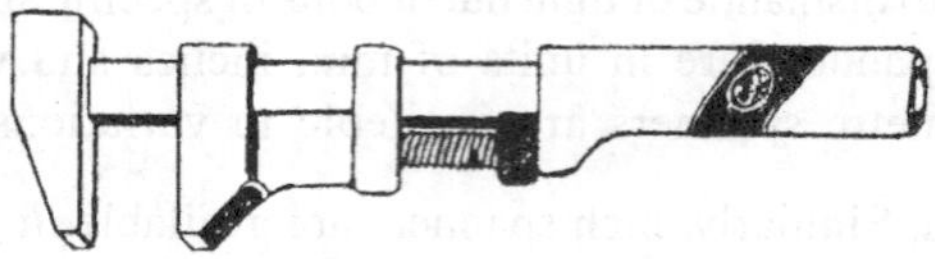

Fig. 9.25. Monkey wrench

Strap Wrench. When we hold pipes and round jobs with pipe wrench it leaves some leruisings scars on the jobs. Therefore strap wrenches are used where damage is caused if such scars are made by the wrenches.

Fig. 9.26. Strap wrench

A leather or canvas belt is provided which is rolled around the job and tightened with the buckle. With the help of its handle the pipe is revolved.

Chain Wrench. In order to fasten or dismantle pipes or round jobs of larger diameter, chain wrench is used. When the job is held in the wrench it is revolved. A plate having cuts in its mouth is fitted, which as joined with a rivet. Chain grips the job very strongly.

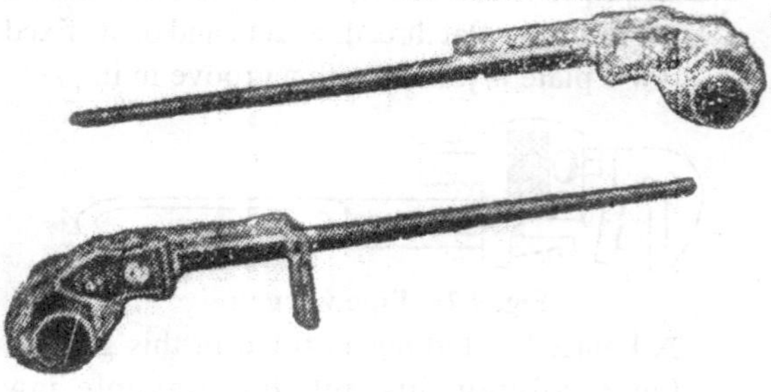

Fig. 9.27. Chain wrench

Hammers

Hammer is a very useful tool. It is used to beat or striking blows on jobs or metals or for driving nails *etc*. It is used to straighten or bend a job made of metal. In addition, it is also used for riveting, chipping and forging jobs.

In other words we can say that hammer is used in the workshops every moment. It is also used in household jobs. Classification of hammers is done according to their pan, face, weight or shape. In workshops and other places mainly the following types of hammers are used :

1. Hand Hammer
2. Sledge Hammer
3. Claw Hammer
4. Soft Hammer

Hand Hammer. These hammers are made of cast steel or carbon steel. Their pan and face are hardened and tempered. The middle body is kept soft. On one end of the body, face and pan are made. An oval shaped hole is made in the body in which the handle is fitted by using wedge. Because of the wedge the hole is somewhat enlarged and there is no risk of handle becoming loose and coming out. The length of hammer depends on its weight. On heavy hammers long handles are used. Contrarily on the light weight hammers shorter handles are used. In hand hammers handles of 8″ to 12″ are used. According to IS 841-1957 the handles used for marking *etc*. have 0.11 to 0.33 kg weight. In the workshops the hammers used by fitter are generally 0.33 to 0.45 kg in weight. Heavy hammers are of 0.91 kg in weight. Hammer has the following parts which have been shown in Fig. 9.28.

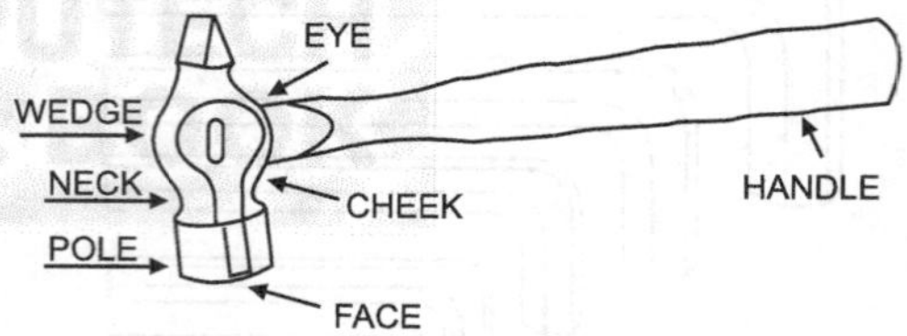

Fig. 9.28. Parts of hammer

1. Face
2. Pole
3. Neck
4. Cheek
5. Wedge
6. Eye Hole
7. Pane

Kinds of Hand Hammer. Based on their utility the hand hammers are of several types. Their classification is done on the basis of their panes and faces. According to the face and pane the hammers are of following types :

1. Ball Pane Hammer
2. Cross Pane Hammer
3. Straight Pane Hammer
4. Double Face Hammer

Ball Pane Hammer. This type of hammer is most widely used in the workshops. On one end of this ball pane hammer a plain face is made and on the other end a pane of $\frac{3}{4}''$ like a round ball is made. It is used for setting rivet. It is also used to strike blows on metal sheet upto certain depth. This type of hammer has been shown in Fig. 9.29. Its weight is between 0.11 to 0.91 kg.

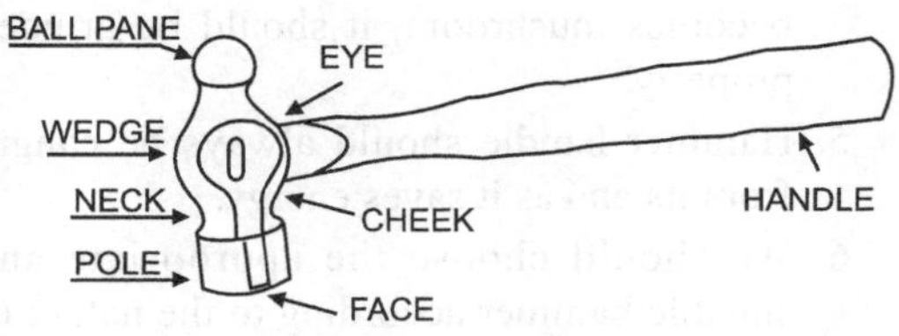

Fig. 9.29. Ball pane hammer

Cross Pane Hammer. This type of hammer has a face on the one end and a pan is made at the right angle of the handle, which is in taper. It has been shown in Fig. 9.30. It is used for making channel "V" grooves, to make inside corner of the job and for expanding metal sheets. Its weight is from 0.22 kg to 0.91 kg.

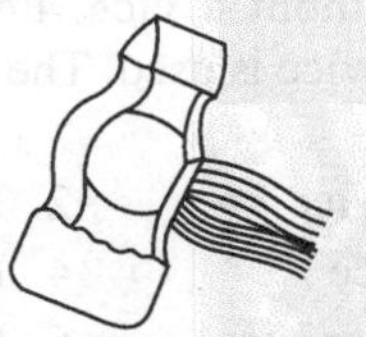

Fig. 9.30. Cross pane hammer

Straight Pane Hammer. This Hammer is almost similar to cross pane hammer but its pan is in straight line to the hammer handle. It is also used like a cross pane hammer for making channel, "V" grooves and expanding the metal sheets. These are of light weight as well. Their weight is 0.11 kg to 0.91 kg. It has been shown in Fig. 9.31.

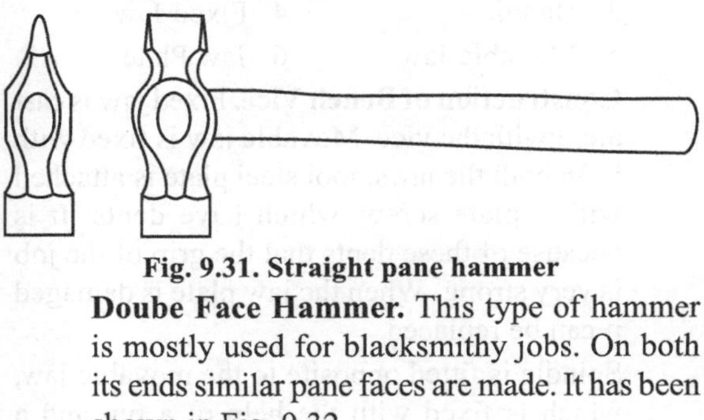

Fig. 9.31. Straight pane hammer

Doube Face Hammer. This type of hammer is mostly used for blacksmithy jobs. On both its ends similar pane faces are made. It has been shown in Fig. 9.32.

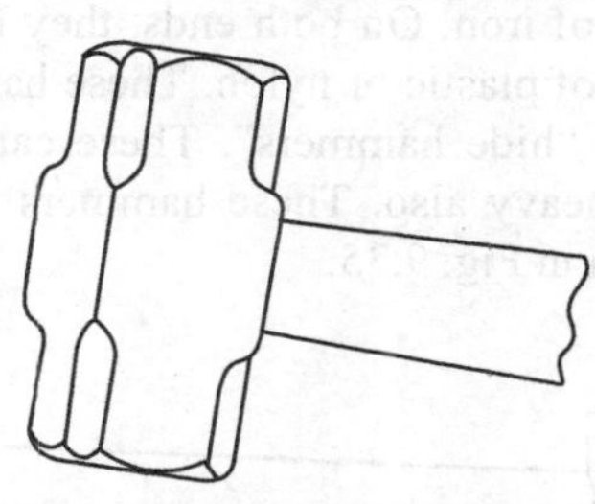

Fig. 9.32. Double face hammer

Sledge Hammer. These are mostly used in blacksmithy for straightening round rods, iron bars, angle iron, channel or flat iron. Its shape is similar to double face hammer. As these are used for heavy jobs their weight is more. Their weight is from 4 kg to 10 kg. It has been illustrated in Fig. 9.33.

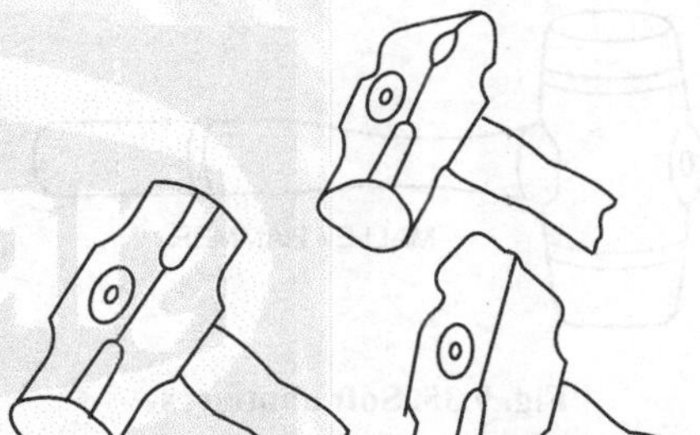

Fig. 9.33. Sledge hammer

Claw Hammer. This is a special type of hammer. On one end of this hammer a round face is made and on the other end its pane is inclined towards the handle. In its centre a slot is cut, with whose help nails *etc.* can be easily extracted (taken out). This hammer is generally used by the carpenters in the carpentry trade. It has been shown in Fig. 9.34.

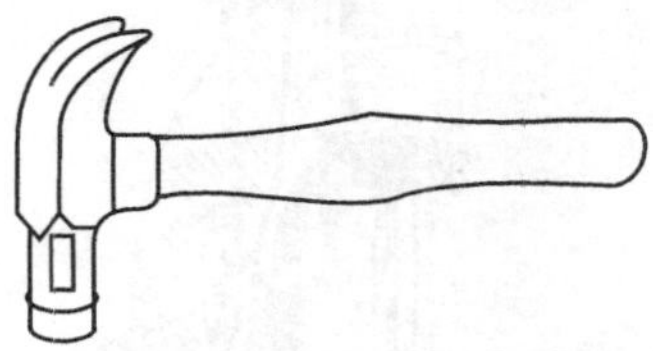

Fig. 9.34. Claw hammer

Soft Hammer. On the jobs which are likely to get scars when we strike a hammer blow, soft hammers are used. These hammers made of wood, backelite, plastic, brass, copper or aluminium. Hammer made of wood is called Mallet. Some hammers of plastic or nylon are made in such a way that from inside they are made of iron. On both ends, they have a cap made of plastic or nylon. These hammers are called "hide hammers". These can be made very heavy also. These hammers have been shown in Fig. 9.35.

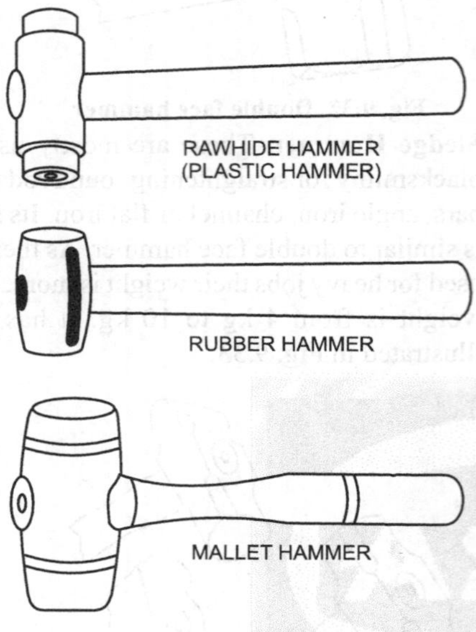

Fig. 9.35. Soft hammers

Power Hammer. For doing the heavy job of forging, bending *etc.* in blacksmithy, these hammers are used. These are not ordinary hammers but are heavy machines as shown in Fig. 9.36. These power hammers are electric or pneumatic hammers. The little effort is required for working on these and they save time.

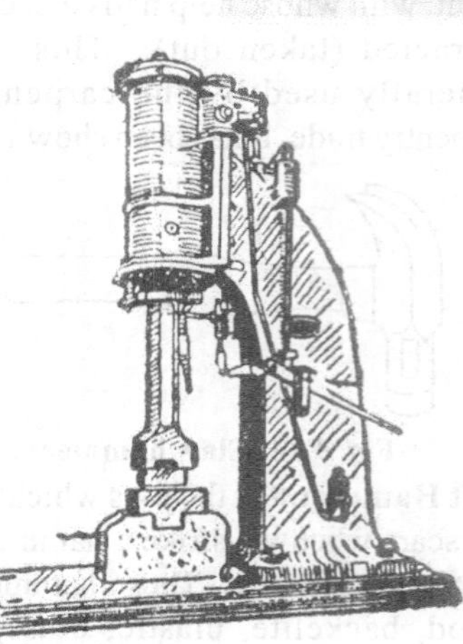

Fig. 9.36. Power hammer

Precautions for using Hammers:

1. We must not use oil, grease or any other oily substance on the handle of hammer and if it is there, it should be properly cleaned.
2. Hammer handle should be plain otherwise it can cause boils on the palm.
3. Hammer handle should be kept tight otherwise from a loose hammer handle would come out and it may cause an accident.
4. If due to excessive use the face of hammer becomes mushroom, it should be grinded properly.
5. Hammer handle should always be caught from its end as it saves energy.
6. We should choose the appropriate and suitable hammer according to the nature of the job.

Vice

In a workshop, it is absolutely essential to hold a job strongly for the purpose of carrying out the various operations like filing, drilling, chipping or milling *etc.* The mechanical contrivance used for holding jobs is called vice. We can say that a workshop is incomplete without a vice. For different jobs, different kinds of vice is used. The following are the main vice :

1. Bench Vice
2. Machine Vice
3. Pipe Vice
4. Leg Vice
5. Carpenter Vice
6. Hand Vice
7. Pin Vice
8. Tool Makers Vice
9. Drill Vice

Bench Vice. The body of this vice is made of cast iron. Both its jaws are made of tool steel. Spindle handle is made of mild steel. This vice is most widely used in a workshop. It contains the following parts :

1. Base
2. Spindle
3. Handle
4. Fixed Jaw
5. Movable Jaw
6. Jaw Plate

Construction of Bench Vice. Fixed jaw is cast alongwith the vice. Movable jaw is fixed with it. In both the jaws, tool steel plate is attached with a plate screw, which have dents. It is because of these dents that the grip of the job is very strong. When the jaw plate is damaged it can be replaced.

Spindle is fitted opposite to the movable jaw, which is fixed with the help of a pin and a spring. This spindle sets in the threaded box nut tightened in the fixed jaw. In the spindle and the box nut square threads are cut. Handle of round rod is fixed in a hole made in the beginning part of the vice. By revolving this handle the movable jaw moves ahead or backwards. Job is held between the two jaws. The size of the vice is taken from its breadth. Vice is tightened on the work table with two or three bolts.

According to the utility and performance, the Bench vice is of the following four types :

1. Simple Parallel Jaw Bench Vice
2. Swivel Base Bench Vice
3. Quick Release Bench Vice
4. Combination Bench Vice

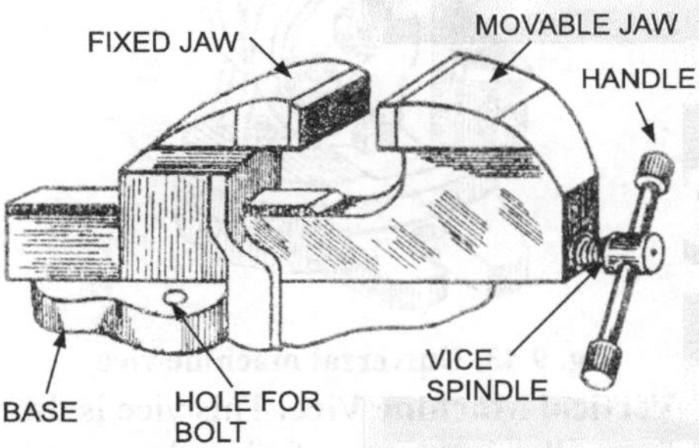

Fig. 9.37. Parallel jaw bench vice

Simple Bench Vice. Complete details of this vice have been given above and it has been shown in Fig. 9.37 above.

Swivel Base Bench Vice. This vice is almost similar to the simple bench vice. But its lower base is constructed in such a way that it could be swivelled. For swivelling it the tightening lever fixed at the base is loosened and after swivelling it as desired, again the lever is tightened. One advantage of using this vice is that having fastened the job once, we can revolve the job in any direction for doing different operations like filing, chipping *etc.* It saves time. This vice has been shown in Fig. 9.38.

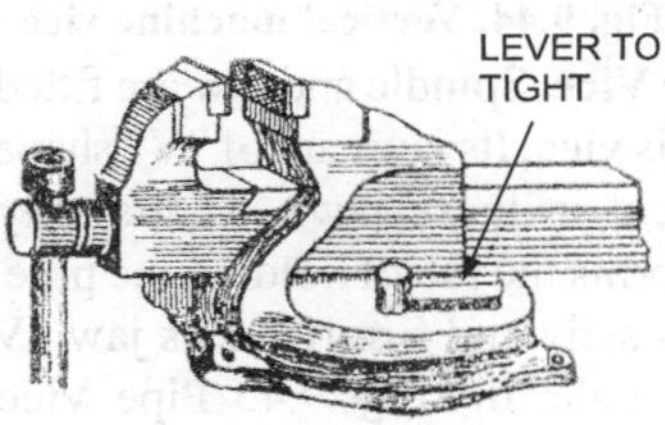

Fig. 9.38. Swivel bench vice

Quick Release Vice. In this type of vice, buttress threads are cut on the spindle and a half nut is used with it. On one side of the spindle a release lever is fixed, which can be pressed to pull out movable job without revolving the spindle. When the lever is pressed half nut is pressed down and the contact between spindle and nut is disconnected. As soon as the pressure from lever is released the nut comes to its previous position with the help of spring and at this time this vice works like an ordinary vice. The main facility provided by this vice is that for carrying out various operations like filing, chipping, scrapping *etc.* job can be frequently fastened or dismentalled. This type of vice has been shown in Fig. 9.39.

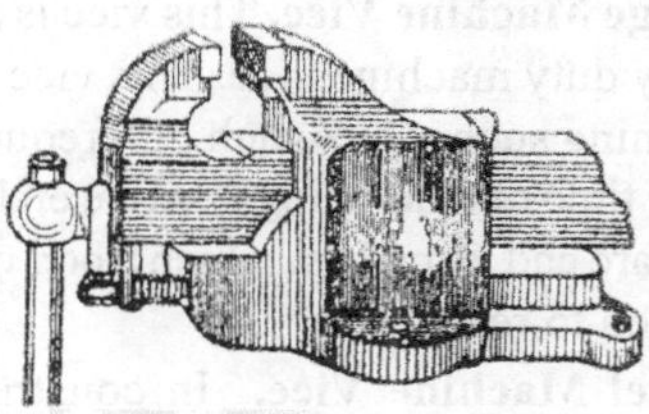

Fig. 9.39. Quick release vice

Combination Vice. It is a verv useful vice. In this vice under both the parallel jaws "V" shaped jaws are also made. Thus, alongwith flat job, round pipes and rods *etc.* can easily be held. It has been shown in Fig. 9.40.

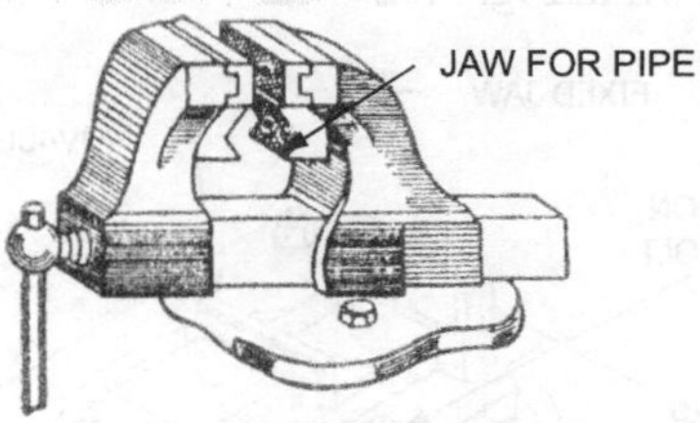

Fig. 9.40. Combination vice

Machine Vice. It is necessary to hold a job strongly for carrying out drilling, milling, slotting or shaping. For holding the job for these operations machine vice is used. This machine vice is fastened on the table. For fastening it on the table "T" bolts are used, which fasten the vice firmly and easily in the "T" slot made in the table. Machine vices are of the following types :

1. Plane Machine Vice
2. Flanged Machine Vice
3. Swivel Machine Vice

4. Universal Machine Vice
5. Vertical Machine Vice

Plane Machine Vice. It has been shown in Fig. 9.41. This machine is used to fasten light jobs. It is also known as light duty machine vice. Its fixed jaw is long in size. On this the movable jaw moves ahead or backward, on revolving the spindle.

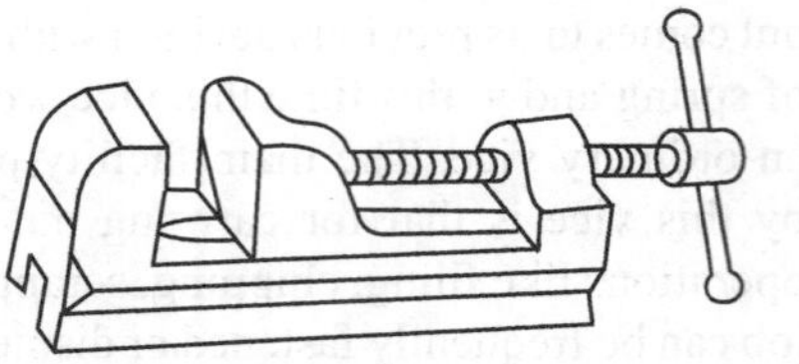

Fig. 9.41. Plane machine vice

Flange Machine Vice. This vice is also called heavy duty machine vice. This vice is used for fastening such jobs which get frequent shocks at the time of machining. On one end of spindle a square end is made in which a box type handle is fixed to revolve it.

Swivel Machine Vice. In construction and shape this vice is similar to flange machine vice but its base is different. With the help of this base the vice can be revolved at any angle. Its advantage is that without separating the job from the vice straight or angular machining can be done. This type of machine vice has been shown in Fig. 9.42.

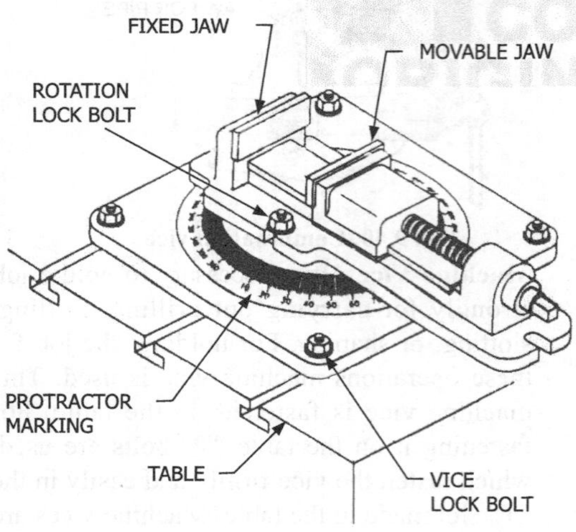

Fig. 9.42. Swivel machine vice

Universal Machine Vice. This is a highly useful machine vice. The speciality of this machine vice is that with it job can be held in vertical, horizontal or angular position. It is mostly used in tool-making. One machine of this type is shown in Fig. 9.43.

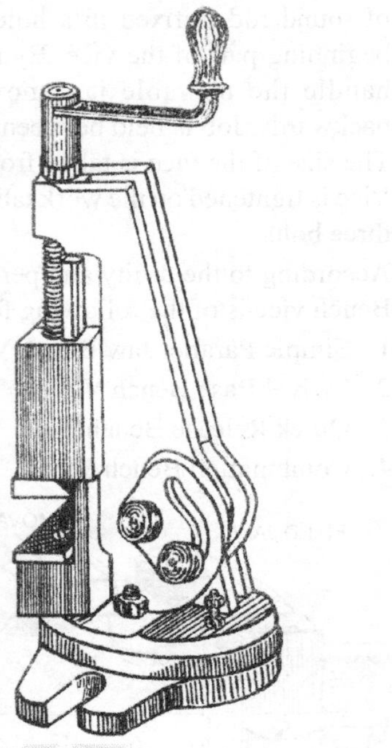

Fig. 9.43. Universal machine vice

Vertical Machine Vice. This vice is different from all other types of vices because in this vice jobs are held in vertical manner. Instead of jaws there are flanges in this vice. With this vice job can be easily held for machining. This type of vice has been shown in Fig. 9.44.

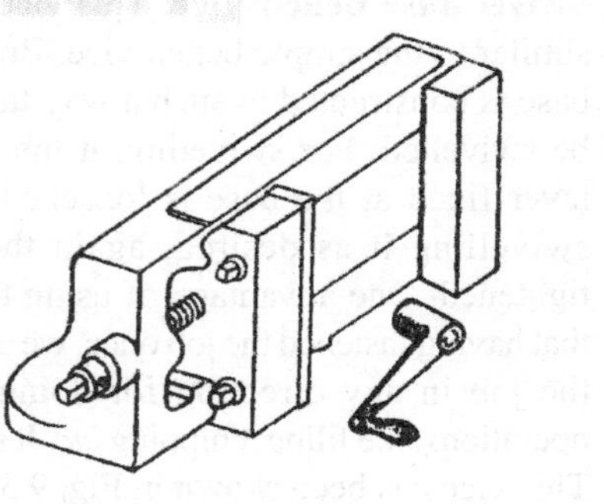

Fig. 9.44. Vertical machine vice

Pipe Vice. Spindle and jaw are fitted vertically in this vice. Its jaws are of "V" shape and dents are cut in these jaws. That's why this vice performs the job of holding the pipe and round job, easily and firmly. In its jaw "V" is made 90° angle. In Fig. 9.45 Pipe Vice has been shown.

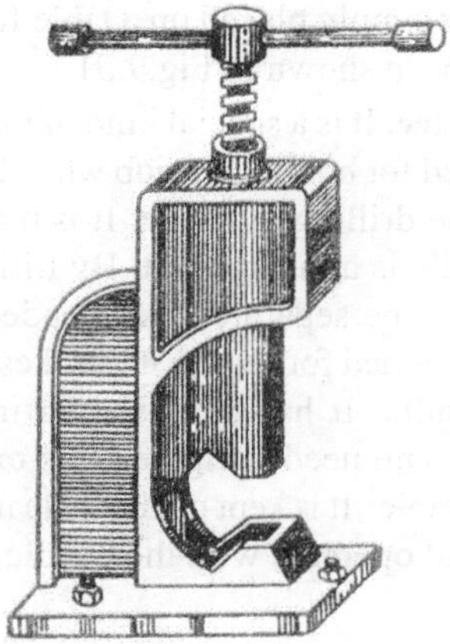

Fig. 9.45. Pipe vice

Leg Vice. It is generally used in black smithy shop. Hot job is fastened in it and blacksmithy operations like forging, bending *etc.* are done. It is fitted in the work bench in a hanging manner. It contains one leg which is straight way placed on wood. Movable jaw and fixed jaw are joined with each other through a hinge. Between these two jaws a strong spring leaf is fixed, with whose help movable jaw handle opens easily when revolved. On the upper side of both the jaws a spindle is fitted in which square threads are cut. A box nut is fitted in the fixed jaw because of this when the handle is revolved, the movable jaw opens towards the outside. This type of vice has been shown in Fig. 9.46.

Fig. 9.46. Leg vice

Its entire body is made of a rought iron. That is why when we strike hammer blows it does not have any bad effect.

Carpenter Vice. This vice is used only for wood works. Its spiders are made of iron but jaws are made of wood. It is used for holding wood and carrying out different operations on it. Buttress threads are cut on its spindle and a spring is fitted in it. This vice also functions almost like the quick release vice.

Hand Vice. This vice is almost similar to the leg vice with a long leg and opens like that vice. Only small jobs can be held in this vice.

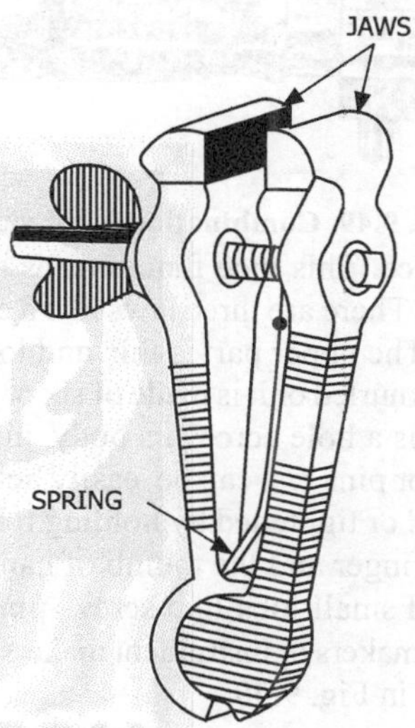

Fig. 9.47. Hand vice

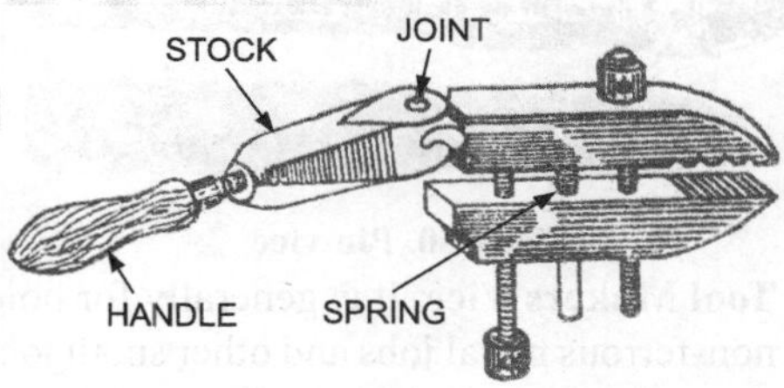

Fig. 9.48. Other types of hand vice

It cannot be fitted on a work bench. As per its name, it is held in hand. Instead of handle a wing nut is used which is attached on the spindle fixed between the two jaws. Between the two legs a spring leave is fixed because of this it opens easily.

Combination Hand Vice. It can be used both in the form of a small bench vice and hand vice. It has been shown in Fig. 9.49. By holding its vice handle it can be used as a hand vice. A base clamp is provided with it. With this clamp it can be fitted on the bench also. In this way it functions as a small bench vice. Its distinguished feature is that by loosening its wing nut, like a swivel vice, it can be fitted at any angle. This vice is made by steel forging process. On its spindle Right Hand and Left Hand threads are cut, so both the jaws open or close simultaneously.

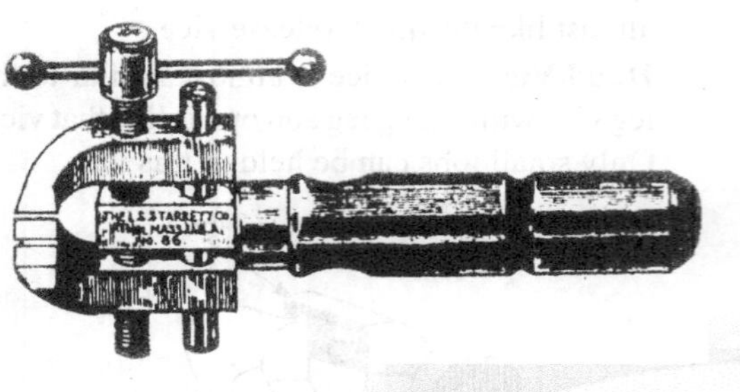

Fig. 9.49. Combination hand vice

Pin Vice. This vice functions as a small drill chuck. There are three jaws like a chuck in this vice. The upper part is thin and long which is either knurled or it is made of six or eight panes. There is a hole across its body, in which long wires or pins *etc*. can be easily held. It can be opened or tightened by holding it between the small finger and the thumb of hand. It is used to hold small jobs like screw, pin *etc*. by the watch makers or instrument makers. It has been shown in Fig. 9.50.

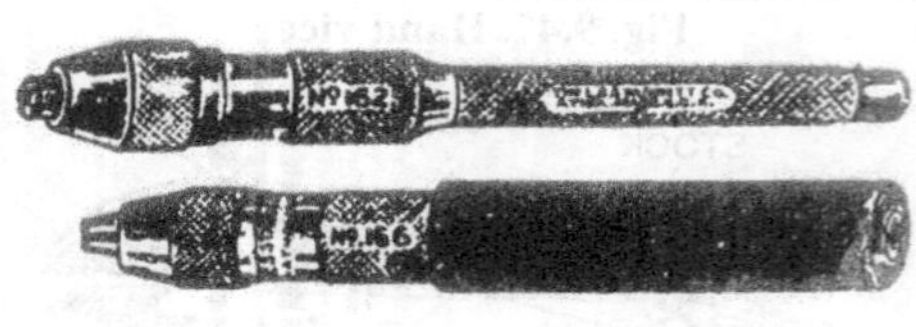

Fig. 9.50. Pin vice

Tool Makers Vice. It is generally for holding non-ferrous metal jobs and other small jobs by the tool makers. Its jaws are made plain, which avoid bruising of the jobs. There is no need to

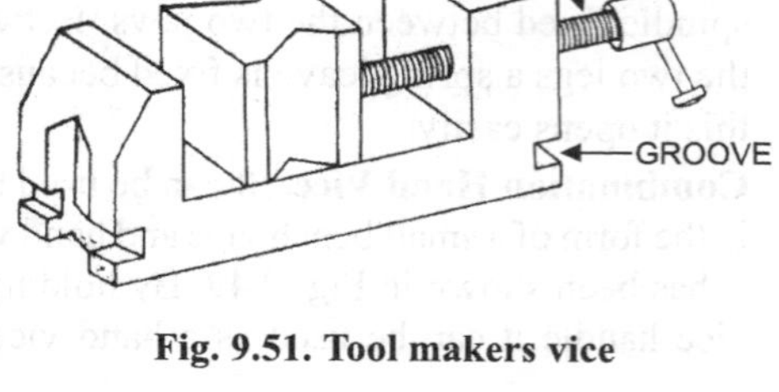

Fig. 9.51. Tool makers vice

fit this vice on the table *etc*. It can be held in hand or simply placed on a table for filing *etc*. It has been shown in Fig.9.51.

Drill Vice. It is a special kind of machine vice. It is used for holding the job while boring holes with the drilling machine. It is made of steel. A handle is attached to it. By lifting it up the jaws can be separated. A threaded spindle is also provided for setting its strokes after lifting the handle. It has been shown in Fig. 9.52. There is no need to tighten this machine drill on the table. It is kept on the table in the normal way and operated with the handle.

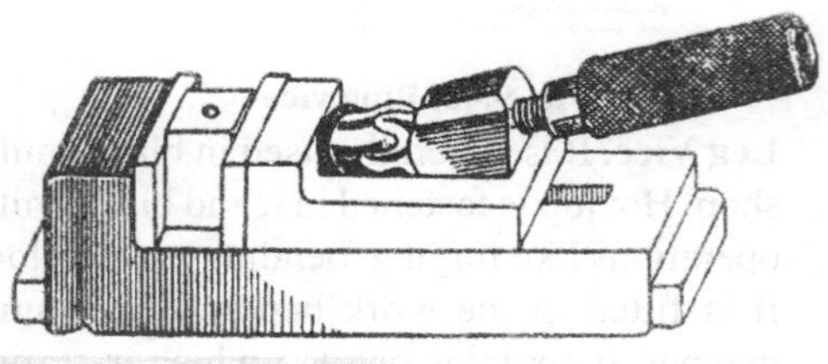

Fig. 9.52. Drill vice

Vice Packing Clamp

In ordinary bench vice parallel jaws are made. These are of hard metal like the tool steel. Slanting dents are cut on it so that the job could be held firmly. But because of these teeth, bruising marks are left on the soft jobs. In order to prevent bruising, vice packing clamp couple is used. The shape of the job can be different therefore these are made in four different designs.

Plain Packing Clamp. This type of clamps are made of copper, brass or aluminium sheets by bending it in the shape of a jaw from the upper side as shown in Fig. 9.53.

It is used for holding square or flat jobs.

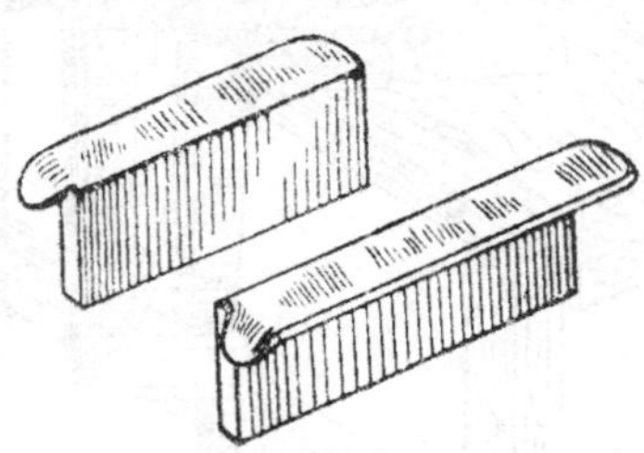

Fig. 9.53. Plain packing clamp

Half Round Packing Clamp. These clamps are made by casting soft metal. In these clamps semi-circular grooves are cut. It is used for holding small rods, pipes *etc*. for cutting threads *etc*. even when it contains parallel jaws.

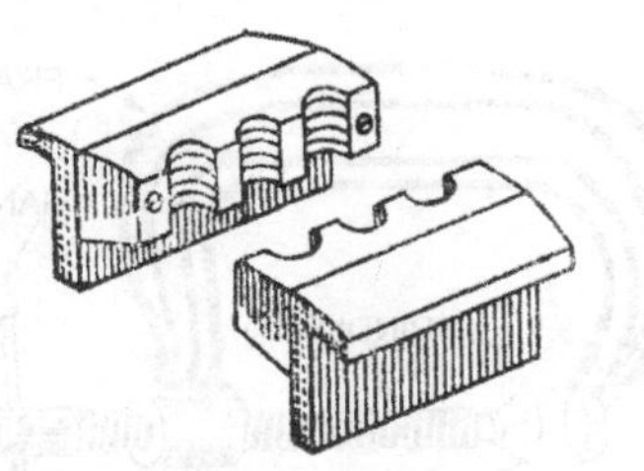

Fig. 9.54. Half round packing clamp

"V" Packing Clamp. This type of clamp is also made in the same process as an half round clamp.

In place of semi-circular grooves "V" shaped grooves are cut in it. With this clamp particularly pipes are firmly held in the vice with parallel jaws.

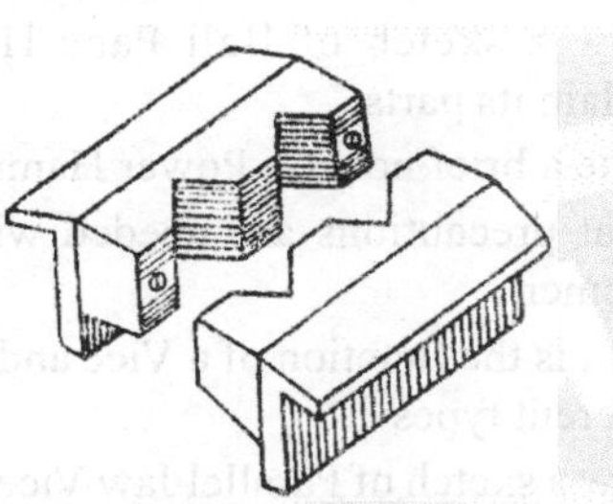

Fig. 9.55. "V"packing clamp

"U" Packing Chimp. This is a different type of clamp. This clamp is made of the shape of English letter "U". It is fitted in the parallel jaw vice as shown in Fig. 9.56. With this clamp round rods and pipes can be held strongly in length. This clamp is needed for making key way in shaft.

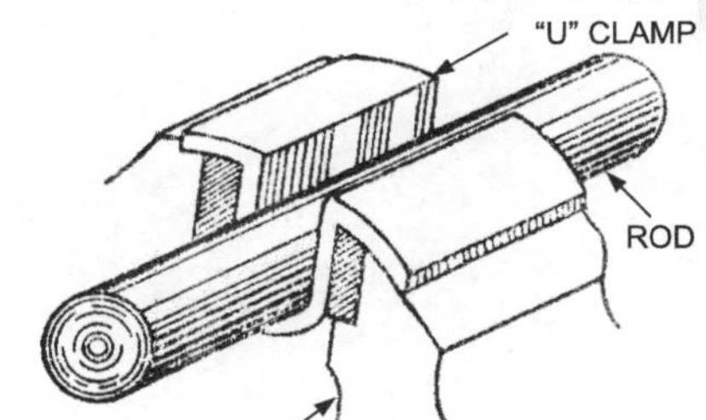

Fig. 9.56. "U" packing clamp

Precautions :

1. Job should be fastened nearly at the centre and it should not be very high from the surface of the vice.
2. While chipping care should be taken to ensure that the blow of hammer should not hit the vice.
3. Job should be tightened in the jaw only by moving the handle manually. A hammer should not be used for this purpose.
4. This job should be held in the jaw with a wood packing otherwise at the time of filing *etc.* chattering takes place.
5. Jobs which have already been finished should be fastened on the vice without packing damp.
6. The height of vice should not be more than the knee of the worker. If the height is less then wooden blocks should be used below the vice.
7. Lubrication must be done in spindle of the vice once a week.
8. After using the vice it should be cleaned. While cleaning it should be ensured that the tiny particles of metal do not go into the spindle.

Clamps

For holding small jobs or two-three machine parts other tools like vice are also used which are called clamps. Mainly the clamps are of the following two types :

(1) Tool-makers Clamp

(2) "C" Clamp

Tool-Makers Clamp. These clamps are in fact similar to the hand vice. These are also known as parallel jaw clamps. Its jaws are plain and two threaded holes are made in which threaded screw and bolts are fitted. In both the jaws these are fitted opposite direction. These jaws are brought closer or their distance is increased by tightening these bolts. These are specially used by the tool makers. Some tool makers clamp's are available in pairs which are used by holding two parts together.

"C" Clamp. Its shape is like the English letter "C". That is why it is known as "C" Clamp. It has the following main parts which have been shown in Fig. 9.57 :

1. Frame
2. Spindle
3. Handle
4. Swivel Tip

All these parts are made of mild steel. One end of the frame is made flat and on the other end threads are cut. It is made round in shape. In this threaded hole spindle is fitted. In the lower end of the spindle, swivel tip and on the upper end, handle is fitted. Job is held between the flat side of the clamp and the swivel tip. With this vice also at a time several parts can be held. These are made several sizes — big and small. According to the height of the clamp, jobs can be held.

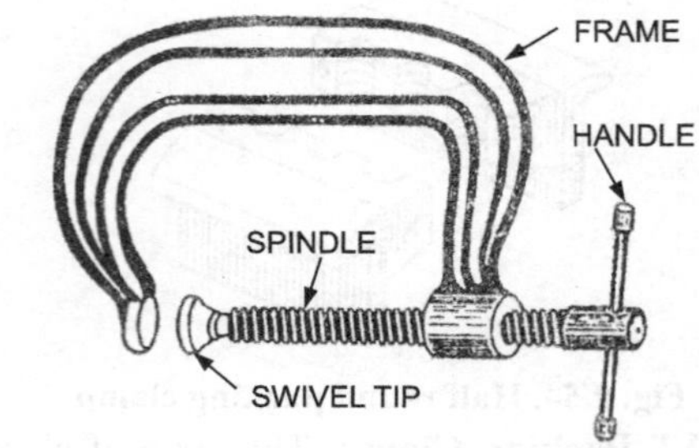

Fig. 9.57. "C" clamp

Questions

1. Name the types of tools used in dismantling and assembling jobs under the fitter shop trade.
2. Draw a sketch of Screw Driver and explain its parts.
3. Comment on Offset screw driver and Philips screw driver.
4. What is the function of a plier and what are its different types ?
5. Write brief comments on Slip Join Plier and Pincer Plier.
6. What is the use of a Spanner and what are its different types ?
7. How is a Ring Spanner different from a Socket Spanner ?
8. Where Hook Spanner and Alien Key are used ?
9. What is meant by measurement of the Spanner ? Explain these measurements.
10. Write brief note on the types of Wrench.
11. What are the different kinds of Hammers ?
12. Draw a sketch of Ball Pane Hammer and explain its parts.
13. Write a brief note on Power Hammer.
14. What precautions are needed while using a hammer ?
15. What is the function of a Vice and what are its different types ?
16. Draw a sketch of Parallel Jaw Vice and explain its parts.
17. What is speciality of Quick Release Vice?
18. Comment on Hand Vice, Pin Vice and Tool Maker's Clamp.
19. What are the different types of Vice Packing Clamps ?
20. What is the use of "C" clamp ?

10

Threads

Threads play a very important role in engineering line for manufacturing various articles of daily use. In this engineering and scientific age, machines are used every moment at every stage. Without threads most of the machines cannot be used.

Definition of Threads. Spiral grooves of equal measurement or shapes made on a round cylindrical article or pipe are known as threads. In other words, spiral grooves of equal pitch and equal depth made on parallel round cylindrical surface or conical round surface are called Threads.

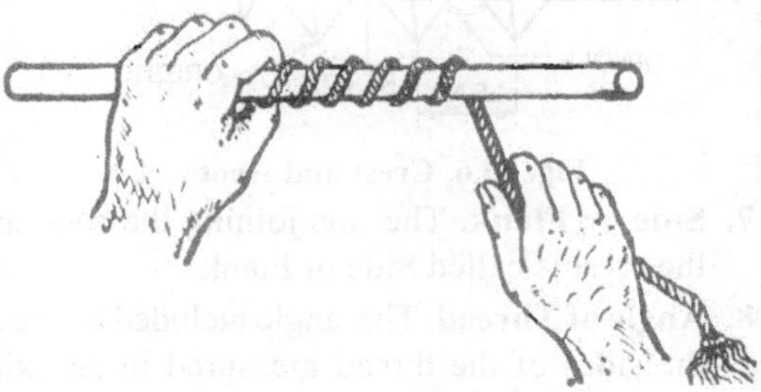

Fig. 10.1. Threads

For example, if we take a round stick and wind a piece of wire in angular indication, the wire's twist would move ahead on the round stick. The path on which the wire moves ahead is called Helix. Like this helix, thread is inclined in an angle on a round surface. Threads may be internal or external. According to their movement, these threads are of the following three types :

1. Right Hand Threads
2. Left Hand Threads
3. Taper Threads

Right Hand Threads. These threads are inclined towards the right hand side. These are tightened in clockwise movement. These are known as Right Hand Threads. These are most widely used.

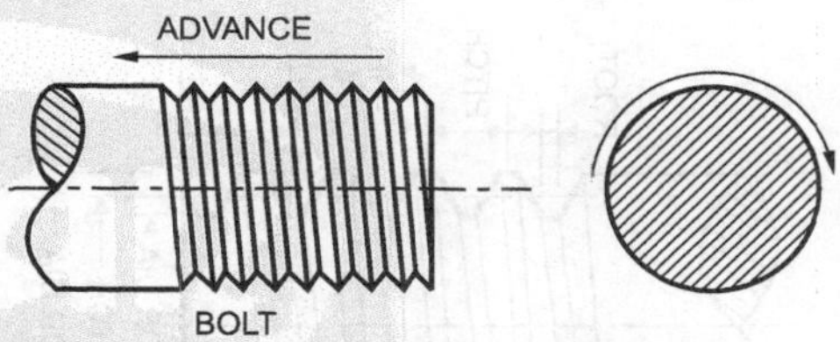

Fig. 10.2(*a*). Right hand threads

Left Hand Threads. These threads are inclined towards left hand. These are tightened in anticlockwise movement. For example, on a screw with left-hand threads, thread is so cut that the bolt, screw or nut has to be turned in a counter-clockwise motion to engage or tighten it. Their use is comparatively less.

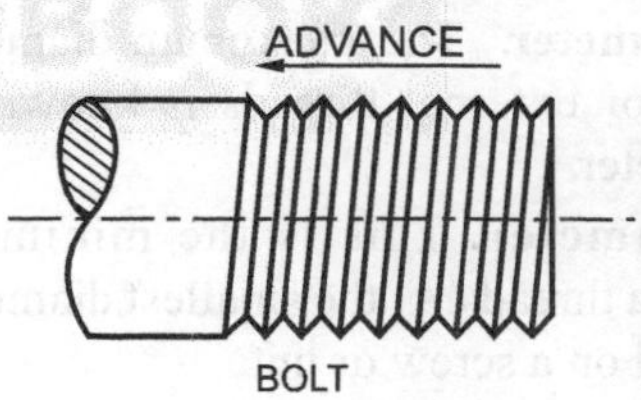

Fig. 10.2(*b*). Left hand thread

Taper Threads. Threads cut on a round but taper surface are called taper threads. These are used for shafts like buffing spindles. These threads can be right-hand or left hand.

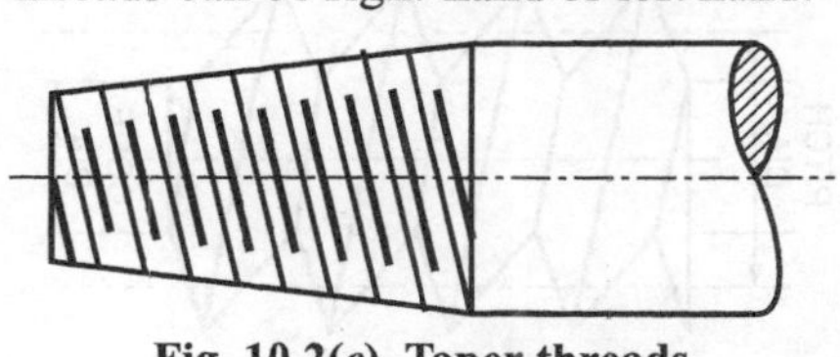

Fig. 10.2(*c*). Taper threads

The above threads are used for the following purposes :

(1) To join two parts of a machine like nut-bolt and stud.

(2) To get mechanical livers for lifting weights, such as chain pulleys, jacks *etc*.

(3) For accuracy in precision instruments like micrometers.

(4) In jobs of power transfer.

(5) To control or reduce speed.

Parts of Threads. In Fig. 10.3 below a shaft having threads has been shown. We can see the different parts of thread in it. Their names are as under :

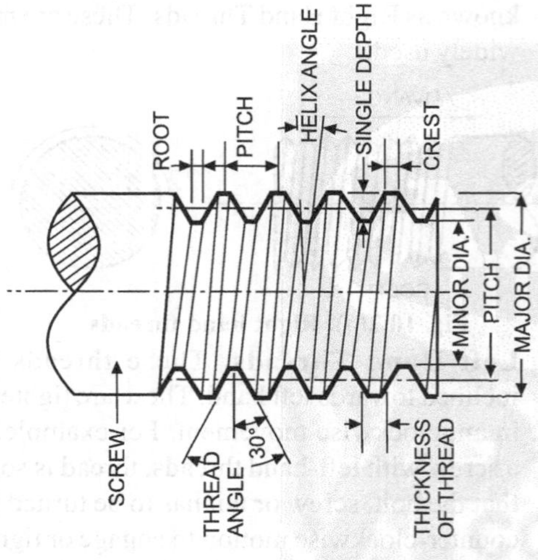

Fig. 10.3. Parts of a thread

1. **Major Diameter.** The maximum diameter of internal or external threads is known as major diameter.
2. **Minor Diameter.** This is the minimum diameter of a thread *i.e.,* the smallest diameter of the thread on a screw or nut.
3. **Pitch Diameter.** The diameter between the centre of a thread to the centre of the thread facing, is called pitch diameter. This diameter cannot be seen but the threads can be counted.

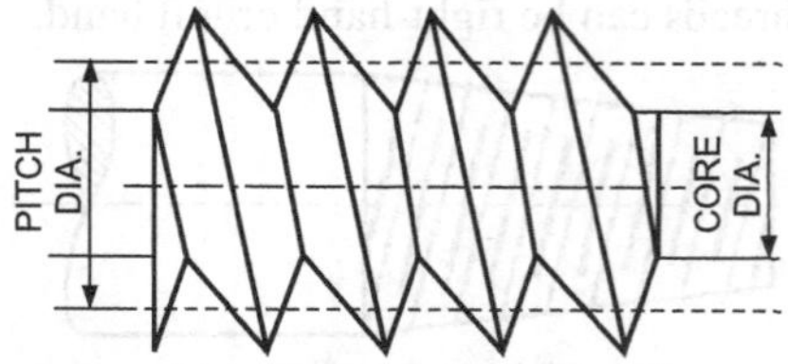

Fig. 10.4. Pitch diameter

4. **Pitch.** It is a term used to denote the number of threads per inch. The distance between the points of two threads measured parallel on the axis line is called the "Pitch". For this purpose if we take creast of a thread, we have to take the crest of the other thread as well.

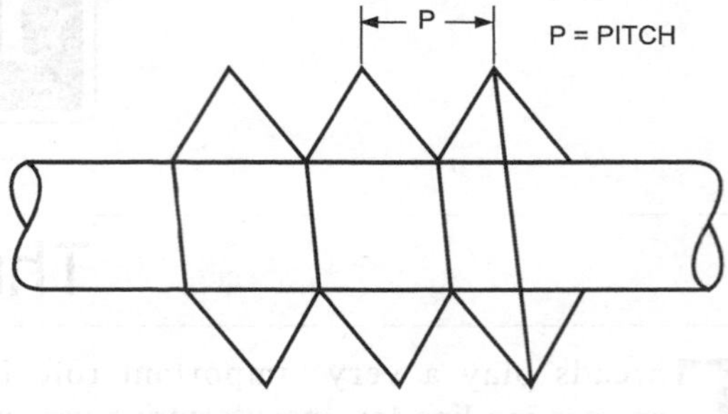

Fig. 10.5. Pitch

5. **Crest.** The top surface joining the two sides of a thread is known as crest.
6. **Root.** The surface of a thread that lies between adjacent threads is called Root.

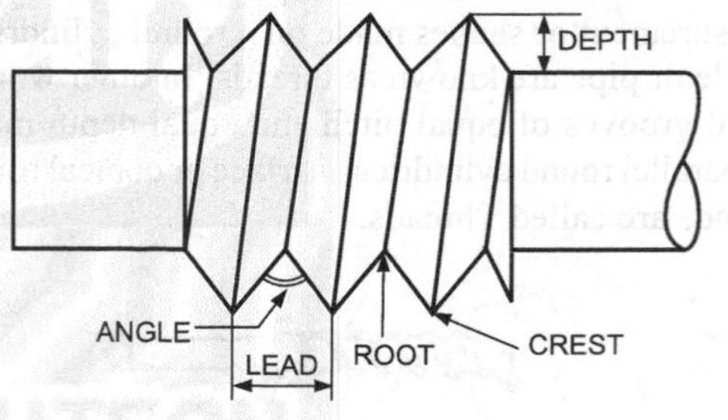

Fig. 10.6. Crest and Root

7. **Side or Flank.** The line joining the root and the crest is called Side or Flank.
8. **Angle of Thread.** The angle included between the sides of the thread measured in an axial plane is called angle of thread.
9. **Depth of Thread.** The distance measured vertical to centre line from crest root is known as Depth of Thread.
10. **Form of Thread.** According to the thread cutting tools, threads are cut in specific shapes such as "V" shape or square shape.
11. **Lead.** The distance a nut or bolt screw advances when given a single complete turn is known as lead.
12. **Helix Angle.** The angle made by the helix of the thread at the pitch diameter with a plane perpendicular to the axis is called Helix Angle.
13. **Thickness of Thread.** The distance between two adjacent sides of threads on pitch line or

parallel threads, is known as Thickness of Thread.

14. **Number of Threads.** The total number of threads per inch is known as Number of Threads.

Form of Threads. As already mentioned above, the shape or size of threads depends upon their utility. Thread cutting tools are also made accordingly. According to their shapes the threads are of the following types :

(1) "V" Shape Threads
(2) Square Threads
(3) Acme Threads
(4) Buttress Threads
(5) Knuckle Threads
(6) Worm Threads

V" Shape Threads. This type of threads are in the shape of English alphabet "V". It is most widely used. This type of threads can be cut or made by tap, die, lathe machine and milling *etc.* These threads are made of different standards. The following types are mostly used :

1. **Metric or International Threads.** This type of thread was originally adopted in 1898 to 1908 in the Central France. With the passage of time, other international countries also started using it. The Indian Standards Institute has also adopted this thread.

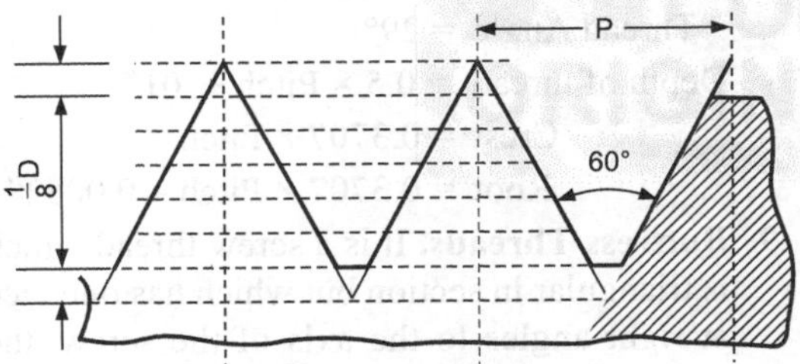

Fig. 10.7. Metric threads

These threads are made on jobs of 0.25 mm to 300 mm diameter. Its angle is at 60°. Its crest is flat and root is round. According to I.S. 1330-1958 these are written prior to the letter M and figure written after "M" indicates pitch such as — M20 × 2.5. It means the number of threads is 20 per inch and its pitch is 2.5 mm.

Thread Angle = 60°

Crest and Root = 0.125 × Pitch

$$\text{Pitch} = \frac{1}{\text{T.P.I.}} \text{ (in mm)}$$

2. **British Standard Whitworth Threads.** This type of threads are originated from Great Britain. Sir Joseph Whitworth, a citizen of Great Britain invented this thread in 1841. This thread was made to provide the facility of interchangeability. It is used in ordinary nut-bolts and other jobs. Its angle is 55°. Its crest as well as root are in round shape. It is known as B.S.W. Thread.

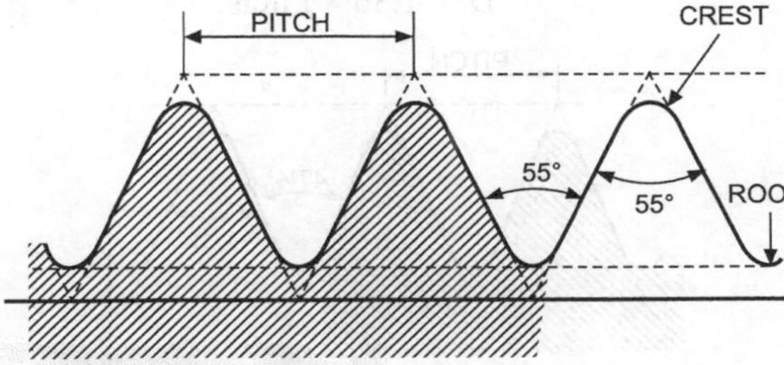

Fig. 10.5. B.S.W. Thread

Thread Angle = 55°

$$\text{Pitch} = \frac{1}{\text{T.P.I.}}$$

Depth = Pitch × 0.6403

Radius = Pitch × 0.1373

Core dia. = D – (1.28 × Pitch)

(D = outer dia. of bolt)

3. **Britsh Standard Fine Thread.** In shape this thread is similar to B.S.W. thread. Angle of this thread is also 55° but the number of threads per inch is more *i.e.,* the thickness of threads is less. This makes the grip more strong. Nut bolts having this thread are used where there is more vibration.

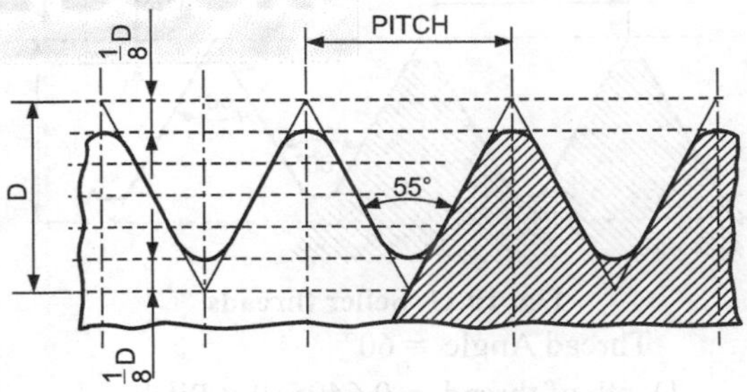

Fig. 10.9. B.S.F. Thread

4. **British Association Threads.** This type of thread is of very thin make-up. It is used in small and tiny electrical and mechanical instruments like radio, television, electrical goods, meters and watches. Angle of this thread is $47\frac{1}{2}$°. These can be used for $\frac{1}{4}$" or 6 mm nut bolts.

These are recognised through numbers which range between 0 to 12. Number 0 = 0.236″ or 6 mm. Number 12 = 0.0511″ or 1.3 mm.

Thread Angle = 47½°

Depth of thread = 0.6 × Pitch

$$\text{Pitch} = \frac{1}{\text{T.P.I.}}$$

$$D = 1.36 \times \text{Pitch}$$

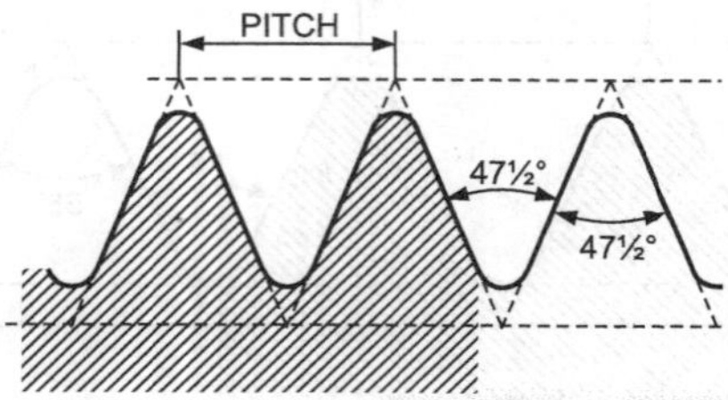

Fig. 10.10. B.A. Thread

5. **British Standard Pipe Threads.** Its angle is at 55° which is cut at $\frac{3}{4}$ taper per foot. It is used in sanitary pipe fittings, steam pipes, gas pipe lines. Because of taper it does not leak.

6. **Seller Threads.** These threads are known by the name of American National Thread. It has been recognised by the American Standards Institute. It is a "V" shape thread. Its angle is at 60°. Its roots and crest are flat. The same standard institute has invented National Fine Thread. This thread is thin. It is used in motor vehicles and aeroplanes *etc.*

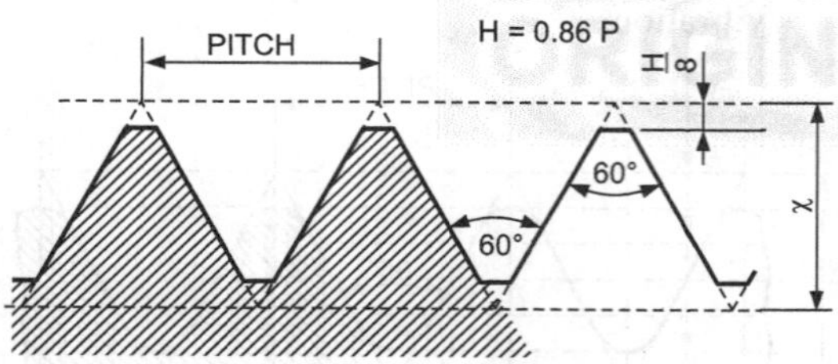

Fig. 10.11. Seller threads

Thread Angle = 60°

Depth of thread = 0.649519 × Pitch

Dia = 0.866025 × Pitch

$$\text{Crest} = \frac{D}{8}$$

Root = 0.125 × Pitch

7. **Square Threads.** This thread has a very powerful root. Its make up is square. These threads are used for lifting heavy loads, transfer of power, to exert pressure, screw jack, lead screw of machines, press machines and vice spindle instruments. Their specific measurement and number per inch is not fixed.

Thread Angle = 90°

Depth of thread = 0.5 × Pitch

Crest and Root = 0.5 × 5

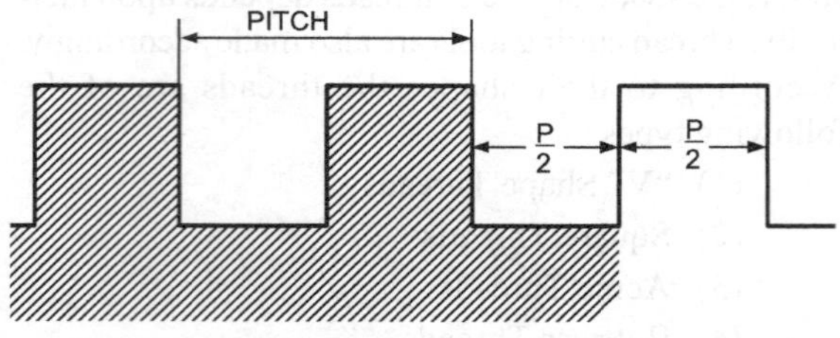

Fig. 10.12. Square thread

8. **Acme Threads.** These threads are more or less like square threads but their shape is in taper *i.e.,* flat from bottom and thin from top. It is comparatively easier to cut it on a job than the square threads. It is also considered stronger. As these threads have slanting ends, it is easier to fix or unscrew split nut on it. There is no backlash in it. This thread is made at 29° angle.

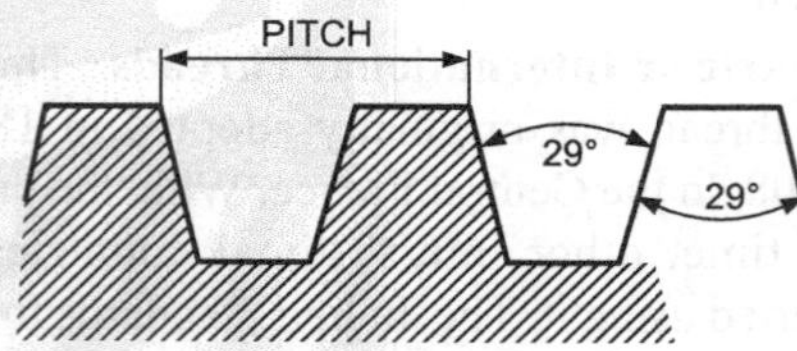

Fig. 10.13. Acme thread

Thread Angle = 29°

Depth of thread = 0.5 × Pitch + .01″

Crest = 0.3707 × Pitch

Root = 0.3707 × Pitch – 0.0052″

9. **Buttress Threads.** It is a screw thread which is triangular in section but which has one face at right angles to the axis of the screw, the second face only being sloped. It has more pulling power than square thread. That is why

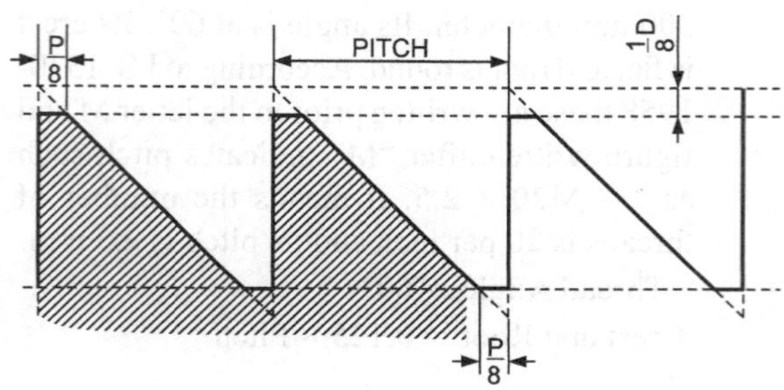

Fig. 1014. Buttress thread

it is used in cases where excessive pull is on one side and it must be absorbed as in a ratchet.

Root and Crest = 0.125 × Pitch

Thread Angle = 45°

Depth = 0.75 × Pitch

10. Knuckle Threads. This thread is also very strong. It is used in heavy and light jobs of rough nature. This thread is half round at both root and crest. It can be cast in a mold.

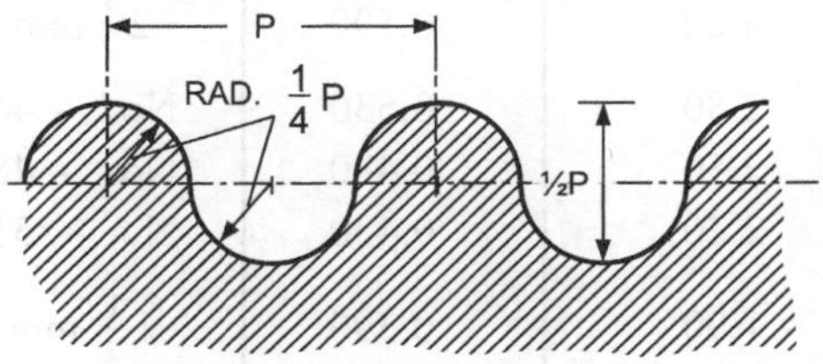

Fig. 10.15. Knuckle thread

Depth of thread = 0.5 × Pitch

Root and Crest radius = 0.25 × Pitch

These threads are specially used for coupling of rail coaches.

11. Worm Threads. Their shape is almost similar to Acme Threads but these are deeper than Acme threads. Their angle is also at 29°. This thread is used in worm wheel of motor vehicles for transfer of power at 90°. As three teeth of worm wheel fit into shaft with worm threads, they fit well.

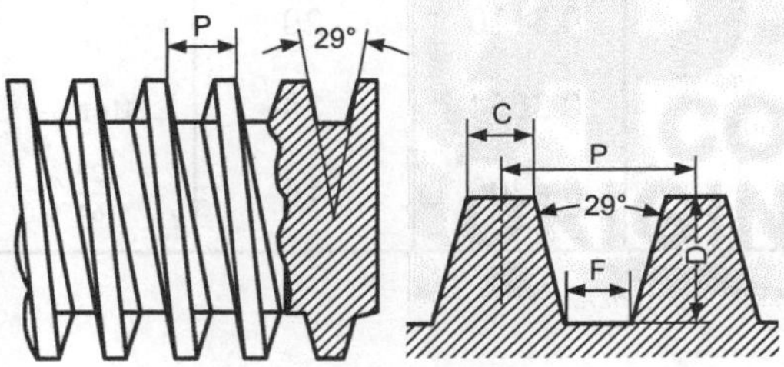

Fig. 10.16. Worm thread

Thread Angle = 29°

Depth of thread = 0.6866 × Pitch

Root = 0.32 × Pitch

Crest = 0.335 × Pitch

12. Cycle Threads. This is a special type of thread. It is mainly used in cycle industry. Its root and crest is round. It is made 24 T.P.I. to 62 T.P.I., 1.5″ to 0.056″ diameter. Its angle is also at 60 degree.

Thread Angle = 60°

Depth of Thread = 0.5327 × Pitch

$$\text{Radius} = \frac{\text{Pitch}}{6}$$

Methods of Cutting Threads. The following methods are used in workshops for making threads according to the jobs and the availability of sources :

1. **By Hand.** For small nut and bolts threads are cut by hand, with the help of tap and die.
2. **By Lathe Machine.** On the lathe machine, besides the lathe work, all kinds of threads can also be cut or made.
3. **By Casting.** This type of threads are made at the tune of casting of the job itself. This method is usually applied in cases where it is not possible to cut threads with other methods as in the case of casting of plastic and glass.
4. **By Milling Machine.** For cutting clear and accurate threads, milling machine is also used.
5. **By Rolling and Pressing.** There are certain jobs in which threads can neither be made by casting nor with cutting tools. These jobs are of thin sheet. Special kind of rollers are pressed on these sheets for making threads. This method is used for jobs like bottle lids.

Table regarding Threads (British Standard Pipe Thread)

Internal size of Pipe (in inches)	*External size of pipe (in inches)*	*Core diameter (in inches)*	*Number of threads per inch*	*Size of Tap Drill*
$\frac{1}{8}$	0.3825	0.3367	28	Letter R
$\frac{1}{4}$	0.5181	0.4506	19	$\frac{29}{64}$″
$\frac{3}{8}$	0.6563	0.5889	19	$\frac{19}{32}$″
$\frac{1}{2}$	0.8257	0.7342	14	$\frac{47}{64}$″
$\frac{3}{4}$	1.041	0.9490	14	$\frac{31}{32}$″
1	1.309	1.192	11	$1\frac{13}{64}$″

Table regarding Threads (B.A. Thread)

No.	*External Dia. (in inch)*	*Core diameter (in inch)*	*No. of threads per inch*	*External diameter (in mm)*	*Pitch (in mm)*	*Size of Tap Drill*
0	0.2360	0.1887	25.40	6.00	1.00	No. — 12
1.	0.2090	0.1665	28.20	5.30	0.900	No. — 19
2.	0.1850	0.1467	31.4	4.70	0.810	No. — 26
3.	0.1610	0.1266	34.8	4.10	0.730	No. — 30
4.	0.1420	0.1108	38.5	3.60	0.660	No. — 34
5.	0.1260	0.0981	43.0	3.20	0.590	$2\frac{1}{2}$ mm
6.	0.1100	0.0849	47.9	2.80	0.530	No. — 44
7.	0.0980	0.0753	52.9	2.50	0.480	No. — 48
8.	0.0870	0.0657	59.1	2.20	0.430	No. — 51
9.	0.0750	0.0565	65.1	1.90	0.390	$1\frac{1}{2}$ mm
10.	0.067	0.0504	72.6	1.70	0.350	No. — 55

Table regarding Threads
(British Standard Whitworth Thread)

External diameter (in inch)	*Core diameter (in inch)*	*Number of Threads (per inch)*	*Size of Tap Drill*
$\frac{1}{16}$	0.0412	60	No. — 56
$\frac{3}{32}$	0.0671	48	No. — 50
$\frac{1}{8}$	0.0930	40	No. — 40
$\frac{5}{32}$	0.1162	32	No. — 31
$\frac{3}{16}$	0.1342	24	$\frac{9}{16}''$
$\frac{7}{32}$	0.1654	24	No. — 18
$\frac{1}{4}$	0.1860	20	No. — 11
$\frac{5}{16}$	0.2414	18	Letter — D
$\frac{3}{8}$	0.2950	16	N
$\frac{7}{16}$	0.3461	14	S
$\frac{1}{2}$	0.3933	12	X
$\frac{5}{8}$	0.5086	11	$\frac{33}{64}''$
$\frac{3}{4}$	0.6220	10	$\frac{5}{8}''$
$\frac{7}{8}$	0.7328	9	$\frac{47}{64}''$
1	0.8400	8	$\frac{27}{32}''$

Table regarding Threads
(British Standard Fine Thread)

External diameter (in inch)	*Core diameter (in inch)*	*Number of Threads (per inch)*	*Size of Tap Drill*
$\frac{1}{4}$	0.2007	26	$\frac{13}{64}''$
$\frac{5}{16}$	0.2543	22	$6\frac{1}{2}$ mm
$\frac{3}{8}$	0.3110	20	$\frac{5}{16}''$
$\frac{7}{16}$	0.3664	18	Letter — U
$\frac{1}{2}$	0.4200	16	$\frac{27}{64}''$

Questions

1. What are the advantages of threads ? Define threads.
2. What is the difference between *Left-hand* threads and *Right-hand* threads ?
3. Comment on the following :
   (*a*) Pitch of threads
   (*b*) Pitch diameter
   (*c*) Minor diameter
   (*d*) Major diameter
   (*e*) Depth of thread
4. Show the above by drawing their figures.
5. What do you understand by pitch of thread and lead of thread ?
6. What are the different standards of thread ?
7. Draw a figure of Acme thread and mention its uses.
8. What is the function of worm threads ?
9. Comment on the following :
   (*a*) Crest
   (*b*) Root
   (*c*) Thread angle
   (*d*) Helix angle
   (*e*) Number of threads
10. Explain in brief the main sources of thread making.

11

Limits, Fits and Tolerances

In the present mechanical age, invention of new machines is on the increase. We need machine in every important work. In each machine, parts of different types and shapes are joined. The efficiency of these machines or equipments depends upon the accuracy of parts used in them. Accuracy of these different parts also depsnds upon the efficiency of workers. While manufacturing such parts the mechanics used to check one or two parts by fitting them on the machines. If they found any defect or difference they used to correct it by filing or by doing suitable machining. But it was uncertain to say that whether these parts work efficiently in other machines. Besides this in case of mass production of parts this method was not found suitable. These machine parts should be so accurate that these could be changed and fitted in any machine of the same type without any difficulty. If a particular part of a machine is worn out or is unfit for use, it should be replaced with ease and without any additional operation by a new part bought from any company. This property of the machine parts is called Interchangeability.

Interchangeability

While repairing a machine if a broken part is to be replaced, we need a new part. Only if, the new part is made of accurately similar measurement, it can be fitted otherwise not. That is why the property of interchangeability is important. If a shaft of 55 mm diameter is to be fitted, it would mean that its basic size is 50 mm. But for manufacturing a shaft of accurate 50 mm diameter, a lot of energy and time will be wasted, which is very difficult in mass production. Therefore, a mechanic is deliberately given concession of some percentage. For a diameter of 10 cm if we give a concession of ±2% the mechanic will manufacture that part either 0.02 cm bigger or smaller. Parts with such concession can fit in any machine of similar size without any difficulty. Thus we can say that mid-changeability is that property, by which even after mass production parts of similar type can have the capacity to change its accuracy, measurement and shape. To make it still simple, the property of interchangeability refers to similar parts so accurate in manufacture that they can be substituted one for another. We can have the following advantages from interchangeability :

1. A similar part from any company can be fitted without any difficulty.
2. It takes little time to change a machine part.
3. It takes less time to fit a machine.
4. Rejection of these parts is less.
5. Production increases and it saves time.
6. The production cost of these parts is less.
7. Wrong setting of machine, wrong use of a tool, defect in measuring tools, defective metal, carelessness of the mechanic, have no effect in the utility of that part.

In order to have the property of interchangeability, it is necessary to keep in mind a few important elements. For these elements a special terminology is used in interchangeability. These have been described as follows :

1. **Shaft.** Under interchangeability male part is called a shaft. A part which is fitted into another part is called a male part. It is an axle or bar, usually cylindrical, used to support rotating pieces, or to transmit power or motion by rotation.
2. **Hole.** Under interchangibility female part is generally called hole. That part in which male part is fitted is called female part.
3. **Basic Size.** It is also known as original theoretical size or nominal size. Treating this

measurement as basis, a part or its blue print is prepared.

4. **Actual Size.** The measurement or shape of a job on which it is prepared by the mechanic is called actual size. This measurement can be slightly more or less than the basic size, which is passed for use.

5. **Limit.** The limit of variation permitted on each side of the correct dimension to give to the job property of interchangeability (in mass production of a part) is called limit. This limit can be given as plus (+) or minus (–) or both. For example, size of a bush is 40 mm and ± 0.03 mm limit of variation is permitted. Then the bush will be made of (40 – 0.03) = 39.97 mm or of (40 + 0.03) = 40.03 mm diameter. This limit is of two types :

(*a*) **High Limit or Maximum Limit.** The maximum variation given on basic size or nominal measurement is known as high limit. In the above example, basic size is 40.00 mm. It can be made of 40.03 mm diameter. Thus here high limit is 40.03 – 40.00 mm = 0.03 mm.

(*b*) **Low Limit.** The minimum variation given on basic size or nominal size is called low limit. In the above example, basic size is 40.00 mm. This bush can be made of minimum diameter of 39.97 mm. Thus its low limit is 40.00 – 39.97 = 0.03 mm.

Tolerance

The difference between high limit of variation and low limit of variation is called tolerance.

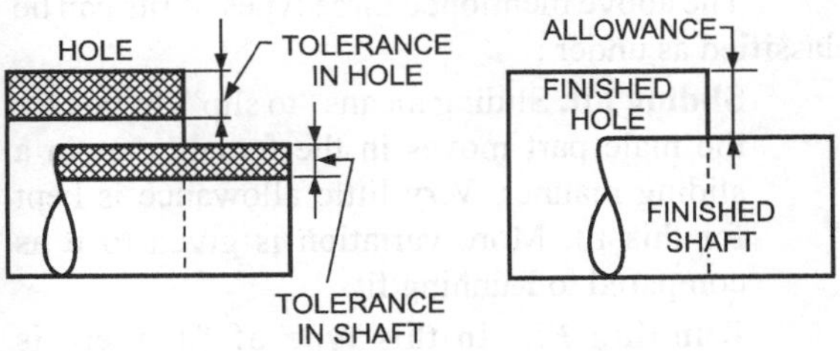

Fig. 11.1. Tolerance

Example. If the basic size of the diameter of a shaft is 25 mm and variation limit of ± 0.02 mm is given then its tolerance would be as under :

Basic Size = 25.00 mm
Limit = + 0.02 mm
Limit = – 0.02 mm
High limits = 25.02 mm
Low limit = 24.98 mm

Thus tolerance = 25.02 – 24.98 = 0.04 mm.

Kinds of Tolerance. Tolerance is given on the basic size of a job in two ways :

(1) Unilateral Tolerance. In this type of tolerance, tolerance is given on one side of the basic size. This tolerance is either (+) or (–).

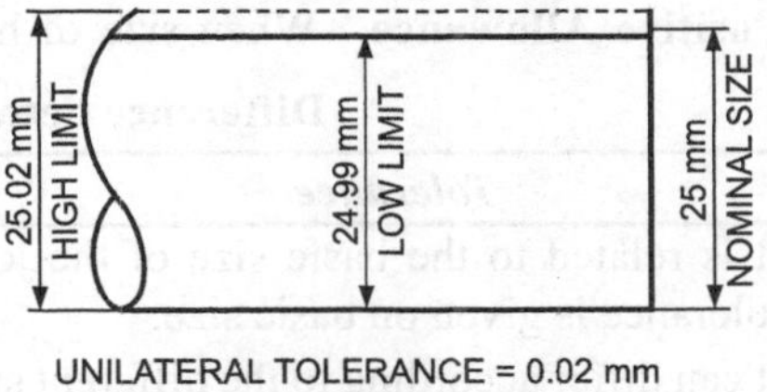

Fig. 11.2(*a*). Unilateral tolerance

For example, if basic size of a job is 25 mm and tolerance is + 0.02 mm, then + 0.02 mm tolerance is only in high limit *i.e.,* that job can be made in high limit of 25 + 0.02 mm = 25.02 mm. It is known as one sided tolerance.

In the same way, if the basic size is 25.00 mm and tolerance given is – 0.02 mm, then the job can be made in low limit of 25.00 – 0.02 mm = 24.98 mm.

(2) Bilateral Tolerance. In this type of tolerance, tolerance is given on both sides of basic size *i.e.* (+) and (–).

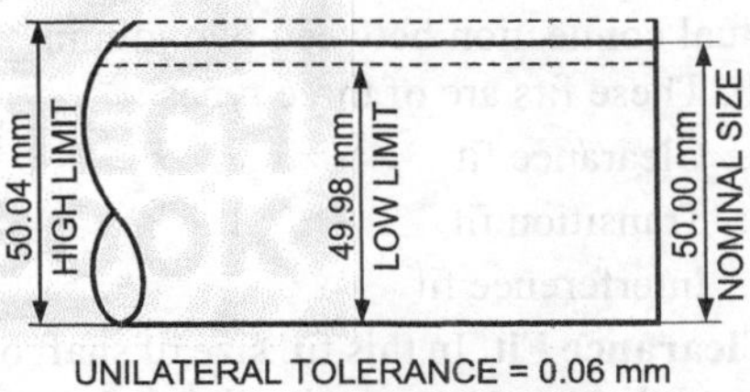

Fig. 11.2(*b*). Bilateral tolerance

For example, if basic size is 25 mm and tolerance of + 0.02 mm and – 0.02 mm tolerance is given then job can be made of the size of 25 + 0.02 = 25.02 mm to 25 – 0.02 = 24.98 mm.

If the limit of variation on basic size of high limit and low limit is equal then size of (±) is indicated on blue print. If the limit of variation on the basic size of high limit and low limit is different then sign of (+) and (–) is written on the blue print.

Allowance

The variation in size which is made in size of

two parts in order to fit them in the desired manner is known as allowance. It is difference between minimum size of male part and the maximum size of female part. It is kept in positive (+) or negative (–). This depends on the shape of fit. If it is not kept there will be difficulty in fitting or working because each part has its own capacity or limit of work. Allowance is of two kinds :

(1) Positive Allowance. When size of hole or female part of a job is more than shaft or male part, the difference between the two will be known as Positive Allowance. This type of allowance is given in running fit.

(2) Negative Allowance. When the size of shaft or male part is more than the size of hole or female part, the difference between their size is called Negative Allowance. This type of allowance is kept to achieve force fit.

Difference between Tolerance and Allowance

Tolerance	*Allowance*
1. It is related to the basic size of the job *i.e.,* tolerance is given on basic size.	It is related to the limit of variation *i.e.,*it depends on the type of the fit.
2. It can differ according to the different sizes of one particular job.	It is given only on two joining parts.
3. It is in High Limit or Low Limit.	For desired fit, it is Positive or Negative.
4. This concession is given intentionally.	It is an actual concession for the fit.
5. It is kept according to drawing or blue print.	It is kept for achieving the desired effect.

Fit

Every machine has a number of parts. These parts are manufactured separately and then assembled together. There are some parts which move by sliding into another parts and there are some parts which fit tightly into other part and move them. For smooth functioning of these parts, it is essential that there should be adequate coordination between these parts. The mutual connection between two joining parts is called fit. These fits are of three types :

1. Clearance fit
2. Transition fit
3. Interference fit

Clearance Fit. In this fit, size of shaft or male part is kept comparatively slightly less than the size of hole or female part so that male part can move in the female part without any obstruction. Running and Sliding fits come under the clearance fit [Fig. 11.3 (*a*)].

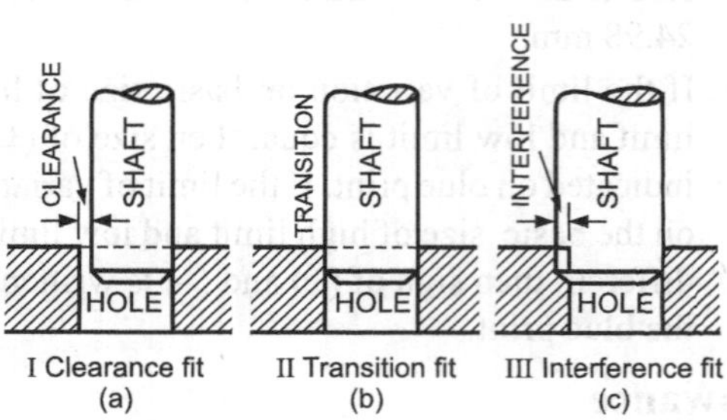

Fig. 11.03.

Transition Fit. In this type of fit, size of male part or shaft is kept comparatively a bit thicker than female part or the hole. But the parts of this type of fit can be fitted with some pressure. Push Fits and Ringing Fits come under this type [Fig. 11.3(*b*)].

Interference Fit. This fit is quite reverse to the clearance fit. In this type of fit size of male part or shaft is bigger than the size of hole or the female part. In order to join two parts or to fit them together great amount of force is used. For this purpose press machines or hydraulic machines are also used. Force fit and Driving fit are included under this fit.

The above mentioned three types of fits can be classified as under :

Sliding Fit. Sliding means "to slip". In this fit, the male part moves in the female part in a sliding manner. Very little allowance is kept for this fit. More variation is given to it as compared to Running fit.

Running Fit. In this type of fit, there is sufficient allowance between two parts such as shaft and hole that male part can revolve in the female part with ease. In this fit the thin layer of lubrication given between the two parts is also taken into consideration. This fit is used in shaft, bush or bearing. The allowance in this fit depends on the part's diameter, hole, length, and its surface.

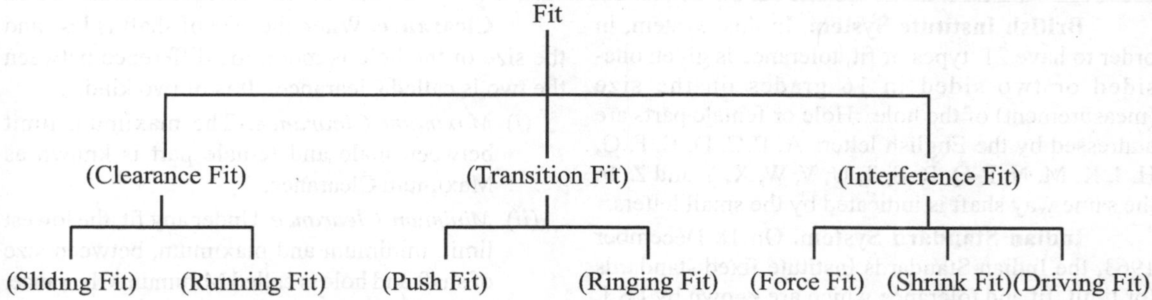

This fit is of three types :

1. Slack running fit
2. Normal running fit
3. Close running fit

In the above fits slack running fit and normal running fit is used for ordinary jobs. Close running fit is used for very accurate jobs.

Push Fit. In this fit allowance is kept less than that of running fit. One part is kept stationary while the other part is pushed with hand or by using a wooden piece and striking it slightly to fit it such as dowel pin, ring gauge *etc*.

Ringing Fit. Ringing means to have friction. In this type of fit female and male parts are found stuck together. If these parts are to be separated, it can be done only by using pressure. This fit is stationary to some extent.

Force Fit. Normally this type of fit is used for round jobs. For example, to fit a shaft in a hole permanently or temporarily. In this fit male part is made slightly bigger or equal in diameter. It is fitted by putting heavy pressure. Machine press or hydraulic press is used for this purpose such as cycle-hub or pulley of a motor.

Shrinkage Fit. In this type of fit female part is kept slightly smaller than the male part. In other words, there is negative allowance in this fit. In order to fit the male part into the female part, the male part is heated in order to fit it in female part, by which its volume increases.

Male part is fitted when the female part is in hot condition. In this way when the female part becomes cool and returns to its normal temperature, it grips the male part permanently. This type of fitting is done to mount iron ring on the wheels with wooden spokes. Besides this, male part can also be fitted by making the male part chilled cold, for example, cylinder liners of motor engines. This fit is called expansion fit.

Driving Fit. In this type of fits a slight difference is kept between male and female parts. These are fitted by striking them with hammer *etc*. It is used in dynamo pulley *etc*.

We can divide this fit into three parts :

1. Light driving fit
2. Medium driving fit
3. Heavy driving fit

While choosing any of the above mentioned fit, the following important points should be kept in mind :

1. Nature of the work of job
2. Length of job
3. Speed of job
4. Lubrication system

Newal System

The world-fame Newal company carried out elaborate research on the tolerance given on different types of fits and they fixed standard tolerance on holes of $\frac{1}{2}$ to 6″ diameter. These standards are used in prominent industries all over the world. Under this system, in order to achieve fit, the size of hole or female part is kept fixed and tolerance is given in shaft or the female part. In this system, holes have been divided into two classes "A" and "B". Class "A" is used in jobs of high accuracy. "B" class is used for general jobs. Under this system there are the following types of fits :

(1) Force fit, (2) Driving fit, (3) Push fit, (4) Ring fit *etc*. In order to indicate these fits on blue print or drawing, letters F, P, D, X, Y and Z are used.

F stands for Force fit

P stands for Push fit

X stands for Slack ring

Y stands for Normal Ring fit

Z stands for Close Ring fit

D stands for Driving fit

British Institute System. In this system, in order to have 21 types of fit, tolerance is given one-sided or two sided in 16 grades on the size (measurement) of the hole. Hole or female parts are addressed by the English letters A, B,C, D, E, F, G, H, J, K, M, N, P, Q, R, S, T, U, V, W, X, Y and Z. In the same way shaft is indicated by the small letters.

Indian Standard System. On 18 December 1963, the Indian Standards Institute fixed standards for limit, fit and tolerance which are known by I.S.I, approval number 919. In order to have different fits in holes and shafts of 3 mm to 500 mm diameters, 16 basic classes have been adopted, which are expressed as ITO^1, ITO^2 and IT^1 to IT^{16}. These have been divided in 25 fundamental deviations. Holes are exhibited through capital letters A, B, C, D, E, F, G, H, Js, J, K, M, N, P, R, S, T, U, X, Y, Z, ZA, ZB and ZC. Similarly, shafts are exhibited by small letters of English language such as a, b, c, d, e, f, g, h, js, j, k, m, n, p, r, s, t, u, v, x, y, z, za, zb and zc.

Terms and their definitions used by Indian Standards Institute :

Size. The unit of a job through which length, breadth and depth are known as its size.

Basic Size. Size of all jobs without the tolerance given to it, is called basic size.

Actual Size. Size of a job, after its completion, is called actual size.

Limit of Size. The ultimate two sizes of a job, having actual size between them, is called the limit of size. This limit is maximum or minimum.

(1) **Maximum Size Limit.** The maximum size between the two limits given on basic size is called maximum size limit.

(2) **Minimum Size Limit.** The minimum size between the two limits given on the basic size is known as minimum size limit.

Deviation. Difference between the basic size of a job shown in blue print and its actual size is known as deviation. It is of two types :

(*i*) *Upper Deviation.* Difference between the basic size of the job and the high limit is called Upper Deviation.

(*ii*) *Lower Deviation.* Difference between basic size of the job, and lower limit is called lower deviation.

Fit. It is the basis of bringing into contact two parts, for doing work according to our desire. Before joining, these parts have different sizes.

Difference of Fit. The mathematical addition of the tolerance of two parts of the fit is called Difference of Fit.

Clearance. When the size of shaft is less and the size of the hole is more, the difference between the two is called Clearance. It is of two kinds :

(*i*) *Maximum Clearance.* The maximum limit between male and female part is known as Maximum Clearance.

(*ii*) *Minimum Clearance.* Under any fit, the lowest limit, minimum and maximum, between size of shaft and hole is called Minimum Clearance.

Fit Hole Basis or Shaft Basis System. In order to obtain proper fit, allowance or clearance is kept in hole or shaft. For achieving this clearance the following two systems can be used :

(1) **Hole Basis System.** In order to achieve the right fit, if diametrical size of a hole is kept equal but diametrical size of shaft only is changed, this process is called Hole Basis System because the basis of size here is hole.

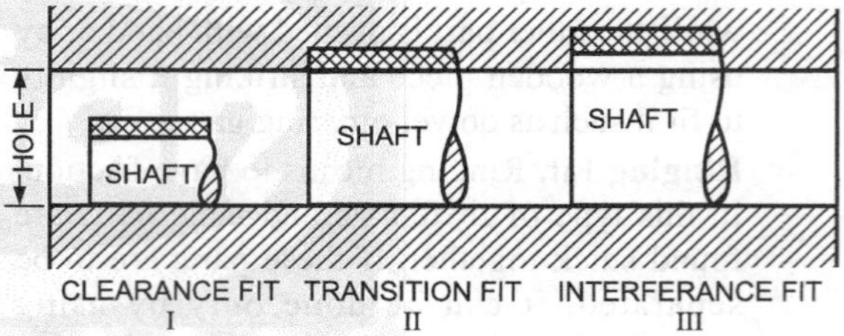

Fig. 11.4. Hole basis system

In Fig. 11.4 only difference in size of the shaft has been exhibited for getting Clearance fit, Transition fit and Interference fit.

(2) **Shaft Basis System.** This system has been shown in Fig. 11.5. In order to get appropriate fit in a job, if the diametrical size of the shaft is kept stable but only the diametrical size of hole is changed, this process is called shaft basis system.

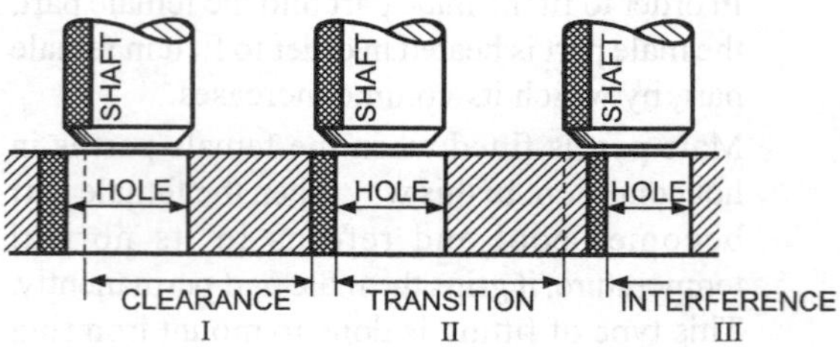

Fig. 11.5. Shaft basis system

Symbol of I.S.I. The following symbols are used by I.S.I. to understand the fits, tolerances *etc.* in drawings. 'E' is used to indicate hole or female part, small 'e' is used to indicate shaft or male part.

ES = Upper deviation of hole

EI = Lower deviation of hole

es = Upper deviation of shaft

ei = Lower deviation of shaft

Similarly, small za, capital ZA, ZB and ZC are used for maximum interference fit.

ab, AB, indicate diameters above 1 mm

J8 is used only for 3 mm diameter

k is used for 3 mm hole

js, JS is an inclusive deviation which is used for all categories of deviation.

Questions

1. What do you understand by interchangeability ? Why it is necessary ?
2. Write definitions of the following :
   (*a*) High Limit and Low Limit.
   (*b*) Tolerance
   (*c*) Allowance.
3. What is difference between unilateral tolerance and bilateral tolerance ?
4. Define "Fit".
5. What are the methods used for "Fit" ?
6. Write comments on the following :
   (*a*) Clearance fit
   (*b*) Transition fit
   (*c*) Interference fit.

12

Fasteners

There are several parts in any machine big or small. These parts are joined in different ways according to their role and position in a machine. Such holding devices as bolts, screws, keys are called fastners. The act of holding together the different parts of a machine is called fastening. Fastening can be of three kinds :

1. Temporary fastening
2. Semi-permanent fastening
3. Permanent fastening

Temporary Fastening. When parts of a machine are joined in such a way that these can be disjoined or joined again easily, it is called temporary fastening. There is no harm to the machine or its parts in temporary fastening. In temporary fastening nut, bolt,, screw, lockpin and washer are used. These things are called fastners. The main temporary fastenings have been explained later in the chapter.

Bolts

This is one of the widely used fastners. Bolt is made from a thin rod of metal.

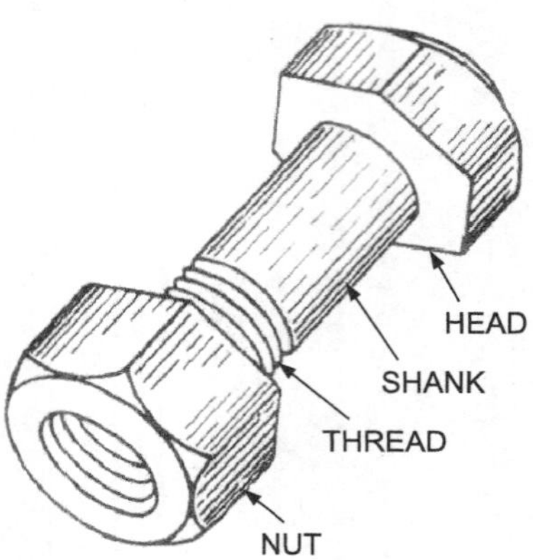

Fig. 12.1. Nut and Bolt

On its upper side, different types of heads are made to fix them. On the remaining part, or a part of it, there are threads. From this side, it can be fixed in a job or a nut can be fitted. Fig. 12.1 shows a nut and a bolt.

According to the type of head, there are following kinds of bolts :

1. Hexagonal head bolt
2. Square head bolt
3. Cheese head bolt
4. "T" head bolt
5. Hook bolt
6. Eye bolt
7. Cup head bolt
8. Counter sunk head bolt
9. Headless taper bolt.

Hexagonal Bolt. This bolt is most widely used. Six equal sides are made on its head. Size of head is standard *i.e.,* it is made according to the diametric thickness of the bolt in different sizes. Its bead is revolved with an ordinary double end or ring spanner *etc*. For covenience its head is chamfered to some extent. One advantage of making head of the size of bolt is that standard spanner fits well in it.

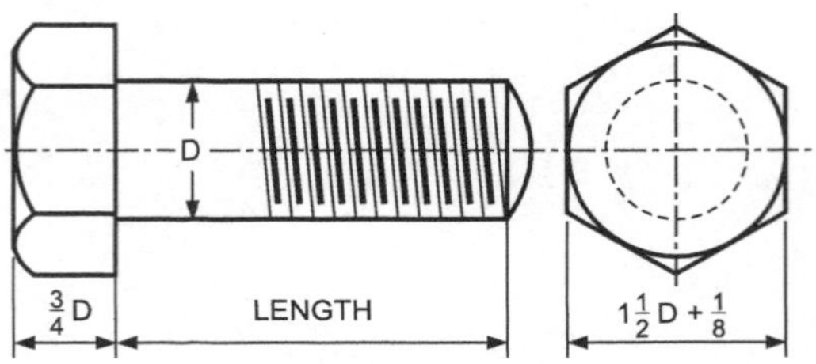

Fig. 12.2. Hexagonal bolt

For example, when the diameter D = normal diameter of bolt then the difference between two sides = $1\frac{1}{2}D + \frac{1}{8}$ and its chamfer will be at 30° angle and chamfer radius will be around $1\frac{3}{8}$ *D*. Thickness of the head would be = $\frac{3}{4}$ *D*.

Square Head Bolt. Head of this type of bolt is square. In common jobs it is used at such places where its head is gripped and neither it moves itself nor allows this part to move. Normally these bolts are fitted in a slot or such a place where square hole is there.

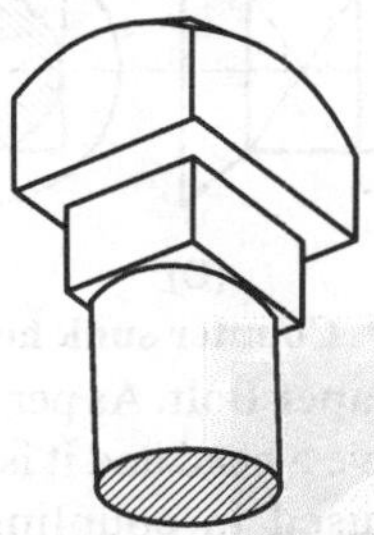

Fig. 12.3. Square head bolt

There are some bolts whose lower part below the square head is also made square. This part fits in the slot or square hole of the job and prevents the job from revolving. The standard of this bolt is as under :

Diameter of the bolt = *D*

Thickness of the head = $\frac{3}{4}D$

Distance between two sides = $\frac{3}{2}D + \frac{1}{8}$

Chamfer radius = $\frac{7}{4}D$

Chease Head Bolt. At those places where there is inadequate space and there is difficulty in fitting the spanner, this type of bolts are used. Their heads are plain or round. But there is a pin below the head which saves it from revolving at the time of tightening the nut.

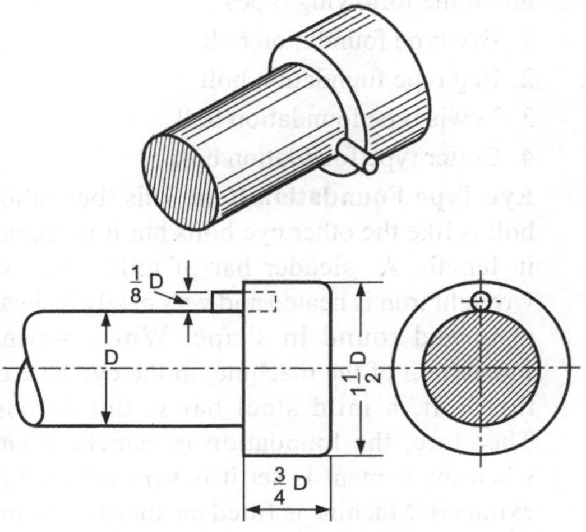

Fig.12.4. Chease head bolt

"T" Head Bolt. This type of bolts are used in machine shop. With the help of this bolt, the job can be fastened straight or with a clamping source to a machine table. Its head is square and under the head square shape is made.

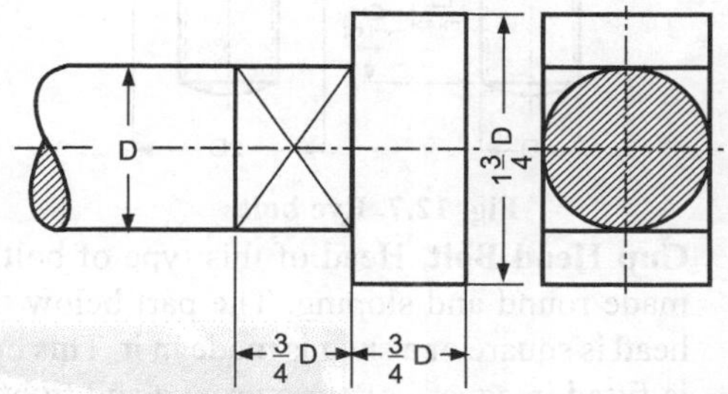

Fig. 12.5. "T" head bolt

Hook Bolt. This is a special type of bolt. In this bolt instead of having a head, there is an unthreaded end bent U shaped or straight at right angles to the body of the bolt. It is used at places where there is a hole on one part and with the other part job is to be held.

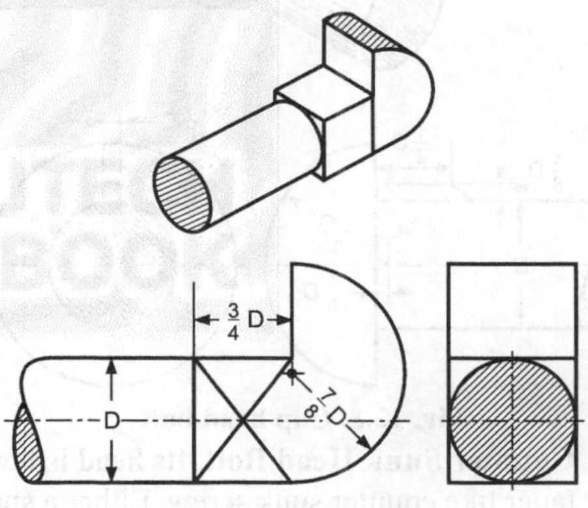

Fig. 12.6. Hook Bolt

Eye Bolt. These bolts are specially fitted in heavy electric motors or other machines. It is a bolt provided with a hole or eye at one end, instead of the usual head. The eye receives a pin, stud, or hook, which takes the pull of the bolt. Their thickness is kept according to the weight of the machine.

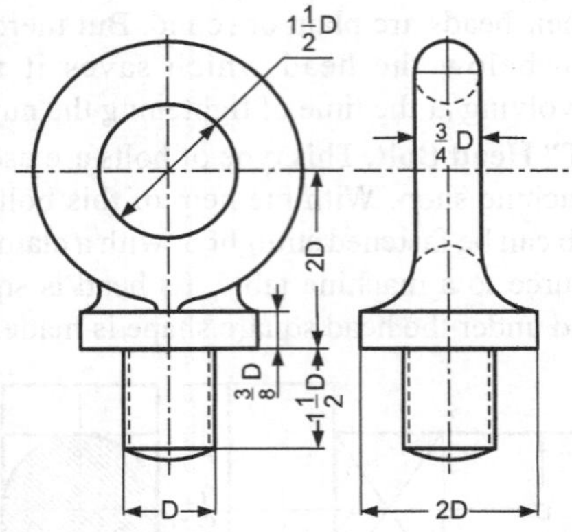

Fig. 12.7. Eye bolt

Cup Head Bolt. Head of this type of bolt is made round and sloping. The part below the head is square or a snug is made in it. This bolt is fitted in square or sung groove and tighten with nut. This type of bolts are often used in wood work. These are also called Rail Track Bolt because they are used on the rail lines.

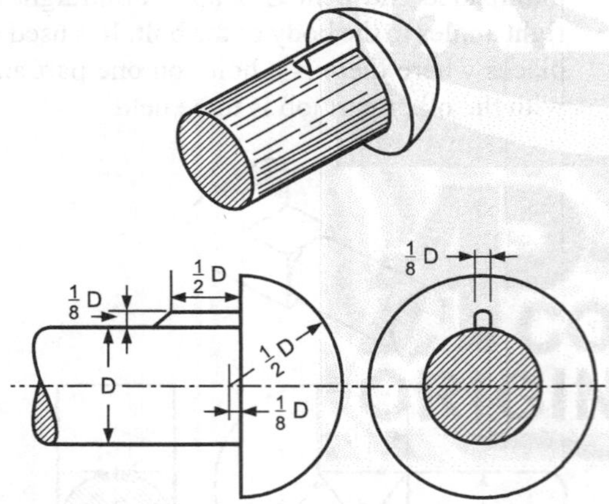

Fig. 12.8. Cup head bolt

Counter Sunk Head Bolt. Its head is built in taper like counter sunk screw. Either a snug is made in its head or the part below head is made square. This type of bolts are used at places where the head is placed inside the surface of the job.

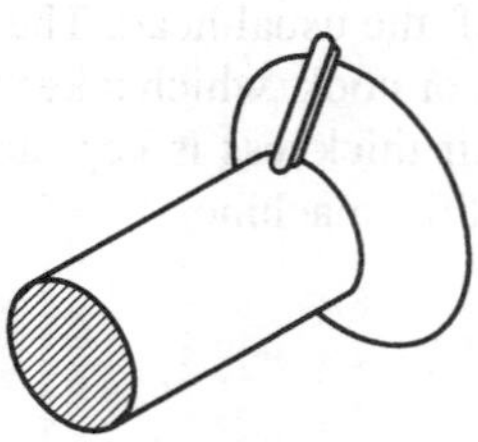

(A)

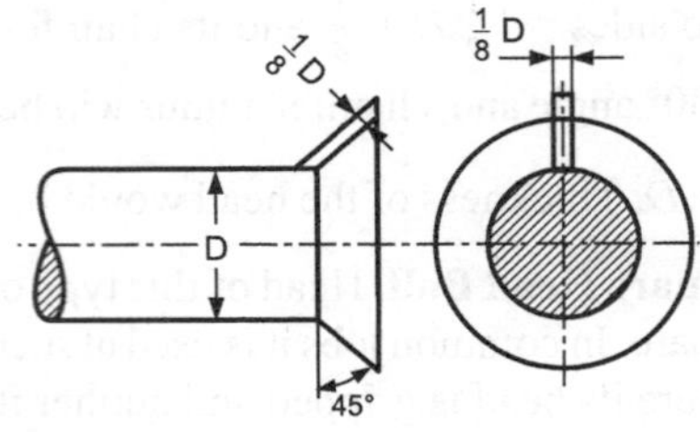

(B)

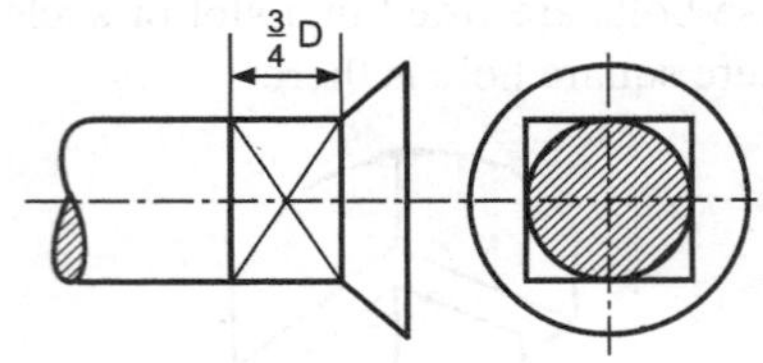

(C)

Fig. 12.9. Counter sunk head bolt

Headless Taper Bolt. As per its name, this bolt does not have a head and it is made in taper. It is mostly used in coupling *etc.* It can be tightened without revolving it.

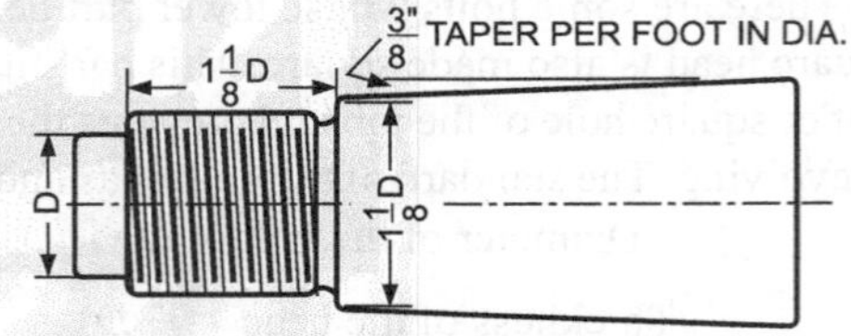

Fig. 12.10. Headless taper bolt

Foundation Bolt. Generally the machines are fixed at appropriate place in the workshops. In order to make them stand in stable manner they are fixed on the ground with the help of the foundation bolts. Bolts used for this purpose are of the following types :

1. Eye type foundation bolt
2. Rag type foundation bolt
3. Lewis type foundation bolt
4. Cotter type foundation bolt.

Eye Type Foundation Bolt. This foundation bolt is like the other eye bolts but it is greater in length. A slender bar of mild steel or wrought iron is heated and very easily its head is turned round in shape. While setting foundation of the machine, in the eye hole of this bolt, a mild steel bar is put across. Therefore, the foundation is cemented and when the cement is set it is very difficult to extract it. Machine is fitted on these bolts and they are tightened with the help of nuts.

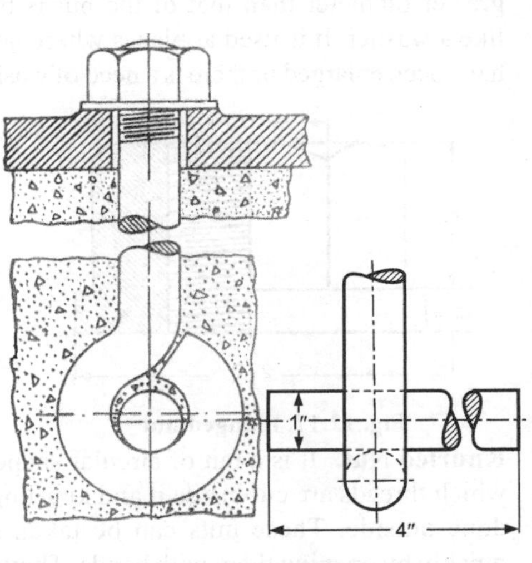

Fig. 12.11. Eye type foundation bolt

Rag Type Foundation Bolt. This type of foundation bolts are used for the foundation of heavy machines. Leaving the threaded portion, it is square in shape and slots are made at its edges as shown in Fig. 12.12 (A). Holes are made in the ground, below the holes of the foot of the machine to be used in foundation and these bolts are hanged with the help of nuts. Mixture of cement and sand or zinc and sulphur is filled around it, which tightly holds to the ground. In order to tight the machine, again the nuts are tightened. Square head bolt or zig-zag type foundation bolts also belong to this category. These have been shown in Fig. 12.12 (B) & (C).

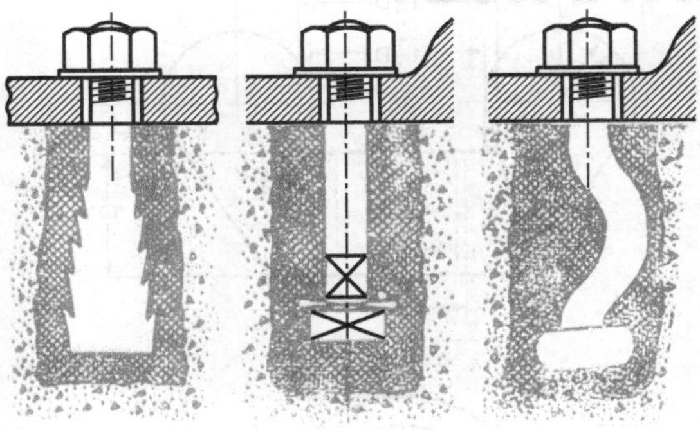

Fig. 12.12. Rag type foundation bolt

Lewis Type Foundation Bolt. In this type of foundation bolt, one side is straight and the other is in taper as shown in Fig. 12.13. On the opposite side of the tapered side a key is fixed. Mixture of cement and sand is filled around it. If foundation bolt of this type is to be taken out, first the key has to be taken out. This key is also somewhat tapered.

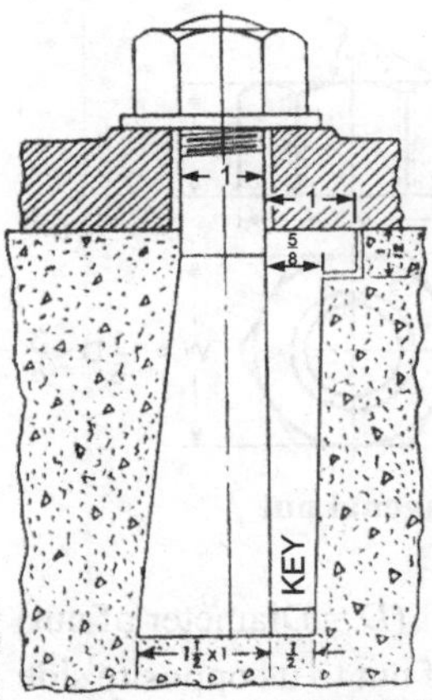

Fig. 12.13. Lewis foundation bolt

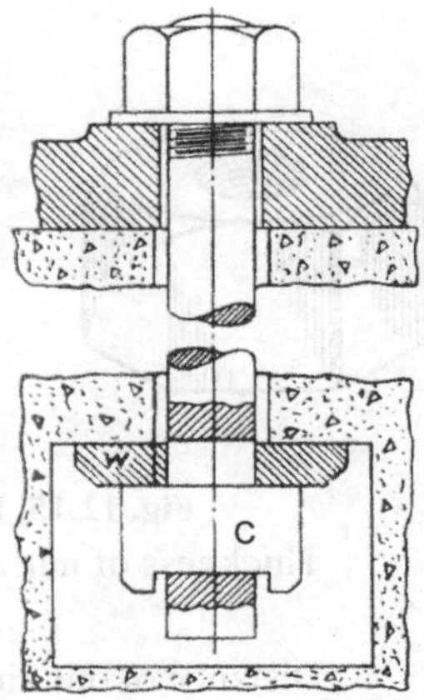

Fig. 12.14. Cotter foundation bolt

Cotter Foundation Bolt. This type of bolts are also used for foundation of heavy machines. These are also of special type. A plate is provided below the bolt in which grooves are cut for fitting cotter. In order to keep the cotter plain washer is also used. This has been shown in Fig. 12.14.

Nut

It is a small block of metal or other material commonly square or hexagonal in shape. It has internal threads to receive a bolt. Bolts are mostly used with the help of nuts. According to their working position these are of the following types :

1. Hexagonal nut
2. Square nut
3. Flanged nut
4. Knurled nut
5. Wing nut
6. Cap nut
7. Dome nut
8. Capstan nut
9. Ring nut
10. Thumb nut

Hexagonal Nut. This is an ordinary six sided form of nut and is most widely used. Because of its hexagonal shape (having six sides) it fits in the spanner easily and there are fewer chances of its slip. Its all sides are at 60° angle. These are chamfered at 30° to 45° angle. Because of this chamfer on the upper part of the nut a circle type is made. Its standard is known in the following way :

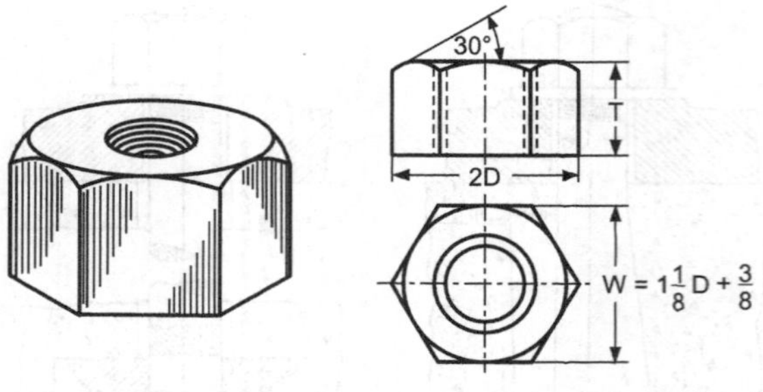

Fig. 12.15. Hexagonal nut

Thickness of nut $T = D$

(D = Diameter of nut)

Distance of one side of nut to its opposite side

$$W = 1\frac{1}{2}\ D + \frac{1}{8}.$$

Distance between two opposite diagonals

$$= 2D$$

Chamfer Radius $= 1\frac{3}{8}\ D$ or $1\frac{1}{2}\ D$ approx.

Square Nut. It is used like square head bolt in normal jobs. Its four sides are made at 90° angle, therefore, there is no possibility of slip of the spanner. This nut is also chamfered. Its standard is of the following type :

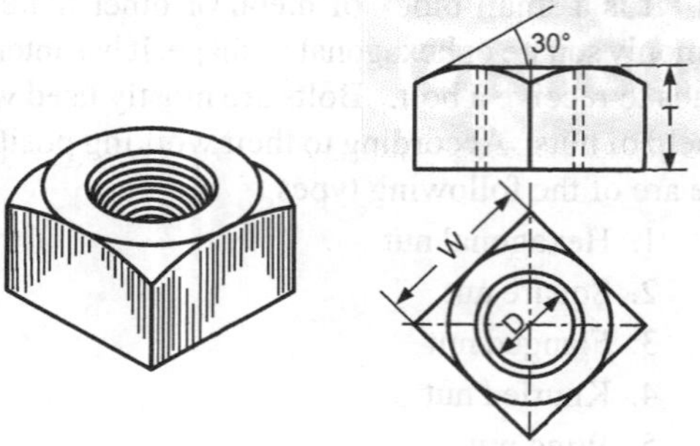

Fig. 12.16. Square nut

Thickness of nut $T = D$ (Diameter of nut)

Distance between one side and the opposite side,

$$W = 1\frac{1}{2} + \frac{1}{8}$$

Chamfer angle =30°

Chamfer radius $R = 2D$ approx.

Flanged Nut. This nut is of normal shape of a hexagonal nut but on its lower side a flange of greater diameter than that of the nut is built like a washer. It is used at places where holes have been enlarged or there is a need of washer.

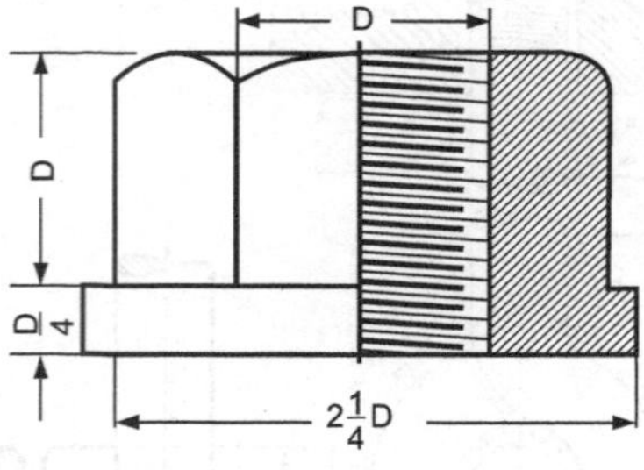

Fig. 12.17. Flanged nut

Knurled Nut. It is a nut of circular shape in which threads are cut inside it and knurling is done outside. These nuts can be taken out quickly by opening them with hands. They are used in measuring tools like micrometer *etc.*

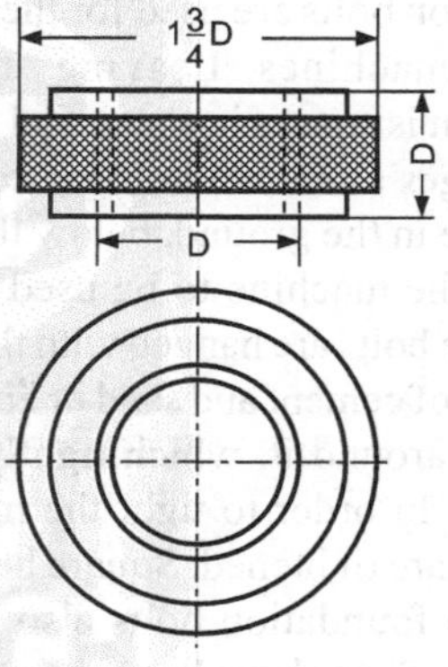

Fig. 12.18. Knurled nut

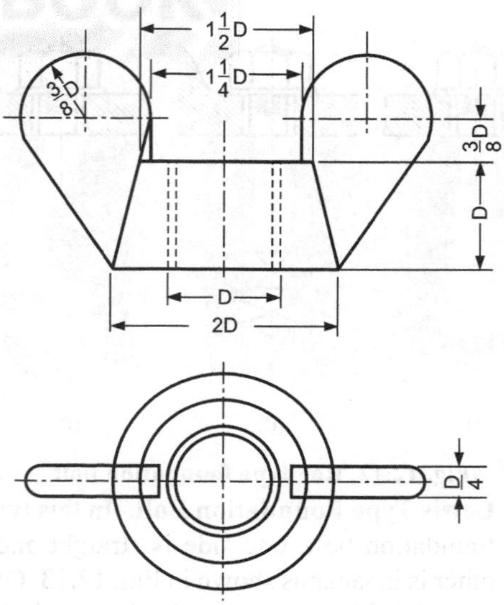

Fig. 12.19. Wing nut

Wing Nut. In this type of nut, on both the ends, a sort of wing is attached. With the help of these wings, these nuts can be easily tightened or loosened. These nuts are also known as fly nuts. These nuts are used at places where there is need to take out these nuts again and again such as in Hexaframe.

Cap Nut. This type of nuts are similar to the ordinary hexagonal nuts but on the top side can is made with a bit small diameter. This types of nuts are used at places where chances of bolt end getting rusted because of water falling there. With the help of this type of nuts even the oil leakage through the threads is also checked.

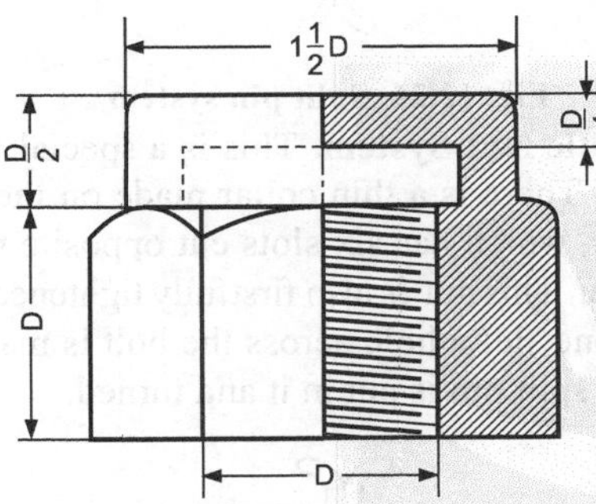

Fig. 12.20. Cap nut

Dome Nut. This type of nuts are also like the cap nut but on their upper side semi-circular dome is made.

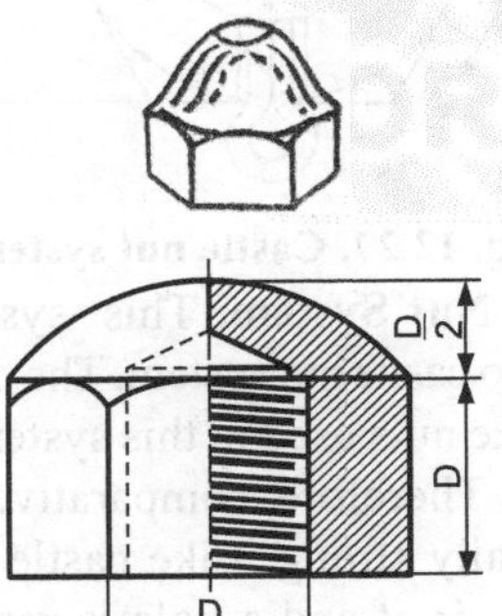

Fig. 12.21. Dome nut

Capstan Nut. This type of nuts are like the knurled nuts nut on their outer side knurling is not done. On the outside diameter four or six drills are made of $\frac{3}{16}$ or of the size needed from top to bottom. These nuts are used to tightened shafts *etc.* For tightening or loosening them pin face spanner is used.

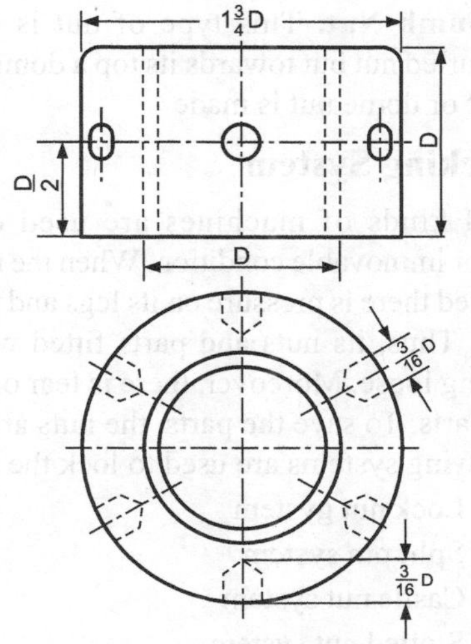

Fig. 12.22. Capstan nut

Ring Nut. This type of nut is similar to the capstan nut but on its outside surface four to six grooves are made. For tightening or loosening this nut crow wrench or hook spanner is used.

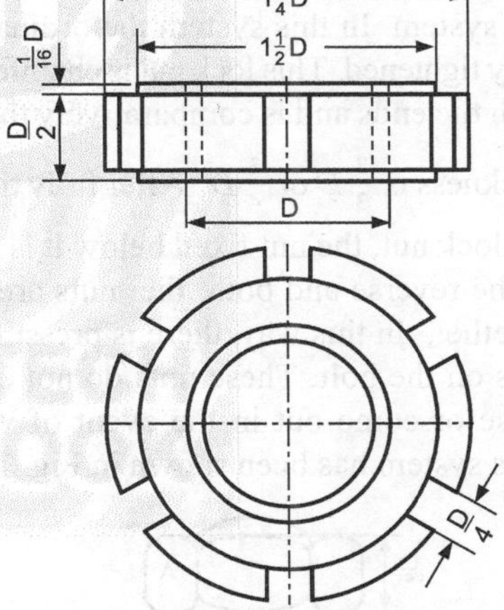

Fig. 12.23. Ring nut

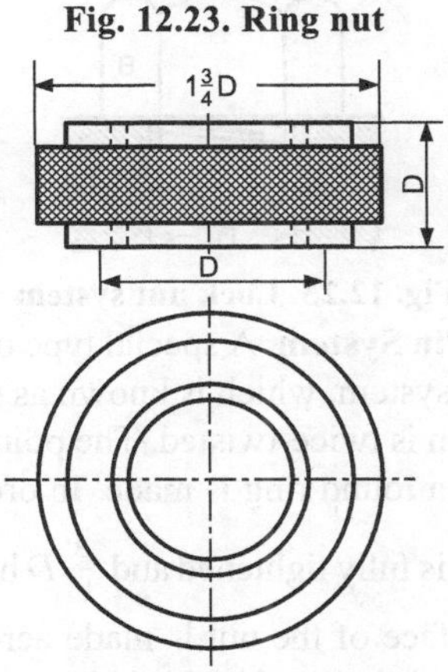

Fig. 12.24. Thumb nut

Thumb Nut. This type of nut is also like knurled nut but towards its top a dome like cap nut or dome nut is made.

Nut Locking System

All kinds of machines are used either in movable or immovable condition. When the machines are operated there is pressure on its legs and they start vibrating. Thus, its nuts and parts fitted with them start getting loose. Moreover, there is fear of damage to those parts. To save the parts, the nuts are locked. The following systems are used to lock the nuts :

1. Lock nut gystem
2. Split pin system
3. Castle nut system
4. Slotted nut system
5. Pin nut system
6. Swan nut system
7. Simmonds lock nut system
8. Spring washer system

Lock Nut System. This is also known as check nut system. In this system the ordinary nut is fully tightened. This lock nut is chamfered from both the ends and is comparatively thinner. Its thickness is $\frac{2}{3}D$ or $\frac{3}{4}D$. After fully tightening the lock nut, the nut fixed below it is revolved in the reverse and both the nuts are brought together. In this way, there is pressure of two nuts on the bolt. These nuts do not easily get loose or come out in the event of vibration. This system has been shown in Fig. 12.25.

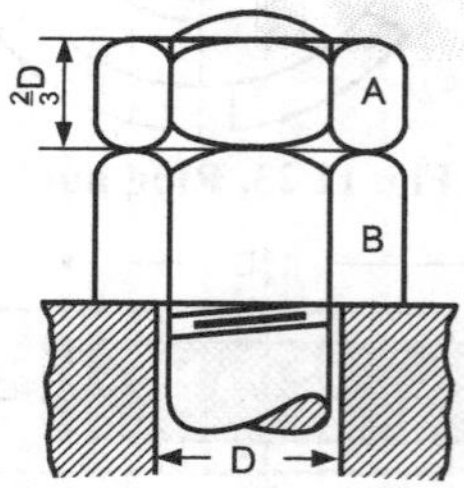

Fig. 12.25. Lock nut system

Split Pin System. A special type of pin is used in this system, which is known as split system. This pin is twice-twisted. The point at which it twists, a round ring is made. In order to use it, the nut is fully tightened and $\frac{3}{16}D$ hole touching the surface of the nut is made across the bolt. This pin is inserted in this hole and on the other end, its ends are turned in their opposite direction as shown in Fig. 12.26. This pin does not allow the nut to revolve in the reverse direction.

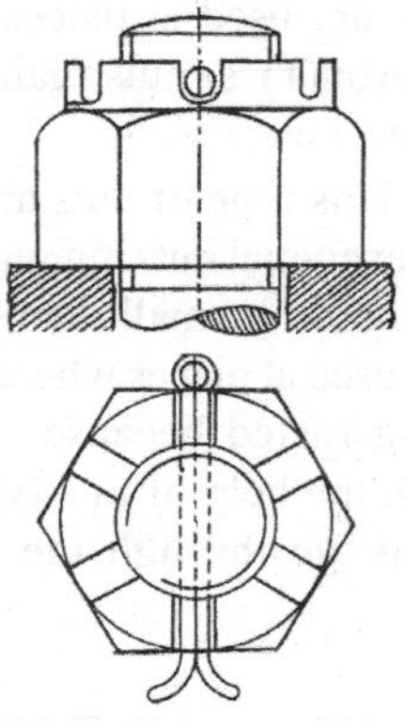

Fig. 12.26. Split pin system

Castle Nut System. This is a special type of nut. There is a thin collar made on the upper side, which has six slots cut opposite to each other. This nut is also firstfully tightened. Then in one slot a hole across the bolt is made and the split pin is put in it and turned.

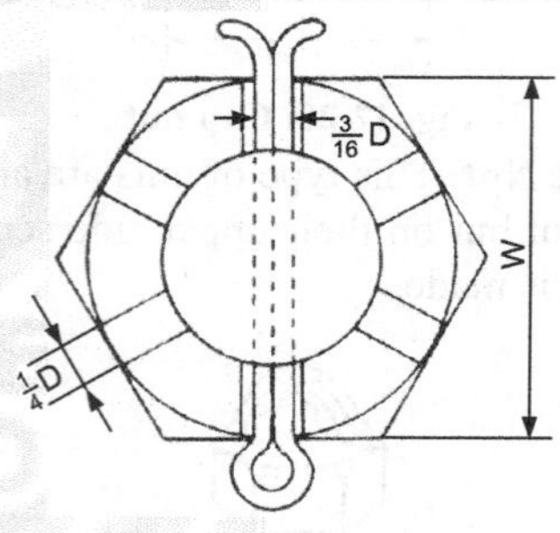

Fig. 12.27. Castle nut system

Slotted Nut System. This system is almost similar to castle nut system. The only difference is that the nuts used in this system do not have a collar. Therefore, comparatively this nut is not equally strong. Like castle nut, slots are also cut in it and a hole is made across the bolt, split pin is inserted in it and then twisted.

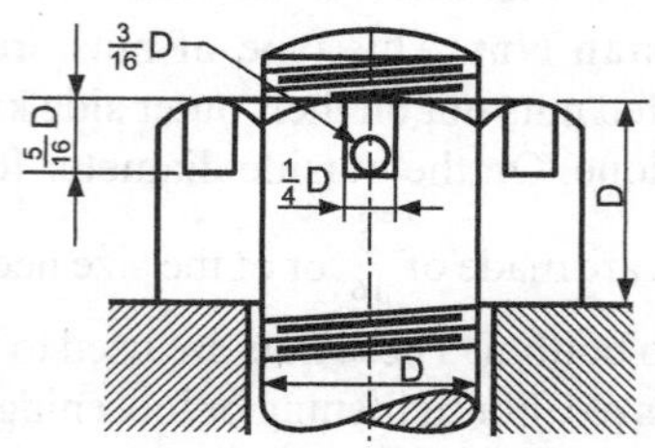

Fig. 12.28. Slotted nut system

Pin Nut System. This system is used at those places where there is sufficient space of surface around the nut after it has been tightened. In this system, after fully tightening the nut, on surface of the job stuck to one side a drill hole is made and a pin is inserted in it as shown in Fig. 12.29. This pin does not allow the nut to revolve. But if the nut is to be further tightened it has to be done after taking out the pin.

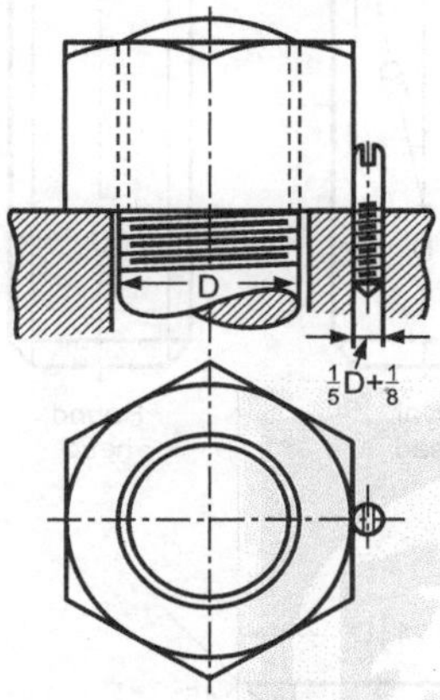

Fig. 12.29. Pin nut system

Swan nut system. In this system a groove is cut on side of the nut. On this side a drill is made towards the upper side and thin threads are cut accordingly. After fully tightening the nut a screw is tightened in the drill hole. By doing so the threads of nut are pressed and the nut is strongly tightened and there is no possibility of its being opened or coming out.

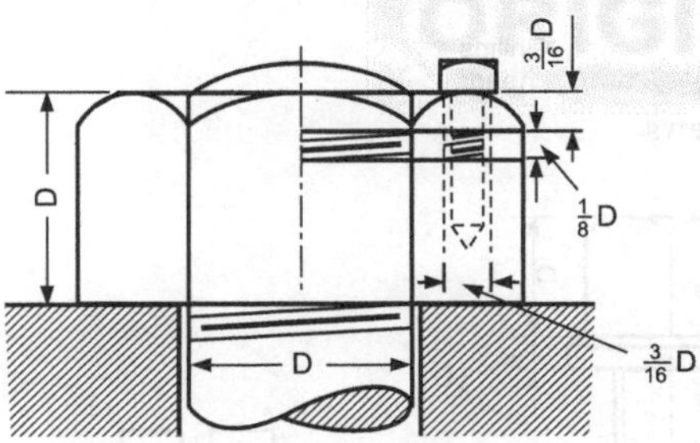

Fig. 12.30. Swan nut system

Simmonds Lock Nut System. In this system a collar is provided on a six sided nut. A round washer of rubber, fibre or nylone *etc.* is fitted in this collar whose inside diameter is somewhat less than the diameter of the bolt. When this nut is tightened washer is cut with the bolt and its material gets fitted in the threads. Thus, when this nut is tight, it neither gets loose nor opens itself.

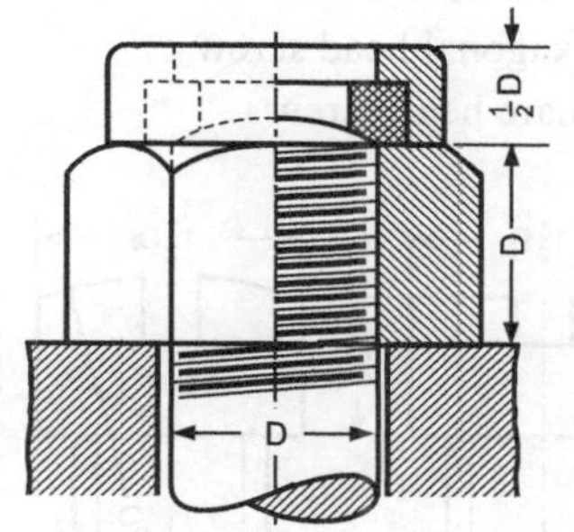

Fig. 12.31. Simmonds lock nut system

Spring washer system. It is also known as lock washer system. A special type of spring washer is used in this system. This washer is made of good quality spring steel. It is cut from one place. Therefore, its cut ends are up and down. This washer is fitted first and then nut is tightened. When nut is fully tightened, with the spring tension alone its both ends come on one surface. Because of tension the nut does not get loose, even if it gets a bit loose both the ends of washer rise in different directions and help in keeping the nut tight.

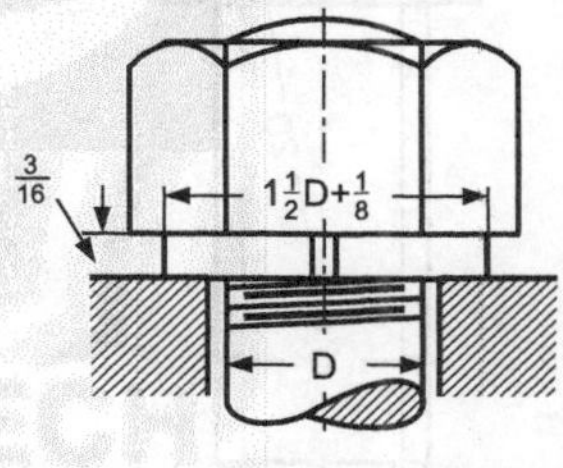

Fig. 12.32. Spring washer system

Screw

Screws are used for joining different parts of machines. Different types of threads are cut on screws. A screw may be considered as a helix wound around a cylinder. Their diameter is comparatively smaller than bolts. Their diameter is upto about $\frac{1}{4}$″. Their heads are of different types. Screw is mainly divided into four parts.

Cap Screw. In this type of screw, there are nine different types of heads or caps and their names have been classified as under. These have been shown in Fig. 12.33.

1. Chease head screw
2. Filister head screw
3. Counter sunk screw
4. Oval head screw

5. Round head screw
6. Hexagonal head screw
7. Square head screw
8. Allen screw
9. Philips screw

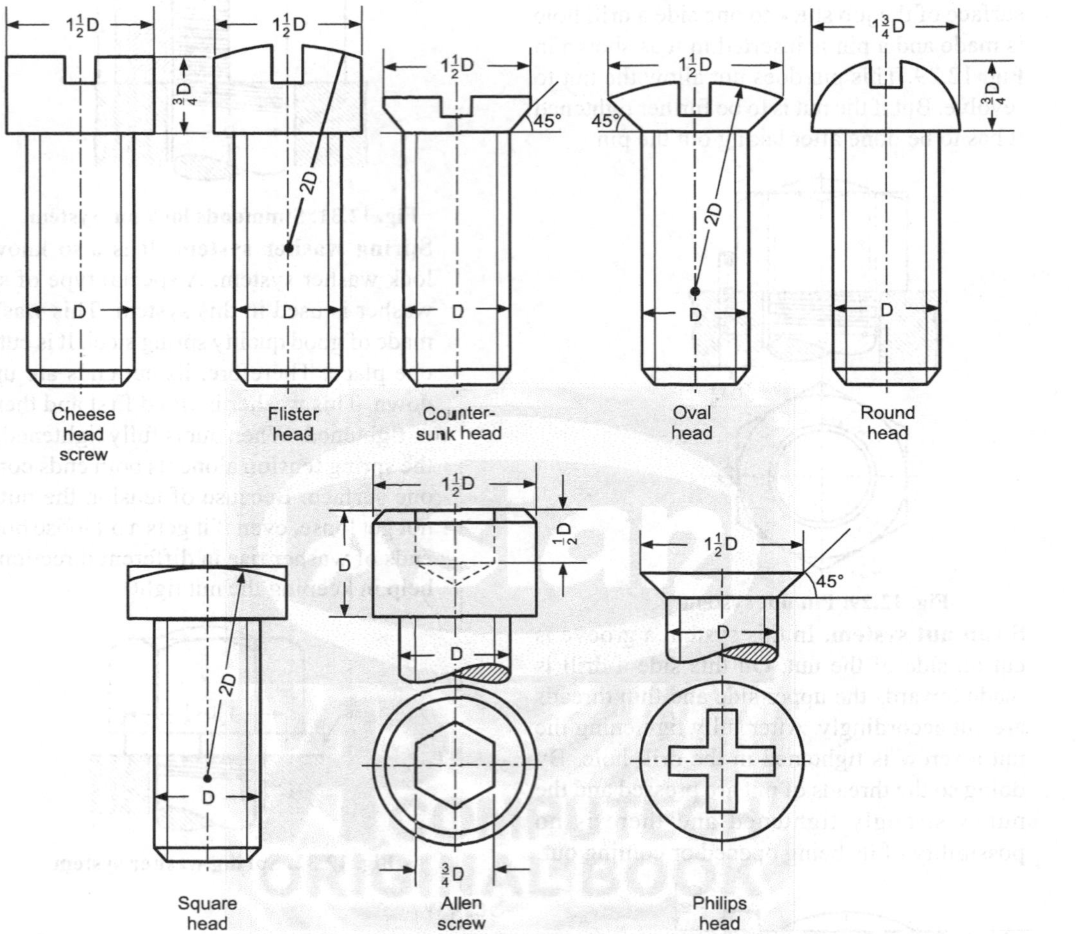

Fig. 12. 33. Cap screws

Among the above mentioned screws Filister head screw and Oval head screw is considered better than the Hexagonal screw because these screws remain stuck to the surface of the job. They can be cleaned easily. But these screws cannot be tightened much. Whereas hexagonal screws can be tightened properly. Allen screws are of special kind. These screws have hexagonal socket in the head. Such screws are adjusted by means of a hexagonal key.

Collar Screw. Heads of this type of screws are hexagonal but a collar is also made below it. That's why these collared screws are used without washer. These are used for clamping of small parts.

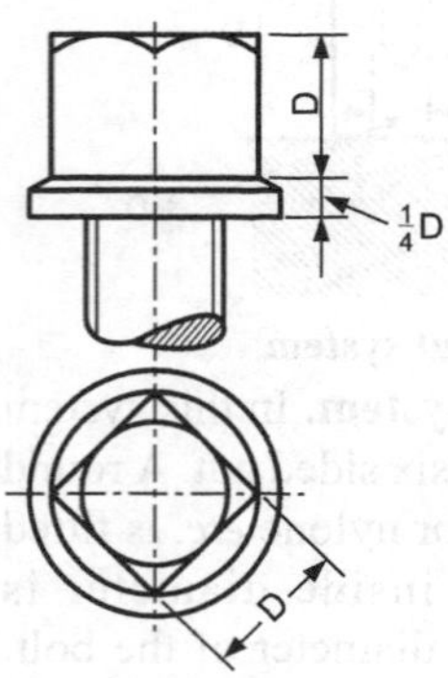

Fig. 12.34.

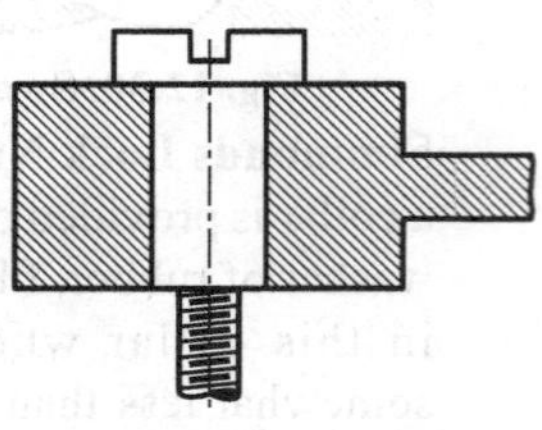

Fig. 12.35.

Shoulder Screw. This type of screw is made in three steps as shown in Fig. 12.34 above. It acts as a pivot pin for levers. There is a plain portion of the diameter between the screw head and the threaded portion, which provides shaft like facility to the moving part.

Set Screw. In working this type of screws are of reverse shape to that of cap screw. It is a plain screw having a square or other shaped head used for tightening purposes, and for locking adjustable parts in position. These are usually heat treated. Cap screw yields pressure on the job but in set screw job is held by the nook of the screw. There are some screws which have only one cut instead of screw head. In Fig. 12.36 the following types of set screws have been shown :

1. Cup point set screw
2. Flat point set screw
3. Half dog point set screw
4. Full dos point set screw
5. Oval point set screw
6. Cone point set screw

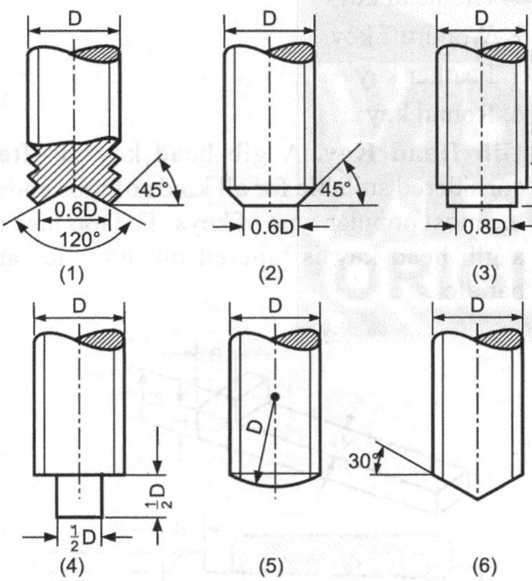

Fig. 12.36. Set screw

Washers

Its shape is like a round ring. Before tightening nut and bolt, it is fitted on stud or bolt. It is used to secure the tightness of a joint, screw *etc.* and it becomes easy to open the nut-bolts and their threads are protected. Even if the diameter of the hole in which bolt is to be fitted is a bit larger than the diameter of the bolt, with the washer's help nut bolt can be tightened easily. As per their utility and function, the washers are of the following types :

1. Spline washer
2. Lock washer
3. Plain washer

Spring Washer. This washer is in the shape of a ring cut by spring steel. Its ends are slightly raised up and down due to spring tension. These washers are placed above or below the nut or bolts and tighten so much that both their ends face each other and becomes levelled.

These washers are used to prevent a nut from loosening. These are used where there is *vibration,* or *jolts* occur. It exerts pressure against the nut and prevents the later (nut) from turning and working loose. There are several forms of spring washers. Each has its own advantage. According to their structure these are of following five forms :

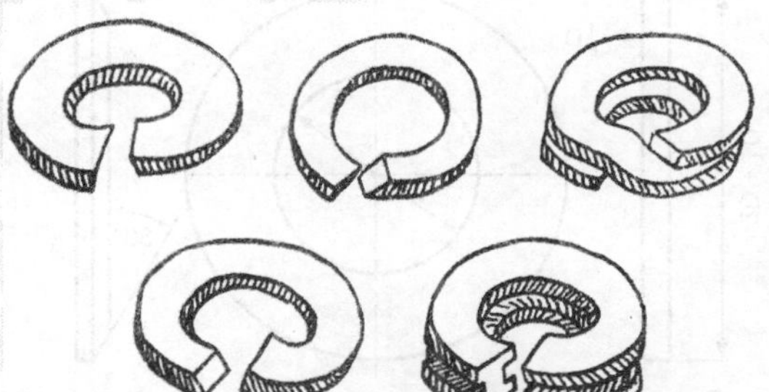

Fig. 12.37. Spring washers

1. Single pattern spring washer
2. Standard pattern spring washer
3. Double pattern spring washer
4. Grip pattern spring washer
5. Girder pattern spring washer

Lock Washer. This form of lock washers are used to lock the nuts and bolts. These are of many forms. Generally six or more leaves are extended beyond the main diameter of the lock

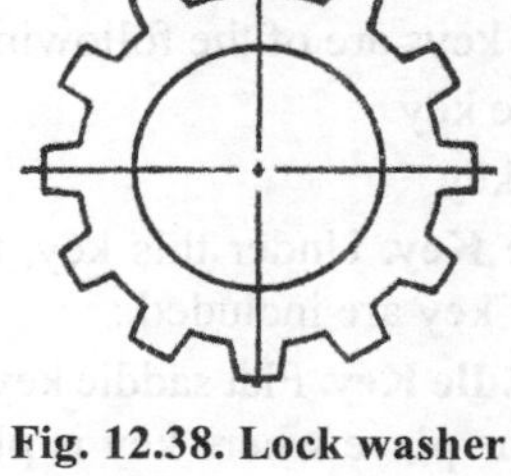

Fig. 12.38. Lock washer

washer. After fixing this washer its leaves are bent on the sides of nut or bolt. Thus, this washer prevents the nut bolts from getting loose. This washer is generally used in cars, trucks, *etc*.

Plain Washer. A plain washer is a flat disc. It has a hole in its centre through which a bolt, stud or set-screw can pass. By using it, the surface below the bolts or nuts becomes plain. In this way, the pressure of the nut is uniform on the entire surface. This washer is of the following standard :

Diameter of the washer $= 2D + \frac{1}{8}$

(D = Diameter of bolt)

Thickness of washer $= \frac{1}{8}\ D$

Angle of chamfer = 30°

Diameter of inner hole = Diameter of bolt

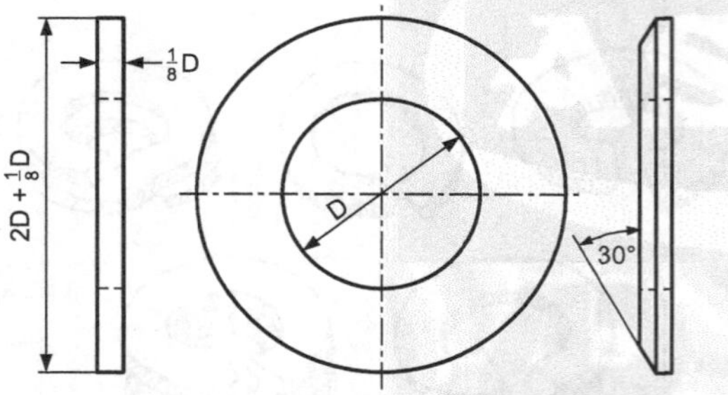

Fig. 12.39. Plain washer

Key and Key-way

We generally use a gear or pulley for moving another shaft through a shaft already in motion. It is used to locate and secure an object in position such as gear or pulley. With the help of key, gear or pulley cannot move on their shaft but the shaft and gear or pulley move together as one unit. A key is inserted between a shaft and a wheel in the key way. This makes the shaft and gear or pulley (or we can use the term "wheel") one unit. Keys are generally made of good quality steel in order to withstand (bear) the stresses. These keys are of the following forms :

1. Saddle key
2. Sunk key

Sadddle Key. Under this key, the following forms of key are included :

Flat Saddle Key. Flat saddle key is fitted over shaft. The place where key is placed is made plain. It rests on this flat surface. This type of key is used only for light loads. This is shown in Fig. 12.40 below.

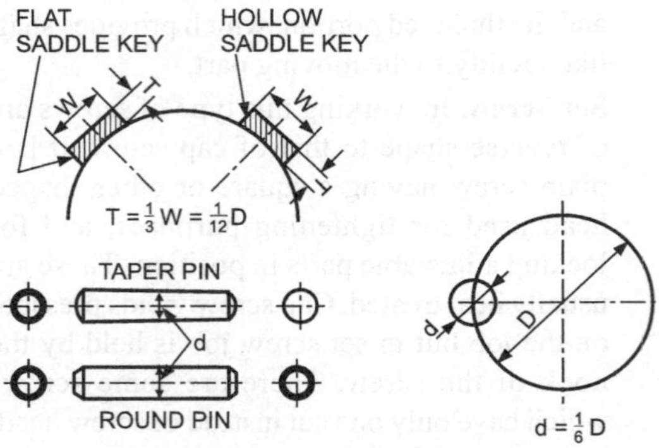

Fig. 12.40. Flat saddle key and hollow saddle key

Hollow Saddle Key. This is also used mostly like a flat saddle key but it is round in shape. Its diameter depends on roundness of the shaft. Screws having threads can also be used as keys. This key is illustrated in the Fig. 12.40 above.

Sunk Key. This includes the following types of keys :

1. Gib head key
2. Woodruff key
3. Feather key
4. Round key

Gib Head Key. A gib head key is often considered suitable for all kinds of jobs and is the most popular type of keys. The top face of a gib head key is tapered but its sides are parallel.

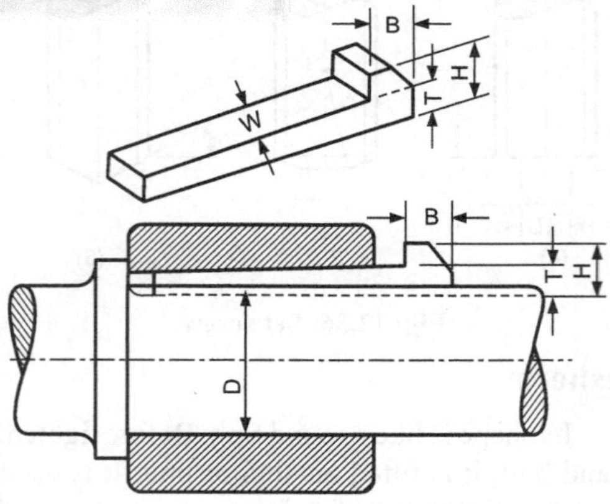

Fig. 12.41. "Gib Head" key

It is of rectangular cross-section. Its head is made towards its thick end, through which it can be easily taken out. It is necessary that it remains fully tight otherwise it can break because of jolts or can come out. It is illustrated in Fig 12.41.

Wood Ruff Key. This differs in shape from other keys previously described. It is plain from one side and in a "half-moon" (or semi-circle) shape from the other side. Shaft contains a key way according to this key. This key is mostly used on small shafts or spindles of fast speed for classes of work. This has been illustrated in Fig. 12.42.

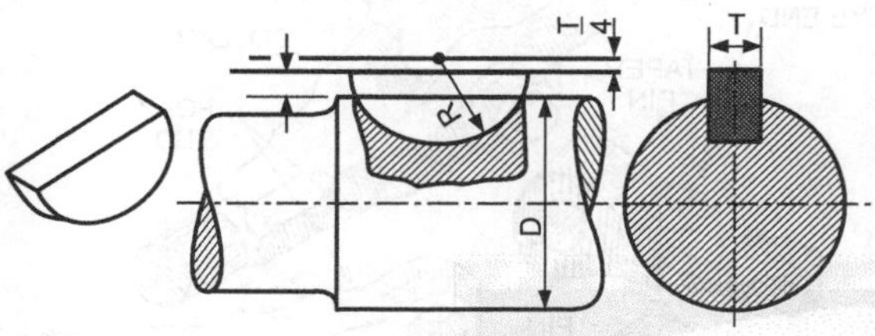

Fig. 12.42. Wood Ruff key

Feather Key. A "Feather" key is of rectangular section and is not tapered. It includes Plain head feather key, Peg feather key, Single head key and Double head feather key. It is fitted into the key-way of a shaft. It has no head.

Plain Head Feather Key. This type of key has been illustrated in Fig. 12.43. Its head is round and these are made long and rectangular.

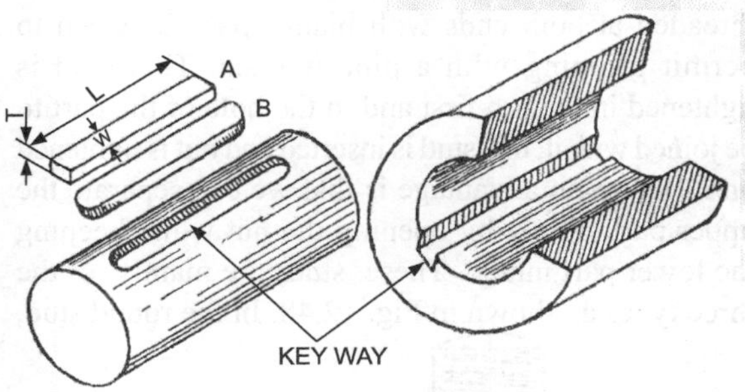

Fig. 12.43. Plain head feather key

Peg Feather Key. This is a different kind of key and is almost similar to plain feather key but its ends are plain. As shown in Fig. 12.44 (A) a peg is made near its centre. This is fitted in the hole made in the shaft so that the key cannot slip from the key-way.

Single Head Leather Key. This key is almost similar to the peg feather key but on its one end a head is made as shown in Fig. 12.44(B). There is a hole in this head in which a screw is tightened which helps in keeping the "key" fixed.

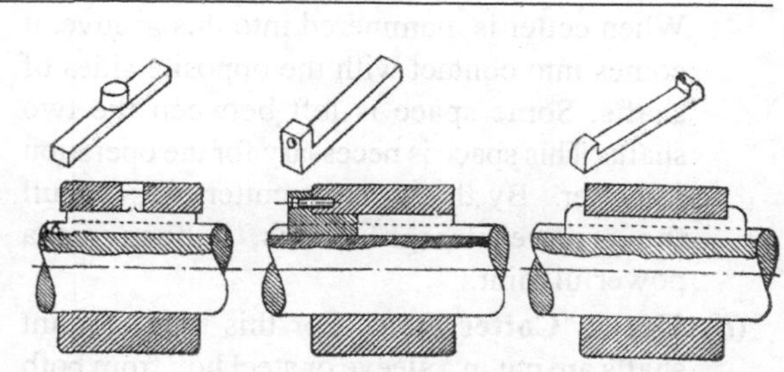

Fig. 12.44.

Double Head Feather Key. In this type of key, heads are made at both the ends. It is used to take help in making the shaft moving with a hub into one unit. This type of key is shown in Fig. 12.45 (C).

Round Key. This key is completely round and long. It fits half in the shaft and half in the hub as shown in Fig. 12.45. These pins can be parallel or in taper but hub and shaft is drilled accordingly.

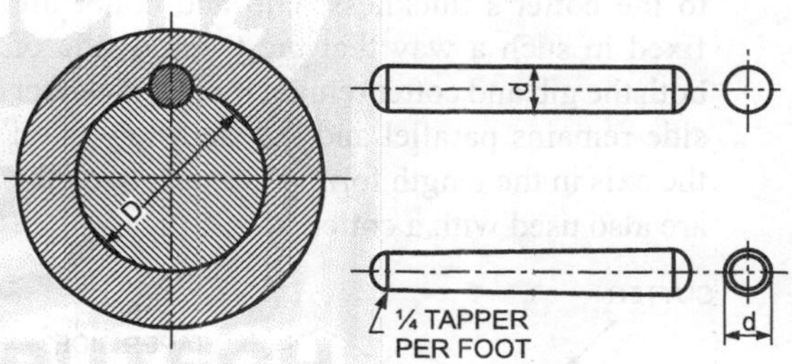

Fig. 12.45. Round key

Cotter and Cotter Joint. It is also used like "key" to join two shafts or parts of a machine. Cotter is a square tapered rod or a pin generally flat in section. These can be made rectangular, square or round. It is fitted to the axis of a rod at 90° angle. At times a cotter pin is also used with it. It is different from key in as much as it is used at places where there is a pressure on rod or shaft. It is fitted at 90° angle where as "key" is fitted at parallel distance and the moving parts are made one unit.

Cotter Joint. For different jobs the following types of joints are used :

(i) Socket and Spigot Cotter Joint. In this type of joint, one end of shaft is made flat and turned into a socket in which the spigot end of the other shaft is fitted. In order to fit cotter grooves are cut at some distance to each other.

When cotter is hammered into this groove, it comes into contact with the opposite sides of shafts. Some space is left between the two shafts. This space is necessary for the operation of cotter. By this process cotter tries to pull the groove straight. Thus, it becomes a powerful joint.

(*ii*) **Sleeve Cotter Joint.** For this type of joint shafts are put in a sleeve or steel box from both the sides cotters are fitted. Two cotters are used separately. These cotters stuck to the shaft and sleeve in opposite direction. In this way the desired space is also left.

(*iii*) **Strap Cotter Joint.** This type of joint is used in square shaped shafts. In this joint one end of the shaft is flat. End of another shaft is fitted in it. For joining, gib is used with cotter as shown in Fig. 12.46. Heads are made on both the ends of the gib. These heads perform almost the same function as a hook and save the flat end of the shaft from becoming loose. Thickness of the head of gib is kept according to the cotter's thickness. Gib and cotter are fixed in such a way that the tapered side of both the gib and cotter remain joined, the outer side remains parallel and the shaft key is on the axis in the length form. At times, two gibs are also used with a cotter.

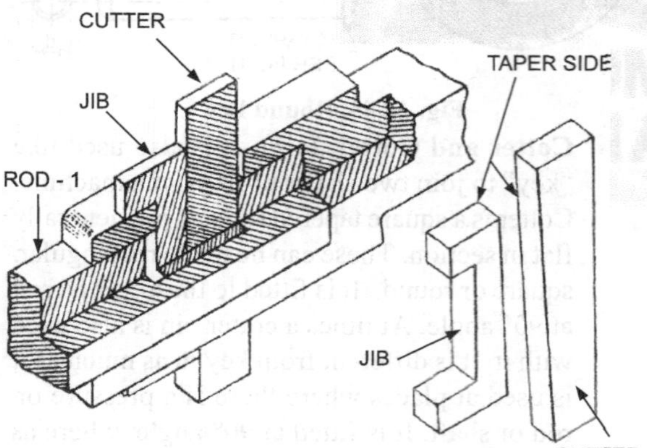

Fig. 12.46. Strap cotter joint

Knuckle Joint. This type of joints are used where two shafts are to be joined to each other at their angles. This type of joints are flexible. For this joint, in one shaft single eye hole is nade and in the other shaft a double eye hole fork is made as shown in Fig. 12.48. These shafts are joined together by fixing a collar type tapered pin or on the opposite end of the cotter a hole is made in which cotter pin is inserted and turned. In this joint, the taper collar pin is kept fixed and the ends of both the shaft remains independent. In short we can say that the Knuckle joint is one in which an eye at the end of a rod is engaged by the forked end of a second rod, the two being connected with a joint pin.

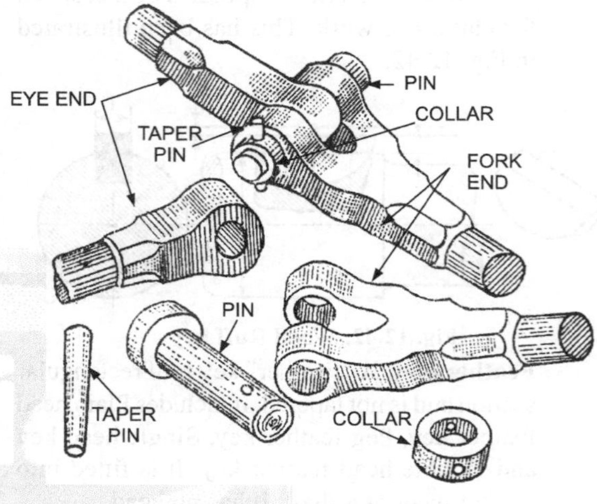

Fig. 12.47. Knuckle joint

Studs

It can be termed as a headless bolt. It is a bolt threaded at both ends with blank space between to permit gripping with a pipe wrench. This stud is tightened in the job first and in the hole of the part to be joined with it, this stud is inserted and nut is tightened on it. Its main advantage is that we can separate the upper part simply by opening the nut while keeping the lower part intact. These studs are mainly of the three types as shown in Fig. 12.48. In the round stud,

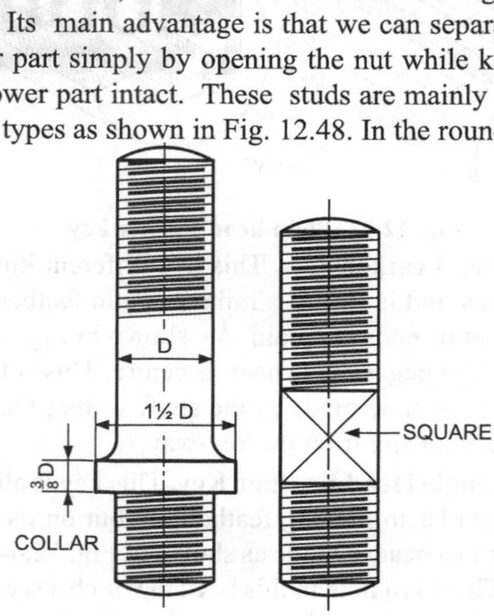

Fig. 12.48. Studs

the middle portion is also round. In square stud the middle portion is kept square. In the third type a collar is made at a little distance from the centre. It is often used in the cylinder head in automobiles.

Rivet and Rivet Joints

In order to join the jobs made of sheets or plates permanently these rivets are used. In the boiler and sheet metal work, it is used for making trunks and buckets. Rivets are generally made of mild steel but at times they are also made of brass, copper and aluminium *etc.* There are three parts of a rivet :

1. **Head.** The upper-most part of rivet is called "head". These are made of different types according to different jobs.
2. **Shank and Body.** The part below rivet is called shank or body. This is round in shape.
3. **Tail.** Part below its centre is called tail. It is somewhat tapered. It is inserted into holes of two plates and head is made by beating their tail. The length of tail is $1\frac{1}{4}$ *D*. A rivet is known by its roundness, length and shape of head.

The rivet heads are of the following shapes :

1. Snap head or cup head rivets
2. Pan head rivets
3. Conical head rivets
4. Counter sunk head rivets
5. Flat head rivets
6. Buffercated head rivets
7. Hollow head rivets.

Snap Head or Cup Head Rivets. Rivets with this kind of heads are used most of all. This type of rivets are shown in Fig. 12.50(A). Its head is of semi-circle in shape. Its diameter is 1.6*D* and its height is 0.7*D*. The joints of this rivet are very strong. That is why it is widely used in bridges made of iron material.

Pan Head Rivets. In heavy engineering pan head rivets are used. These have been shown in Fig. 12.50 (B). Height of its head is 0.7 *D* and its diameter is 1.6 *D*. The upper portion of rivet head is flat and taper. Small diameter of head is equal to the diameter of the rivet.

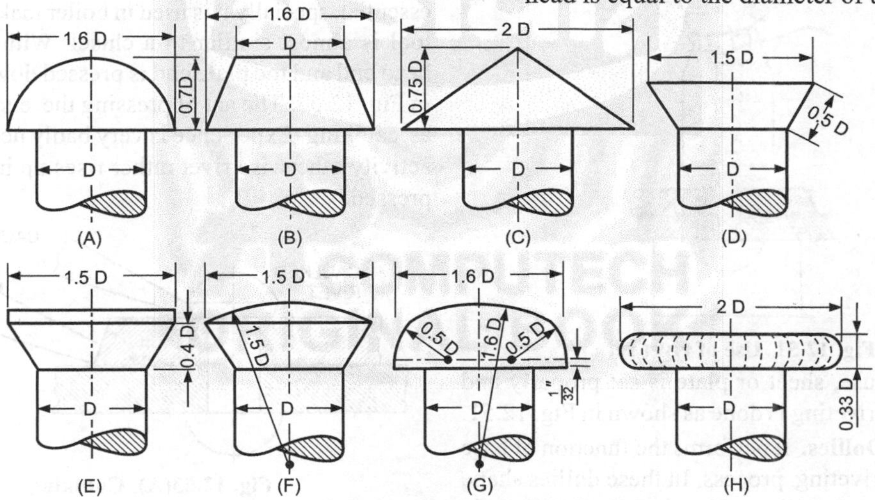

Fig. 12.50. Different kinds of rivet heads

Conical Head Rivets. This rivet is shown in Fig. 12.50(C). These rivets are used for light jobs. Conical shape is given to the head by a hammer. The diameter of its head is 0.75 *D* and height of its head is 2*D*.

Counter Sunk Head Rivets. At places where it is necessary to keep the surface plane even after fixing a rivet, this type of rivets are used. The diameter of its head is 1.5*D*, taper side is 0.5*D* and taper angle is 60°. These are of three kinds as shown in Fig. 12.50 (D, E, F).

Flat Head Rivets. For small and light jobs of sheet metal, flat head rivets are used. These are generally used in non ferrous metals and thin sheets. Its head is flat. The diameter of its head is 2*D* and height is 0.33*D*. This rivet is shown in Fig. 12.50 (H).

Buffercated Rivets. This type of rivets are different from other rivets. These are used for joining chain *etc.* in place of pins.

Hollow Rivets. Hollow rivets are used where a part of machine moves and it is also necessary to keep this part attached to the machine.

Method of Riveting. The act of putting rivet into the hole in a job made of plate or sheet and then making a head on its tail side is known as riveting. There are several methods of riveting, such as by striking hammer blows with hands. Under this method, head side is kept on a hard metal and tail is turned into head or made flat by striking hammer blows on it. Besides ordinary hammers, steam hammers, pneumatic hammer or hydraulic hammers are also used for this purpose. In the Fitter trade riveting is often done with the hand hammer. For riveting, following three types of tools are used :

1. Revet set, 2. Revet dollies, 3. Revet snap.

Rivet Set. It is a steel punch with a hollow or cupped face, used in the setting of rivets.

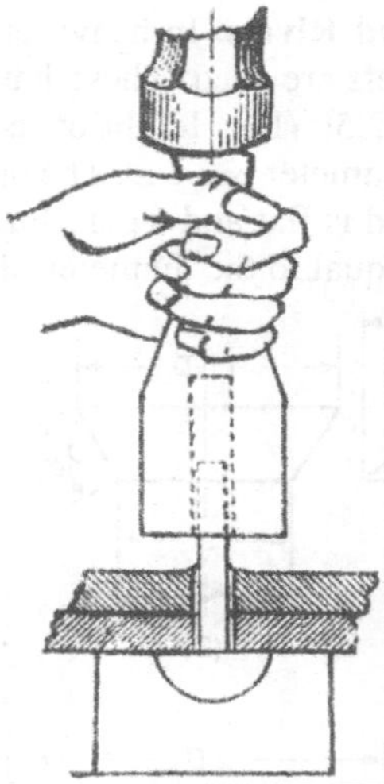

Fig. 12.51 Use of rivet set

By its use, sheet or plate is set properly and proper riveting is done as shown in Fig. 12.51.

Rivet Dollies. It performs the function of base in the riveting process. In these dollies shape is made according to its rivet head. It is held against heads of rivets while riveting. It saves rivet head from damage.

Rivet Snap. This tool is used to provide proper shape and finishing to the head made by hammer on the tail side of the rivet. Use of this tool is shown in Fig. 12.52.

In the riveting act, cold rivet of tail side is beaten to make its head. But rivet is fully heated or only tail is heated to make head. Fixing a cold rivet is called cold riveting. When it is fully heated it is called hot riveting. If only tail is heated, it is called partially hot riveting.

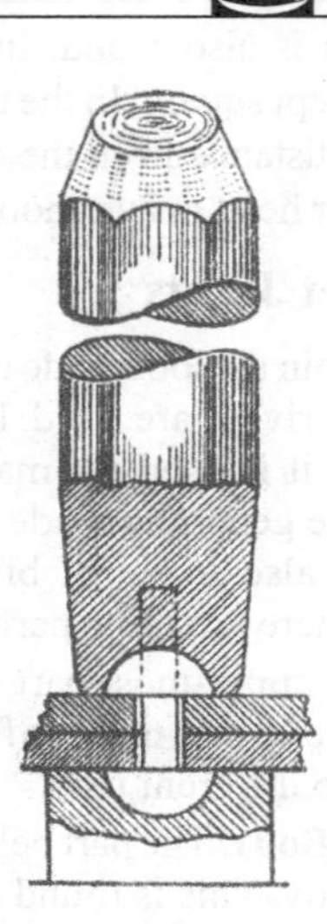

Fig. 12.52. Use of rivet snap

Caulking and Fullering

For the jobs which are required to be made, air-tight or water-tight, caulking and fullering tool is essential, specially it is used in boiler making *etc.* This tool is almost similar to a chisel. With it, the rivet head end and the plate end is pressed down as shown in Fig. 12.53. The act of pressing the ends is known as caulking. Experience is very badly needed for this activity otherwise rivet rather rises up instead being pressed.

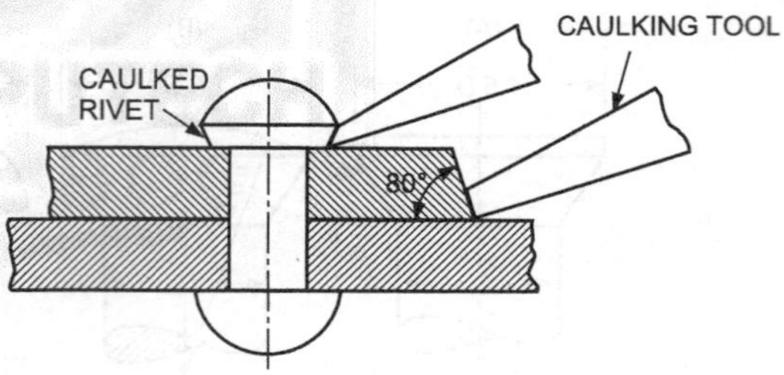

Fig. 12.53(A). Caulking

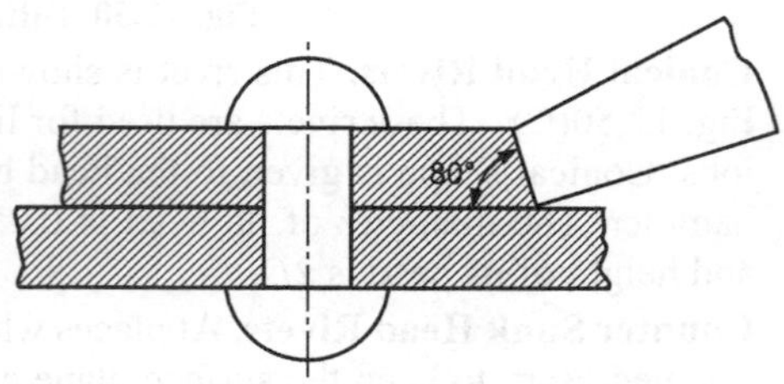

Fig. 12.53 (B) Fullering

Fullering is another activity like caulking. This activity is comparatively easy. Thickness of this tool is approximately the same as the thickness of the plate. In this activity the plate ends are already made at 80°

angle. After fullering the angle increases further. For doing the above two activities in the big workshops pneumatic or other type of power hammers are used.

Selection of Rivet

Right selection of rivet is essential for making the riveting process easy, strong and good. Riveting depends on the right selection of rivet. Selection of rivet depends on the sheet or plate to be riveted.

1. In order to find the thickness of rivet the following formula should be used :

   Formula —

   Diameter of Rivet = Thickness of plate × $1\frac{1}{2}$

2. If a rivet is to be made of an iron bar, we can know the length of the bar with the following formula :

   Formula —

   Number of plates × thickness of plates + 3.5 diameter

3. For finding out the length of the rivet the following formula should be used :

   Formula —

   No. of plates × thickness of plates

4. Size of the hole for a rivet is found out by using the following formula :

   Formula —

   Diameter of the Rivet × Diameter × $\frac{1}{16}$.

Various Rivet Joints

The joints made by rivets are called rivet joints. These rivet joints are of two types based on the distance and direction of joint :

1. Lap joint
2. Butt joint

1. Lap Joint. In this type of joints, two sheets of metal are joined by keeping them one over the other. Under this type of joint, three different ways of riveting can be done.

(i) **Single Riveted Lap Joint.** Under this arrangement the entire rivets are fixed in one line. It has been shown in Fig. 12.54. How much should the plate be in width over one another ? For this it should be ensured that this size should be three times more than the diameter of the rivet.

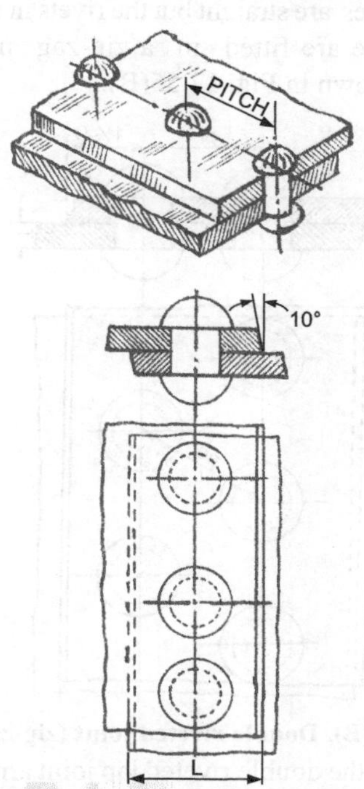

Fig. 12.54. Single riveted lap joint

(ii) **Double Riveted Lap Joint (Chain Type).** Under this arrangement instead of one line, rivets are fixed in two lines as shown in Fig. 12.55(A). If the length of the job is more, three lines can also be made. This arrangement is known as chain type double riveted joint.

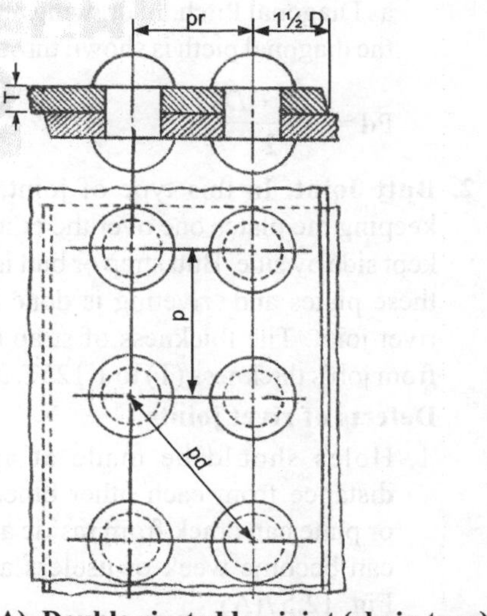

Fig. 12.55(A). Double riveted lap joint (chain type)

(iii) **Double Riveted Joint (Zig-zag Type).** When there is need for fixing rivets in two or more lines then this arrangement is resorted to. In this arrangement all rivet

lines are straight but the rivets in the parallel line are fitted in a zig-zag manner as shown in Fig. 12.55(B).

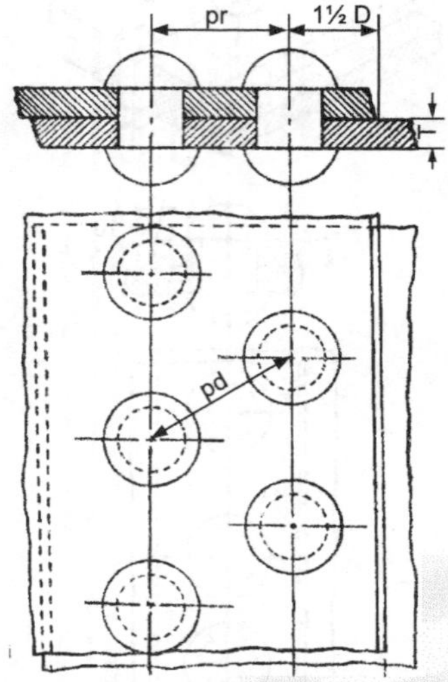

Fig. 12.55(B). Double riveted joint (zig-zag type)

In the double riveted lap joint arrangement, the central distance between one row and the other is known as Row Pitch, which is indicated in the drawing or blue print as Pr.

In the chain arrangement, $Pr = 2D + \frac{1}{4}''$ and in the zig-zag arrangement the distance from the centre of rivet of one row to the centre of rivet in the second row is known as Diagonal Pitch. In drawing and blue print the diagonal picth is shown through Pd. This

$$Pd = \frac{2P + D}{2}.$$

2. **Butt Joint.** In this type of joint, instead of keeping the plates one over the other, these are kept side by side. Butt strap or butt is kept under these plates and riveting is done like double rivet joint. The thickness of strap (T_1) is kept from job's thickness (T) to 1.125T. (Fig. 12.56).

Defects of rivet joints

1. Holes should be made at appropriate distance from each other otherwise sheet or plate can crack from inside and the joint can become week or useless as shown in Fig. 12.57(A).
2. Hole should not be made at the brink of the sheet otherwise at the time of riveting the plate can torn from the end as shown in Fig. 12.57(B).

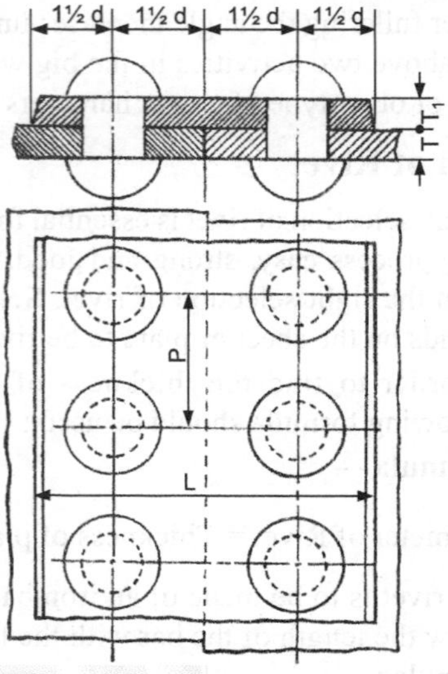

Fig. 12.56 Butt Joint

3. Thickness of the rivet should be according to the holes made in the job. If the rivets are loose in the holes, the joint in the job would also be loose and there are chances that rivet would be cut. This has been shown in Fig. 12.57(C).
4. The thickness of rivet should not be more than the hole otherwise rivet would damage the surface and the joint would become loose as shown Fig. 12. 57(D).

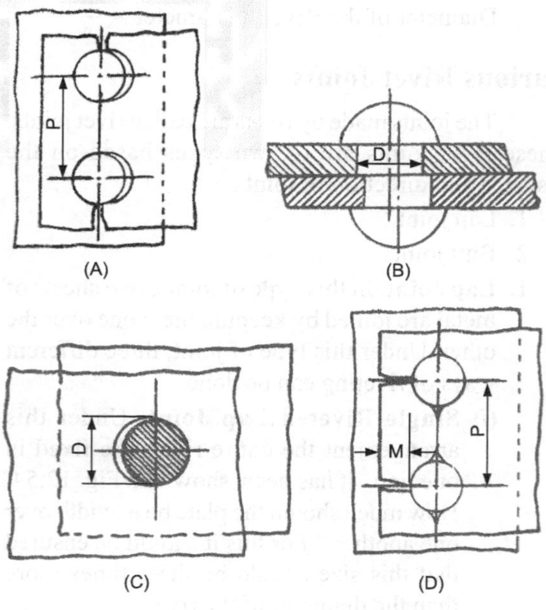

Fig. 12.57. Defects in rivet joints

Method of Riveting and Precautions :

1. Clean the plates which are to be riveted.
2. Mark the point with a centre punch where a rivet hole is to be made.
3. While making holes, plate or sheet should be held properly so that the holes are straight.
4. The holes should be according to the thickness of the rivets.
5. After making holes their mouths should be properly cleaned.
6. In order to save the dented sheets from rusting, we should apply red oxide on it.
7. For convenience holes should be made one by one and bolts should be tightened in them and then bolts should be opened one by one and then riveting should be done.
8. First we should make a head of the tail side with a hammer and then finishing should be done with a snap.
9. Rivets of thickness above $\frac{3}{8}''$ should be heated before fitting them.
10. The length of the rivet should be according to the formula.

Questions

1. What is the use of Fasteners in engineering line ?
2. How many types of Fasteners are there ?
3. Draw a figure of Bolt and Nut and explain its parts.
4. Explain a Foundation Bolt with examples.
5. Write in brief the different types of Nuts.
6. Explain the main methods of Nut-lock, giving suitable examples.
7. Write brief comments on Screw and Washer.
8. What is meant by "Key" and "Keyway" ?
9. How many kinds of "Key" is used ?
10. Why Knuckle Joint is used ?
11. Where Studs are used ?
12. How many types of Rivet Joints are there ?
13. Draw figures of main Rivet Heads.
14. Write about the main tools used for riveting.
15. What are the causes of defects in Rivet Joints ? Explain.

13

Jigs and Fixtures

There has been tremendous progress in the field of engineering in the present age. Machines of different types, useful for different purposes, have been invented. Large scale production of different parts of these machines is being undertaken. It is essential to have interchangeability of these parts in the machines. In the old days, each part of a machine was made by hands, one after another. But that used to take a lot of time. It would not be an exaggeration to say that the development of engineering was very slow. Now-a-days a large variety of machines are available to increase production and various kinds of resources, ways and means are also applied for this purpose. With the help of these sources, it is possible to increase production by using interchangeable parts. In using these parts, however it is not essential that we need only highly experienced technicians. Even semi-skilled or apprentices can also give higher production, with the use of these sources and ways. These sources and combinations have been given the name of Jigs, Fixtures and Templates. For mass production different types of gauges are used but gauges can only check the accuracy of the jobs. We cannot inspect the holes, grooves and related jobs with the gauges. For example, if there are two holes of two inch diameter and their distance from each other is one inch, we can check the diameter of holes easily with the help of gauges but in order to check their distance we will have to apply some other source. The following are the uses of jigs, fixtures and templates :

1. Through their use the production increases and we need not do marking on the job or measure it.
2. After setting the job once we can do a number of operations.
3. Semi-skilled or less experienced technicians can also increase production.
4. Jobs acquire the property of interchangeability.
5. Jobs produced with their help can be easily assembled.
6. Cost of production is less.

Difference between Jigs and Fixtures

Jig	***Fixture***
1. Jig is such a source which holds the job strongly and also guides the tool.	Fixture is a source which can only hold the job strongly.
2. It eliminates the need for marking on the job.	Marking on the job has to be done while using fixture.
3. Jigs are used for drilling, reaming and tapping *etc.*	It is used for turning, milling and shaping *etc.*
4. These are light in weight. These can be used either by fastening them with the table or holding then in hand.	Their weight is comparatively more. It is essential to tie them to the table.
5. Even an ordinary technician can use them.	Some experience is needed for using them.

Jigs

Jigs are used for drilling, reaming, tapping *etc*. These are of the following types, according to their function :

1. Plate Jig
2. Angle Jig
3. Channel Jig
4. Box Jig
5. Diameter Jig
6. Ring Jig
7. Leaf Jig
8. Vice Jig
9. Indexing Jig
10. Jig Bushing

Plate Jig. For boring in a job made of plate, plate jig is used. This jig is made of plate and its shape is according to the job. Hard bushes are used with this jig. This jig guides the cutting tool.

Angle Jig. Its shape is like angle plate. This jig is tied to the machine from one side. On the other side of the plate, there is another plate in which right type of bush drills are fixed as shown in Fig. 13.1. Job is fixed in such a manner that the place where hole is to be made, the drill bush goes under the plate. This type of jig is used for drilling of cone, pulley *etc*.

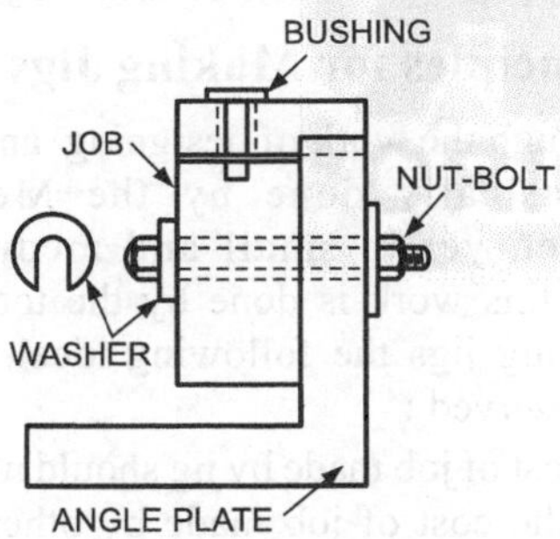

Fig. 13.1. Angle jig

Channel Jig. This jig is made of channel section. Ordinary bushing and means of fastening *etc*. are used. Only rectangular jobs are held and drilled (Fig. 13.2).

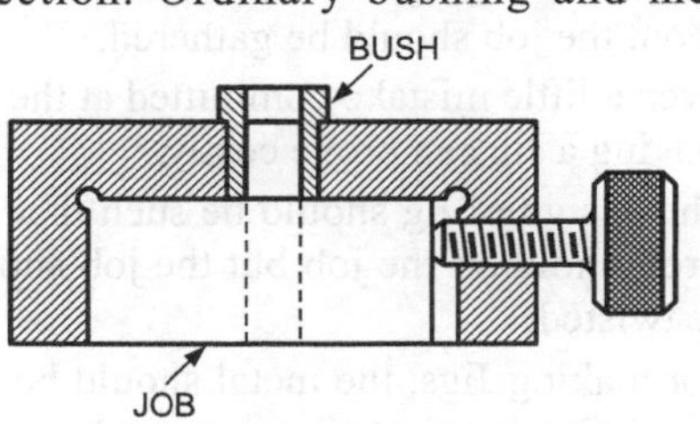

Fig. 13.2. Channel Jig

Box Jig. The shape of this type of jig is like a box. Job is closed in this box and it sticks to its place.

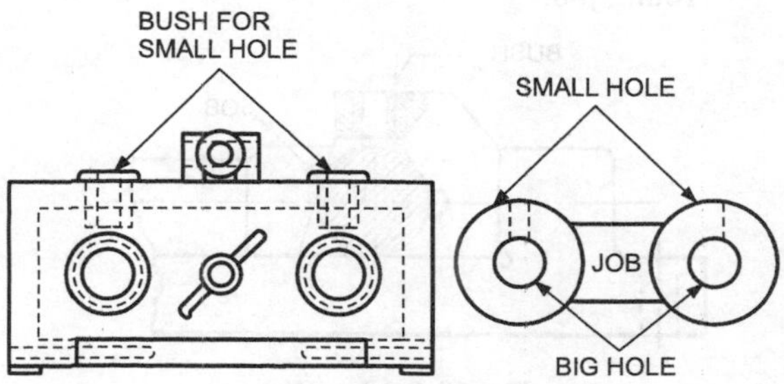

Fig. 13.3. Box jig

This jig is used for such jobs where bores are to be drilled at different places.

Diameter Jig. This type of jig has been illustrated in Fig. 13.4. It is used for drilling in cylindrical jobs.

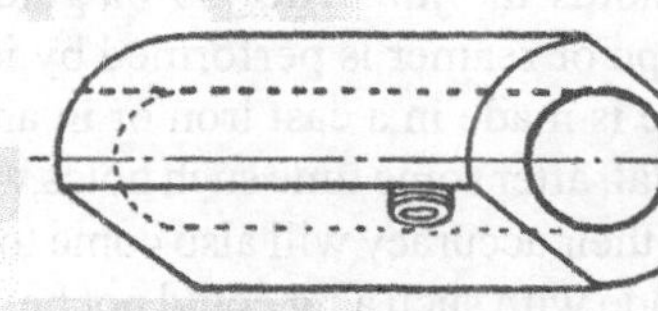

Fig. 13.4. Diameter jig

Ring Jig. This type of jig is used for drilling in cylindrical flange or pipes. This type of jig is shown in Fig. 13.5.

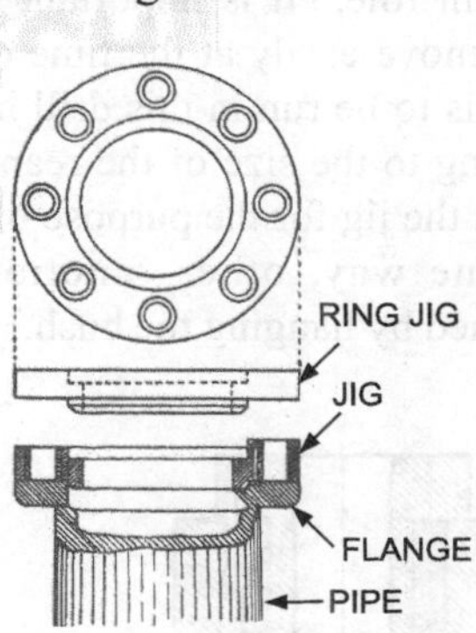

Fig. 13.5. Ring jig

Leaf Jig. This jig is considered to be the best one for drilling in different jobs. There is a hinged lid in this jig. This lid is used for keeping or taking out the job. Bushes are fixed in this lid itself. When it is used after closing the lid, the bushing fixed in it guides the cutting tool. One major fault in this type of jig is that there is no provision for outlet of small metal chips, As a result, the hinges of the lid become defective or become loose easily and there is a possibility of drilling being done at a wrong place.

Vice Jig. This type of jig has been shown in Fig. 13.6. It is used mainly to hold and drill a round job.

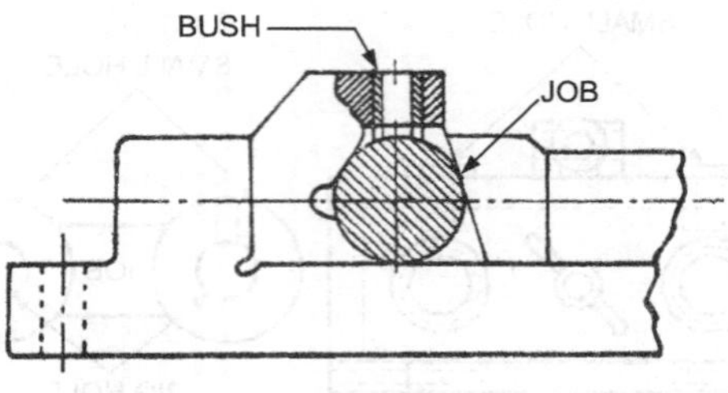

Fig. 13.6. Vice Jig

Indexing Jig. This type of jigs are used where a number of holes of the same size are to be made in a job. This jig holds the job as well as guides the cutting tools.

Jig Bushing. In fact jig is simply a device which holds the job. The job of guiding the drill, tape or reamer is performed by its bush. If a hole is made in a cast iron or in any other soft metal, after some time such holes will wear out and their accuracy will also come to an end. Jobs made with such a jig could not be perfect. Therefore hardened steel bushing is inserted in the face of a jig to serve as a guide for drills. In these bushes tool clearance plays an important role. It is important that the drill should move easily at the time of drilling. If reamer is to be run in this drill hole, bushing according to the size of the reamer has to be fitted in the jig for the purpose of reaming. In the same way, other functions are also performed by hanging the bush.

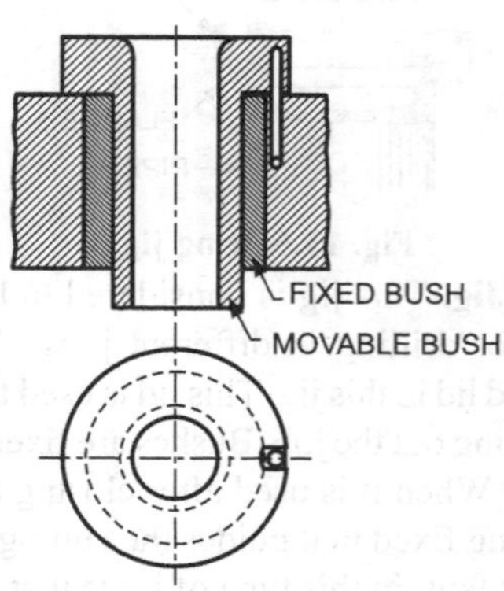

Fig. 13.7. Fixed bush

Jig bushes are made of the following kinds :

1. Fixed Bush, 2. Slip Bush, 3. Movable Slip Bush.

Fixed Bush. Fixed Bush has been shown in Fig. 13.7 above. When both the Jig and bush are of the same strength, then fixed bush is filled in the Jig. This bush is fitted in the plate holes by pressing it.

Slip Bush. This type of bush is shown in Fig. 13.8. This bush is fitted in the Jig hole with a pin or screw. This bush can be changed when it wears out.

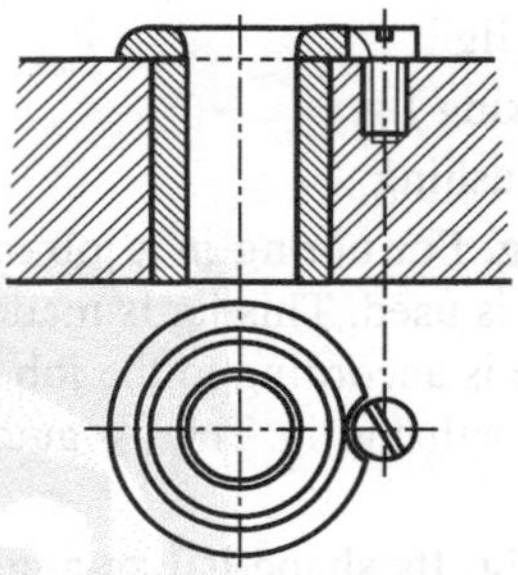

Fig. 13.8. Slip bush

Movable Slip Bush. This type of bush is used where a number of operations such a drilling, reaming and tapping are to be performed. In this bush, a slip bush is also fixed inside the fixed bush. This bush is changed according to the cutting tool. With it a number of operations can be performed after setting the job once.

Ideal Principles for Making Jigs

Although the work of designing and drawing work is basically done by the Mechanical Draughtsmen yet in small and medium class workshops this work is done by the tool makers. While making jigs the following ideal principles should be observed :

1. The cost of job made by jig should not be more than the cost of job made by other tools. In other words, if the cost of making jig is high, it is better to use ordinary tools.
2. While making jigs all the relevant information about the job should be gathered.
3. Even a little mistake committed at the time of making a Jig can prove costly.
4. The design of jig should be such that it has a strong hold on the job but the job should not be twisted.
5. For making Jigs, the metal should be light in weight but have adequate strength also.

6. Important parts of the job should be easily visible to the technicians while fitting in the jig.
7. The design of the Jig should provide appropriate outlet for the small chips.
8. There should be proper provision for withstanding the shocks given by the cutting tools when they are in operation.
9. The structure of the jig should be simple so that even ordinary technicians can use it.
10. There should be adequate provision for supplying coolants or lubricants to the cutting tools.

Fixture

It is a general term used for devices used to tie a job to the table. Their design depends on the design of the job and the machine to be used. These can be of several types. Some fixtures are made in round or flat shapes. These can be fitted in ordinary vice and jobs can be held or tied accordingly. In addition, angle plate, parallel stepped blocks, stepped "V" block and "T" bolt *etc.* are also used as fixtures. In Fig. 13.9 some samples of fixtures have been shown.

As already mentioned, fixtures are used on different machines for holding jobs. Therefore, fixtures are manufactured according to the design of the machine and the shape of the jobs. These fixtures are named after these machines, such as grinding fixture, milling fixture, slotter fixture, plainer fixture *etc.* The fixture should be designed in such a way that it should be able to hold the jobs strongly and after once fitting the job a number of operations can be performed.

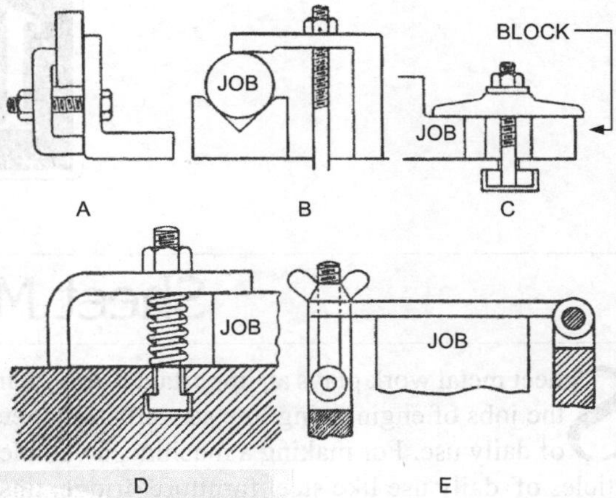

Fig. 13.9. Fixture

Template

By means of template at a time a number of similar jobs can be used for marking. As jig is used for performing several operations on similar jobs, in the same way by means of template for mass production quick marking can be done. These are made with thin metal sheets according to their drawings. In other words we can say that it is a plate by which work is either marked out, or a by which its accuracy is checked.

Questions

1. What is the use of Jigs and Fixtures ?
2. What is the difference between Jigs and Fixtures ?
3. What kinds of Jigs are available ?
4. What are the important points to be borne in mind while designing Jigs and Fixtures ?
5. What is meant by Jig bushing ?
6. Name the different kinds of Jig-bushing.
7. What is a Fixture ?
8. Why Templates are used ?

14

Sheet Metal Work

Sheet metal work plays an important role both in the jobs of engineering line as well as gadgets of daily use. For making a machine, a vehicle, articles of daily use like steel furniture, fridge, tins, boxes *etc*. sheet metal is used. Those who make such articles of sheet metal are called sheet metal workers. In the absence of an efficient sheet metal worker an engineering workshop remains incomplete. A sheet metal worker uses sheets made of different metals for making different articles. Main tools and instruments used by a sheet metal worker are as under :

These can be broadly divided into three categories :

1. Sheet metal hand tools
2. Sheet metal bench tools
3. Sheet metal machine tools

Sheet Metal Hand Tools. Sheet metal worker does most of his job with the help of hand tools. These hand tools are :

1. Sheet metal hammer
2. Scriber
3. Rule
4. Divider
5. Trammel
6. Steel square
7. Chisel
8. Punch
9. Pliers
10. File
11. Snip
12. Shears

Sheet metal hammers. Different kinds of hammers are used in different sheet metal processes, according to the needs of the jobs. Their names are according to their shape and its use. Following kinds of sheet metal hammers are used :

1. **Hollowing Hammer.** This type of hammers are used for beating the heavy and thick metal sheets. In appearance these hammers look like Ballpan hammer but they have round balls on both the phases, as shown in Fig. 14.1(A).
2. **Cross Pan Hammer.** Details about cross pan hammer are given in the chapter on Dismentalling, Assembling and other Tools.
3. **Planishing Hammer.** Planishing hammer's both phases are flat. These hammers are used for providing finish to sheets and jobs made from sheets. This hammer is shown in the Fig. 14.1(B).

(A) Hollowing hammer

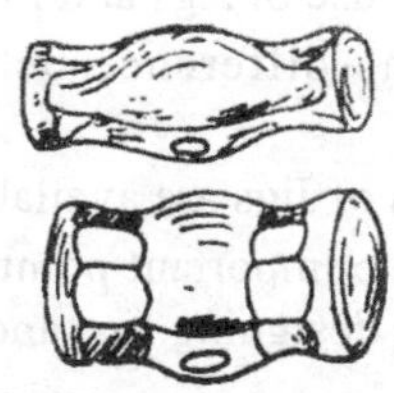

(B) Planishing hammer

(C) Bullet head hammer

(D) Scrubing hammer

Fig. 14.1.

4. **Bullet Head or Bullet Face Hammer.** This type of hammer is shown in Fig. 14.1 (C). These hammers are used to make the jobs made of light sheets hollow.

5. **Scrubing Hammer.** This hammer has been shown in Fig. 14.1(D). Its pan is flat from one end and of cross shape at the other end. It is used for riveting and making slots.
6. **Riveting Hammer.** This hammer is of a special shape. This is shown in Fig. 14.2(A) below. This hammer is used for rivet-joint jobs in sheet metal work.

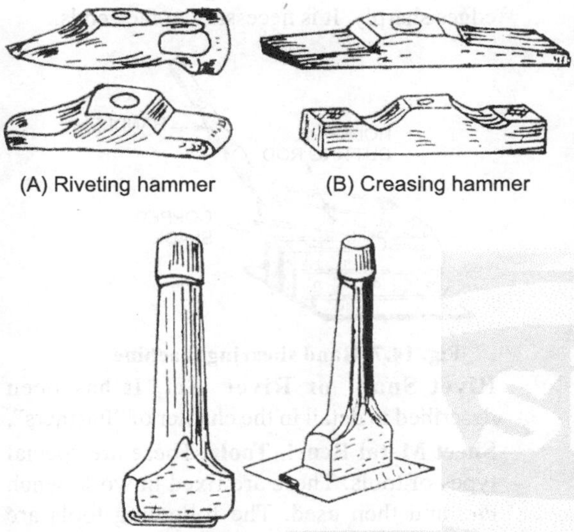

(A) Riveting hammer (B) Creasing hammer

(C) Panning hammer

Fig. 14.2.

7. **Creasing Hammer.** This type of hammer has been shown in Fig. 14.2(B) above. It is used for preparing wire edge for making groove in sheet metal jobs.
8. **Panning Hammer.** These are also known as blacking hammers. With the help of panning hammers sheet metal joints are strengthened. This has been shown in Fig. 14.2(C).
9. **Mallet.** These are generally similar to the hammers made of wood. These are used for making metal sheets plainer to turn or bend them.

   Mallet does not make dents on metal sheets. This has been shown in Fig. 14.3.

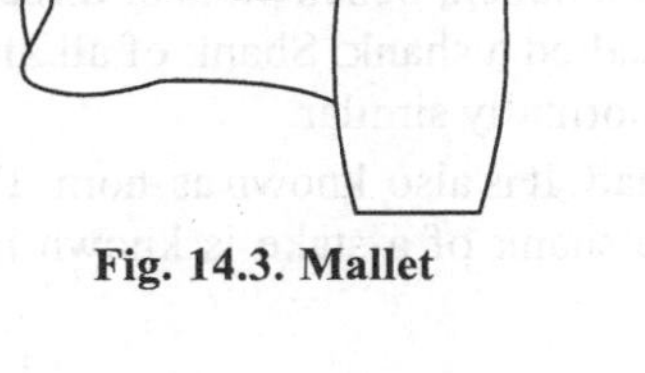

Fig. 14.3. Mallet

Scriber. This tool is used for marking in sheet metal jobs.

Rule. In sheet metal jobs a number of rules are used for measuring purposes. These have been discussed in detail in the chapter on measuring tools.

Divider. Divider is used in sheet metal jobs for circle marking. With the divider we can also do marking the parts of a job.

Trammel. This is also a marking tool which has been discussed in the chapter on "Marking Tools'"

Steel Square. For right angle marking in sheet metal jobs steel square is used. In addition, this is also used for checking the right angle of the jobs.

Chisel. Several types of chisels are used for cutting metal sheets in different ways. These have been discussed in details in chapter on "Cutting Tools'.

Punch. Punch is used in sheet metal jobs for punching or deep marking. Their detailed description is given in the chapter on "Marking Tools".

Pliers. Pliers are used for holding or cutting small jobs or wires *etc*. These have been described in detail in the chapter on "Dismentling, Assembling and other Tools".

File. Several types of files are used for smoothing metal sheets. We can read about them in detail in the chapter on "Cutting Tools".

Snip. This tool used for cutting thin metal sheets before or after marking, according to the jobs, is called Snip. It is like scissors used by tailors. It is made of steel and its cutting blades are hardened and tampered. Their edge is grinded at 80° angle. According to their use, these are of the following two types :

1. Straight Snip
2. Bent Snip

Straight Snip. Its blades are quite straight as shown in Fig. 14.4.

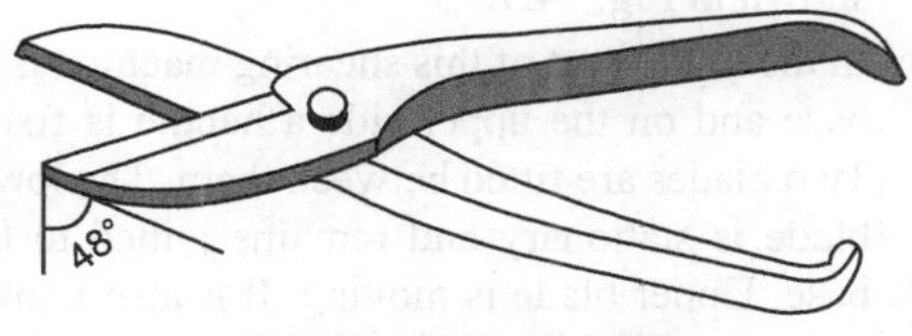

Fig. 14.4. Straight snip

This type of snip is widely used in sheet metal jobs. We can cut a sheet in a straight line or for outside roundness of jobs.

Bent Snip. According to its name, the blades of this type of snip are bent as shown in Fig. 14.5. With this snip we can cut inside and outside roundness of job with small roundness.

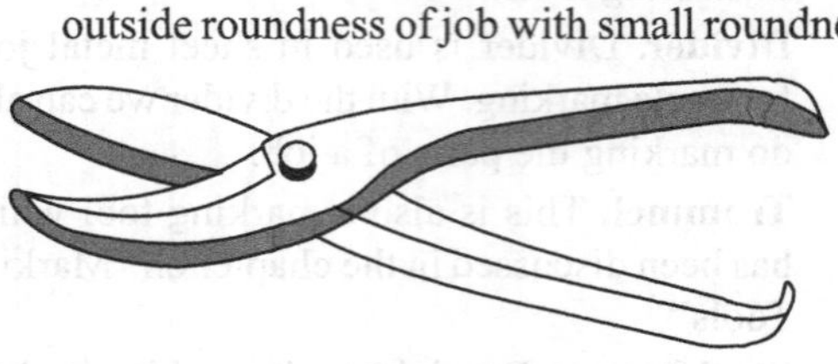

Fig. 14.5. Bent snip

Shears. This is also used like snip for cutting metal sheets but it is used to cut thick sheets as compared to snip. This is of two types :

1. **Stock Shear.** This type of shear has been shown in Fig. 14.6. This is almost like a straight snip but is larger than that. Its cutting blades are straight.

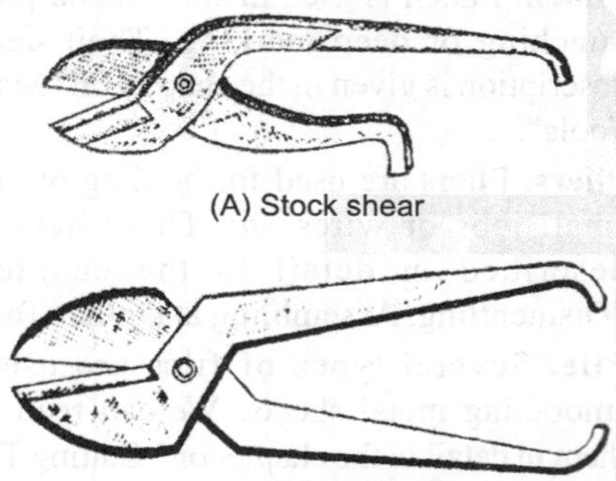

Fig. 14.6.

2. **Block Shear.** This type of shear has been illustrated in Fig. 14.6(B). One of its legs is like a stock shear but the other one is slightly short and is bent at 90° angle at its end. The small handle or leg is fitted into vice or any other means and the other leg is pressed with hand to cut the sheet.

Hand Shearing Machine. This type of shear is fixed on the work bench with a bolt. It is shown in Fig. 14.7.

In the lower part of this shearing machine is its base and on the upper side a handle is fixed. Two blades are fitted between them. The lower blade is stationary and remains joined to the base. Upper blade is moving. It is also known as cropper. With this hand shearing machine iron sheets of $\frac{1}{4}''$ thickness and $\frac{3}{8}''$ thick rods can be cut. For cutting rods a hole is made on the upper side. The size of the machine is known according to the length of its blade. Generally, these blades are 8 foot long. Length of handle depends upon the length of the blades. This machine is helpful in doing the job quickly, clearly and in less time. But it does not cut the edges sharply. It is necessary to face ends.

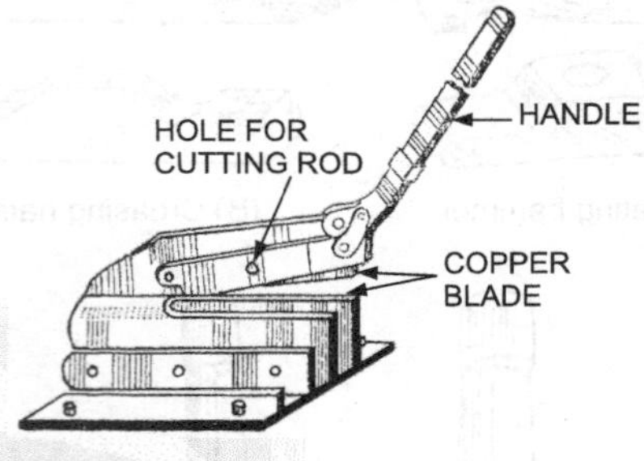

Fig. 14.7. Hand shearing machine

Rivet Snap or Rivet Set. It has been described in detail in the chapter of "Fastners".

Sheet Metal Bench Tools. These are special types of tools. These are fixed in work bench *etc.* and then used. The following tools are included among the tools :

1. Vice
2. Stakes
3. Groover
4. Bench plate

Vice. Vice is used in sheet metal works for holding sheets or jobs. Normally, parallel jaw vice is used in sheet metal works. This has been discussed in detail in the chapter "Fastners".

Stakes. In different kind of jobs along with hand tools some special anvils are also used for sheet bending, grooving, reveting and hollowing *etc.* These anvils are called stakes. Stake is a very important bench tool in sheet metal trade. A sheet metal worker does most of his work with the stake. Stakes are of several kinds but mainly they are of the following three types :

Shank. That part of a stake which is fixed into work bench, bench plate or direct into ground is called a shank. Shank of all kinds of stakes is normally similar.

Head. It is also known as horn. The part above the shank of a stake is known head or horn.

The job is placed over them and operation is carried out. According to their heads or horns, stakes are of the following types :

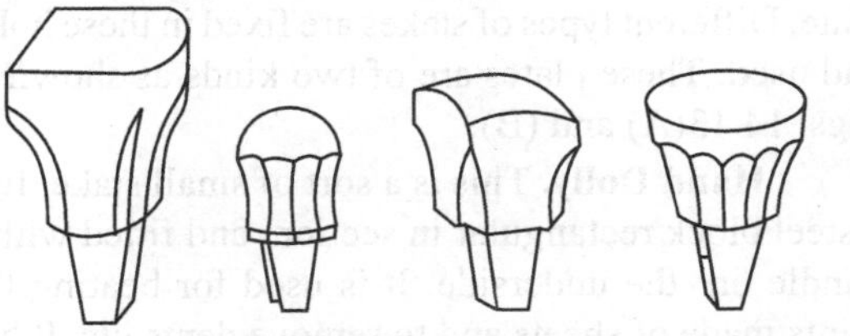

Fig. 14.8.

These all are included in the anvil type stake category. These have been shown in Figs. 14.8 (A), (B), (C) and (D). These are used to give shape according to their head to sheet.

Hatchet Stake. It is used for bending the sheets at any angle. It has been shown in Fig. 14.9 (A).

Funnel Stake. This stake is highly used. With its help sheet can be given the shape of a funnel. This has been illustrated in Fig. 14.9(B).

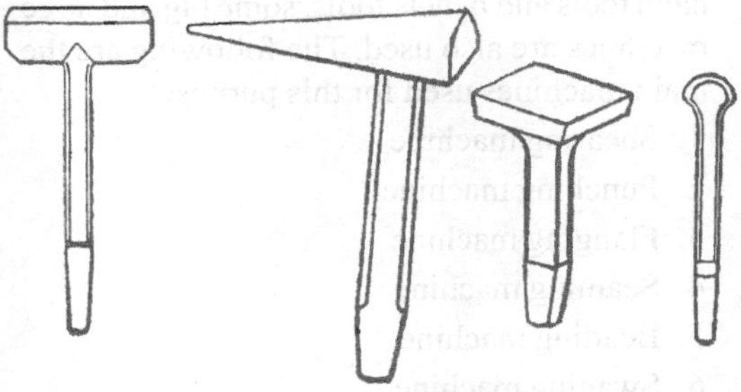

Fig. 14.9.

Square Stake. It has been shown in Fig. 14.9(C). With it we can bend the sheet at 90° angle.

Halfmoon Stake. In shape it looks like halfmoon. It is used for bending the sheet in semi-circle shape.

Pipe Stake. It has a horn on one side, which is in semi-circular shape from the top. It is used for making jobs like pipes *etc.* It has been shown in Fig. 14.10 (A).

Side Stake. For preparing different types of sides of jobs, this type of stake is used. Ends prepared with it are clear. This is shown in Fig. 14.10(B).

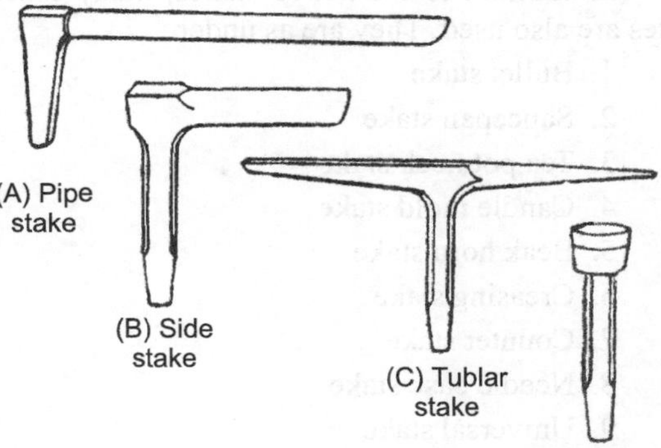

Fig. 14.10.

Tubler Stake. In this type of stake, horn is thin and lengthy. Jobs of round tubes are prepared with this stake. It has been shown in Fig. 14.10(C).

Bottom Stake. In this type of stake horn is somewhat bevel. It is used for making bottoms. We can also define it as an upright bar with the working edge at the upper end. It has been shown in Fig. 14.10(D).

Horse Stake. In this type of stakes square holes are made in the horn on one side or both the sides. Other type of tools are fitted in these holes and different operations are performed. It has been shown in Fig. 14.11(A).

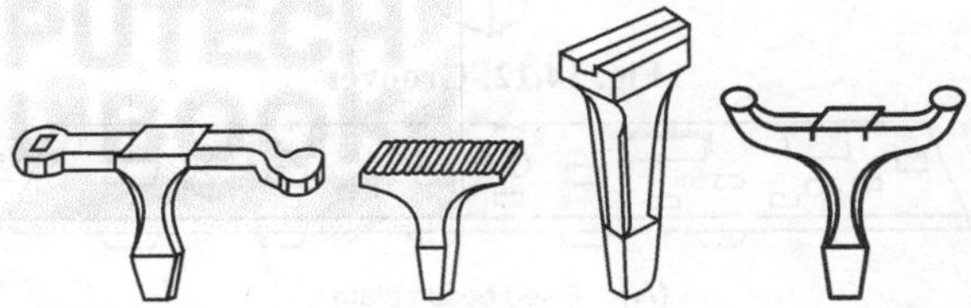

Fig. 4.11.

Grooving Stake. Different types of slots are cut over the horn in this type of stakes. It is used for cutting slots for swaging. It has been shown in Fig. 14.11(B).

Tea Kettle Stake. Its shape is like the bottom of a tea kettle. It is shown in Fig. 14.11(C).

Double Seam Stake. This stake has a long and a flat horn. It is used for seam joint or seaming works in long jobs. We can see it in Fig. 14.11(D).

In addition to the above stakes, many other stakes are also used. They are as under :

1. Bullet stake
2. Saucepan stake
3. Tea pot neck stake
4. Candle mold stake
5. Beak horn stake
6. Creasing stake
7. Counter stake
8. Needle case stake
9. Universal stake
10. Blow horn stake

Groover. This is a very useful tool. It is made of carbon steel and is then hardened and tampered. These are of different sizes. These are used for locked joints in sheet metal works making wire edges and slots. This is shown in Fig. 14.12.

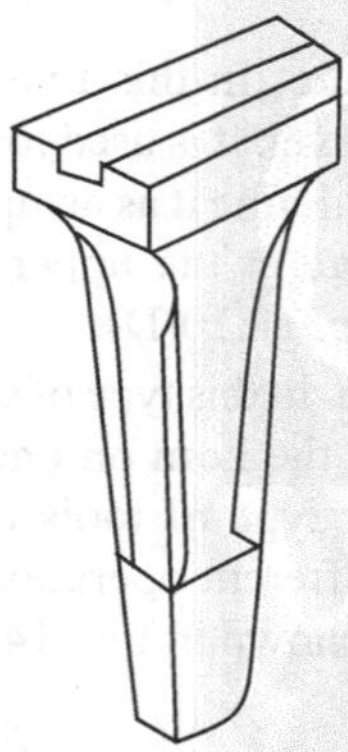

Fig. 14.12. Groover

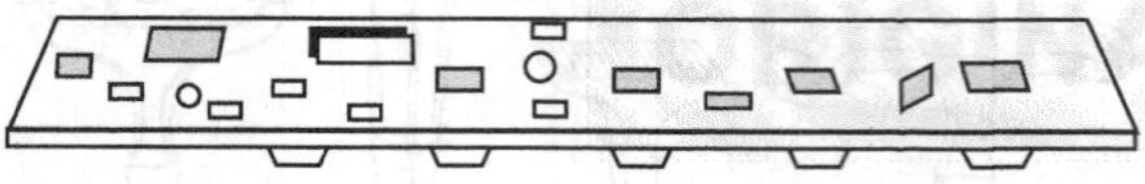

(A) Fixed bench plate

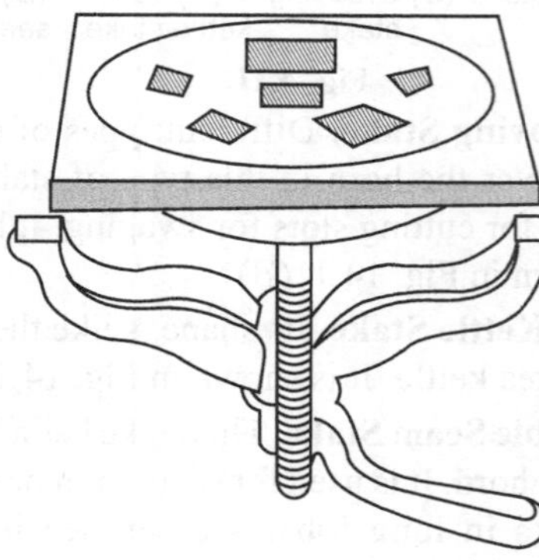

(B) Revolving bench plate

Fig. 14.13.

Bench Plate. This is a special type of plate made of carbcn steel. Different types of holes, round, square, in different shapes and sizes are made in this plate. Different types of stakes are fixed in these holes and used. These plates are of two kinds as shown in Figs. 14.13(A) and (B).

Hand Dolly. This is a sort of small stake. It is a steel block rectangular in section, and fitted with a handle on the underside. It is used for beating the joints made of sheets and to remove dents *etc*. It has been shown in Fig. 14.14.

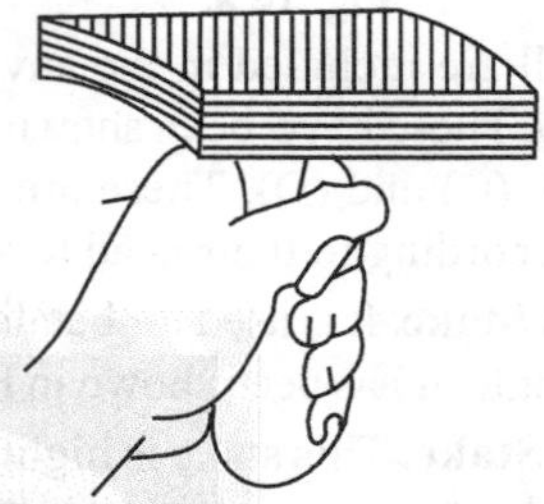

Fig. 14.14. Hand dolly

Machine Tools. In sheet metal works besides hand tools and bench tools, some big and large machines are also used. The following are the main machines used for this purpose:

1. Shearing machine
2. Punching machine
3. Flanging machine
4. Seaming machine
5. Beading machine
6. Swaging machine
7. Power press
8. Rivetting machine
9. Spinning machine
10. Engraving machine
11. Notching machine
12. Blanks and dyes.

Sheet Metal Operations

In order to make a job through sheet metal, the following operations are performed :

1. **Marking.** Before making a job, lines and points are drawn on the sheet according to the drawing so that the sheet is cut as per the required size. These 1ines and points are known as marking. Accuracy of the job depends to a large extent on the marking operation.
2. **Cutting.** After marking on the sheets they are cut according to the drawing with the help of

proper cutting tools. This act is known as cutting.

3. **Grooving.** In order to join the sheet metal jobs their ends are grooved with the help of grooving tools. This act is called grooving.
4. **Swaging.** In order to provide strength to the sheet metal jobs, slots are cut in them. By doing so, elasticity almost ends in these jobs. This operation is essential particularly for the thin sheets. Alongwith strength swaging provides beauty to the jobs as well.
5. **Hollowing.** The act of hollowing a sheet metal for making a sheet metal job is called hollowing.
6. **Wiring.** In order to provide strength to edge of sheet metal jobs its edges are turned and a wire is placed in the groove so prepared. This act is known as wiring. It also adds to the beauty of the job.

   Besides this, in sheet metal jobs, shearing, backing, piercing, punching, blanking and seaming *etc.* is done with the help of machines.
7. **Shearing.** Cutting sheet metal into pieces with machines or by hands is called shearing.
8. **Blanking.** Cutting a sheet according to the job from a flat sheet is called blanking. This work is done by snip or a die.
9. **Piercing.** To make a round, square or any other kind of hole in a sheet, with the help of a machine is called piercing.
10. **Punching.** The making of a hole through sheets by means of a punching machine is called punching.
11. **Seaming.** A sheet-metal joint in which the edge of piece is folded or turned over the edge of another is called seaming operation.
12. **Notching.** For cutting the corners of square pans, *etc.* of blanks of pieced sheet-metal work, notching is done by means of dies.

Sheet Metal Joint

For joining the sheet metal job, several types of joints are used. Among these, the following are prominent ones :

1. **Butt Joint.** This kind of joint is often used for thick sheets. Two pieces of metal sheets are stuck together. Later coating is done through brazing. Brazing is done on one or both sides. Soldering of this joint should be done on thin sheets only because it is not very strong.
2. **Lap Joint.** This type of joint can be used for all kinds of sheets. Two pieces of sheets are overlapped according to their thickness and size of the job. Afterwards, on both the edges soldering or brazing is done. These joints are stronger than the butt joints. Major fault of this type of joint is that its thickness is greater.
3. **Sunk Lap Joint.** This type of joint is almost similar to lap joint. But in this joint the edges of sheet which are to be lapped are tappered either by beating them or by rubbing. Its main advantage is that the thickness of this joint remains almost at the job's level.
4. **Grooved Joint.** This type of joints are widely used. Their strength is very reliable. The joining edges of the sheet are bent in the form of hooks. After bending them they are fixed into each other and pressed by hitting them with a hammer. Soldering or brazing is not needed in this type of joints. But if we want to make this joint water leak proof then soldering is necessary.
5. **Pan Down Joint.** This type of joint is generally used for making bottoms of round jobs made of thin sheets. The end at the long part is turned in "J" form. This joint is soldered too.
6. **Cramped Joint.** This type of joints are made for round or cylindrical jobs.These are used especially for brass, copper *etc.* non-ferrous metals. In this joint grooves are cut at both the ends of the job and these grooves are intermingled like a corn and soldering or brazing is done afterward. This joint is very clear. It can only be made on thick sheets conveniently.
7. **Locked Joint.** This type of joint is used for cylinderical jobs such as pipes and drums. Hooks are made at both ends of the jobs. These hooks are then joined together and are pressed down with the hammer.
8. **Rivet joint.** In this type of joint, both the ends of the job are placed like lap joint and then joined with a revet. This joint is used for strong joints, this has been discussed in detail in the chapter "Fastners".

Soldering and Brazing

When we join pieces of metal under proper heat, it is known as soldering. In order to make the jobs especially of thin sheets, water-proof, the soldering is done. In this process, for soldering generally soft alloy metals are used. This is called solder. It is usually an alloy of equal parts of lead and tin. By changing the ratio of these metals solder is made for different metals. Solder has been divided into two parts :

1. **Soft Solder.** This solder is used for the light jobs or those jobs which do not get much load or shocks. In this solder the metals are mixed in the following proportion :

Name of Solder	*Lead*	*Tin*	*Melting*	*Flux*	*Remarks*
Tin main solder (coarse)	50%	50%	205°C	Zinc chloride	
Tin main solder (fine)	40%	60%	192°C	Zinc or Ammonium chloride	
Plumber solder	66%	34%	240°C	Zinc chloride	
Electrician solder	5%	95%	220°C	Zinc chloride or rasin	
Copper or brass solder	66%	34%	225°C	Ammonium chloride	
Gun-metal solder	63%	37%	220°C	Rasin	

2. **Hard Solder.** Jobs pined with soft sole are often weak. For strong joints hard sole is used. Copper + zinc, zinc + copper + 4 to 8% silver or 66% tin and 34% antimony are mixed for hard solder. Melting point of hard solder is 350°C to 600°C.

Flux

In order to prevent deposit of layer of oxide at the soldering point, flux is used. It not only helps in protection from oxidation but also in melting the sole quickly as well as making the joint stronger. Flux is of the following two types :

(1) **Non-corrosive Flux.** This type of flux does not harm the metal of the job even if it is left on the job after soldering or brazing. Borex, rasin and turpentine oil come under this flux.

(2) **Corrosive Flux.** If this type of flux is allowed to remain on the job, it harms the metal of the job. Zinc chloride, amonium chloride, hydrochloric acid and sal-ammoniac come under this flux. After making the joint it should be washed with water.

Soldering Iron

In the soldering process the tool which is used to melt solder is called soldering iron. Soldering irons are of the following types :

1. **Copper Bit Soldering Iron.** That part of the soldering iron which is heated, is called its bit. In this type of soldering irons small and big several sizes of bits are used. There is provision for fixing rod having handle or shanks to these bits. Only bit is heated and soldering is done by using handle. One special feature of this iron is that it heats the joining part quickly because it is made of copper. It also helps in making a joint quickly. This has been shown in Fig. 14.15(A).

2. **Hatchet Soldering Iron.** Normally, this type of soldering iron is used by the sheet-metal work. Its shape is similar to an axe. Its bit and shank is made of a piece of iron. When it is hot, it is used with a handle. This has been illustrated in Fig. 14.15(B).

(A) Copper bits soldering iron

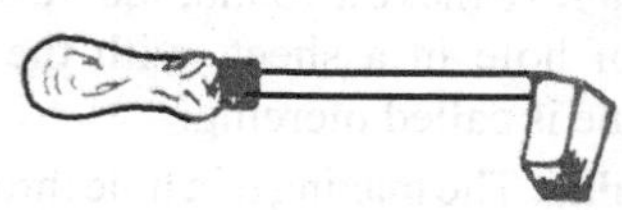

(B) Hatchet soldering iron

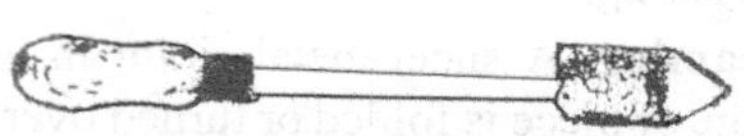

(C) Adjustable soldering iron

Fig. 14.15.

3. **Adjustable Soldering Iron.** This type of soldering iron has been shown in Fig. 14.15(C). Copper bit is used in this soldering iron. This bit is joined to the shank through a hinge, on which handle can be used. This copper bit can be turned at any angle and soldering can be done.

4. **Electrical Soldering Iron.** For heating this type of soldering iron, an electric element is fitted inside its bit, which are connected with electric wire. Its bit is made of copper, which is fitted in a special type of shank with a handle. It is used for joints in radio, T.V. *etc.*

Tinning of bit. Bits made of copper are coated with tin, otherwise they would not work efficiently. For tinning, bits are properly heated at appropriate temperature and then coated with tin. If the tin flows down from the bit while tinning, then bits should be slightly cooled and then tinning should be done. If the tin is not being coated, it may be because the bit is not adequately heated. Unless tin coated bit is over-heated the tin coating cannot be removed.

Method of Soldering. First of all the parts to be joined should be properly cleaned with a file, scraper or acid and then flux should be applied. We should now arrange to hold these parts in proper position. After heating at appropriate temperature soldering iron should be applied flux and then soldering should be done. The hot bit should be quickly moved on the joint. If solder is inadequate we should add some more solder to the joint and move the soldering iron. It should be ensured that the metal being joined also get heated to some extent by the soldering iron otherwise the joint would not be strong enough. If sheet is thick, the joining parts should be heated with blow lamp or furnace.

Method of Soldering with Silver. This type of joint is fixed with hard soldering, which makes the joint strong. The parts to be joined should be so heated that they become red. Borax is applied to it as flux. Melted solder is poured on it and spread with the soldering iron.

Brazing

It is the process of joining two or more pieces of metal with an alloy. Generally brass is used for this purpose. This brass is used in the form of spleter. The melting point of spleter is 600°C. Therefore, brazing cannot be done on those metals which melt at less temperature. For brazing the joint of job is heated to red point. The piece of spleter or brass is kept on the joint and heated with blow lamp or in a furnace. When the spleter melts and spreads on the joint, it should be allowed to cool down. It is important to ensure that in order to have protection from oxidation proper flux is used. Brazing can generally be done in the following four ways :

1. **Torch Brazing.** This type of brazing is done by the gas welding process. Job and the brass rod is heated by burning oxygen and acetylene.
2. **Dip Brazing.** Under this process, some special types of jobs are dipped in boiling spleter or brazing rod is kept beside and heated.
3. **Electric Brazing.** Under this method, the process of heating the brazing rod and the job is performed like electric welding.
4. **Furnace Brazing.** Heating is done with furnace or a blow lamp.

Note : In both the processes of soldering and brazing, flux is used and therefore it is essential to wash the joints after joining is over. Otherwise, flux can cause damage.

Difference between Soldering and Brazing

Soldering	*Brazing*
1. Joint is often made with solder.	1. Joint is often made with brass.
2. These joints are not very strong.	2. This type of joints are very strong.
3. This joint can dis-joint at less tempera-ture also.	3. This joint can dis-joint only at high temperature.
4. Soldering can be done even without much experience.	4. It requires experi-ence.
5. This joint is made with electric current and very simple instrument is used.	5. Costly instrument is required for brazing with electricity.
6. Ammonium chloride is used as a flux.	6. Ash is used as a flux.
7. It costs less.	7. It is a costly joint.
8. It is not necessary to heat the joint or job.	8. It is necessary to heat the job with a blow lamp or furnace.
9. Temperature of 300°C is adequate for soldering.	9. For brazing tempera-ture at 700°C is necessary.
10. Soldering is done only on thin sheets.	10. Brazing is often done on thick sheets.

Sheet Metal

Sheets made of different metals are used in sheet metal jobs. Some of them are as follows :

1. **Iron Sheets.** Iron sheets are used maximum in the sheet metal jobs. These sheets are made of iron or steel and are generally thin. For protecting these sheets from rust they are galvanised and known as G.I. sheets. Those sheets which are not galvanised are known as Black Iron sheets. These G.I. sheets are made plain or in pipes. These are in different sizes. Their thickness is known from their gauge

numbers. Their number are either according to British Standards wire or according to sheet gauges. The greater the number the thinner would be the sheet. There is danger of the black iron sheet getting crack when turned so these sheets are given annealing treatment.

2. **Stainless Steel Sheets.** Sheet metal trade has shown tremendous progress since the invention of steel. For making stainless steel, metal sheets besides other metals chromium is also mixed. Because of this the metal acquires special properties and it does not get damaged by acids, fruit juices, and rust. Both in the engineering line as well as in our daily life stainless steel is being widely used.

3. **Copper Sheets.** Copper sheets are particularly used in household utensils, jewellery and for decoration. These are made by rolling the copper rods. Their distinct quality is that they are soft as well as strong. These can be turned in any way and they can be engraved. These can be beautified by pasting them with tin or choromium. They can be conveniently soldered or brazed.

4. **Aluminium Sheets.** Aluminium sheets are used almost in every field. These sheets are available in different sizes and thickness. These sheets are very light in weight. They can be provided full strength by mixing other metals with aluminium while keeping them light too. Various operations on these sheets can be performed through spinning and dyes. Beautiful and decorative articles can be made with these sheets which can be given different colours through anodizing.

5. **Brass Sheets.** The main alloy of copper is brass. It is mixed with copper or zinc. These sheets can be conveniently turned or moulded in any shape. Like copper sheets, these sheets can also be painted with chromium or tin. These sheets are used in household utensils, decoration pieces and electric appliances *etc*. These sheets are available in different sizes and thickness.

6. **Lead Sheets.** Lead is an old metal. Lead sheets are used in chemical factories *etc*. Waterproof covers of electricity wires are made with it because water does not have any adverse effect on these. These sheets are heavy in weight. Pipes made of lead sheets are used in sanitary jobs.

Besides the above types of sheets, sheets of gold and silver are also made. These are used to make jewellery, costly gifts and decorative articles.

Questions

1. What are the main tools used by sheet metal worker ?
2. What is the function of stakes in sheet metal works ? What are the different types of stakes ?
3. What are the different operations that are performed under Sheet Metal trade ?
4. Which are the commonly used sheet metal joints ?
5. What is the difference between hard solder and soft solder ?
6. Solder of what proportion is used by a sheet metal worker ?
7. How brazing is done ?
8. What is the difference between brazing and soldering ?

15

Blacksmithy and Forging

Normally work relating to iron is known as blacksmithy. Forging means to give desired shape to any job of metal by heating or cooling it and then striking it either with an ordinary hammer or by using any special machine meant for this purpose. Small forging jobs can be done by striking it with an ordinary hammer but heavy jobs of forging are done only by machines. Forging can be done in three different ways :

1. Hand forging
2. Machine forging
3. Drop forging

Hand Forging. To give shape to a job by striking it with a hammer is called hand forging or smithing.

Machine Forging. To give desired shape to a job with the help of a forging machine is called machine forging. Press machine, rolling machine and various kinds of power hammers are included in this category.

Drop Forging. For jobs of same size and similar shape drop forging process is used. In this process drop hammer is used. The top dye is raised to adequate height through mechanical devise and then dropped to hit the hot metal kept at the bottom dye. Thus, the hot metal takes the shape of dye. Wrench and other ordinary things are made through drop forging.

It is not possible to change the shape of metals when they are cold. It is therefore necessary to heat the metal in fire. By heating the metal, it becomes soft and acquires the property of plasticity. As such, it can be bent or moulded in any shape.

Advantages of Forging :

1. Tensile strength of metal is reduced and it acquires the property of plasticity which enables us to give desired shape to the metal.
2. With the help of the properties of plasticity and malleability, drawing out, jumping and bending operations can be easily performed.
3. It is easy to give finish to a forged job because its shape is almost ready and it takes less time.
4. After forging on a hard metal, other machine activities can be easily carried out on the job.
5. There is little wastage of metal.
6. Structure of metal becomes proper through hot forging.
7. There is little scope of stresses and cracks on the metal.

Disadvantages of Forging :

1. When metal is heated oxidation takes place, which harms the metal.
2. Brittle metals cannot be forged.
3. Finishing is not possible in forging process.
4. There is a change in job's size.

Cold Forging. To give desired form or shape to the metal by hammering it but without heating is called cold forging. This process is easy only for soft metals.

Hot Forging. To give desired form or shape to metal by hammering it after heating, it is called hot forging. This process can be applied on solid or hard metals also. After heating the metal, it acquires the property of plasticity which enables us to turn or bend it in any direction.

Forge

In hot forging process, several types of forges

(Blacksmith's Hearth) are used. Under this method, forges of hard coke are mostly used. Gas or electricity is used in some forges also. Of whatever type a forge might be, it should have maximum forging facilities. A modern Forge or Blacksmith's Hearth in which hard coke is used has been illustrated in Fig. 15.1.

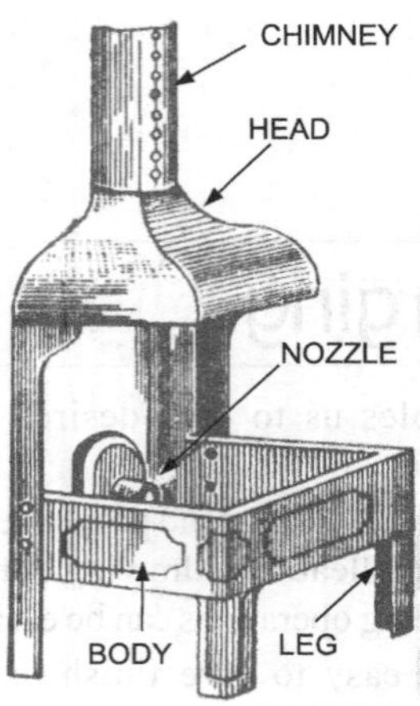

Fig. 15.1.

This forge has all the necessary facilities. It has the following main parts :

1. **Chimney.** This is the upper most part of the forge, through which smoke is provided an outlet at an appropriate height.
2. **Head.** There is a head built over the forge, which is also known as hood. This prevents fumes and ash from spreading in all directions.
3. **Body.** Its body is generally 2′ in length and 2′ in width. A nozzle is provided to the body which provides air. The nozzle is attached to the lower pipe. Fire brick or fire clay is used in the body.
4. **Ash Pot.** The pot used for collection of burnt ash is called ash pot. It is kept below the forge.
5. **Water Tank.** A tank (or bosh) is attached to the body, where water is stored. Tool or job is dipped into this water, in case there is a need to cool them.
6. **Air Regulator.** In order to regulate or control air between blower and the forge, an air regulator is fixed. Air regulator lets the air pass according to requirement.
7. **Coal Tray.** For keeping coal, a coal tray is generally built either below or on one of its sides.
8. **Legs.** The body of the forge rests on four legs, which are of 2′ height each.
9. **Blower.** A blower provides blast of air and helps in quickly setting the fire and in maintaining it at the required temperature. It is electrically operated.

Apart from the above forge, small work is usually hand-forged and a hand forge is used for this purpose. It is a small and movable forge. It can be moved to any place and used there. A hand blower is attached to it, which is operated by hands. It has been shown in Fig.15.2 below.

Fig. 15.2. Hand forge

Forge Tools

A number of forge tools are used to control fire in the forge. Broadly these are of the following four types :

Shovel. For putting coal into the forge a shovel is used.

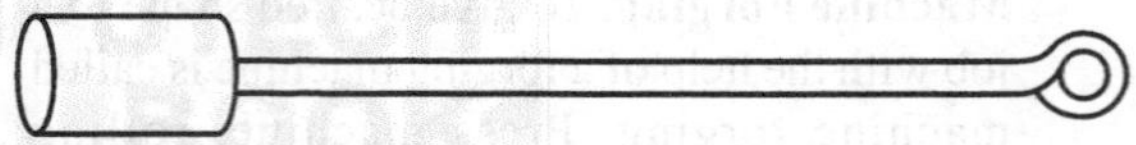

Fig. 15.3. Shovel.

Poker. Poker is a rod made of mild steel. It is about one meter in length and 1 cm in thickness. It is used to shed the fire-ash of the forge. On one end, it is conical and on the other there is a ring to handle it.

Fig. 15.4. Poker

Swoop. It is almost similar to a poker. One of its ends is made flat and then turned. It helps in keeping the burning coal at the required place in the forge.

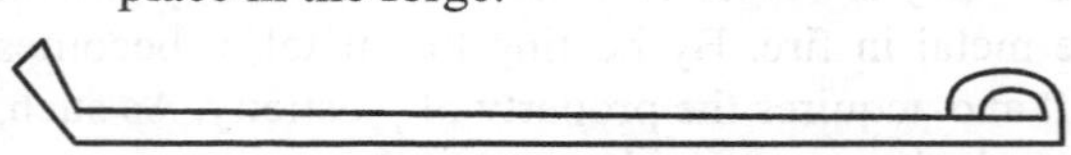

Fig. 15.5. Swoop

Sprinker. It is a water tin, having numerous small holes. It is used to control fire by filling it with water and sprinkling the fountain of water produced by it.

Anvil. In blacksmithy workshops, jobs are struck with light or heavy hammers, while forging. Anvil is the main tool which provides base for this purpose. It is a block made of cast or wrought iron, upon which forging is done. Its weight varies from 80 kg to 200 kg. Jobs are given shape by keeping them on the anvil and striking them with hammers.

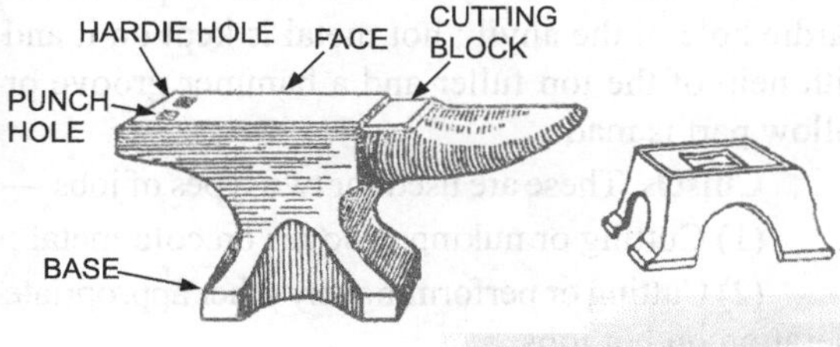

(A) Anvil (B) Anvil stand

Fig. 15.6.

It is generally kept on a stand, which is shown in Fig. 15.6(B). Its measurement is calculated on the basis of width of platform for work that is available on it. An anvil has the following six parts, which have been shown in Fig. 15.6 (A).

1. **Beak.** The pointed portion of the anvil is known as beak. Hot metal is kept on it to turn it and give the metal a circular shape.
2. **Cutting Block.** Cutting block and edges are used for cutting the metal pieces. This part is made at the beak and the rear of the body.
3. **Face.** This is the main part of the anvil and all forging jobs are done on it. Its surface is plain, which should not be spoiled.
4. **Punch Hole.** On the one corner of face of an anvil, there is a round hole, which is used for punching holes in the sheet. The metal sheet is kept over it and a punch is used to make holes.
5. **Hardie Hole.** On the opposite side of punch hole on the face, there is a square hole. It is known as Hardie Hole. It is used to fit hardy bottom, fuller bottom and swage in it and then metal is cut over it.
6. **Base.** The lower part of anvil is called base. It is fitted into the ground upto a certain level or fitted on a stand.

Swage Block

It is a large rectangular block of cast iron or cast steel. On all its four sides there are "V" grooves and semicircular slots. It has numerous holes both round and square in section, for reception of work which requires smouldering.

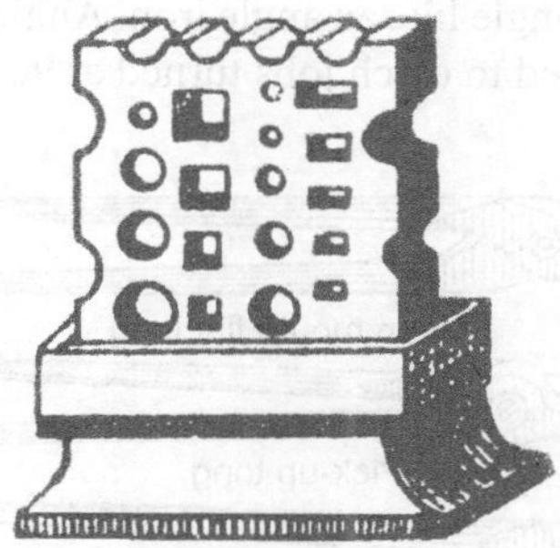

Fig. 15.7. Swage block

Through these holes jobs are given shapes or holes are made in metals. We should not do work with sledge hammer because by doing so it can crack. Swage blocks are kept on the stands built for this purpose. These are available in the following sizes :

1. 12″ × 12″ × 4″
2. 14″ × 14″ × 5″
3. 18″ × 18″ × 6″
4. 20″ × 20″ × 6½″

Tongs

It is a two legged instrument used for picking hot jobs or for help in heating a job in a forge as well as in performing several other forging jobs. It is generally made of mild steel.

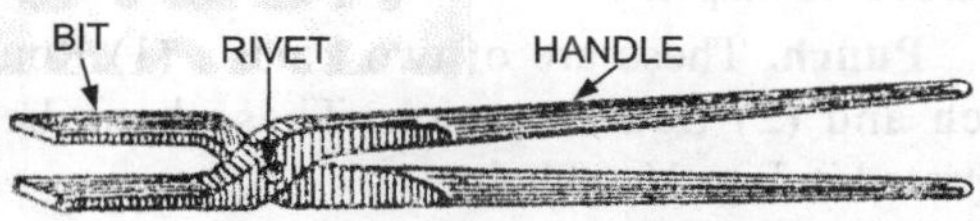

Fig. 15.8. Open mouth tongs

This type of tongs and its parts has been shown in Fig. 15.8 above. In order to catch different types of jobs firmly and with ease, the following types of tongs are used :

(1) **Open Mouth Flat Tongs.** Jobs of square and flat shape and mediun size are caught by these tongs.

(2) **Pick-up Tongs.** This tong is used to pick-up small round jobs such as rivets and pieces of thin rods.

(3) **Close Mouth Flat Tongs.** Flat jobs thin metal are caught with this type of tong.

(4) **Round Nose Tongs.** This type of tong is used to catch round or hexagonal jobs.

(5) Rivet Tongs. The end of Rivet tong which picks up things is round in shape. Rivet tongs are used to catch round jobs like bolts and rivets.

(6) Angle Iron Tongs. One of its bits is turned at right angle like an angle iron. Angle iron tongs are used to catch jobs turned at 90° angle.

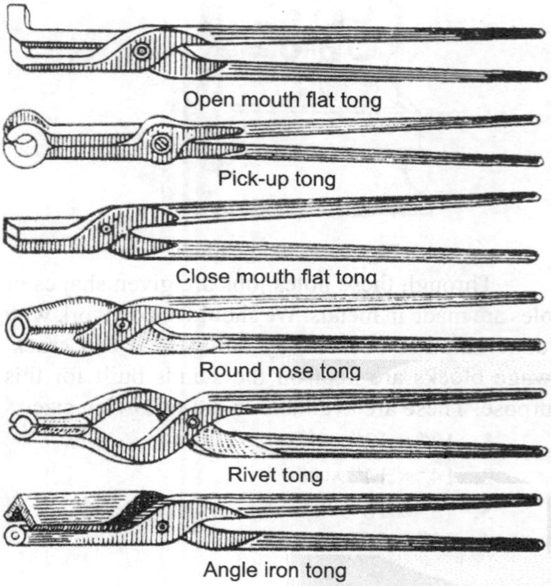

Fig. 15.9. Tongs

Hammers. In blacksmithy, for jobs of light nature, four kinds of hammers are used. For heavy jobs sledge hammers are used. These have been discussed in chapter 9.

Punch. These are of two kinds : (1) Round punch and (2) Square punch. These have been illustrated in Fig. 15.10 below :

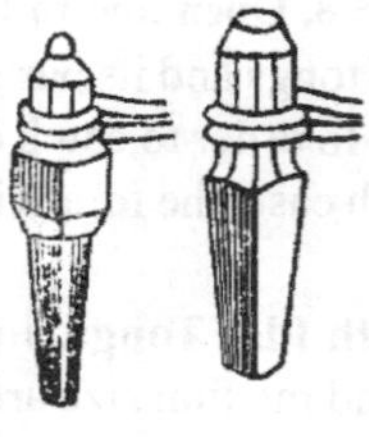

Fig. 15.10. Round and square punch

These are used to make holes in jobs of hot metal of round or square shape.

Hardie. It is fitted in the hardie hole of anvil, hot metal is kept on it and cut by striking at it. It is shown in Fig. 15.11.

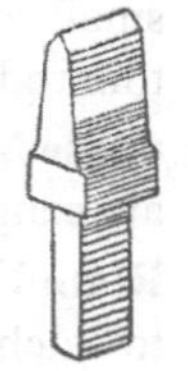

Fig. 15.11. Hardie

Fullers. These are available in sets. One set consists of one bottom fuller and one top fuller. These have been shown in Fig. 15.12.

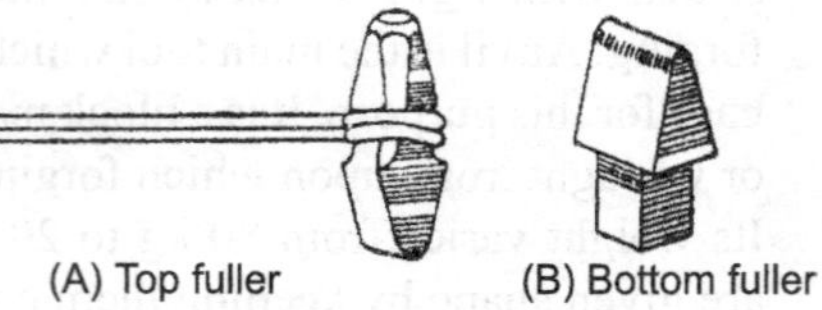

Fig. 15.12.

In order to use it, bottom fuller is put in the Hardie hole of the anvil ; hot metal is kept on it and with help of the top fuller and a hammer groove or hollow part is made.

Chisels. These are used for two types of jobs —

(1) Cutting or nuking grooves on cold metal ;

(2) Cutting or performing any other appropriate operation on hot jobs.

Chisels used for cutting cold metals are called cold chisels. These are also known as cold set because a handle of thin rod is also attached to these. Similarly chisels used for cutting hot metals are called hot chiseis or hot sets. Cold sets are used for marking on the cold jobs or for making grooves. Hot sets are used for hot jobs.

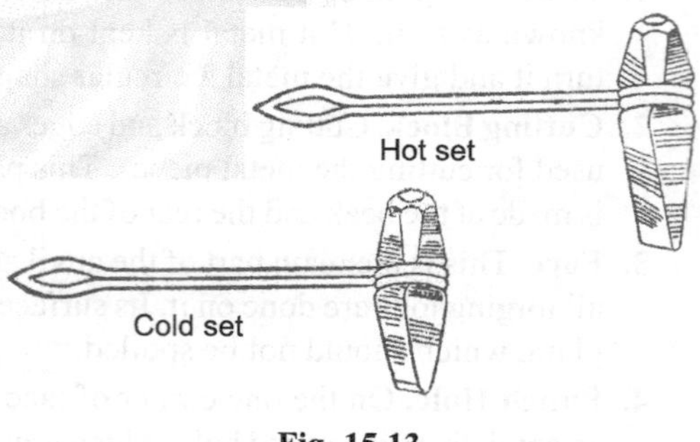

Fig. 15.13

Swage. These are also available in the forms of sets. One set consists of a bottom of swage and one top swage. A handle of thin rod is attached to the top swage. These are used for finishing of round jobs. Bottom swage is fitted into the hardie hole of the anvil. Hot metal is kept on it. Proper shape is given to the hot metal by keeping it on the swage and top swage is kept on the round job.

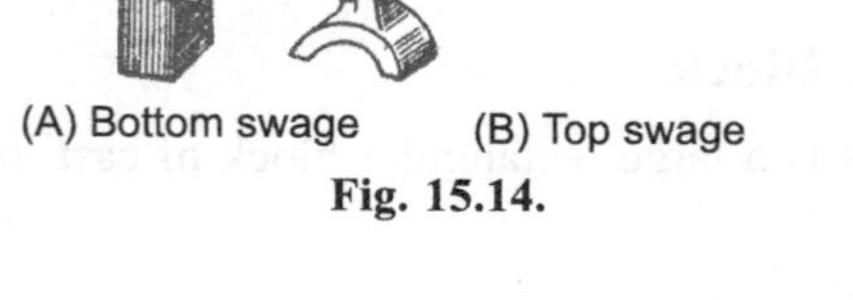

Fig. 15.14.

Flatter. This is a finishing tool. The surface of plain jobs is finished by the flatter. This makes the surface of the job plain.

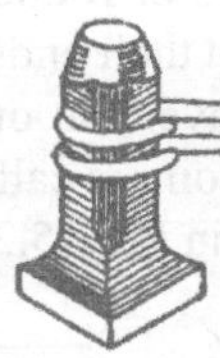

Fig. 15.15. Flatter

Gouge. Gouge is a cutting tool. It is a cutting chisel which has either a concave convex cutting surface.

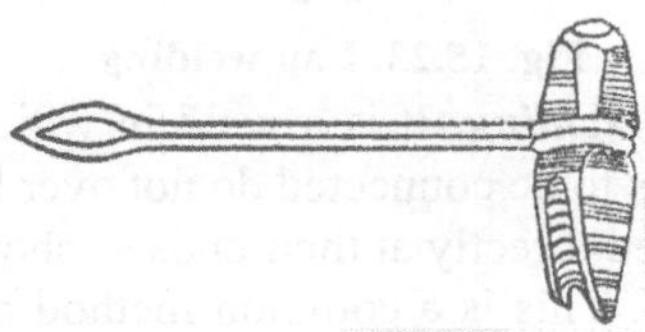

Fig. 15.16. Gouge

Drift. It is a cylindrical tapered tool. It is used to enlarge the holes in a hot metal.

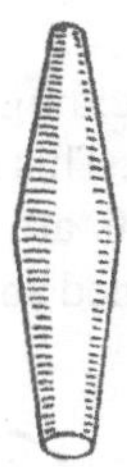

Fig. 15.17. Drift

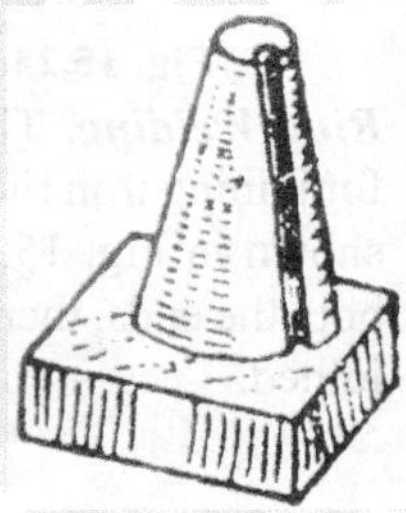

Fig. 15.18. Cone

Cone. It is used to make round rings of different sizes (measurements). It is a tapered steel rod, having a base.

Forging Operations :

(1) Marking
(2) Cutting
(3) Drawing out
(4) Jumping
(5) Bending
(6) Punching or Drifting
(7) Setting down
(8) Forge welding

(1) Marking. Before performing any other operation related to forging it is essential to make marking on the metal according to the drawing. For this purpose brass rules, tri-square, centre punch *etc.* are used.

(2) Cutting. To make small parts of long metal rods and plates is known as cutting. This can be done both in cold or hot condition. For cold metals, chisel of 45° to 65° cutting angle is used. For hot metals, chisel of 30° cutting angle is used. Metal beyond thickness of 20 mm should be cut only after heating it.

(3) Drawing out. To increase metal's length is called "Drawing out". This has been shown in Fig. 15.19 below.

Fig. 15.19. Drawing out

The metal is heated at a temperature between 950°C to 1300°C and hammer is struck at the beak of the anvil. Fuller is also used for this purpose.

(4) Jumping. To shorten and thicken a piece of metal after heating it is called "jumping" or "upsetting". By jumping the length of the metal can be reduced to almost half. Jumping is done in three ways :

(*i*) **Head Jumping.** This has been shown in Fig. 15.20(A). Jumping of one end of a round rod is called "Head jumping" such as rivet head.

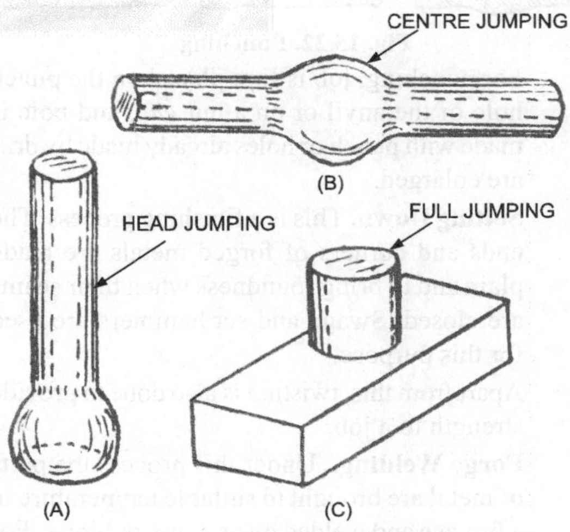

Fig. 15.20.

(*ii*) **Centre Jumping.** This has been illustrated in Fig. 15.20 (B). In this category, jumping is done in any other part except the two corners of the round metal rod. Example : Tap handle.

(*iii*) **Full Jumping.** This has been shown in Fig. 15.20 (C) above. The metal is completely heated and its length is reduced.

Bending. To turn or bend a piece of metal in round or angular form is called ""bending". This has been shown in Fig. 15.21 below.

Round rings *etc*. are made through this operation.

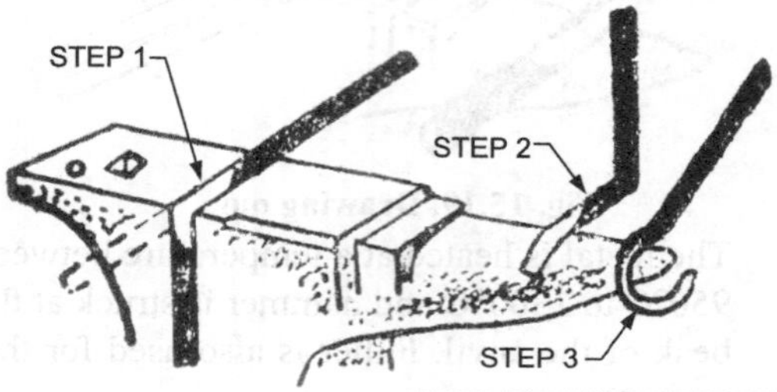

Fig. 15.21. Bending

Punching. This has been shown in Fig. 15.22. In this operation hole is made in hot metal with the help of a punch.

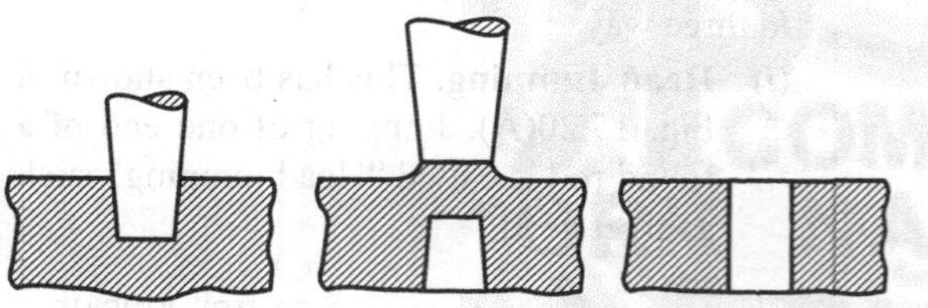

Fig. 15.22. Punching

For punching, job is first placed on the punch hole of the anvil or on a nut *etc*., and hole is made with punch or holes already made by drift are enlarged.

Setting Down. This is a finishing process. The ends and corners of forged metals are made plain and to bring roundness when their seams are closed. Swage and set hammers are used for this purpose.

Apart from this, twisting is also done to provide strength to a job.

Forge Welding. Under this process the parts of metal are brought to suitable temperature in a furnace and welded by pressure or blows. For forge welding, the ends of the pieces of metals are made scarf through jumping. The following types of joints are made by forge welding :

Lap Welding. In this type of joints, whether these are flat bars or round bars, jumped and scarfs are made at their ends. Then these scarfs are placed one over the other and joined by striking it. This joint is called "lap joint" This has been shown in Fig. 15.23.

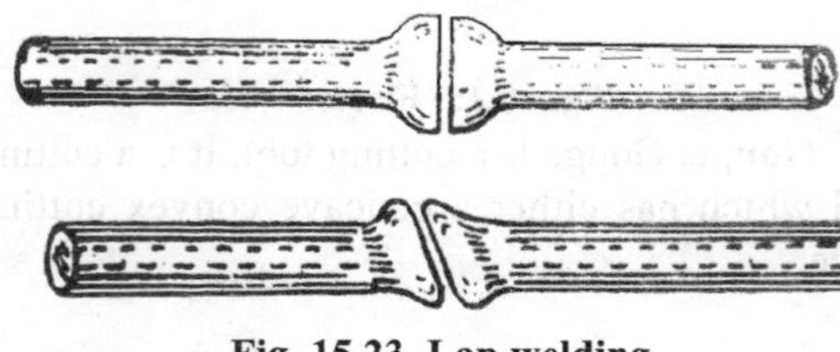

Fig. 15.23. Lap welding

Butt Welding. It is a weld in which the two pieces to be connected do not over lap but are welded directly at their ends as shown in Fig. 15.24. This is a common method of welding rods by an electric rods.

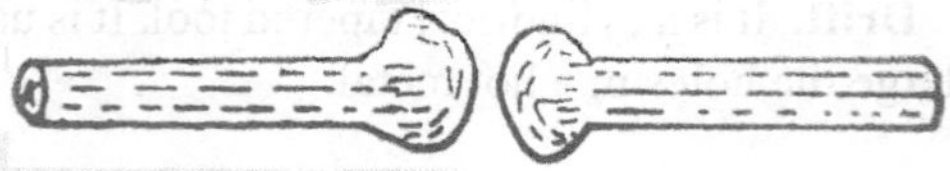

Fig. 15.24. Butt welding

Ring Welding. This type of welding is done for joining iron rings, chains *etc*. This has been shown in Fig. 15.25. First scarfs are made at both the ends, then the rod is turned and finally joined.

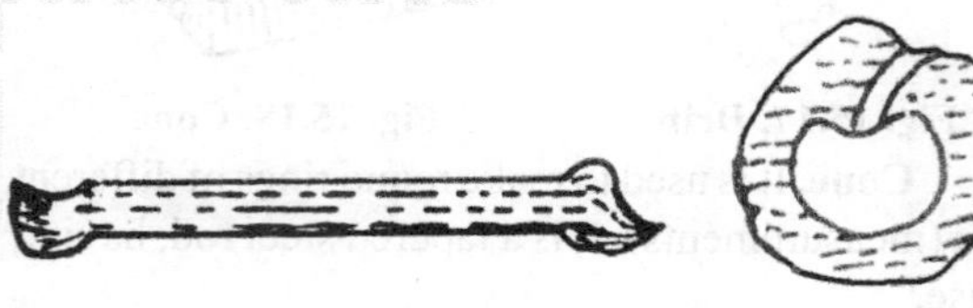

Fig. 15.25. Ring welding

Split Welding. When two pieces of metal are joined to increase length, it is known as split

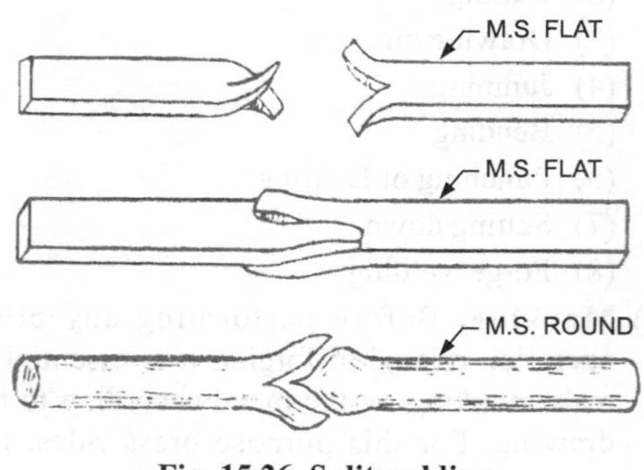

Fig. 15.26. Split welding

welding. For this purpose, different types of scarfs are made, which have been shown in Fig. 15.26.

Angle Welding. This type of welding is done to join the metal at angle, as shown in Fig. 15.27.

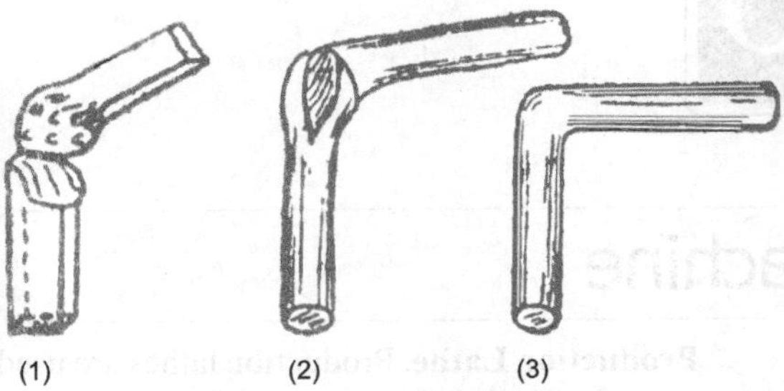

Fig. 15.27. Angle welding

"T" Welding. "T" welding is done where load is heavy as shown in Fig. 15.28.

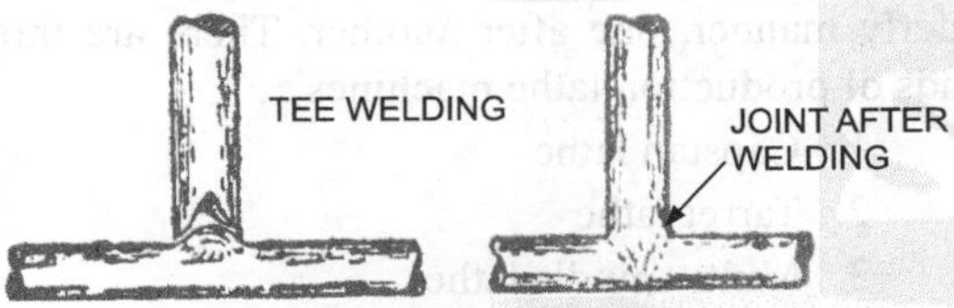

Fig. 15.28. "T" welding

Heat. In blacksmithy the entire work depends on the temperature of heat used. Different types of temperatures are needed for performing different jobs because melting point of different metals arrives at different degrees of temperature. Mild steel or wrought iron can be heated at greater temperatures but great precaution is necessary while heating carbon steel. If carbon steel is given excess heat, its carbon would be burnt and it can break into pieces when struck with a hammer. Heat required for some metals has been discussed below :

1. **Low Red Heat.** This is also known as blood heat. In this heat as soon as the metal becomes red the operation should be carried out.
2. **Bright Red Heat.** This is also called "Cherry Red Heat". It is appropriate for turning or bending mild steel anil wrought iron.
3. **White Heat.** This type of heat is appropriate for jumping work of mild steel and wrought iron.
4. **Welding Heat.** This heat is suitable for melting the metal. Blue flames are clearly visible in this heat. It is appropriate for use in forge welding job, especially metal of mild steel.

Questions

1. What do you understand by forging ? What are the different kinds of forging ?
2. Which facilities should be there in a good forge ?
3. What are the forge tools ? What are the uses of forge tools ?
4. Draw an outline of an Anvil and describe its parts.
5. What is the function of Swage Block ?
6. Which are the main tools used in blacksmithy ?
7. What forging operations are done in blacksmithy ?
8. What is meant by forge welding ? What are different types of forge welding?

16

Lathe Machine

Brief History of Lathe Machine

Nature has helped man in inventing several machines. Many scientists observed natural phenomena, thought over them and after experiments made useful inventions. In 1700 AD, a scientist of France once saw that a stone which fell from a high mountain became round. Thus he observed that if a moving soft thing is scraped with a hard material, the soft material can be turned round in shape. This imagination led to the invention of a "Tree Lathe" machine by that scientist. Later in 1740 AD, the improved lathe was made, which we see today. The act of cutting threads on lathe also started. But the real credit of designing lathe goes to an American engineer Mr. Henri Moudslay, who introduced the basic principle of thread-cutting lathe machine, in which it became possible to cut threads on a lathe by changing gears on spindle and main screw.

In real sense, any workshop is incomplete without the presence of a lathe machine. Lathe machine helps in making several other machines. That is why this machine is known as "mother of machines". An efficient fitter should have full knowledge about a lathe machine.

Types of Lathe Machines

Lathe machines used in workshops can be divided into the following sections :

Centre Lathe. This is also known as S.S. and C. Lathe. It is used for surface turning and screw cutting. Fine types of Lathe machines are available under this type :

1. Hand lathe
2. Bench lathe
3. Foot lathe or Tradle lathe
4. Tool room lathe
5. Engine lathe.

Production Lathe. Production lathes are used when a particular job is to be produced in large quatitity. A special feature of these lathe machines is that one particular job has been set on the lathe machine, the various operation can be performed in orderly manner, one after another. There are three kinds of production lathe machines :

1. Capstan lathe
2. Tarret lathe
3. Multi-spindle lathe.

Special Lathe. As is evident from the name itself, special lathe machines are made and used for a specific purpose. For example, relieving lathe, which are used for providing relief to milling cutters or tap. Three types of lathes are available under this section :

1. Wheel and axle turning lathe
2. Copying lathe
3. Relieving lathe.

Engine Lathe. This is highly prevalent lathe machine. This lathe machine is normally used by a fitter in workshops. When electric motors were not invented, these machines were operated with steam engines. That was why it was named as Engine Lathe. This lathe has almost all the qualities of a good lathe machine. There is full provision in its head stock for moving its spindle at various speeds. Cutting tool can be run in longitudinal and cross-section. Carriage can be moved by hand or with the lead screw itself. Their classification is done on the basis of their functions. These are made with cast-iron. Its main parts are as under :

1. **Leg.** The heavy lathe machines which are fixed on the ground, legs are used by fixing them to the machine bed and the ground. All the parts of the lathe machine are fixed to it. Guideways are made on both the longitudinal ends. One

of them is outerway and the other is innerway. Saddle of the carriage slides on the outerways and on the innerway base of the tail stock slides.

These ways are made of two types. (See Figs. 16.1 and 16.2)

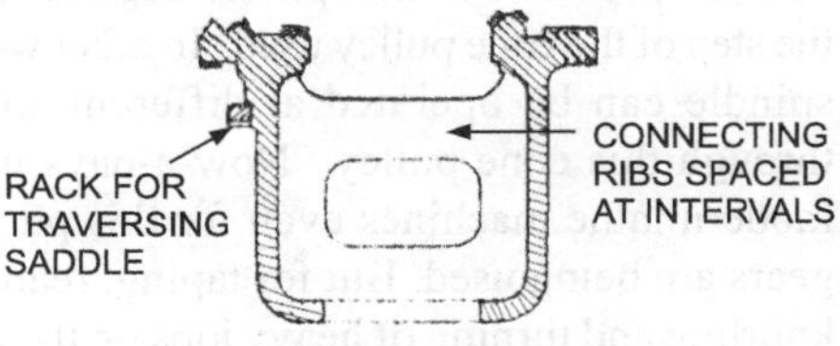

Fig. 16.1. "V" bed ways

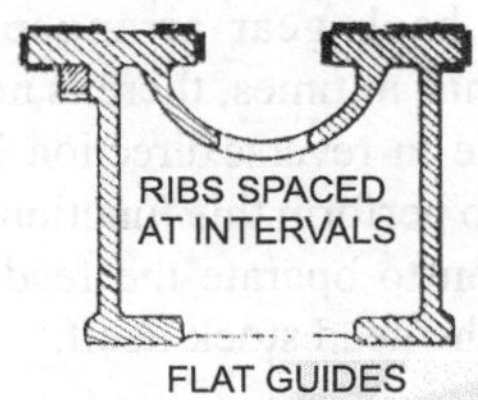

Fig. 16.2. Flat bed ways

(*i*) **"V'Bed.** This type of beds are used for small machines.

(*ii*) **Flat Red.** This type of beds are used for lathe machines meant for heavy jobs. In this type of bed the contact of the surlace which provides base to the saddle is more because of wide and flat guide ways.

2. **Carriage.** Literal meaning of "carriage" is to carry. Through carriage, a job can be brought in contact with the cutting tool or withdrawn from such a contact. It operates on bed ways between tail stock and head stock, it contains five sub-parts :

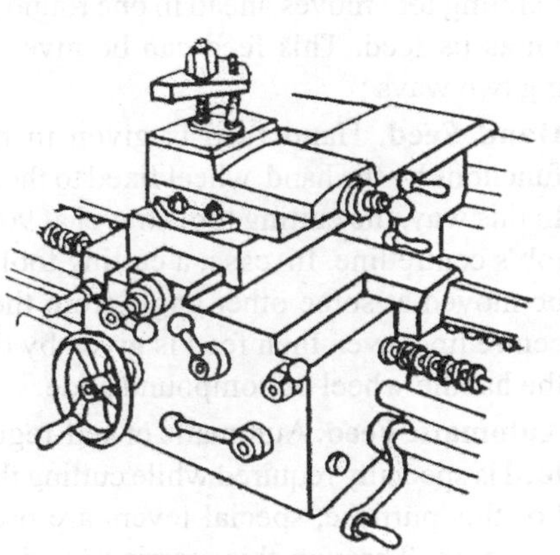

Fig. 16.3. Carriage.

1. Saddle
2. Cross slide
3. Compound slide
4. Tool post
5. Apron.

Saddle. "H" shaped part, fitted on the bed of the lathe machine is called "Saddle". There is a provision of hand wheel to move it on the bed way. Its main function is to bring the tool mounted on it into contact with the job in right direction. For this purpose, cross slide, compound slide and tool post is fixed on the saddle itself.

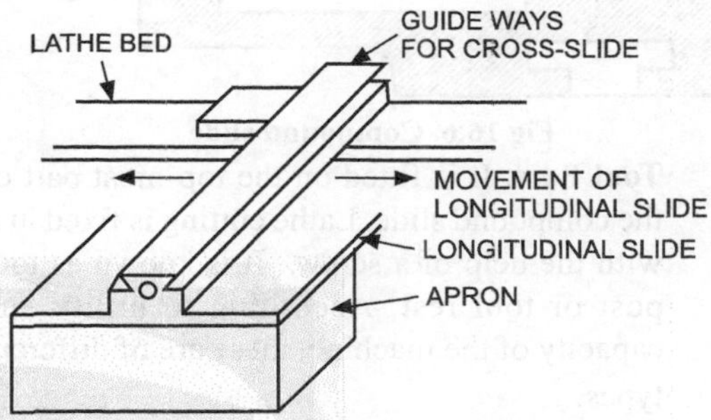

Fig. 16.4. Saddle

Cross Slide. Its cross-section has been shown in Fig. 16.5. It is a transverse section at right angles with the longitudinal axis of the work through which the section is taken. In the lathe it is on the upper side of the saddle, in the form of dovetail. A provision is made to drive the cross slide with a head wheel.

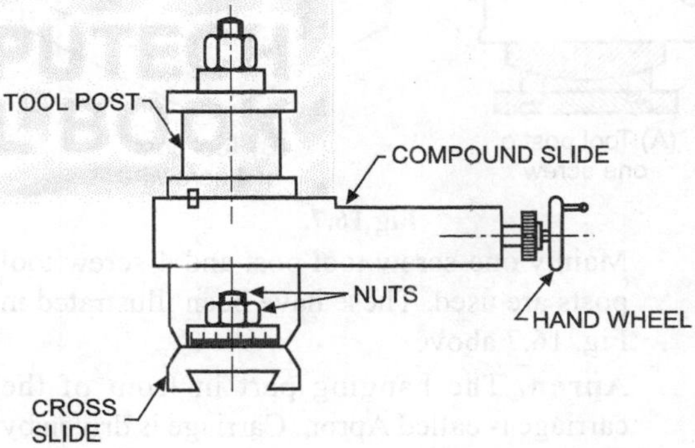

Fig 16.5. Cross slide

For having the necessary knowledge about feed, graduation is indicated near handle wheel, close to shaft. With its help depth is given to the tool. A round groove is cut on it and compound slide is fitted in it with the help of a screw.

Compound Slide. It is also known as tool post slide because tool post is fitted on this compound slide. It is fitted over the cross slide, on a turn table by using a set screw. On its base there are signs of degrees, which help in taper turning and thread-cutting. A provision of separate hand wheel is made for moving this compound slide. It can only be driven with hand and automatic speed cannot be given to it.

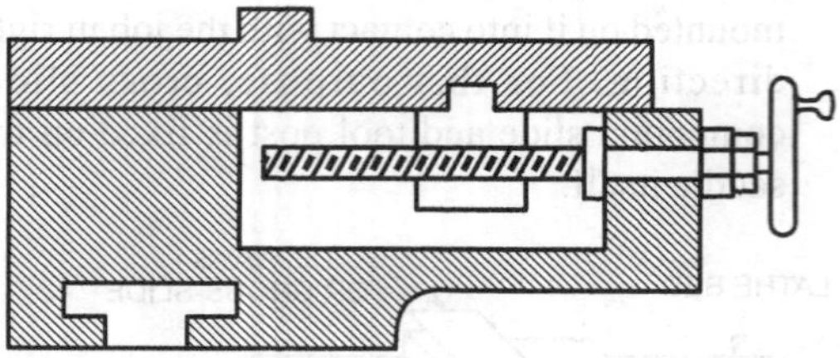

Fig 16.6. Compound slide

Tool Post. It is fitted on the top-most part of the compound slide. Lathe cutting is fixed in it with the help of a screw. It is known as tool post or tool rest. According to utility and capacity of the machine, these are of different types.

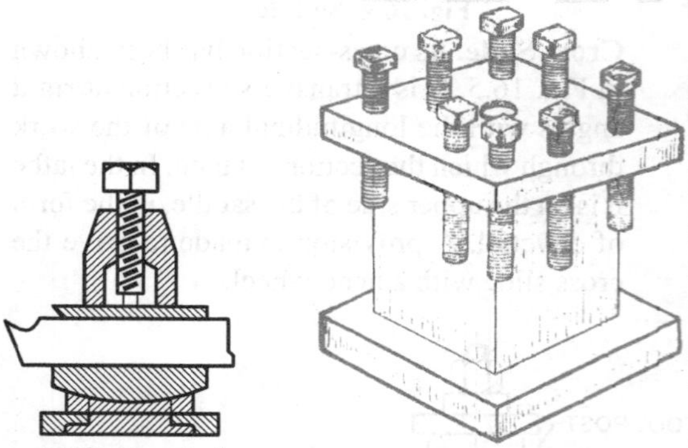

(A) Tool post of one screw

(B) Tool post of 4 screws

Fig 16.7.

Mainly one-screw tool post and 4-screw tool posts are used. These have been illustrated in Fig. 16.7 above.

Apron. The hanging part in front of the carriage is called Apron. Carriage is driven by hand with the help of hand wheel fixed on it. A few gears and a split half-nut is fitted in a hosing in it. Besides this, there are some other levers in the apron, which help in providing automatic speed and thread cutting. We can also define apron as a vertical plate, in the front part of the carriage of a screw cutting lathe to which the split nut is attached.

Head Stock. Head stock is fitted on lathe bed on the left-hand side of the lathe operator. The required gear and cone pulley is fitted in it for driving the lathe's spindle. Cone pulley remains free on spindle. It is moved by the belt. On the front side of the spindle, a large gear is fitted with the help of a spindle "key". Its contact provides speed through catching pin via pulley. The run provided to the spindle depends upon the step of the cone pulley used. In other words, spindle can be operated at different speeds through this cone pulley. Now-a-days in the modern lathe machines even for this purpose gears are being used. But for taping, reaming, knurling and turning of heavy jobs on the lathe machines, very slow speed is needed. For this purpose, back gear arrangement is used. Besides this, at times, there is need to operate the spindle in reverse direction. Tumbler gears are used to perform this function. There is also a provision to operate the feed rod and lead screw in the head stock itself.

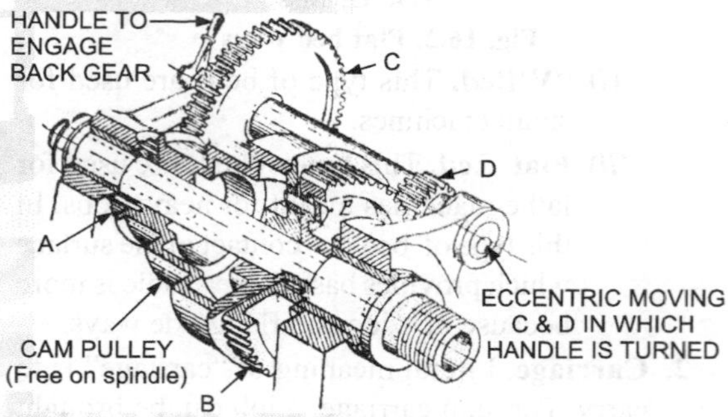

Fig. 16.5. Head stock

Feed Mechanism

While doing turning of a job, the extent to which a cutting tool moves ahead in one round of job, is known as its feed. This feed can be given in the following two ways :

1. **Hand Feed.** Hand feed is given in normal functions by the hand wheel fixed to the apron. In this way, the cutting tools travel at 90° from job's centre line. In case, a cutting tool has to be moved at some other angle from the job's centre line, even then feed is given by driving the handle wheel of compound slide.
2. **Automatic Feed.** Automatic or self-regulating feed is specially required while cutting threads. For this purpose, special levers are provided on apron. Through this, carriage is driven at the equal speed of head stock spindle. Power transmits from the spindle, travels through

several gears and drives the lead screw gear which drives the carriage.

Tail Stock

Tail stock is fitted on the lathe machine's bed, on the right hand side of the lathe machine operator. It can be moved to any desired space on the lathe bed, in case of need. It is used for centre to centre turning of lengthy jobs and for carrying out different operations such as taping, drilling, reaming *etc.* In short we can define tail stoke as, the movable head of a lathe as distinguished from the head stock, which is fixed. Tail stock has the following main parts :

1. Body
2. Base
3. Spindle
4. Hand wheel
5. Clamping unit
6. Tail stock offsetting screws
7. Spindle locking lever.

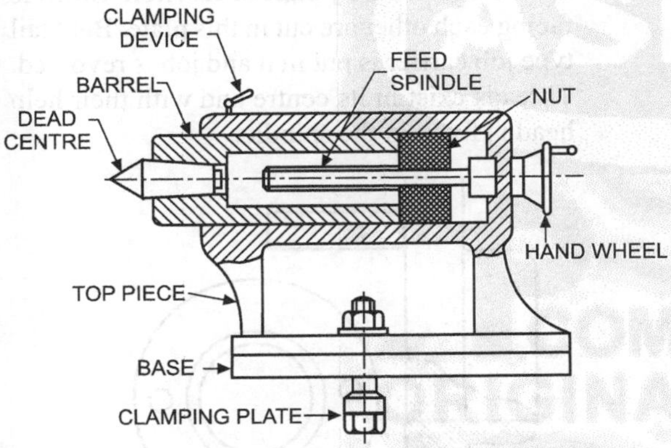

Fig. 16.9. Tail stock

Lathe Accessories

The means or source used for handling or providing support to a job in lathe machine are included under this head. Out of these, the following are the main accessories :

1. Lathe centre
2. Chuck
3. Catch Plate
4. Carriers
5. Face plate
6. Steady rest
7. Mandrel

Lathe Centre. To provide support to lengthy jobs on lathe machines, centres are used. These are used by fitting them into tail stock's spindle and head stock's spindle. These are made of carbon steel or alloy steel, solid, tapered or conical as illustrated in Fig. 16.10 below. Its nose is generally built at 60° but for heavy jobs 75° centres are used. These can be divided into two parts :

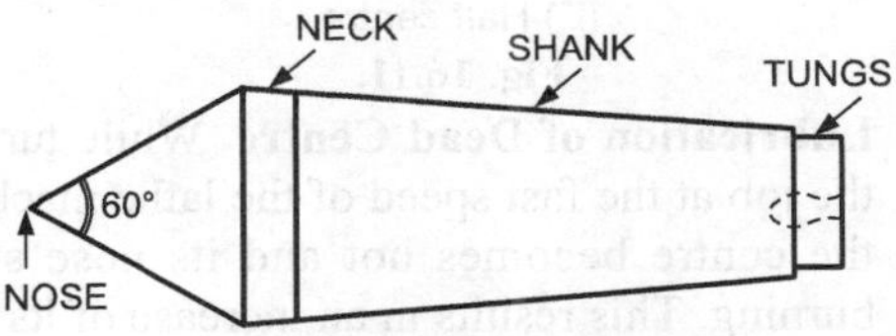

Fig. 16.10. Lathe centre plain.

1. **Live Centre.** These are fitted in head stock's spindles. These are driven with the power of the machine. That is why these are called as live centres.
2. **Dead Centre.** These centres are fitted in centre tail stock spindle and they provide support to the other end of the job. They do not get any power from the lathe machine. Therefore, these are called "Dead centres". These are of following types, which are used according to the shape of the job and their operations. Some of the main centres have been illustrated in Fig. 16.11.

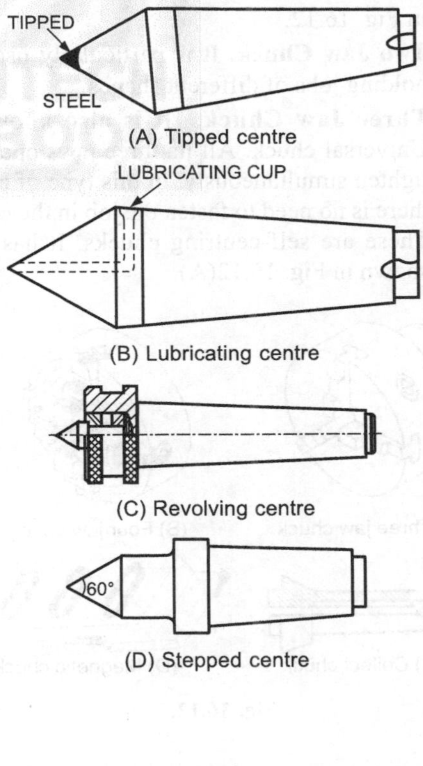

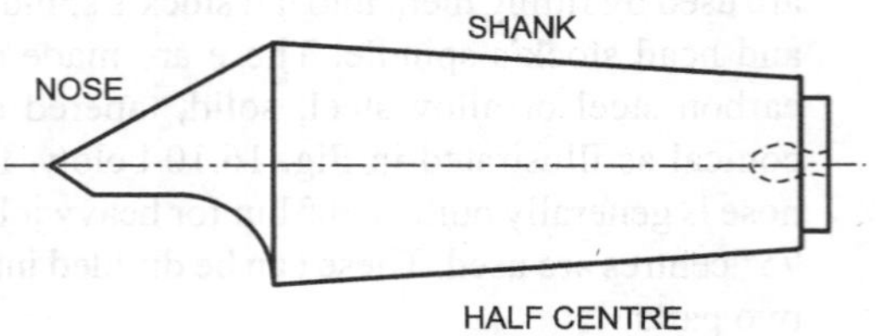

(E) Half centre

Fig. 16.11.

Lubrication of Dead Centre. While turning the job at the fast speed of the lathe machine, the centre becomes hot and its nose starts burning. This results in an increase of its area and there is a risk of mistake in its accuracy. Thus, it is necessary to lubricate the centres with tallow or graphite mixed grease.

Chuck. Chuck is normally used to provide a strong grip to catch the job on the lathe machine. These are easily fitted on the thread cut on the end of head stock spindle. According to the utility of the job, these are of the following kinds :

1. Two jaw chuck
2. Three jaw chuck
3. Four jaw chuck
4. Collet chuck
5. Magnetic chuck.

The above mentioned chucks have been shown in Fig. 16.12.

Two Jaw Chuck. It is particularly used for holding jobs of different shapes.

Three Jaw Chuck. It is also known as Universal chuck. All its three jaws open and tighten simultaneously. In this type of chuck, there is no need to fasten the job in the centre. These are self-centring chucks. It has been shown in Fig. 16.12(A).

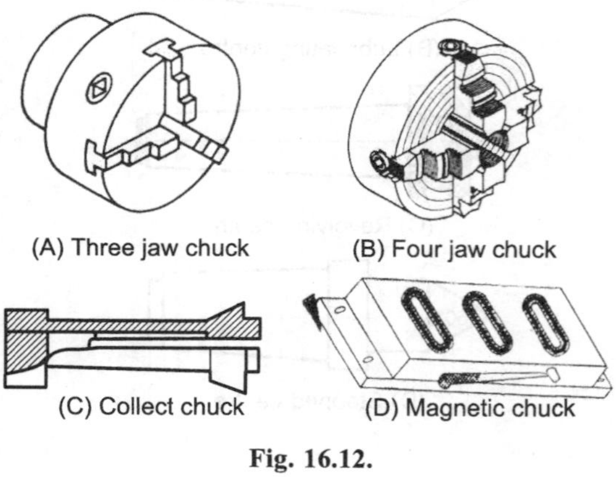
(A) Three jaw chuck (B) Four jaw chuck (C) Collect chuck (D) Magnetic chuck

Fig. 16.12.

Four Jaw Chuck. This type of chuck has been shown in Fig. 16.12 (B). Its each jaw can be opened or tightened separately. That is why it is also known as independent jaw chuck. This chuck can also be used from the reverse side. It is helpful in holding big jobs of different shapes. In order to fasten the job from the centre, round lines are made on its face at equal distance.

Collet Chuck. This chuck is used to hold lengthy jobs of same type in production jobs. These are attached to tapered sleeve fitted in the spindle of the machine. This chuck has been shown in Fig. 16.12 (C).

Magnetic Chuck. This type of chuck has been shown in Fig. 16.12 (D). With this chuck jobs are held with the magnetic power. It is used for holding small and little jobs. Permanent magnets and temporary electric magnets are used for this purpose.

Catch Plate. It is also known as Driving Plate. It is a round ordinary plate of cast iron. Grooves facing each other are cut in this plate. Bent tail type job carrier is put in it and job is revolved. Threads exist in its centre and with their help head is fixed in the spindle.

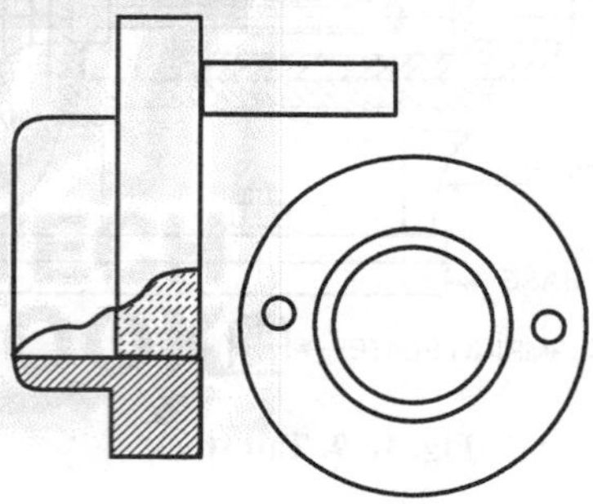

Fig. 16.13. Catch plate or driving plate

If straight tail type job carrier is to be used with it, a pin is fixed in a groove and this plate is fitted there.

Carrier. It is also known as Dog. It is used with the catch plate. The job is tied in the carrier and fitted in the catch plate in such a way that when the catch plate is revolved by the spindle the job tied in the carrier also revolves.

Carriers are of four types : (*i*) Straight tail carrier, (*ii*) Bent tail carrier, (*iii*) Double head bent tail carrier, (*iv*) Adjustable carrier. Normally, Straight tail carriers and Bent tail carriers are mostly used (Fig. 16.14).

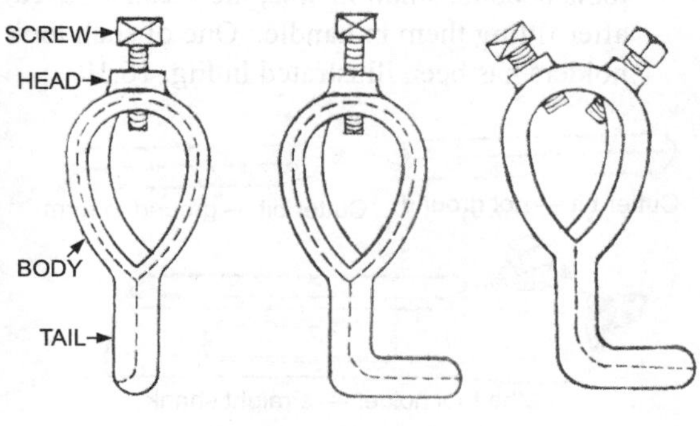

Fig. 16.14.

Face Plate. There are a number of jobs of such a shape that these can not be fitted into the centres or clamped with the help of chucks for the purpose of turning. Such jobs are gripped by the face plate. This plate is also like the catch plate but it has a number of grooves on it. With the help of these grooves or slots a job can be tightened or tied (Fig. 16.15).

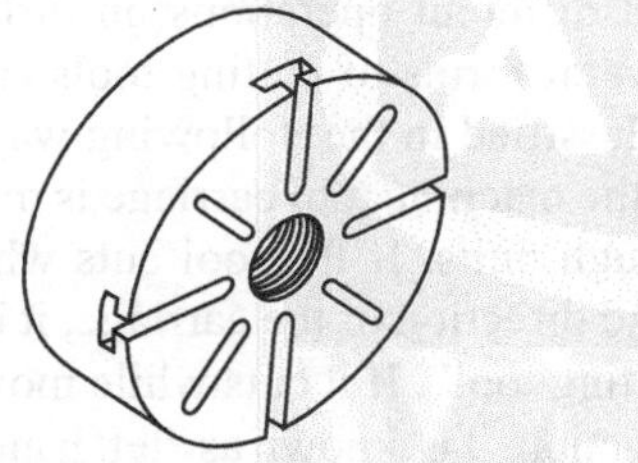

Fig. 16.15. Face plate

Steady Rest. Steady rest is used for such cylindrically long jobs which are likely to get resilient at the time of turning. These are of two types :

Fixed Steady Rest. This has been shown in Fig. 16.16 below. It is attached to the ways of a lathe bed for supporting long slender jobs while it is being machined. In case of long or thin job, two steady rests can also be used. The job gets support from three pins.

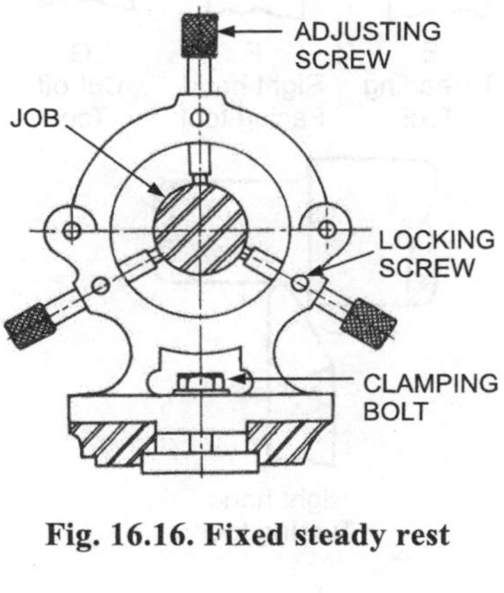

Fig. 16.16. Fixed steady rest

Travelling Steady Rest. It is also known as follower steady rest. It is related to the carriage cross slide with two bolts. That's why it travels (moves) along with the cutting tool and provides support to elasticity caused by pressure of the tool by remaining near it. This has been shown in Fig. 16.17.

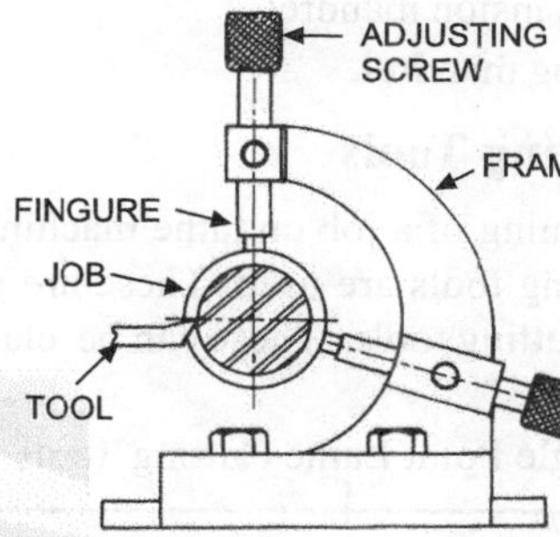

Fig. 16.17. Travelling steady rest

Mandrel. It is like a long, straight stake of steel. It has a rounded face for the greater portion of its length, terminating in a short, flat anvil. It has drill holes at both the ends and its surface which comes into contact is hard and smoothly finished.

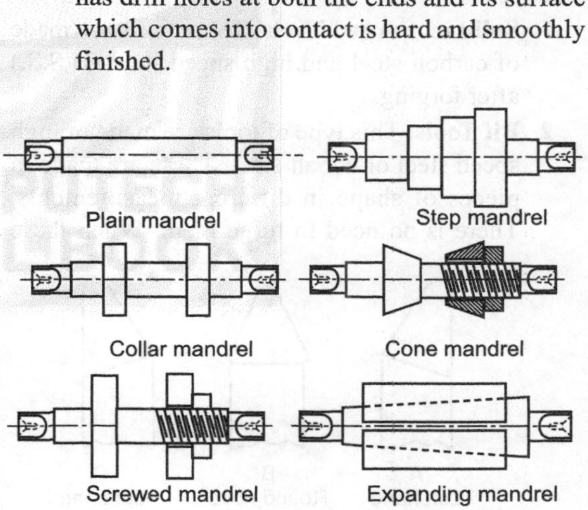

Fig. 16.18.

A mandrel is used for the following types of jobs on which holes have already been bored :

1. When job is to be turned in its complete length.
2. External turning is to be done on the centre line of a bored job.
3. The external diameter of bored jobs having same size is to be made of same size.

4. To quicken the process of production.

For different types of functions, different kinds of mandrels are used. Some of these are shown in Fig.16.18.

1. Plain mandrel
2. Stepped mandrel
3. Taper mandrel
4. Cone mandrel
5. Thread mandrel
6. Expansion mandrel
7. Gang mandrel.

Lathe Cutting Tools

For turning of a job on lathe machine several kinds of cutting tools are used. These are generally single point cutting tools. These can be classified in three ways :

Single Point Lathe Cutting Tools

- According to shape
- According to their function
- According to metal

Lathe Cutting Tools according to Shape. Shape-wise lathe cutting tools are of the following three types :

1. **Solid or Forged Tools.** These tools are made of carbon steel and high speed steel (H.S.S.) after forging.
2. **Bit Tools.** This type of tools are made of high speed steel or cobalt steel. These are made in pieces of shape in different measurements. There is no need to forge them. When these tools become small in size, these can be used after fitting them in handle. One of such tool holders has been illustrated in Fig. 16.19.

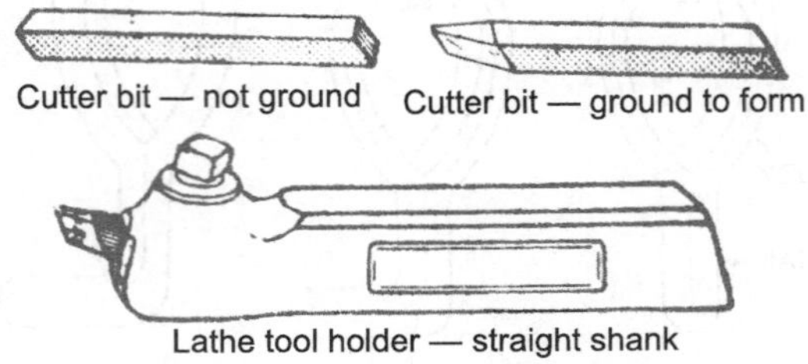

Fig. 16.19. Lathe tool holder

3. **Tipped Tool.** In this type of tools, a small piece of cutting meta1 is joined by brazing on the tool shank built by soft steel. These tips are made of carbide steel, molybdenum steel *etc*. This is a very valuable metal. As such, only tips made of this metal are used to keep the price of the tools low.

Lathe Cutting Tools according to Work. To carry out different operations on different types of jobs, several forms of cutting tools are used. These can be classified in the following ways. For cutting of the lathe machine tool carriage is moved right and left through units. If the tool cuts while moving in right hand direction of the carriage, it is called "right hand cutting tool". If it cuts while moving in the left hand direction, it is known as "left hand cutting tool".

On the basis of operations carried out by the lathe, cutting tools are of the following types, which have been illustrated in Fig. 16.20.

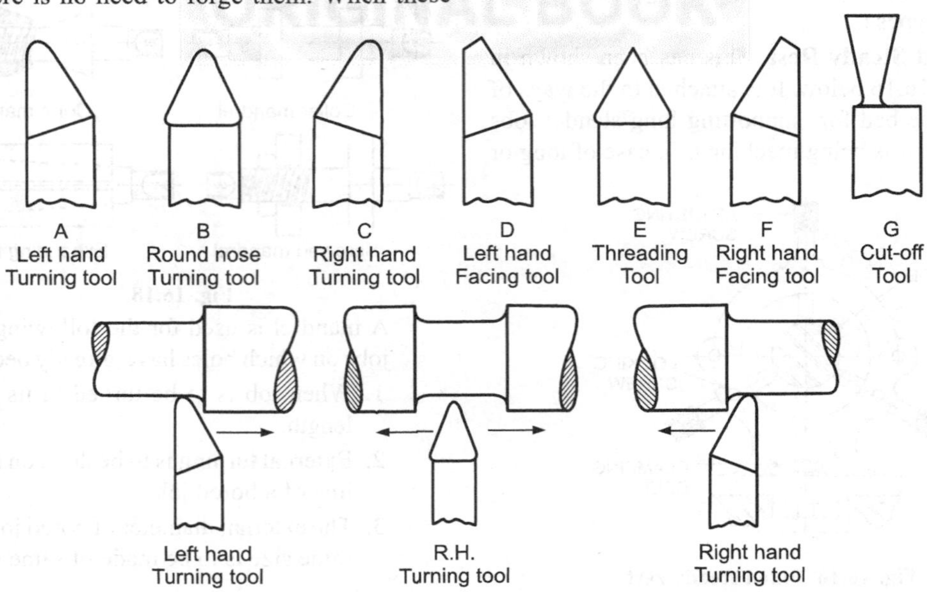

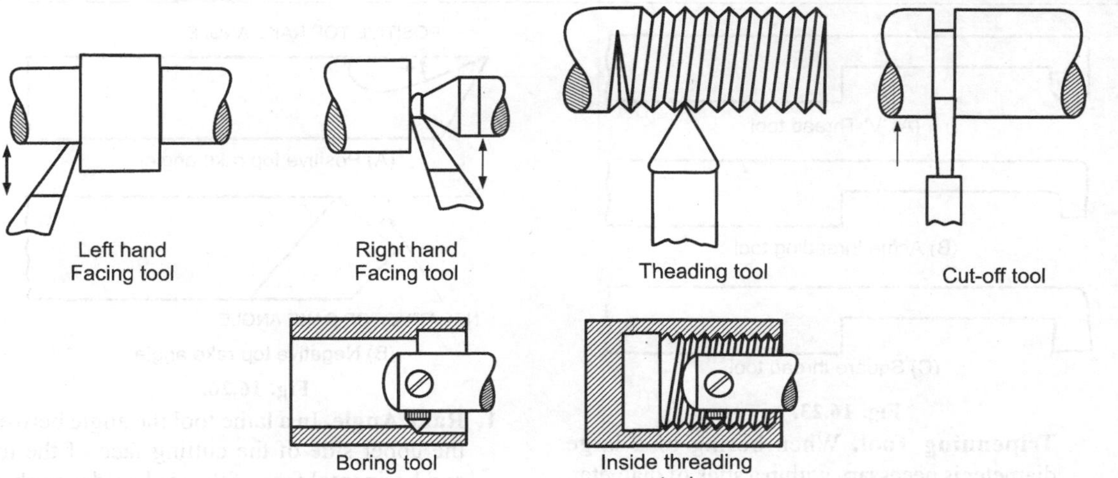

Fig. 16.20. Different types of lathe cutting tools

1. **Facing Tool.** Facing tools are used for facing the actual longitudinal ends of the job and to make its both ends at 90° from the centre line. Its shape is like a knife. It is used both as left hand and right hand tool.
2. **Rough Turning Tools.** It is used to remove the excess metal from the job by cutting it. Its front part is some what round and only a side rack angle is made. This is also right hand and left hand.
3. **Finishing Tool.** This is almost like a rough tool but its point is a bit more round. It is given top rake angle along with side rake angle.
4. **Parting Off Tool.** This type of cutting tool is used to divide (cut) the job into two parts. Its angle is back clearance angle.
   Because of this its edge does not get stuck into the groove, a chip breaker is also made over it in the form of a groove.
5. **Radius Tool.** Jobs which require round cutting are done with this radius tool. These are of two types :
   (A) Concave radius tool
   (B) Convex radius tool.
6. **Form Turning Tool.** In jobs where both concave and convex turnings are necessary, form turning tool is used. It is made of opposite shape to the job. This is shown in Fig. 16.21.

Boring Tools. Several jobs require lathe operations to be performed inside the jobs. For such jobs, boring tool is used.

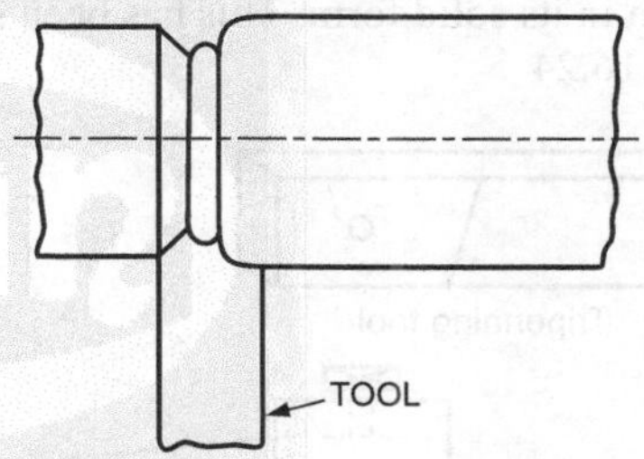

Fig. 16.21. Form tool

Operations are carried out in the bores made by drills. According to work they perform and their shape, boring tools are of the following four types, which have been shown in Fig. 16.22.

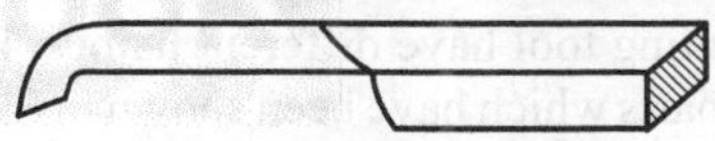

Fig. 16.22. Boring tool

1. Plain boring tool
2. International threading tool
3. Internal left side cutting tool
4. Internal square grooving tool.

External Threading Tools. For the jobs which need external threading, cutting part of tools are made according to the specific shape of the thread as shown in Fig. 16.23.

These are of the following three types :

1. "V" threading tool
2. Acme threading tool
3. Square threading tool.

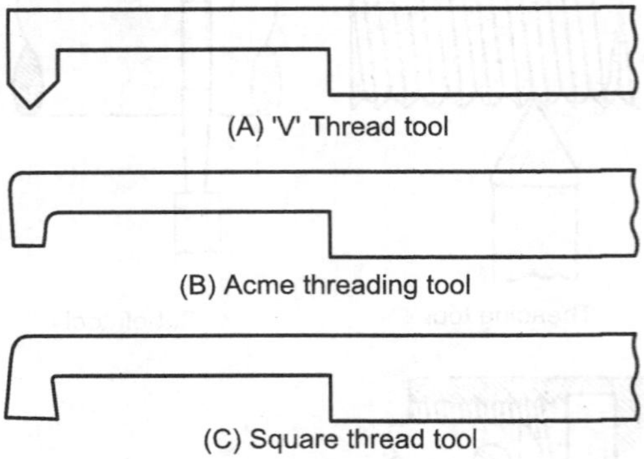

Fig. 16.23.

Tripenning Tool. When boring of a large diameter is necessary within a stick of diameter, tripenning tool is used. Its special feature is that through tripenning tool a metal can be cut even in its solid form. This has been shown in Fig.16.24.

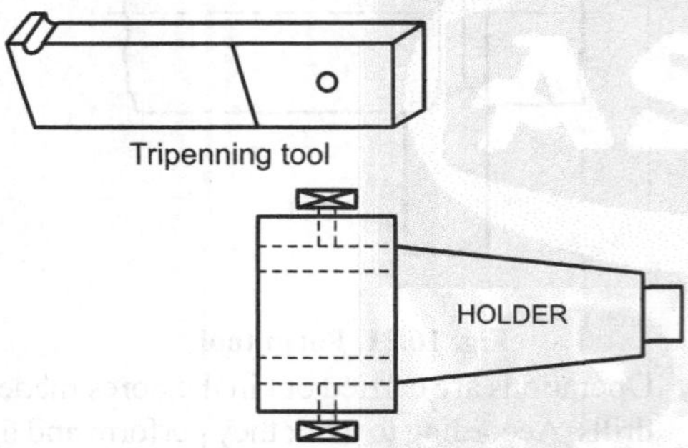

Fig. 16.24. Tripenning tool

Parts of Lathe Cutting Tool. Different parts of lathe cutting tool have different names. It has the following parts which have been shown in Fig. 16.25.

(*i*) Base
(*ii*) Shank
(*iii*) Face
(*iv*) Nose

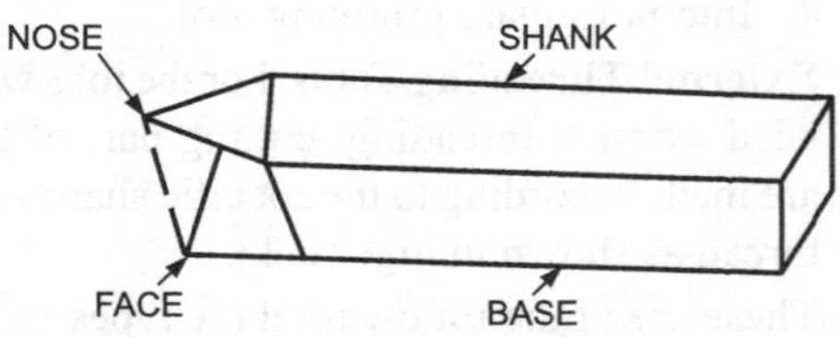

Fig. 16.25. Lathe cutting tool's parts

Lathe Cutting Tool Angles. For full efficiency of lathe cutting tools some angles are made. Metal can be cut with them easily, cutting is clear and edge of the tool works for longer. Lathe cutting tool has the following angles :

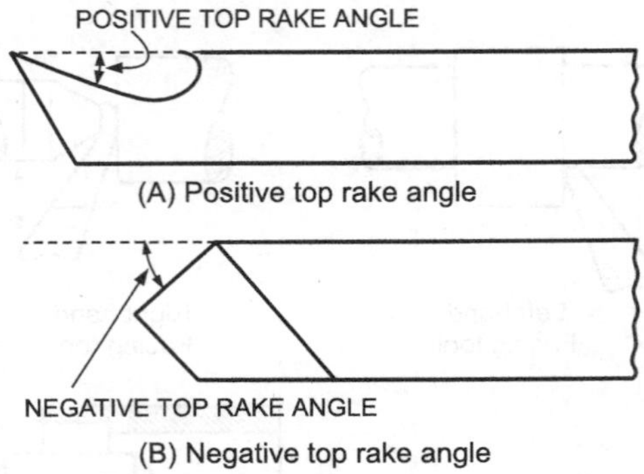

Fig. 16.26.

1. **Rake Angle.** In a lathe tool the angle between the upper side of the cutting face of the tool and horizontal face of the tool holder or shank is known as rake angle. These are of the following two types :

   (A) Top Rake Angle. It is made by drawing lines on the nose of the tool prallel to the base. This includes Positive Top Rake and Negative Top Rake Angles, which have been shown in Fig. 16.26.

   (B) Side Rake Angle. The top rake angle of the job is given slope from the edge under some special circumstances. It is known as side rake angle. Because of this the cutting chips are longer, which are in the shape of skein.

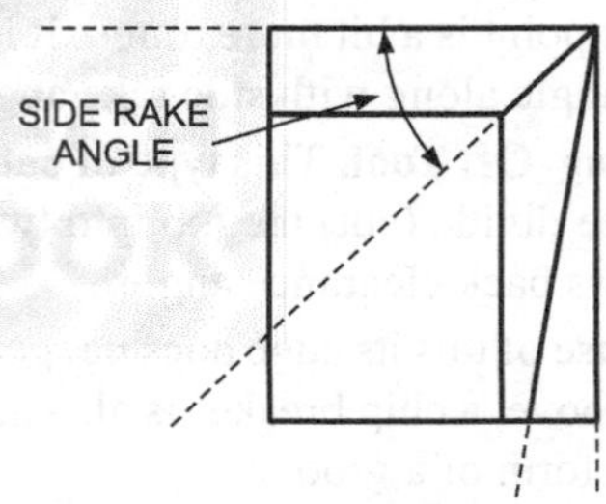

Fig. 16.27. Side rake angle

2. **Clearance Angle.** In a lathe tool, the angle between the cutting edge and vertical position of the work, is called clearance angle. This angle is kept in the following ways :

   (A) Front Clearance Angle. This angle is formed with the line drawn in length from

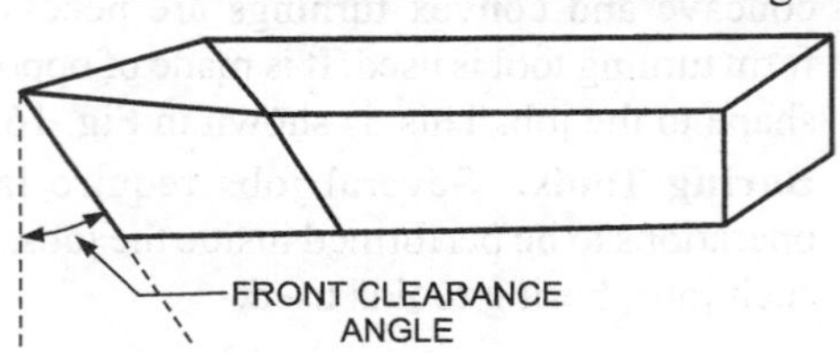

Fig. 16.28. Front clearance angle

the nose of the cutting tool towards the base and the line of the grinded surface of tool as shown in Fig. 16.28.

(B) *Front Side Clearance Angle.* An angle formed with the longitudinal line drawn from one point to the base, on the edge of the cutting tool which is towards the job, is called front side clearance angle. This has been shown in Fig. 16.29.

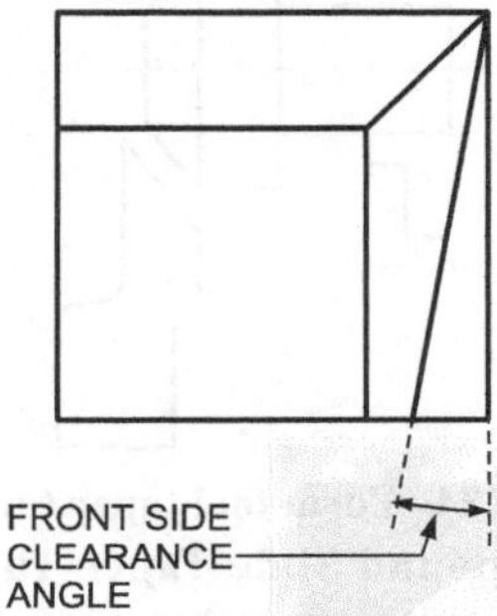

Fig. 16.29. Front side clearance angle

(C) *Back Side Clearance Angle.* An angle formed on the opposite direction to the front side clearance angle which is of similar type, is known as back side clearance angle. This has been shown in Fig. 16.30.

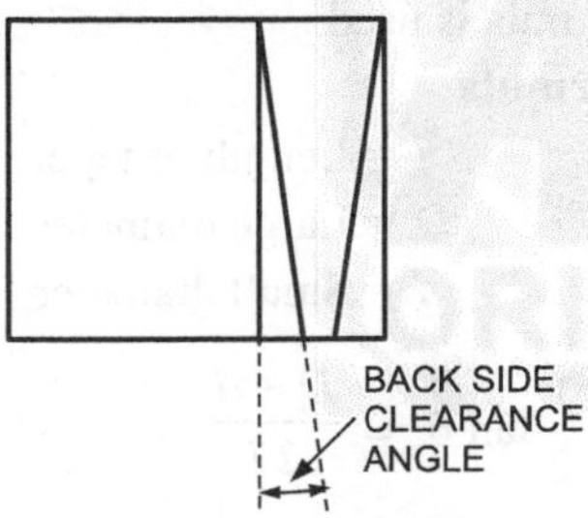

Fig. 16.30. Backside clearance angle.

(D) Back Clearance Angle. This type of angle has been shown in Fig. 16.31. This is formed only in parting off tools. This makes the front side of the toll flat and it does not entabgle in the grooves.

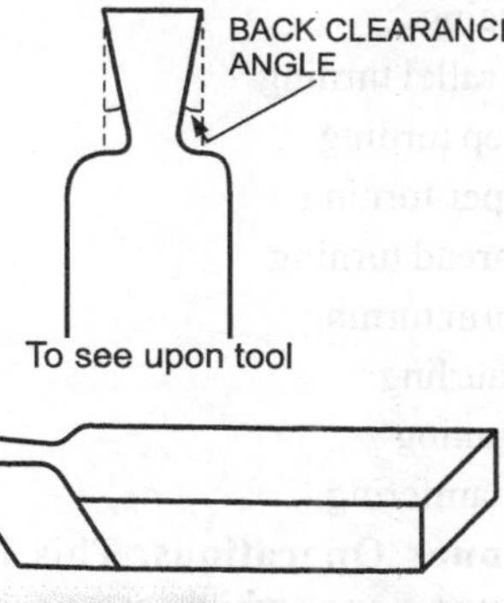

Fig. 16.31. Back clearance angle

3. Cutting Angle. After making the front clearance angle and top rake angle, the third angle left on the tool is called cutting angle. It has been shown in Fig. 16.32.

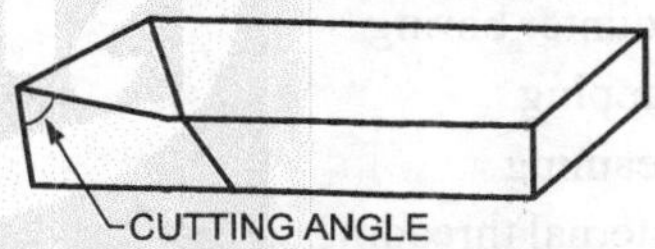

Fig. 16.32. Cutting angle.

4. Profile Angle. This angle has been shown in Fig. 16.33. When both the sides of the cutting tool are grinded and they meet at the nose, cutting angle is formed.

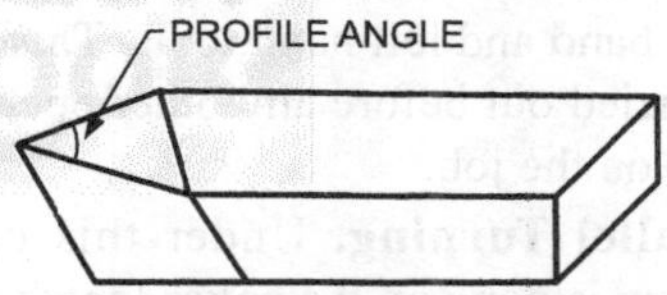

Fig. 16.33. Profile angle

Angles in High Speed Steel Metals

Metal of the job	*Front Clearance Angle*	*Side Clearance Angle*	*Top Rake Angle*
(A) Brass	6°	6°	0°
(B) Aluminium	8°	15°	20° to 40°
(C) Bronze	6°	6°	0°
(D) Cast iron	10°	12°	10°
(E) Mild steel	5° to 10°	20°	10° to 20°
(F) High carbon steel	6°	20°	10°
(G) Alloy steel	6°	14°	8°

Lathe Operations

Normally, the lathe operations can be divided into the following two parts :

(A) Outer Operations. This includes the following operations :

1. Facing
2. Parallel turning
3. Step turning
4. Taper turning
5. Thread turning
6. Form turning
7. Knurling
8. Panning
9. Chamfering.

(B) Inner Operations. This includes the following operations, which are performed after drilling or with drilling :

1. Drilling
2. Boring
3. Taper boring
4. Counter boring
5. Tapping
6. Reaming
7. Internal threading.

Facing. The act of making equal and plain ends of a job in their actual length is called facing. Tools are placed at the centre line of the job and feed is gradually given through cross slide. It can be done according to the job, both on right hand and left hand tools. This operation is carried out before any other operations are done on the job.

Parallel Turning. Under this operation, turning is done on the entire length of the job according to its maximum diameter.

Step Turning. To make smaller diameter on a plain round shaft than the diameter of the shaft is called step turning. This operation is done after the facing and parallel turning operations.

Taper Turning. When one side of a job with parallel diameter, is cut turned completely or partially, to reduce its diameter, by lathe machine, is called taper turning. The angle of taper is made according to the need, more or less internal or outer. The following four methods are used for taper turning :

1. **Form Tool Taper Turning.** Small sized outer taper are cut with these tools, as shown in Fig. 16.34. With these tools, tapers are made in length.

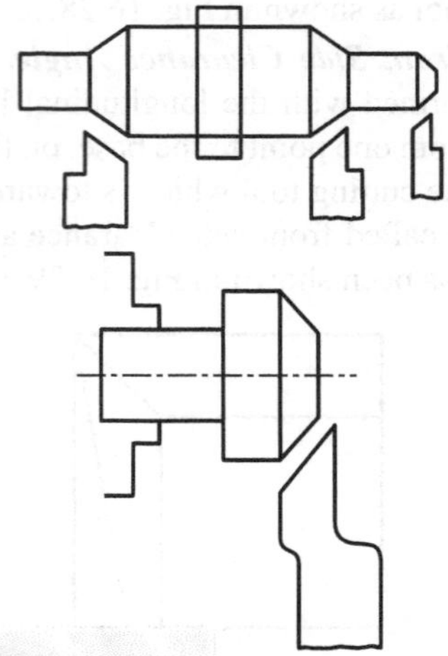

Fig. 16.34. Form tool taper turning

2. **Compound Slide Taper Turning.** In this process, compound rest is set by revolving it on half angle of taper angle. For setting on the determined angle, below the compound rest marking at 0° to 90° angle is indicated. With this process tapers cannot be cut with complete accuracy. But we can cut internal as well as outer taper with it. For finding out the taper, the following formula is used :

Formula

l = Length of taper

D = Large diameter

d = Small diameter

$$\frac{1}{2}\tan\theta = \frac{D-d}{2l}$$

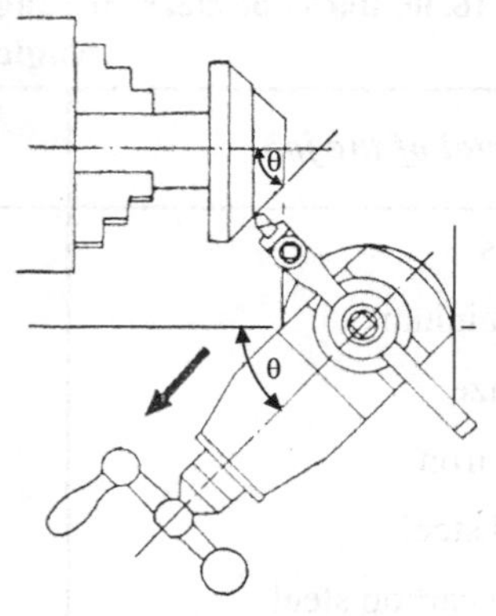

Fig. 16.35. Compound slide taper turning

3. Tail Stock Offset Taper Turning. With this process only external taper can be cut. First job is tied on both the sides between the centres. Tail stock is tied outside the centre and then taper is done. Self regulating feed is given. The following formula is used to find out set over :

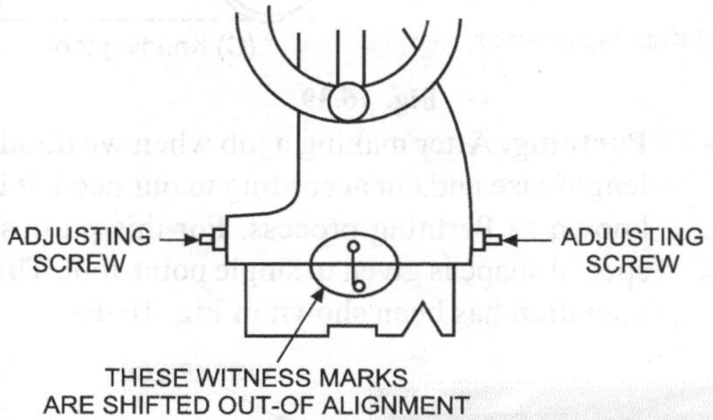

Fig. 16.36. Tail stock offset turning

1. Set over

$$= \frac{\text{Taper per foot}}{2} \times \frac{(\text{Length of job in inches})}{12}$$

2. Set over

$$= \sin\frac{\theta}{2} \times \text{Length of job in mm}$$

3. Set over

$$= \frac{D-d}{2} \times \frac{\text{Length of job in mm}}{\text{Length to be cut in mm}}$$

4. Taper Turning Attachment. In the workshops where there is need for cutting tapers frequently, taper turning attachment is used. This attachment is fixed behind the carriage. While cutting tapers the cross slide is loosened.

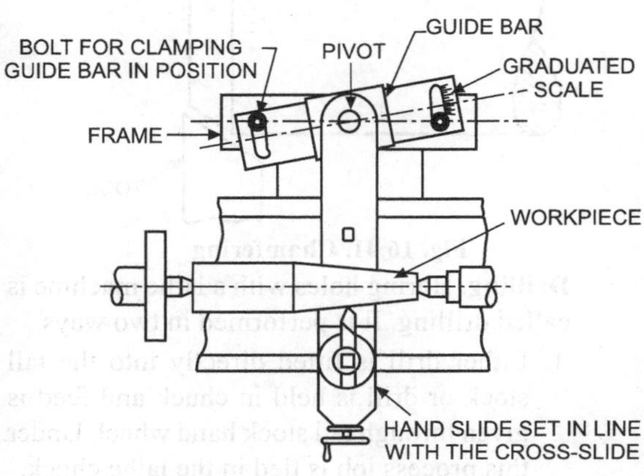

Fig. 16.37. Taper turning attachment

The angle at which the guide bar of the attachment is set, tool post is fixed at the same angle and the tool moves in length along with the carriage. Automatic or self regulating feed can be given in this process but taper cannot be cut at more than 10° angle.

Thread Cutting

Cutting threads on a job on lathe machine is called thread cutting. In this method, threads of desired pitch, greater angle *etc.* can be cut. There is need to give feed to the carriage as desired. This feed is provided by lead screw or feed gear box. For cutting threads only feed screw is used. Three acts are performed for this purpose :

1. Selection of those gears which can provide feed, as per requirement.
2. Cutting tool should be made according to the threads.
3. Arrangement should be made in such a way that every time the tool should travel on the same track *i.e.* takes up one thread only.

The most important work involved in cutting threads is selection of gears, which is also known as gear train. Two points are known to us : (A) Number of thread per inch on the lead screw, and (B) Number of threads per inch to be cut on the job. We can find out the desired speed through the proportion of these two. For this purpose the following formula is used :

Formula :

$$\frac{\text{Lead screw threads per inch}}{\text{Per inch threads to be cut in the job}} = \frac{\text{Driver gear}}{\text{Driven gear}}$$

$$\textit{i.e.,} \quad \frac{\text{stud gear}}{\text{lead screw gear}}$$

Example 1. Determine the number of gears for cutting 8 T.P.I. on a 4 T.P.I. lead screw machine.

Solution. Formula :

$$\frac{\text{T.P.I. of lead screw}}{\text{T.P.I. to be cut}} = \frac{\text{Driver gear}}{\text{Driven gear}}$$

$$\frac{4}{8} = \frac{1}{2} = \frac{\text{Driver gear}}{\text{Driven gear}}$$

In this way, we came to know that stud gear and lead screw are in the 1 : 2 proportion. With the same proportion, we can use driver gear of 20, 30 or 40 dents and driven gear of 40, 60 or 80 dents.

Example 2. Count the number of gears if the lead screw's pitch is 0.250″ and with this machine threads of 0.1″ pitch are to be cut.

Solution. $\frac{0.1''}{0.250''} = \frac{1}{10} \times \frac{100}{25} = \frac{2}{5}$

Thus there is proportion of 2 : 5 between driver gear and driven gear *i.e.*, driver gear with 20 dents and driven gear with 100 dents.

Gear Train

The arrangement ot thread cutting gears is called gear train. This arrangement of gear train is done in the following two ways:

1. **Simple Gear Train.** Its gear proportion is very simple. This is simple proportion of driver and driven gears. For changing the speed of the machine either one or both of them is changed.
2. **Compound Gear Train.** When we fail to get gears of right proportion for gear counting this train is used. The gear proportion is in compound *i.e.,* two driver and two driven gears are used.

Idler Gear. This gear has no concern with the gear proportion. It is used in the centre between driver and driven gears. In this process, the direction of the gears can be changed without changing their speed.

Form Turning. There are certain jobs on which both concave and convex shapes are to be made. Form turning is done on such jobs. For making this shape cutting tool is made exactly of the opposite shape as shown in Fig. 16.38 and job is cut accordingly. Beside this, form turning can also be done by giving cross-feed or by template and copying attachment.

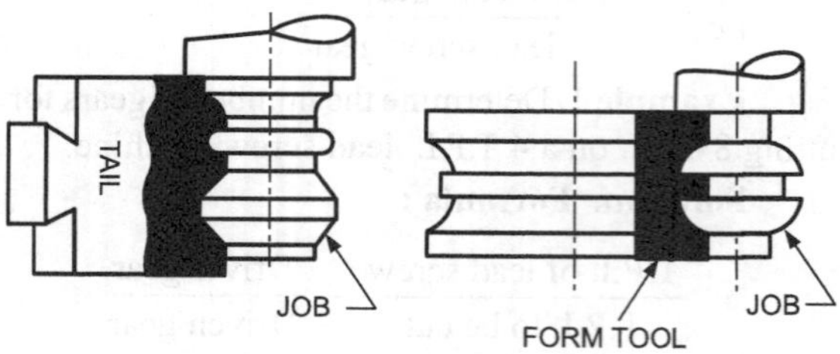

Fig. 16.38. Form turning

Knurling. Drawing slanting or square projecting lines on the surface of a job in order to have better grip is known as knurling. For this purpose a special knurling tool is used. Knurling operation has been shown in Fig. 16.39.

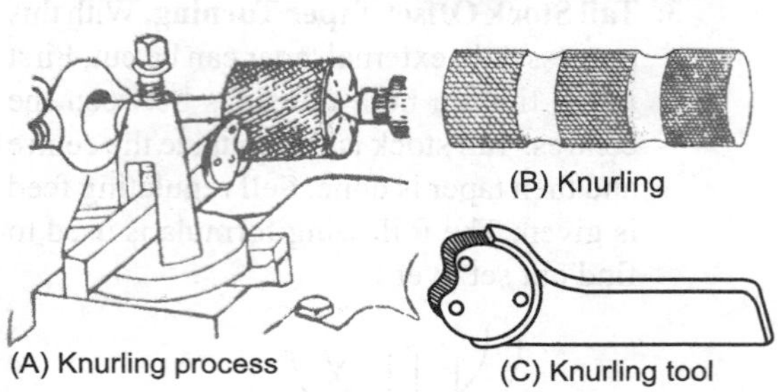

Fig. 16.39.

Partning. After making a job when we divide lengthwise and cut according to our need, it is known as Partning process. For this purpose special shape is given to single point tool. This operation has been shown in Fig. 16.40.

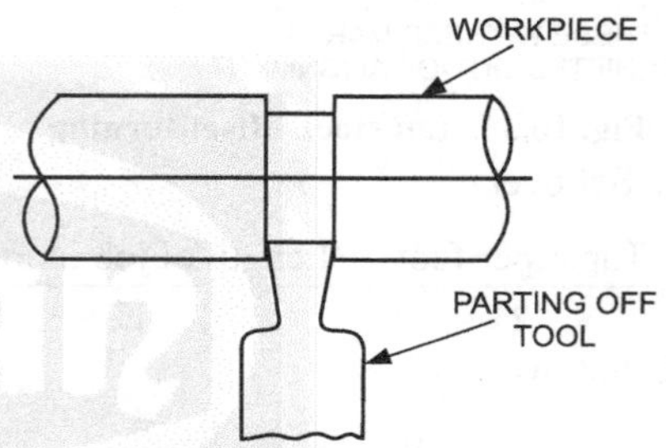

Fig. 16.40. Partning

Chamfering. Tapering of a small part of a job at its edge or corner is known as chamfering. With this process the burs of that part ends. It adds to the beauty of the shaft and it becomes easy to fit it. Chamfering is done after boring, knurling *etc.* has been done on the nut, bolt *etc.*

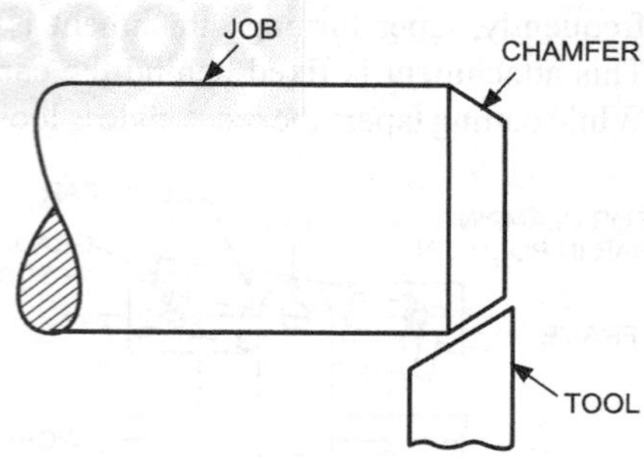

Fig. 16.41. Chamfering

Drilling. Boring holes with a lathe machine is called drilling. It is performed in two ways.

1. Either drill is fitted directly into the tail stock or drill is held in chuck and feed is given through tail stock hand wheel. Under this process job is tied in the lathe chuck.
2. Either drill is directly held in the lathe chuck or it is held with the help of drill chuck and

it is held in the tail stock of the job with the help of centre and with the point of the drill. Under this process feed is also given with the tail stock hand wheel.

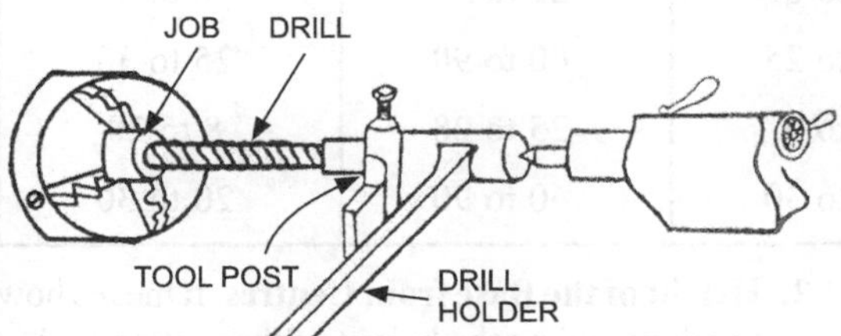

Fig. 16.42. Drilling

Boring. To finish or enlarge a hole already drilled with the lathe machine is called boring. A special type of boring tool is used for this purpose. If the holes are very deep their boring bar is also used.

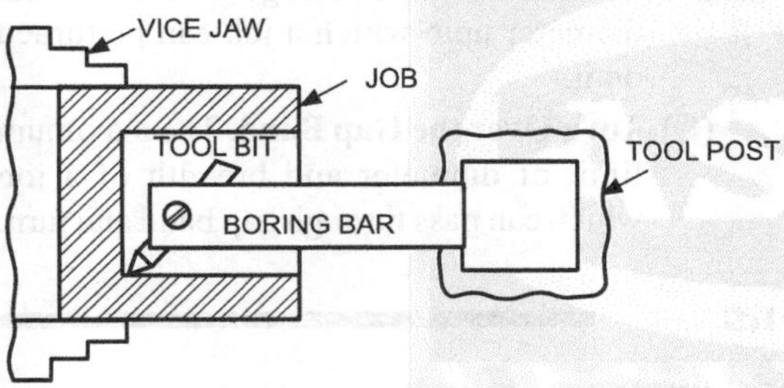

Fig. 16.43. Boring

Taper Boring. This process is similar to the normal boring. But it is also necessary to use processes similar to taper turning.

Counter Boring. To enlarge a hole through part of its length by boring is known as counter boring. With the help of counter boring we can have plain surface in a job even after nut bolts have been fixed in it.

Reaming. A hole bored with a drill used in a lathe machine does not have good finishing. For smoothing enlarging and tapering such holes a reamer is used by fixing it in a tail stock. This operation is known as reaming.

Tapping. Tapping is done to make internal threads in small jobs. Under this process, tap is held in a tail stock and job is held with the help of lathe chuck, face plate *etc*. Tap is given feed with the hand wheel of the tail stock. After the threads have been cut, the tap is withdrawn by rotating it in reverse order.

Internal Threading. In jobs where tapping cannot be performed, threads are cut with the help of internal threading tool. Special tool are made for this purpose.

Speed, Cutting Speed and Feed. Different jobs cannot be made by giving them, same speed, cutting speed or feed because their metals, size and shapes are different. Therefore, it is necessary to have knowledge about them.

Speed. The rate at which a body moves per unit of time *i.e.,* the distance covered in per unit of time. It is known from the following formula :

Formula : $\dfrac{\text{Distance covered}}{\text{Time}}$

Example. We say about a vehicle that it is moving at 45 km per hour. It means that the vehicle is covering 45 km distance in an hour. In fixed machines, we count the rotation of the gears and wheels per minute and determine their speed according to their periphery.

Cutting Speed. In those machines on which cutting operation is carried out, at the time of cutting, the job comes into contact with the cutting point or cutting point rotates on the job. In other words we can say that the distance a surface of job covers with the cutting point in a minute is its cutting speed. The following formula is used to find out the speed :

1. Cutting Speed

$$= \frac{\pi \times \text{Diameter} \times \text{R.P.M.}}{1000}$$

= Meter per minute

2. Cutting Speed

$$= \frac{\pi \times \text{Diameter (cm)} \times \text{R.P.M.}}{100}$$

= Meter per minute

3. Cutting Speed

$$= \frac{\pi \times \text{Diameter (in inches)} \times \text{R.P.M.}}{12}$$

= Foot per minute

Example. A job is of 35 mm diameter and it is being cut at rate of 200 R.P.M. Find out its cutting speed.

Solution. Formula

$$= \frac{\pi \times \text{Diameter (mm)} \times \text{R.P.M.}}{1000} \text{ meter / min.}$$

$$= \frac{\frac{22}{7} \times 35 \times 200}{1000} = \frac{22 \times 5 \times 2}{10}$$

= 22 meter per minute.

Average Cutting Speed of High Speed Steel

Metal	***Turning***	***Threading***	***Drilling***	***Reaming***
Mild steel	25 to 31	9 to 10	28 to 35	10 to 25
Cast Iron	15 to 20	7 to 8	22 to 31	6 to 8
Brass	60 to 90	20 to 25	60 to 90	25 to 30
High carbon steel	20 to 25	8 to 9	25 to 28	8 to 20
Aluminium	120 to 130	25 to 30	60 to 90	20 to 30

Feed. In a turning operation, rate of tool travel across a surface cutting it, is called feed. It is indicated in three ways :

1. Feed per round, such as 0.005″ per round
2. Feed per minute, such as 5.5 mm per minute
3. Cut per inch or per mm such as 50 cut per inch or 10 cut per mm.

Size of Lathe Machine. Size of the lathe machine is known from its following distances :

1. **Length of Base.** It includes the length of its entire base. It tells us that how much space is needed to fix that machine.
2. **Height of the Base from Centres.** It means how much would be the height of the cutting tool.
3. **Length of Lathe Bed.** It means the length of the job which can be turned on the machine.
4. **Swing.** It is of three kinds :

(A) Turn Over the Bed. The maximum diameter upto which a job can be turned.

(B) Turn Over the Carriage. The maximum diameter upto which a job can be turned on it.

(C) Turn Over the Gap Band. The maximum limit of diameter and breadth of a job which can pass through gap band and turn.

Questions

1. How do we classify lathe machines ?
2. Explain the major parts of an engine lathe machine.
3. What are the different kinds of lathe cutting tools ?
4. What are the different angles on lathe cutting tools and why ?
5. What are the jobs that can be done on a lathe machine ?
6. What are the various methods of taper turning ?
7. What is meant by gear train ? Why its selection is necessary ?
8. What are the different types of gear train ?
9. Why knurling is done ?
10. What is meant by speed, cutting speed and feed ?

17

Grinding and Grinding Machines

In the present age, every day new machines are being invented. These machines include machines useful in our daily life as well as those related to invention of new machines. Whatever machines we have, their success depends upon the efficient working of the parts fitted in them. A number of jobs are performed to make these parts. In order to cut a metal, often we have to make use of some hard metal. These tools have one or more than one cutting edge. But in grinding innumerable cutting edges are used. These innumerable cutting edges are provided by the grinding wheel. Besides clean and good cutting it saves time also. Because of these benefits, now-a-days grinding is being used in more and more jobs of making new machines. Main advantages of grinding are as follows :

1. Machine parts made by grinding are of accurate size.
2. These parts have fine finishing.
3. Unnecessary cutting and wastage of metal is saved.
4. It saves time.
5. Cost of production is less and production is more.

Grinding Wheel

Grinding wheel is a tool for metal, cutting with innumerable cutting edges. Success of grinding largely depends on suitable manufacturing of grinding tools according to the needs of the jobs. If we look at a grinding wheel through a magnifying glass we shall notice that there are innumerable tiny particles on the grinding wheel, which act as different cutting edges. These particles are called abrasives. The material used to glue (paste) these particles is called "bond". Some grinding wheels have very thin particles and some have thick ones. On the basis of these particles these are known according to their grades. Edges of these particles also get blunt. There is no need to sharpen their edge because they keep on falling from the grinding wheel. This depends on the grip of the abrasive particles. Those grinding wheels whose abrasive particles have strong grip are called hard wheels. And those grinding wheels whose abrasive particles do not have strong hold are called soft wheels.

Construction of Grinding Wheel. Different types of grinding wheels are made for different jobs using various materials. For their classification, the following elements are considered :

Abrasive. Abrasive is a very hard substance. Like diamond, if we break abrasive it results in innumerable cutting edges and particles. Abrasive is made of small particles. These are also known as grains. Abrasives are of the following two types :

1. Natural abrasive
2. Artificial abrasive.

Natural Abrasive. Under the natural abrasive we have Emery, sand stone and quartz. But these abrasives contain a lot of impurities. For example, we find 35% impurity in Emery. These impurities are not useful for cutting purposes. They prove hurdle in cutting jobs. Therefore, instead of natural abrasives, artificial abrasives are used.

Artificial Abrasive. Under this category of abrasive, we have main two types of abrasives :

1. Aluminium oxide
2. Silicon carbide.

This abrasive is made in the furnace according to the required properties and standards, which ensure efficient grinding.

Aluminium Oxide Abrasive. Chemical symbol of this abrasive is Al_2O_3. This type of abrasive is hard and of sharp grains and is widely used in grinding or cutting materials of high tensile strength such as alloy and high speed steels, annealed malleable iron, tough bronze *etc*. This is made by baking bauxite (a white to red earthy aluminum hydroxide) in arc-type furnace. This bauxite is the principal source of the metal aluminium. Coke and iron is also mixed in it in some percentage. When it is baked in the furnace, its impurities get mixed with the iron and drop down with it. Granular aluminium oxide is left in the form of a lump, which is considered as one of the hardest metals. This lump is broken into small particles and separated by filtering into different standards. Tensile strength of this abrasive is 9.6 while that of diamond is 10.

Aluminium oxide is of the following two types :

1. **Regular Aluminium Oxide.** Its symbol is "A". It is generally used for heavy jobs like snag steel casting, grinding of welding joints and for off-hand grinding of mild steel. It should not be used on heat-sensitive metals like stainless steel, nickel steel and tungsten *etc*.
2. **White Aluminium Oxide.** Its symbol is "AA" "VA" and "WA". This is made colourless by removing all the impurities of regular aluminium oxide. Its distinct feature is that it has the capacity of doing free and cold cutting. Cutters, cuttery tools and surgical instruments are grinded with it.

Silicon Carbide. Its chemical symbol is S.C. It is also one of the hardest metals and is sharp edged. Its tensile strength is 9.87, which is even more than that of the aluminium oxide. This is generally used for grinding material of low tensile strength such as cast iron, bronze, brass, aluminium, copper and non-magnetic like rubber, marble, glass, celluloid and tungsten carbide *etc*. This abrasive is made by mixing two elements (1) silicon (2) carbon. Silica sand and coke is heated in resistance type electric furnace at 2200°C for 30 hours. Through this chemical process, carbon comes out from coke and silicon from the silica sand comes out in the form of gas while the remaining matter is left in the form of lump of particles. This is silicon carbide. This lump is reduced to particles. Through magnetic process these are purified and through different filters separated in different sizes. Silicon carbide is prepared in two colours (1) Shiny black (2) Green. On this basis these are divided into two parts :

1. **Black Silicon Carbide.** Its sympol is "C". Jobs of less tensile metal are grinded and cylindrical grinding, centreless grinding, surface grinding, internal grinding and snaging grinding is done with this carbide.
2. **Green Silicon Carbide.** Its symbol is "GC". It is light green in colour. It is used particularly for cemented carbide tip tools grinding. Solid and chilled casting is grinded with it.

Grain or Grit. All kinds of abrasives are broken and reduced to the grain ton and then is completely cleaned and purified. These purified grains of abrasive are filtered through sieves of different sizes. First it is filtered through sieve of 8 holes per inch. Grain filtered through this sieve are of 8 grain. It means 8×8 = grains filtered through 64 hole. This has been shown in Fig. 17.1.

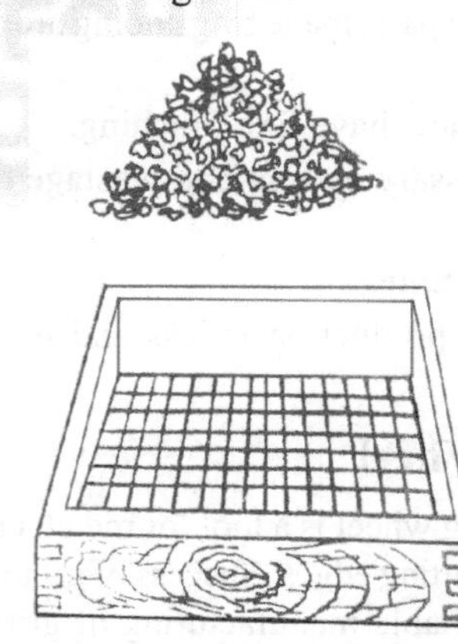

Fig. 17.1. 8-Grain and sieve

Table 1

Coarse grain	8	10	12	14	16	20	Very thick grains
Medium grain	24	30	36	46	54	60	Grains of medium thickness
Fine grain	70	80	90	700	120	150	Thin grains
Very fine grain	180	220	240	280	320	—	Very thin grains
Very thin grain	400	500	600	—	—	—	Grains thin like flour

Grains filterad through this sieve also contain 10 grains and these again filtered through sieve of 10 grains. Grains which cannot be filtered through this sieve, these are actually of 8 grains. Normally size of 8 to 600 grain is used which can be known from the previous table.

Grade. Grade of grinding wheels means the measurement of their power to hold the abrasive grain. It tells us the extent of the resistance offered by the grinding power (which tries to break the grain particles or wears out the wheels) *i.e.*, the combined power of bond and abrasive grains at the time of grinding. This depends upon the kind of bond and the quantity of binding meterial. Through this we come to know the hardness and softness of the grinding wheels. These are divided on the basis of grades. Grades are known by English alphabets, which are from "A" to"Z". Wheel of "A" grade is considered the most soft and that with "Z" indication is considered the hardest grinding wheel. In the same way, the hardness of grinding wheels is known by other letters, which has been shown in the following table :

Table 2

Highly soft	A	B	C	D			
Soft	E	F	G	H			
Medium	I	J	K	L	M		
Hard	N	O	P	Q	R	S	
Very Hard	T	U	V	W	X	Y	Z

Structure. By structure of grinding wheel we mean the blank space between grains (spacing) and density. While making grinding wheels of same type of abrasive and bond their density is increased or decreased. For example, in two grinding wheels, the mixture of abrasive and bond is 800 gm and 600 gm. If this mixture of abrasive and bond is moulded in same size, in heavy grinding wheel abrasive grains would be close to each other. On the basis of distance (spacing) of grains in grinding wheels these can be divided into the following three sections :

(1) Open, (2) Medium and (3) Dense. These have been shown in Fig. 17.2.

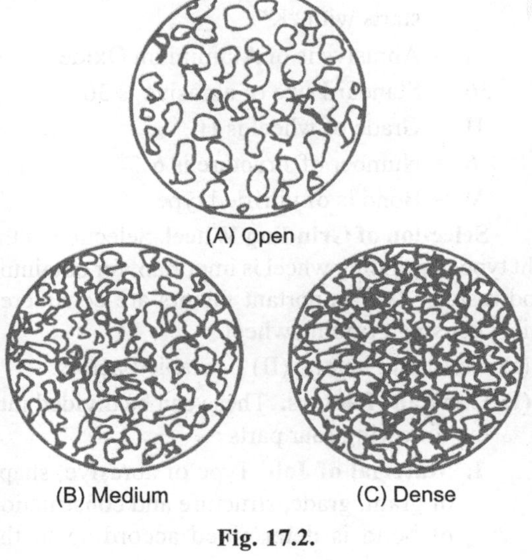

Fig. 17.2.

Structure or construction can be known by numbers 1 to 15 as given in the follwing table :

Table 3

Dense	1	2	3	4	5	6	7	8	(very dense)
Medium	6	7	8	9	10				(medium)
Open	11	12	13	14	15				(very open)

Bond. By bond we mean a binding agent *i.e.*, material used to hold particles of a abrasive together in a grinding wheel. After use if a grain becomes blunt, this binding material ends its holding power and allows it to fall down. Instead of that grain, a new grain below that starts grinding. This material (bond) does not perform any cutting action itself. The quantity of bond acts as the bast for making the grinding wheel hard or soft because in the grinding wheels made of one type of abrasive grains the difference between their hardness can be brought only by the bond. These bonds are of the following seven types :

S. No.	*Name of Bond*	*Symbol*
1.	Vitrified Bond	"V'
2.	Resinoid Bond or Bakelite Bond	"B'
3.	Shellac Bond	"E'
4.	Silicate Bond	"S'
5.	Rubber Bond	"R
6.	Oxichloride Bond	"OXY"
7.	Metallic Bond	"M"

Vitrified Bond. About 75% of the grinding wheels are made of this type of bond. The grinding wheels of this type do not have any impact of water, oil, acid and normal temperature on them. A specific proportion of clay is mixed with this bond and this mixture is moulded with this press machine and it is freezed after melting it at 3000°F temperature. With this type of grinding wheels heavy materials can be cut.

Grinding wheels which are made of bond and aluminium oxide are known by the symbols

"V 23", "VN", "VVE" and "V 99". Grinding wheels of silicon carbide made of this bond are known by the symbols "V 17" and "VK.".

Resinoid Bond. This is a sort of synthetic compound with which several types of grinding wheels like hard, dense and thick wheels are made. This compound contains mixture of Backelite which is pressed with the abrasive grains and heated at comparatively lower temperature. These grinding wheels work in cold condition. They perform quick cutting of metal. They can be operated at high speed. These are used for table grinding, roll grinding, cam grinding *etc*. These grinding wheels are known by the symbols : "BL_1", "BL_2", "BL_3", "B_4", "B_5", "B_9" and "B_{12}".

Shellac Bond. The grinding wheels made with this type of bond are made by heating shellac and abrasive grains. These are used for grinding of cam shaft, crank shaft, safety razor *etc*. These grinding wheels cannot be used for heavy jobs. These wheels are known by the symbols "E_6" and "E_7".

Silicate Bond. The grinding wheels of this bond are made by heating the silicate soda and abrasive grains at low temperature. Their grains fall down quickly as compared to the vitrified bond wheels. These wheels are used where the heat produced by grinding can be kept low. This type of grinding wheels are made in large sizes for tough jobs. These wheels are known by the symbol "S".

Rubber Bond. This type of grinding wheels are made by rolling synthetic rubber and abrasive grains. First they take the shape of sheet. Then different types, shapes and sizes of wheels are cut out of these wheels and valcanised. These wheels can be made thin to the extent of 0.003". These are used for grinding such jobs which need good finishing. While using these wheels coolants should be used. These grinding wheels are known by the symbols "Rso" and "Rsi" and only "R".

Oxy-chloride Bond. This type of bond is used for those grinding wheels with which jobs like grinding of safety razor blade are ground. These wheels are indicated by the symbols of "OXY".

Metallic Bond. Grinding wheels of this type of bond are made by melting soft metal and abrasive through dye-casting process. These are used for grinding of very hard metals. These are made in different shapes and sizes. When their abrasive become blunt these are made loose by a special type of wheel dresser. In this way, the abrasive grains with sharp edges come up from below.

Standard Marking of Grinding Wheels. In order to facilitate selection of grinding wheels, their manufacturing companies have adopted some standard. Through these standards, their qualities are indicated through some letters on the grinding wheels. First letter indicates the name of the manufacturer. Second letter indicates the type of abrasive. At third place number is indicated. They indicate the standard of the grain. At the fourth place "A" to "Z" any letter is indicated which indicates the hardness of the grinding wheel. At the fifth place again numbers 1 to 15 are written, which indicates the distance or spacing (structure) of the abrasive grains. At the sixth place letter indicating the type of bond is written.

We can know the above standard from the following details :

1. First Place — Letter of the name of manufacturer.
2. Second Place — Type of abrasive.
3. Third Place — Number of the grain class.
4. Fourth Place — Grade or hardness of grain.
5. Fifth Place — Structure.
6. Sixth Place — Type of bond.

Example. What is meant by K A 36 H 6 V indicated on the grinding wheel ?

K = The name of manufacturing company starts with "K"

A = Abrasive is of Aluminium Oxide

36 = Standard size of abrasive is 36

H = Grade of wheel is H

6 = Number of structure is 6

V = Bond is of vitrified type.

Selection of Grinding Wheel. Selection of the right type of grinding wheel is important for obtaining good results. Two important factors are considered while choosing grinding wheel.

(I) Constant Factors, (II) Variable Factors.

(I) Constant Factors. These can be divided into the following four parts :

1. Material of Job. Type of abrasive, shape of grain, grade, structure and construction of bond is determined according to the material of which the job is made and then selection of grinding wheel is done. For this purpose the following points should be borne in mind :

(1) For steel and steel alloy grinding wheel of aluminium oxide and cast iron should be chosen and for non-ferrous metal and non-metallic materials silicon carbide grinding wheel should be choosen.

(2) For hard and brittle metals thin grinder should be choosen and for soft and ductile metals grinding wheel of thick grain should be chosen.

(3) For hard metals, soft grinding wheel should be taken and for soft metals hard wheel should be chosen.

(4) For hard and brittle metals, dense wheel should be chosen and for ductile metals wheel with open structure should be selected.

2. **Finishing of the Job.** Type of grain and bond depends upon the accuracy with which job is to be finished. The following points should be considered in this regard :

(1) For fast cutting grinding wheel of thick grain and for fine cutting thin grains wheel should be used.

(2) For rough and ordinary finishing vitrified bond and for high or finishing resinoid rubber shellac bond grinding wheel should be used.

3. **Contact Area of Job.** Area of contact affects grain, grade and structure in the wheel. In this connection, the following points should be kept in mind :

From less area thin grain, for large thick grain, for less area dense structure and for large area open structure should be used.

4. **Type of Grinding of the Job.** By this we only decide the bond. For accurate grinding vitrified bond and for greater accuracy, resenoid, rubber or shellac bond wheel is selected.

(II) Variable Factors. These factors are also divided into the following parts :

(1) Speed of the Grinding Wheel. This is related to the bond of the wheel. We must ensure that for high speed, soft wheels are used.

(2) Rate of feeding. This is related to the grade of the wheel. In this connection, it should be ensured that when more pressure is to be exerted on the wheel, hard wheel should be used.

(3) Capacity of Grinding Machine. Hard grinding wheel should be used for the old machines and whose spindle has become loose.

Capacity of the Grinding Man. If the worker is not an experienced one and he has to do small jobs, off and on, on the grinding machine, it is better to use a hard wheel.

Selection of Grinding Wheel

	Job or Metal to be grinded	*Abrasive*	*Grain*	*Grade*
(A)	**For outside grinding :**			
	Soft steel	Aluminium Oxide	36	M
	Hard steel	"	46	K
	Drill, reamer *etc.* cutting tool	"	80	K
	Cast iron and bronze	Silicon Carbide	46	L
(B)	**Inside cylindrical grinding :**			
	Soft steel	Aluminium Oxide	46	I
	Hard steel (Roughing)	"	46	J or K
	Hard steel (Polishing)	"	80	J or K
	Brass (Roughing)	Silicon Carbide	36	H or I
	Brass (Polishing)	"	80	H
(C)	**Surface grinding :**			
	Hard steel	Aluminium Oxide	46	H
	Hard carbon steel	"	60	G or U
	Cast iron	Silicon carbide	36	M

Grinding Speed. The speed of rotation of circumference of a grinding wheel is called grinding speed. It is found out by surface speed per minute or surface speed meter per second. By this speed we come to know the rate at which the point is moving on the grinding wheel. This rate of rotation of wheel is directly related to the capacity. If the speed is slow, without adequate grinding abrasives would be destroyed. Contrarily, if the speed is too high even then grinding would not be proper and there would be risk of breaking of the wheel. Generally, for different jobs the speed of grinding wheel is from 1500 to 7000 surface speed foot per minute (S.F.P.M.) or 20 to 80 surface speed meter per second (S.M.P.S.). Speed of some special jobs can be known from the following table :

Grinding Speed

Type of grinding	*Safe speed (S.F.P.M.)*	*Safe speed meter/second*
Tool and cutter grinding	1500 to 2000	20 to 25
Cylindrical grinding	1800 to 2250	25 to 43
Internal grinding	1500 to 2000	20 to 35
Surface grinding	1700 to 2500	30 to 40
Diamond wheel grinding	5000 to 7000	20 to 25
Disc grinding	4000 to 5500	20 to 28

In order to know the S.F.P.M. of a grinding wheel, the following formula is used :

$$\text{Surface speed} = \frac{r \times \text{diameter of wheel} \times \text{rounds per minute}}{12}$$

(In F.P.S. system)

$$\text{Surface speed} = \frac{r \times \text{diameter of wheel} \times \text{rounds per minute}}{1000}$$

(In M.K.S. system)

Example. If the diameter of a grinding wheel is 200 mm and it is rotating at 3500 R.P.M., find out the S.S.M./sec.

Solution. As per the above formula

$$\text{S.S.M. / sec} = \frac{22 \times 200 \times 3500}{7 \times 1000}$$

$$= 2200 \text{ S.S.M. / sec.}$$

Grinding Wheel Feed. Whether the pressure of the job is towards the wheel or the pressure of the grinding wheel is towards the job, the rate of this pressure is known as grinding wheel feed. Normally, for rough jobs this speed is from 0.025 mm to 0.102 mm and for finishing jobs, it is kept upto 0.01 mm. It is directly related to the speed of the wheel. In this connection the following two points should be borne in mind :

1. If the grinding wheel starts wearing out quickly at the time of grinding, we should think that speed is slow and we should reduce the feed.
2. If the grinding wheel makes the job hot at the time of grinding, feed should be increased and, the speed of wheel should be reduced.

Shape and Use of Grinding Wheels. As different materials are used for making grinding wheels for different jobs, in the same way their shape also differs. Grinding wheels have the following shapes :

1. Straight
2. Recessed one side
3. Recessed two sides
4. Offset
5. Counter sunk dovetail
6. Raised dovetail
7. Tapered one side
8. Tapered two sides
9. Ring or cylindrical
10. Straight cup
11. Double cup
12. Flaring cup
13. Dish
14. Saucer
15. Cutting off and sliting.

Grinding Wheel Dressing. When the small and thin grains of metal get stuck into the cutting surface of the grinding wheel or when because of continued use of the grinding wheel, its abrasive grains fall down from the soft surface and dents are formed in it, or their ends wear out and become round, such grinding wheels are dressed with the steel cutters. This act is also known as truing. This dressing is done in two ways : (1) Hestington Dresser, (2) Diamond Dresser.

Hestington Dresser. This type of dresser is shown in Fig. 17.3. Three or four cutters of hard steel are provided in this dresser. For dressing, tool's handle is held and pressed on the face of grinding wheel gradually. With this the abrasive at uneven surface of the face starts falling. When cutter wheel starts touching the entire face equally, we should consider that face is all right. It is also known as star dresser. It is used for dressing hand grinding wheel and pedestal grinding wheel.

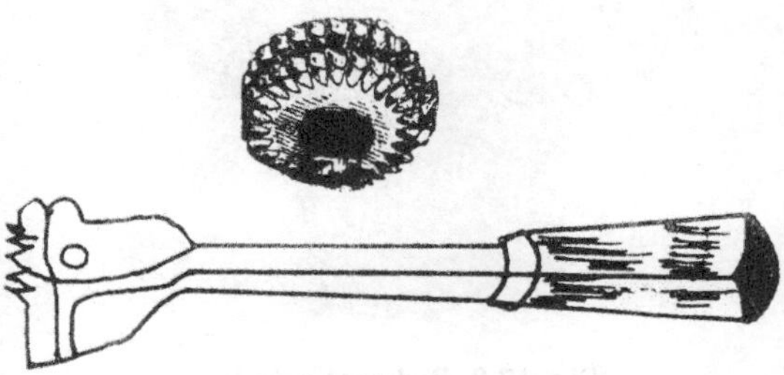

Fig. 17.3. Hestington wheel dresser

Diamond Dresser. This type of dresser has been shown in Fig. 17.4. It is like a stick of steel. On one end of this there is a diamond point. For doing wheel dressing with the diamond dresser, the dresser is pressed in an angular state on the face of the grinding wheel. It should be moved on the face of the grinding wheel with equal pressure. First light cuts should be taken and when the face becomes allright, face should be dressed properly. It is used for wheels for grinding of precision tools.

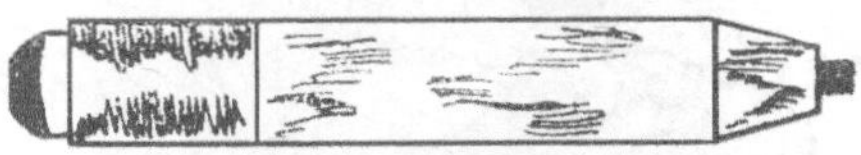

Fig. 17.4. Diamond dresser

Fastening of Grinding Wheel on Machine Spindle. Fastening of grinding wheel is an important act. First of all wheel should be checked. Bore of wheel should be 0.005" larger than the spindle and plastic lead bushing should fit in well into it. Before fitting the wheel the inside flange should be fitted with the "key" and wheel should be mounted on the spindle and then outside flange should be fitted. We must use rubber packing at the wheel side of the inside flange and at wheel side of the outside flange. After fitting, the wheel nut should be tightened. It should be ensured that the size of flange should be at least half of the wheel. We should never tight the wheel only with nut, without the flange. After fitting the wheel, it should be operated on trial and see that there is no twist or trembling in it. If it is there it should be stopped.

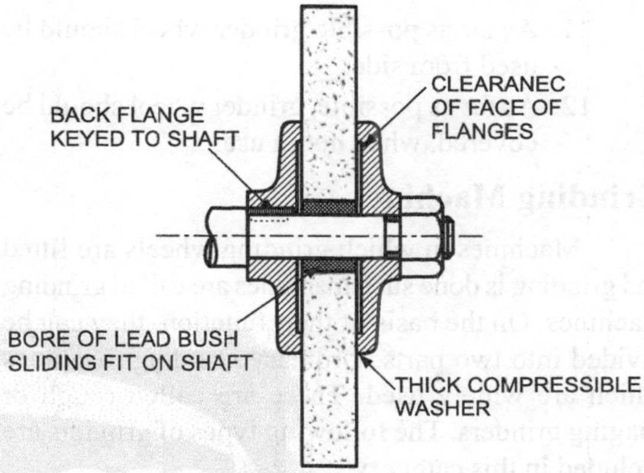

Fig. 17.5. Fastening of grinding wheel

Grinding Wheel Balancing. For quality finishing on any job it is essential that the grinding wheel should be properly balanced. Wheels are checked on the balancing stand. If there is any shortcoming in its balancing, it is set right by providing lead packing. Sometimes, the balance is disturbed because of loose bore or bushing. Lead bushes are used for this purpose.

Safety and Care of Grinding Wheels :

1. Before fitting a new grinding wheel, it should be verified that there are no cracks. This can be done by having the wheel and striking with a piece of wood, of it should give sound "tune". In no case, a crack wheel should be used.
2. Grinding wheel can get broken in case of a fall. Therefore these should be handled carefully.
3. Don't keep heavy loads on the wheels.
4. Grinding wheels should not be used without flange.
5. While using wheel dress alertness should be observed else they would be broken.
6. If the flanges of the wheel are very tight or very thick they can be broken.
7. Grinding machine should be fitted properly. If there is a vibration in the grinding machine its wheel can be broken.

8. Job should be placed at the tool rest and then grinded otherwise there are chances that it can be broken by getting entangled between tool rests of thin jobs and wheel.
9. Grinder should not be moved at more than the fixed speed.
10. The face of the grinder wheel should be plain.
11. As far as possible grinder wheel should be used from side.
12. As far as possible, grinder wheel should be covered, when not in use.

Grinding Machines

Machines in which grinding wheels are fitted and grinding is done such machines are called grinding machines. On the basis of their function, they can be divided into two parts. Ordinary grinding machines which are widely used. These are called rough or snaging grinders. The following types of grinders are included in this category :

1. **Bench Grinder.** This type of grinder is fixed on a work bench or table. Gear or pulley is fitted in it. For rotating the big size gear or pulleys a handle is also fixed. It contains one or two grinding wheels. Edges of cutting tools can be made with this grinder. Provision can be made to operate these with power also (Fig. 17.6).

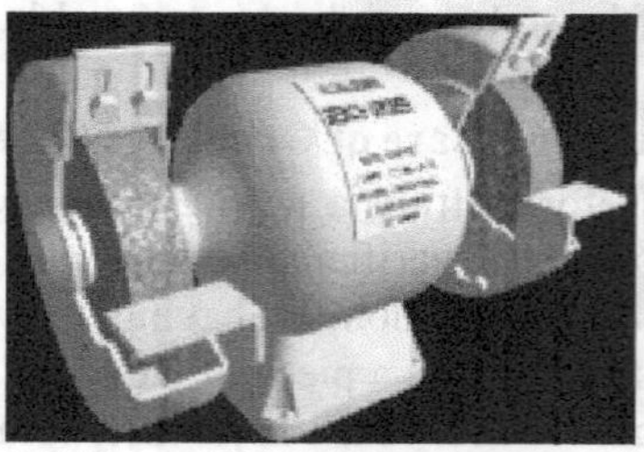

Fig. 17.6. Bench grinder

2. **Hand Grinder.** This grinder is also fixed on the work bench or table. There is a provision of moving the grinding wheels with a lever as shown in Fig. 17.7.

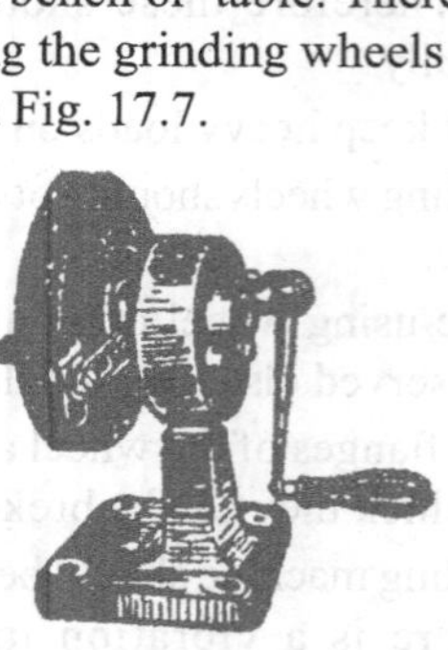

Fig. 17.7. Hand grinder

3. **Pedestal Grinder.** This type of grinder is operated with electric power. This is fitted on a pedestal frame separately on the ground. A grinding wheel is fitted each on both the sides of the shaft of the electric motor. Tool restes are also provided with them. These are most widely used in the workshops. Edges of all types of cutting tools are made with these grinders. Apart from this, moulded articles can also be cleaned with it.

Fig. 17.8. Pedestal grinder

4. **Portable Grinder.** This is a small grinder operated with electric power. It can be easily carried anywhere. Grinding can be done by holding it in hand. It is used for cleaning the heavy welding jobs. On one end of the motor shaft a grinding wheel is fitted and on the other end a handle or switch for operating the machine is fixed according to convenience. It should be used carefully since there is possibility of getting electric shock.

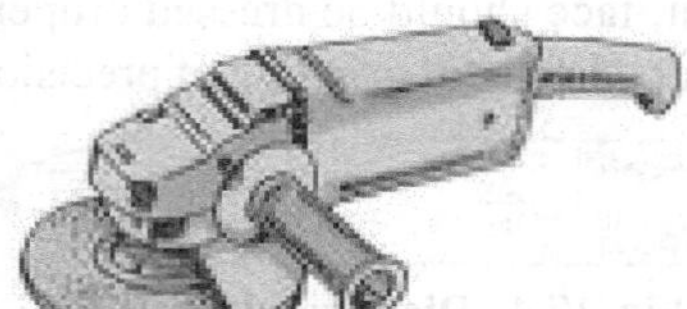

Fig. 17.9. Portable grinder

Flexible Grinder. This type of grinder is shown in Fig. 17.10. The electric motor in this grinder is fitted on such a basis that it can be moved in any direction. A flexible shaft is fitted on the motor shaft with the help of a coupling. On one end of this shaft a grinding wheel and handle is provided. Large jobs can be easily grinded with this grinder.

Fig. 17.10. Flexible grinder

Precision grinder. In this type of grinder a movable spindle is fitted in the grinding wheel. This spindle is fitted on a table along with its motor. With this spindle the grinding wheel can be turned in forward, backward, left or right direction in running condition. Jobs of excellent finish and accuracy are grinded with it. These grinders are of the following types :

1. Cylindrical grinder
2. Plung cut grinder
3. Form grinder
4. Internal grinder
5. Centreless grinder
6. Surface grinder
7. Universal grinder
8. Tool and cutter grinder.

1. **Cylindrical Grinder.** The surfaces which have been made plain by shaper or plainer are grinded with this grinder. The cylindrical surfaces are grinded with a machine in which grinding wheel is fitted on the shaft of a free electric motor, in this type of grinders, the grinding wheel is fitted on machine's work table, which can be given cross feed and the entire surface of the job can be grinded.

   These are of the following three kinds :

   (*i*) **Plain Cylindrical Grinder.** In this type of grinders job is rotated in chuck or centre and the entire cylindrical surface of the job is grinded. With this grinder finishing of sleeves, pins, rods, taper pins *etc.*

   (*ii*) **Roll Grinder.** This type of grinders are used in steel mills, printing presses *etc.* for grinding heavy rollers

   (*iii*) **Piston Grinder.** Pistons of I.C. engines are required to be grinded not in round shape but in oval and taper shape so that when their size increases due to heat these may not get deposited in the cylinder. This grinder is specifically made for grinding of these shapes.

2. **Plunge Cut Grinder.** These grinders are used to grind small shafts. The diameter of the grinder is much more than that of the job. Crank shafts of motor vehicles are grinded with this grinder. These are also called crank shaft grinding machines. This type of grinder is also made in a different form for cam shaft grinding. In order to save the shaft from becoming flexible, steady rests are used.

3. **Form Grinder.** Grinding wheels of different shapes are made under this type of grinders. These wheels are given feed and accurate grinding is done as per the shape of the grinding wheel on the moving cylindrical surface. Under this category, three types of grinders are included. These are :

   (*i*) **Ordinary Form Grinder.** These grinders are used for grinding jobs of ordinary shape. Principle of an ordinary form grinder is shown in Fig. 17.11 below.

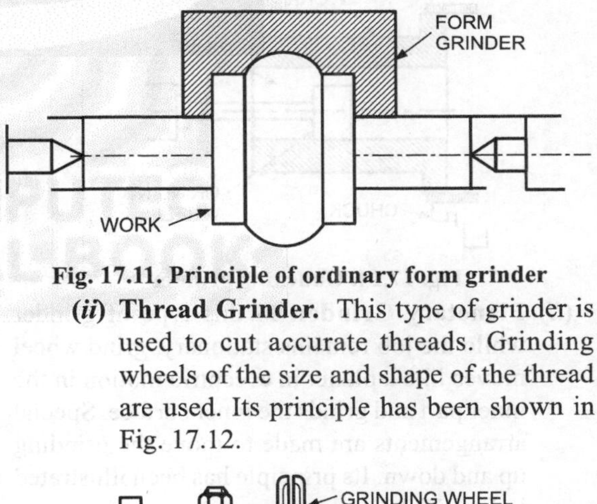

Fig. 17.11. Principle of ordinary form grinder

   (*ii*) **Thread Grinder.** This type of grinder is used to cut accurate threads. Grinding wheels of the size and shape of the thread are used. Its principle has been shown in Fig. 17.12.

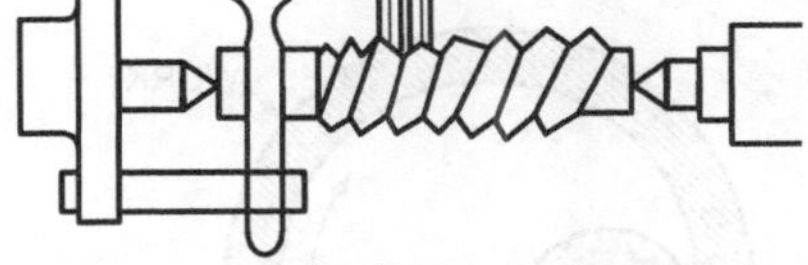

Fig. 17.12. Principle of thread grinder

   (*iii*) **Gear Grinder.** Principle of gear grinder is shown in Fig. 17.13. Grinding wheels of different forms are used in this grinder to cut dents of different sizes and shapes.

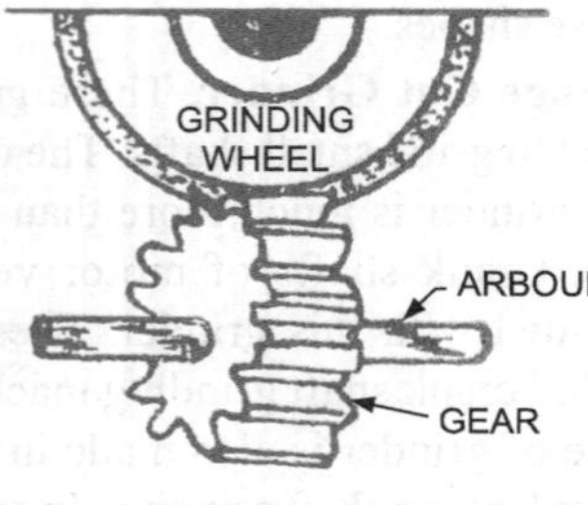

Fig. 17.13. Principle of gear grinding

4. **Internal Grinder.** These grinders are used for grinding round and hollow jobs whether the internal surface of these jobs is completely round, ditched round, or is in taper. Small grinding wheels of 3 cm to 5 cm are used in such grinders. Sometimes grinding wheels of special shape 0.2 cm to 0.3 cm. These grinders can be divided into two parts :

(*i*) **Chucking Grinder.** In this type of grinder, job is held in the chuck. The grinding wheel makes the job accurate through grinding of its hollow part.

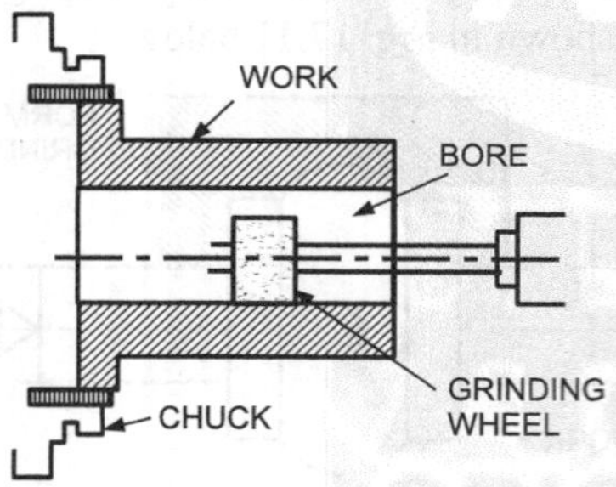

Fig. 17.14. Chucking grinder

(*ii*) **Planetary Grinder.** In this type of grinder while the job remains stationary, grind wheel moves like a planet in eccentric motion in the inner part and grinds the inner surface. Special arrangements are made to move the grinding up and down. Its principle has been illustrated in Fig. 17.15.

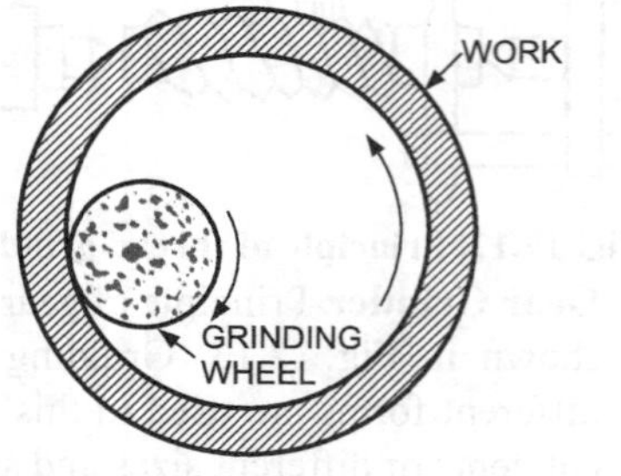

Fig. 17.15. Planetary grinder

5. **Centreless Grinder.** In this type of grinder, for holding the job no chuck is used. The job is moved through the medium of a grinding wheel and a regulating wheel. There are four main parts of this grinder : (1) Grinding wheel, (2) Work rest, (3) Regulating wheel, (4) Guide. Their principle has been explained through Fig. 17.16. Guides

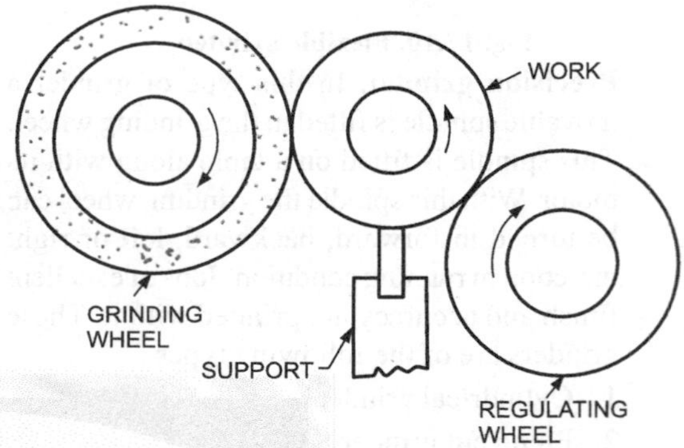

Fig. 17.16.

have not been shown in this figure. Job keeps on touching the work rest blade because of the pressure of grinding wheel. The regulating wheel forces the job to spin at an equal speed. In this way, the regulating wheel and the grinding wheel start moving in one direction. The job gets automatic forward speed. The rate of movement of job depends upon the inclination and speed of the regulating wheel. It can be adjusted according to the requirement. This type of grinder is used in the modern workshops for mass production. Jobs of glass, porcelain, wood, rubber, plastic, iron and steel and alloy are polished and finished with this grinder. The job can be placed in their positions :

1. Above the centre
2. In the centre
3. Below the centre.

These are shown in Fig. 17.17.

(*i*) **By Keeping the Job Above Centre.** Job axis remains above the axis of grinding wheel and regulating wheels.

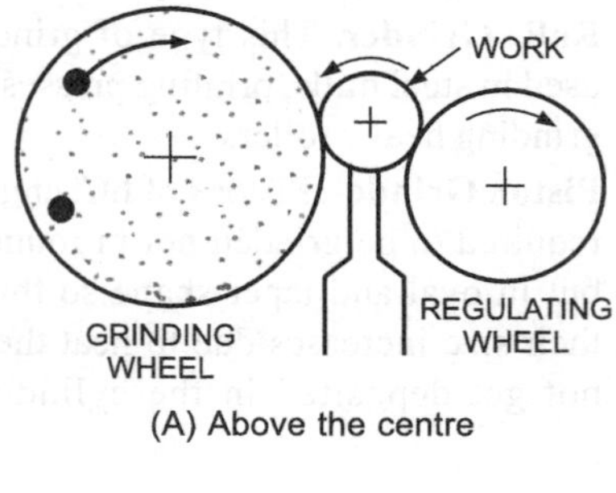

(A) Above the centre

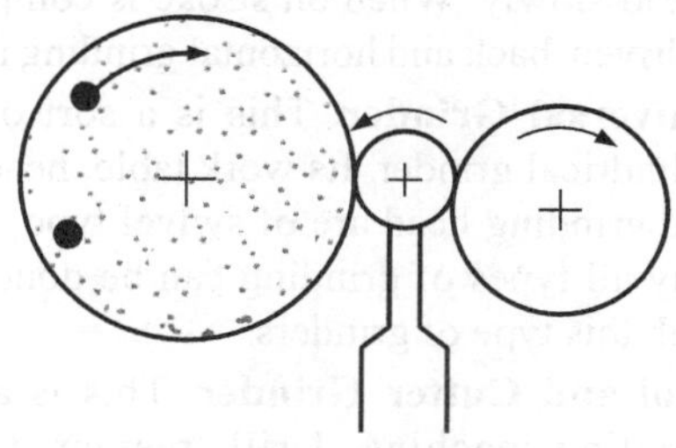
(B) In the centre

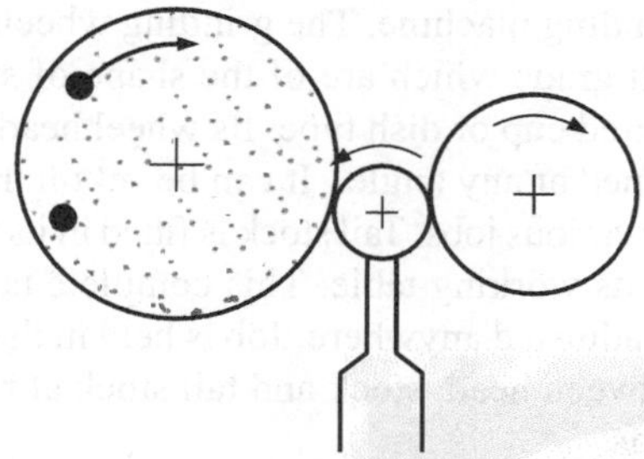
(C) Below the centre

Fig. 17.17.

(*ii*) **By Keeping the Job in the Centre.** In this position, zig-zag or irregulation shape of the job is grinded.

(*iii*) **By Keeping the Job Below the Centre.** By keeping the job below the centre, the job is grinded by remaining on the lower side. This type of grinder is used for those jobs which are not straight.

Internal Centreless Grinding. As external grinding is done on the job similarly internal centreless grinding is also done. The principle of this type of grinding is explained in Fig. 17.18.

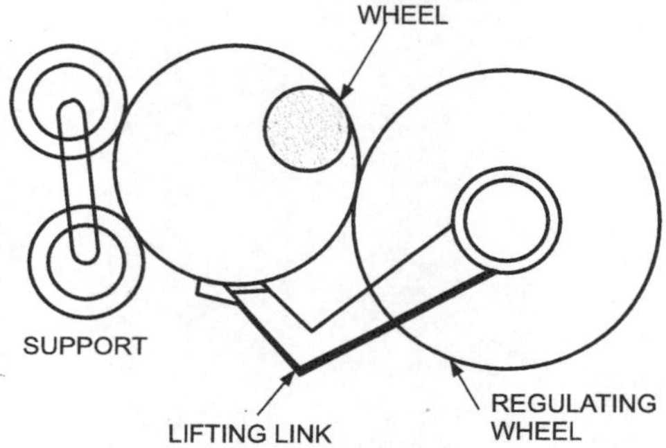

Fig. 17.18 Principle of internal centreless grinding

In the above figure, (P) regulator wheel is pressing the job. Rollers rotate on their axes. Grinding wheels grind the surface like the planetory grinding. After the job has been grinded it is pushed above with the help of left link.

6. **Surface Grinder.** Flat surfaces are accurately grinded with this type of grinders. For this grinder the job is held directly by magnetic chuck or work table. Race-protecting table of plaining or shaping machine is also used in form of table. Their classification is done in two ways :

(A) According to the table, they are of two types :

(*i*) Rotary table

(*ii*) Reciprocating table

(B) According the spindle, they are of the following types :

(*iii*) Vertical spindle grinder

(*iv*) Horizontal spindle grinder

(*i*) **Rotary Table Surface Grinder.** This type of grinder has been shown in Fig. 17.19. The work table rotates on its axis and arrangement is also made for feeding this table :

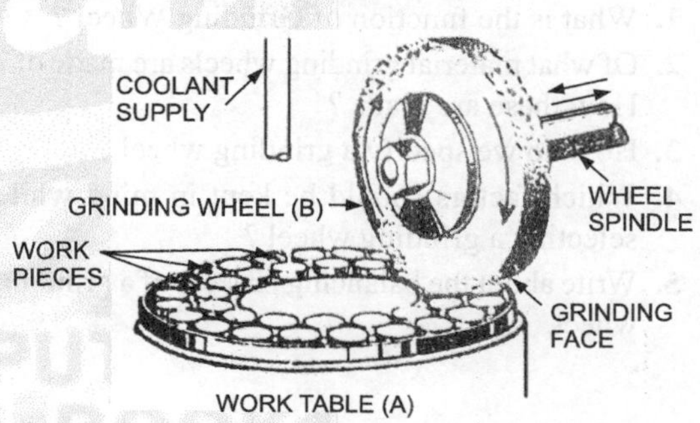

Fig. 17.19. Rotary table surface grinder

(*ii*) **Reciprocating Table Surface Grinder.** This type of grinder has been shown in Fig. 17.20 below. In this work table reciprocate like plainer or shaper machine.

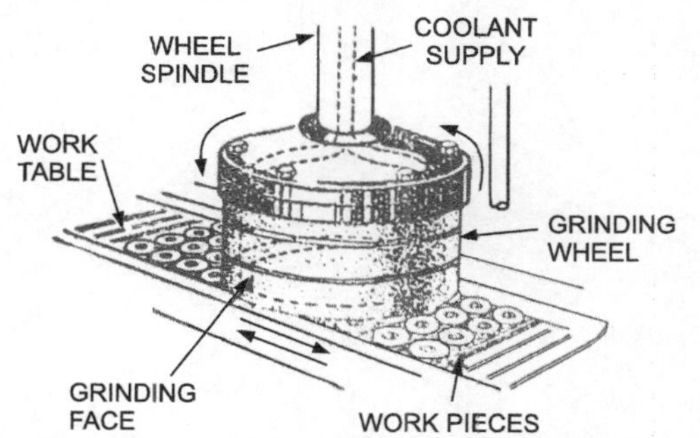

Fig. 17.20. Reciprocating table surface grinder

(*iii*) **Vertical Table Surface Grinder.** In this type

of grinder, grinding wheel is fixed vertical to the machine table or job as shown in Fig. 17.21.

(iv) Horizontal Spindle Surface Grinder. A horizontal spindle surface grinder is shown in Fig. 17.21. The spindle of the grinding wheel is fitted in horizontal direction. Wheel is moved

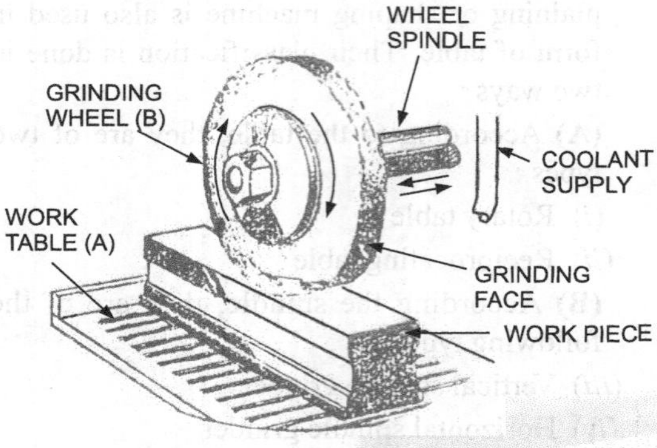

Fig. 17.21. Horizontal spindle surface grinder

ahead slowly. When on stroke is complete, it is driven back and horizontal grinding is done.

(7) Universal Grinder. This is a sort of plain cylindrical grinder. Its work table, head stock and grinding head are of swivel type. That is why all types of grinding can be done easily with this type of grinders.

(8) Tool and Cutter Grinder. This is a small grinding machine. Drill, reamer, tap and particularly milling cutter is grinded with this grinding machine. The grinding wheels are of soft grade which are of the shape of straight, flaired cup or dish type. Its wheel head can be turned at any angle. It can be set on the table for various jobs. Tail stock is fitted in its "T"slot on its working table. This complete table can be adjusted anywhere. Job is held in the centre between head stock and tail stock at both the ends.

Questions

1. What is the function of Grinding Wheel ?
2. Of what material grinding wheels are made of? How these are made ?
3. How do we specify a grinding wheel ?
4. Which factors should be kept in mind while selecting a grinding wheel ?
5. Write about the balancing process of a grinding wheel.
6. What do we mean by grinding wheel safety ?
7. What are the different types of grinder machines ?
8. Comment on the following :
   (*a*) Plane cylindrical grinder
   (*b*) Thread and gear grinder
   (*c*) Centreless grinder
   (*d*) Surface grinder
   (*e*) Universal grinder.

18

Honing, Lapping and Surface Finishing

As a result of various operations performed on each job, some scars or marks are left on it, even if these operations are done through lathe machine, shaper, milling, slaughter or drill machine. Because of such markings on the job, its surface becomes rough. Such rough surfaces are made plain and polished through honing or lapping operations. These marks or roughness is created by cutting tools. Therefore some allowance is given in the size of the jobs while making them.

Honing

Honing is performed on a job to make it of the proper size by removing marks and roughness left on a job by the cutting tools. By honing we get the following advantages :

1. There is no friction in the job.
2. The jobs rotate easily.
3. Surface becomes plain, which is not possible by any other operation.

Special honing attachments are fixed for honing. A flexible electrical drilling machine and a honing stone is used. Honing stone is made of aluminium oxide, silicon carbide or diamond dust, which are selected according to the metal of the job. The honing stones are of different size and shape such as round, square or triangular. Selection of honing stone depends upon the following considerations :

1. The metal of the job which is to be given honing treatment.
2. Hardness of the job.
3. The quantum of extra material left on the job.
4. The type of surface finishing required for the job.
5. The type of coolant to be used for the job.
6. Whether rough, medium or fine honing is required.

Honing Attachment. This tool is almost similar to large size adjustable reamer. Three, four, five or six honing stones are fixed in it. The number of honing stones is determined accordmg to the job. These stones can be easily fixed or removed. These can be stretched or shrinked to a limited extent. These can also be adjusted according to the job. This attachment can be turned up and down in a flexible drill machine.

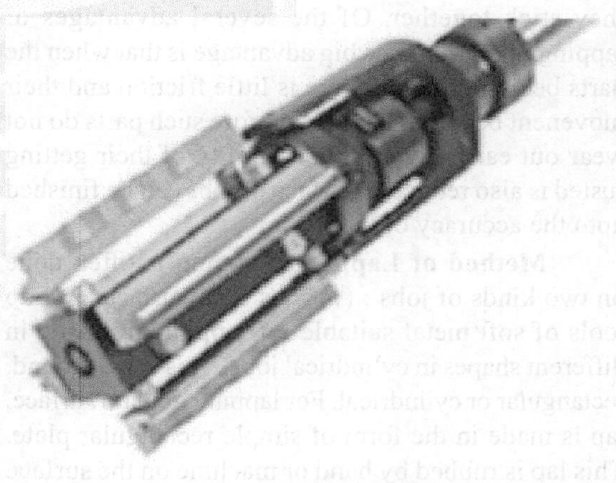

Fig. 18.1. Honing tool

Honing Operation. To clean a metal by removing roughness from its hole or bore made by a honing tool is called honing operation. This operation is conducted in the following two ways :

1. **Dry Honing.** Jobs which require rough finishing or from which more extra metal is to be removed, are given dry honing treatment. In other words, collant is not used. Stones used for the dry honing are of 90 to 120 abrasive grain.
2. **Wet Honing.** Jobs which require fine finishing

or from which less extra metal is to be removed are given wet honing treatment. Honing stone of 120 to 130 abrasive grain are used and for polishing suitable coolant is also used. But with this typs of honing metal can be cut only to the extent of 0.005″.

Kinds of Honing Abrasive. The following three kinds of abrasive honing stones are used in honing :

1. **Rough Hone Stone.** In order to remove the boring signs left by the boring tool after the normal boring, rough hone stone is used.
2. **Medium Hone Stone.** In order to do medium finishing, this type of hone stone is done.
3. **Fine Hone Stone.** For finishing on the surface of various jobs, particularly on automobile cylinders, fine hone stone is used.

Lapping

The finishing of external or internal surfaces either by hand or machine is called lapping. For this purpose, special type of pastes and grinding abrasives are used. They provide fine finishing to the jobs, and small spots also vanish. Surface becomes so smooth and plain that a vacuum is created between them and they stick together. Of the several advantages of lapping operation, one big advantage is that when the parts become smooth there is little friction and their movenent becomes easy. Therefore such parts do not wear out early. Even the possibility of their getting rusted is also reduced. Surface of jobs can be finished upto the accuracy of 0.0001″.

Method of Lapping. Lapping is often done on two kinds of jobs : (1) Jobs with surface (2) Lap tools of soft metal suitable for lapping are made in different shapes in cylindrical jobs. This can be round, rectangular or cylindrical. For lapping of plain surface, lap is made in the form of simple rectangular plate. This lap is rubbed by hand or machine on the surface of the job after applying lapping paste *etc.* When lap and job start sticking to each other it should be considered as proper lapping. When a cylindrical job like an automobile engine's cylinders are required to be lapped, aluminium piston of smaller size than the size of cylinder is used as lap. Paste is applied to the piston and a stick is moved up and down. For making lap, cast iron, aluminium, copper, glass or wood is used.

The following precautions should be taken while carrying out the lapping operations :

1. Metal of job should be softer than the lap metal.
2. Before lapping scraping or honing should be done.
3. Adequate material should be used for lapping.
4. Proper lubricant or coolant should be used while lapping.
5. Measurement and shape of the lap should be according to the job.
6. After lapning the job should be cleaned with a soft cloth.

Charging Material of Laps. Materials used for lapping are known as charging materials of laps. These are of two kinds :

1. **Natural Abrasive.** This type of abrasives are found in the form of minerals after mining operation. Diamond, carborundum, emery and chromium oxide are the main ones. Small particles of these material is fixed with oils to make lapping paste.
2. **Artificial Abrasive.** This type of abrasives are artificially made from aluminium oxide and silicon carbide. Paste prepared with silicon carbide does not give good finishing. High quality finish is possible with the paste prepared with a aluminium oxide abrasive and it also gives shining to the surface.

Abrasives of all types are used after grinding them like flour. They have different grades according to their flour sizes. For making lapping paste, suitable abrasive is put in the the oil. Heavy and dirty abrasive settles down but the light abrasive remains on the upper surface. This oil having powdered abrasive is used for lapping. Oils in the form of mobile oil, hard oil, kerosene oil, turpentine oil or other suitable alcohol are used.

Difference between Honing and Lapping

Honing	*Lapping*
1. Size of job is set right after removing the marks of matching through honing.	1. By lapping surface of the job is made smooth like that of glass or polished surface.
2. It is certain that there is difference in the size of the job after the honing operation is carried out.	2. There is not much difference in the size of the job after lapping.

3. For honing operation, honing attachment and flexible drill machine is essential.	3. Lapping can be done through the medium of hands.
4. For the honing operation both adequate coolant and lubricant are needed.	4. For lapping, oil mixed in paste is enough.
5. In the honing operation, honing attachment is to be revolved on the job speedily in one direction alone.	5. In the lapping operation, lap is moved at slow speed or rubbed.
6. Honing stone is used for honing.	6. Paste made with abrasive and oil is used for lapping.

Surface Finish

Different operations are performed to complete a job. Particularly while performing cutting operations some rough marks are left on the job. In order to remove this roughness and marks, honing and lapping is done. This makes the surface of the job smooth and polishing. How far surface has to be finished depends on the utility of the job. The marks left by cutting tools are called "Hills" and "Vallies" and it is necessary to remove them. This increases their working capacity as well as their beauty.

It is necessary to have high quality finishing of the surfaces of those parts which produce friction while they move. This would lessen friction.

Surface finishing of a job can be known or judged in the following ways :

1. **By Touching.** By touching the surface of a job we can know the smoothness or roughness of a job.
2. **By Looking at it.** We can examine the surface by looking at a job. Magnifying glass can also be used for this purpose.
3. **By Comparison.** Surface of a new job can be compared with a smooth, beautiful and polished job.
4. **By profiteometer.** This is an exceedingly accurate instrument for measuring the smoothness or roughness of a surface. With this instrument hills and valleys can be measured up to 0.455 mm.

Words Related with Surface Finish. Unit of surface finish is R.M.S. (Root, Mean, Square), (A.A.R.) or C.L.A.

Surface. That part of a job which can be easily seen or touched by hand is called, surface whether this surface is outer or inner.

Roughness. While casting, (moulding) or cutting a job some hills and valleys are formed on the job. The irregularity or disorder which results in because of these hills and valleys is known as roughness.

Smoothness. Where the possibility of friction is comparatively the least, that job is called smooth. In other words, a job which has no hills and valleys is called smooth surface.

Finish Surface. The surfaces whose hills and valleys have been finished according to the utility of the job through honing or lapping are known as "Finish Surface"

In order to know the extent of rougnness of a job we keep the instrument parallel to the centre line of the job and take five readings above and five readings less. There are several ways of taking reading with instruments but the Indian Standard Institute (ISI) has adopted (M) method. Centre is taken as basis for reading purpose under this method on arithmetical average. Roughness is taken as "R". Several grades of roughness have been made in "N" numbers. Roughness of the surface of the job is indicated on the basis of the following table :

Roughness Grade	***Value of Roughness (R)***	***Roughness sign***
N. 12	50	×
N. 10 to 11	15.5 to 25	△
N. 7 to 9	1.6 to 6.3	△△
N. 4 to 6	0.2 to 0.8	△△△
N. 1 to 3	0.025 to 0.1	△△△△

19

Engineering Metals

Metal is a very important element in engineering line as well as for use in every day life that without it several jobs would remain incomplete. It would not be an exageration to say that because of metal so much progress has been achieved in the world. Metal is the basic element in things right from a tiny needle or nail upto an aeroplane. Metal is solid, it has weight, it is opaque, and it is good conductor of heat. For various purposes, different kinds of metals are used. Metal contains the following three main properties :

(*i*) Physical Properties
(*ii*) Mechanical Properties
(*iii*) Chemical Properties.

Physical Properties. A metal is recognised by the following six physical properties :

(1) Colour. Each metal has its own distinct colour with which that metal is recognised such as iron is light black, silver is bright white and copper has red colour.

(2) Weight. Each metal has it own weight. Some metals are light in weight, others are heavy. For example, iron is heavy in weight but aluminium in comparatively very light. Metal is weighed in per cubic centimetre or as per cubic inch. Weight of some metals can be known from the following table :

Name of Metal	*Weight in cubic inch*	*Weight in cubic foot*
Aluminium	0.097 lbs.	160 lbs.
Copper	0.320 lbs.	655 lbs.
Brass	0.304 lbs.	520 lbs.
Cast iron	0.260 lbs.	480 lbs.
Lead	0.412 lbs.	712 lbs.
Nickel	0.310 lbs.	535 lbs.
Steel	0.283 lbs.	489 lbs.

(3) Structure. Each metal has a different inner composition. It can be known after breaking the metal. For example, the inner structure of tin and wrought iron is fibrous. The inner composition of cast iron is granular. Zinc's inner structure is zig-zag granular.

(4) Fusibility. The readiness with which a metal passes from the solid into the liquid form is known as fusibility. There is a specific degree of temperature at which the solid metal changes liquid form, therefore, it differs from metal to metal. Because of this property, the impurities of a metal can be removed after melting it and it can be cast in the desired shape. The temperature at which a metal starts melting is called its melting point. For example, wrought iron melts at 1000°C. Melting points of some other metals are shown in the following table :

Name of Metal	*Melting point in Centigrade*	*Melting point in Fahrenhite*
Steel	1615°C	2915°F
Nickel	1520°C	2712°F
Copper	1083°C	1844°F
Brass	962°C	1760°F
Aluminium	648°C	1200°F
Zinc	415°C	824°F
Lead	327°C	608°F
Tin	230°C	446°F
Cast iron	1260°C	2282°F

(5) Magnetic Effect. That property of a metal because of which a metal is attracted towards a magnet is called magnetic effect on the metal. This property is found only in iron. Non-ferrous metals do not get attracted towards the magnet.

(*6*) **Conductivity.** Each metal has the ability to carry an electrical current or heat. But non-metallic things like wood *etc*. are non-conductor of heat and electricity. For examples if a metallic wire is heated from one end or electric current is given by touching one end, the other will soon start getting hot or the electric current will pass on to the other end also. On the contrary, if a piece of wood is burnt from one end or is given electric current neither the other end would receive heat nor electric current would reach the other end.

(7) **Opaque.** We cannot see through metals. All metals have this property.

Note. Every metal except mercury is in solid form. Only mercury is found in liquid form.

Mechanical Properties. That particular property of a metal by which it can be given a desired shape either by heating it, pressing it or both by heating or pressing is known as its mechanical property. Mechanical properties include the following qualities. Selection of a metal for a particular job is made on the basis of these properties.

(A) Elasticity. That property of a metal by which it can be brought back to its old form after applying force on it, is known as elasticity. In other words when force is applied, the metal is deformed and returns to its original shape when such force is withdrawn. For example, if we stretch a wire, it can be stretched to a certain extent and when we withdraw / remove the force, if it returns to its original shape it can be said that this wire has the property of elasticity. This property can be easily seen in rubber. Metals which contain less quantity of carbon will have more elasticity. On the other hand, metals with more quantity of carbon are considered solid. For steel measure of elasticity limit is 2580 kg/cm^2.

(B) Tensity. That property of metal which enables it not to break when it is stretched is called tensity. The following points are covered under this property :

(*i*) ***Yield Point.*** When pull is applied to a metal and that metal does not return to its original shape after having been stretched to a certain point, this is known as yield point.

(*ii*) ***Tensile Strength.*** The amount of directly applied pull which a part will stand before it breaks is called its tensile strength. That is, if it is stretched more, its tensile strength will break.

(*iii*) ***Ultimate Tensile Stress.*** The highest unit of stress that a metal can sustain *i.e.,* at which point it gets broken is called its ultimate tensile stress.

(*iv*) ***Fatigue Resistance.*** That property of metal which sustains it from breaking at ultimate tensile stress is known as "Fatigue Resistance."

(*v*) ***Permanent Set.*** When a metal is stretched and it remains there permanently *i.e.,* the metal does not return to its ordinal shape, it is known as permanent set.

Working Load. It is the ordinary load to which a metal is subjected. We cannot stretch or lay stress on a metal to such an extent that it crosses the yield point and gets broken, therefore, load from 1/4 to 1/3 part of a metal's tensile strength is applied to it. This load is known as working load.

Safety Factor. Proportion between tensile strength and working load is called "Safety Factor".

Strain. Proportion between the increased length of a metal, after it is loaded, and its original length is called "Strain".

$$\text{Strain} = \frac{\text{Change in length}}{\text{Original length}}$$

$$\text{Stress} = \frac{\text{Load}}{\text{Area of cross section}}$$

$$\text{Working load} = \frac{\text{Ultimate tensile load}}{4}$$

(C) Toughness. That property of a metal by which it does not break or deform even after bending or twisting, is called "toughness". For example, wrought iron does not break quickly even when it is bent.

(D) Ductility. That property of metals by virtue of which they can be drawn into wires is known as "ductility". This property remains in the metal in both hot as well as cold conditions.

(E) Malleability. That property of metals by virtue of which they can be hammered or rolled out, without breaking or cracking is called "Malleability." Gold and lead have this property comparatively in good measure. Gold is the most malleable and ductile of all metals.

In the following table Tensile Stress and Compressible Stress of some metals are given :

S. No.	*Name of Metal*	*Tensile strength lbs. / sq. inch*	*Compressible stress lbs. / sq. inch*
1.	Brass	4000	3000
2.	Copper	4000 to 6000	6000
3.	Gun metal	6000	6000
4.	Steel	18,000 to 20,000	18,000 to 20,000
5.	Cast iron	4000	16,000
6.	Wrought iron	12,000 to 14,000	14,000
7.	Bronze (phosphur)	10,000	10,000
8.	Bronze (manganese)	12,000	—
9.	Navel bross	8000	—
10.	Muntz metal	7000	—

(F) Hardness. That property of metals by virtue of which they cannot be easily cut or wornout by other substances but on the contrary they can cut other metals, is known as "hardness" of metals. Cutting tools are made keeping in view this particular property of metals.

(G) Brittleness. That property of metals by virtue of which they break and disintegrate into pieces, when their shape is changed, is called "brittleness". If the quantity of carbon is more in steel, it becomes brittle and gets broken upon hitting.

Some Properties of Metals

(*a*) Hardness :

1. Hard steel
2. White cast iron
3. Rail steel
4. Wrought iron
5. Platinum
6. Copper
7. Aluminium
8. Silver
9. Zinc
10. Gold
11. Tin
12. Lead

(*b*) Ductility :

1. Gold
2. Platinum
3. Silver
4. Iron
5. Copper
6. Aluminium
7. Nickel
8. Zinc
9. Tin
10. Lead

(*c*) Malleability :

1. Gold
2. Silver
3. Aluminium
4. Copper
5. Tin
6. Platinum
7. Lead
8. Zinc
9. Iron
10. Nickel

Chemical Properties. That property of metal by virtue of which their shape can be changed by chemical action is known as chemical property. These properties can be known through chemical methods.

Metal and Non-metal. Whatever things we see in the world can be divided into the following two categories :

(*i*) Metal

(*ii*) Non-metal

(*i*) **Metal.** It is solid like iron, copper, gold or silver *etc.*

(*ii*) **Non-metal.** These are available in the form of solid, liquid or gasses such as wood stone *etc.*

Difference between Metal and Non-metal

Metal	*Non-metal*
(*i*) It is solid, coloured and heavy.	(*i*) It is solid, liquid, in form of gas, coloured or colourless and light in weight.
(*ii*) Metals have shining.	(*ii*) Non-metals do not have shining.
(*iii*) Metals have high density.	(*iii*) Non-metals have less density.
(*iv*) When we strike metals they give particular sound.	(*iv*) Non-metals do not give such particular sound.
(*v*) Metals remain solid at low temperature.	(*v*) Non-metal somewhat changes its form at low temperature.
(*vi*) Metals can be forged.	(*vi*) Non-metals cannot be forged.
(*vii*) Metals are good conductor of electricity.	(*vii*) Non-metals are good conductor of heat.

Ferrous and Non-Ferrous Metals. Metals have been divided into two forms — Ferrous and Non-ferrous metals.

(*i*) **Ferrous Metals.** Metals which have iron, which can be attracted by magnets, which can get rust, all these are included in ferrous metals. Such as, pig iron, mild steel, carbon, steel, manganese steel and nickel steel *etc.*

(*ii*) **Non-Ferrous Metals.** Metals which do not contain parts of iron, which cannot be attracted by magnet and which cannot be rusted, are called non-ferrous metals, such as gold, silver, copper, aluminium, tin, platinum, zinc, mangenese and antimony.

Difference betwen Ferrous and Non-ferrous Metals

Ferrous Metals	*Non-ferrous Metals*
(*i*) They contain grains of iron.	(*i*) They do not contain grains of iron.
(*ii*) These are of light grey or black colour.	(*ii*) These are of different colours.
(*iii*) They melt at high temperature.	(*iii*) They melt at low temperature.
(*iv*) They can get rusted.	(*iv*) They do not get rust.
(*v*) They have very little shrinkage.	(*v*) They do get shrinked.
(*vi*) They become brittle in cold condition.	(*vi*) These are petulant in condition.
(*vii*) These are very good conductors of heat.	(*vii*) These are also very good conductors of heat.

Iron and Iron Ore. Iron is a highly useful metal, which is used in maximum jobs. It is found in crude form from mines, after mining. It contains impurities of phosphorous, sulphur, soil and oxygen. These impurities are known as gangue. Gangue is mixed with 60% to 75% of iron particles. Combined form of both these is known as "Iron Ore". This is iron and mineral. It is used in production of iron. Iron is found in the world in the following forms :

1. Magnetite
2. Hematite
3. Siderite
4. Limonite
5. Pyrite
6. Clay Iron Stone

Magnetite. In India, it is found in Salem in Madras and among foreign nations it is found in Canada, America *etc.* It contains 73% of iron. Its specific centre of gravity is from 5.1 to 6.1. Because of excess magnetic property, it is difficult to derive iron from it.

Hematite. It is the best iron-ore of the world. In India it is found in Gwalior, Bihar, Mysore, Bisawar (Madhya Pradesh) and among foreign countries it is found in Canada, America, Brazil and China. It is of two kinds :

(*i*) *Red Hematite.* It contains pure iron from 47% to 72%. Its colour is like red soil.

(*ii*) *Brown Hematite.* It contains 52% to 85% pure iron and its colour is brown.

Siderite. It is found in England, Germany and Australia. It contains about 50% pure iron. Its specific centre of gravity is from 3.8 to 3.9.

Limonite. It is found in Germany, France, Beleium and South America. It contains about 60%

of pure iron. Its specific centre of gravity is from 3.6 to 4.0.

Pyrite. It is mainly found in Italy. This type of mineral is considered inferior to all minerals because it contains a huge quantity of sulphur. Therefore, the iron oxide which we get after sulphur is separated from it, is used for making iron.

Clay Iron Stone. It is found in abundance in India in Raniganj and Jharia areas. It contains 40% pure iron. It is found in the form of stone.

When iron ore is derived from the mines it contains impurities of carbon, silicon, sulphur, phosphorus and soil *etc.* To clean or purify iron ore, three methods are used :

(*i*) Washing. (*ii*) Roasting, (*iii*) Megnatic separation.

Washing. Iron ore is almost grinded and washed in fast flow of water. Impurities which are light get washed away with the water but because of its weight, the iron settle down. In this way, pure iron is found.

Roasting. Under this process, iron ore is heated on an iron plate below which fire is put on. Thus the impurities get burnt.

Magnetic Separation. In this method, mineral iron is grinded and kept near moving magnetic belts. The magnetic belts attract the pure iron, which is collected separately.

Even after applying the above methods of removing impurities, some of them remain. These are removed by melting the iron. Iron ore is melted in the blast furance by using hard coke, lime and air pressure. Hard coke provides heat while lime stone acts as flux. All types of iron is found only from iron ore. Iron is divided in separate sections on the basis of other materials which come along with iron. First of all, we make pig iron.

Blast Furnace. Iron ore is reduced into small pieces which are melted in the blast furnace. This furnace is like a round drum. Its diameter is from 6 to 9 metres and height is from 25 to 40 metres. Its external surface is built of thick iron sheet. In the inner circle of the blast furnace fire bricks of $1\frac{1}{4}$ to $1\frac{1}{2}$ meter thick are fixed, making the inner wall. A special mixture is used for fixing these bricks. This contains the heat within the furnace and does not allow it to have its effect outside. A tapping hole is built on the lower side of the furnace from which the melted iron flows out. A little above this hole, there is another hole known as slag hole. Impurities of iron come out from this hole in the form of foam. On the lower part of the furnace about 12 to 16 stone nozzles are fixed through which blast hot air is given to the furnace. That is why the furnace is called blast furnace. Its mouth can be closed at the top by using a double cup. For depositing iron ore, lime and hard coke in the furnace, an automatic convey is used. At a time iron ore from 800 to 1200 tonne can be melted in this furnace. Chemical reaction takes place between iron ore and lime and the impurities are driven out in the form of foam through the slag hole. The remaining iron is called pig iron. It contains carbon from 2% to 5%, 3% silicon, 0.1% phosphorus, 0.3% sulphur and 1% mangnese and the rest pure iron.

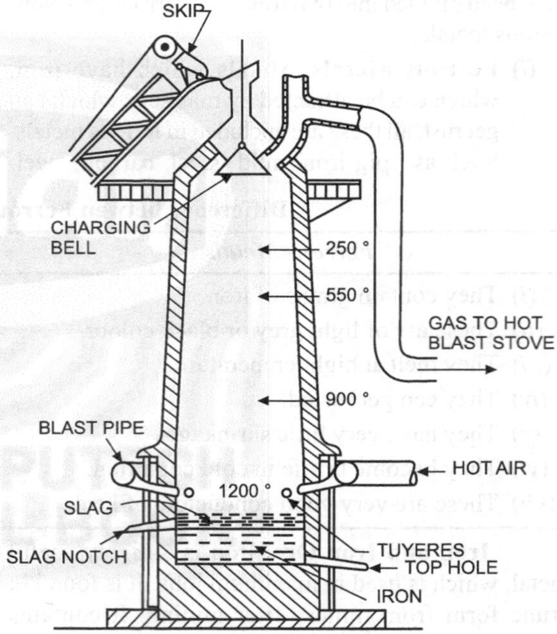

Fig. 19.1. Blast furnace

Pig Iron. This is the second form of iron next to its original form.

It cannot be used in the engineering line. It is of the following three kinds :

(*i*) Grey Pig Iron

(*ii*) White Pig Iron

(*iii*) Molted Pig Iron.

In engineering line, for various commercial uses, pig iron is classified in different numbers is under:

(*i*) According to composition

(*ii*) According to use

(*iii*) According to the method of its manufacture.

According to Composition. These are available in Nos. 1 to 6. No. 1 pig iron is the best. Pig iron is known by its grains. It is broken and then known through its grains.

According to Use. Pig iron can be divided into the following three sections :

(*i*) ***Bessemer Pig Iron.*** This pig iron is used for making steel in Bessemer convenor.

(*ii*) ***Malleable Pig Iron.*** This pig iron is used for malleable casting.

(*iii*) ***Foundry Pig Iron.*** For common casting foundry pig iron is used.

No. 1 Pig Iron. If we break it, we will notice that it is of fast grey colour from inside and is very hard. It contains 3.75% graphite and 0.3% carbon. It is for line casting.

No. 2 Pig Iron. If it is broken we notice that it is light grey from inside and is harder than No. 1 pig iron. It contains a 4% mixed carbon. Therefore, the property of fluditiy is comparatively less in it.

No. 3 Pig Iron. Its colour is lighter even than No. 2 pig iron but it contains greater quantity of carbon. It has greater power to sustain stretch and lesser property of fluidity.

No. 4 Pig Iron. Its colour is very light grey. It contains 1% combined carbon. If is used for casting of rough jobs.

All the four types of pig iron mentioned above are used in the iron foundry for common jobs.

No. 5 Pig Iron. Its colour is grey from inside and bright, shiny grains are visible. It is also called Molted Pig iron. It contains from 1.5% upto 2% carbon and graphite in equal quantities.

No. 6 Pig Iron. It is also known as white pig iron. It has the properties of hardness and brittleness. If we break it, we can see bright and shiny grains. It starts melting at low temperature. It is used for making wrought iron.

Cast Iron

Making other steels from pig iron is a very costly affair. But from pig iron cast iron is produced at minimum cost which is used maximum. It is made by melting the pig iron once again. For this purpose Cupola Furnace or Crucible Furnace is used. In Crucible Furnace less quantity of cast iron is made. For greater production of Cast-iron Cupola Furnace is used, which has been shown in Fig. 19.2.

Height of Cupola Furnace is 5 to 10 metres, diameter is from 1 to 2 metres. Its round tank is made

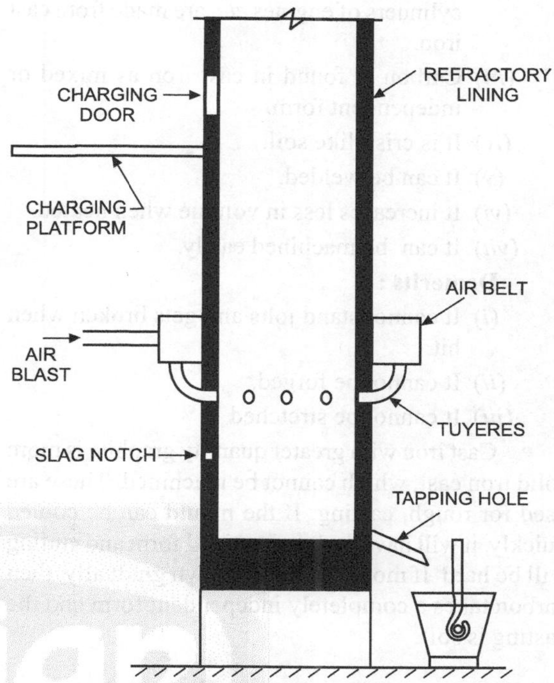

Fig. 19.2. Cupola furnace

with iron sheets of 6 mm to 10 mm thickness. At one time, about 28 tonne cast iron can be prepared in this furnace. Temperature inside the furnace is from 1260° to 134o°C. This temperature is adequate to melt any type of pig iron. In this furnace also there are holes for drawing out the melted iron and slag. Fire bricks are fixed inside the furnace.

First pig iron mixed with metal chips are laid in the furnace. Then layers of hard coke and lime are laid. Layers are kept one over the other. Fire is set in the furnace and air is provided through the blower. By this process the pure cast iron settles down after it gets melted and then flows out from the molting hole. Its sulphur comes out in the form of slag. The melted iron is filled in laddles and then put in different moulds (dies) and given the desired shape. This is known as cast iron. It contains impurities of carbon from 3% to $4\frac{1}{2}$ %, silicon from 0.8% to 3%, phosphorus 0.5%, sulphur 0.1% to $1\frac{1}{2}$ % and 0.5% to 1 % manganese.

Properties of Cast Iron :

(*i*) Cast iron is a strong and cheap metal. In melted form, it can easily flow. That is why it can be cast in any shape.

(*ii*) It has a comprehensive strength of 6250 km per sq. cm. Therefore machine beds, cylinders of engines *etc*. are made from cast iron.

(*iii*) Carbon is found in cast iron as mixed or independent form.

(*iv*) It is crisp like soil.

(*v*) It can be welded.

(*vi*) It increases less in volume when heated.

(*vii*) It can be machined easily.

Demerits :

(*i*) It cannot stand jolts and gets broken when hit.

(*ii*) It cannot be forged.

(*iii*) It cannot be stretched.

Cast iron with greater quantity graphite is more solid iron cast, which cannot be machined. These are used for rough, casting. If the mould can be cooled quickly, it will have carbon in mixed form and cutting will be hard If mould is cooled down gradually, then carbon takes a completely independent form and the casting is soft.

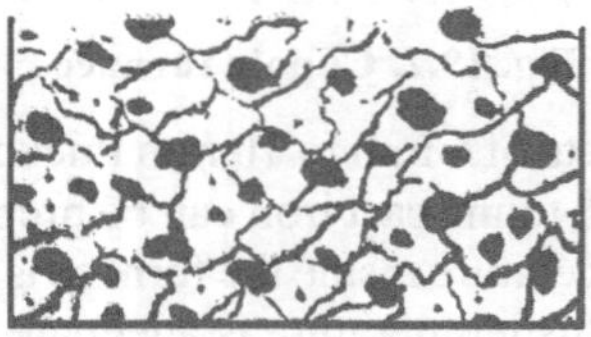

Fig. 19.3. Composition of Cast Iron

Kinds of Cast Iron :

(*i*) Grey Cast Iron

(*ii*) White Cast Iron

(*iii*) Mottled Cast Iron

(*iv*) Alloy Cast Iron

(*v*) Malleable Cast Iron.

Grey Cast Iron. In this type of cast iron there is 3% to 4% carbon, out of which 1% is combined carbon and 2% to 3% of pure carbon. Therefore it looks grey with slightly red colour. In comparison to other types of cast iron it is soft and weak. Its machining can be done easily. Its melting point is less. Graphite which is available in independent form, because of this there is no need for lubrication separately. It is used for making machine frames, brackets, pipe *etc*. after casting.

White Cast Iron. Its structure is fibrous and of shiny grains. It contains mixed carbon from 2% to 4% and about 1% to 2% independent carbon. It is made solid by abruptly cooling it. It cannot be cut or machined, it is used for making jobs, which do not require machining such as fire bars, covers for manhole, water pipes, *etc*.

Mottled Cast Iron. It is a mixed form of grey cast iron and white cast iron. It contains the quantity of carbon 50% combined and 50% independent form. Besides this it contains 0.4% to 3% silicon, 0.3% to 0.35% sulphur, 0.2% to 1.5% phosphorus and 0.05% to 1.5% manganese.

Alloy Cast Iron. In this type of cast iron, pig iron and chromium, nickel, vanadium, silicon, and molybdenum are mixed to prepare alloy cast iron. Its internal structure and tensile strength becomes very good. At times, copper or aluminium is mixed in the alloy.

Malleable Cast Iron. This type of cast iron is made from good quality of white cast iron. Its special feature is that it can be easily machined because it contains softness. Sometimes, steel scrap from 15% to 40% is also mixed. By doing so it acquires the properties of wrought iron. Two methods are used for making malleable cast iron.

(*i*) White Hearth Process

(*ii*) Black Hearth Process

White Hearth Process. Under this process white cast iron is kept below the hematite iron ore in the furnace. It is melted in the furnace. By this process the quantity of carbon is reduced to seme extent and it becomes machinable cast iron.

Black Hearth Process. Under this process, white cast iron is kept in a box along with silica. The box is closed and kept in the furnace and heated for 60 hours at a temperature between 1500°F to 1600°F. Thus that cast iron is case hardened. It is cooled slowly and it becomes machinable.

Wrought Iron

It is given the name of pure iron. White pig iron is melted in Puddling Furnace in order to remove all its impurities. It is approximately 99.8 % pure iron. Only 0.01 % to 0.02% carbon and slag is left. It is very soft iron. It can easily be bent in any direction by heating it. Its construction is fibrous. It cannot be hardened or tempered. Chains, farming implements, water pipes, nails *etc*. are made with iron.

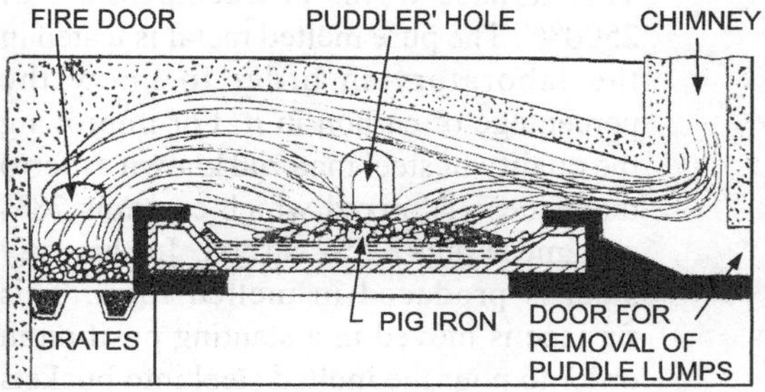

Fig. 19.4. Puddling furnace

Powder of cast iron and pig iron is used for making it. It is heated in the puddling furnace in indirect way. On ore side fire is put on in the furnace and the hot air produced is blown in the hearth. This hot air melts the powder of cast iron and pig iron is melted in the paste form. In this melted form of iron there is no quantity of carbon because carbon turns into carbonic acid and silicon *etc.* come up in the form of oxide and then flow out in the form of slag. When the above impurities are removed wrought iron is prepared in the form of sponge.

Properties of Wrought Iron :

(*i*) Even after heating it slightly, it can be easily twisted or bent.

(*ii*) Its compressive strength is 20 tonne to 30 tonne per square inch. Therefore, it can be given any shape by heating, without any damage.

(*iii*) It melts at 1600°C temperature.

(*iv*) Because of its properties of malleability, it can be used for making bars, sheets or wires.

(*v*) Its fibres are long and thus it can be forge welded easily.

(*vi*) It can be used both in the construction as well as technical jobs.

(*vii*) It cannot be hardened or tempered out, it can be case hardened.

(*viii*) Because of its purity, it contains more magnetic property as compared to other types of iron. That is why it is used as a core in motor dynamo *etc.*

(*ix*) All types of operations can easily be done on it.

(*x*) It is 99 % pure iron.

Steel

In the present age steel is used in one or the other form almost in all jobs. Pure iron is used in the engineering line but it cannot meet all its needs. Therefore carbon is mixed with iron to make it hard. In steel carbon can be considered as the main element because on this basis different types of steels are made. Carbon is present in the steel in combined form. For special uses, sulphur, phosphorus, silicon, manganese *etc.* are mixed in different proportions. Steel can be divided into two parts *i.e.* plain carbon steel and Alloy steel :

(i) Plain Carbon Steel. This type of steel is made by mixing carbon in iron. The hardness of this type of steel depends upon the quantity of carbon. Because of this factor, carbon is considered to be the main element. On this very basis, plain carbon steel is divided into three parts :

(1) Low Carbon Steel

(2) Medium Carbon Steel

(3) High Carbon Steel.

(1) Low Carbon Steel or Mild Steel. In this type of steel the percentage of carbon is 0.07% to 0.25%. In the steel with very little percentage of carbon is called as Dead Mild Steel. This steel is ductile and it can be easily forged. Some hardness can be provided to it by case hardening. Steel with 0.1% to 0.25% carbon is called mild steel. It can also be made hard by case hardening. Wires, iron sheets, angle and 'T' iron *etc.* are made with this iron. Nut bolt, screw *etc.* is made with thin steel.

(2) Medium Carbon Steel. The percentage of carbon in this steel is 0.3 to 0.7%. It is a bit more hard than the mild steel. It can be hardened and tempered. It is used for making drop forging, shafts of machines, axis of vehicles, ordinary tools *etc.* Leaf springs of motor and wheels of railway trains are made of this steel.

(3) High Carbon Steel. The percentage of carbon in this type of steel is 0.7 to 1.5%. Therefore, comparatively it is more brittle. But its hardness is more. It can be hardened as well as tempered. It is used for things where hard metal is needed. Mainly it is used for cutting tools. With the steel having 0.75% to 1.0% carbon, tools meant for cutting wood, all types of hammers, dies for forging, spring, centre punch and drifts are made. With high carbon steel having 1.1% to 1.3% carbon, milling machine cutters, dies for pressing machines, drills and files *etc*. are made. With the steel having 1.4% to 1.5% carbon, lathe cutting tools, milling cutters, gauges, reamers, files and thick sheets and cutting shearing machine blades are made.

All types of steels are made by mixing carbon with iron in different proportions. There are six different ways of making steel. They are as under :

(*i*) Bessemer Method
(*ii*) Cementation Method
(*iii*) Open Hearth Method
(*iv*) Crucible Method
(*v*) Electric Method
(*vi*) High Frequency.

Bessemer Method. In this method a special furnace known as Bessemer converter is used. Its shape is almost similar to a small pappaya. Inside this furnace fire bricks are fixed. A special feature of this furnace is that in case of need it can be set at any angle. With its help melted cast iron is supplied to the furnace. There is arrangement for air blast under this furnace. This air is passed through melted cast iron which removes all its impurities in the form of hot bubbles because these impurities become oxide.

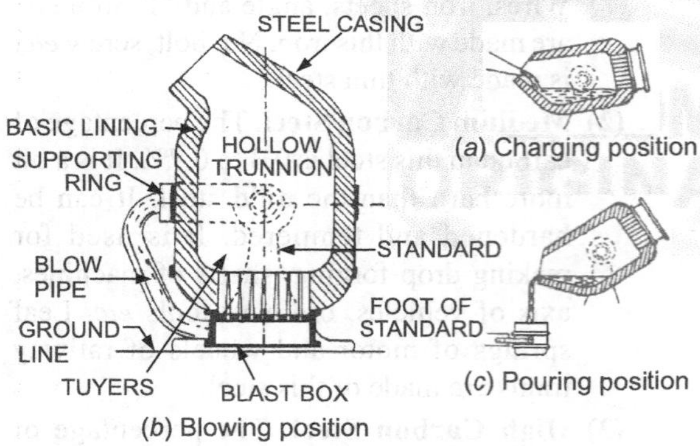

Fig. 19.5. Bessemer method

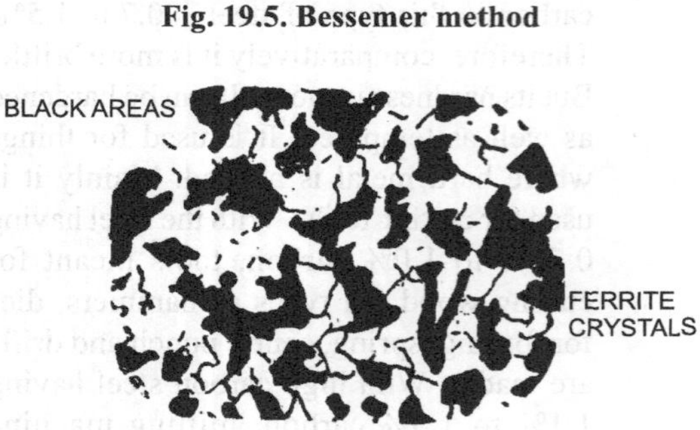

Fig. 19.6. Composition of mild steel

This furnace works at a temperature of 2500°C. The pure melted metal is tested in the laboratory in order to know the percentage of carbon in it. For improving the quality of steel material known as ferro manganese is mixed which contains 78% mangnese and 8.5% carbon. In this way steel is produced in melted form. This furnace is moved in a slanting position in order to pour the melted steel into buckets *etc*. and then put in the grooves and allowed to become cold. In Fig. 19.6, composition of mild steel has been illustrated.

Cementation Method. This method is used for producing steel in small quantity. Under this method steel is produced with wrought iron. For making steel, bars of wrought iron or plates and charcoal is arranged in a box-type furnace and closed. While arranging the wrought iron in the box it is ensured that it is covered with the charcoal from both up and down. This box is air tight. This box or furnace is heated at 1600°C for 48 hours. In this way, carbon gets combined with the wrought iron in the form of carbon gas. When this furnace becomes cold, several spots of carbon are visible on wrought iron. Steel produced with this process is known as Blister steel. When this steel is heated once again and rolling *etc*. is done, carbon is mixed into the entire wrought iron. Steel produced in this way is known as "Shear Steel". It is used for making all kinds of cutting tools *etc*.

Open Hearth Method. It is known as open Hearth Method because an open furnace is used in this method. First of all this method was used by a German scientist named Simons. This method is best for heating the iron uniformly and constantly. For making steel, melted iron and iron scrap is put in the furnace. It is given hot air which is controlled by a valve. With the hot air let out by this valve, chemical reaction starts taking place in iron and scrap. As a result, the iron gets melted. At that time its temperature is 1800°C.

In the iron melted at this degree, some lime stone is mixed as a flux. Within two-three hours after mixing lime stone the impurities in the form of mangnese, carbon or dirt gets separated from the iron. After testing the pure iron in the laboratory and ferrosilicon and ferromengnese is mixed in appropriate quantity in order to make steel of different grades. The melted steel is put into the grooves and allowed to become cold.

Crucible Method. Steel produced by the above cited method is not of high standard because these methods are used for producing steel in bulk . For producing steel of very good quality this method is used. This method was invented by watch maker of England, named Benjauin Aunts Man. For making steel under this method, bristle steel and hard coke is fitted into small earthen granery. These pots are specially made of graphite and fire clay for heating purpose. These pots are kept in the crucible furnace and hard coke is filled round these pots. Fire is put on under the furnace to melt the iron. When it is boiled two three times, all impurities start floating, which are taken out. The remaining melted iron is mixed with mangnese and some percentage of aluminium. This mixed metal is put into grooves or moulds. This is a costly method therefore it is used only for making quality steel in small quantities.

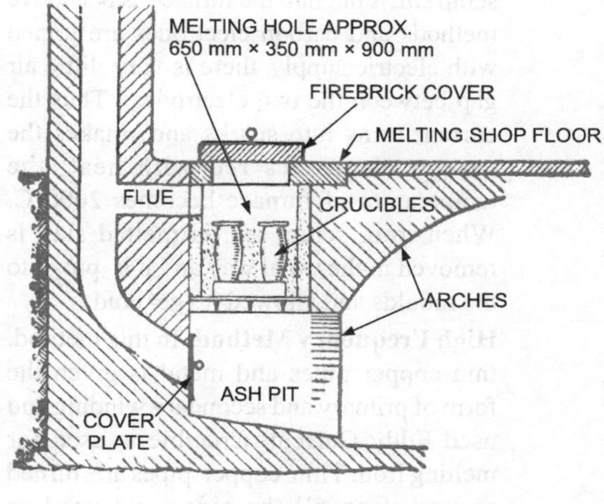

Fig. 19.7. Crucible method

Electric Method. Under this method, electric arc is used for melting iron. Carbon electrodes are used for producing arc which are supplied A.C. (Alternating current). In this method base of the furnace is made in round shape which can be easily moved on rollers and set at any angle. Inside this furnace a layer of Dolomite or Magnesite is built. In this way there is no impact of heat outside the furnace. For producing steel, iron,

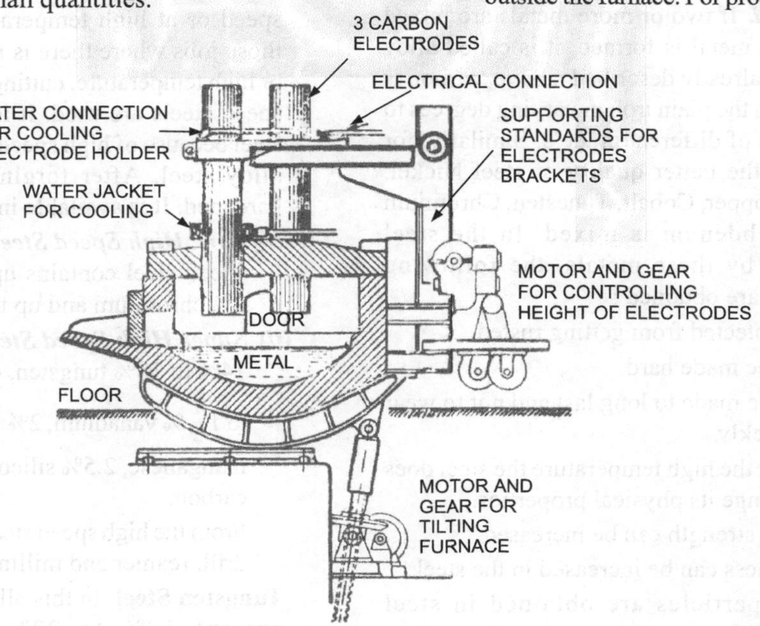

Fig. 19.8. Electric method

scrap *etc.* is put into the furnace as per above methods and carbon electrodes are joined with electric supply, there is very little air gap between the two electrodes. Thus the current turns into sparks and makes the carbon electrodes red with heat, the temperature of furnace becomes 2000°C. When iron, scrap, *etc.* is melted slag is removed in the usual way and it is put into the moulds and allowed to get cold.

High Frequency Method. In this method, thin copper pipes and metal is given the form of primary and secondary winding and used Eddy Current. Crucible is used for melting iron. Thin copper pipes are turned around it on all the sides and used as primary winding. These pipes pass the current and also perform the function of effecting water as well. The material kept inside the crucible performs the function of secondary winding. When high frequency current passes through it, eddy current is produced by mutual induction. With this temperature the iron kept in crucible is melted and in the usual ways cited above, it is filled in moulds and allowed to get cold.

(ii) ***Alloy Steel.*** If two or more metals are mixed and a new metal is formed, it is called alloy Metal. As already described above, carbon is mixed with the plain iron in varying degrees to make steel of different grade's. Similarly, for obtaining the better quality of steel Nickel. Silicon, Copper, Cobalt, Tunesten, Chromium and Molybdenum is mixed. In the steel produced by these metals, the following properties are obtained :

(*i*) It is protected from getting rusted.

(*ii*) It can be made hard.

(*iii*) It can be made to long last and not to wear out quickly.

(*iv*) Even at the high temperature the steel does not change its physical properties.

(*v*) Tensile strength can be increased.

(*vi*) Toughness can be increased in the steel.

(*vii*) Their particles are obtained in steel composition.

Alloy steel is named after the metal which is mixed in maximum quantity. In engineering line the following types of alloy steels are used for various purposes :

Chromium Steel. This alloy is mainly based on chromium metal. It contains 0.60% to 4% Chromium and 0.15% Carbon. It is a very hard metal. It can be heat treated. It is used for making cutting tools, ball bearings, parts of watches, files *etc.*

Stainless Steel. This metal is white shining alloy steel. It contains 1% to 2% Carbon, 8% Nickel and 18% Chromium and rest iron. It is used for making utensils of daily use, shaving blades, fine cutting tools, surgery equipments, parts of motor vehicles and parts of aircrafts.

Nickel Steel. This metal is also white shining alloy steel. It is used for manufacturing precision measuring tools, decoration articles used in military, parts of motor vehicles, parts of aircraft *etc.* In ordinary nickel steel there is 3.5% of nickel and up to 0.3% Carbon. It has the property of protection from rust. But those parts which remain constantly in water for longer periods are made by using 30% Nickel. For tiny measuring tools used for accurate measurement, Nickel mixed alloy steel up to 35% is used.

High Speed Steel. Cutting tools of high carbon steel cannot be used constantly on high speed or at high temperature. Therefore for those jobs where there is need for high speed or high temperature, cutting tools made of high speed steels are used. It is called high speed steel because of high speed. This is a very hard alloy steel. After forging it, it can be air hardened. It is available in two proportions.

(*i*) ***Low High Speed Steel.*** This type of high speed steel contains up to 14% tungsten, 4% chromium and up to 0.6% carbon.

(*ii*) ***Super High Speed Steel.*** It contains from 14% to 18% tungsten, 4% chromium, 1 % to $1\frac{1}{2}$ % vanadium, 2% to 3% cobalt, 30.2% manganese, 2.5% silicon and 0.6% to 0.7% carbon.

From the high speed steel, lathe cutting tool, drill, reamer and milling cutters are made.

Tungsten Steel. In this alloy steel tungsten is present 18% to 22%. It is used for manufacturing cutting tools of lathe machines. Drill, reamers and milling cutters of good quality are also made with this steel. It is also used in filament of the electric bulbs.

Cobalt Steel. It is a very hard alloy steel. It is made by mixing cobalt metal from 30% to 35% in high carbon steel. It is used for making bits for lathe cutting tools. Hardness in this steel is three times more as compared to tungsten steel and eight times more as compared to high carbon steel.

Manganese Steel. Its colour from inside is that of black grain. This alloy steel is hard even without heat treatment. It contains manganese from 10% to 15% and carbon 1%. If its machining is required then its annealing is essential. It is used for railway lines and other heavy jobs. It cannot be tempered or case hardened. Sometimes manganese is mixed with silicon, to produce manganese silicon alloy. It contains 3% silicon, 0.8% manganese, 1.2% carbon and rest iron. It is used for making generators, electric motors, spring *etc*.

Molybdenum Steel. In this type of alloy steel chromium and nickel is mixed. It is available in the following three proportions :

(*i*) 0.15% to 0.25% molybdenum and 0.5% to 0.8% nickel.

(*ii*) 0.3% to 0.4% molybdenum and 0.5% to 0.8% chrominum, 1.5% to 2% nickel.

(*iii*) 0.2% to 0.3% molybdenum and 1.65% to 2% nickel steel.

Gears, bearing and motor parts are made with this alloy.

Vanadium Steel. This type of alloy steel contains 0.15% to 2.5% vanadium, 0.9% chromium and rest iron. Its special feature is that it can absorb shocks easily. That is why spring are made of this steel. It can beeasily forged or machines.

Apart from the above types of alloy steel, some new metals have been discovered. These metals are produced in electric fumaces for sharp cutting tools. Some of these modern metals are described below :

Stelite. This is a special type of alloy. In this alloy 45% to 55% cobalt, 30% to 35% chromium, 12% to 17% tantalum of tungsten and 1 % to 2% carbon is mixed. It does not come under the category of ferrous metals because of toughness it can neither be turned nor rolled. It is a very hard alloy. It is use for heavy cutting tools at high speed.

Cemented Carbide. When all types of alloy steels prove useless in cutting the hardest metal, cutting tools of cemented carbide are used. Even the hardest metal can be cut with this metal. Its cutting tools are available in the form of tips. These are joined to the mild steel shank near the cutting edge with brazing. The cutting capacity of these tools is very high. Because there is very little wear out there is no need to grind it again and again. This type of tip tools are made by grinding carbon, tungsten, cobalt into thin rain and melted in electric furnaces. Temperature of l500°C to 1600°C is given. In order to keep their grains together some amount of Molybdenum is also mixed. It is available according to the number of cobalt bonds *i.e.*, K-10, K-20, K-30, K-40 *etc*.

Ceramic tools. This type of tools are also available in tip form. It is made of aluminium oxide. This type of tools are used by holding them with tool holders. Their edge is made at the time of making itself. This edge cannot be provided again.

Inner Structure of Steel. The inner structure of each steel is different and it depends on the quantiry of carbon mixed in them. Mainly six kinds of structures are found :

(*i*) ***Cementite.*** In its grains elements of iron and carbon are mixed which is known as iron carbide. It is in the form of plates. It is very hard and brittle.

(*ii*) ***Pearlite.*** Iron is used in pure form and carbon is available in combined form. Its tesile strength is 70 tonne per square centimeter. The structure of its grain depends upon its rate of making it cold.

(*iii*) ***Martensite.*** In this type of steel, iron is available in two forms viz. alpha and gamma. It is a solid solution of iron and carbon. It is very hard.

(*iv*) ***Austenite.*** It is in the solid solution of iron and carbon. For producing it steel is heated up to the critical point. It is mixed solution of cementite and Ferrite. But it is not as hard as these metals.

(*v*) ***Graphite.*** The steel in which the quantity of carbon is present in an independent form is known as graphite.

(*vi*) ***Ferrite.*** In this type of steel carbon present in combined form. It is a pure form of iron. It is very soft, malleable and ductile. It is difficult to make it hard. It contain magnetic properties in quite a good proportion.

Forms of Steel. Steel is available in the market in the following forms :

(*i*) Blooms : These are of 36 sq. inch.

(*ii*) Billets : These are of 4″ to 30″ crosssection.

(*iii*) Slabs : These are available in rectangular form.

(*iv*) Strip : It is less than $\frac{1}{4}$″ in thickness and wide up to 2 feet.

(*v*) Sheet : It is less than $\frac{1}{4}$″ in thickness and more in breadth than strip.

(*vi*) Plate : It is more than $\frac{1}{4}$″ in thickness and more than 6″ in breadth.

(*vii*) Bar : It is more than $\frac{1}{4}$″ in thickness and more than 6″ in length.

(*viii*) Round Bar : Its radius is more than 0.734″.

(*ix*) Rod : It is of 0.207″ to 0.734″ in radius.

(*x*) Wire : It is of less than 0.207″ in diameter and is in the form of a wire.

Non-ferrous Metals. In the engineering jobs, beside ferrous metals several non-ferrous metals are also used. These metals have their own specialities. Their most important feature is that they do not get rusted. These metals are also used in pure forms or it is mixed with two or more than two metals and used as alloy Metal. These are of the followirg types :

Copper. It is extracted from the mines in the form of ore. This ore contains impurities in the form of oxide, sulphide, sulphate and silicate. First of all some of the impurities are separated and it is melted in the blast furnace. Thus its impurities come up in the form of slag, which are separated. Pure copper is red. It can be easily twisted, turned or rolled. It is a very soft metal. It contains the properties of ductility and malleability. If it is heated in excess, it becomes brittle. Its melting point is 1083°C. It does not get rusted. It is mixed with other metals to produce brass, bronze, monal metal and German silver. Copper is a very good conductor of heat and electricity. It is mostly used in electric equipments, water boilers, decoration materials *etc*. It is produced in the form of sheet, plate, round bar and wire.

Zinc. It is a bluish white metal. It is a very malleable and ductile metal. Sheets and bars of zinc are made through rolling and drawing. It is known as granular metal. Its quality depends on granular grains shining. It gets melted in acid of water and salt. It is rustproof. It becomes soft at 110°C to 150°C temperature and becomes brittle at 200°C temperature. It is mostly used for galvanising. Water pipes and motor parts are also made of zinc.

Lead. It is the heaviest and most soft metal. It can be easily cut or scrapped. It is produced from the ore obtained from the mines. Its ores are of three kinds :

(*i*) Galena, (*ii*) Carbonate of lead, (*iii*) Sulphate of lead. Its ore is purified by floatation and smeltering process. By this process it becomes pure upto 99.9%. It melts when heated at 380°C. Pipes, plates and wires are made of this metal. It is mixed with other metals to make alloy metals like solder, paint and bearing metal *etc.*

Tin. It is obtained in the form of ore from the mines alongwith iron, silver and arsenic. Its impurities are known as wolfram. It is purified through the electro-magnetic process. It is not used in its pure form because it is a very soft and malleable metal. It is used in the form of alloy metal after mixing it with other metals. Slabs, sheets and pipes are made with this metal. It is also used for coating on copper and brass. Its melting point is 230°C and it is rust-proof.

Aluminium. This is also found in the mines in the form of ore. Its ore is of two kinds :

(*i*) Bauxite

(*ii*) Cryolite

It is very light metal. Its weight is approximately 0.09 lbs. per sq. inch. Its tensile strength is very low. It is a cheap metal. Its colour is white bluish. It is a good conductor of heat and electricity. That is why in electrical jobs and as utensils, aluminum is widely used. It can be melted at 650° temperature. It is mixed with other metals to make it hard and used for making pistons of motor vehicles and for making parts of other machines. It can be changed into various beautiful colours through anodizing. It can be forged as well as rolled. Maximum use of aluminium is made in aeroplanes. It would not be an exaggeration to say that aluminium is used in all industries.

Silver. Its colour is bright white. It contains the properties of ductility and malleability

Therefore it can be used for making thin fine leaves and wires. It is an excellent conductor of heat and electricity. Its melting point is 960°C. It is used for making coins, ornaments *etc.*

Gold. Its colour is bright golden. Its melting point is 1060°C. It is the most malleable and ductile of all metals. Copper is generally mixed with it to make ornaments. It is also used in liquid form for polishing jobs. We can easily make thin sheets and wires of gold.

Antimony. Its colour is bluish black. It melts at 632°C. It is highly brittle and acids do not have any effect on it. For castings, it is used by mixing some other metals. Type letters for printing are made with antimony.

Nickel. Its inner composition is fibrous. It's white in colour like silver. It is mixed with other metals and used. Its specific gravity is of 8.63. Its chief uses are for nickel plating and the forming of alloys.

Chromium. It is a grayish-white metallic element. Its melting point is 2930°F. It is used in alloy steels and in plating.

Cadmium. It is bluish white metallic element. It is used for plating of various parts of machines. Its melting point is 321°C.

Platinum. It is a costly metal. It is more ductile and malleable in comparison to other metals. It is used in manufacture of jewellery, for scientific apparatus and in certain industrial processes. Its melting point is 1773°C.

Non-Ferrous Alloys. When non-ferrous metals with adequate properties are not available, the non-ferrous alloy metals are used. In such non-ferrous alloys, two or more non-ferrous metals are mixed. These are used in the engineering jobs in the ways mentioned below :

Brass. It is a metal having yellow colour. Mainly copper or zinc is mixed. Its colour and solidity depends on the quantity of zinc mixed in it. Copper is also used in the mixture sometimes. On this basis, brass is of the following types :

(A) **Muntz Metal Brass.** It has 60% copper and 40% zinc. It is used in jobs only after forging because in cold condition it is not malleable. It has a great tensile strength. It is used in articles of daily use such as water taps, electric condensers and water and air pumps.

(B) **Yellow Brass.** This includes 65% copper and 35% zinc. Screws, rivets and other parts of machines are made with this metal.

(C) **Brazing Brass.** It contains 75% copper and 25% zinc. It is mostly used for permanent solder of brass. In addition, it is also used for musical instruments and artificial jewellery. It is very soft and has golden shining.

(D) **Red Brass.** It contains maximum quantity of copper. That's why it is reddish in colour. It has 85% copper and 15% zinc. It is very little ductile and soft. Machining can be done on it easily even in cold condition. It is used for manufacturing radiators of motor engines, pipe and condenser bodies.

(E) **Cartridge Brass.** It contains 70% copper and 30% zinc. It has high tensile strength. But it is very rough or soft. It is used for manufacturing caps of cartridges, radiators, reflector pipes, *etc.*

(F) **Neval Brass.** It contains 62% copper, 31% zinc, and 7% tin. Its speciality is that it does not get damaged even after remaining in water for several days. Therefore, it is used for ships. Because of tin mixed in it, it acquires some toughness and its strength increases.

(G) **Silicon Brass.** It has 78% copper, 20% zinc and 2% silicon. It has great tensile strength. It is used in fire fighting equipment, parts of refrigerators and for other casting jobs.

(H) **Aluminium Brass.** It has 76% copper, 22% zinc and 2% aluminium. Its colour is wheatish yellow. It is used for manufacturing condenser tubes, pipe rods *etc.*

(I) **Forging Brass.** It contains 68% copper, 30% zinc and 2% lead.It is considered as a very strong brass. It is used in casting jobs.

(J) **Clock Brass.** There is a mixture of 55% copper, 34% zinc, and 1% lead. It is used for manufacturing parts of watches.

Bronze. Ordinary bronze is made by mixing tin and copper. Tin and other metals are also used in different percentages in bronze as well. On this basis, bronze is of the following type :

(A) **Phosphorous Bronze.** It contains 93.7 % copper, 6% tin and 0.3% phosphorus. It is used in gears, large bearings, nut bolts, special type of screw and welding rods.

(B) Silicon Bronze. This bronze is used for manufacturing tanks, boilers and parts of ships. It has 94% copper, 3% silicon and 3% zinc.

(C) Manganese Bronze. This type of bronze is used for manufacturing worm wheel, bush, pump rod and propeller blades. It contains 56% copper, 39.9% zinc, 1% tin, 0.8% manganese, 1.4% iron and 0.30% aluminium. Its tensile strength is 30 tonne per square inch.

(D) Bell Bronze. It contains 70% to 75% copper and 20% to 25% tin. If it is struck gives a very sweet sound. Therefore, it is used for making bells.

(E) Bearing Bronze. This type of bronze is mainly used for bush bearing and pipe fittings. It has 86% to 88% copper, 9% to 11% tin, 0.5% to 1.5% lead and 1.25% to 5% zinc.

Gun Metal. It contains 85% copper, 10% tin and 5% zinc. It is mainly used for bush bearing, boiler casting and for making part of guns.

White Metal. It has 85% tin, 2% copper, 8% zinc and 2% lead. It is chiefly used for filling bearings of motor vehicles and engines.

Duralumin. Aluminium is a very soft metal but in order to make it solid it is given the name of Duralumin. It contains 90% aluminium and 10% other metals. It is used in ships and aeroplanes.

Tin Alloy. It is used for soldering. It is also used for coating other metals for making them beautiful. It contains 45.5% tin, 52% lead and 2.5% antimony.

Solder. For joining metals with solder the following types of solders are used :

(A) Tin Smith Solder. It contains a mixture of 49% to 51% tin, 3% antimony and rest lead.

(B) Plumber Solder. It is a mixture of 29% to 31% tin, 1.7% to 2% antimony and rest lead.

(C) Hard Solder. 41% tin, 3% antimony and rest lead

(D) Electric Solder. 95% tin and 5% antimony.

Questions

1. What are the properties of a metal ? Describe physical and mechanical properties of a metal.
2. What do you understand by ferrous metals and non-ferrous metals ? What is the difference between the two ?
3. What is iron-ore ? What are its different kinds ?
4. How iron-ore is purified ?
5. How iron is prepared in a blast furnace ?
6. What is pig-iron ? How pig-iron is made ?
7. What are the properties of cast-iron ? How cast-iron is made ?
8. What are the different types of cast- iron ?
9. What do you understand by White Hearth Process and Black Hearth Process ?
10. What are the different types of steel ? What are the uses of high carbon steel ?
11. What do you understand by independent and combined form of carbon in steel ?
12. Explain the Bessemer method of making steel.
13. What is meant by Alloy Steel ? What are the main branches of engineering in which it is used ?
14. What are the different metals used in high speed steel and what is the percentage of each metal in the mixture prepared for high speed steel ?
15. What is the use of cemented carbide alloy steel ?
16. What are the Non-ferrous metals ?
17. What is meant by Non-ferrous alloy metals? Of how many kind these are?
18. Write brief comments on the following :
    (*a*) Copper
    (*b*) Bronze
    (*c*) White metal.

20

Heat Treatment

In the previous chapter we studied the properties and characteristics of metals. Every metal has its own special properties and characteristics. In order to change the properties and characteristics metals are either heated or cooled. This process is known as heat treatment. In other words carefully controlled heating and cooling of steel to bring it to its highest efficiency is called heat treatment. The treatment prescribed for any particular kind of metal must be rigidly followed as different metals require different treatment. Through heat treatment the internal structure of the metal is changed according to our needs and change is brought in its mechanical properties. The following are the main advantages of heat treatment :

1. Hard metal can be soften.
2. Soft metal can be hardened.
3. The metal can be made workable for machining.
4. The mechanical properties of the metal such as tensile strength, compressible stress *etc.* can be increased or reduced.
5. By heat treatment the internal structure of the metal can be changed. For example, if steel having 1.1% carbon is cooled in the normal way, its austenite structure would change into pearlite and cementite structure. Similarly, if that steel is cooled from 700° temperature to 300°C abruptly, its structure would first change into martensite and later on into pearlite and cementite structure. In the same way, when metal is heated or cooled down there is change in its structure according to the degree of heating or cooling.

Critical Point

Steel has a special quality, if it is heated up to a specific degree of temperature, the temperature stops rising. A special change takes place in the internal fibres of the steel in this case, iron and carbide becomes one. This point of temperature is called upper critical point. After some time, the temperature of steel starts rising again but now the rate of increase in temperature is reduced and the temperature rises only to a limited extent. Again a change takes place in it and the fibres in the internal structure of steel get separated. The point of temperature at which this action takes place is known as "Lower Critical Point". Temperature between upper critical point and the lower critical point is called, "Critical Range".

In this way, if steel is heated in a furnace to such a degree that it becomes red *i.e.* upto upper critical point and at that stage if it is cooled in water or oil, it acquires special properties.

Under the heat treatment special changes in metals can be brought by the following processes :

(*i*) Annealing
(*ii*) Normalising
(*iii*) Hardening
(*iv*) Tempering
(*v*) Case Hardening.

Annealing. Heating a defective and hard matal especially high carbide steel to a critical temperature and cool it slowly in order to soften it, reduce brittleness and more workable for machining is called annealing. For annealing the steel is first heated at upper critical point. Then, it is cooled slowly in the ash of the furnace sand or in a room. When steel is heated to upper critical point, carbon mixed in it changes into liquid form. When it cools down gradually, its structure passes through pearlite and makes the metal ductile and soft. Fuel used for heat treatment is hard coke, oil, gas or electric furnace. Barometer is used to know the right temperature. Annealing temperature of all the metals depends on the quantity of carbon mixed in it. In the following table temperature is given on the basis of quantity of carbon :

TABLE

S. No.	*Quantity of Carbon*	*Annealing Temperature*
1.	Below 0.12%	875°C to 925°C
2.	From 0.12% to 0.25%	840°C to 870°C
3.	From 0.3% to 0.5%	815°C to 840°C
4.	From 0.5% to 0.9%	780°C to 810°C
5.	From 0.9% to 1.3%	760°C to 780°C

Normalising. While using a metal when we beat it in hot or cold condition, a change takes place in the structure of its internal fibres. The action of heat treatment done to again make it normal is called normalising. This action is generally performed for machining of a part after it has been forged. For normalising metal or any metal part is heated to upper critical point (*i.e.* when it becomes red) and for some time it is kept at the same temperature. Then it is allowed to get cool in the normal air independently. By this act the steel acquires adequate tensile strength and yield point. Stress is removed and the structure becomes of good fibres. Change in the structure of steel depends upon the quantity and the rate of cooling it.

Hardening. Heating a steel in a normal way and then making it hard by cooling it is known as hardening. For hardening, steel is heated at temperature of 750°C to 850°C and then it is abruptly cooled in oils, water, or other suitable solutions. This steel becomes very hard. Hardness of steel depends on the quantity of carbon mixed in it. The higher the quantity of carbon, the more hard the steel would become on cooling it. Besides this hardening of steel mainly depends on the following factors :

(*i*) Temperature
(*ii*) Grain size
(*iii*) Quenching medium
(*iv*) Speed of cooling.

The rate of cooling is kept as 18°C per second. Those steels which have quantity of carbon more than 0.83% should first be normalised.

Quenching. The dipping of heated steel into water, oil, or other bath, to impart necessary hardness is known as quenching. It is of following types :

(*i*) *Water Quenching.* Cutting tools are dipped and cooled in cold water because water affects quickly. It makes high speed steel and high carbon hard.

(*ii*) *Water and Caustic Soda.* In this method, solution for cooling steel is prepared by mixing water and caustic soda. Medium steel is hardened by this method.

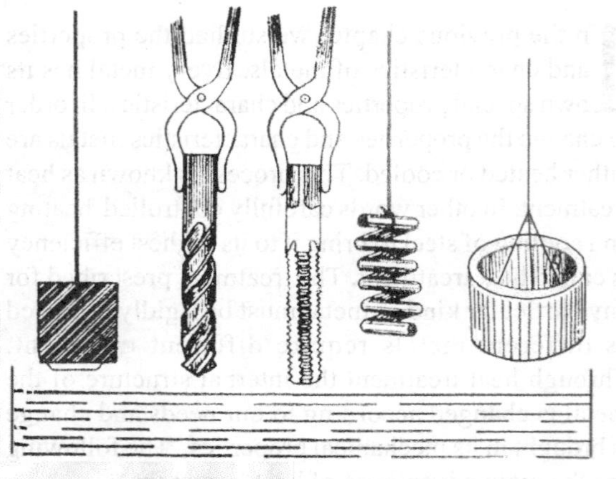

Fig. 20.1. Quenching method

(*iii*) *Oil Quenching.* Under this method, steel is heated and then dipped and cooled in different oils.

Precautions. While quenching parts of steel, it should be ensured that the long parts such as drill, reamer, tap and spring *etc.* are dipped vertically into the quenching solution. In the same way, plates, milling cutters *etc.* should be dipped at ends only as shown in Fig. 20.1.

Hardening Aluminium and Copper. Aluminium and Copper can also be hardened. These metals are first heated at 1450°F and then cooled in open air. Again it is heated at 600° to 900°F and it is cooled down. Air circulation furnace is used to heat it. This method is called Off Hardening.

Tempering. Hardening treatment makes a steel hard but it becomes brittle. As such, there is fear of breaking of such a steel, when it is hammered.

In order to remove this shortcoming it is essential to change its Martensile structure into turasite structure. For this purpose, a part of hardened steel is heated at 230° to 580°C and cooled in water or any other tempering material two or three times. This action is called tempering. It is important to note that, it is not necessary to dip the complete piece but only that part should be dipped which has an edge *etc.* made on it. Immediately after dipping it, we should watch and notice the change in its colour. A special colour on that part is visible. For different metals temperature is of different degrees as shown in the following table.

TABLE

Temperature	*Description of Job*	*Colour*
230°C	Grinding wheel dresser	Light yellow
235°C	Hexa blade, Shaving blade, Soft cutting tool	Yellow
240°C	Lathe cutting tool, Milling cutter, drill and File	Fast yellow
255°C	Scissors, punch die and tape	Brownish yellow
256°C	Hard metal lathe cutting tool, hammer, snip *etc.*	Reddish brown
275°C	Rivet set, knife, chisel, *etc.*	Purple
285°C	Chuck-key, vice jaw, spanner *etc.*	Purple
295°C	Tool of blacksmithy *etc.*	Blue
310°C	Shearing machine blade, cold chisel, *etc.*	Light blue
330°C	Screw driver, spring, *etc.*	Grey

Tempering is mainly done to provide cutting ability and to remove brittleness of the cutting tools. The following are main methods of tempering :

(*i*) Single Heat Tempering

(*ii*) Double Heat Tempering

(*iii*) Lead Bath Tempering

(*iv*) Sand Bath Tempering.

Single Heat Tempering. This method is also known as point tempering. Part of the tool to be tempered is heated to upper critical point (*i.e.* when it becomes red) and its essential parts like its edge *etc.* are dipped in water or oil. By this gradual change in the colour of the remaining part starts taking place. When required temperature is given, complete part or tool is dipped in water and cooled in the open air.

Double Heat Tempering. This method is also called "Hot plate tempering". Under this method, alongwith the tool a plate of hard metal is also heated to red point. Now both are taken out of the furnace. Cutting edge of the tool is again kept on the plate and is given heat. When right colour is visible, then that part is dipped in water or oil. When it gives proper colour, the complete tool is dipped in water. Finally, it is cooled in the air.

Lead Bath Tempering. Under this method besides tool lead is also heated. When the part or tool is heated at appropriate temperature, its cutting edge is dipped into hot lead. When the required colour is visible on the complete part, it is dipped into water and cooled or is dried in the air.

Sand Bath Tempering. This method is generally used for small jobs. Sand is heated in a pot of wide opening and the heated part is put into it. In this way, the part gets heat as well as air. When the required colour appears it is cooled and then dried.

Case Hardening. Case hardening is done to harden the upper surface of steels having less quantity of carbon such as mild steel. Because of less quantity of carbon in it, it cannot be hardened completely since even after heating and then cooling the job its structure does not become Martensite. Case hardencd steel acquires strength to tolerate hammering upto a limited extent. Usually, the following ways are used for case hardening :

(*i*) Carburising Method

(*ii*) Syniding

(*iii*) Nitriding

(*iv*) Induction Hardening

(*v*) Flame Hardening.

Carburising Method. Parts made of low carbon steel or mild steel do not have hardness because of little quantity of carbon in them. After finally making such parts, quantity of carbon on their surface is increased and thus these parts are hardened. This action is known as carburising. Therefore, it is also called Surface Hardening. It is of three kinds :

(A) **Pack Carburising.** In this method, a box of cast iron is used, which has fire clay or fire brick fixed on all the four sides. Inside this box, parts of mild steel are inserted into mixture of Potassium Ferosynide, cuttings of the hoofs of animals, bone powder soft coke *etc*. things containing carbon. All the parts are kept in this box in such a manner that these are surrounded by things having carbon. The box is then properly closed and heated in the furnace at 900°C to 1000°C temperature. In this way, carbon enters the surface of those parts and makes it hard. The extent of carbon's depth depends on the time for which it is heated. If the box is heated for longer period, the carbon will enter deeply. After heating box for adequate duration, it is allowed to get cold gradually. Through this process, while the inner structure remains of mild steel, its surface becomes of carbon steel. To what extent carbon affects at different temperatures can be known from the following table :

TABLE

Sl. No.	*Time*	*Depth*
1.	From 4 to 5 hours	0.4 mm to 0.7 mm
2.	From 5.5 to 6.5 hours	0.6 mm to 0.9 mm
3.	From 6.5 to 10.5 hours	0.8 mm to 1.2 mm
4.	From 8.5 to 11.5 hours	1.0 mm to 1.4 mm
5.	From 10 to 14 hours	1.2 mm to 1.6 mm
6.	From 11.5 to 16 hours	1.4 mm to 1.6 mm
7.	From 14 to 19 hours	1.6 mm to 2.0 mm
8.	From 16 to 22 hours	1.8 mm to 2.2 mm
9.	From 19 to 24 hours	2.0 mm to 2.4 mm

Material to be used in pack carburising and their percentage quantity can be known from the following table :

TABLE

Sl. No.	*Name of Material*	*Percentage Quantity*
1.	Charcoal Barium carbonate Sodium carbonate Calcium carbonate Molasses	74% to 78% 12% to 15% 1.0% to 1.5% 3% to 5% 4.5% to 5%
2.	Charcoal Sodium carbonate	90% 10%
3.	Charcoal Barium carbonate	90% 10%
4.	Peat coke Sodium carbonate	85% to 90% 15% to 20%

(B) **Gas Carburising.** In this method, carburising can be done upto the depth of 0.8 mm to 1.0 mm. Mild steel's job is heated at temperature of 850°C to 1050°C in muffle furnace or by electric heat of gas. When the job becomes hot, carbon monoxide, Butane, Ethane, Town Gas and Methane gases are blown with pressure into the chamber of the furnace. This makes the outer surface of the job hard.

(C) Liquid Carburising. With this method carburising can be done upto the depth of 0.8 mm. For this purpose a chemical mixture is used, which includes sodium chloride, sodium cyanide, sodium carbonate and potassium cyanide. A job of mild steel is dipped into this mixture for about four hours. With the chemical reaction, the outer surface becomes hard.

Cyaniding. It is considered better than pack carburismg. Sodium cyanide 55% and sodium carbonate 45% are mixed to prepare a solution, which is heated at a temperature of 900°C. Then the job which is to be cyanided is dipped into this solution. This process is known as cyaniding. When the same mixture is given the form of gas, it is known as gas cyaniding. In addition, the above mixture is also used by spray process. For this purpose the job is heated upto upper critical point and the mixture is sprayed two or three times.

Nitriding. Under this process, for surface hardening, Nitrogen gas is used. In this process only the surface of alloy steel is hardened. For this purpose, the job is deposited in an anti-heat box, vacuum is created in this box and ammonium gas is filled in it. This box is heated at a temperature of 510°C to 640°C. By this method, after becoming hot ammonium gas gets separated into hydrogen and nitrogen gas. After mixing with alloy steel the nitrogen gas becomes nitirte and harders the surface.

Induction Hardening. Under this process surface hardening of the job is done by the electrical induction. For this purpose the surface of the job is heated and induction coils are used. A.C. current is supplied in these coils. By this process, a magnetic area is formed between the hot surface of the job and the coil. The outer surface's contact with magnetic effect it produces eddy current. At this moment, the job is made cool with the cold water.

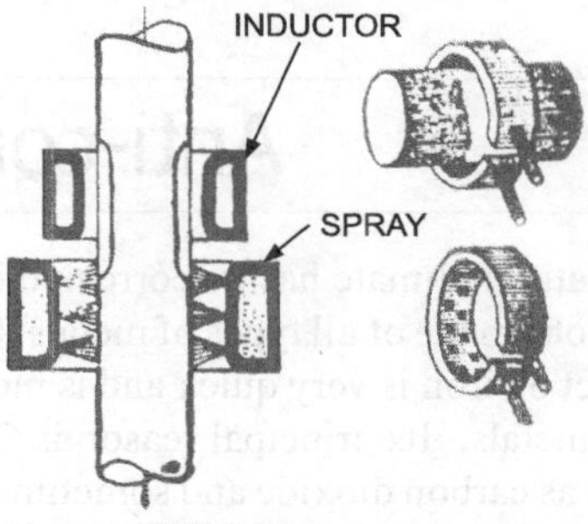

Fig. 20.2. Induction hardening

Flame Hardening. Very often for outer surface hardening of the medium carbon steel jobs, this process of surface hardening is used. The job is heated by moving it on fire from all the sides. When it is heated at the appropriate heats, it is sprayed with water which makes it cold. Now the outer surface of the job becomes hard. For flame, blow lamp gas welding equipment is used.

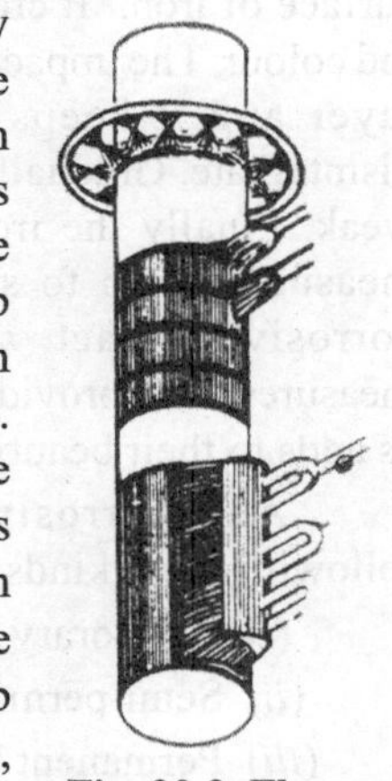

Fig. 20.3. Flame hardening

Questions

1. What is meant by Heat Treatment ? What are its uses ?
2. What is a critical point? What is meant by critical range ?
3. Under heat treatment, in what different ways change in the properties of a metal is brought ?
4. What do you understand by Annealing and Normalising ? What is difference between annealing and normalising ?
5. In what ways hardening is different from tempering job ?
6. Explain different types of Quenching.
7. Why tempering is done and what are the types of tempering ?
8. Name the metal which can be given case-hardening treatment.
9. Explain clearly the process, need and uses of pack carburising.
10. Write brief comments on :

    (*a*) Cyniding (*b*) Nitriding

    (*c*) Induction Hardening (*d*) Flame Hardening.

21

Anti-corrosive Treatment

The natural climate has its corrosive impact on the jobs made of all types of metals. Corrosive effect on iron is very quick and is more severe than other metals. Its principal reason is Oxidation. Gases such as carbon dioxide and sometimes sulphur dioxide mixed in the air, have its effect on the outer surface of iron. It creates a weak layer of brownish red colour. The impact of oxidation is even inside this layer and it keeps on letting the upper layer disintegrate. Gradually the strength of iron becomes weak. Finally the iron is reduced to powder. The measures taken to save metals from rusting and corrosive impact, are known as anti corrosive measures. This provides longer life to the jobs as well as adds to their beauty.

Anti-corrosive treatment can be of the following three kinds :

(*i*) Temporary Treatment

(*ii*) Semi-permanent Treatment

(*iii*) Permanent Treatment

Temporary Treatment. Anti-corrosive treatment which is done to protect the jobs from corrosion for short period is known as temporary treatment. For temporary anticorrosion treatment the metals are applied any kind of oil, grease or varnish.

Semi-permanent Treatment. Anti-corrosive treatment which protects the metals from corrosive for longer periods is known as semi-permanent treatment. These include colouring, tinning, painting and galvanising *etc*.

Colouring. Colouring is done in different ways for different types of metals. The following are the main methods :

(*a*) Colouring of Iron and Steel through Heat. Under this method, first the metal is heated at appropriate temperature, then it is cooled down in oil. Through this treatment metal *i.e.,* iron or steel can be coloured as yellow, purple, brown and blue. Colour depends on heat and oil. In addition for colourirg the metal as black or blue black lead, lead acetate, sodium thiosulphate and water are mixed in 1, 1, and 10 ratio respectively and metal is boiled in this mixture for about half and hour.

(B) Bronze Coating Colouring. For this type of colouring bronze powder is mixed with Banana oil and then applied to the metal like paint.

(C) Brass Colouring. For brass colouring a number of chemicals are mixed and with this liquid several colours are possible. For example, Hydraulic sodium, white arsenic potasium-sulphate and cold water are mixed and metal is dipped in it to get grey colour. In order to get brown colour on the metal, ferrous nitrate, sodium thiosulphate are mixed with cold water. Green colour can be had by mixing Ammonium Chloride, cream of tar-tar and Copper nitrate.

(D) Copper Colouring. For copper colouring also different chemicals are used such as potassium sulphide or ammonium sulphite and water are mixed to get blue or near-black colour. By mixing ammonium chloride, cream of tar-tar salt and copper nitrate, in water we get light green colour on copper.

Tinning

The process of coating iron plates with tin or

coating of a soldering iron with solder prior to its use is known as tinning. Any metal and particularly sheet metal is made anti-corrosive by tinning. These metals are washed and put in acids of water and salt. After this, these are dipped in solution of melted tin. In case of sheets, these are passed through rollers to shed extra tin. For other jobs tin is split over them. For drying of the sheets and other jobs as also for bringing shinning over them, wooden dust is rubbed by means of moving drums. In this way, metals and sheets look beautiful as well as get anti corrosive treatment.

Painting. Of all the anti-corrosive treatments, painting is the most popular method. First the metal job is properly cleaned then with the help of a brush or spray varnish mixed paint or enamel is applied. This paint or enamel forms a layer on the job and helps in providing anti-corrosive treatment to it, to a great extent. This adds to the beauty of the job. Red lead also provides anti corrosive treatment.

Galvanising. To coat iron with zinc is known as galvanising. It is not usually an electrical process but consists simply of dipping the iron in molten zinc. First the job is cleaned with acid of salt then it is washed with water and dipped in molted zinc solution and taken out. For shedding the extra zinc wire brush or wire rollers are used. This kind of sheets and jobs are called G.I. Sheet and G.I. bolt respectively.

Permanent Treatment. The treatment given to metals in order to protect metals from corrosive action permanently, is known as permanent treatment. This primarily includes Electroplating. Through electroplating jobs made of metals are given thin layers of chromium, nickel, silver and gold *etc.*

Electroplating. The act or process of depositing metal by electric means is called electroplating. To make the definition more clear we can add that the process of applying a thin layer of a metal over a job made of another metal is called electroplating. Before electroplating the job is first cleaned and then thoroughly cleaned with buffing. Adequate solution is filled in a tank for the purpose of pasting it on the metal. For example, if we want to do copper plating on brass, we will fill copper sulphate in the tank. In the same way, for different metals solution of different metallic salts are used. Two copper plates are hanged in this tank and then the brass job too is hanged in it. Treating the copper plates as anode and brass plates as cathode, we will connect them Direct Current (D.C. supply) and give current of 2 to 3 volts. By doing this, copper will start melting from copper plates and starts depositing on brass plates. The extent of thickness of the metal layer depends upon the current supply and the duration for which the job has been dipped into the solution.

After electroplating, the job is washed with bare water and then put in wooden dust. This process brings shinning to the job. For the purpose of shinning, buffing is done again.

Note. (*i*) It is very important that before electroplating any job it should be properly cleaned. Kerosene oil, caustic soda, salts acid, sulphuric acid and fine emery paper or wire brush is used for cleaning the job.

(*ii*) While making solution of acid it should be ensured that acid is added to water slowly and in appropriate quantity.

(*iii*) Never put in your bare hands in acid solution. For handling a job, tongs, pliers and proper glooves should be used.

Questions

1. What do you understand by corrosive process ?
2. What are the different types of anti-corrosive treatment ?
3. What is the process of tinning and galvanising ?
4. What do you understand by electroplating and how it is done ?
5. Comment on the following :
   (*a*) Iron and steel colouring.
   (*b*) Brass colouring.
   (*c*) Green colouring on copper.

22

Lubricants and Coolants

Lubrication and Lubricants

If two things are brought together and rubbed, they generate heat. For example, during winter we often rub our hands, which generate heat and we feel warm. In the same way, there are several parts in a machine which touch each other while the machine is in motion and cause friction. When friction takes place between two parts made of metal they generate heat. Due to this heat these parts expand bit in size and pose hinderance in their smooth movement. Such friction in a machine causes noise as well as the parts start getting worn out. Because of increase in temperature the natural properties of the metal are destroyed. There is therefore, need for making a thin layer or film of some sticky and greasy substance. These substances are known as lubricants. The process or act of putting the lubricant at places of friction between different parts of machines is called lubrication. According to the nature of machines and their parts, various types ol lubricants are used, depending upon their need and utility.

Lubricant

As alraady pointed out, the substances used for lubrication are called lubricants. When these lubricants create a thin film between two parts of a machine their temperature does not increase and these parts do not wear out easily. The machine operates smoothly whithout creating any noise. Lubricants are of three kinds :

(1) Liquid Lubricant

(2) Semi Solid Lubricant

(3) Solid Lubricant

1. **Liquid Lubricant.** Lubricants in the form of liquids like oils are called liquid lubricants. In this category the following three kinds of oils are included:

(*a*) Vegetable Oil

(*b*) Mineral Oil

(*c*) Fats Oil

(a) Vegetable Oil. The oils extracted from fruits, vegetables and seeds are called vegetable oils. Even in this catagory two types of oils are available :

(*i*) *Drying Oil:* Oils which become dry in normal temperature and their greasiness ends, called drying oils. These oils are used to protect precision measuring tool from moisture. Turpentine oil is generally used in this oil.

(*ii*) *Non-drying Oil.* Oils which do not get dried easily and their greasiness remains in tact are non-drying oils. These oils are used in light machines. Under these oils come Coconut oil, Mustard oil, Cotton-seed oil, Castor oil, Olive oil, Palm oil *etc*. which contain adequate greasiness.

(b) Mineral Oil. These are natural oils. Such oils are extracted from mines like other minerals. These mineral oils are purified in the refineries and different kinds of oils are produced, such as petrol, diesel, mobile oil, kerosene oil and gear oil.

(c) Fats Oil. Oils extracted from fats of water animals and other animals are called fats oils. These oils are used in all kinds of machines. Mainly fats oil is extracted from fats of Pigs and Fish *etc*. In addition, oils made from fats of other animals are also used.

2. **Semi-solid Lubricant.** Grease and Vaseline are often termed as semi-solid lubricants. Grease in a thick substance which contains stickness and greasiness. This can be generally divided into two parts :

   (i) ***Soft Grease.*** Soft Grease is used at such places where it is difficult to make a film from other lubricants or where it is difficult to do lubrication daily. For lubrication with soft grease, grease cap and nipple are used. Grease is made from mixture of mineral oils and other substances. The quantity of mineral oils is from 65 to 90 percent. Grease is specially prepared for different purposes of lubrication, for example, bearing grease, chesis lubrication grease *etc*. There are other types of greases which melt in excess temperature or grease which melts in low temperature.

   (ii) ***Hard Grease.*** For protecting precision instruments and small cutting tools from rust, hard grease is used. Hard grease is also of different types. After melting it this is applied to the tools and machine parts is allowed to get dry. This grease does not melt at normal temperature and remains stuck to the machine parts and tools.

3. **Solid Lubricant.** Where liquid and semi-solid lubricants cannot be used solid lubricants are used. Wax, graphite, Talac, Mica *etc*. come under this category. These substances are good lubricants itself.

Properties of Lubricant. All types of lubricant mentioned above have their own properties. Their classification and selection is made on this very basis. Lubricants should be chosen on the basis of their following properties :

Viscosity. The property of flow in a liquid is called viscosity. The thin liquids have low viscosity and thick oils have more viscosity. The viscosity of lubricants is reduced due to temperature in the operation of machines. According to machine, lubricant of appropriate viscosity should be used. If the lubricant is of low viscosity, it would flow out as a thin layer between the two parts of a machine. On the other hand, if lubricant with high viscosity is used it would not be able to reach between the two parts of a machine easily. Viscosity is known by numbers.

Table showing Viscosity number of some Special Machine Oils

S. No.	*Machine oil*	*Viscocity*
1.	Light machine oil	180, 210
2.	I.C. Engine oil	260
3.	Compressor oil	275
4.	Cylinder oil	2000, 3500
5.	Pump oil	300, 375
6.	Motor oil	1200, 3000
7.	Diesel oil	600, 900
8.	Turbo oil	145, 150

Oiliness. The property of making the surface wet and producing greasiness is called oiliness. That is why it creates a layer of greasiness between two parts.

Flash Point. Temperature at which oil turns into steam and evaporates is called Flash Point.

Fire Point. The point at which the steam of oil starts burning is called Fire Point. It is usually more than the Flash point by 15 to 20°.

Pour Point. Temperature at which oil stops flowing and starts freezing is known as Pour Point. It is important in air-conditioners and refrigerators.

Emulsification. If a lubricant or oil gets mixed with water it is against the properties of a lubricant. The oil must have the quality of not dissolving in the water.

Acidity. Any kind of acidity in oil is against its properties. There should be no acid in water else it would have an adverse impact on the jobs.

Specific Gravity. The property of oil which enables it to gain weight and remain below the water, when it is mixed with water, is known as specific gravity.

Lubrication Methods

Lubrication between two parts of a machine is done in various ways. Some of the prominent methods are as under :

(i) **Gravity Feed Method.** Under this system oil is kept in a pot at a height from the machine. This lubricant is supplied with the help of cotton wicks through the principle of gravity.

(ii) **Splash Method.** Under this method oil is kept in a pot inside or outside a machine. When a certain part of machine is operated (moves) oil

drops are splashed or it is done by ring method. These splashed drops of oil reach the machine parts and perform lubrication appropriately.

(iii) **Forced Feed Method.** Under this method oil is kept in a container outside or inside the machine, which is regularly supplied to the different parts through the various oil channels with adequate pressure. Oil is also supplied through oil gun or oil can.

Lubricators

The sources with whose help lubricant is supplied between the two parts in operation are called lubricators. Generally the following lubricators' arrangement is done :

Wick Lubrication Arrangement. There are some machines and its parts, which need constant lubrication drop by drop. An oil container and wicks are used as shown in Fig. 22.1. These wicks are made of woollen stuff and remains dipped in oil from one end. Oil gets absorbed in the wick and falls in drops from the other end on shaft or other parts.

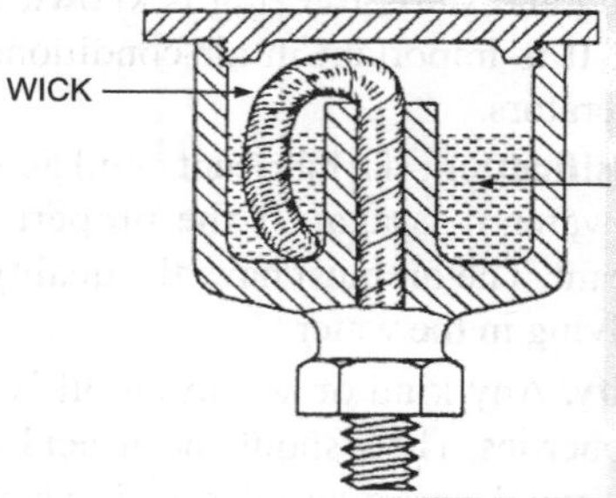

Fig. 22.1. Wick lubrication arrangement

Liveness Glass Lubrication Arrangement. This arrangement has been shown in Fig .22.2. This arrangement is usually used in oil engines

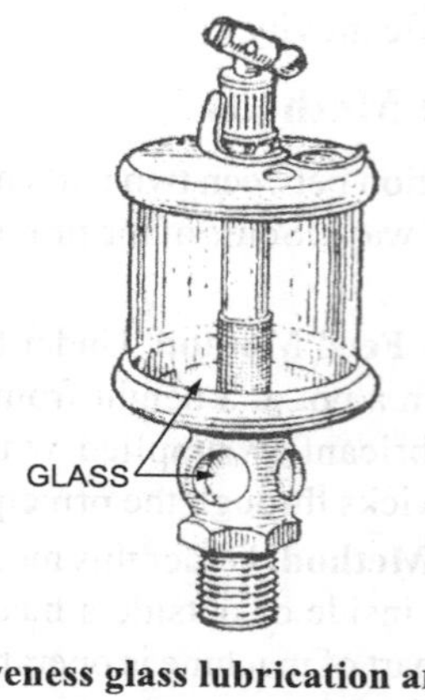

Fig. 22.2. Liveness glass lubrication arrangement

etc. Oil is filled in a container like a glass tumbler. Oil is controlled by a valve. When the engine operates valve gets opened and the oil falls on the shaft in drops. When engine is put off, the valve also closes and no oil comes out.

Oil Cup Lubrication Arrangement. Under this arrangement a small gun metal cup is used. It is particularly used in vertical steam engines. It can also be fitted on other machines in case of need. Under this arrangement also lubrication is in drops and is regular.

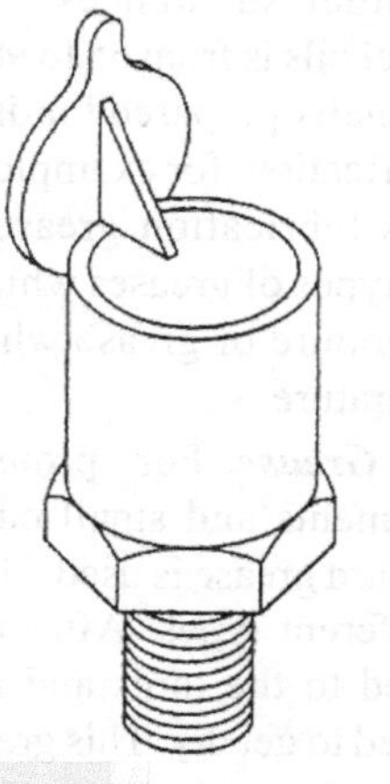

Fig. 22.3. Oil cup lubrication arrangement

Oil Can Arrangement. This is the easiest arrangement for lubrication on externals parts. An oil container is used for lubrication purposes. It has been shown in Fig. 22.4. When we press its pressure button, oil comes out from the nozzel in the desired quantity, according the pressure.

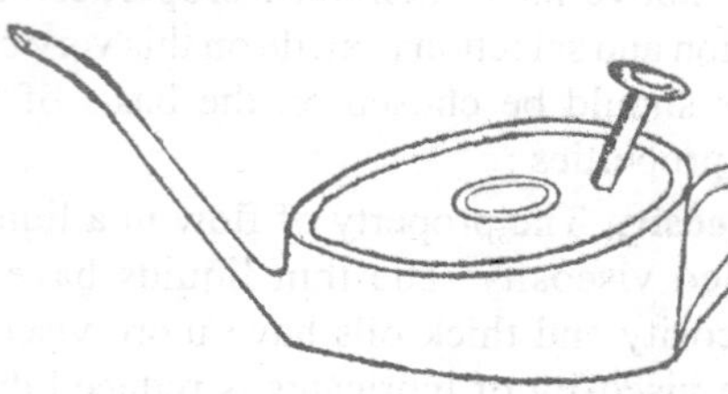

Fig. 22.4. Oil can

Oil Gun Arrangement. It is used for lubrication of those parts where lubrication is not possible with the oil can. This oil gun is similer to an ordinary syringe, which contains a flexible nozzle. In sonic oil guns arrangements are made to exert pressure on oil through compressed air.

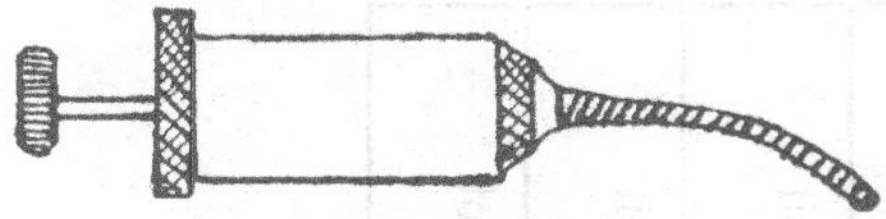

Fig. 22.5. Oil gun lubrication

Grease Gun Arrangements. At places where greasing is necessary as per a fixed schedule, greasing gun is used. It looks like a syringe. A piston and a nozzel is used in it. With this greasing can be done with proper pressure. At places where there is need for greasing with great pressure, there is provision for providing pressure of compressed air.

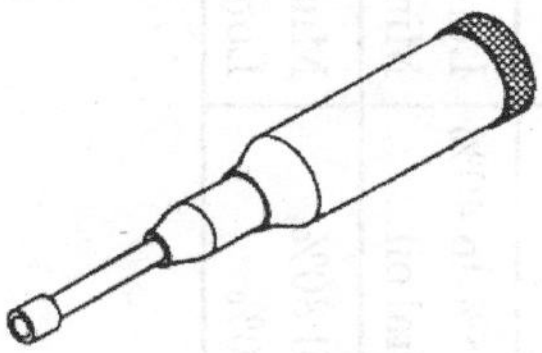

Fig. 22.6. Grease gun

Ring Lubrication Arrangement. In order to lubricate the shafts of some machines, ring lubrication arrangement is used. Under this arrangement oil is filled in a container kept below the shaft. Two rings are provided near the shaft bush. These rings rotate with the shaft and bring up oil for lubrication.

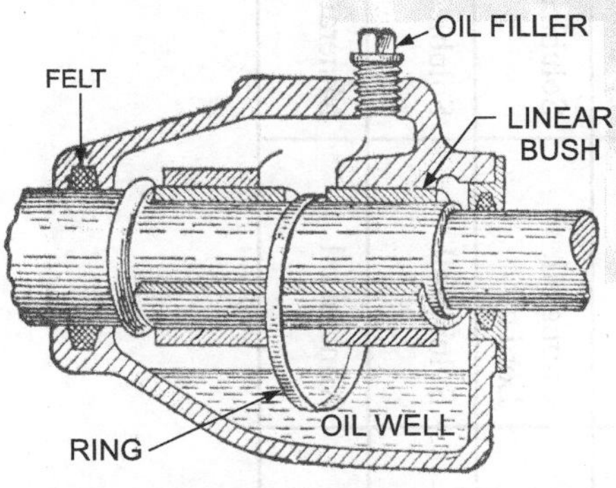

Fig. 22.7. Ring lubrication arrangement

Coolant

When metal is cut with a cutting tool, because of friction between the metal and the tool, heat is produced. Although the cut chips absorb this heat yet some heat has to be borne by cutting tools and jobs. However job may not be damaged by this heat but the cutting tool can be damaged. With heat the temper of cutting tools wears out and the cutting capacity is also reduced. Finishing clean and quick cutting cannot be done with these cutting tools. Coolants are used for protecting these cutting tools. In the old days, only water was used as a coolant but in the modern age tremendous progress has been achieved in engineering. As a result number of effective coolants have been invented, which are known by the name of the cutting fluids. Cutting fluids have the following advantages in addition to being coolants.

Advantages of Cutting Fluids :

(*i*) It performs lubrication between the job and the cutting tool.

(*ii*) It keeps the jobs and the cutting tool at normal temperature and save them from burning.

(*iii*) It saves the job, tool and cutting chips from blending.

(*iv*) It saves the job from rust.

(*v*) Increases the life of the tool.

(*vi*) Keeps the tip or edge of the tool away from the chips.

(*vii*) It brings good finishing on the job cutting.

(*viii*) The rate of cutting increases.

Kinds of Cutting Fluids. For different jobs different kinds of fluids are used. These can be divided into two parts :

(*i*) Mineral and animal oil

(*ii*) Soluble oil.

Mineral and Animal Oil. There are certain jobs and spaces, where the coolant water can harm the machine, instrument or the job. At such places fluid without water is used. These fluids include kerosene oil, animal oil, diesel, turpentine oil, or mobile oil. They function as coolants and lubricants.

Soluble Oil. This type of cutting fluid is prepared from animal oils, vegetable oils, mineral oils and chemicals. These materials are soluble in water and these are mixed with water and used as coolants. The ratio of water and oil is 6 : 1.

Properties of Cutting Fluids. A good cutting fluid should have the following properties :

(*i*) Lubricant. Cutting fluid should have the quality of functioning as a lubricant besides cutting.

(*ii*) Coolant. Cutting fluid should save the jobs and cutting tools from getting hot.

(*iii*) Welding Resistance Properly. Cutting fluid should not let the cutting tools, job and cutting chips weld with each other.

Metals, Operations and Proper Cutting Fluids

Mineral	*Drilling*	*Reaming*	*Threading*	*Tapping*	*Tinning*	*Milling*
Aluminium	Soluble oil 10 to 25%, water 75 to 90%	Kerosene oil, Mineral oil, Lord oil	Cutting oil, Kerosene oil, Dry	Lord oil, Service oil	Soluble oil, Mineral oil	Soluble oil, Mineral oil
Brass	Soluble oil 25% Water 75%	Cutting oil, Dry	Lord oil, Cutting oil	Mineral oil 80% to 90%, Lord oil 10% to 20%	Mineral oil 75%, Sulphur base oil 25%	Soluble oil, Mineral oil 90%
Bronze	Soluble oil	Mineral oil, Dry cutting oil	Lord oil, Cutting oil	Lord oil 20%, Mineral oil 10%	Soluble oil	Lord oil, Mineral oil
Cast Iron	Dry	Dry	Dry	Dry	Dry	Dry
Cast Steel	Soluble oil	Soluble oil	Soluble oil	Soluble oil	Soluble oil	Soluble oil
Alloy Steel	Cutting oil	Mineral oil	Mineral oil	Lord oil, Mineral oil	Sulphur base oil 25%, Mineral oil	Lord oil 10%, Mineral oil 90%
Maleable Iron	Soluble oil	Soluble oil	Soda water, Lord oil	Cutting oil	Soluble oil	Soluble oil
Mild Steel	Cutting oil, Mineral oil	Cuting oil, Lord oil	Solubleoil	Soluble oil	Soluble oil	Solubleoil
Tool Steel and Low Carbon Steel	Soluble oil	Soluble oil	Solubleoil	Lord oil 25% to 40% with Mineral oil	Lord oil 25%, Mineral oil 75%	Solubleoil
Magnesium	Mineral oil	Mineral oil	Mineral oil	Mineral oil 80%, Lord oil 20%	Mineral oil 90%, Lord oil 10%	Mineral oil

(*iv*) **Rust Resistance Property.** Cutting fluids are often made by mixing water. Therefore, they should be rust resistance and should not allow the job, machine and tool to get rusted.

Soda Water Cutting Fluid. In the absence of appropriate cutting fluid, mixture of soda water can be used as cutting fuid. One kg soda is mixed in 80 kgs water. In order to bring lubricating property in it one kg animal oil or any other soluble oil should be mixed in it.

Dry Machining of Cast Iron. From the Lubricant Coolant Table on the next page it is obvious that cast iron can be machined without the use of any coolant because of the following reasons :

(*i*) In the cast iron, carbon is present in great quantity in the form of graphite. Graphite itself acts as a lubricant.

(*ii*) Crystals are of big size in the cast iron. That is why friction of cutting tool is comparatively very little.

(*iii*) Another reason for not using coolant in cast iron is that its particles mix with water and form sticky solution. It poses difficulty in machining.

Difference between Lubricants and Coolants

Lubricant	***Coolants***
1. Thin layer of this fluid between two machine parts helps in keeping them cool.	1. It helps to cool down the job and cutting tool while cutting operations are carried out.
2. It gives long life to machine parts.	2. It gives long life to cutting tools.
3. It saves machines from rust.	3. It saves job from rust.
4. It helps in the smooth running of machines and its parts.	4. Cutting is done easily with its use.
5. It protects the machine parts from becoming jam.	5. It protects the job and tools from becoming jam.
6. It helps in keeping the machine fit and in good working condition.	6. It helps in giving fine finishing on the jobs.

Questions

1. Why lubrication is necessary ?

2. What are the different kinds of lubricants ?

3. What are the different ways of lubrication ?

4. What are the essential properties of a good lubricant ?

5. List the types of lubricators.

6. What is the function of coolant ?

7. List the properties needed in a good coolant.

8. What are the different types of coolants ?

9. What is the difference between lubricant and coolant ?

10. Why no coolant is used while machining cast iron ?

23

Mechanical Power Transmission

Transfer of mechanical power from one place to another is necessary for operating a machine. This process is known as "Mechanical Power Transmission". All machines are operated with one or the other power. This power is made availible through electric motor or automotive engines, which include steam engines, diesel engines, and petrol engines. The power generated by these engines is transferred through one or the other mediums. Generally the following mediums are applied for this purpose :

(*i*) Gears
(*ii*) Pulley and Belts
(*iii*) Chain and Sprocket
(*iv*) Clutch
(*v*) Shaft and Coupling
(*vi*) Cam
(*vii*) Rope.

Power Transmission by Gears

Power transmission by gears can be done at such places where the distance between two shafts is not much. In this medium gears made of cast iron, steel and gun-metal are used. Gear is made like a round wheel. Hole is made in the centre of gears to fit them on shafts. In some gears, there are grooves in this hole. On the periphery of the wheel teeth of similar shape are cut at equal distance. On the basis of their structure gears can be divided into the following five parts :

(*i*) Spur Gear
(*ii*) Bevel Gear
(*iii*) Helical Gear
(*iv*) Worm Gcar
(*v*) Rack and Pinion Gear.

Spur Gear. Spur gears are normally used at all places. Teeth of similar shape are cut on its complete periphery at equal distance, parallel to the shaft. In other words, it is a gear wheel whose teeth are on the outer diameter and at right angles with the sides of the wheel. Through this gear the speed of power can be increased or decreased or can be transmitted from one place to another. But for heavy works these gears are not used. In the gearbox lathe machine, this type of gears are used.

Fig. 23.1. Spur gear

Structure of Spur Gear. Spur gears can perform the function of pushing each other in the proper manner only if they are designed in

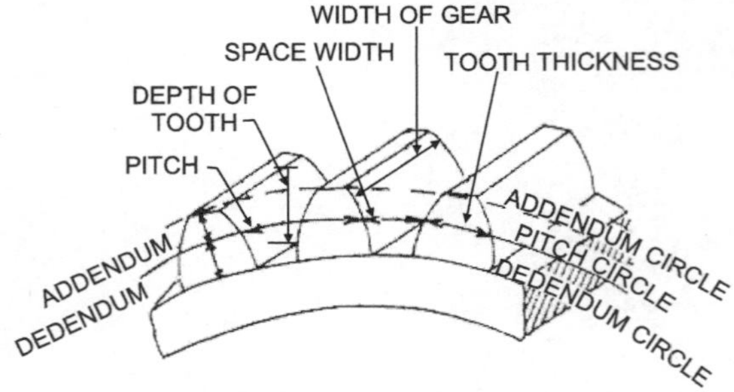

Fig. 23.2. Parts of gear

a particular shape. If there is a difference in their profile they would get stuck to each other. Their teeth do nor set in complete in fillets of the other gears, there is some clearance in them.

Terms used in connection with gears. It is essential to have knowledge about the technology used with regards to gears. Some of them have been defined below :

(1) Outer circle. The outer diameter of gear is known as "Outer Circle".

(2) Root circle. The circle made on the fillet of the gear is called Root Circle.

(3) Pitch circle. It is also known as Pitch diameter. The circle of contact in meshed gears is called Pitch Circle.

(4) Fillet. The conclave curve at the root of a teeth in a gear, which is the difference between total depth and the depth in use, is called Fillet.

(5) Flank. The side of gear teeth lying below the pitch line is called flank.

(6) Face. The face of a gear wheel indicates the breadth of the teeth. In other words, space between the pitch circle and the outer circle on its both sides is called Face.

(7) Top. The upper most part of teeth is known as Top.

(8) Circular pitch. The distance from the centre of one tooth to the centre of the next measured on pitch line is called Circular Pitch

(9) Diametral Pitch. The relation, or ratio, existing between the number of teeth on a gear and its pitch diameter is called diameteral pitch. If a gear has 40 teeth and its pitch diameter is 10, the diameteral pitch is 4.

(10) Module. This is as proportionate part of the pitch as a circular pitch is a portionate part of the periphery of the pitch.

(11) Pitch diameter. Diameter of pitch circle is called "Pitch Diameter".

(12) Addendum. The point or portion of the tooth of a gear wheel lying outside the pitch circle is called Addendum. The outer circumference of a gear wheel is called addendum circle.

(13) Dedundum. That portion of a gear tooth lying between the pitch and the root lines is known as dedundum.

(14) Whole depth. The total depth of one gear tooth is called Whole Depth.

(15) Working depth. The depth of a tooth from addendum line to clearance line *i.e.,* the total depth minus the clearance.

(16) Clearance. The amount of space, open or free between adjacent teeth of gears.

Bevel Gear. Where power is to be transmitted at 90° angle, this type of gear is used. For example, drilling, plainer machines *etc*. The shape of this gear is like a cone. These are of the following types :

(*i*) Straight bevel gear

(*ii*) Zeerol bevel gear

(*iii*) Spiral bevel gear.

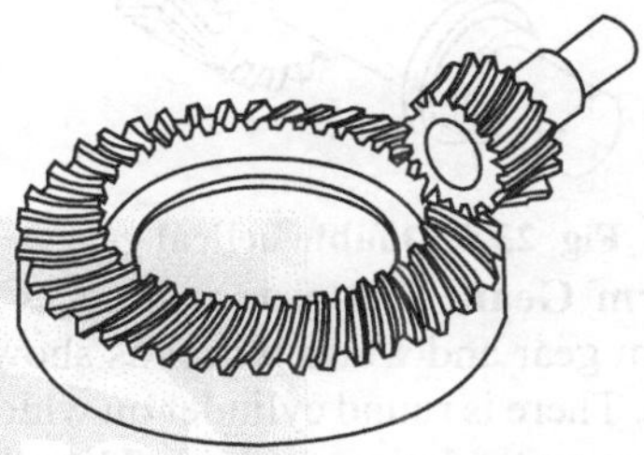

Fig. 23.3. Bevel gear

Straight Bevel Gears are mostly used in ordinary jobs. The shape of Zeerol Bevel Gear's teeth is circular. Teeth of Spiral Bevel gear are circular and slanting. Power transmission through these gears is slow but constant.

Helical Gear. This type of gear has been shown in Fig. 23.4. It is a tooth gear in which wheel teeth, instead of being at right angles with their faces, are set at some other angle there with. These may be used to transmit power between (1) parallel shafts, (2) shafts at right angles and not intersecting, (3) shafts inclined at any angle and not intersecting. It gives greater strength and smoother operation, but develops considerable end thrust.

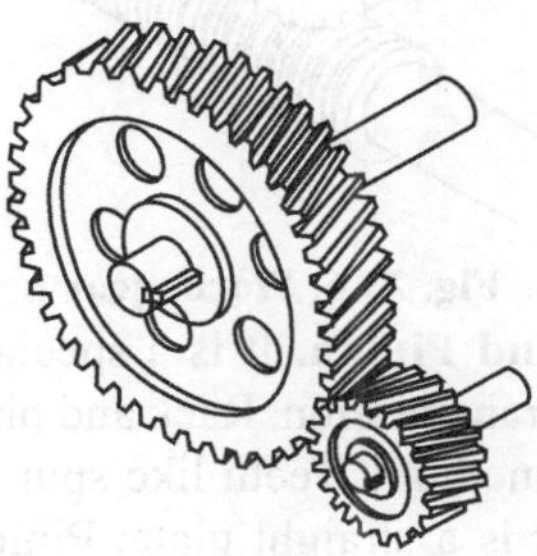

Fig. 23.4. Helical gear

These gears are made in two ways :

(1) In the form of straight helical gears, which are known as single helical gears.

(2) Double helical gear, which is also known as Harring Bone gear. It contains double rows of helical teeth. Halical gear is used where fast speed is to be provided.

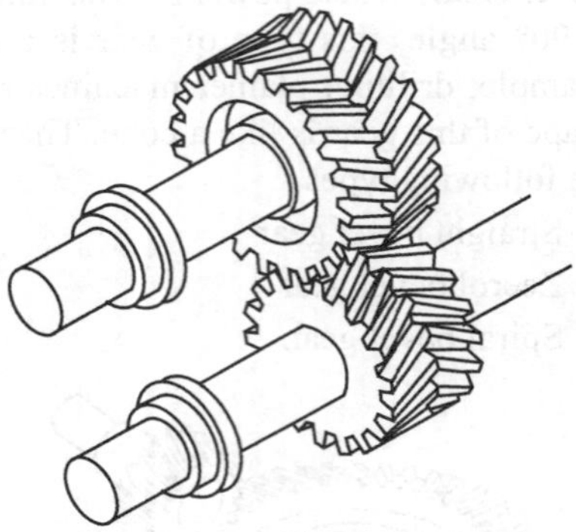

Fig. 23.5. Double helical gear

Worm Gear. This gear is used as a pair of worm gear and worm wheel as shown in Fig. 23.6. There is round cylinder on which threads are cut on the lathe machine. The other part is a round wheel. Teeth according to its threads are cut on its periphery. These gears are used at places where speed is slow but pressure is more. *e.g.,* dividing head and differential of motor vehicle. A special feature of this gear is that in heavy jobs it performs the function of speed reduction efficiently. For this purpose necessary ratio is maintained between the teeth and threads of worm wheel and worm gear.

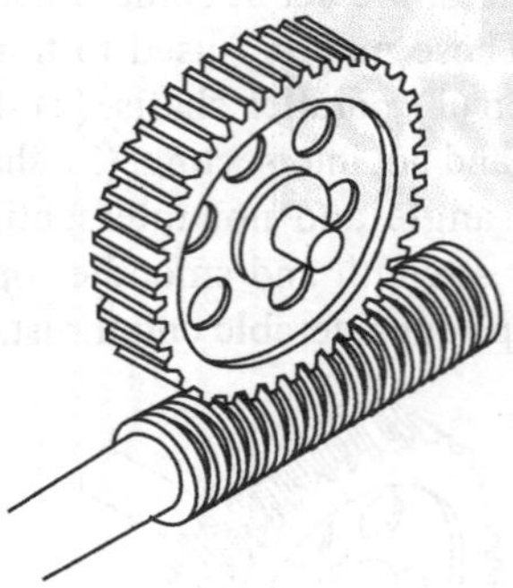

Fig. 23.6. Worm gear

Rack and Pinion. It is a special medium of power transmission. Rack and pinion are used in this medium. Teeth like spur gears are cut on it. It is a straight plate. Pinion is a small round gear. It is used for light job *e.g.* elevating screw *etc.* It has been shown in Fig. 23.7.

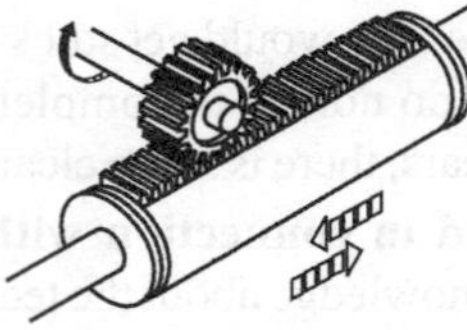

Fig. 23.7. Rack and pinion

Uses of Gears. Using two or more gears for power transmssion has several advantages and disadvantages.

Advantages :

(*i*) Power transmission takes place easily and noiselessly.

(*ii*) Speed can be had in less or more ratio.

(*iii*) Direction of speed can be changed.

(*iv*) This medium functions for a long time without any obstructions.

Disadvantages :

(*i*) Power transmission at distant places is very costly.

(*ii*) Gear fitting can be done only by an experienced technician.

Terms used in connection with speed of gears :

Driver Gear. When power is transmitted through two or more gears, the gear connected with the electric engine or machine is called Prime mover or Driver gear.

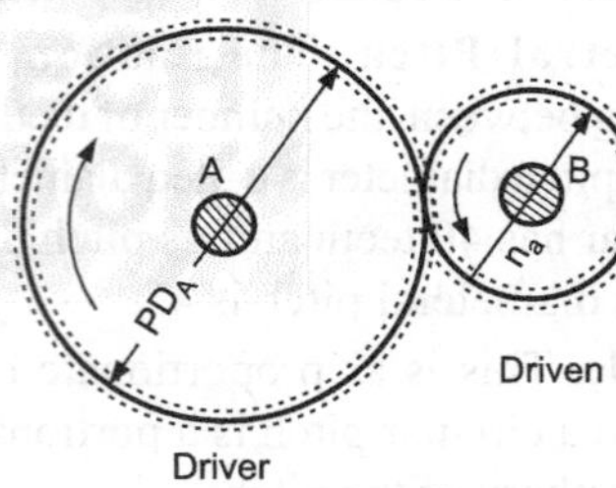

Fig. 23.8. Contact of gears

Driven Gear. The gear driven by the driver gear is called Driven Gear. Its speed depends on the ratio of teeth cut on the gear. This gear moves in the opposition direction of the driver gear.

Idler Gear. When there is need to move the Driven gear in the same direction in which the Driver gear is moving, in such cases a third gear is used between the two gears. This gear is known as Idler Gear. Its use has been shown in Fig. 23.9.

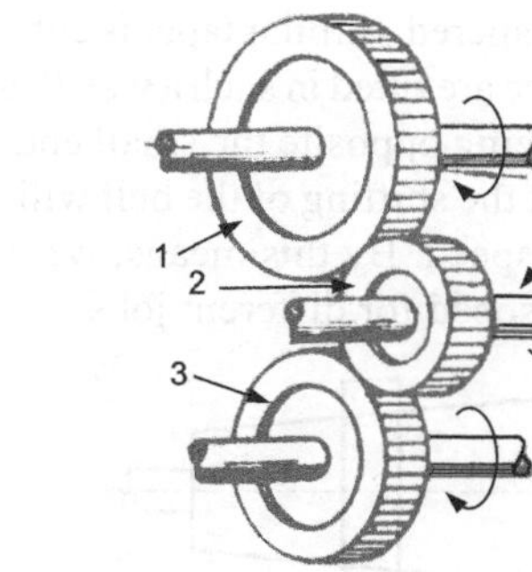

Fig. 23.9. Use of idler Gear

Gear Law. As per the principle of gear, if a small gear drives a bigger one, the speed of the bigger would be less than the smaller gear. Contrarily if a smaller gear is driven by a bigger gear, the speed of the small gear would be more than the bigger gear. Two gears 'A' and 'B' have been shown in Fig. 23.10. "A" gear is taken as a driver gear, which has ten teeth and if it is rotating at 300 R.P.M. then the driven geal "B" which has 30 teeths would rotate at 100 R.P.M. On the other hand, if "B" gear is taken as driver gear and its speed is 300 R.P.M. then gear "A" would rotate at a speed of 900 R.P.M. In this way we can calculate the speed of driver and driven gears, if we know the number of their teeth and there speed.

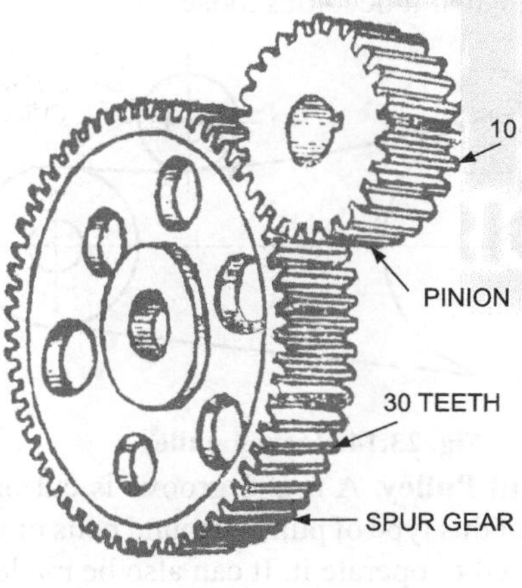

Fig. 23.10. Gear law

Example. We take a driver gear which has 100 teeth and the driven gear with 300 teeth. And if the driven gear rotates at 200 R.P.M., find out the speed of the driver gear.

Formula:

R.P.M. of Driver Gear

$$= \frac{\text{No. of teeth of gear} \times \text{RPM of driven gear}}{\text{Teeth of the driver}}$$

$$= \frac{300 \times 200}{100} = 600 \text{ R.P.M.}$$

Pulley and Belts

The most easy and common medium of power transmission is "pulley and belts". Pulleys are available in small and big sizes. These are operated with the help of the belts. Pulley fixed on the shaft or pulley which moves other pulleys are called driver pulleys. The pulley moved by the driver pulley are called Follower Pulleys. Pulley is like a round wheel, which is fitted on the shaft. We can increase or reduce the speed of power transmission as in the case of gears and shafts by using big and small pulleys. Pulleys contains the following parts as shown in Fig. 23.11.

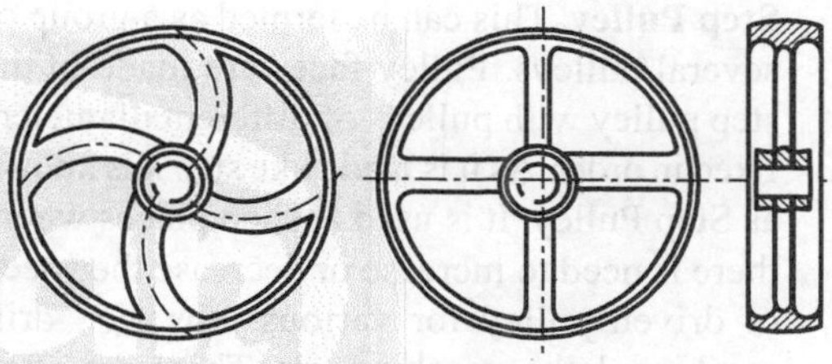

Fig. 23.11 Pulley

(*i*) Face, (*ii*) Hub, (*iii*) Arms, (*iv*) Bore

Face. The part containing periphery of the pulley is called "Face". It is slightly bulging from the centre and is descending from sides. The protruding middle part is called Crown. Face is either plain or "V" groove is built on it.

Hub. The central part of a pulley, which has a bore for the shaft, is called Hub. These are of three types :

(*i*) *Solid hub.* In this type of hub only shaft of one particular size is fitted. For shafts of different sizes, it is used with different bores.

(*ii*) *Slotted hub.* This type of hub is slotted from one side which is tightened with a nut and bolt after fitting the shaft. It is also made in one piece, it can be used with shafts of different diameter.

(*iii*) *Split hub.* This type of hub is made in two pieces (parts). For fitting these two parts on the shafts two nuts and bolts are used. Their faces are made of two pieces. These can be used for big and small shafts of the same type.

Arms. The joining parts which joins pulleys face and hub, is called Arms. Their number is according to the diameter of the pulley and its use. It may be four, six or eight.

Bore. Hole in the hub is called "bore". A key way is cut in the hole. With the "key" shaft and pulley is locked.

Types of Pulleys. For different machines and jobs the following types of pulleys are used :

(*i*) Step Pulley
(*ii*) "V" Groove Pullev
(*iii*) Split Pulley
(*iv*) Cone pulley
(*v*) Jockey Pulley
(*vi*) Round Pulley
(*vii*) Fast and Loose Pulley
(*viii*) Drum Pulley

Step Pulley. This can be termed as a group of several pulleys. Pulley faces are made in the step pulley with pulleys of different diameters fixed in order. As it is made like step it is known as Step Pulley. It is used at such places where there is need to increase or decrease the speed of driven pulley for various jobs *e.g.,* drill machine, lathe machine *etc.* These are often used in pairs.

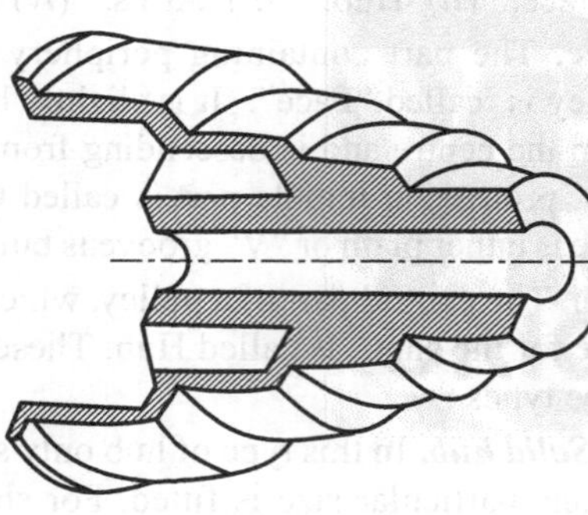

Fig. 23.12. Step pulley

"V" Groove Pulley. A groove like the English letter "V" is cut in the face of this pulley. It is used in electric motors and automobiles. A special "V" shape belt is used with these pulleys. In some pulleys more than one "V" grooves are cut. This type of pulleys are used for power transmission for heavy jobs. With the use of more than one "V" belt there are less chances of slip of power.

Split Pulley. This type of pulleys are made in two parts of face and hub. Its speciality is that it can be used on the pulleys of different sizes, big and small. It is used in saw machine.

Cone Pulley. It is used in a set of two pulleys (pairs). It is tapered. Similar taper is cut on two pulleys. These are fitted in such a way that large end of one being opposite the small end of the other, so that the shifting of the belt will make a change of speed. By this means, we can get appropriate speed for different jobs.

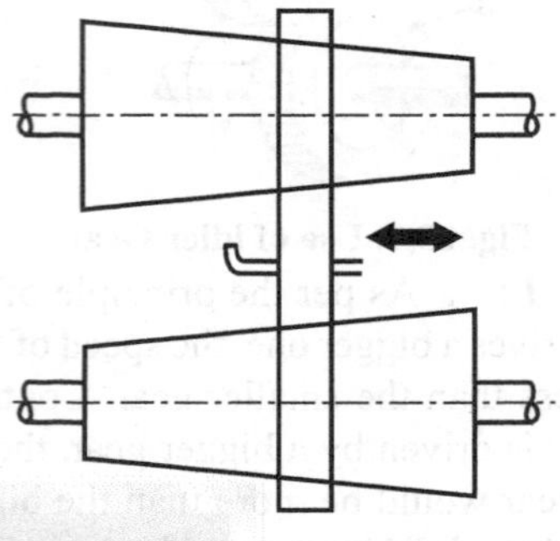

Fig. 23.13. Cone pulley

Jockey Pulley. One problem which we usually come across while using pulleys is that after some time their belts get loose and start slipping, which results in loss of power. In order to overcome this problem a third pulley is used with the pair of two pulleys as shown in Fig. 23.14. It is called jockey pulley. This pulley is self controlled pulley which keeps the belt tight, when it becomes loose.

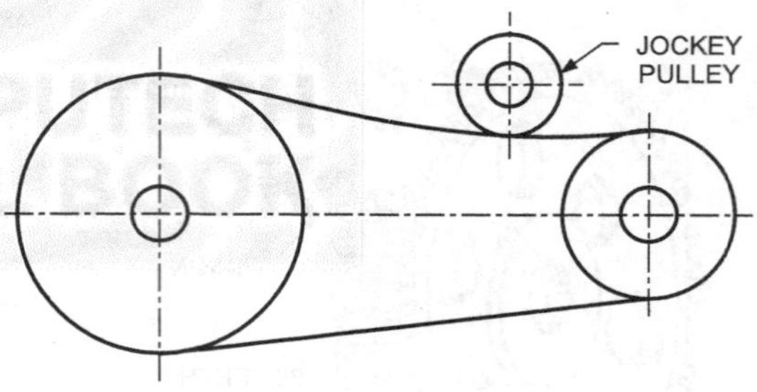

Fig. 23.14. Jockey pulley

Round Pulley. A round groove is cut on the face of this type of pulley. Round belts or ropes are used to operate it. It can also be made like the step pulley.

Fast and Loose Pulley. These pulleys are used for the machines which are quicklystarted or put off. These are used in pairs of two small pulleys, which are fitted on a counter shaft. One pulley is tightened on the conter shaft with a 'key' or some other medium and other pulley is fitted through a provision for free rotation. When the machine is to be operated, the belt is mounted on the tight pulley. This pulley is known as fast pulley. When machine is to be put off, the belt is slipped on to the independent pulley, which is known as loose pulley. Its major advantage is that we can put off the machine yet the main shaft being run with the electric motor or oil engine keeps on rotating. A lever is provided for slipping the belt.

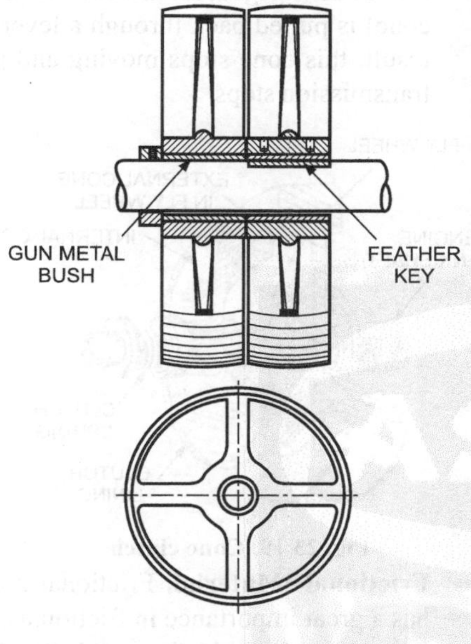

Fig. 23.15. Fast and loose pulley

Drum Pulley. This pulley is used as a driver pulley on the counter shaft of those machines which are operated by one single electric motor or oil engines and by one counter shafts. Their faces are made appropriately broad, and flat belts are used.

Chain and Sprocket

This method is also used like gears in power transmission. But in this method, gears which are called sprockets are fitted separately on the shafts, are run by a chain. This method can be used in places where two shafts are not fitted at longer distance from each other. The length of chain is at the most 40 times of its pitch. We find the use of chain and sprocket for power transmission in bicycles and timing gears of motor vehicles. In Figs. 23.16 (A, B) uses of this method have been shown in two different ways. On the sprockets a tooth like projection is made so as to engage with the links of a chain. Different types of chains are used for this purpose. The prominent chain have been described as under :

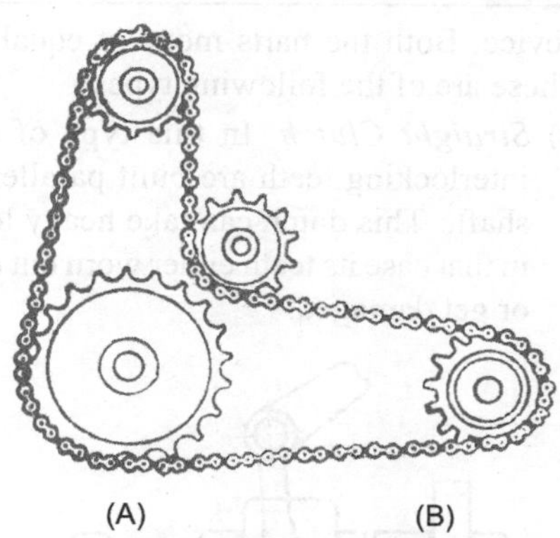

Fig. 23.16. Chain and sprocket

Roller Chain. This type of chain is most widely used. In this chain links are built with cylinders or rollers to reduce noise and friction and help in power transmission as in a bicycle chain. This chain is built in one or more rows. Chain of more than one row is used with a sprocket of double teeth.

Silent Chain. It is a transmission chain, each link of which is made up of a number of thin plates inter-locked with the plates of the adjoining links and connected with pins or rivets. This chain makes the minimum noise. It is much used for timing gear drive on automobiles and in many other places where only short lengths are required.

Block Chain. In this chain links are made like hooks. These hooks are interconnected with each other to form a chain. This chain can be quickly increased or reduced in lenght. This should not be used in sprockets of diameter of 1: 6. This chain is used for light jobs as in bicycles.

Bush Chain. This chain is almost similar to the roller chain but in these chains instead of rollers, bush is used. These are used for power transmission at lower speed.

Clutch

Clutch is a device which makes temporary connection between pieces of shifting *etc*. Clutch can engage or disengage connection between two pairs of a shaft or gears or pulleys mounted on them, on one line. If the clutch is engaged then both the parts move together as one unit. When clutch is disengaged both the parts become independent. There are four kinds of clutchs. These are :

(*i*) **Positive Clutch.** In this type of clutch inter-locking principle is used as a mechanical device. Both the parts move at equal speed. These are of the following types :

(*a*) *Straight Clutch.* In this type of clutch, interlocking teeth are built parallel to the shaft. This dutch can take heavy load but in that case its teeth either worn out quickly or get damaged.

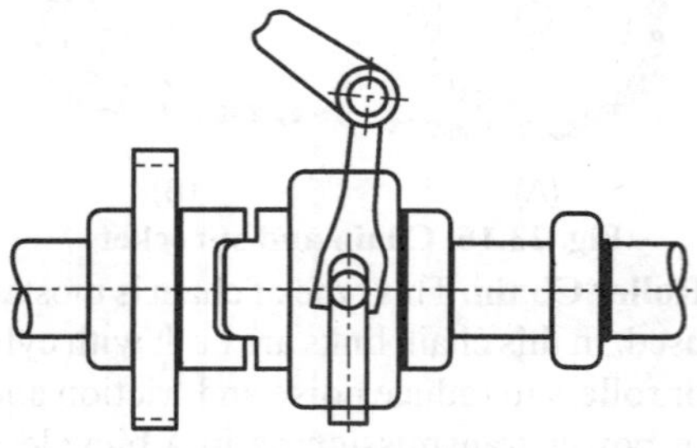

Fig. 23.17. Straight clutch

(*b*) *Saw Teeth Clutch.* In saw teeth clutch interlocking teeth are used like auto. The biggest draw back in this clutch is that in the event of excess load, it starts slipping.

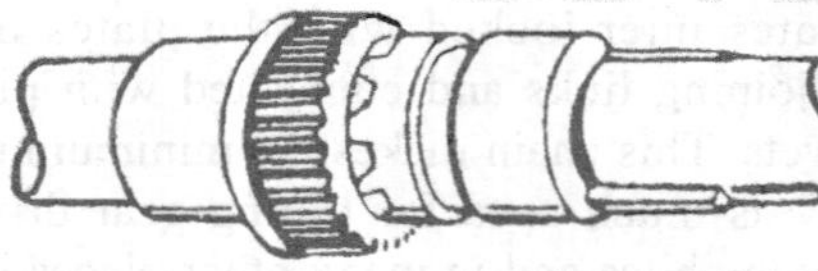

Fig. 23.18. Saw teeth clutch.

(*c*) *Automatic Machine Clutch.* Its interlocking teeth are built at 90° angle. It can be engaged or disengaged easily. It is used in a number of machines.

(*ii*) **Friction Clutch.** A special feature of this clutch is that it takes load gradually and in case of necessity it disengages two parts. These are of the following types :

(*a*) *Disc Clutch.* There is a driver plate in this clutch or it has a pressure plate. A clutch plate is fixed between them. This plate remains pressed towards the driver plate. When the driver plate starts moving it also makes the clutch plate move which is related to (connected with) driven shaft. In order to disengage clutch, pressure plate is pushed back by the lever against the pressure of the spring, in this way pressure is removed from clutch plate and it stops moving with driver plate. As such power transmission stops. This type of clutch is used in motor cars, motor cycles *etc.*

(*b*) *Cone Clutch.* In this type of clutch a pair of outer and inner cone is used. External cone is fixed on the driver shaft and internal cone is fitted on the driven shaft. Frictional material is fitted inside external cone and outside the internal cone. Both the cones remain stuck together through the pressure of a spring and when driver cone moves it moves the driven cone also. When clutch is to be disengaged, the driver cone (internal cone) is pulled back through a lever. As a result, this cone stops moving and power transmission stops.

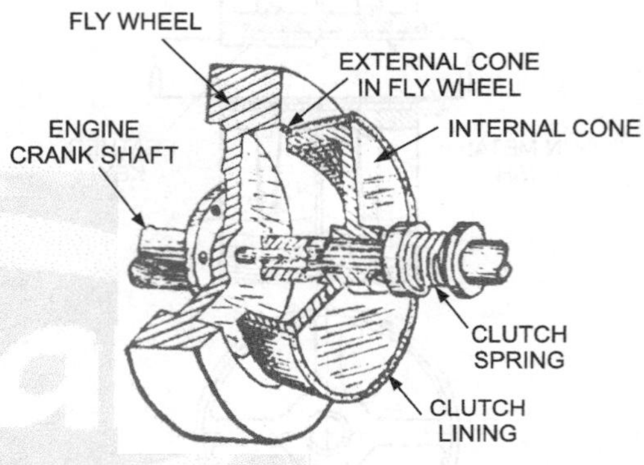

Fig. 23.19. Cone clutch

Frictional Material. Frictional material has a great importance in frictional clutch. For this purpose leather, cork, hard fibre and wood is used.

(*c*) *Magnetic Clutch.* Magnet is used in this type of clutch. The driving plate is magnetised after completing the electric circuit. As soon as this plate is magnetised it attracts the driven plate towards it.Thus the clutch is engaged. When this clutch is to be disengaged, the electric magnet is finished by putting off the electric switch and both the plates become independent.

(*d*) *Hydraulic Clutch.* In place of conventional solid or frictional clutch, now-a-days hydraulic clutch is more in use. With this clutch power transmission is carried out easily and noiselessly. It looks like a bowl. It has a driven member and a driving member. Both members have been built inside them. Both the members remain closed in a case, in which oil is filled. Driving member is connected with the shaft of an electric engine or oil engine and driven member is linked to the gear or pulley which drives the machine. When the motor or engine starts, driving member produces centrifugal force by moving into the oil in its front and by churning in it. If the speed of the driving member is reduced, the slip is 100%.

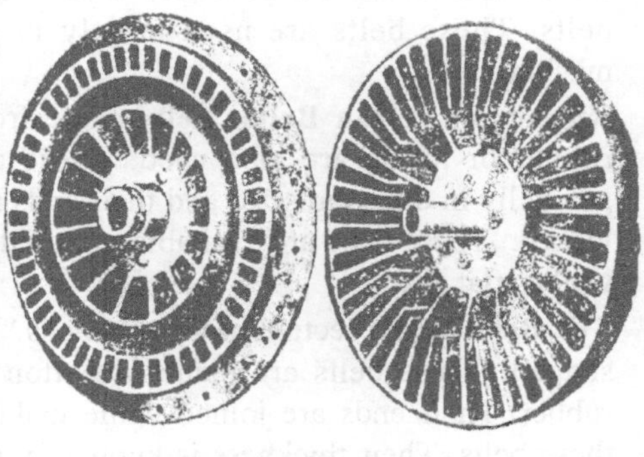

Fig. 23.20. Hydraulic clutch

Shaft Coupling

In order to save energy in most of the workshops several machines are operated by one motor or engine. For this purpose, the maximum length of a shaft used is 6 meters. If the length is to be increased then more than one shafts are joined. The method used for joining these shafts, is known as coupling. In order to provide support to the several kinds of bearings are used. Coupling can be divided into the following two parts :

(*i*) *Hard Coupling.* It includes three types of coupling :

(*a*) **Flange Coupling.** This type of coupling is shown in Fig. 23.21. Two flanges are used to join two shafts. A hole is made in these, according to shafts. These flanges are fitted tight on shafts. Sometimes key is used. Both the flanges are lightened together with the help of ordinary nut-holts or taper holts.

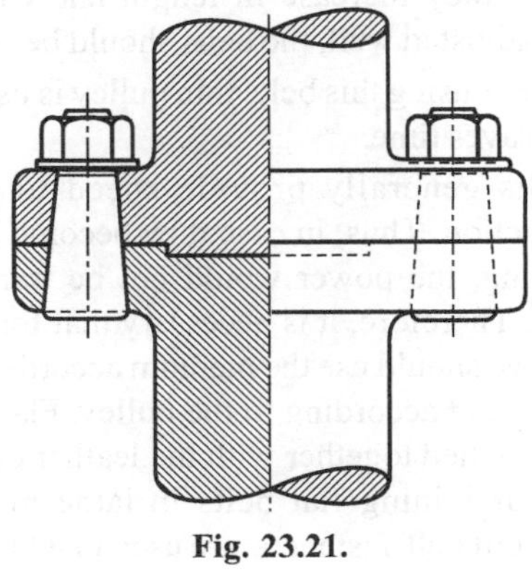

Fig. 23.21.

(*b*) **Muff Coupling.** Two pieces of iron are used to join two shafts in this type of coupling. One piece is kept over the other. Both the pieces are tightened with nut and bolt. It takes considerable amount of time to untie or tighten it.

(*c*) **Compression Coupling.** In this type of coupling taper bush is used, which contains cast iron shell. Shells are tightened with the help of nut, bolt or stud, by which there is pressure on the bush and bush grips the shaft firmly.

(*ii*) ***Flexible Coupling.*** Flexible coupling is used, where it is not possible to keep the shafts in one line or where they are not in alignment. This type of coupling includes following :

(*a*) **Chain Coupling.** This type of coupling has been illustrated in Fig. 23.22. Even if both the shafts are not in alignment, power transmission is possible.

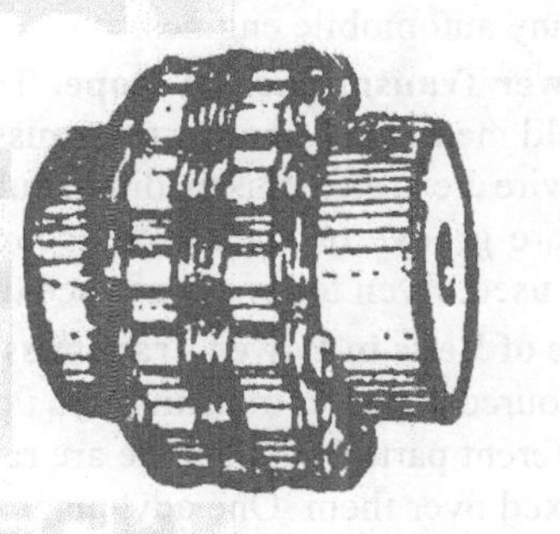

Fig. 23.22. Chain coupling

(*b*) **Fabric Coupling.** This type of coupling is used where alongwith flexibility it is also necessary to absorb jolts. In thes couplings, flexible material or rubber is used on coupling face, which provides flexibility.

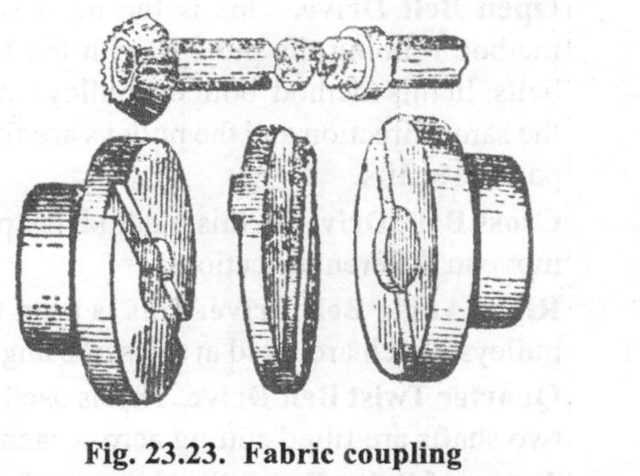

Fig. 23.23. Fabric coupling

(*c*) **Old Ham Coupling.** In this kind of coupling internal grooves are cut on the face, a plate is fitted among them. On both sides of this plate, projected parts are built accordingly. This type of coupling is shown in Fig. 23.24.

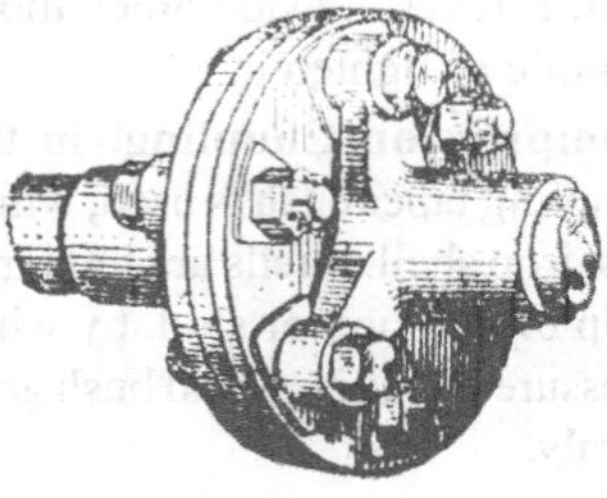

Fig. 23.24. Old ham coupling

Cam

It is a device mounted on a revolving shaft used for transposing rotary motion into an alternating, reciprocating or back and forth motion. It is used where there is need of interrupted power transmission — such as for the purpose of opening the valve on motor or any automobile engines.

Power Transmission by Rope. This is one of the very old mediums of power transmission. Ropes of jute or wire are used in this medium. Pulleys having one or more groove on their face according to the ropes, are used. Even today we can see this.

Use of Belts in Power Transmission. This is the main source of power transmission. Pulleys fixed on the different parts of a machine are run with help of belts fixed over them. One advantage of the belts is that in case there is excess load on the machine, the belt start slipping and thus machine is saved from any damage. Secondly, power can be transmitted to any distance. Thirdly, through the belts and use of pulleys power can be transmitted in any direction. Belt drives are of the following kinds :

Open Belt Drive. This is the most suitable method running the pulleys with the help of belts. In this method both the pulleys move in the same direction and the pulleys are fixed on parallel shafts.

Cross Belt Drive. In this method the pulleys move in different directions.

Right Angle Belt Drive. This is used for the pulleys winch are fixed at the same angle.

Quarter Twist Belt Drive. This is used where two shafts are fitted cutting across each other.

Types of Belts. For different types of pulleys and jobs, the following types of belts are used :

Leather Belts. These belts are made of one or more layers of leather. These belts of 5 mm to 8 mm thickness can bear the load of 10 kg per minute. On this basis, the layers are determined.

Canvas Belts. Canvas and cotton is used in these belts. These are generally used as flat belts. These belts are used mostly in all machines.

Rubber or Nylon Belts. Belts made from rubber or nylon are also used. These are generally in different sizes and their ends are locked. These belts are available in round as well as flat shape.

"V" Belts. Cross section of these belts is "V" shaped. These belts are made of cotton or rubber. Their ends are joined while making these belts. Their thickness is known by the grades such as A, B, C, D *etc*. Their length is measured on the basis of their inner circumference. The grade as well as length is indicate on these belts itself by the company, such as B-80, C-60 *etc*.

Advantages and Precautions of "V" Belts

(*i*) Power is fully transmitted only when the belt is tight. In this way, there is no wastage of power as well.

(*ii*) For power transmission at a greater scale, more than one belt can be fixed on a pulley, having provision for more than one belt on it. In such cases, care should be taken that all the belts are from the same company and are of the same measurement.

(*iii*) This belt transmits power without noise or jolts because it does not slip. But it should be ensured that sides of these belts are in complete touch with the pulley-side.

(*iv*) These belts have strong joints. But in case if they increase in length and cannot be adjusted well, the belts should be changed.

(*v*) For using this belts thin pulley is use which saves time.

Belts generally provide speed to pulleys through friction. Thus, in case they become loose or start slipping, the power would not be transmitted efficiently. Therefore, it is necessary that for joining their ends we should use the medium according to the job, weight and according to the pulley. Flat pulleys are often stitched together with the leather or canvas thread. For joining flat belts in lathe machines, specially built belt-fasteners are used in which comb of bent dents and a pin is used. Broad, thick and heavy belts are joined with counter sunk bolts and nuts.

Length of Belts. The percentage of power transmission through pulley and belt largely depends on the length of belts. If the belt is tight, the pulley will also run lightly. Its bush bearings shall also worn out easily. On the other hand, if length of a belt is in excess of the need, it will slip frequently and result in loss of power. In order to determine the right length of belt, the following formulae are applied :

Indications :

L = Requisite length of the belt
C = Distance from the centre
D = Diameter of the larger pulley
d = Diameter of the small pulley
R = Radius of larger pulley
r = Radius of the small pulley.

Formula. (*i*) For finding out length of open belt (for pulleys of equal diameter).

$$L = \frac{(D+d)}{2}\pi + 2C$$

or $$L = D\pi + 2C$$

Formula. (*ii*) For finding out length of open belt (of pulleys of different diameter).

$$L = \frac{\pi D}{2} + \frac{\pi d}{2} + 2\sqrt{C^2 + \left(\frac{D-d}{2}\right)^2}$$

Formula. (*iii*) For finding out the length of cross belt (of pulleys of equal diameter)

$$L = \pi D + 2\sqrt{[D]^2 + [C]^2}$$

Formula. (*iv*) For finding out the length of cross belt (of pulleys of different diameter).

$$L = \frac{\pi}{2}[D + d] + 2\sqrt{C^2 + \left(\frac{D+d}{2}\right)^2}$$

Characteristic of Belt. Next to the length of belt, the second important thing about a belt is its quality. If the quality of the belt is good its length would remain stable, stable power transmission would be possible and there would be minimum belt slips. Contrarily, if the belt is not of good quality, its length would soon increase, it would frequently slip and result in wastage of power. In addition, a loose belt is likely to dismount frequently. Therefore, we must use a belt, having the following essential qualities :

(*i*) Belts must have elasticity.

(*ii*) Thickness in a belt should be uniform (same) throughout its length.

(*iii*) Belt should have the capacity to turn, in case of need.

(*iv*) Thickness, breadth and length of the belt should be according to the machine, load and speed.

Slip of Belt. When the speed of driven pulley becomes less than the driven pulley, because of the belt, it is known as 'Slip of Belt". The slip is caused on account of (*i*) excess length of the belt, (*ii*) because of excess use of the belt.

Besides these reasons, in the beginning, when one pulley tries to move the other pulley, slips occur. As a result, power transmission at constant velocity ratio is not possible.

Creep of Belt. Elasticity is one of the qualities of a belt. But it has some disadvantage also. Initially, when the driver pulley tries to move the driven pulley because of pressure the lower length of the belt increases and the upper length gets loose. Because of this we do not get constant velocity ratio. This is known as creep of belt. It has got no relation with the slip of belt.

Questions

1. What is meant by power transmission ? Why do we need it ?
2. Describe the different mediums used for power transmission.
3. (*i*) How can speed be increased or decreased by using gears ?
   (*ii*) In what way the direction of a driven gear can be changed ?
   (*iii*) How the speed of a driven gear can be known at the time of power transmission ?
4. Describe the types of pulleys.
5. What is meant by "Jockey Pulley" ?
6. What is meant by fast and loose pulley ?
7. What are the advantages of chain and sprocket in power transmission ?
8. Where do we use flexible coupling ?
9. In what different ways belts are used on pulleys and when ?
10. What do you understand by creep of belt ?

24

Bearings

In the previous chapter, we read about the power transferring processes. In all types of machines power is transmitted through the above mentioned mediums. In these mediums or methods different types of shafts — big and small, are used. Besides this, there are several such parts in a machine, in which big and small shafts are used. Bearing is used to give support to these shafts while they are in motion. In addition to providing support, these bearings also provide base to long shafts. Broadly there are the following advantages of bearings :

(*i*) Shaft gets strong base.
(*ii*) It provides stable speed.
(*iii*) Lubrication becomes possible between the base and the shaft
(*iv*) Speed of the machine increases.
(*v*) Parts of the machine do not wear out early.
(*vi*) It saves time and power

Types of Bearings

Bearings can be divided into three types :

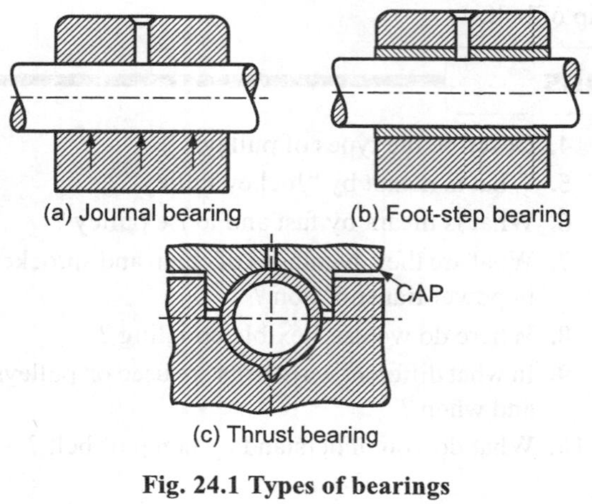

Fig. 24.1 Types of bearings

(*i*) Journal Bearing
(*ii*) Foot-Step Bearing
(*iii*) Thrust Bearing.

Journal Bearing. It is supporting portion of a shaft *i.e.* the part which revolves in the bearing. It is of the following three kinds :

(*a*) Solid Bearings. This is the easiest means of bearing. It has been shown in Fig. 24.2. It is a one-piece rigid bearing. Its use is limited as it must be slipped over the end of the shaft which is to support. If it wears out it can not be set right by adjusting it.

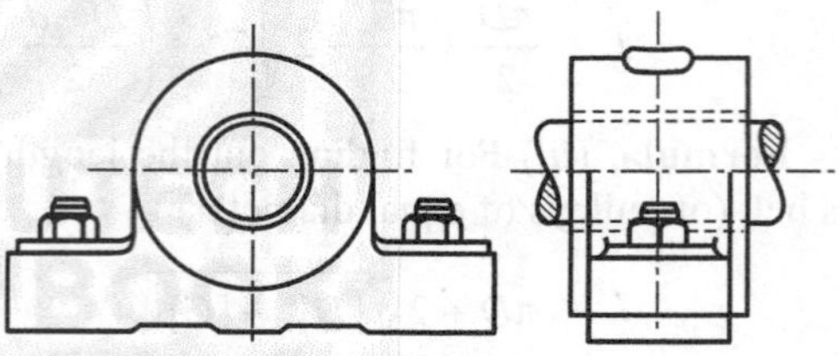

Fig. 24.2. Solid bearing

(*b*) Bush Bearing. This can be called as the improved form of solid bearing. A bush made of brass or gun metal is used in this bearing. When the bush wears out, it can be easily changed.

(*c*) Plumber Block or Pedestal Bearing. This bearing is used for large size and fast moving mild steel shafts. Bushes of brass, bronze or gun metal or two pieces stone bushes are used. These are fixed in stationary blocks of cast-iron and then fitted with nut bolts. These are generally called as "brass". We can have provision for lubrication in these bearings. Provision is also made to see that bearing does not slip in left, right, ahead or backward directions.

This type of bearing has been shown in Fig. 24.3.

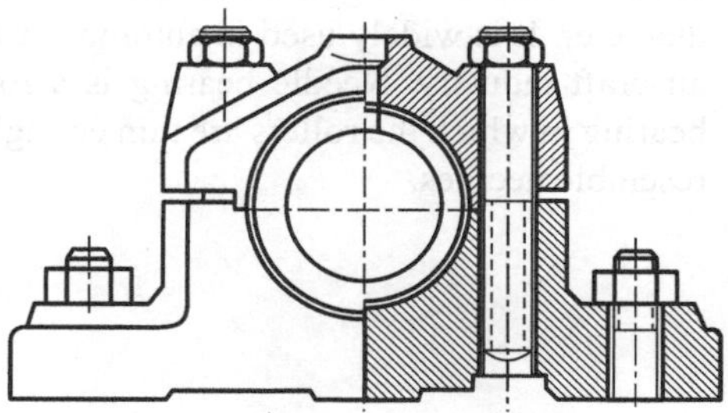

Fig. 24.3. Plumber block

Foot-Step Bearing. It is also known as Pivot Bearing or Two-bearing. These are used where there is need to provide support to the shaft in standing position. In short it is used at the lower end of a vertical shaft or spindle to carry the end thrust. Bushes of brass, bronze or gun-metal are fixed in the blocks of cast-iron to make use of this bearing. In order to protect the end of shaft, its face is slightly hollowed. This type bearing has been shown in Fig. 24.4.

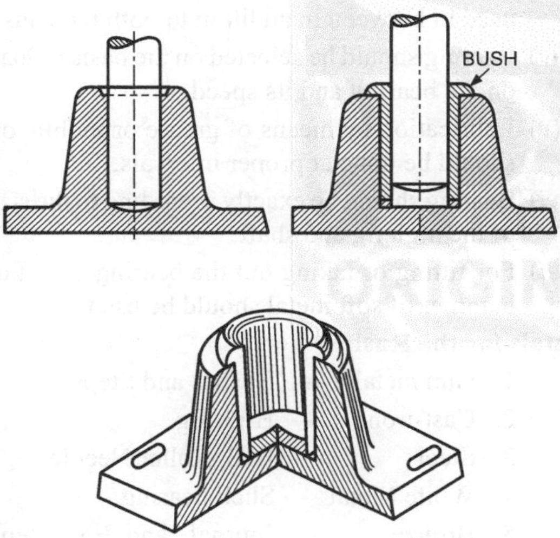

Fig. 24.4. Foot-step bearing

Thrust Bearing. This bearing is used to receive the longitudinal thrust or pressure of a shaft. They absorb pressure through the collars made on the shaft. Its main advantage is that the shaft rotates at a fixed point. This has been shown in Fig. 24.5.

The above mentioned bearings are called frictional bearings. There are some anti-frictional bearings also. The rolling shaft has a very slight touch

Fig. 24.5. Thrust bearing

with the contact point of bearing. Ball roller, taper roller and needle are often used between the outer and the inner race. These are of the following types :

Ball Bearing. In this type of bearing hardened steel balls are used. These steel balls are of equal size and of fine finishing. These are fitted between the outer and inner race of the bearing. Provision for keeping the balls exist inside the outer race and in the outer side or the inner race. A cage is used to keep the balls at equal distance. Contact of area of these balls is very limited. That is why these balls continue to roll without getting hot. The inner race should be a "drive fit" on the shaft, so as to rotate with it. The "outer race" should not rotate, but should fit tightly into a "housing" of similar construction to a light-type pedestal body.

Fig. 25.6. Ball bearing

In this way, when the shaft rotates it rotates the inner race balls of the bearing and it also starts rotating, thus friction is almost negligible in some part of the balls. This keeps the run of the shaft free and smooth. If grease is applied in these bearings once, there is no need for lubrication for several days.

Keeping the above facts in view, we can sum up the main advantages of the anti-frictional bearings as under :

(*i*) Even at a high speed, the friction is very limited, and thus smooth running is ensured.

(*ii*) By using these bearings the shaft can be protected from wearing out.

(*iii*) These can be easily changed in case of need.

Ball bearings are of various types such as Single Row Balls, Double Row Balls which contain provision for centre-contact, angular-contact and radial contact balls. In addition to these, there are some other types of ball bearings also like self alignment ball-bearings and thrust ball bearings.

Roller Bearing. These bearings are also like the ball bearings with the difference that instead of round steel balls, a bearing made of hardened steel rollers are used. Other types of roller bearings are called taper roller bearings. These have rollers of slightly tapered formation held in position in a specially shaped cage. Their distinct advantage is that we can easily adjust the play of shafts in which these are used. Such bearings are used in high class general engineering work and are also widely used in the motor car industry.

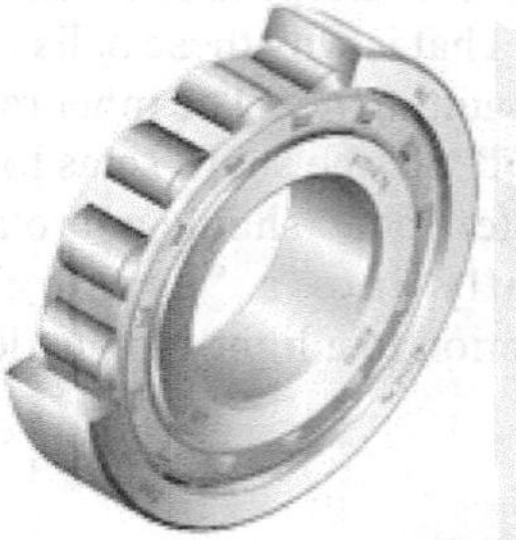

Fig. 24.7. Roller bearing

Needle Bearing. In a way, these can be called Frictional Bearings because their thin needles have friction with the job in complete length. On both sides of the needle a cage in the form of a ring is provided. In this cage, there are holes at equal distance in which the point of needle is fixed. Needles keep on rotating in these holes. In this way, most of the shaft is protected from having friction with the bearing and it can rotate at a high speed. The needle used in this bearing is of 2 mm to 8 mm diameter. It is widely used in automobile and air-craft industry. Needle bearing is a roller bearing in which the rollers are thin enough to resemble needles.

Fig. 24.8. Needle bearing

Some important points :

(*i*) Small size bearing should first be fitted on the shaft and then it should be fitted in high jig.

(*ii*) Large bearing is first fixed in the high jig and later shaft should be fixed in it.

(*iii*) For thin and long shafts, bearings should be used in between in addition to both the ends.

(*iv*) Bearing should be selected on the basis of load on the bearing and its speed.

(*v*) Lubrication by means of grease or mobile oil should be done at proper intervals.

(*vi*) Bearing should be exactly according to the size of the high jig and shaft.

(*vii*) For fitting or taking out the bearings, drift or hammer of soft metal should be used.

Metals for the Rush

1. Gun metal — Bushes and Steps
2. Cast-iron — High Jig
3. Steel — Ball, Roller Needle
4. White Metal — Shell bearing
5. Bronze — Journal and Foot-step bearings.

Questions

1. Where the bearings are used ?
2. What are the advantages of bearings ?
3. What are the kinds of bearings ?
4. Of what metal bush bearings are made and where these are used ?
5. What is meant by anti-frictional bearing ?
6. Describe in brief the kinds of anti-frictional bearing.
7. What precautions are needed for selection and fitting of bearings ?
8. Where are the needle-bearings used ?

25

Pipe and Pipe Fittings

Pipe, as we all know, is the medium through which air, smoke, water or oil *etc.* are taken from one place to another in covered manner. Pipes are used for the above purposes in residential buildings, offices, workshops and various kinds of machines. These are also known as tubes. Through pipes or tubes liquids or gases are transferred from one place to another without any risk or harm. Normally, there does not appear to be any big difference between a pipe and a tube. But, in fact, there are three basic differences between a pipe and a tube :

(*i*) Measurement of a pipe is always taken from the inside diameter of a pipe, no matter however thick metal sheet has been used in making it. On the other hand, a tube's measurement is taken from its outside diameter, however thick rubber is used for making the tube.

(*ii*) Pipes are available in the market in lengths according to diameter while tubes are sold in coils according to their diameter. These coils are made in difierent lengths.

(*iii*) Pipes are generally of greater diameter than tubes and often thin tube sheet is used in tubes. More pipes are used at different places than tubes. For different jobs, the following kinds of pipes are used :

(A) As per work :

(*i*) Pipes used for water
(*ii*) Pipes used for oils
(*iii*) Pipes used for gases or steam.

(B) As per metal :

(*i*) Cast-iron pipe (*ii*) Wrought-iron pipe
(*iii*) Copper pipe (*iv*) Brass pipe
(*v*) Galvanised iron pipe
(*vi*) Lead pipe

(C) As per manufacturing process :

(*i*) Butt-welded pipe (*ii*) Lap welded pipe
(*iii*) Brazed pipe (*iv*) Riveted pipe
(*v*) Casted pipe (*vii*) Drill-hole pipe

(D) As per joint :

(*i*) Threaded pipe (*ii*) Flanged pipe.
(*iii*) Socket or Collar pipe

(E) As per strength :

(*i*) Standard or ordinary pipe
(*ii*) Pipes for heavy jobs
(*iii*) Pipe of extra ordinary capacity.

Cast Iron Pipe. Normally cast iron pipes are used for draining out dirty water and for supply of drinking water. These pipes are made of cast-iron. In order to save these pipes from getting rusted, a special paint known as Dr. Angus Smith solution is coated on the pipes. Diameter of these pipes is from 2 inches to 6 feet. Their length is on the basis of their joining ends. For example, socket and collar cast-iron pipes are of 9′, 12′ and 18′ length. Pipes with flanges are 6′ and 9′ in length. Pipes in which there is a socket on one end and spigot is built on the other end, are joined with the melted lend. Pipes, in which flanges are made, are joined with nut and bolt by giving rubber packing.

Some pipes are made of good milleable cast iron. These are particularly used in water supply lines because for domestic water connections threads can be cut on these pipes easily. Their casting is also flowless, which rules out the possibility of leakage.

Wrought Iron Pipe. These pipes are made, keeping in view the properties of wrought iron. These pipes are used for transferring hot liquid materials and hot gases at low pressure, from one place to another, such as in boiler *etc*. These pipes are made long and minimum number of joints are provided in these pipes. Their length ranges between 18′ to 36′. Flanges are made on both their ends in order to join them with each other. Asbestos packing is provided and these are tightened with nut and bolts. In pipes of different sies flanges are also of different sizes. Their standards can be known from the following table :

TABLE

Internal Diameter of pipe	*Diameter of bore of the flange*	*External diameter of the flange*	*Diameter of bolt*	*Pitch of bolt*	*Size of drill*	*Diameter of bolt*	*Thickness of flange*
$\frac{3}{8}''$	$\frac{11}{16}''$	$3\frac{3}{4}''$	$2\frac{5}{8}''$	4″	$1\frac{9}{6}''$	$\frac{1}{2}''$	$1\frac{9}{6}''$
$\frac{1}{2}$	$\frac{27}{32}$	$3\frac{3}{4}$	$2\frac{5}{8}$	4	$1\frac{9}{6}$	$\frac{1}{2}$	$1\frac{9}{6}$
$\frac{3}{4}$	$1\frac{1}{16}$	4	$2\frac{7}{8}$	4	$1\frac{9}{6}$	$\frac{1}{2}$	$\frac{5}{8}$
1	$1\frac{11}{32}$	$4\frac{1}{2}$	$3\frac{1}{4}$	4	$1\frac{9}{6}$	$\frac{1}{2}$	$\frac{11}{16}$
$1\frac{1}{2}$	$1\frac{29}{32}$	$5\frac{1}{4}$	$3\frac{7}{8}$	4	$1\frac{9}{6}$	$\frac{1}{2}$	$\frac{13}{16}$
2	$2\frac{3}{8}$	6	$4\frac{1}{2}$	4	$\frac{11}{16}$	$\frac{5}{8}$	$1\frac{1}{4}$
$2\frac{1}{2}$	3	$6\frac{1}{2}$	5	4	$\frac{11}{16}$	$\frac{5}{8}$	$1\frac{1}{4}$
3	$3\frac{1}{2}$	$4\frac{1}{4}$	$5\frac{3}{4}$	4	$\frac{11}{16}$	$\frac{5}{8}$	
4	$4\frac{1}{2}$	$8\frac{1}{2}$	7	4	$\frac{11}{16}$	$\frac{5}{8}$	
5	$5\frac{1}{2}$	10	$8\frac{1}{4}$	8	$\frac{11}{16}$	$\frac{5}{8}$	

Galvanised Iron Pipes (G.I. Pipes). These pipes are used for domestic water supply and irrigational equipments. Their diameter ranges between $\frac{1}{2}''$ to 6″. These are made with mild steel and butt welding is done on them. As these pipes remain in contact with water so there is risk of their getting rusted. In order to protect them from rust / zinc coating is done on these pipes. For joining these pipes with each other, threads are cut on both their ends. Type of these threads is called British Standard Pipe Threads. The pipes are joined by providing socket. The special type of threads act on the pipes are also cut on the sockets. The number of threads per inch required on pines of different size can be known from the following table :

TABLE

Diameter of Pipe		*Threads in Pipe*	
Inner diameter of pipe	***Outer diameter of pipe (Approx.)***	***Threads per inch***	***Depth of Threads in inches***
$\frac{1}{8}$	$\frac{13}{32}$	28	0.0230
$\frac{1}{4}$	$\frac{17}{32}$	19	0.0335
$\frac{3}{8}$	$\frac{11}{16}$	19	0.0335
$\frac{1}{2}$	$\frac{27}{32}$	14	0.455
$\frac{3}{4}$	$1\frac{1}{16}$	14	0.0455
1	$1\frac{11}{32}$	11	0.0580

$1\frac{1}{4}$	$1\frac{11}{16}$	11	0.0580
$1\frac{1}{2}$	$1\frac{29}{32}$	11	0.0580
2	$2\frac{3}{8}$	11	0.0580
$2\frac{1}{2}$	3	11	0.0580
3	$2\frac{1}{2}$	11	0.0580
$3\frac{1}{2}$	4	11	0.0580
4	$4\frac{1}{2}$	11	0.0580
$4\frac{1}{2}$	5	11	0.0580
5	$5\frac{1}{2}$	11	0.0580
$5\frac{1}{2}$	6	11	0.0580
6	$6\frac{1}{2}$	11	0.0580
7	$7\frac{1}{2}$	10	0.0640
8	$8\frac{1}{2}$	10	0.0640
11	$11\frac{1}{2}$	8	0.0800
12	$12\frac{1}{2}$	8	0.0800

As there are standard sizes for diameters of pipes, similarly there are standard sizes for their lengths. Often the producers make these pipes in lengths of 19′, 20′ or 21′ feet. In a good G I. pipe weight should be according to the following table. If the weight is less we should consider that the pipe is of inferior quality :

Diameter of pipe	*Outer diameter*	*Length of pipe*	*Weight (approx.)*
$\frac{1}{2}$″	$\frac{19}{16}$″	20′	6.50 kg
$\frac{3}{4}$″	$1\frac{1}{16}$″	20′	8.50 kg
1″	$1\frac{5}{16}$″	20′	10.50 kg

Stone Ware Glazed Pipe (S.W.G P). This is also known as soil pipe. It is made with China clay or Fire clay. It is usually used for draining out the waste water from the building in the form of drains. These are very weak pipes and break with slight blow. These pipes are used underground. Their length is 60 cm. On one end of such pipes a spigot is made and on the other end a socket and these are joined with cement.

Asbestos Cement Pipe (A.C.P.). These pipes are made by mixing asbestos and cement. These pipes are used as drains to drain out the rain water. These pipes are even weaker than S.W.G. pipes. These are used in erect drains. These can be easily joined with cement. Their length is from 2 meters to 3 meters. Their diameter is between 8 cm to 10 cm.

Copper Pipe. Their diameter is usually $\frac{1}{8}$″ to 1″. These are made as coils in different lengths. Generally there is no effect of heat on them. Therefore, these pipes are used in boilers and steam engines *etc*. Thin copper pipes are used for supplying oil from one part to the other in automobiles. For joining these pipes, union made of brass or steel and nipple is used.

Lead Pipe. This type of pipes are used in the flushing cisterns in the bath rooms and wash basins. These are made with almost pure lead. These are used in acid jobs because acids do not have any effect on them.

Conduit Pipe. This type of pipes are used for electrical jobs painted with Dr. Angus Smith's solution of black paint. With these pipes both underground and open wiring can be done. Now these pipes are also being used in steel furniture jobs. These are made of thin steel sheets, which have thickness of less or more gauges. Their length is 10′ and diameter is $\frac{1}{2}$″ to 2″. For joining them, bend, socket and junction box are used, which are tightened with the help of threads or screws.

Thread Table for Conduit Pipe

Sl. No.	*Outer diameter of pipe*	*Thread per inch*
1.	$\frac{1}{2}$″	28
2.	$\frac{5}{8}$″	20
3.	$\frac{3}{4}$″	20
4.	$\frac{7}{8}$″	18
5.	1″	18
6.	$1\frac{1}{2}$″	18

In addition to the above mentioned pipes, in some other jobs, the following types of pipes are also used :

Flexible Pipe. Flexible Pipes are generally used in wiring of machines, oil pipe lines *etc.*

Fibre Pipe. These pipes are used in aeroplanes and electrical works.

Canvas Pipe. Canvas pipes are generally used for temporary water supply. These pipes are mostly used by the Fire Brigades for extinguishing fire.

Rubber Pipe. Generally these pipes are used for temporary water supply, automobile gardening *etc.*

Alvin Pipe. Alvin pipes are used for water supply in hilly areas and stony areas.

Hose Pipe. Hose pipes are made from rubber and cambric. These are used in railway bogies and automobile radiators.

Armer Pipe. This is a rubber pipe having wiring over it. Mainly it is used for tempowater supply of large volume.

Alckathin or Polythin Pipe. These pipes are now being used in electrical wiring and water supply.

Porcelain Pipe. These pipes are used for underground electrical wiring or for taking electrical wires from one room to another.

Pipe Accessories

We have just read about different types of pipes, which are made from different materials and are meant for different purposes. In the same way, pipe accessories are also made for their joining, bending and other jobs. These are also made of different materials and serve specific purposes.

Cast-iron, S.WG. Pipe, A.C. Pipe Accessories. For these pipes, generally the following types of accessories are used :

(*i*) "Y" Junction (*ii*) "T" Junction
(*iii*) Rain water head (*iv*) Slotted vent cowl
(*v*) Shoe (*vi*) Cone cap cowl
(*vii*) Short bend (*viii*) Lone bend
(*ix*) Swan neck

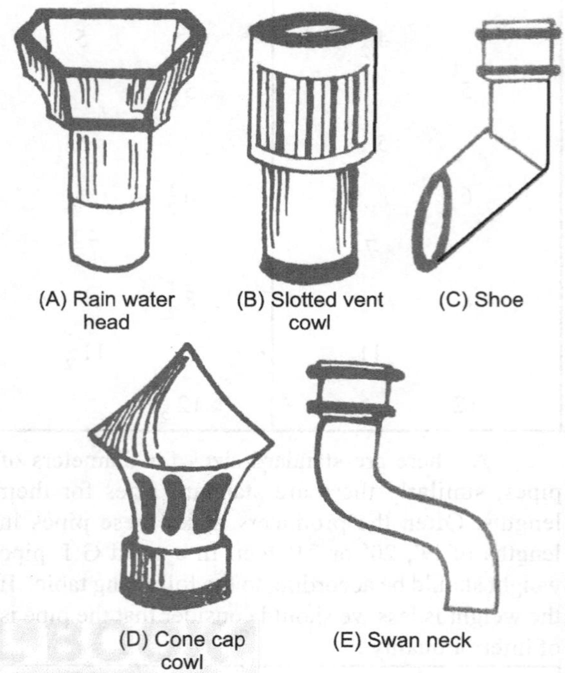

Fig. 25.1.

G.I. Pipe Accessories. G.I. Pipes are generally used for water supply in houses or for transfer of oil or gas from one place to another. Their fitting is done by using different types of accessories depending upon the place and use of these pipes. The main accessories used in these jobs are as follows :

1. **Socket.** Its outer diameter is somewhat larger than the diameter of the pipe. Its inside diameter is equal to that of the pipe's. On its full length internal threads are cut accoording

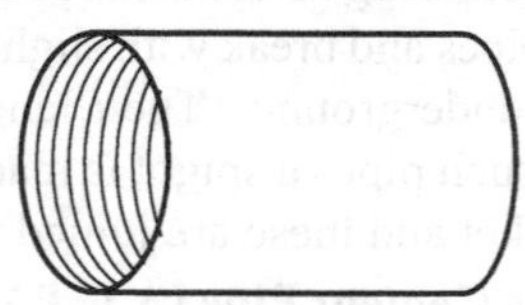

Fig. 25.2 Socket

to the pipe. These are used to bring two pipes in a straight direction.

2. **Elbow.** Its internal and outside diameter is similar to the socket. In appearance it looks like elbow of hand as shown in Fig. 25.3. It is used for fitting two pipes at right angles. It is also used for joining pipes at 55° and 45°. Internal threads are cut in the elbows.

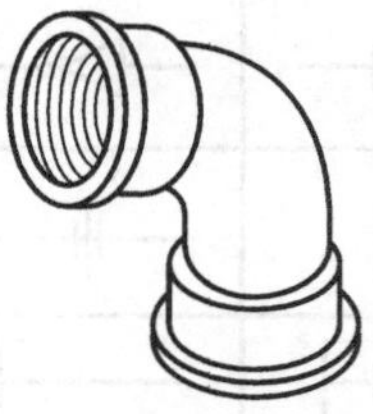

Fig. 25.3. Elbow

Fig. 25.4. Bend

3. **Bend.** Its diameter is equal to the size of the pipe. It is used at corners in pipe fitting jobs. On both its ends threads are cut one inch on each end as in a pipe. These are joined to the socket and pipe. The advantage of bend is that the water pressure does not become low. It is used where there is adequate space (Fig. 25.4).

4. **"T".** It is similar in shape to the English letter "T". It is used for giving connection to branch line from the main pipe line. With its help besides the supply line two lines can also be joined (Fig. 25.5).

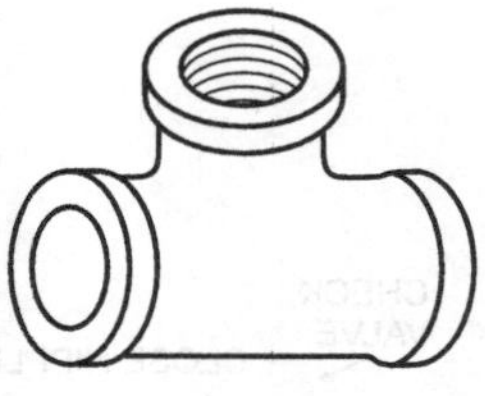

Fig. 25.5. "T"

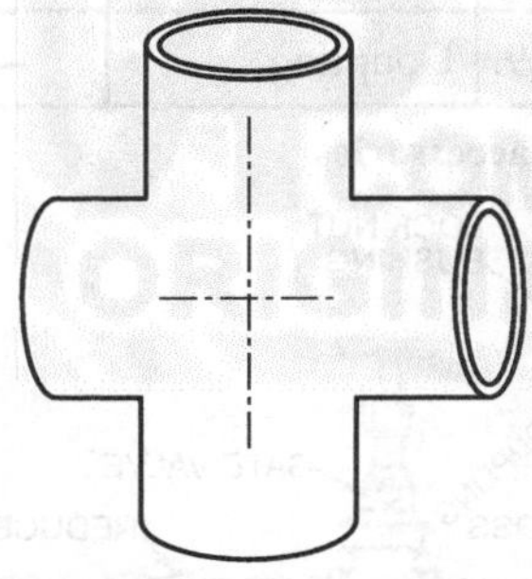

Fig. 25.6. Four way cross

5. **Four-way Cross.** Its shape is like the plus sign (+). It is used where there is need for fitting pipe in Four directions. On all its four edges, threads are cut as on a pipe (Fig. 25.6).

6. **Valve.** Pipes can be joined with valves and according to our needs we can stop water, oil, gas *etc.* flowing in these pieps, for passing on to the other side. The main advantage of a valve is that in case of fitting of a number of lines, we can stop or put on any particular pipe. Pipes are generally made of copper or gun-metal. For different kinds of jobs the following types of valves are used. (A wheel valve has been shown in figure 25.7) :

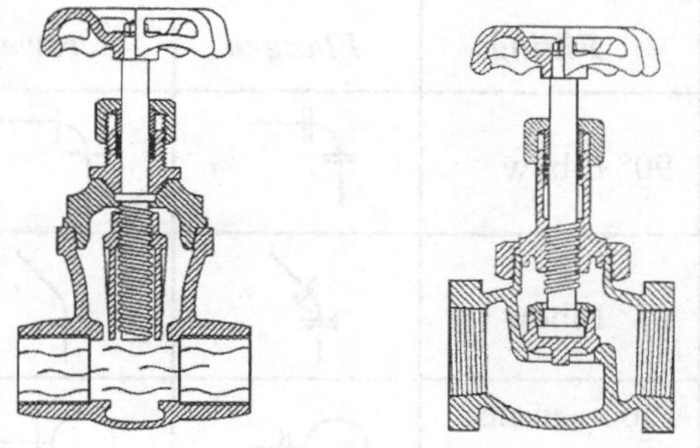

Fig. 25.7. Valve

(*a*) Wheel Valve	(*b*) Check Valve
(*c*) Safety Valve	(*d*) Silence Valve
(*e*) Full or Gate Valve	(*f*) Needle Valve
(*g*) Non Return Valve	(*h*) Globe Valve
(*i*) Ball Valve	(*j*) Hidden Valve
(*k*) Air Release Valve	

7. **Cock.** We generally know it as a tap. A cock serves the purpose of putting off or on the flowing water, oil or gas in a pipe. In our houses we use it for taking water or stopping the flowing water from a tap. These are made from copper, gun metal, plastic or cast-iron *etc.*, according to the needs. At its top there is provision for starting the flow of water and inside there is a cock. That is why it is also called "Bib Cock". In addition, the following kinds of cocks are used :

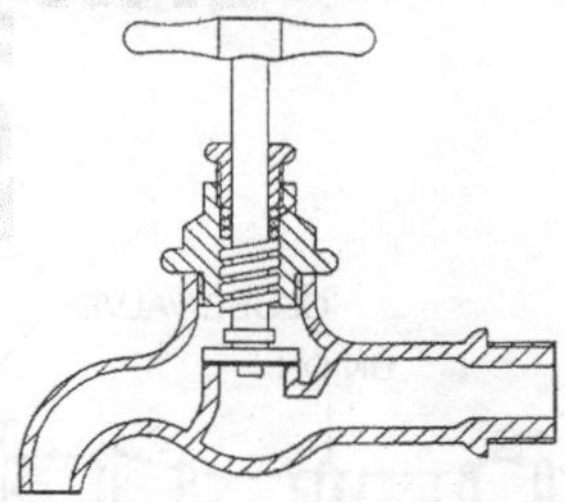

Fig. 25.8. Bib cock

(*a*) Bib Cock	(*b*) Stop Cock
(*c*) Push Cock	(*d*) Combination Cock
(*e*) Plug Bib Cock	(*f*) Locking Cock
(*g*) Peot Cock	(*h*) Pillar Cock
(*i*) Surgeon Cock	(*j*) Plug Stop Cock

Tools and Signs of Pipe Fitting. While fitting pipes the following tools are used :

(A) Pipe vice	(B) Pipe Dye
(C) Hacksaw Frame	(D) Pipe Cutter
(E) Pipe Wrench	(F) Chain Wrench

In the blue print or drawing the various accessories have been shown through the symbols (Fig. 25.9)

S. No.	*Fittings*	*Flanged*	*Screwed*	*S. No.*	*Fittings*	*Flanged*	*Screwed*
1.	90° Elbow			10.	Reducing elbow		
2.	45° Elbow			11.	Reducer		
3.	Elbow turned Up			12.	Union		
4.	Elbow turned Down			13.	Cap		
5.	Tee			14.	Bushing		
6.	Tee outlet Down			15.	Globe valve		
7.	Tee outlet Up			16.	Gate valve		
8.	Cross valve			17.	L Globe valve		
9.	Lateral			18.	Check Valve		
				19.	Coupling		

Fig. 25.9. Pipe accessories

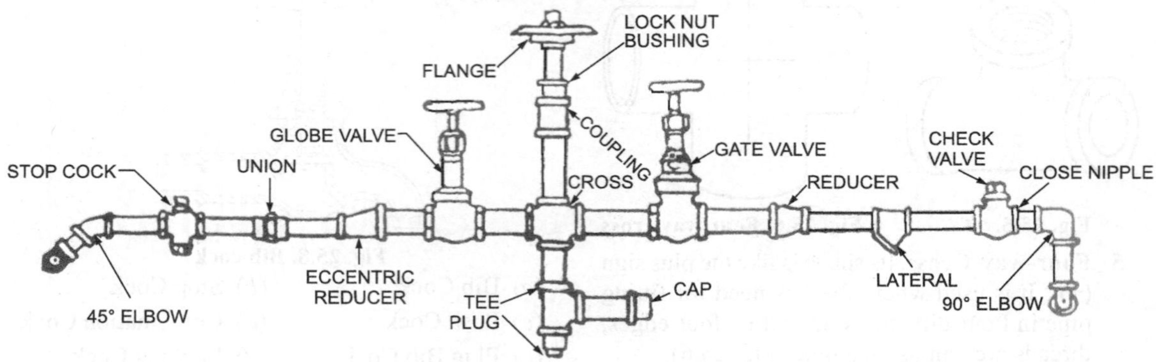

Fig. 25.10. Accessories used in pipe fitting

Questions

1. What is the difference between a pipe and a tube ?
2. Which metals are used for manufacturing pipes ?
3. Which accessories are used in G.I. pipes ?
4. What is the difference between a valve and a cock ?

26

Welding Process and their Introduction

Welding is a process of joining two similar or dissimilar metal pieces. In this process, the two metallic pieces are joined by the application of heat. There are various methods of welding. The welding technology has developed upto a great extent during past decades. In fact, welding is a quick, cheap and simple technique of joining the metallic pieces.

Welding Methods

All welding methods can be classified into following two main classes :

(*a*) **Autogeneous Welding.** In this method, two pieces of the same metal are joined with or without the application of a filler rod of the same metal.

(*b*) **Heterogeneous Welding.** In this method, two pieces of different metals are joined by applying a filler rod. The melting point of the filler metal is kept lower than that of the metals to be welded so that the filler metal can make a quick joint by melting itself within the gap between the two weldable pieces.

In addition to the above classification, the welding methods can be classified on the basis of the principle involved in the welding :

(*a*) **Pressure or Plastic Welding.** In this method the two weldable metallic pieces are heated upto a *semi-molten state or a plastic state* and then joined together by applying a pressure. The method includes forge welding, resistance welding and chemical welding.

(*b*) **Non-pressure or Fusion Welding.** In this method, two weldable metallic pieces are heated upto their melting points and they are allowed to cool down so as to form a firm joint. No pressure is applied in this method. The method includes gas welding and arc welding.

Gas Welding

It is the most popular method of welding and it is used widely in the field of engineering. In this method, the weldable metal is melt with the heat developed by the flame of a fuel gas and oxygen. The molten metal pieces get welded after becoming cool. A filler metal rod may also be used in this method too.

In gas welding, the flame is generally formed by acetylene and oxygen gases but hydrogen, propene or butane gas may be also be used together with the oxygen gas.

Oxy-acetylene Welding

In this method of gas welding, the flame is produced by a mixture of oxygen and acetylene gases. Oxygen gas helps in burning. Two gases are supplied to users by filling them in cylinders at a high pressure. The two gases are mixed at the nozzle of the welding torch after passing through the regulators and flexible pipes clamped to the cylinders. The fuel gas burns in the presence of oxygen gas and produce heat. The chemical equation of combustion is as follows :

$$\underset{\substack{\text{Acetylene} \\ \text{(2 part)}}}{2C_2H_2} + \underset{\substack{\text{oxygen} \\ \text{(5 part)}}}{5O_2} \longrightarrow \underset{\substack{\text{carbon} \\ \text{dioxide}}}{4CO_2} + \underset{\text{steam}}{2H_2O} + \text{heat}$$

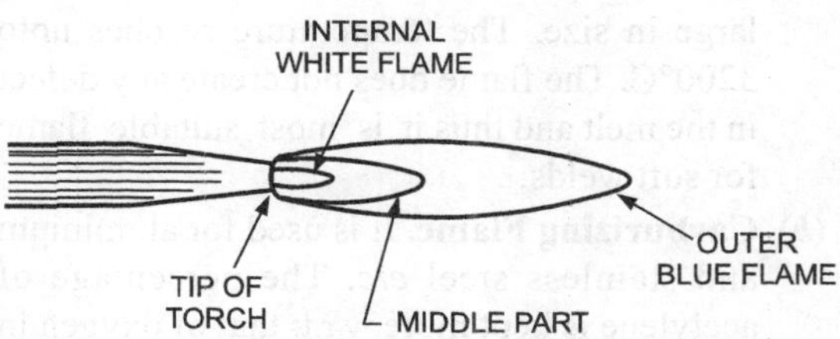

Fig. 26.1. Oxy-acetylene gas flame

The above equation shows that one part of acetylene gas requires 2.5 parts of oxygen gas for its complete combustion. Different metallic jobs require different type of flames depending on their thickness. Regulator valves and gas controlling knobs provided on the welding torch are meant for producing different types of flames.

The ratio of the oxygen and acetylene gases used in combustion is controlled by their respective gas controlling knobs. The combustion of the acetylene gas takes place in two stages. The chemical action which takes place of the tip of the nozzle of welding torch is as follows :

$$\underset{\text{acetylene}}{C_2H_2} + \underset{\text{oxygen}}{O_2} \longrightarrow \underset{\substack{\text{carbon}\\\text{mono-oxide}}}{2CO} + \underset{\text{hydrogen}}{H_2} + \text{heat}$$

In this way, a bright internal white flame is produced near the tip which is called *inner cone.* This is the hottest part of the flame. The chemical action of the second stage of combustion of the acetylene gas is as follows :

$$4CO + 2H_2 + 3O_2 \longrightarrow 4CO_2 + 2H_2O + \text{heat}$$

Thus, the *outer* blue part of the flame is called *outer cone* or *outer envelope.* The temperature of the outer cone is lower than that of the inner cone.

Types of Oxy-acetylene Flame. Following three different types of flames are used for different welding purposes :

(*i*) Neutral flame

(*ii*) Carburizing flame

(*iii*) Oxidising flame

(*i*) **Neutral Flame.** It is used for ordinary metals and general purposcs. The flame has equal quantities of oxygen and acetylene gases. The white cone of the flame has a clear and regular shape, as shown in Fig. 26.2(*a*).

Fig. 26.2. (*a*) Neutral flame

The outer part of the flame is colourless and large in size. The temperature reaches upto 3200°C. The flame does not create any defect in the melt and thus it is most suitable flame for soft welds.

(*b*) **Carburizing Flame.** It is used for aluminium and stainless steel *etc*. The percentage of acetylene is kept more w.r.t. that of oxygen in this type of flame. The white cone of the flame has a feather shape. The length of the flame can be adjusted by increasing or decreasing the quantity of acetylene. The temperature of the flame reaches upto 3100°C, see Fig. 26.2(*b*).

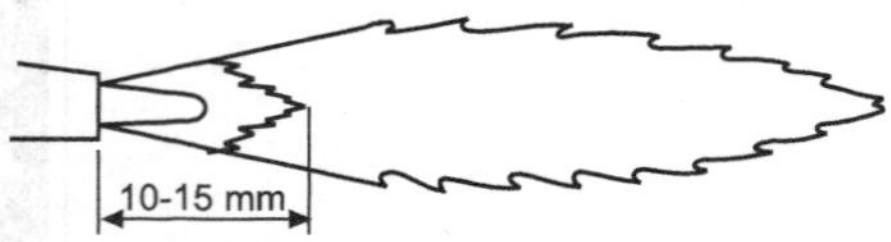

Fig. 26.2. (*b*) Carburizing flame

(*c*) **Oxidizing Flame.** It is mainly used for the non-ferrous metals. The percentage of acetylene is kept a little lower w.r.t. that kept in the carburizing flame. The flame can be easily identified by its sharp edged cone and small size of the flame as shown in Fig. 26.2 (*c*). The temperature of the flame re aches upto 3300°C.

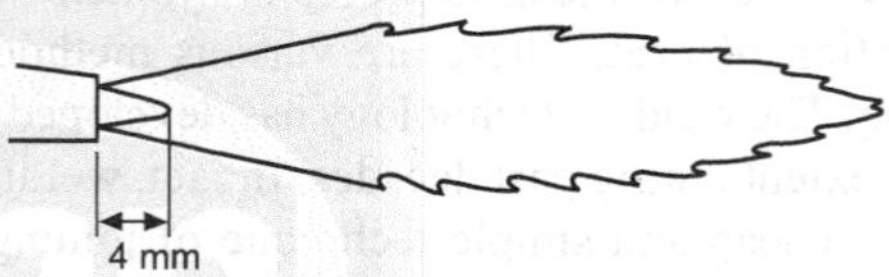

Fig. 26.2. (*c*) Oxidizing flame

Ferrous Metals and Types of Flames

Metal or Alloy	*Types of Flame*
1. Wrought iron	Neutral flame
2. Cast iron	Neutral or low percentage oxidizing flame
3. Chromium steel	Neutral flame
4. Cast steel	Neutral flame
5. High carbon steel	Carburizing flame
6. Mangncse steel	Low percentage oxidizing flame

Non-ferrous Metals and Types of Flames

Non-ferrous metal or Alloy	*Types of Flame*
1. Brass	Low percentage oxidizing flame
2. Bronze	Neutral flame or Low percentage oxidizing flame
3. Copper	Neutral flame or Low percentage oxidizing flame
4. Lead	Neutral flame
5. Nickel	Low percentage oxidizing flame

27

Gas and Arc Welding Tools

Welding Tools

The common tools used for gas welding purposes are as follows :

(*a*) **Spanner.** A double ended spanner is used for tighting and opening the nuts of the welding apparatus and jobs, see Fig. 27.1.

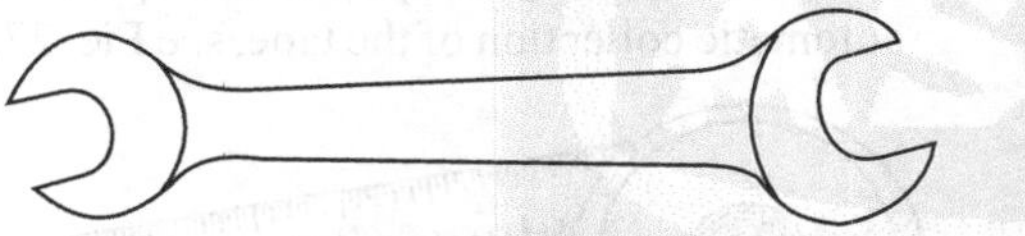

Fig. 27.1. Open-mouth double ended spanner

(*b*) **Hammer.** It is used for shaping the job. Normally a 500 grams hammer is used for the purpose. There are three types of hammers — Ball-pane, Cross-pane and Straight-pane. For large sized jobs a sledge hammer may be used. Various types of hammers are shown in Fig. 27.2.

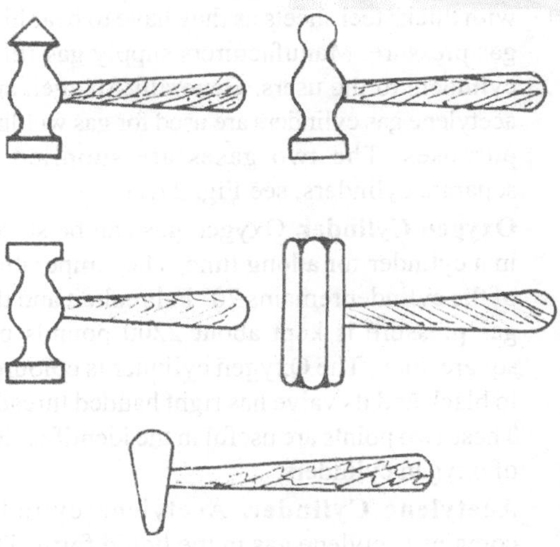

Fig. 27.2. Different types of hammers

(*c*) **Chisel.** It is used for cutting the jobs and for cleaning the slug, spatter and surplus metal from the job after welding, see Fig. 27.3

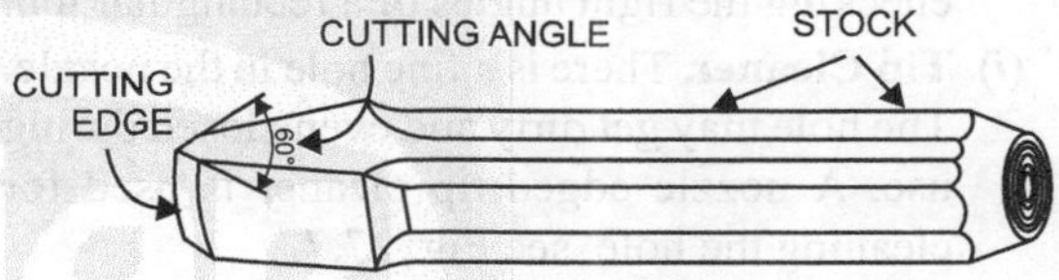

Fig. 27.3. Chisel

(*d*) **Tongs.** Tongs of various shapes and sizes are used for holding a job while welding, see Fig. 27.4.

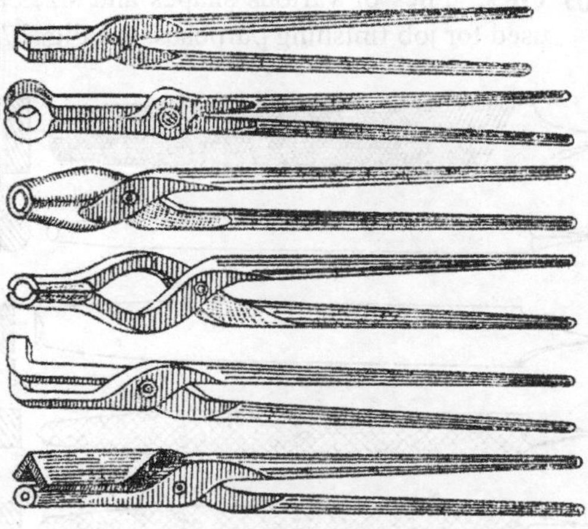

Fig. 27.4. Different types of tongs

(*e*) **Cyiinder Key.** It is used for opening and tighting the spindle valve of the gas cylinder, see Fig. 27.5.

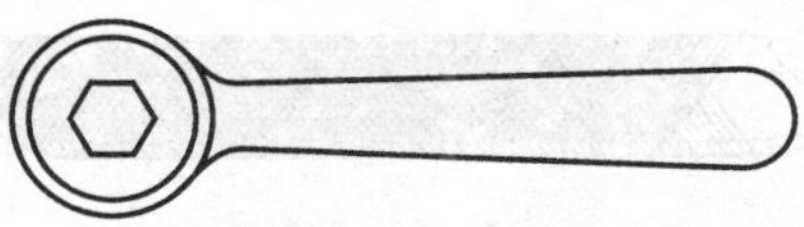

Fig. 27.5. Closed-mouth wrench

(*f*) **Wire Brush.** It is used for cleaning the job before and after welding. It is made of steel wire, see Fig. 27.6.

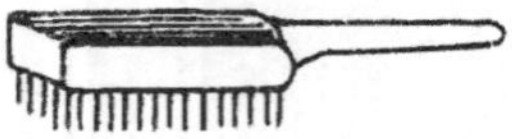

Fig. 27.6. Wire brush

(*g*) **Spark Lighter.** It consists of a sharp edged stone piece which produces a spark when it is rubbed with a hatched cast-iron wheel. It is used for lighting the gas released from the welding torch.

(*h*) **Try Square.** It is a L-shaped measuring instrument. Its blade is usually graduated in centimeters and the same is used for job measurement purpose. It is also used for checking the right angles of a rectangular job.

(*i*) **Tip Cleaner.** There is a fine hole in the nozzle. The hole may get dirty and even closed during use. A nozzle edged tip cleaner is used for cleaning the hole, see Fig. 27.7.

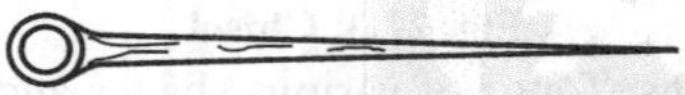

Fig. 27.7. Tip cleaner

A tip cleaner may also be used for removing slag from the job after welding.

(*j*) **Files.** Files of various shapes and sizes are used for job finishing purposes, see Fig. 27.8.

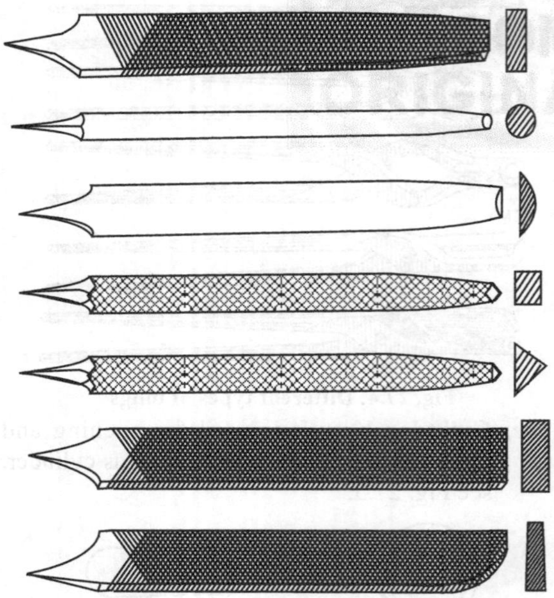

Fig. 27.8. Files

(*k*) **Centre Punch.** It is used for marking on a job piece before cutting the same into a desired shape.

(*l*) **Scale and Weld-gauge.** Scale is used for measuring the size of a job and the weld-gauge is used for measuring the depth of the weld, see Fig. 27.9.

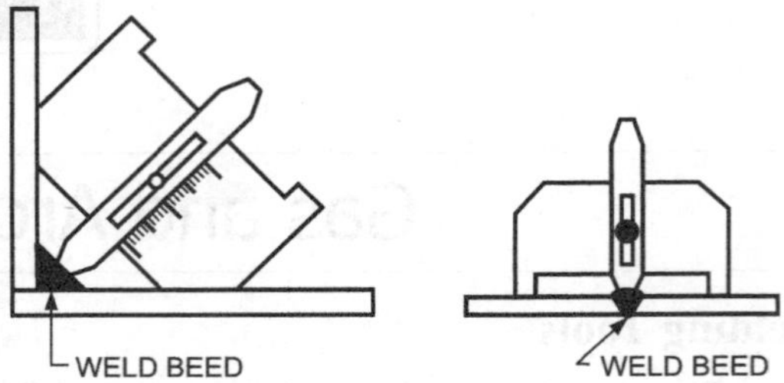

Fig. 27.9. Weld-gauge

(*m*) **Steel Tape.** Long jobs are measured by a steel tape. It is marked in inches and centimeters and it is housed in a steel or plastic case. The spring of the assembly helps in the quick and automatic collection of the tape, see Fie. 27.10.

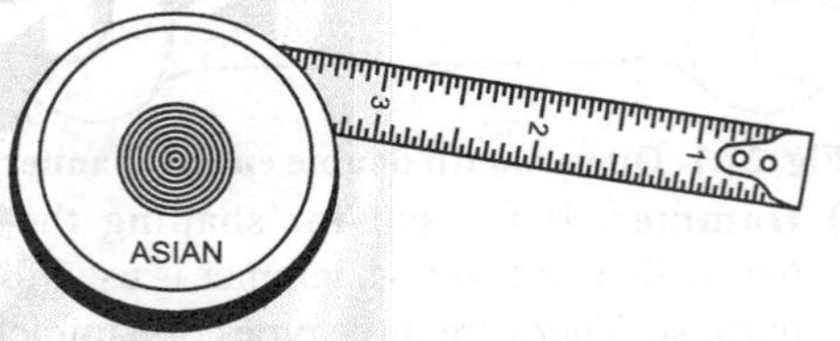

Fig. 27.10. Steel tape roll.

Welding Equipments

The equipments used in welding are as follows :

Gas Cylinder. Welding gas cylinders are made with thick steel sheets as they have to bear high gas pressure. Manufacturers supply gas filled cylinders to the users. Generally, oxygen and acetylene gas cylinders are used for gas welding purposes. The two gases are supplied in separate cylinders, see Fig. 27.11.

Oxygen Cylinder. Oxygen gas can be stored in a cylinder for a long time. The temperature of the cylinder remains 70° Fahrenheit and the gas pressure is kept about 2200 pounds per square inch. The Oxygen cylinder is coloured to black and its valve has right handed threads. These two points are useful in the identification of oxygen cylinders.

Acetylene Cylinder. Acetylene cylinder contains acetylene gas in the liquid form. The temperature of the cylinder remains

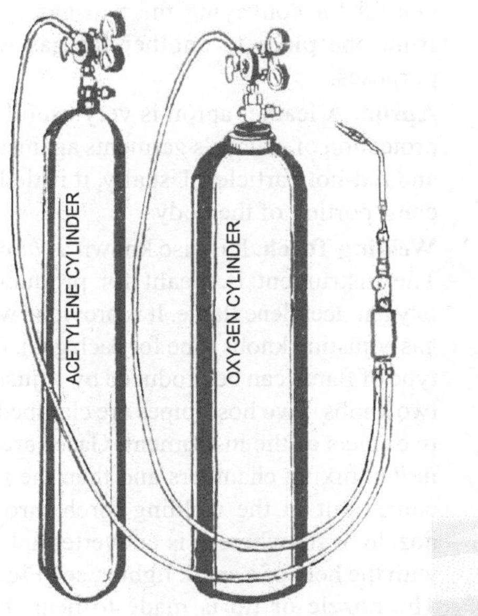

Fig. 27.11. Gas cylinders

70° Fahrenheit and the gas pressure is kept about 250 pounds per square inch. Before filling the gas some quantity of dry porous material (charcoal) and then acetone are filled in the the cylinder. Now acetylene gas is filled in the cylinder at about 250 pounds per square inch pressure and finally the cylinder is rotated for some time. Acetylene cylinder is coloured to dark red and its valve has left handed threads. These two points are useful in the identification of acetylene cylinders. There are two safety valves also which are mounted in the bottom of the cylinder. Both the cylinders are provided with safety caps. The acetylene cylinder shouldn't be used in its lying state.

Gas Regulator. For welding, the oxygen and acetylene gases reach the welding torch through gas regulalators. There are two main functions of a regulator :

(*i*) to maintain necessary gas pressure during the course of welding.

(*ii*) to supply the gas to the welding torch at a low pressure. Regulator's body is made of brass.

(1) Single Stage Regulator. It mainly consists of the following parts :

(*a*) diaphragm (*b*) spring (*c*) control valve (*d*) body (*e*) pressure gauge (*f*) pressure adjusting screw.

Regulator has two ways (*i*) inlet — through which the gas at a high pressure enters the regulator from the cylinder, (*ii*) Outlet — through which the gas at a low pressure is supplied to the welding torch through the hose pipe, see Fig. 27.12.

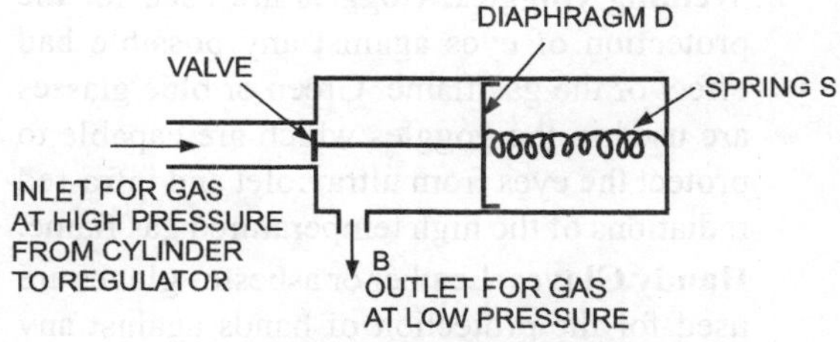

Fig. 27.12. Single stage regulator

The gas enters the regulator at a high pressure through the inlet and exerts a pressure on the diaphragm. The diaphragm is supported by a spring which is also is also used as a pressure adjusting device with the help of a screw. Regulator's valve and the disphragm reduce the gas pressure and supply the same to the welding torch via hose pipe from the outlet.

(2) Double Stage Regulator. In this type of regulator the pressure of the gas is reduced from high to low in two steps. The device consists of two gas chambers (*i*) Main chamber (*ii*) Auxilliary chamber . There are two springs and two diaphragms in the device, see Fig. 27.13.

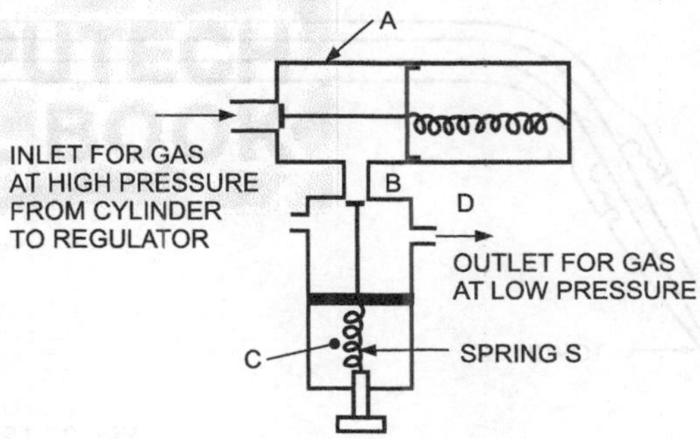

Fig. 27.13. Double stage regulator

The gas enter's the main chamber and its pressure reduced to some extent. The gas then enters the auxiliary chamber from the main chamber at a reduced pressure. Here, the gas pressure is reduced further and the same reaches the welding torch through hose pipe at the working pressure.

Hose-pipe. Hose pipe is the medium through which the gas is supplied to the welding torch from the regulator. Separate hose pipes are used for the oxygen and acetylene gases. These are made of a fine quality rubber and are fitted with the help of clamps to their respective regulators and the welding torch. Generally, a black or green pipe is used for oxygen gas while a red pipe is used for acetylene gas.

Welding Goggles. Goggles are used for the protection of eyes against any possible bad effect of the gas flame. Green or blue glasses are used in the goggles which are capable to protect the eyes from ultraviolet and infra-red radiations of the high temperatured gas flame.

Handy Gloves. Leather or asbestos gloves are used for the protection of hands against any possible burn during welding.

Anvil. An anvil is used for hammering a hot job as required. It is made of steel so as to have sufficient toughness, see Fig. 27.14.

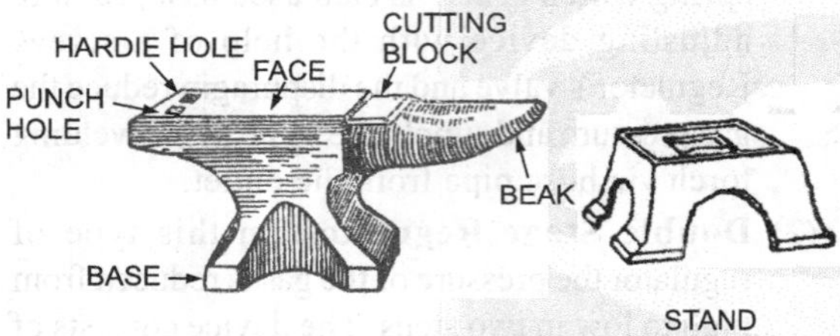

Fig. 27.14. Anvil

Cylinder Trolly. A cylinder trolly is very helpful for conveying the two gas cylinders from one place to another for gas welding purposes.

Apron. A leather apron is very useful for the protection of welder's garments against sparks and red-hot particles. Usually, it is tied on the chest portion of the body.

Welding Torch. It is also known as *blow-pipe.* The instrument is meant for producing the oxygen-acetylene flame. It is provided with two gas adjusting knobs (one for each gas). Desired type of flame can be produced by adjusting the two knobs. Two hose-pipes are clamped on the two inlets of the instrument. Gases are mixed in the mixing chambers and then the mixture comes out of the welding torch through its nozzle or tip where it is converted into flame with the help of a spark lighter, see Fig. 27.15. The nozzle or tip is made to bear the high temperatures. The size of a nozzle depends on the size of its hole and they are replaceable. The size is marked on the nozzle which indicates the thickness of the metallic sheets to be welded with that nozzle.

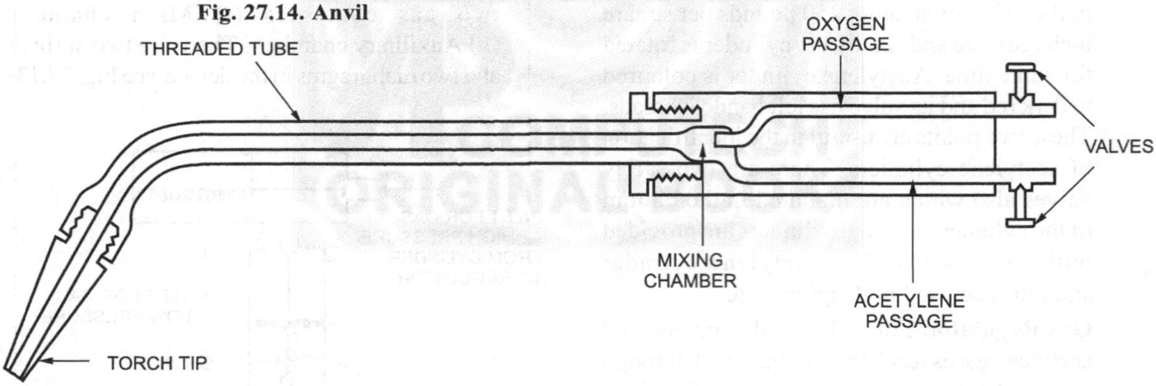

Fig. 27.15. Welding torch

Tip Table

1.	0.3	to	0.5	mm
2.	0.5	to	1.0	mm
3.	1	to	2	mm
4.	2	to	4	mm
5.	4	to	6	mm
6.	6	to	9	mm
7.	9	to	14	mm
8.	14	to	20	mm
9.	20	to	30	mm

There are two main types of welding torches :

(*a*) **Low Pressure Welding Torch.** In this type of torch the pressure of oxygen gas is kept about 10 to 40 pounds per square inch, whereas, the pressure of acetylene gas is kept about 1 to 2 pounds per square inch. The tip of this type of torch can only be replaced together with its neck.

(*b*) **Medium Pressure Welding Torch.** In this type of torch the pressure of the oxygen is kept about

1 to 24 pounds per square inch, whereas, the pressure of acetylene is kept about 1 to 15 pounds per square inch. The tip of this type of welding torch can be replaced without the replacement of its neck.

Arc Welding Equipments

In addition to most of the gas welding equipments, the following equipments are required for arc welding :

(1) Welding machine, (2) Welding cables, (3) Electrode holder, (4) Earth clamp, (5) Welding table, (6) Cable connector, (7) Chipping hammer, (8) Files, (9) Centre punch, scale and weld gauge.

(1) Electric Source and Welding Machine. There are following types of electric sources and machines :

(*a*) **D.C. Motor Generator.** This type of machine provides D.C. The armature of the generator is rotated in the electro-magnetic field by an electric motor, diesel engine *etc.* The armature is rotated at 1400, 1800 or 3600 R.P.M. so as to obtain the required amount of current. Usually, this machine provides 24 to 400 amperes of current at 40 to 80 volts. Any one terminal out of the two can be treated as positive and other negative of the machine and it is its speciality.

(*b*) **A.C. Transformer.** A welding transformer converts the high voltage and low amperes supply to a low voltage and high amperes supply. It consists of two windings of copper wire which are called primary and secondary windings. The output voltage of the transformer rests between 80 to 100 volts.

(*c*) **A.C. Transformer/D.C. Rectifier.** This machine can provide A.C. or D.C. supply as per requirement by employing a rectifier for converting the A.C. into D.C.

(2) Welding Cable. Welding cable is used to connect the job with the earth line and the electrode holder with the main line (or phase line). Highly insulated aluminium or copper cables are used for the purpose.

(3) Electrode Holder. It consists of a handle and a jaw. The electrode can be fitted in the jaw at any desired angle, see Fig. 27.16.

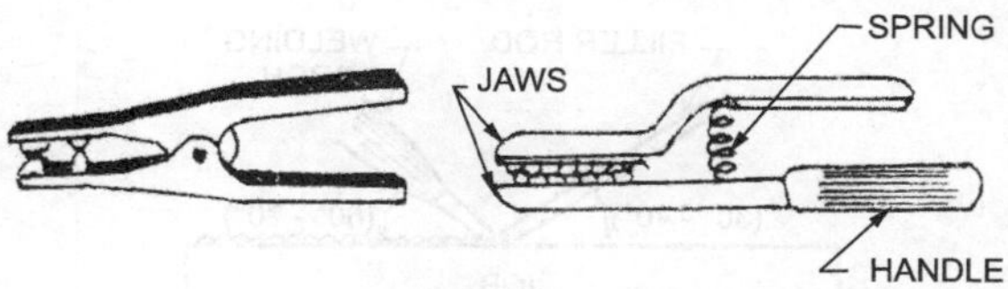

Fig. 27.16. Electrode holder

(4) Earth Clamp. It is fitted on the earth line terminal. It completes the electric circuit through the jobby earthing the later, see Fig. 27.17.

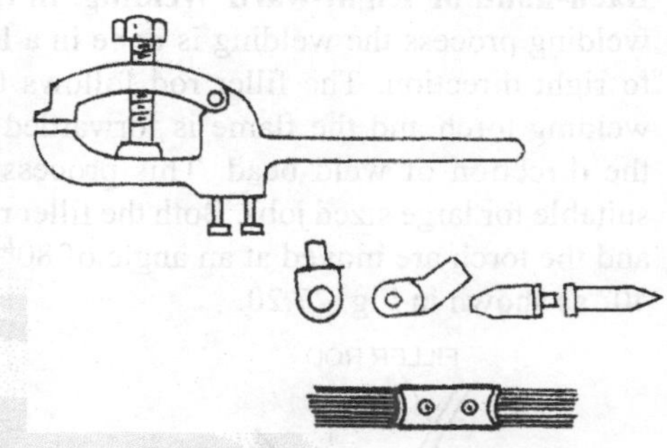

Fig. 27.17. Earth clamp and cable connectors

(5) Cable Connector. Many types of cable connectors are used for joining two cable pieces, see Fig. 27.17.

(6) Welding table. A welding table is used for the welding of small size jobs.

(7) Clamp. A clamp is used for holding the job properly as per job requirements, see Fig. 27.18.

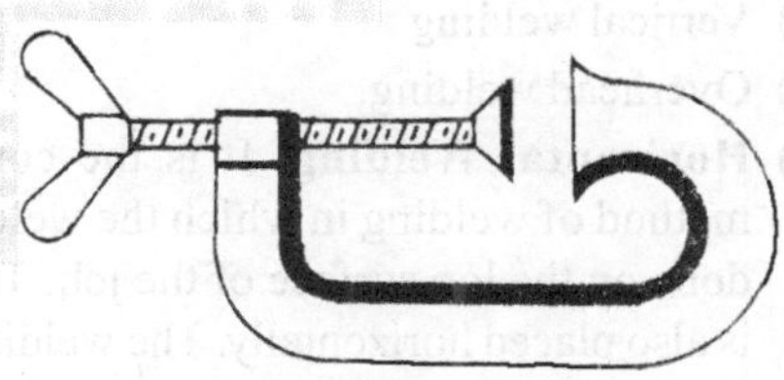

Fig. 27.18. Clamp

Welding Methods

In gas welding, the filler rod is melted and moved in accordance with the job requirement. The welding process can be divided into two types on the basis of the movements of welding torch filler rod.

(*i*) **Fore-hand or Left-ward Welding.** In this welding process, the flame follows the completed bead and the filler rod follows the flame. The welding is done in a right to left direction. The blow pipe is movied at an angle of 60° to 70° and the filler rod is moved at an angle of 30° to 40° as shown in Fig. 27.19.

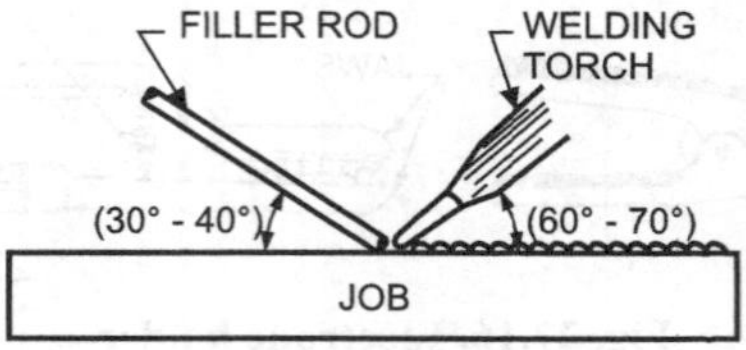

Fig. 27.19. Fore-hand welding

This welding process is suitable for upto 3 mm thick sheets and for other general purposes.

(*ii*) **Bach-hand or Right-ward Welding.** In this welding process the welding is done in a left to right direction. The filler rod follows the welding torch and the flame is forwarded in the direction of weld bead. This process is suitable for large sized jobs. Both the filler rod and the torch are moved at an angle of 80° to 40° as shown in Fig. 27.20.

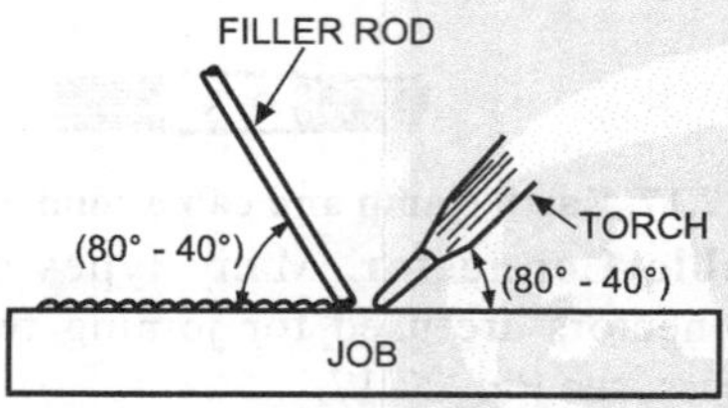

Fig. 27.20. Back-hand welding

Welding should be done in accordance with the position of job. On this basis there are following three types of welding :

(1) Horizontal welding

(2) Vertical welding

(3) Overhead welding.

(1) Horizontal Welding. It is the common method of welding in which the welding is done on the lop surface of the job. The job is also placed horizontally. The welding can be done in left-ward or righl-ward direction.

(2) Vertical Welding. This method of welding is adopted for erected job. The welding can be done in upward or downward direction in accordance to the convenience of the mechanic as shown in Fig. 27.21.

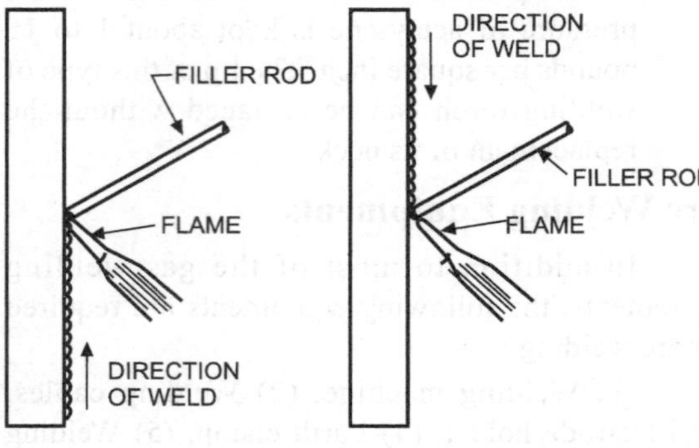

Fig. 27.21. Vertical welding

(3) Overhead Welding. Sometimes, a mechanic has to weld a job above his head which is called overhead welding. It is a tough process and requires experience. The welding can be done in rightward or leftward direction whichever is convenient as shown in Fig. 27.22.

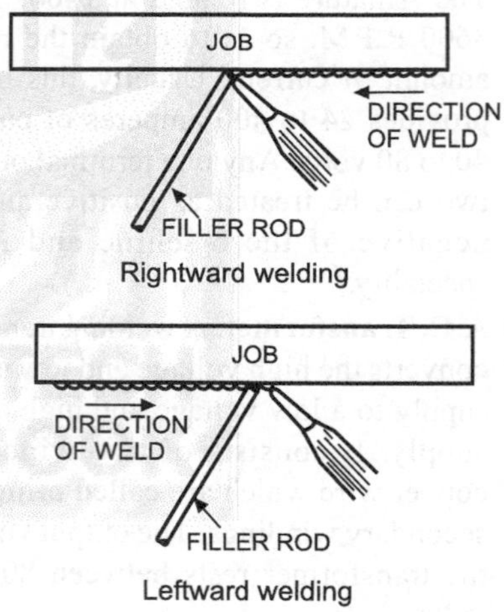

Fig. 27.22. Overhead welding

28

Electric Arc Welding Processes

An electric arc produces heat. For producing an arc, two current carrying conductors are slightly separated from each other. In the potential difference and current are maintained then heat and light are poduced in the air gap between the two conductors. The temperature of the spark gap reaches upto 6200°C which melts the metal and prepare a molten pool near the joint to be made. The molten pool becomes a joint on cooling. Electrodes and filler rods are used for the purpose as per requirements see Fig. 28.1.

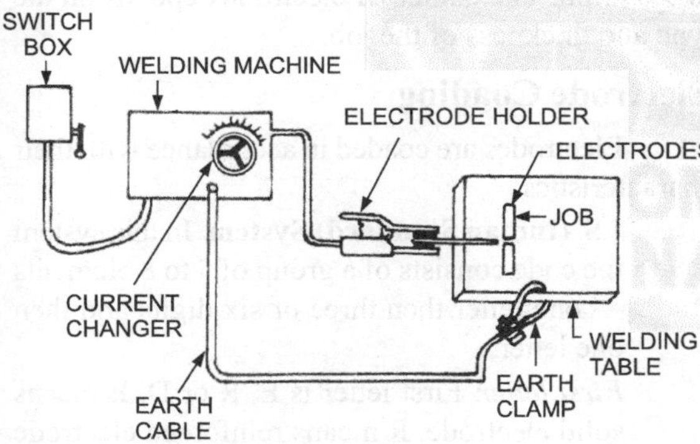

Fig. 28.1. Arc Welding.

There are many methods of electric arc welding out of which main methods are as follows :

(*a*) Carbon arc welding
(*b*) Metal arc welding.
(*c*) Atomic hydrogen welding
(*d*) Submerged arc welding
(*e*) Electric resistance welding

(*a*) Carbon Arc Welding. In this method, a carbon electrode is used for producing an arc. The arc produced between the job and the electrode or between two electrodes. A filler rod is also used in this method. Carbon electrodes are called non-consumable, even though, they consume slowly due to evaporation.

(*b*) Metal Arc Welding. In this method, the arc is produced between the job and a metallic rod. The metallic rod is called the electrode. Welding can be done on A.C. or D.C. Usually, the metallic rod or electrode is coated with suitable flux which helps in welding by cleaning the weldable surface.

(*c*) Atomic Hydrogen Welding. This method is used for hardening the face of a ferrous or non-ferrous job. It is a sort of non-pressure fusion method. In this system, the arc is produced between the two non-consumable tungsten electrodes and hydrogen gas is passed through the arc at a pressure of about 0.4 kg/cm^2. High temperature of the arc decomposes the hydrogen molecule into two atoms and a temperature of 2900°C is developed due to this reaction. A.C. supply is required for the above stated process.

(*d*) Submerged Welding. It is an automatic arc welding process. It is suitable for *Butt welding* of thick metallic sheets. In this system arc produced between a consumable bare electrode and the job. A granular flux is applied on the joint during welding so that the hot-joint remains covered.

(*e*) Electric-resistance Welding. In this system both the temperature and pressure are aligned in welding. Temperature is developed by passing a amount of current through the joint to be welded and the pressure is applied to shape the joint as per requirements. No filler rod is used in this method. Related principal methods are as follows:

(*i*) Spot welding

(*ii*) Seam welding

(*i*) Spot Welding. This method is employed for the welding of thin sheets and wires. For this, the job is placed between the two electrodes and a high amperes current is applied at a low voltage. One electrode rests fixed and the other one is employed for exerting pressure on the job. For this purpose, the movable electrode is operated through a lever. In this way, the process of jointing becomes identical to forging, see Fig. 28.2.

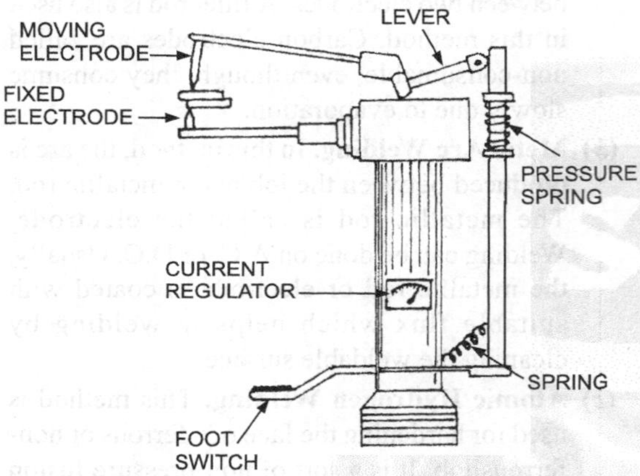

Fig. 28.2. Spot welding

(*ii*) Seam Welding. In this system, high temperature is developed by passing a current through the resistance of job. This system employes a wheel type electrode made of copper alloy. In comparison to the spot welding, the welding process of this system is continuous. This method is used for welding two sheets by keeping them one over the other.

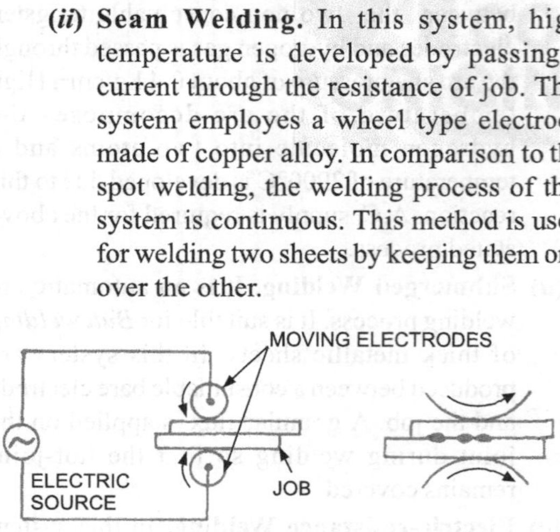

Fig. 28.3. Seam welding

The job is put between the two rotating eletrodes. The electrode circuit is completed through the first electrode, the job and the second electrode. The heat is produced by the resistance of the job and the pressure of the two electrodes prepares the joint. The magnitude of current and electrode pressure both are adjustable in accordance with the job requirements, see Fig. 28.3.

Arc Welding Electrode

An electrode is an essential part of electrode arc welding. The electrode may be a bare metallic rod or a flux coated metallic rod. These two types of electrodes are called (*i*) Bare electrode (*ii*) Flux coated electrode. All types of electrodes can be classified into following two classes :

(1) Consumable electrode

(2) Non-consumable electrode

The first type of electrodes are metallic electrodes whose length goes on reducing during the cource of welding. These electrodes are usually flux coated. Their types are as follows :

(1) Light coated electrode (2) Heavy coated electrode (3) Cast-iron electrode (4) Alloy-steel electrode (5) Mild-steel electrode.

The wire or rod used in the electrode is called *core.* The thickness is usually kept between 1.6 mm to 9.00 mm. The choice of electrode depends on the type and thickness of the job.

Electrode Coading

Electrodes are coaded in accordance with their characteristics.

I.S. (Indian Standard) System. In this system the code consists of a group of 5 to 8 elements — one letter then three or six digits and then one letter.

First letter. First letter is E, R or D, E means solid electrode, R means reinforced electrode and D means dipped electrode. Thus, first letter indicates the method of coating.

First digit. First digit may be 1 to 6 or 9.

1 = Superfluity of cellulose (it produces less ash and smoke)

2 = Superfluity of titania (it produces a thick slag)

3 = Proper quantity of titania (it produces fluid slag)

4 = Superfluity of iron/silicate (it produces spongy slag)

5 = Superfluity of iron oxide (it produces heavy and solid slag)

6 = Superfluity of calcium carbonate and fluoride (it produces less quantity of hydrogen)

9 = Special characteristic other than those stated above

Second digit. Second digit may be 1 to 7.

1 = For all positions such as horizontal, vertical, tilted *etc*

2 = For flat and horizontal surfaces

3 = Only for flat surfaces

4 = For flat, horizontal and tilted surfaces

5 = For flat, horizontal and overhead surfaces

6 = For vertical and overhead surfaces

7 = For any other position other than those stated above

Third digit. Third digit may be 0 to 7 or 9.

0 = D + Direct current reversed polarity

1 = D + A95 (A.C. Open circuit voltage 95 V)

2 = D – A 70 (A.C. Open circuit voltage above 70 V)

3 = D – A45 (A.C. Open circuit voltage above 45 V)

4 = D + A75 (A.C. Open circuit voltage above 75 V)

5 = D ± A 95 (Direct current reversed polarity above 95 volts)

6 = D ± A 70 (Direct current reversed polarity above 70 volts)

7 = D ± A45 (Direct current reversed polarity above 45 volts)

9 = other than those stated above.

Fourth digit. Fourth digit may be 1 to 8. It indicates the tensile strength of the weld metalin kg per mm^2. 1 = 31, 2 = 41, 3 = 44, 4 = 48, 5 = 52, 6 = 56, 7 = 68, 8 = 69.

Fifth digit. Fifth digit maybe 1 to 5. It indicates the tension powder of weld metal.

1 = 14%, 2 = 18%, 3 = 27%, 4 = 26%, 5 = 30%

Sixth digit. Sixth digit may be 1 to 9. It indicates the impact power of the weld metal.

1 = 4.1, 2 = 5.7, 3 = 7.00, 4 = 8.90, 5 = 10.40, 9 = other than those stated above.

Last letter. The last letter may be P, H or J.

P = Deep penitration electrode

H = Low-hydrogen electrode

J = Iron powder coated electrode

Example. D 245324 J

D = Dipped electrode

2 = Superfluity of titania in the electrode

4 = For flat, horizontal and tilted surfaces

5 = D + A95 (direct current reversed polarity above 95 V)

3 = 44 kg per mm^2 tensile strength

2 = 18% tension power type

4 = 8.90 impact power type

J = Iron powder coated electrode.

Difference in Welding and Brazing

Welding	***Brazins***
1. It is done by gas or electric.	1. It is done by blow lamp or stoves.
2. It requires many equipments.	2. It requires only few equipments
3. A sodium carbonate is used as flux.	3. Borox is used as flux.
4. It requires 3000°C temperature.	4. It requires 500°C to 700°C temperature.
5. Filler rod or wire is used.	5. Spelter is used.
6. Weld slag has to be cleaned off.	6. No slag is produced.
7. Safety precautions are to be observed.	7. Comparatively less safety precautions are to be observed.
8. It is costly process.	8. It is a cheap process.
9. Joints are strong enough.	9. Joints are weak and may open.
10. It requires experience.	10. It can be accomplished without experience.

29

Welding Joint, Bead and Preparation of Edges

Welding Joint

For joining two metallic pieces by welding process, first of all they are placed properly as per job requirements. If necessary, a clamp may be used for holding the job pieces so as to make the weld joint quickly and easily. The types of weld joints which can be made as per the position of job as shown in Fig. 29.1, are

(*i*) Lap joint
(*ii*) Butt joint
(*iii*) T-joint
(*iv*) V-joint
(*v*) Corner joint
(*vi*) Edge joint

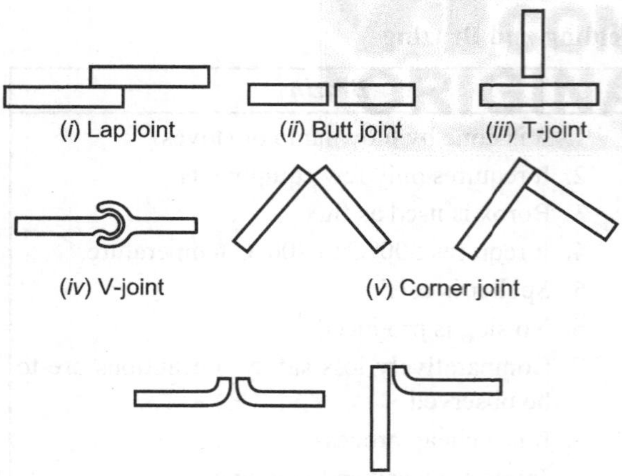

Fig. 29.1. Weld joints

Amongst all the weld joints, the lap joint is considered to be the strongest one and the butt joint is considered as the most suitable type of joint for welding. A corner joint is preferred in case of a heavy job and it is strong enough too.

Types of Weld Joints. There are many types of weld joints but the same is selected as per job requirements. Common types of weld joints are shown in Fig. 29.2.

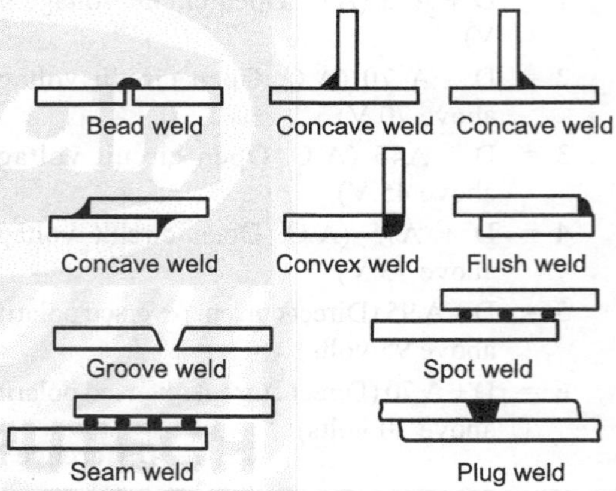

Fig. 29.2. Types of weld joints

Types of Weld Beads. The shape taken by a weld joint is known as weld bead. A welder prepares the same in accordance with his experience. The shape of a weld bead also depends on the direction and speed of welding. A defective bead creates *incomplete fusion* defect. Some popular weld beads are shown in Fig. 29.3 (*a*). The main reasons of a defective bead are the change in welding speed and inexperience of the welder, see Fig. 29.3 (*b*).

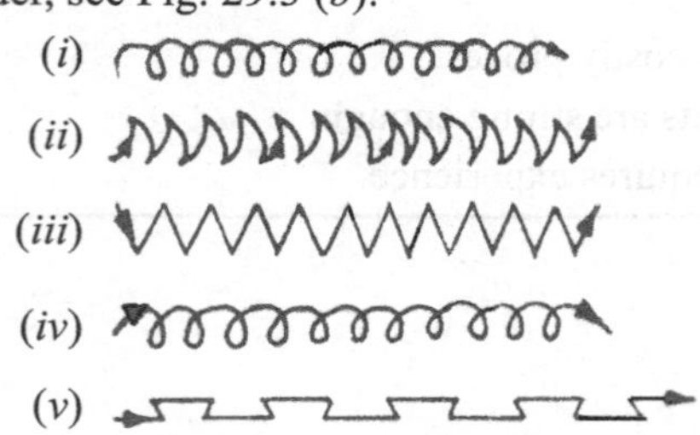

Fig. 29.3 (*a*) Weld beads

(vi) 

(vii) 

Fig. 29.3 (*b*). Defective weld beads

Preparation of Job Edges. The edges of job pieces are prepared especially and carefully before starting the actual welding. For this purpose, the edges of the job pieces are shaped to a proper pattern. It results in a complete penetration even in the butt joiny and T-joint. The shape patten of the edges of job pieces depends on the thickness of the job. In lap-joint the job pieces are placed one above the other for welding, therefore, there is no need of preparing job edges.

The procedure of preparing the job edges in case of butt joint and T-joint is shown in Fig. 29.4.

Advantages of Edge Preparation :

(*i*) The weld so made becomes strong.

(*ii*) Least internal stress develops.

(*iii*) Penetration becomes complete.

(*iv*) Protection from any possible distortion.

(*v*) The weld looks beautiful.

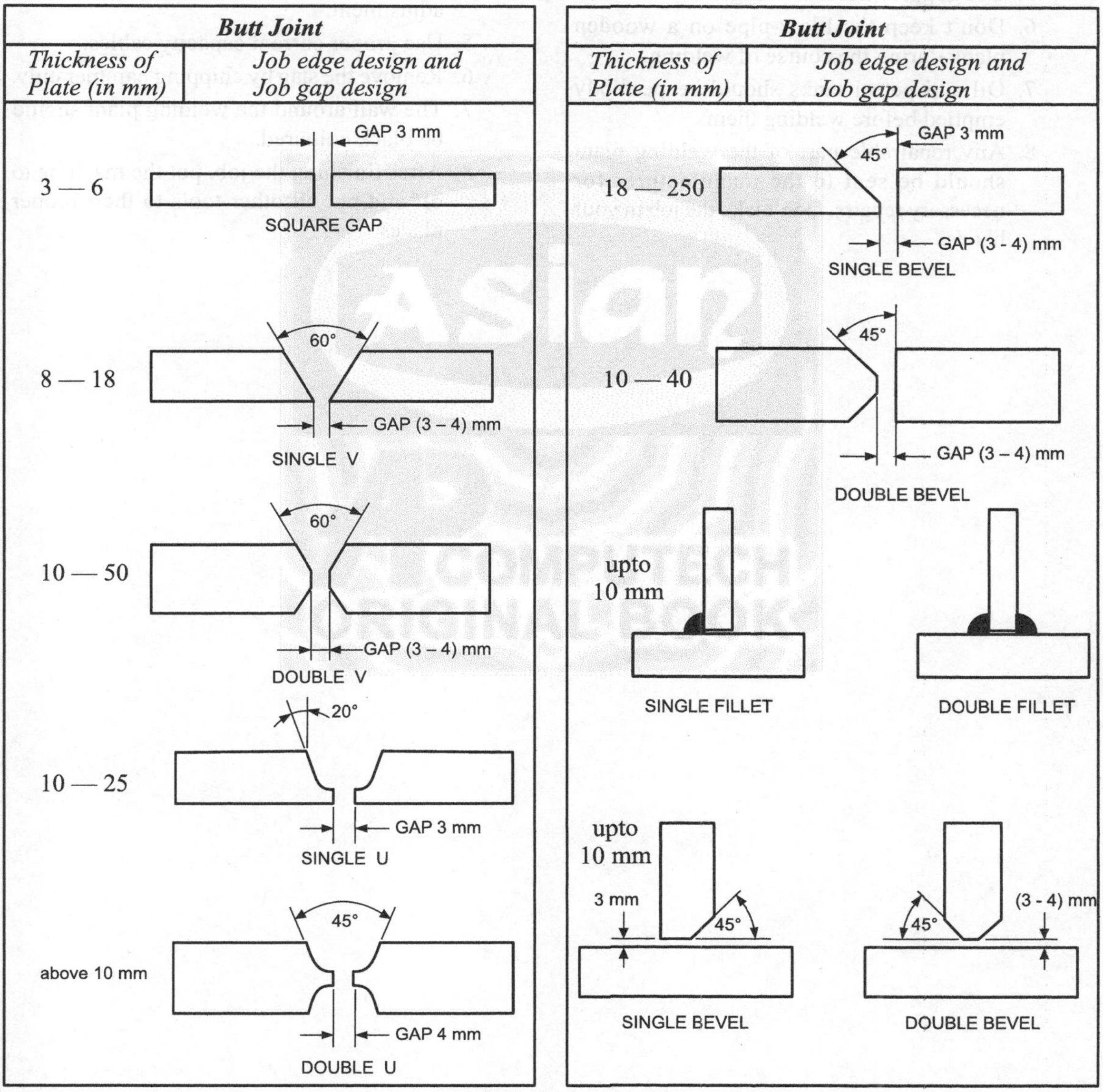

Fig. 29.04. Preparation of job edges

Safety Precations

(*a*) Safety precautions for gas welding:

1. As far as possible use a spark lighter for lighting the flame.
2. Oil, petrol and other explosives should be kept away from the welding plant.
3. Don't use any grease *etc.* for fitting the hose pipe to regulator.
4. Don't use hammer in setting up of the welding plant.
5. Use goggles while welding.
6. Don't keep the blow-pipe on a wooden plank during the course of welding.
7. Oil and petrol tanks should be perfectly emptied before welding them.
8. Any repairable part of the welding plant should be sent to the manufacturer for necessary repairs. Don't take the job in your hands.
9. Use proper tools for each job at the welding plant.
10. Put the welding plant to off after use in every time.

(*b*) Safety precautions for arc welding :

1. Use well understood welding machine.
2. No welding apparatus should be wet or damp.
3. The arc should only be observed through a shied or goggles.
4. Put the machine to off before any current adjustment.
5. Use proper current capacity cables.
6. Remove the slag by chipping hammer only.
7. The wall around the welding plant should be black coloured.
8. After finishing the job, put the machine to off and put all other tools to their proper places.